CIVIL WAR BOOKS

A Critical Bibliography

I

VOLUME ONE

CIVIL
WAR
BOOKS
A Critical Bibliography

edited by

ALLAN NEVINS
JAMES I. ROBERTSON, JR.
BELL I. WILEY

Published for the U.S. Civil War Centennial Commission by

LOUISIANA STATE UNIVERSITY PRESS
BATON ROUGE

PREFACE

The Civil War has been the subject of more publications than any other episode in American history. Although the exact number of books and pamphlets on the war is unknown, authoritative estimates place the total at between 40,000 and 60,000 volumes. The ever-increasing number of books is proof of a deep-seated interest, and it seems unlikely that this interest will diminish appreciably in the foreseeable future.

Such a mass of printed work is more than staggering; it is baffling. This is particularly true because not once since the war has the steadily mounting volume of writing been accurately catalogued or systematically organized. Hence, it has not been fully utilized by researchers and scholars. Civil War literature forms a flood of such magnitude that those who brave its depths soon take refuge on the few printed islands they recognize and/or respect. In marked contrast to most other areas of history, the Civil War is one in which the sources tend to overwhelm the searchers.

Our knowledge and divination of this epochal war has accordingly suffered. No full history of a subject can be written without some mastery of its historiography. Because so little attention has been given to this axiom in the area of the Civil War, thousands of volumes on that period have been repetitious, restricted in scope, and limited in value.

Books and monographs on the solitary figure of Abraham Lincoln run into the thousands; a veritable library exists on the single overworked battle of Gettysburg. Yet less than half a dozen volumes attempt to deal with any considerable part of bibliography, and these few but commendable attempts to assimilate portions of the war's literature are outdated, incomplete, or little-known. Illustrative of such works are John R. Bartlett's *The Literature of the Rebellion* (Boston, 1866) and John P. Nicholson's *Catalogue of Library of Brevet Lieutenant Nicholson . . . Relating to the War of Rebellion, 1861-1866* (Philadelphia, 1914). Notable exceptions to the handful of neglected listings are E. Merton Coulter's selective but descriptive *Travels in the Confederate States* (Norman, Okla., 1948) and Charles E. Dornbusch's meticulous but as yet incomplete *Regimental Publications & Personal Narratives of the Civil War: A Checklist* (New York, 1961).

For years researchers and writers have lamented this lack of what they agree Civil War history most needs: an annotated, critical bibliography of the major works in the field. Late in 1963 the United States Civil War Centennial Commission in Washington, D.C., decided to try to bridge this unfortunate gap. With the endorsement of all members of the commission, its officers, Allan Nevins (Chairman), James Robertson (Executive Director), and Bell I. Wiley (Chairman of the Executive Committee) established such a reference guide as one of the commission's major goals. Nevins and Wiley agreed to handle problems of organization and promotion; Robertson took on the duties as managing editor of the entire project.

The editors realized at the outset that the scope of this undertaking would be enormous. This fact in itself explained why a bibliography such as they envisioned had never been undertaken by one person. Nevins, Robertson, and Wiley therefore decided to break down the Civil War field into fifteen subjects — following the basic outline of the bibliography in the standard work by James G. Randall and David Donald, *The Civil War and Reconstruction* (Boston, 1961). Next, the editors had to find fifteen historians willing to act as compilers for the various sections.

This appeared to be anything but an easy task. Bibliographical compilation is tedious, time-consuming, and exacting. Finding competent historians who on the one hand were specialists in each of the fifteen categories and who on the other hand were not already hard at work on other endeavors involved a painstaking search of college campuses and research libraries. To complicate matters, the Centennial Commission could offer little enticement to those invited. Royalties could not be promised (since the original assumption was that the government would print the bibliography in the public domain); remuneration could not be granted (since the sponsor was a government agency with severely limited appropriations); public recognition was, at most, a hope; and controversy was inevitable with critics who assuredly would take issue with compilers' evaluations of certain works. The only reward that the commission could insure the compilers was the gratitude of every Civil War student and scholar who would use the bibliography in the years to come.

Fifteen historians promptly accepted the commission's invitation. Their enthusiasm for the project, their conscientious approach to the task, and their indefatigable labors can neither be underestimated nor over-praised.

With the personnel ready, the next step of the editors was to establish guidelines for the bibliography. On March 7, 1964, with Dr. Wiley presiding, a conference of compilers convened for an all-day meeting in Washington. Six of the seventeen persons involved in the project discussed all aspects of what should be, and what should not be, included in the compilation. Wiley and Robertson then consulted David Donald, Richard Harwell, and other authorities on final details of the listing. Shortly thereafter, each compiler received itemized instructions on procedure and mechanics; an order for thousands of printed title-cards went to the Card Division of the Library of Congress; and in late spring, 1964, work on the various sections began in earnest by compilers scattered from Louisiana to Minnesota.

Progress was slow but steady. Of necessity several compilers traveled to major depositories in order to examine scarce works in their sections. A constant stream of correspondence flowed between compilers in the hinterland and the managing editor, Dr. Robertson, in Washington. Queries on individual points were numerous; many title-cards first assigned to one section were, on reflection,

reassigned to another category; Library of Congress cards, and blank file cards for the annotations, passed to and fro in the mails.

Early in 1965 the first completed sections began arriving at the Centennial Commission offices. Robertson began the slow task of editing each entry: condensing and reworking annotations to bring them into general conformity; comparing entries in one section with those of an allied section to avoid duplication of titles; ordering title-cards for entries inadvertently omitted; and superintending the retyping of all annotation cards to obtain clean copy.

Notwithstanding several limitations placed on the titles to be included in the final listing, it was soon obvious that the total number of entries was too great for incorporation into a single volume. By January, 1966, with half the sections submitted and edited, the editors resolved to issue them as Volume I of a two-volume work. Volume I consists of the following bibliographical categories:

> Military Aspects — Mobilization, Organization, Administration, and Supply
> Military Aspects — Campaigns
> Military Aspects — Soldier Life
> Prisons and Prisoners of War
> The Negro
> The Navies
> Diplomacy

Volume II will include these remaining sections (with compiler's name in parenthesis):

> General Works (E. B. Long)
> Biographies, Memoirs and Collected Works of Important Leaders and Key Personalities (Robert W. Johannsen)
> The Confederacy — Government and Politics (Martin Abbott)
> The Confederacy — State and Local Studies (Malcolm C. McMillan)
> The Confederacy — Social and Economic Studies (May S. Ringold)
> The Union — Government and Politics (Rodney C. Loehr)
> The Union — State and Local Studies (William E. Parrish)
> The Union — Economic and Social Conditions (John T. Hubbell)

This bibliography is designed to serve both scholars and general readers. It is restricted to literature bearing solely on the war years. Works treating of the causes, results, and subjects not closely related to the Civil War had to be omitted. The entries are further confined to titles for which Library of Congress cards exist and to titles accessible to the respective compilers.

Owing in large part to limitations of time and money, the bibliography lists only books and pamphlets. Other source material was omitted for reasons given below.

Manuscripts were excluded because: (1) their inclusion would lead to an unevenness of the various segments of the compilation — since manuscripts abound for some sections (e.g., Soldier Life) and rarely exist for others (e.g., The Negro); (2) in many instances the manuscripts are so widely scattered that compilers would have been unreasonably burdened if they had attempted to include them; and (3) for the most part, users of manuscripts are professional historians who already know where and how to gain access to these sources.

Articles are excluded since they are of such quantity and varying worth as to demand a separate bibliography. In one or two instances, a group of articles was included here when it appeared in one publication and contributed richly to a single topic. (For example, see *Civil War History* under "Prisons and Prisoners of War.")

Doctoral dissertations and masters' theses were excluded because of the difficulty of locating them and because of the assumption that the best of these studies have been or will be published.

Poetry, drama, fiction, and juvenile, satirical, and tongue-in-cheek works are excluded for the reason that they are not history in the more conventional sense.

Volume I contains more than 2,700 annotated titles, divided into seven divisions. The critiques will show that it contains bad works as well as good ones. The overall aim of the project was to analyze those volumes familiar and unfamiliar, general or limited, indispensable or useless, for the benefit of anyone delving into the literature of the Civil War. If for one reason or another a title does not appear in the listing, this does not necessarily mean that it has no value.

Volume II, encompassing the remaining eight sections, will include approximately 3,000 titles. It will also contain a cross-referenced index to facilitate use of both parts of the bibliography.

Many persons helped in many ways to make this publication possible. Space does not permit public acknowledgment of indebtedness to everyone who aided the undertaking. However, the editors wish to express particular thanks to the following: the compilers, whose unselfish labors are a testimonial to their devotion to history; Edmund C. Gass, final director of the U.S. Civil War Centennial Commission, who attended to a host of minor but all-important details; the Louisiana State University Press, for its interest in and publication of this listing; James V. Murfin, who diligently supervised the long and tedious preparation of camera copy; the staff of the Centennial Commission; the ever-helpful personnel in all divisions of the Library of Congress; the many scholars who gave encouragement and advice throughout the early stages; and, most of all, the American people, whose moral and financial support of the U.S. Civil War Centennial Commission enabled it to make this contribution toward a better understanding of our common heritage.

ALLAN NEVINS
JAMES I. ROBERTSON, JR.
BELL I. WILEY

COMPILERS

FRANK BYRNE is associate professor of history at Kent State University. He is the author of *Prophet of Prohibition: Neal Dow and His Crusade* and editor of *The View from Headquarters: Civil War Letters of Harvey Reid.*

DUDLEY T. CORNISH is professor of history at Kansas State College at Pittsburg. He is best known for his study *The Sable Arm: Negro Troops in the Union Army, 1861-1865.*

NORMAN FERRIS is associate professor of history at Middle Tennessee State University. He is completing a multi-volume biography of the diplomat Charles Francis Adams.

WARREN W. HASSLER, JR., is professor of history at Pennsylvania State University. He has written *Commanders of the Army of the Potomac* and a biography of General George B. McClellan.

ARCHER JONES is chairman of the Department of History and Political Science at Virginia Polytechnic Institute. He is the author of *Confederate Strategy from Shiloh to Vicksburg.*

JAMES I. ROBERTSON, JR., formerly executive director of the U.S. Civil War Centennial Commission, is now associate professor of history at the University of Montana. His writings include *The Stonewall Brigade* and *One of Jackson's Foot Cavalry.*

THOMAS WELLS is associate professor of history at Northwestern State College of Louisiana. He is the author of *Commodore Moore and the Texas Navy.*

CONTENTS

CIVIL
WAR
BOOKS

A Critical Bibliography

I

MILITARY ASPECTS
Mobilization, Organization, Administration and Supply

Archer Jones

Abdill, George B
    Civil War railroads. ₁1st ed.₁ Seattle, Superior Pub. Co. ₁1961₁

      192 p. illus. 22 x 28 cm.

A topical photographic history with full captions; illustrative of equipment and methods of destruction.

Abel, Annie Heloise, 1873–
    The American Indian as participant in the civil war, by Annie Heloise Abel ... Cleveland, The Arthur H. Clark company, 1919.

      403 p. incl. front. (facsim.) port., double map, 2 fold. facsim. 24½ cm. (*Her* The slaveholding Indians, vol. II)

The first two volumes of this scholarly work explain the source and extent of Indian support for the Confederacy.

Adams, George Worthington.
    Doctors in blue; the medical history of the Union Army in the Civil War. New York, H. Schuman ₁1952₁

      xii, 253 p. illus. 22 cm.

A complete scholarly treatment covering administration, hospitals, ambulances and nursing, as well as medical affairs.

Albaugh, William A   1908–
    Confederate edged weapons. Illustrated by Carl J. Pugliese. New York, Harper ₁1960₁

      198 p. illus. 29 cm.

A comprehensive and well-illustrated account with much information on sources of supply, both foreign and domestic.

Albaugh, William A   1908–
    Confederate handguns: concerning the guns, the men who made them, and the times of their use. By William A. Albaugh, III, Hugh Benet, Jr. ₁and₁ Edward N. Simmons. Philadelphia, Riling and Lentz, 1963.

      xix, 250 p. illus., ports., maps. 29 cm.

Complete and well-illustrated, with much information on foreign and domestic supplies.

Albaugh, William A   1908–
    The original Confederate Colt; the story of the Leech & Rigdon and Rigdon-Ansley revolvers, by William A. Albaugh, III, and Richard D. Steuart. New York, Greenberg ₁1953₁

      62 p. illus., map. 27 cm.

A brief fragmentary history of the firm that made the first Confederate colt.

Albaugh, William A   1908–
  A photographic supplement of Confederate swords ₁Washington? ᶜ1963₁

  xv, 205 p. illus., ports. 26 cm.

An illustrated effort to identify each sword used in the Confederacy and to determine its manufacturer.

Albaugh, William A   1908–
  Tyler, Texas, C. S. A. Harrisburg, Pa., Stackpole Co. ₁1958₁

  235 p. plates, maps. 23 cm.

A history of the Confederate ordinance works at Tyler; largely extracted from official correspondence.

Albert, Alphaeus Homer, 1891–
  Buttons of the Confederacy; a descriptive and illustrated catalog of the buttons worn by the troops of the Confederates ₁sic₁ States of America, 1861–65. ₁1st ed. Hightstown, N. J.₁ 1963.

  xvii, 93 p. illus., facsims. 23 cm.

Illustrated description, organized by branch of service and states.

Amann, William Frayne, *ed.*
  Personnel of the Civil War. New York, T. Yoseloff ₁1961₁

  2 v. 22 cm.

Includes much information on designations of both Union and Confederate organizations and commands, and lists of general officers; Marcus J. Wright was one of the compilers.

Anderson, Charles Carter, 1867–
  Fighting by southern federals, in which the author places the numerical strength of the armies that fought for the Confederacy at approximately 1,000,000 men, and shows that 296,579 white soldiers living in the South, and 137,676 colored soldiers, and approximately 200,000 men living in the North that were born in the South, making 634,255 southern soldiers, fought for the preservation of the Union. By Charles C. Anderson. New York, The Neale publishing company, 1912.

  408 p. front. (map) 20½ cm.

A detailed treatment of individual military activities on behalf of the Union by southerners and northerners born in the South; covers a total of more than 600,000 Union troops.

Andrews, Edmund, 1824–1904.
  The primary surgery of Gen. Sherman's campaigns. By E. Andrews … and J. M. Woodworth … Chicago, G. H. Fergus, printer, 1866.

  cover-title, 20 p. 21½ᶜᵐ.

Statistics comparing surgical results in Sherman's army with those in other Civil War armies.

Barnard, John Gross, 1815–1882.
  Report of the engineer and artillery operations of the Army of the Potomac, from its organization to the close of the Peninsular campaign. By Brig.-Gen. J. G. Barnard, chief engineer, and Brig.-Gen. W. F. Barry, chief of artillery … New York D. Van Nostrand, 1863.

  1 p. l., ₁5₁–230 p. 5 pl. (incl. front.) 13 maps and plans (part fold.) 24½ᶜᵐ.

Reports of McClellan's Chief Engineer and Chief of Artillery.

Barton, George, 1866–1940.
  Angels of the battlefield. A history of the labors of the Catholic sisterhoods in the late civil war. By George Barton. Philadelphia, Pa., The Catholic art publishing company, 1897.

  xvi, 302 p. illus., 15 pl. (incl. front.) 2 port. 25 cm.

Discursive and anecdotal account of the nursing and hospital work of the Catholic sisterhoods.

Bates, David Homer, 1843–1926.
  Lincoln in the telegraph office; recollections of the United States military telegraph corps during the civil war, by David Homer Bates, manager of the War department telegraph office, and cipher-operator, 1861–1866. New York, The Century co., 1907.

  viii, 432 p. incl. plates, ports., facsims. front. 21½ᶜᵐ.

Contains information on the organization, operation, and role of the military telegraph service.

Beale, James, 1844?–   *comp.*
  The battle flags of the Army of the Potomac at Gettysburg, Penna. July 1st, 2d, & 3d, 1863. Philadelphia, J. Beale, 1885.

  35 l. 32 col. pl. 30½ x 26ᶜᵐ

Each flag is illustrated in color.

Beale, James, 1844?–   *comp.*
Tabulated roster of the Army of the Potomac at Gettysburg, Penna., July 1, 2, 3, 1863. Arranged by states, showing the brigade, division, and corps with which each organization served during the battle. Philadelphia, Comp. and pub. by James Beale [c1888]
32 p.   16 x 13 cm.

An indexed order of battle tables, organized by regiment.

Black, Robert C   1914–
The railroads of the Confederacy. Chapel Hill, University of North Carolina Press [1952]
xiv, 360 p.   illus., ports., maps (1 fold.) facsims.   25 cm.

An able and detailed treatment of the management, difficulties, and significance of Southern railways, with emphasis on the railways themselves.

Bradlee, Francis Boardman Crowninshield, 1881–1928.
Blockade running during the civil war and the effect of land and water transportation on the Confederacy, by Francis B. C. Bradlee ... Salem, Mass., The Essex institute, 1925.
xii, 340 p.   front., plates, ports., maps, facsims.   24 cm.

The title is misleading because almost half of the volume is devoted to an anecdotal treatment of Confederate railroad, postal, telegraph and express service.

Brockett, Linus Pierpont   1820–1893.
The philanthropic results of the war in America. Collected from official and other authentic sources, by an American citizen. Dedicated by permission to the United States sanitary commission. New York, Sheldon & co.; [etc., etc.] 1864.
160 p.   15½ cm.

Contains a brief account of the work of the Sanitary Commission on the home front.

Bruce, Robert V
Lincoln and the tools of war. Foreword by Benjamin P. Thomas. [1st ed.] Indianapolis, Bobbs-Merrill [1956]
xi, 368 p.   illus., ports.   23 cm.

Interesting, scholarly study of Union equipment from rifles to ships, showing Lincoln's strong interest in all kinds of weapons.

Buckeridge, Justin O
Lincoln's choice. [1st ed.] Harrisburg, Pa., Stackpole Co. [1956]
254 p.   illus.   23 cm.

An account, journalistic in style, of the operations of troops armed with the Spencer repeater.

Chisolm, Julian John, 1830–1903.
A manual of military surgery, for the use of surgeons in the Confederate States Army; with an appendix of the rules and regulations of the Medical department of the Confederate States Army. By J. Julian Chisolm ... 2d ed.—rev. and improved. Richmond, Va., West & Johnson, 1862.
xii, 514 p. incl. forms.   fold. form.   19 cm.

A widely circulated and standard work in the Confederacy.

Clements, Bennett Augustine, *d.* 1886.
Memoir of Jonathan Letterman ... by ... Brevet Lieut.-Colonel Bennett A. Clements ... [New York, Press of G. P. Putnam's sons, 1883?]
cover-title, 38 p.   24 cm.

Eulogizes Letterman's work as Medical Director of the Army of the Potomac.

Coggins, Jack.
Arms and equipment of the Civil War. Illustrated by the author. [1st ed.] Garden City, N. Y., Doubleday, 1962.
160 p.   illus.   29 cm.

A well-illustrated, basic introduction that includes everything from ships to tents.

Colby, Carroll B
Civil War weapons: small arms and artillery of the Blue and Gray. New York, Coward-McCann [1962]
48 p.   illus.   28 cm.

Composed largely of illustrations with descriptions of small arms and artillery.

Confederate States of America. *War dept.*
General orders from Adjutant and Inspector-General's office, Confederate States army, from January, 1862, to December, 1863, (both inclusive) In two series. Prepared from files of head-quarters, Department of S. C., Ga., and Fla. With full indexes. Columbia, Presses of Evans & Cogswell, 1864.

2 v. in 1. 18ᶜᵐ.

Covering everything from a court martial for drunkenness to impressment and instructions for engineering and quartermaster officers.

Confederate States of America. *War dept.*
Regulations for the army of the Confederate States, 1863. With a full index. By authority of the War department ... Richmond, West & Johnston, 1863.

xxx, 432 p. pl. 19ᶜᵐ.

An annual publication whose contents ranged from requisition forms to the conduct of sieges.

Confederate States of America. *War dept.*
Regulations for the Medical department of the C. S. army. Richmond, Ritchie & Dunnavant, printers, 1863.

76 p. 18ᶜᵐ.

Detailed regulations for surgeons and stewards. Includes compensation, medical qualifications of officers, forms, menus, cooking directions and supply tables for hospitals.

Cornish, Joseph Jenkins.
The air arm of the Confederacy; a history of origins and usages of war balloons by the Southern armies during the American Civil War. Richmond, Richmond Civil War Centennial Committee, 1963.

48 p. illus., ports., maps. 24 cm. (₍Richmond. Civil War Centennial Committee₎ Official publication 11)

A brief treatment of Confederate military ballooning.

Cunningham, Horace Herndon, 1913–
Doctors in gray; the Confederate medical service. Baton Rouge, Louisiana State University Press ₍1958₎

xi, 338 p. plate, ports., facsims. 24 cm.

A scholarly treatment of hospitals, supply, and administration; some data on medical personnel.

Dyer, Frederick Henry, 1849–
A compendium of the war of the rebellion, comp. and arranged from official records of the Federal and Confederate armies, reports of the adjutant generals of the several states, the Army registers, and other reliable documents and sources, by Frederick H. Dyer ... Des Moines, Ia., The Dyer publishing company, 1908.

1796 p. 32 cm.

Contains Union mortality tables and departmental organization throughout the war, with constituents' units and their commanders.

Ellett, Charles, 1810–1862.
The Army of the Potomac, and its mismanagement; respectfully addressed to Congress. By Charles Ellet, jr. ... Washington, 1861.

19 p. 24ᶜᵐ.

A brief logistical criticism of McClellan's strategy in the fall of 1861.

Elliott, Ezekiel Brown, 1823–1888.
... On the military statistics of the United States of America, by E. B. Elliott ... Berlin, Printed by R. v. Decker, 1863.

3 p. l., 44 p. 3 diagr. 27 x 22½ᶜᵐ.

A statistical study of the mortality, age, and physical measurements of U. S. troops.

Flint, Austin, 1812–1886, *ed.*
Contributions relating to the causation and prevention of disease, and to camp diseases; together with a report of the diseases, etc., among the prisoners at Andersonville, Ga. Ed. by Austin Flint, M. D. New York, Pub. for the U. S. sanitary commission, by Hurd and Houghton, 1867.

vii p., 1 l., ix–xi, ₍ix₎–xviii, 667 p. 24½ cm. (*Half-title:* Sanitary memoirs of the war of the rebellion. Collected and pub. by the United States sanitary commission. ₍v. 1₎)

A description of the medical results of the war with respect to camp diseases, etc.

Forman, Jacob Gilbert
The Western sanitary commission; a sketch of its origin, history, labors for the sick and wounded of the western armies, and aid given to freedmen and Union refugees, with incidents of hospital life. St. Louis, Pub. for the Mississippi valley sanitary fair, R. P. Studley & co., 1864.

144 p. front., pl. 23 cm.

A careful and thorough history of the work of the Commission in the West through 1863.

Foster, Ethan.

The conscript Quakers, being a narrative of the distress and relief of four young men from the draft for the war in 1863. By Ethan Foster. Cambridge, Printed at the Riverside press, 1883.

29 p. 15½cm.

An account of the author's efforts to secure the exemption of four Quaker draftees.

Foster, G   Allen.

The eyes and ears of the Civil War. New York, Criterion Books ₁1964, ᶜ1963₎

168 p. illus., ports. 22 cm.

This brief work surveys communication and observation activity on the Union side, with emphasis on intelligence work.

Fowler, W   H

Guide for claimants of deceased soldiers; being instructions to army officers and to claimants, with a collation of the laws of Congress and the orders from the War department, and the rules of practice in the offices of the second auditor and the comptroller of the Treasury concerning the settlement of the claims of deceased officers and soldiers. By Col. W. H. Fowler ... Rev. and approved by the second auditor and comptroller of the Treasury, and adapted to general use. Richmond, Va., G. P. Evans & co., printers, 1864.

72 p. 19cm.

Treats eligibility and evidence required; includes complete information on pay and allowances in the Confederate army.

Fox, William Freeman, 1840–1910.

Regimental losses in the American civil war, 1861–1865. A treatise on the extent and nature of the mortuary losses in the Union regiments, with full and exhaustive statistics compiled from the official records on file in the state military bureaus and at Washington. By William F. Fox ... Albany, N. Y., Albany publishing company, 1889.

vi, 595 p. 30cm.

A statistical analysis of Union casualities together with histories of Union units.

Fuller, Claud E   1877–

Firearms of the Confederacy; the shoulder arms, pistols and revolvers of the Confederate soldier, including the regular United States models, the imported arms and those manufactured within the Confederacy. ₁By₎ Claud E. Fuller and Richard D. Steuart. Huntington, W. Va., Standard publications, inc., 1944.

3 p. l., vi, ₁8₎, 333 p. 1 illus., plates, ports., facsims. 24¼ cm.

Included in this study are quantities, sources, and manufacturing activities.

Fuller, Claud E   1877–

The rifled musket. Harrisburg, Pa., Stackpole Co. ₁1958₎

302 p. illus., facsims. 29 cm.

A complete description of the models (1861–1864) and their manufacturers; includes reproductions of the manual and targets.

Gavin, William G

Accoutrement plates, North and South, 1861–1865; an authoritative reference with comparative values. Foreword by Stephen V. Grancsay. Philadelphia, Riling and Lentz, 1963.

xvii, 217 p. illus., ports. 23 cm.

A scholarly, thorough, and well-illustrated effort to describe accoutrement plates of the Federal, Confederate and state forces.

Goldsmith, Middleton, 1818–1887.

A report on hospital gangrene, erysipelas and pyæmia, as observed in the departments of the Ohio and the Cumberland, with cases appended. Published by permission of the surgeon general, U. S. A. By M. Goldsmith ... Louisville ₁Ky.₎ Bradley & Gilbert, 1863.

94 p. tables (part fold.) 22½cm.

A collection of case reports, with statistics of wounds and treatments.

Gould, Benjamin Apthorp, 1824–1896.

Investigations in the military and anthropological statistics of American soldiers. By Benjamin Apthorp Gould ... actuary to the U. S. sanitary commission. New York, Pub. for U. S. sanitary commission, by Hurd and Houghton, 1869.

3 p. l., ₁v₎–xiv, 655 p. incl. illus., tables, fold. diagrs. 24½cm. (Half-title: Sanitary memoirs of the war of the rebellion. Collected and pub. by the United States sanitary commission. ₁New York, 1869. v. 2₎)

A complete statistical survey covering vision, height, weight, complexion, age, etc.

Grace, William.

The army surgeon's manual, for the use of medical officers, cadets, chaplains, and hospital stewards, containing the regulations of the Medical department, all general orders from the War department, and circular from the Surgeon-general's office ... 1861 to ... 1865. By William Grace ... 2d ed. ... New York, Bailliere brothers, 1865.

2 p. l., ₁7₎–225 p. 18½cm.

Regulations, general orders and circulars relating to medical matters, including chaplains and hospital stewards.

Greenbie, Marjorie Latta (Barstow) 1891–
... Lincoln's daughters of mercy. New York, G. P. Putnam's sons [1944]

x, 211 p. 21½ cm.

An account of the Sanitary Commission, with emphasis on individual participants, particularly nurses.

Hackley, F   W
A report on Civil War explosive ordnance. Indian Head, Md., U. S. Naval Propellant Plant [1960?]

iv, 44 l. illus. 27 cm.

A brief description, with diagrams and photographs, of the more common types of army explosive ordnance.

Hammond, William Alexander, 1828–1900.
A statement of the causes which led to the dismissal of Surgeon-General William A. Hammond from the army; with a review of the evidence adduced before the court. [New York, 1864]

73 p. 23ᶜᵐ.

Hammond's explanation of why he should not have been dismissed.

Hardesty, Jesse.
Killed and died of wounds in the Union army during the civil war, by Jesse Hardesty, formerly of Co. "B," 7th O. V. I. ... San Jose, Cal., Press of Wright-Eley co. [ᶜ1915]

34 p. 15½ᶜᵐ. $0.25

An analysis for each regiment, as well as data on the number of regiments supplied by each state.

Harlow, Alvin Fay, 1875–
Brass-pounders: young telegraphers of the Civil War. Denver, Sage Books [1962]

159 p. illus. 23 cm.

A light and anecdotal account of the activities of union telegraphers.

Haurowitz, Harry Valentin von, 1799–1882.
Das militärsanitätswesen der Vereinigten Staaten von Nord-Amerika während des letzten krieges, nebst schilderungen von land und leuten; von dr. H. V. Haurowitz ... Stuttgart, G. Weise, 1866.

viii p., 1 l., 350 p. 23ᶜᵐ.

A description of the organization and functions of the Sanitary Commission, sickness and mortality figures, and information on quartermaster and commissary activities.

Hayden, Howard K
Billy Yank, soldier of the North [by] Howard K. Hayden. Illustrated by Daniel I. Hennessey. [Long Branch, N. J., Drum Press, 1965]

52 p. illus., facsims., port. 25 cm.

An illustrated children's book about Union soldiers' equipment.

Haydon, Frederick Stansbury, 1908–
Aeronautics in the Union and Confederate armies, with a survey of military aeronautics prior to 1861, by F. Stansbury Haydon. Baltimore, The Johns Hopkins press, 1941–

v. plates (part fold.) ports., facsims., diagrs. 23½ cm.

A scholarly study of the material, organization, and employment of balloons in the first year of the war.

Henry, Guy Vernor, 1839–1899.
Military record of civilian appointments in the United States army. By Guy V. Henry ... New York, Carleton; [etc., etc.] 1870–73.

2 v. 23ᶜᵐ.

Service records of officers of the Union army.

Hokanson, Nels Magnus, 1885–
Swedish immigrants in Lincoln's time, by Nels Hokanson, with a foreword by Carl Sandburg. New York and London, Harper & brothers [ᶜ1942]

xviii p., 1 l., 259 p. front. (map) pl., ports., facsims. 22½ᶜᵐ.

Biographical in emphasis, noting contributions of individuals in military and civil life; includes some information on raising Swedish regiments for the Union army.

Howe, Samuel Gridley, 1801–1876.

A letter on the sanitary condition of the troops in the neighborhood of Boston, addressed to His Excellency the governor of Massachusetts, by S. G. Howe ... Printed by request of the Advisory committee. Washington, Govt. print off., 1861.

16 p. 22½cm.

A letter to the governor of Massachusetts reporting the results of an inspection.

Johnston, Angus James.

Virginia railroads in the Civil War. Chapel Hill, Published for the Virginia Historical Society by the University of North Carolina Press, 1961.

xiv, 336 p. illus., maps, tables. 24 cm.

A scholarly study of the logistical and strategic place of railroads in the Virginia campaigns.

Jones, Joseph, 1833–1896.

Researches upon "spurious vaccination", or the abnormal phenomena accompanying and following vaccination in the Confederate army during the recent American civil war, 1861–1865. By Joseph Jones ... Nashville, Tenn., University medical press, 1867.

164 p. 22½cm.

The results of Dr. Jones' investigation of "untoward results . . . and a number of deaths" following vaccinations in the Confederacy.

Kane, Harnett Thomas, 1910–

Spies for the Blue and Gray. [1st ed.] Garden City, N. Y., Hanover House [1954]

311 p. 22 cm.

Sprightly accounts of spy exploits on both sides.

Katz, Irving I

The Jewish soldier from Michigan in the Civil War. Detroit, Wayne State University Press, 1962.

62 p. illus. 22 cm.

Includes a list of Jewish participants from Michigan and a brief treatment of national Jewish participation.

Kaufmann, Wilhelm, 1858–

Die Deutschen im amerikanischen bürgerkriege ⟨sezessionskrieg 1861–1865⟩ von Wilhelm Kaufmann; mit 36 karten und plänen. München und Berlin, R. Oldenbourg, 1911.

xii p., 1 l., 588 p. illus. (maps, plans) 23½ cm.

A general history with emphasis on the role of participants of German extraction.

Kelley, William Darrah, 1814–1890.

Lincoln and Stanton; a study of the war administration of 1861 and 1862, with special consideration of some recent statements of Gen. Geo. B. McClellan; by Wm. D. Kelley, M. C. New York & London, G. P. Putnam's sons, 1885.

1 p. l., 88 p. 20 cm. (*On cover:* Questions of the day. 29)

A rebuttal to McClellan; very critical of McClellan and eulogistic of Lincoln and Stanton.

Kniffin, Gilbert Crawford.

... Estimated effective strength of the Union and Confederate armies, and their respective losses during the war of the rebellion. By Companion Lieutenant-Colonel Gilbert C. Kniffin ... Read at the stated meeting of November 1, 1911 ... [Washington, 1911]

24 p. front. (port.) 23½ cm. (Military order of the loyal legion of the United States. Commandery of the District of Columbia. War papers. 84)

A very brief work primarily devoted to developing an estimate of the total forces engaged on each side.

Korn, Bertram Wallace.

American Jewry and the Civil War. With an introd. by Allan Nevins. Philadelphia, Jewish Publication Society of America, 1951.

xii, 331 p. illus., ports. 25 cm.

A good account of Jews in the Civil War, with emphasis on Jewish chaplains and Jewish rights.

Lewis, Berkeley R

Notes on ammunition of the American Civil War, 1861–1865. Washington, American Ordnance Association, 1959.

unpaged. illus. 26 cm.

Excellent brief description of all types of small arms and artillery ammunition with clear explanations of technical details. Includes tables of quantities of different classes of ordnance used by the Union armies.

Livermore, Thomas Leonard, 1844–1918.

Numbers and losses in the Civil war in America, 1861–65; by Thomas L. Livermore ... [2d ed.] Boston and New York, Houghton, Mifflin and company, 1901.

viii p., 1 l., 150 p., 1 l. 24ᶜᵐ.

The standard work; a complete statistical account based largely on official records.

Livermore, Thomas Leonard, 1844–1918.

Numbers & losses in the Civil War in America, 1861–65. Introd. by Edward E. Barthell, Jr. Bloomington, Indiana University Press, 1957.

150 p. illus. 21 cm. (Civil War centennial series)

Identical to the 1901 edition but with the addition of a biographical sketch of Livermore by Edward E. Barthell, Jr.

Lonn, Ella, 1879–

... Desertion during the civil war, by Ella Lonn ... New York, London, The Century co. [c1928]

vii, 251 p. front. (fold. map) 23ᶜᵐ.

A brief but comprehensive treatment of desertion, including causes, impact and prevention, and evasion and recapture methods.

Lonn, Ella, 1879–

Foreigners in the Confederacy [by] Ella Lonn ... Chapel Hill, The University of North Carolina press, 1940.

xi p., 1 l., 566 p. front., ports. 24 cm.

Scholarly account of the military and civilian role of foreigners in the Confederacy.

Lonn, Ella, 1879–

Foreigners in the Union Army and Navy. Baton Rouge, Louisiana State University Press [1952, c1951]

viii, 725 p. port. 25 cm.

A definitive and thorough coverage of the sources of one fifth of the enlistments in the Union forces.

Lord, Francis Alfred, 1911–

Civil War collector's encyclopedia; arms, uniforms, and equipment of the Union and Confederacy. [1st ed.] Harrisburg, Pa., Stackpole Co. [1963]

360 p. illus. (part col.) facsims. 29 cm.

A well-illustrated, detailed description of all items of equipment, including everything from pontoons to epaulettes.

Lord, Francis Alfred, 1911–

They fought for the Union. [1st ed.] Harrisburg, Pa., Stackpole Co. [1960]

375 p. illus., ports., map, facsims., tables. 29 cm.

A scholarly treatment, fully explaining army organization, administration and conditions-- including training, supply and equipment, technical services, etc.

McClellan, George Brinton, 1826–1885.

... Letter of the Secretary of war, transmitting report on the organization of the Army of the Potomac, and of its campaigns in Virginia and Maryland, under the command of Maj. Gen. George B. McClellan, from July 26, 1861, to November 7, 1862. Washington, Govt. print. off., 1864.

1 p. l., 242 p. 23 cm.

McClellan's official report, containing much information on the initial organization of the Army of the Potomac.

McCrady, Edward, 1833–1903.

"Formation, organization, discipline and characteristics of the Army of northern Virginia." An address before the Association Army of northern Virginia delivered in the hall of the House of delegates, Richmond, Va., Thursday, Oct. 21, 1886, by Col. Edward McCrady, jr. ... Richmond, W. E. Jones, printer, 1886.

41 p. 24ᶜᵐ.

A short account of the formation of the Army of Northern Virginia, with some observations on discipline and other characteristics.

McKim, Randolph Harrison, 1842–1920.

The numerical strength of the Confederate army; an examination of the argument of the Hon. Charles Francis Adams and others, by Randolph H. McKim ... New York, The Neale publishing company, 1912.

71, [1] p. 19ᶜᵐ.

Contends that T. L. Livermore's figures for total Confederate forces are too high.

Major, Duncan Kennedy, 1876–

Supply of Sherman's army during the Atlanta campaign. By Duncan K. Major, jr., 27th infantry, and Captain Roger S. Fitch, 2d cavalry. Fort Leavenworth, Kan. [Army service schools press] 1911.

108 p. 20ᶜᵐ.

A collection of material from the <u>Official Records</u>, with some connecting narrative.

Martin, Bessie, 1891–

Desertion of Alabama troops from the Confederate army; a study in sectionalism, by Bessie Martin ... New York, 1932.

2 p. l., 7–283 p. illus. (maps) 22½ᶜᵐ.

A scholarly study of the military, political, economic, and social causes of desertion; includes a treatment of measures to prevent desertion and recover deserters.

Massachusetts. *Surgeon-general's office.*

Annual report.
Boston, 1862–

v. 23½ᶜᵐ.

Primarily reports of the state agents who visited and aided state troops and arranged bounties for reenlistments.

Maxwell, William Quentin.

Lincoln's fifth wheel: the political history of the United States Sanitary Commission. Pref. by Allan Nevins. [1st ed.] New York, Longmans, Green, 1956.

xii, 372 p. 22 cm.

A scholarly and comprehensive narrative, covering all aspects of the treatment of the sick.

Meneely, Alexander Howard, 1899–

The War department, 1861; a study in mobilization and administration, by A. Howard Meneely ... New York, Columbia university press; London, P. S. King & son, ltd., 1928.

400 p. front. (port.) 23 cm. (*Half-title:* Studies in history, economics and public law, ed. by the Faculty of political science of Columbia university, no. 300)

A scholarly and thorough treatment of the War Department in Buchanan's last days and of the initial mobilization effort under Cameron.

Moore, Albert Burton, 1887–

Conscription and conflict in the Confederacy, by Albert Burton Moore ... New York, The Macmillan company, 1924.

ix p., 2 l., 367 p. 22½ cm.

A detailed account and excellent evaluation of Confederate and state conscription activity.

Moss, Lemuel, 1829–1904.

Annals of the United States Christian commission. By Rev. Lemuel Moss, home secretary to the commission. Philadelphia, J. B. Lippincott & co., 1868.

752 p. front. (port.) illus., plates. 24ᶜᵐ.

A semi-official account of the Commission's work: food parcels and books supplied; hospital and religious activity, as well as fund-raising.

Nagle, John Thomas, 1842–

An appeal to President Roosevelt for justice to a class of acting assistant surgeons of the United States army, who served in the civil war, by John T. Nagle ... [New York, M. B. Brown press, 1908]

xiv, 194 (i. e. 215) p. front. (2 port.) 23½ᶜᵐ.

Contains some information on the status of acting assistant surgeons.

Nagle, John Thomas, 1842–1919.

The status of acting assistant surgeons of the United States army, who served in the late civil war, being a reply to the ruling of the War department ... By John T. Nagle ... New York, M. B. Brown, printer, 1893.

90 p. port. 24ᶜᵐ.

Correspondence relating to the author's eligibility, as an acting assistant surgeon, to receive a Medal of Honor.

New York (*State*) *General agent for the relief of sick and wounded soldiers.*

Annual report.

Albany, 186

v. plates, plans. 23½ᶜᵐ.

Reports of the agents which the State of New York stationed around the country to assist wounded and furloughed New York soldiers.

New York (*State*) *Governor, 1863–1865 (Horatio Seymour)*

Communication from the governor, and report of the commission appointed by the President to determine and ascertain the quota of this state, under the different calls for troops. Transmitted to the Legislature March 1, 1864. Albany, Comstock & Cassidy, 1864.

cover-title, 18 p. 23ᶜᵐ.

An investigation of the unequal incidence of the draft of New York.

New York. Committee to recruit the Ninth army corps.

Report of Committee to recruit the Ninth army corps. February to August, 1864. Prepared by the secretary. New-York, J. W. Amerman, printer, 1866.

16 p. 23ᶜᵐ.

This committee collected and paid out bounty money and engaged in various recruiting activities.

New York (*State*) *Military board of state officers, 1861.*

... Communication from the governor transmitting the report of the Board of state officers named in the act of April 16, 1861, entitled, "An act to authorise the embodying and equipment of a volunteer militia and to provide for the public defence" ... January 9, 1862 ... [Albany, 1862]

214 p. 23ᶜᵐ. ([Legislature, 1862] Assembly [doc.] no. 15)

Minutes, correspondence, etc. relating to the organization and equipment of New York state forces in 1861.

New York medical association for the supply of lint, bandages, etc. to the United States army.

Final report of the New York medical association for the supply of lint, bandages, etc. to the United States army. Presented July 25th, 1861. New York, The Association, 1861.

cover-title, 32 p. 22¼ᶜᵐ.

Lists receipts and disbursements of clothing, bandages, etc.

Nichols, James Lynn.

Confederate engineers. [Limited ed.] Tuscaloosa, Ala., Confederate Pub. Co., 1957.

122 p. port. 21 cm. (Confederate centennial studies, no. 5)

A scholarly study of the Confederate Engineer Bureau, of engineer supplies and operations in coast and seige operations.

Nichols, James Lynn.

The Confederate quartermaster in the Trans-Mississippi, by James L. Nichols. Austin, University of Texas Press [1964]

vii, 126 p. illus. 24 cm.

Treats clothing, equipment, transportation, finance, and aspects of the Mexican trade.

North Carolina. *Confederate Centennial Commission.*

A guide to military organizations and installations, North Carolina, 1861–1865, compiled by Louis H. Manarin. [Raleigh, 1961]

1 v. 28 cm.

Designations of Confederate units and a list of North Carolina military installations.

Norton, Herman Albert.

Rebel religion; the story of Confederate chaplains. St. Louis, Bethany Press [1961]

144 p. illus. 23 cm.

A scholarly and readable account of the work of Confederate chaplains, with an alphabetical roster of chaplains.

O'Brien, John Emmet.

Telegraphing in battle; reminiscences of the civil war, by John Emmet O'Brien ... Scranton, Pa. [The Raeder press, Wilkes-barre, Pa.] 1910.

xi p., 2 l., 3–312 p. front., plates, ports., maps. 21½ᶜᵐ. $2.00

Some light is shed on military telegraph operations by the author's collection of short reminiscences from many who served with him.

Ohio. *Surgeon-general's office.*

Annual report.
Columbus, 18

v. 23½ᶜᵐ.

Primarily a medical treatise on diarrhea; includes a brief report on surgeons in Ohio regiments.

Ordronaux, John, 1830–1908.

Manual of instructions for military surgeons, on the examination of recruits and discharge of soldiers. With an appendix, containing the official regulations of the Provost-marshal general's bureau, and those for the formation of the invalid corps, etc., etc. Prepared at the request of the United States sanitary commission, by John Ordronaux ... New York, D. Van Nostrand; London, Trübner & co., 1863.

238 p. incl. front. 19^{cm}.

Descriptions of disqualifying and non-disqualifying infirmities.

Otis, George Alexander 1830–1881.

... Reports on the extent and nature of the materials available for the preparation of a medical and surgical history of the rebellion. Philadelphia, Printed for the Surgeon general's office by J. B. Lippincott & co., 1865.

1 p. l., 166 p. incl. illus., tables, diagrs. col. plates. 30½ x 25^{cm}. (Circular no. 6. War department, Surgeon general's office)

A survey of records available for an analysis of wounds, amputations, sickness, etc.

Pennsylvania. *Surgeon-general's office.*

Report of the surgeon general. [Harrisburg, 18

v. 24^{cm}.

Just as in similar reports for other states, this work consists primarily of lists of units and names of individuals, with casualty figures, etc. added.

Peterson, Harold Leslie, 1922–

Notes on ordnance of the American Civil War, 1861–1865. Drawings by Robert L. Miller. Washington, American Ordnance Association, 1959.

unpaged. illus. 26 cm.

An excellent brief listing with specifications and descriptive text.

Phisterer, Frederick, 1836–1909.

The communities of New York and the Civil War; the recruiting areas of the New York Civil War regiments. Compiled by C. E. Dornbusch from Phisterer's New York in the War of the Rebellion, 1861–1865. New York, New York Public Library, 1962.

31 p. 26 cm.

List of counties and communities, with names of units recruited from these areas.

Phisterer, Frederick, 1836–1909.

... Statistical record of the armies of the United States, by Frederick Phisterer ... New York, C. Scribner's sons, 1883.

viii, 343 p. 19 cm. (Campaigns of the civil war. Supplementary vol. [XIII])

A reference work containing lists of armies, corps, departments, engagements, and general officers.

Pinkerton, Allan, 1819–1884.

The spy of the rebellion; being a true history of the spy system of the United States Army during the late rebellion. Revealing many secrets of the war hitherto not made public. Comp. from official reports prepared for President Lincoln, General McClellan and the provost-marshal-general. By Allan Pinkerton ... New York, G. W. Carleton & co., 1883.

[ix]–xxxii, 33–688 p. illus., 24 pl. (incl. front.) 24 cm.

Pinkerton's account of his Secret Service Department under McClellan, with emphasis on incidents and the exploits of individual agents.

Pitts, Charles Frank.

Chaplains in Gray; the Confederate chaplains' story. Nashville, Broadman Press [1957]

166 p. 21 cm.

An account of the organization, activities, and influence of chaplains with detailed treatment of the work of some individual chaplains.

Plum, William Rattle.

The military telegraph during the civil war in the United States, with an exposition of ancient and modern means of communication, and of the federal and Confederate cipher systems; also a running account of the war between the states. By William R. Plum ... Chicago, Jansen, McClurg & co., 1882.

2 v. front., illus., port., maps, facsim. 23½^{cm}.

Stresses the role of the telegraph in each campaign; includes much information on operators, plus a section on cryptography.

Porcher, Francis Peyre, 1825–1895.

Resources of the southern fields and forests, medical, economical, and agricultural. Being also a medical botany of the Confederate states; with practical information on the useful properties of the trees, plants, and shrubs. By Francis Peyre Porcher ... Prepared and published by order of the surgeon-general, Richmond, Va. Richmond, West and Johnston, 1863.

xxv, 594 p. 23^{cm}.

A notable work on Southern plants and trees; tells where they are found and analyzes their medicinal and industrial use.

Rains, George Washington, 1817–1898.
History of the Confederate powder works, by Col. (General) Geo. W. Rains ... An address delivered by invitation before the Confederate survivors' association, at its fourth annual meeting, on Memorial day, April 26th, 1882. Augusta, Ga., Chronicle & constitutionalist print, 1882.

30 p. 22ᶜᵐ.

A good brief history of Confederate powder-making at Augusta, with strong emphasis on details of manufacturing and supply of raw materials.

Rhode Island. *Adjutant-general's office.*
... Report on the physical condition of the Rhode Island regiments, now in the field, in Virginia and in the vicinity of Washington, D. C., also on the condition of the hospitals in and around Washington: made to His Excellency Governor Sprague, and presented to the General assembly, of Rhode Island, January session, A. D. 1863, by Lloyd Morton ... commissioner. Providence, A. Anthony, printer to the state, 1863.

21 p. 26ᶜᵐ. (Public document. Appendix. no. 2)

A report on Rhode Island troops in Virginia in December, 1862, with emphasis on clothing, food, and medical attention.

Rolph, Gerald Vern, 1927–
The Civil War soldier, by G. V. Rolph and Noel Clark. Washington, Historical Impressions Co., 1961.

24 p. illus. 23 cm.

A short pamphlet illustrated with photographs explaining equipment, food, and clothing.

Shannon, Fred Albert, 1893–
The organization and administration of the Union army, 1861–1865, by Fred Albert Shannon ... Cleveland, The Arthur H. Clark company, 1928.

2 v. fronts. (port., v. 2) plates. 25 cm.

The standard work on the subject, though the author devoted more space to early demoralization than to later efficiency.

Simonhoff, Harry.
Jewish participants in the Civil War. New York, Arco Pub. Co. [1963]

336 p. illus. 21 cm.

Primarily devoted to biographical sketches of the more important Jewish participants.

Smaridge, Norah.
Hands of mercy; the story of sister-nurses in the Civil War. Illustrated by Albert Micale. New York, Benziger Bros. [1960]

180 p. illus. 22 cm. (A Banner book [13])

A light survey of the Catholic sisterhoods in the Civil War.

Smith, George Winston.
Medicines for the Union Army; the United States Army laboratories during the Civil War. Madison, Wis., American Institute of the History of Pharmacy, 1962.

119 p. illus. 25 cm.

Scholarly study of the Union army's medicine supply, with considerable emphasis on the manufacturing laboratories.

Speed, Thomas, 1841–1906.
Who fought the battle. Strength of the Union and Confederate forces compared. An address by Capt. Thos. Speed before the Army corps society of Louisville, Ky., January 26, 1904. [Louisville, Ky., Press of F. G. Nunemacher, 1904]

cover-title. 31 p. 23½ᶜᵐ.

A judicious comparison of the totals of Union and Confederate armies.

Statistical pocket manual of the army, navy, and census of the United States of America. Together with statistics of all foreign nations ... Boston, D. P. Butler [ᶜ1862]

2 v. 16ᶜᵐ.

Includes much miscellaneous information, such as pay rates and a list of general officers and their staffs.

Stern, Philip Van Doren, 1900–
Secret missions of the Civil War; first-hand accounts by men and women who risked their lives in underground activities for the North and the South, woven into a continuous narrative. Chicago, Rand McNally [1959]

320 p. illus. 22 cm.

A collection of original accounts of assorted Civil War incidents, many related to intelligence activities.

Summers, Festus Paul, 1895–

The Baltimore and Ohio in the civil war, by Festus P. Summers ... with 16 illustrations and 8 maps. New York, G. P. Putnam's sons [ᶜ1939]

xii p., 1 l., 15–304 p. illus. (maps) plates, 2 port. (incl. front.) 23ᶜᵐ.

A scholarly study of a strategic railroad in the war, with considerable attention to affairs in West Virginia.

Thompson, Samuel Bernard.

Confederate purchasing operations abroad, by Samuel Bernard Thompson. Chapel Hill, The University of North Carolina press, 1935.

ix, 137 p. 24 cm.

A detailed account of overall management, purchasing and financing; includes a special section on the Trans-Mississippi and Mexico.

Thruston, Gates Phillips, 1835–1912.

The number and rosters of the two armies in the civil war, by Gen. Gates P. Thruston of Nashville, Tenn. [Nashville, 1911?]

1 p. l., 13 p. 26ᶜᵐ.

A judicious discussion of the total of Union and Confederate soldiers.

Tucker, John, *of New York.*

Reply to the report of the Select committee of the Senate on transports for the War department. By John Tucker, (late assistant secretary of war) February 27, 1863. Philadelphia, Moss & co., 1863.

57 p. 22½ᶜᵐ.

A former Assistant Secretary of War's reply to allegations of overpayment and of other irregularities in connection with troop transports.

Turner, George Edgar.

Victory rode the rails; the strategic place of the railroads in the Civil War. Maps by George Richard Turner. [1st ed.] Indianapolis, Bobbs-Merrill [1953]

419 p. illus., ports., maps. 25 cm.

A capable study of the impact of Union and Confederate railroads on military operations, with emphasis on particular campaigns and theaters of operations.

U. S. *Adjutant-general's office.*

... Itinerary of the Army of the Potomac, and co-operating forces in the Gettysburg campaign, June 5–July 31, 1863; organization of the Army of the Potomac and Army of northern Virginia at the battle of Gettysburg; and return of casualties in the Union and Confederate forces. Comp. under the direction of Brigadier-General Richard C. Drum ... <3d ed.> Washington, Govt. print. off., 1888.

69 p. 25½ᶜᵐ.

Includes Union casualties by unit.

U. S. *Adjutant-general's office.*

List of synonyms of organizations in the volunteer service of the United States during the years 1861, '62, '63, '64, and '65. Comp. under the direction of Brigadier General Richard C. Drum, adjutant general United States army, by John T. Fallon ... Washington, Govt. print. off., 1885.

301 p. 23½ᶜᵐ.

An exhaustive list arranged alphabetically and by state.

U. S. *Adjutant-general's office.*

... Medals of honor awarded for distinguished service during the war of the rebellion. Comp. under the direction of Brigadier General Richard C. Drum, adjutant general U. S. Army, by Frederick H. Stafford ... Washington, 1886.

32 p. 23ᶜᵐ.

An alphabetical list of recipients with their unit, date, and place of action, and occasion for the award.

U. S. *Adjutant-general's office.*

Official Army register for 1861–[1865] ... Washington, Adjutant general's office, 1861–65.

7 v. fold. tables. 19½–21½ cm.

Lists of officers in regular army; especially useful for 1861.

U. S. *Adjutant-general's office.*

... Organization of the Army of the Cumberland, commanded by Major General W. S. Rosecrans, at the battle of Chickamauga, Ga., September 19–20, 1863, and return of casualties. Comp. under the direction of Brigadier General Richard C. Drum, adjutant general U. S. army. Washington, 1886.

25 p. 23½ᶜᵐ.

The table of organization for the battle of Chickamauga.

U. S. *Allotment commissioners for the state of New York.*

United States allotment system. Report to the President of the United States of the commissioners for the state of New York. Theodore Roosevelt, Wm. E. Dodge, jr., Theodore B. Bronson, commissioners. New York, G. F. Nesbitt & co., printers, 1862.

19, [3] p. 22ᶜᵐ.

A good brief explanation of the system of voluntary soldier pay allotments.

U. S. *Army.*

Military correspondence relating to the war of the rebellion. 1860–1865. Arranged in chronological order, in accordance with an act of Congress approved June 23, 1874, under the direction of the adjutant general of the army, by Mr. S. R. Davis ...
Washington, Adjutant general's printing office, 1875–

v. 24ᶜᵐ.

Most of the correspondence in the one volume published relates to 1861 army organization and administration.

U. S. *Army.*

Telegrams received by Major Gen. H. W. Halleck, while general-in-chief and chief of staff ... Washington, War department printing office, 1877.

5 v. in 6. 24ᶜᵐ.

Alphabetically arranged by sender.

U. S. *Army.*

Telegrams sent by Major Gen. H. W. Halleck, while general-in-chief and chief of staff. Washington, War department printing office, 1877.

4 v. 24ᶜᵐ.

Alphabetically arranged by recipient.

U. S. *Army. Corps of Engineers.*
Military maps. [Washington, 1879]

[25] plates (chiefly fold. maps, part col.) 78 cm.

Colored maps of Western battles and fortifications; dispositions are shown.

U. S. *Army. Corps of Engineers.*
Military maps of the United States. [Washington, 1883]

[36] maps (1 fold., part col.) 77 cm.

Maps of campaigns, showing routes and dispositions.

U. S. *Army. Corps of Engineers.*
Military maps illustrating the operations of the armies of the Potomac & James, May 4th 1864 to April 9th 1865, including battlefields of the Wilderness, Spottsylvania, Northanna [sic], Totopotomoy, Cold Harbor, the Siege of Petersburg and Richmond, battle-fields of Five Forks, Jetersville & Sailor's Creek, Highbridge, Farmville & Appomattox Court-house. [Washington] War Dept., Office of the Chief of Engineers, 1869.

[1] l., [16] maps (part fold., part col.) 61 cm.

Colored maps showing forts and battle areas.

U. S. *Army. Dept. of the Cumberland.*
General orders and circulars.
Louisville, Ky. [etc.]

v. in   20 cm.

General orders of the Department of the Cumberland during January-October, 1863. They shed light on administration and supply.

U. S. *Army. Dept. of North Carolina.*
General orders.
Raleigh [etc.]

v. 20 cm.

Largely composed of court martial orders, but provides data on administrative matters in Schofields' army in the last days of the war.

U. S. *Army. Dept. of the Ohio.*
General orders. Aug. 23, 1862–
[Knoxville, Tenn., etc.]

v. 20 cm.

Primarily concerns court martials.

U. S. *Coast and Geodetic Survey.*
Selected Civil War maps, reproduced from originals made by the U. S. Coast Survey, 1861–1865. [Washington, 1961]

20 plates (including illus., maps) 79 cm.

Maps of various cities, forts, and geographical regions; no dispositions are shown.

U. S. *Coast and geodetic survey.*
... Military and naval service of the United States Coast survey 1861–1865. Comp. from official records and pub. by the U. S. Coast and geodetic survey, E. Lester Jones, superintendent ... Washington, Govt. print. off., 1916.

72 p. 25ᶜᵐ. (Special publication no. 37)

Considerable correspondence and a brief account of the engineer service rendered by coast survey personnel.

U. S. *Military railroad dept.*
United States military railroads. Report of Bvt. Brig. Gen. D. C. McCallum, director and general manager, from 1861 to 1866. [Washington, 1866]

48 p. 20ᶜᵐ.

A short report by the Director General of the United States Military Railroads; summarizes equipment, operation, and construction activities.

U. S. *Military secretary's dept.*
... Memorandum relative to the general officers in the armies of the United States during the Civil war—1861–1865. (Compiled from official records) 1906 ... Washington, Govt. print. off., 1908.

cover-title, 73 p. 23ᶜᵐ. ([U. S.] 60th Cong., 1st sess. Senate. Doc. no. 245)

A list of general officers by rank with date of rank; includes an alphabetical index.

U. S. *Provost-marshal-general's bureau.*
Annual report of the provost marshal general. Washington, 1863–

v. 23ᶜᵐ.

A report of the operation of the draft organization and of rejection for physical reasons.

U. S. *Provost-marshal-general's bureau.*
Appendix to the provost marshal general's report. November 7, 1863. [Washington, 1863]

27 p. incl. tables. 23ᶜᵐ.

A report on the number of draftees rejected as physically unfit; includes comparative figures from European armies.

U. S. *Quartermaster's Dept.*
General orders. 1865–68. Washington.

4 v. in 3. 20 cm.

Assignments, instructions, and reorganization orders.

U. S. *Quartermaster's Dept.*
Letter of the Secretary of War in answer to a resolution of the Senate of the 30th day of January in relation to the vessels purchased or chartered for the use of the War Department since the 1st day of April last. [Washington, 1862]

15 p. 21 cm. (37th Cong., 2d sess. Senate. Ex[ecutive] doc[ument] no. 37)

A list of ships chartered and purchased from April 1, 1861, through January 30, 1862.

U. S. *Quartermaster's dept.*
Military commanders and designating flags of the United States army, 1861–1865. [Philadelphia, Burk & McFetridge, printers, 1888]

88 l. 89 col. pl. 39½ x 30ᶜᵐ.

Colored plates of flags designating the headquarters of armies, corps, divisions and brigades, and an alphabetical listing of commanders and their units.

U. S. *Quartermaster's dept.*
Roll of honor. Names of soldiers who died in defence of the American union, interred in the national cemeteries at Washington, D. C., from August 3, 1861, to June 30, 1865 ... Washington, Govt. print. off., 1865.

viii, [9]–294c (i. e. 194c) p. 22½ᶜᵐ.

Lists of Union soldiers, arranged by cemetery.

U. S. *Quartermaster's dept.*

Statement of the disposition of some of the bodies of deceased Union soldiers and prisoners of war whose remains have been removed to national cemeteries in the southern and western states ... Washington. Govt. print. off., 1868–69.

4 v. 22½cm. (Quartermaster general's office. General orders no. 8, 21, 33, 1868: no. 12, 1869)

Lists of original and final graves.

U. S. *Quartermaster's dept.*

Tabular statements showing the names of commanders of army corps, divisions and brigades, United States army, during the war of 1861 to 1865. Compiled from data on record in the office of the quartermaster-general of the army. 1887. Philadelphia, Burk & McFetridge, printers and lithographers [1887]

43 l. 48½ x 60½cm.

Included in the earlier work which reproduced flags.

U. S. *Record and pension office.*

... Missouri troops in service during the civil war. Letter from the secretary of war, in response to the Senate resolution passed on June 14, 1902, transmitting a paper prepared by the chief of Record and pension office of the War department, showing various classes of Missouri volunteers, militia, and home guards in service during the civil war, and the laws, etc., under which they were raised; also what classes of such are recognized by the War department as being in the military service of the United States and what classes are not so recognized. June 18, 1902.—Laid on the table and ordered to be printed. Washington, Govt. print. off., 1902.

335, [1] p. 23cm. (57th Cong., 1st sess. Senate. Doc. no. 412)

Contains much pertinent state, Federal, and Confederate correspondence concerning the mobilization and organization of Missouri troops on both sides.

U. S. *Surgeon-general's office.*

The medical and surgical history of the war of the rebellion. (1861–65). Prepared, in accordance with the acts of Congress, under the direction of Surgeon general Joseph K. Barnes, United States Army. Washington, Govt. print. off., 1870–88.

3 v. in 6. illus., plates (part col. and mounted) maps, diagrs. 29½ cm.

A compilation of elaborate statistics and numerous reports on various diseases and wounds.

U. S. *War Dept.*
Military railroads.
Washington [etc.]

v. 20 cm.

A collection of laws, general orders, instructions, and letters relative to military railroads.

United States Christian commission.

United States Christian commission, for the **army and navy.** Work and incidents. First[–fourth] annual report. Philadelphia, 1863–66.

4 v. in 1. illus., pl., map, tables (part fold.) 22½cm.

Covers the reports of branches, the finances of the commission, and such activities as numbers of packages shipped, Bible classes, reading matter, etc.

United States Christian commission. *Committee of Maryland.*

Report ... Baltimore, Printed by J. Robinson, 1862–66.

5 v. maps (part fold.) 22½cm. (v. 1: 18½cm.)

Details of the religious and philanthropic work of the commission in different parts of Maryland.

United States sanitary commission.

Documents of the U. S. sanitary commission. vol. I–[III] numbers 1–96. [1861–1866] New York [etc.] 1866–71.

3 v. 22½ cm. (v. 3: 23 cm.)

Includes a wide assortment of material: reports, instructions, histories of commission activities, etc.

United States sanitary commission.

Bulletin. vol. 1–3. numbers 1–40. [Nov. 1, 1863–Aug. 1, 1865] New York, 1866.

3 v. illus. 24".

The Sanitary Commission newspaper; contains news of the Commission's activities, as well as appeals for funds.

United States sanitary commission.

History of the United States sanitary commission, being the general report of its work during the war of the rebellion. By Charles J. Stillé. New York, Hurd and Houghton, 1868.

xviii, 17–553 p. 23½cm.

A comprehensive, chronological history with special attention to organization, finance, actuarial service, etc.

United States sanitary commission.

Military, medical and surgical essays prepared for the United States sanitary commission. 1862–1864. Washington, D. C., 1865.

[448] p. illus., plates. 22ᶜᵐ.

Monographs on vaccination, scurvy, amputations, camp sanitation, etc.

United States sanitary commission.

Minutes of the U. S. sanitary commission. [Washington? D. C., 1865?]

239 p. 23ᶜᵐ.

Minutes of the Commission's meetings - reports received, funds voted, committees appointed, etc.

United States sanitary commission.

The Sanitary commission of the United States army; a succinct narrative of its works and purposes. New York, Pub. for the benefit of the United States sanitary commission, 1864.

vi, [3]–318 p. incl. pl. 22½ᶜᵐ.

An explanation of the agency's origin, and a detailed report of its work-- with heavy emphasis on letters and summaries.

United States sanitary commission.

Surgical memoirs of the war of the rebellion. Collected and published by the United States sanitary commission. [New York, U. S. sanitary commission; Cambridge, Riverside press, 1870–71]

2 v. col. plates. 24ᶜᵐ.

A study of amputations, gangrene, etc.

Vandiver, Frank Everson, 1925–

Ploughshares into swords; Josiah Gorgas and Confederate ordnance. Austin, University of Texas Press, 1952.

xiv, 349 p. port. 24 cm.

This scholarly account of Gorgas' activities amounts to a complete history of Confederate ordnance.

Wasson, Robert Gordon, 1898–

The Hall carbine affair; a study in contemporary folklore. [Rev. ed.] New York, Pandick Press, 1948.

x, 190 p. illus., port., facsims. 24 cm.

A detailed analysis of the sale of the defective Hall Carbine to the U. S. Government and of J. P. Morgan's alleged role in the affair.

Weber, Thomas, 1916–

The Northern railroads in the Civil War, 1861–1865. New York, King's Crown Press, 1952.

318 p. 21 cm.

A careful, scholarly work emphasizing the impact of the war on the railroads.

Weist, Jacob R

"The medical department in the war." A paper read before the Ohio commandery of the Military order of the loyal legion of the United States, October 6, 1886. By Companion J. R. Weist ... Cincinnati, H. C. Sherick & co., 1886.

22 p. 23ᶜᵐ.

Brief discussion of the initial difficulties of the medical service in the field.

Willard, Sylvester David, 1825–1865.

Conservative surgery, with a list of the medical and surgical force of New York in the war of the rebellion, 1861–2. To which is added a brief notice of the hospitals at Fortress Monroe and White House, Virginia. By Sylvester D. Willard ... Albany, C. Van Benthuysen, printer, 1862.

41 p. 23ᶜᵐ.

A plea against an "eagerness to cut"; includes a copy of the examination for surgeons and an alphabetical list of New York surgeons.

Willard, Sylvester David, 1825–1865.

Regimental surgeons of the state of New York, in the war of the rebellion, 1861–3. By Sylvester D. Willard ... [Albany? 1863]

cover-title, 33 p. 23ᶜᵐ.

A list of New York regimental surgeons with some information about each, such as medical school attended and date of appointment.

Wormeley, Katharine Prescott 1830–1908.

The United States sanitary commission. A sketch of its purposes and its work. Compiled from documents and private papers. Published by permission. Boston, Little, Brown and co., 1863.

xiii, 299 p. 18½ᵐ.

A contemporary treatment of the Commission's origin and operation through the fall of 1863; emphasis is on work with the armies.

Wright, Edward Needles, 1897–

Conscientious objectors in the civil war, by Edward Needles Wright. Philadelphia, University of Pennsylvania press; London, H. Milford, Oxford university press, 1931.

vii, 274 p. illus. (facsims.) 23½ cm.

A complete study of the objectors, their motives, attitudes toward them, and their treatment.

MILITARY ASPECTS
Campaigns

Warren W. Hassler, Jr.

Abbot, Willis John, 1863–

Battle fields and camp fires. A narrative of the principal military operations of the civil war from the removal of McClellan to the accession of Grant. (1862–1863) By Willis J. Abbot ... Illustrated by W. C. Jackson. New York, Dodd, Mead & co. [ᶜ1890]

xii, 349 p. incl. front., illus., pl., maps. 23½ x 19½ᶜᵐ.

A popular, overwritten story of operations from the beginning of the Second Manassas campaign through Chattanooga and the bombardment of Fort Wagner.

Abbot, Willis John, 1863–

Battle-fields of '61; a narrative of the military operations of the war for the union up to the end of the Peninsular campaign, by Willis J. Abbot ... With illustrations by W. C. Jackson. New York, Dodd, Mead & co. [ᶜ1889]

xii, 356 p. incl. front., illus., pl., maps. 23½ x 19½ᶜᵐ.

An undocumented and at times inaccurate narrative of the war through Malvern Hill; written for popular consumption.

Allan, William, 1837–1889.

The Army of Northern Virginia in 1862, by William Allan ... with an introduction by John C. Ropes ... Boston and New York, Houghton Mifflin and co., 1892.

x, 537 p. front. (port.) fold. maps. 22½ cm.

An early, balanced, documented study in detail of the operations of Lee's army in the year 1862; by a former officer under Jackson.

Allan, William, 1837–1889.

Stonewall Jackson's campaign in the Shenandoah Valley of Virginia, from November 4, 1861, to June 17, 1862; by William Allan ... London, H. Rees, ltd., 1912.

xv, 284 p. 8 maps (1 in pocket) 22 cm. (*On cover:* The Pall Mall military series)

A persuasive, albeit at times over-enthusiastic, study of Jackson's Valley operations by the chief ordnance officer of the Confederate 2nd Corps.

21

Anderson, John H
American civil war, the operations in the eastern theatre from the commencement of hostilities to May 5, 1863, and in the Shenandoah valley from April 1861 to June 1862, by J. H. Anderson, F. R. HIST. SOC. ... London, H. Rees, ltd., 1910.

120 p. 14 fold. maps. 22ᶜᵐ.

A tersely written, generally accurate outline; designed for British officers for the promotions examination.

The **Annals** of the war written by leading participants north and south. Originally pub. in the Philadelphia weekly times. Philadelphia, The Times publishing company, 1879.

1 p. l., iv, ii p., 1 l., 17–800 p. illus. 23 cm.

A valuable collection of subjective articles written by such leading wartime commanders as Beauregard, J. E. Johnston, Longstreet, and Pleasonton.

Anthony, William, *ed.*
Anthony's History of the battle of Hanover (York county, Pennsylvania) Tuesday, June 30, 1863, compiled from writings of George R. Prowell and others by William Anthony, editor, printer and publisher. Hanover, Pa., 1945.

4 p. l., 160 p. incl. front., illus., pl., ports. 23½ᶜᵐ.

A rambling, ill-organized collection of vignettes pertaining to a cavalry engagement; valuable only for the articles of George R. Prowell.

Archer, W   P
History of the battle of Atlanta, also Confederate songs and poems. Knoxville, Ga., C. B. H. Moncrief [ᶜ1940]

35 p. incl. front. (port.) plates, port. 19½ᶜᵐ.

A brief, vividly written, popular series of sketches of the battle for Atlanta.

Ashby, Thomas Almond, 1848–1916.
The Valley campaigns, being the reminiscences of a non-combatant while between the lines in the Shenandoah valley during the war of the states, by Thomas A. Ashby ... New York, The Neale publishing company, 1914.

327 p. 21ᶜᵐ.

A personal, eyewitness account of Valley operations and their impact upon the countryside and its people.

Badeau, Adam, 1831–1895.
Military history of Ulysses S. Grant, from April, 1861, to April, 1865. By Adam Badeau ... New York, D. Appleton and company, 1885.

3 v. front. (port.) 22½ cm.

A detailed and overly sympathetic account of Grant's campaigns; written by his military secretary and aide.

Ballard, Colin Robert, 1868–1941.
The military genius of Abraham Lincoln; an essay, with a pref. by Fletcher Pratt. Photos. from the Meserve Collection. [1st American ed.] Cleveland, World Pub. Co. [1952]

viii, [10], 246 p. ports., maps. 22 cm.

A British brigadier's analysis and warm defense of Lincoln as a military strategist; undocumented, but with maps and illustrations.

Barnard, John Gross, 1815–1882.
The C. S. A. and the battle of Bull Run. (A letter to an English friend.) By J. G. Barnard ... New York, D. Van Nostrand; [etc., etc.] 1862.

2 p. l., [3]–136 p. fold. maps, fold. plans. 23ᶜᵐ.

An untrustworthy and pretentious revamping of published reports and accounts by a chief engineer of the Army of the Potomac.

Barnard, John Gross, 1815–1882.
The Peninsular campaign and its antecedents, as developed by the report of Maj.-Gen. Geo. B. McClellan, and other published documents. By J. G. Barnard ... New York, D. Van Nostrand, 1864.

96 p. 18½ᶜᵐ.

A distorted, anti-McClellan tract of little use.

Barrett, John Gilchrist.
Sherman's march through the Carolinas. Chapel Hill, University of North Carolina Press, 1956.

viii, 325 p. maps (on lining papers) 24 cm.

Bibliography: p. [282]–309.

A solidly researched and entertaining study of Sherman's operations following the capture of Savannah.

Bates, Samuel Penniman, 1827–1902.
 The battle of Chancellorsville. By Samuel P. Bates ... Meadville, Pa., E. T. Bates, 1882.
  261 p. incl. maps. front. (port.) 23½ cm.

An undocumented, discursive but not uninformed account of Hooker's May, 1863, meeting with Lee.

Bates, Samuel Penniman, 1827–1902.
 The battle of Gettysburg. By Samuel P. Bates ... Philadelphia, T. H. Davis & co., 1875.
  336 p. front., pl., ports., maps (1 fold.) plan. 23½ cm.

Although somewhat unreliable and turgidly written, this undocumented story of the Pennsylvania campaign nonetheless contains some information not readily found elsewhere.

Battine, Cecil William, 1867–
 The crisis of the confederacy; a history of Gettysburg and the Wilderness, by Cecil Battine ... London, New York [etc.] Longmans, Green, and co., 1905.
  xv, [1], 424 p. col. front., 6 fold. maps. 23½ cm.

An accurate, almost day-by-day narrative of Gettysburg and the Wilderness; by a British officer.

The **battle** of Chancellorsville and the Eleventh army corps. New York, G. B. Teubner, printer, 1863.
  48 p. 22½ cm.

While this is a rapidly argued defense of the Eleventh Corps and a condemnation of Howard, a number of telling points are made.

Baxter, William, 1820–1880.
 Pea Ridge and Prairie Grove; or, Scenes and incidents of the war in Arkansas. By William Baxter. Cincinnati, Poe & Hitchcock, 1864.
  262 p. 18 cm.

A delightful personal story of wartime activities in Arkansas.

Beauregard, Pierre Gustave Toutant, 1818–1893.
 A commentary on the campaign and battle of Manassas, of July 1861 ... with a summary of the art of war, by Gen. G. T. Beauregard. New York, London, G. P. Putnam's sons, 1891.
  xiv, 187 p. fold. maps. 20 cm.

Repetitious of Beauregard's earlier writings and purporting to answer several of J. E. Johnston's views; only partially convincing.

Beecham, Robert K 1838–
 Gettysburg, the pivotal battle of the civil war, by Captain R. K. Beecham ... with illustrations and map. Chicago, A. C. McClurg & co., 1911.
  5 p. l., 9–298 p. front., plates, ports., fold. map. 21½ cm.

An overly-lyrical, impressionistic story of the battle, by a former Federal officer who was a lieutenant at Gettysburg.

Bellah, James Warner, 1899–
 Soldiers' battle: Gettysburg. Pref. by Henry Graff. New York, D. McKay Co. [1962]
  204 p. illus. 22 cm.

A well-written but mediocre account of the battle, in which the author was highly selective about those events upon which he chose to elaborate.

Bigelow, John, 1854–1936.
 The campaign of Chancellorsville, a strategic and tactical study, by John Bigelow, jr. ... with maps and plans. New Haven, Yale university press; [etc., etc., ᶜ1910]
  xvi, 528 p. maps (part fold.) plans (1 fold.) 29¼ cm.

A masterful study -- one of the very finest ever written on an American campaign; thoroughly documented and notably impartial.

Bowen, John Joseph, b. 1839.
 The strategy of Robert E. Lee, by J. J. Bowen ... New York, The Neale publishing company, 1914.
  256 p. front., ports. 21 cm.

A poorly organized potpourri of quotations from official reports and other accounts of the major Confederate operations in the East.

Boykin, Edward Carrington, 1889–
    Beefsteak Raid.   New York, Funk & Wagnalls [1960]
    305 p. illus. 22 cm.

The September, 1864, provision raid by Confederate cavalryman Wade Hampton near Petersburg; undocumented and thin, but entertaining.

Boynton, Henry Van Ness, 1835–1905.
    Sherman's historical raid. The Memoirs in the light of the record. A review based upon compilations from the files of the War office. [By] H. V. Boynton ... Cincinnati, Wilstach, Baldwin & co., 1875.
    276 p. facsim. 22 cm.

A hard-hitting, sometimes convincing attack on Sherman, his Savannah campaign, and his memoirs.

Breihan, Carl W   1915–
    Quantrill and his Civil War guerrillas. Denver, Sage Books [1959]
    174 p. illus. 24 cm.

A short, popular but well-written narrative of Quantrill and his guerrilla activities; includes a valuable list of men who at one time or another served with Quantrill.

Britton, Wiley.
    The civil war on the border ... by Wiley Britton ... New York and London, G. P. Putnam's sons, 1890–99.
    2 v. front., illus. (plans) plates, port., maps (part fold.) 23½ cm.

A useful though confusingly written narrative of campaigns in Arkansas, Kansas, Missouri, and the Indian Territory; based upon official reports and personal observations.

Brown, Dee Alexander.
    Grierson's Raid. Urbana, University of Illinois Press, 1954.
    261 p. illus., ports., maps. 24 cm.

A thorough and interestingly written study of the 1863 raid through Mississippi to Baton Rouge; well illustrated, though needing more maps.

Brownlee, Richard S
    Gray ghosts of the Confederacy; guerrilla warfare in the West, 1861–1865.   Baton Rouge, Louisiana State University Press [1958]
    274 p. illus. 23 cm.

A competent, documented study of the military activities of the guerrillas west of the Mississippi; contains useful illustrations but an inadequate index.

Brunker, Howard Molyneux Edward, 1844–
    Story of the campaign in eastern Virginia, April, 1861 to May, 1863. Including "Stonewall Jackson's" operations in the valley ... By Lieut.-Colonel H. M. E. Brunker ... 2d ed. London, F. Groom & co., ltd., 1910.
    xxvii, 109 p. 13 fold. maps. 22½ᶜᵐ.

A generally accurate, outline-type description and analysis of the major operations in the East through Chancellorsville, by a British officer.

Buell, Don Carlos, 1818–1898.
    Statement of Major General Buell, in review of the evidence before the military commission, appointed by the War department in November, 1862. Campaign in Kentucky, Tennessee, northern Mississippi and north Alabama in 1861 and 1862. [n. p. 1863]
    cover-title, 71, [1] p. 23ᶜᵐ.

Though strongly stated, Buell's testimony adds up to a fairly convincing defense of a bulk of his operations.

Cannon, John.
    History of Grant's campaign for the capture of Richmond (1864–1865) ; with an outline of the previous course of the American civil war. By John Cannon. London, Longmans, Green and co., 1869.
    xi, 470 p. 19½ᶜᵐ.

An early narrative by a British officer; moderately successful as a modest, largely objective account of the war.

Catton, Bruce, 1899–
    The centennial history of the Civil War. E. B. Long, director of research. [1st ed.] Garden City, N. Y., Doubleday, 1961–
    v. col. maps, col. diagrs. 25 cm.

A well-balanced, entertainingly written general story of the war; good on evaluation of leaders, both civil and military, though weaker on non-military events.

Catton, Bruce, 1899--
    Grant moves south. With maps by Samuel H. Bryant. [1st ed.] Boston, Little, Brown [1960]
      x, 564 p. port., maps. 22 cm.

Based largely on the research of Lloyd Lewis, this is a well-written, generally accurate, pro-Grant narrative of that general's campaigns through Vicksburg.

Catton, Bruce, 1899–
    Mr. Lincoln's Army. Garden City, N. Y., Doubleday [1962]
      xiii, 363 p. maps. 22 cm. (*His* The Army of the Potomac, v. 1)

A popular, opinionated account of the Army of the Potomac under McClellan's command; colorful, but only lightly documented.

Catton, Bruce, 1899–
    Glory Road. Garden City, N. Y., Doubleday [1962, ᶜ1952]
      x, 389 p. maps. 22 cm. (*His* The Army of the Potomac, v. 2)

A well-written, popular narrative of the stresses on Union soldiers in the Fredericksburg, Chancellorsville, and Gettysburg campaigns.

Catton, Bruce, 1899–
    A stillness at Appomattox. Garden City, N. Y., Doubleday [1962, ᶜ1953]
      x, 438 p. 22 cm. (*His* The Army of the Potomac, v. 3)

Based largely on regimental histories, this is a simple yet vivid story of Grant and his men in the 1864-1865 operations against Lee.

Chesney, Charles Cornwallis, 1826–1876.
    Campaigns in Virginia, Maryland, etc., etc., by Capt. C. C. Chesney, R. E. ... 2d ed. rev. and enl. London, Smith, Elder and co., 1864–65.
      2 v. fold. front., maps (part fold.) 20½ cm.

A rather precise early account by a professor at the British Staff College.

Cist, Henry Martyn, 1839–1902.
    ... The Army of the Cumberland, by Henry M. Cist ... Subscription ed. New York, C. Scribner's sons [ᶜ1885]
      viii p., 1 l., 289 p. illus., 2 port. (incl. front.) fold. map. 20½ cm.

One of the weaker volumes in the Scribner's "Campaigns of the Civil War" series; this book treats operations in Kentucky and Tennessee in an unimaginative fashion.

Colton, Ray Charles, 1907–
    The Civil War in the western territories: Arizona, Colorado, New Mexico, and Utah. [1st ed.] Norman, University of Oklahoma Press [1959]
      ix, 230 p. illus., ports., maps. 24 cm.

A first-rate, documented introduction to wartime activities in the Southwest; includes information on the attitudes of the Indians in that region.

Confederate States of America. *War dept.*
    Southern history of the war. Official reports of battles, as published by order of the Confederate Congress at Richmond. New York, C. B. Richardson, 1863.
      578 p. front. (port.) 22½ᶜᵐ.

A convenient compilation of the official reports of Confederate officers, covering operations-- chiefly in the West-- of the first year of the war.

Connelley, William Elsey, 1855–1930.
    Quantrill and the border wars, by William Elsey Connelley ... Cedar Rapids, Ia., The Torch press, 1910.
      542 p. front., illus. (incl. ports., facsim.) fold. map, fold. plan. 24½ cm.

Strongly hostile to everything about Quantrill, the author has put together a badly organized but pungent story of the guerrillas.

Cox, Jacob Dolson, 1828–1900.
    ... Atlanta, by Jacob D. Cox ... New York, C. Scribner's sons, 1882.
      vii p., 1 l., 274 p. illus. (maps) 19 cm. (Campaigns of the civil war. IX)

A terse, adequate account -- in the Scribner's series -- of Sherman's campaign against the Georgia city; by a Union corps commander.

Cox, Jacob Dolson, 1828–1900.
   The battle of Franklin, Tennessee, November 30, 1864. A monograph, by Jacob D. Cox ... New York, C. Scribner's sons, 1897.

   x, [2], 351 p. 4 maps (2 fold.) 21ᵐ.

Informed and well organized, this is a generally convincing study of Schofield's successful delaying action against Hood.

Cox, Jacob Dolson, 1828–1900.
   ... The march to the sea; Franklin and Nashville, by Jacob D. Cox ... New York, C. Scribner's sons, 1882.

   ix p., 1 l., 265, [1] p. incl. maps. 19 cm. (Campaigns of the civil war. x)

A concise, balanced story of Sherman's actions after Atlanta, and Hood's sortie into Tennessee; possibly not sufficiently appreciative of General Thomas.

Crawford, Samuel Wylie, 1829–1892.
   The genesis of the civil war; the story of Sumter, 1860–1861, by Samuel Wylie Crawford ... New York, C. L. Webster & company, 1887.

   xxiv, 486 p. front. (8 port.) illus. (incl. plans, facsims.) double plan. 23½ cm.

The standard, thorough study of the fall of Fort Sumter, by a Federal eyewitness inside the fort.

Crist, Robert Grant.
   Confederate invasion of the West Shore—1863. A paper presented before the Cumberland County Historical Society and Hamilton Library Association on March 23, 1962. Lemoyne, Pa., Lemoyne Trust Co., 1963.

   44 p. illus., facsims. (incl. plans) fold. map. 24 cm.

A brief, well-illustrated, documented, and popular study of the farthest Confederate advance eastward in the Gettysburg campaign.

Cunningham, Edward, 1940–
   The Port Hudson campaign, 1862–1863. [Baton Rouge] Louisiana State University Press [1963]

   174 p. illus. 24 cm.

An able and well-researched monograph on Gen. N. P. Banks' 1863 campaign against the Confederate stronghold below Vicksburg.

Cunningham, Frank, 1911–
   General Stand Watie's Confederate Indians. San Antonio, Naylor Co. [1959]

   242 p. illus. 23 cm.

A popular, undocumented but interesting story of the use of Indians by the Confederates in the Southwest.

Davis, Burke.
   To Appomattox; nine April days, 1865. New York, Rhinehart [1959]

   433 p. illus. 24 cm.

A detailed, popularly written account of the final Appomattox campaign.

Deaderick, Barron, 1886–
   Strategy in the civil war, by Barron Deaderick ... Harrisburg, Pa., The Military service publishing company, 1946.

   6 p. l., 200 p. illus. (ports., maps, plans) 21½ cm.

A brief, thin, opinionated survey of the war's major campaigns, by an historian of the Sons of Confederate Veterans.

Deaderick, John Barron, 1886–
   The truth about Shiloh. [Memphis, Press of S. C. Toof, 1942]

   36 p. illus., maps. 16 cm.

This pamphlet is a popularly written, succinct, and generally accurate narrative of Shiloh.

Dodge, Grenville Mellen, 1831–1916.
   The battle of Atlanta and other campaigns, addresses, etc., by Major-General Grenville M. Dodge. Council Bluffs, Ia., The Monarch printing company, 1910.
   183 p. incl. front., illus., plates, ports. 23 cm.

A potpourri of articles and speeches by a Federal general and bridge builder.

Dodge, Theodore Ayrault, 1842–1909.

A bird's-eye view of our civil war, by Theodore Ayrault Dodge... Boston, J. R. Osgood and co., 1883.

xi, 346 p. illus., maps (part fold.) 23½ cm.

Succinctly written by a reputable military historian of the late 19th Century, this is a balanced narrative and good analysis of the operations in all theaters of the war.

Dodge, Theodore Ayrault, 1842–1909.

The campaign of Chancellorsville, by Theodore A. Dodge. Boston, J. R. Osgood and co., 1881.

vi p., 1 l., 261 p. fold. maps. 23ᶜᵐ.

A usually reliable, knowledgeable, general account of Hooker's disastrous campaign against Lee.

Doubleday, Abner, 1819–1893.

... Chancellorsville and Gettysburg, by Abner Doubleday ... New York, C. Scribner's sons, 1882.

xi p., 2 l., 243 p. incl. maps, diagrs. 19 cm. (Campaigns of the civil war. VI)

A participant in these two campaigns provided a chronicle of limited use, marred by some errors and by the author's hostility to O. O. Howard.

Doubleday, Abner, 1819–1893.

Reminiscences of forts Sumter and Moultrie in 1860–'61, by Abner Doubleday ... New York, Harper & brothers, 1876.

184 p. incl. front., map. 19½ᶜᵐ.

This charming story, by a then-captain of artillery inside the two forts, is a memoir of merit because of the aura of its immediacy and intimacy.

Dowdey, Clifford, 1904–

Death of a nation; the story of Lee and his men at Gettysburg. [1st ed.] New York, Knopf, 1958.

383 p. illus. 22 cm.

An undocumented, dynamically written, but at times thin and inaccurate story of Lee's defeat in Pennsylvania.

Dowdey, Clifford, 1904–

Lee's last campaign; the story of Lee and his men against Grant—1864. With maps by Samuel H. Bryant. [1st ed.] Boston, Little, Brown [1960]

415 p. illus. 22 cm.

A spirited though undocumented account of the Grant-Lee overland campaign of 1864.

Downey, Fairfax Davis, 1893–

Clash of cavalry; the Battle of Brandy Station, June 9, 1863. New York, D. McKay Co. [1959]

xv, 238 p. illus., ports., maps, music. 22 cm.

A colorful and unflaggingly interesting story of the Civil War's largest cavalry battle.

Downey, Fairfax Davis, 1893–

The guns at Gettysburg. New York, D. McKay [1958]

290 p. illus. 22 cm.

A popular but knowledgeable narrative of the Federal and Confederate artillery, and their commanders, in the battle which saw the war's heaviest artillery duel.

Downey, Fairfax Davis, 1893–

Storming of the gateway; Chattanooga, 1863. New York, D. McKay Co. [1960]

303 p. illus. 22 cm.

An interestingly written though hardly profound tale of operations around Chattanooga.

Drake, Samuel Adams, 1833–1905.

... The battle of Gettysburg, 1863; by Samuel Adams Drake ... Boston, Lee and Shepard, 1892 [1891]

178 p. incl. front. (port.) diagr. 17½ᶜᵐ. (Decisive events in American history)

Though brief and sketchy, this beautifully written little volume contains a number of perspicacious analyses and assessments.

Driscoll, Frederick.

The twelve days' campaign. By Frederick Driscoll. An impartial account of the final campaign of the late war. Montreal, Printed by M. Longmoore & co., 1866.

103 p. fold. map. 22^{cm}.

A series of brief dispatches, written by a British observer with the Army of the Potomac, treating of the Appomattox campaign.

Dudley, G   W

The lost account of the Battle of Corinth and court-martial of Gen. Van Dorn, by an unknown author. Introd. and informal essay on the battle by Monroe F. Cockrell. Jackson, Tenn., McCowat-Mercer Press, 1955.

78 p. Illus., ports., fold. map (in pocket) 25 cm.

A popular recital of the 1862 battle at Corinth and the ensuing court-martial of Confederate cavalryman Earl Van Dorn.

Dufour, Charles L

The night the war was lost. [1st ed.] Garden City, N. Y., Doubleday, 1960.

427 p. illus. 25 cm.

An able if somewhat overdrawn study of the struggle for control of the mouth of the Mississippi River and New Orleans.

Duke, Basil Wilson, 1838–1916.

The great Indiana-Ohio raid by Brig.-Gen. John Hunt Morgan and his men, July 1863; an authentic account of the most spectacular Confederate Cavalry raid into Union territory during the War Between the States ... the capture and subsequent escape of Brig.-Gen. Morgan, as seen and told by Basil W. Duke, Orlando B. Willcox, and Thomas H. Hines. With an introd. and commentary notes by Don D. John. Louisville, Ky., Priv. print., Book Nook Press [1955]

32 p. illus. 25 cm.

A short, popularly written pamphlet, comprising three eyewitness accounts by participants.

Du Pont, Henry Algernon, 1838–1926.

The campaign of 1864 in the valley of Virginia and the expedition to Lynchburg, by H. A. Du Pont ... New York, National Americana society, 1925.

5 p. l., 3–188 p. front. (port.) maps. 23½^{cm}.

Personal observations by a Federal artillery officer with strong opinions.

Dupuy, Richard Ernest, 1887–

The compact history of the Civil War [by] R. Ernest Dupuy [and] Trevor N. Dupuy. With battlefield maps designed by T. N. Dupuy and C. G. Dupuy. [1st ed.] New York, Hawthorn Books [1960]

445 p. illus. 24 cm.

Though generally accurate as to statements of fact, this book contains highly opinionated views of a number of Civil War commanders.

Early, Jubal Anderson, 1816–1894.

The campaigns of Gen. Robert E. Lee. An address by Lieut. General Jubal A. Early, before Washington and Lee university, January 19th, 1872. 2d rev. ed. Baltimore, J. Murphy & co.; New York, E. J. Hale & son, 1872.

47 p. 23^{cm}.

A gracefully written though forceful address, defending all of Lee's actions and assigning censure elsewhere for Confederate failures.

Early, Jubal Anderson, 1816–1894.

Jackson's campaign against Pope, in August, 1862. An address by Lieut. Gen'l Jubal A. Early before the first annual meeting of the Association of the Maryland line, together with the proceedings at the third annual banquet of the Society of the army and navy of the Confederate States, in the state of Maryland. [Baltimore, Foley bros. printers, 1883?]

52, 38 p. front., port. 23^{cm}.

A knowledgeable though opinionated speech covering the highlights of Jackson's August, 1862, operations.

Eisenschiml, Otto, 1880–

The celebrated case of Fitz John Porter; an American Dreyfus affair. Maps by Barbara Long. [1st ed.] Indianapolis, Bobbs-Merrill [1950]

344 p. illus., ports., maps. 23 cm.

A lightly documented, strongly argued, but on the whole convincing brief on behalf of Porter.

Eisenschiml, Otto, 1880–

The story of Shiloh. Pub. under the auspices of the Civil War Round Table and decorated by Joseph Trautwein. [Chicago, Norman Press, 1946]

89 p. plates, ports., maps. 24 cm.

A brief, highly opinionated account of Shiloh.

Emilio, Luis Fenollosa, 1844–

The assault on Fort Wagner, July 18, 1863. The memorable charge of the Fifty-fourth regiment of Massachusetts volunteers. Written for "The Springfield republican," by Captain Luis F. Emilio ... Boston, Rand Avery company, 1887.

16 p. 23½ᶜᵐ.

Vivid and thrillingly written, this eyewitness story is a bit overdone but nonetheless impelling.

Feuerlicht, Roberta Strauss.

Andrews' raiders. Illustrated by Angelo Torres. [1st ed.] New York, Collier Books [1963]

127 p. illus., maps. 18 cm. (A Collier books original)

A vivid though overwritten and thin story of the famous Chattanooga Railroad Expedition of 1862.

Fiebeger, Gustave Joseph, 1858–

Campaigns of the American civil war, by G. J. Fiebeger ... West Point, N. Y., United States military academy printing office, 1914.

iv, [1], 432 p. 23½ᶜᵐ. *and* atlas of 1 p. l., 7 numb. l., 46 maps. 17½ x 25½ᶜᵐ.

Although outlinish in form, and written without grace or color, this technical account by a West Point instructor is generally balanced and accurate.

Fisher, Horace Newton, 1837–1916.

"The Harris letter" outlining Bragg's plan of campaign for the invasion of Kentucky in 1862. [Dedham? Mass.] ᶜ1953.

[1] l., facsim.: 3–15 l. 29 cm.

A short letter giving the major features of Bragg's and Buell's campaign plans for 1862 operations in Kentucky.

Fiske, John, 1842-1901.

The Mississippi valley in the civil war, by John Fiske ... Boston and New York, Houghton, Mifflin and company, 1900.

xxv, 368 p. front., maps, plans. 20 cm.

A sweeping narrative of the war in the West, by one of America's most widely read popular historians of the late 19th Century.

Fitch, Michael Hendrick, 1837–

... The Chattanooga campaign, with especial reference to Wisconsin's participation therein, by Michael Hendrik Fitch ... [Madison] Wisconsin history commission, 1911.

xiii, 255 p. 6 maps (incl. front.) 23½ cm. (Wisconsin history commission : Original papers, no. 4)

Gracelessly written and only lightly documented; nevertheless, a useful account of the battle of Chattanooga.

Force, Manning Ferguson, 1824–1899.

... From Fort Henry to Corinth, by M. F. Force ... New York, C. Scribner's sons, 1881.

vii p., 2 l., 204 p. incl. maps. 19 cm. (Campaigns of the civil war. II)

An unadorned, businesslike chronicle written by the Federal commander of the 1st Division, XVII Corps.

Formby, John.

The American civil war, a concise history of its causes, progress, and results, by John Formby ... New York, Charles Scribner's sons, 1910.

xiii p., 1 l., [xv]–xvii, 520 p. *and* atlas of 2 pl., 66 maps on 50 fold. pl. 22½ cm.

Although cursorily covering the pre- and post-war events, this book is chiefly an accurate study of the military campaigns in all theaters.

Foster, Eli Greenawalt.

The civil war by campaigns, by Eli G. Foster ... Topeka, Kan., Crane & company, 1899.

286 p. illus. (plans) double maps. 19½ᶜᵐ.

An undocumented, turgidly written account of the major operations of the war; of limited merit.

Fout, Frederick W

The dark days of the Civil War, 1861 to 1865 : The West Virginia Campaign of 1861. The Antietam and Harper's Ferry Campaign of 1862. The East Tennessee Campaign of 1863. The Atlanta Campaign of 1864. [St. Louis] Printed by F. A. Wagenfuehr, 1904.

422 p. plates, ports., maps. 25 cm.

A sketchy, but not often inaccurate narrative by an Indiana officer.

Franklin, Robert M
   Battle of Galveston, January 1st, 1863, by Robert M. Franklin. ₍Galveston, Tex., The Galveston news, 1911₎
   cover-title, 2–11 p. port. 24ᶜᵐ.

A terse personal account by a Confederate "Horse-marine" of the Southern attack on Federal troops and ships at Galveston.

Freeman, Douglas Southall, 1886–
   Lee's lieutenants, a study in command, by Douglas Southall Freeman ... New York, C. Scribner's sons ₍1946₎
   4 v. illus. (incl. ports.) maps (part fold.) 24 cm.

The ablest descriptive and evaluative study of the leading generals (and their campaigns) in Lee's army; massively documented, movingly written, highly authoritative, and faintly smug.

French, Samuel Livingston.
   The Army of the Potomac from 1861 to 1863: an inside view of the history of the Army of the Potomac and its leaders as told in the official dispatches, reports and secret correspondence; from the date of its organization under General George B. McClellan in 1861, until the supersedure of General Hooker, and the assignment of General Meade to its command in 1863. By Samuel Livingston French. ₍New York₎ Publishing society of New York, 1906.
   1 p. l., 17–375 p. illus. (map) 7 port. (incl. front.) 23½ᶜᵐ.

A strongly biased tract, amounting almost to a diatribe; the author is as violently hostile to McClellan as he is friendly to Burnside and Hooker.

Fry, James Barnet, 1827–1894.
   Operations of the army under Buell from June 10th to October 30th, 1862, and the "Buell commission." By James B. Fry ... New York, D. Van Nostrand, 1884.
   201 p. front. (port.) fold. map. 18½ cm.

An able, succinct account of Buell's major operations; sympathetic to Buell.

Gard, Ronald Max, 1913–
   Morgan's Raid into Ohio. Lisbon, Ohio, 1963.
   62 p. illus. 24 cm.

A thin, surface account of Morgan's raid; lacks documentation, bibliography, and index.

Geer, Walter, 1857–
   Campaigns of the civil war, by Walter Geer ... illustrated with thirty-three maps. New York, Brentano's, 1926.
   xxii, 490 p. front., maps (part fold.) 24ᶜᵐ.

While not highly original, this account of the major operations of the war is assessive, well-organized, and generally reliable.

Gibson, John Mendinghall.
   Those 163 days; a southern account of Sherman's March from Atlanta to Raleigh. New York, Coward-McCann ₍1961₎
   317 p. illus. 22 cm.

A readable narrative of Sherman's operations from Atlanta to the end of the war; by a Southerner still somewhat hostile to the Federal general.

Gillmore, Quincy Adams, 1825–1888.
   Engineer and artillery operations against the defences of Charleston harbor in 1863; with a supplement. By Q. A. Gillmore ... Illustrated by eighty-three plates and views. New York, D. Van Nostrand, 1868.
   viii, 7–314, 172 p. col. front., plates (part col.) fold. maps, fold. plans. 24 cm. (Professional papers, Corps of engineers, no. 16)

A professionally detailed and technical collection of accounts of unsuccessful efforts to recapture Fort Sumter.

Glazier, Willard, 1841–1905.
   Battles for the union: comprising descriptions of many of the most stubbornly contested battles in the war of the great rebellion, together with incidents and reminiscences of the camp, the march and the skirmish line ... By Captain Willard Glazier ... Hartford, Conn., Gilman & company, 1878.
   xix, ₍1₎, 21–417 p. front. (port.) 8 pl. 19¼ᶜᵐ.

An unbalanced and oftentimes personal story of selected actions of the war.

Gordon, George Henry, 1825?–1886.
   History of the campaign of the Army of Virginia, under John Pope ... from Cedar mountain to Alexandria, 1862. By George H. Gordon ... Boston, Houghton, Osgood and company, 1880 ₍1879₎
   xiv, 498 p. fold. maps. 23½ cm.

A useful, but opinionated account of the Second Manassas campaign, by a Federal brigade commander; marred somewhat by the author's hostility to Pope.

Gough, John Edmond, 1871–

Fredericksburg and Chancellorsville, a study of the federal operations, by Colonel J. E. Gough ... With an introduction by Brig.-General H. H. Wilson ... London, H. Rees, ltd., 1913.

xvi, 285 p. 17 fold. maps (1 in pocket) diagr. 22cm. (The Pall Mall military series)

A terse and mediocre study of the operations conducted by Burnside and Hooker; for pre-World War I British Army officers.

Gracie, Archibald, 1858–1912.

The truth about Chickamauga, by Archibald Gracie ... Boston and New York, Houghton Mifflin company, 1911.

xxxii p., 2 l., 462 p., 1 l. front., plates, ports., maps (part fold.) plans. 24m.

A rather elaborate, informed but opinionated story of Chickamauga; includes useful maps.

Greene, Francis Vinton, 1850–1921.

... The Mississippi, by Francis Vinton Greene ... New York, C. Scribner's sons, 1882.

ix p., 1 l., 276 p. front., fold. maps. 19 cm. (Campaigns of the civil war. VIII)

One of the best written, most analytical, and thorough volumes in the Scribner's "Campaigns" series.

Hall, Granville Davisson.

Lee's invasion of northwest Virginia in 1861, by Granville Davisson Hall ... [Chicago, Press of the Mayer & Miller company] 1911.

3 p. l., 9–164 p. 20cm.

An awkward assemblage of letters and reports by participants; unsympathetic toward Lee.

Hall, Martin Hardwick.

Sibley's New Mexico campaign. Austin, University of Texas Press [1960]

xv, 366 p. illus., ports., maps, facsims. 24 cm.

Lightly documented but a detailed and thoughtfully written study of Sibley's invasion and Canby's defense of the New Mexico Territory.

Hamlin, Augustus Choate, 1829–1905.

... The battle of Chancellorsville; the attack of Stonewall Jackson and his army upon the right flank of the Army of the Potomac at Chancellorsville, Virginia, on Saturday afternoon, May 2, 1863. By Augustus Choate Hamlin ... Bangor, Me., The author, 1896.

viii, [5]–196 p. 9 maps (2 double) 22cm.

A detailed study of Jackson's flanking movement; the author defends Howard's XI Corps.

Hanover, Pa. Chamber of Commerce. *Historical Publication Committee.*

Encounter at Hanover: prelude to Gettysburg; story of the invasion of Pennsylvania culminating in the Battles of Hanover and Gettysburg, June and July, 1863; with a bicentennial view of the town founded by Colonel Richard McAllister in 1763. [Hanover] 1963 [c1962]

274 p. illus. 24 cm.

An ill-organized, rambling but somewhat useful collection of information regarding the cavalry at Hanover, Pa.

Hanson, Joseph Mills, 1876–

Bull Run remembers ... The history, traditions, and landmarks of the Manassas (Bull Run) campaigns before Washington, 1861–1862. [Prepublication subscribers ed.] Manassas, Va., National Capitol Publishers, 1953.

ix, 194 p. illus., maps. 23 cm.

Though intimate and informed, this is a poorly organized potpourri of essays by the late superintendent of the Manassas battlefield.

Haskell, Franklin Aretas, 1828–1864.

The battle of Gettysburg.

(*In* Dartmouth college. Class of 1854. A history of the class of 1854. Boston, 1898. 24cm. p. [69]–131)

One of the classic eyewitness accounts in all military annals; by a Federal officer at the storm center of Gettysburg.

Haskell, Franklin Aretas, 1828–1864.

The Battle of Gettysburg. Edited by Bruce Catton. Boston, Houghton Mifflin, 1958.

xviii, 169 p. maps. 22 cm.

A reissue of the preceding title; rendered less useful by the deletions of the editor.

Hassler, Warren W
    Commanders of the Army of the Potomac. Baton Rouge,
Louisiana State University Press [1962]
        281 p. illus. 24 cm.

A documented study of the Federal army commanders in the East, their campaigns, and their
relations with Washington authorities.

Hay, Thomas Robson.
    Hood's Tennessee campaign, by Thomas Robson Hay ...
New York, W. Neale, 1929.
        xv, [1], 17-272 p. maps (2 fold., incl. front.) 24^{cm}.

A thoroughly researched though unimaginatively
written monograph on Hood's 1864 counter-thrust
into Tennessee.

Henderson, George Francis Robert, 1854-1903.
    ... The campaign in the Wilderness of Virginia. Lec-
ture delivered by Lieut.-Col. G. F. R. Henderson, January 24th, 1894. 2d ed. London, H. Rees, ltd., 1908.
        40 p. 4 fold. maps. 18½^{cm}.

A brief, incisive evaluation of the Lee-Grant
confrontation in 1864.

Henderson, George Francis Robert, 1854-1903.
    The campaign of Fredericksburg, Nov.-Dec., 1862. A
tactical study for officers. By Brevet-Major G. F. R. Henderson ... 3d ed., with coloured maps. London, Chatham, Gale
& Polden [1891]
        xviii p., 1 l., 145 p. 2 pl., 4 maps (part fold.) 18½^{cm}. (*On cover:* Gale
and Polden's military series)

A study of merit regarding Lee's 1862 operations
against Burnside; designed primarily for British
army officers of the last century.

Heysinger, Isaac Winter, 1842-1917.
    Antietam and the Maryland and Virginia campaigns of
1862 from the government records—Union and Confederate—
mostly unknown and which have now first disclosed the truth;
approved by the War department, by Captain Isaac W. Heysinger ... New York, The Neale publishing company, 1912.
        322 p. 19^{cm}.

Rambling, highly opinionated, and undocumented;
strongly pro-McClellan and anti-Stanton.

Hinton, Richard Josiah, 1830-1901.
    Rebel invasion of Missouri and Kansas, and the cam-
paign of the army of the border against General Sterling
Price, in October and November, 1864. By Richard J.
Hinton ... 2d ed. Chicago, Church & Goodman; Leavenworth, Kan., F. W. Marshall, 1865.
        2 p. l., ii, [3]-351 p. incl. maps. front., port. 22½^{cm}.

A personal narrative, by an officer of a Kansas
colored unit; emphasizes the service of Kansas
militiamen.

Hoehling, Adolph A
    Last train from Atlanta. New York, T. Yoseloff [1958]
        558 p. illus., ports., map, facsims. 24 cm.

A popular, detailed, and readable story of the
Atlanta campaign, and especially of the impact
of the siege and fighting upon the people.

Hoke, Jacob, 1825-1893.
    The great invasion of 1863; or, General Lee in Pennsyl-
vania. Embracing an account of the strength and organization of the armies of the Potomac and northern Virginia;
their daily marches with the routes of travel, and general
orders issued; the three days of battle; the retreat of the
Confederates and pursuit by the Federals; analytical index,
... with an appendix containing an account of the burning of
Chambersburg, Pennsylvania, a statement of the General
Sickles controversy, and other valuable historic papers. By
Jacob Hoke. Dayton, O., W. J. Shuey, 1887.
        xxxi, [33]-613 p. front., illus., port., fold. plan. 22¼ cm.

While somewhat rambling, this assessment of
the Gettysburg campaign by a civilian contains
useful information.

Holcombe, Return Ira, 1845-1916.
    An account of the Battle of Wilson's Creek, by Holcombe
and Adams. Centennial ed. Springfield, Mo., Springfield
Public Library, 1961.
        111 p. illus. 23 cm.

While brief and overwritten, this popular chronicle of Lyon's defeat in Missouri does contain
pertinent data on Wilson's Creek.

Holmes, Prescott.
    The battles of the war for the union, being the story
of the great civil war from the election of Abraham Lincoln to the surrender at Appomatox. By Prescott Holmes
... Philadelphia, H. Altemus [c1897]
        338 p. incl. front., illus., port. 20^{cm}.

This turgidly written narrative of the principal
military operations of the war is sparing of in-
tense value judgements.

Horn, Stanley Fitzgerald, 1889–
    The Army of Tennessee. Norman, University of Oklahoma Press [1953, °1941]

    503 p. illus., ports., maps, facsims. 25 cm.

    Bibliography: p. 483–487.

A well-written, documented, standard history of the main Confederate army in the Western theater.

Horn, Stanley Fitzgerald, 1889–
    The decisive battle of Nashville. Baton Rouge, Louisiana State University Press [°1956]

    181 p. illus. 21 cm.

A thorough study of Hood's ill-fated campaign, but marred by the author's unconvincing overstatements regarding the decisiveness of the battle in relation to the war as a whole.

Hull, Augustus Longstreet.
    The campaigns of the Confederate army, by Augustus Longstreet Hull ... Atlanta, Ga., Foote & Davies co., 1901.

    107 p. pl., 2 maps (1 fold.) 19½ cm.

Originally prepared as lectures by the secretary of the University of Georgia, these mediocre essays report the major Confederate military operations of the war.

Humphrey, Willis C
    The great contest: a history of military and naval operations during the civil war in the United States of America, 1861–1865. By Willis C. Humphrey ... Detroit, C. H. Smith & co., 1886.

    xii, 13–691 p. 3 port. (incl. front.) map. 24 cm.

A popularly written, unexciting survey of the chief operations of the war.

Humphreys, Andrew Atkinson, 1810–1883.
    ... The Virginia campaign of '64 and '65; the Army of the Potomac and the Army of the James, by Andrew A. Humphreys ... New York, C. Scribner's sons, 1883.

    x p., 1 l., 451 p. fold. maps. 19 cm. (Campaigns of the civil war. XII)

Though dull and gracelessly written, this is one of the best and most accurate surveys of the Lee-Grant operations in Virginia.

Humphreys, Andrew Atkinson, 1810–1883.
    From Gettysburg to the Rapidan. The Army of the Potomac, July, 1863, to April, 1864. By Andrew A. Humphreys ... New York, C. Scribner's sons, 1883.

    viii, 86 p. 3 fold. maps. 19 cm.

A brief, authoritative description of the maneuvering and skirmishes of the armies of Meade and Lee.

Hunt, Aurora.
    The army of the Pacific; its operations in California, Texas, Arizona, New Mexico, Utah, Nevada, Oregon, Washington, Plains Region, Mexico, etc., 1860–1866. Glendale, Calif., A. H. Clark Co., 1951 [°1950]

    455 p. 17 plates (incl. ports.) fold. map. 25 cm.

A thin, lightly documented, overly long story of Civil War activities from the Mississippi to the Pacific.

Jenkins, Paul Burrill, 1872–
    The battle of Westport, by Paul B. Jenkins ... Kansas City, Mo., F. Hudson publishing co., 1906.

    193 p. incl. front., plates, ports., maps. 20½ cm.

A mediocre though not uninformed story of Price's Confederate 1864 raid into Missouri.

Johnson, John, 1829–1907.
    The defense of Charleston harbor, including Fort Sumter and the adjacent islands. 1863–1865. By John Johnson ... With original papers in appendix, full official reports, maps, and illustrations. Charleston, S. C., Walker, Evans & Cogswell co., 1890.

    276, clxxxvi p. illus., plates (part fold.) ports., maps (part fold.) plans (part fold.) 24 cm.

A meritorious collection of data, with useful documents and maps.

Johnson, Ludwell H
    Red River campaign; politics and cotton in the Civil War. Baltimore, Johns Hopkins Press [1958]

    317 p. illus. 22 cm.

Wide and thorough research, good organization, and suspenseful writing make this study of Banks' peripheral campaign of 1864 the best available.

Johnson, Rossiter, 1840–1931.
   The fight for the republic; a narrative of the more note-worthy events in the war of secession, presenting the great contest in its dramatic aspects, by Rossiter Johnson; with maps and battle plans ... New York and London, G. G. Putnam's sons, 1917.

   xii p., 1 l., 404 p. front., plates, ports., maps (part fold.) plans (part fold.) 23½ cm.

A mediocre story of the major events of the war, rendered less useful by some over-writing and distortions.

Johnston, Robert Matteson, 1867–1920.
   Bull Run; its strategy and tactics, by R. M. Johnston ... Boston and New York, Houghton Mifflin company, 1913.

   xiv p., 1 l., 293, [1] p. fold. maps. 22½ cm. $2.50

A generally accurate and objective analysis of the preliminary plans, the conduct of the campaign and battle, and their results.

Jones, Archer, 1916–
   Confederate strategy from Shiloh to Vicksburg. Baton Rouge, Louisiana State University Press [1961]

   xxi, 258 p. 3 maps. 23 cm.

A good overall analysis and evaluation of the evolution of Confederate grand strategy from early 1862 through mid-1863.

Jones, Samuel, 1819–1887.
   The siege of Charleston and the operations on the south Atlantic coast in the war among the states, by Samuel Jones ... New York, The Neale publishing company, 1911.

   295 p. front. (port.) 21 cm.

This study contains information of value regarding Federal amphibious operations against the Confederacy's Atlantic littoral.

Jones, Virgil Carrington, 1906–
   Eight hours before Richmond. Introd. by Robert Selph Henry. Illustrated with photos. [1st ed.] New York, Holt [1957]

   180 p. illus. 22 cm.

A popularly written, somewhat thin but readable story of the Kilpatrick-Dahlgren Raid.

Jones, Virgil Carrington, 1906–
   Gray ghosts and Rebel raiders; with an introd. by Bruce Catton. [1st ed.] New York, Holt [1956]

   431 p. illus. 22 cm.

A detailed, interestingly written, documented study of guerrilla warfare in Virginia.

Jordan, Thomas, 1819–1895.
   The campaigns of Lieut.-Gen. N. B. Forrest, and of Forrest's cavalry ... By General Thomas Jordan and J. P. Pryor. New Orleans, New-York [etc.] Blelock & company, 1868.

   xv p., 1 l., [17]–704 p. incl. front., illus., plates, ports., fold. maps. 22 cm.

An early, detailed account of Forrest's operations; written by strongly sympathetic admirers.

Kearsey, Alexander Horace Cyril, 1877–
   A study of the strategy and tactics of the Shenandoah valley campaign, 1861–1862, with six maps. Illustrating the principles of war, battles described. By A. Kearsey ... Aldershot, London [etc.] Gale & Polden, ltd. [1930]

   3 p. l., 70 p. 6 fold. maps. 22 cm.

A useful but not profound survey of Jackson's Valley operations.

Keller, Allan.
   Morgan's Raid. Indianapolis, Bobbs-Merrill [1961]
   272 p. illus. 24 cm.

A thin but colorfully written narrative of the 1863 raid into Ohio by John Hunt Morgan.

Kellogg, Sanford Cobb, 1842–
   The Shenandoah valley and Virginia, 1861 to 1865; a war study, by Sanford C. Kellogg, u. s. a. New York & Washington, The Neale publishing company [1903]

   247 p. 20½ cm.

Although brief and undocumented, this is a useful outline of the major campaigns in the Valley of Virginia.

Kerby, Robert Lee.
   The Confederate invasion of New Mexico and Arizona, 1861–1862. Los Angeles, Westernlore Press, 1958.

   159 p. illus., ports., maps, facsims. 21 cm. (Westernlore Great West and Indian series, **13**)

A well documented though unnecessarily dull study of the Sibley invasion of New Mexico.

Key, William, *d.* 1958.
   The Battle of Atlanta and the Georgia campaign. New York, Twayne Publishers [1958]

   92 p. illus. 24 cm.

An uncritical narrative of the 1864 Union and Confederate operations in Georgia.

Kniffin, Gilbert Crawford, 1832–1917.
   ... Army of the Cumberland and the battle of Stone's River. Prepared by Companion Lieutenant-Colonel Gilbert C. Kniffin ... and read at the stated meeting of April 3, 1907. [Washington, 1907]

   24 p. 23ᶜᵐ. (Military order of the loyal legion of the United States. Commandery of the District of Columbia. War papers. **68**)

This short essay is well-written and has an air of immediacy about it.

Kniffin, Gilbert Crawford, 1832–1917.
   ... The Army of the Cumberland at Missionary Ridge. Prepared by Companion Lieutenant-Colonel Gilbert C. Kniffin ... and read at the stated meeting of December 5, 1900. [Washington, 1900]

   28 p. 23ᶜᵐ. (Military order of the loyal legion of the United States. Commandery of the District of Columbia. War papers. **37**)

Though undocumented, this essay is dynamically written and is, on the whole, an accurate narrative.

Kremer, W[esley] P[otter] 1841–
   100 great battles of the rebellion; a detailed account of regiments and batteries engaged — casualties, killed, wounded and missing, and the number of men in action in each regiment; also, all the battles of the revolution, war of 1812–5, Mexican war, Indian battles, American-Spanish war, and naval battles. State rosters from the several northern states, giving the enrollment, number killed, wounded, died and deserted from each organization during the war, by W. P. Kremer. Hoboken, N. J., 1906.

   366 p. illus. 18ᶜᵐ.

A convenient compilation of numbers and losses suffered in many battles; taken chiefly from the <u>Official Records</u> and adjutant general reports.

Lewis, Oscar, 1893–
   The war in the Far West: 1861–1865. [1st ed.] Garden City, N. Y., Doubleday, 1961.

   263 p. 22 cm.

An entertaining though rambling story of the Civil War in the West.

Lloyd's battle history of the great rebellion, complete, from the capture of Fort Sumter, April 14, 1861, to the capture of Jefferson Davis, May 10, 1865, embracing General Howard's tribute to the volunteer ... and a general review of the war for the union. New York, H. H. Lloyd & co.; Boston, B. B. Russell & co.; [etc., etc.] 1865.

   1 p. l., viii, [3]–566 p. front., plates, ports., maps (part fold.) 24ᶜᵐ.

An early, turgidly written but calm survey of the principal operations of the war.

Longstreet, Helen (Dortch)
   Lee and Longstreet at high tide; Gettysburg in the light of the official records, by Helen D. Longstreet. Gainesville, Ga., The author, 1904.

   346 p. front., plates, ports., facsims. 25 cm.

Although painfully defensive in tone, this justification of Longstreet's conduct at Gettysburg is, in most respects, convincing, though at times overdrawn.

Lytle, Andrew Nelson, 1902–
   Bedford Forrest and his critter company. Rev. ed. with an introd. by the author. New York, McDowell, Obolensky [1960]

   402 p. illus. 24 cm.

In the main, a fairly accurate narrative with an air of immediacy about it.

McCann, Thomas H
   The campaigns of the civil war in the United States of America, 1861–1865, by Thomas H. M'Cann ... [Hoboken, N. J., Hudson observer, 1915]

   223, 9 p. illus. (ports.) 24ᶜᵐ.

A terse outline account of the major operations of the war.

McClellan, Carswell, 1835–1892.
The Personal memoirs and Military history of U. S. Grant versus the record of the Army of the Potomac; by Carswell McClellan ... Boston and New York, Houghton, Mifflin and company, 1887.

3 p. l., 278 p. fold. maps. 20½ cm.

An incisive account of Grant's command in the East in 1864-1865; sharply critical of Grant.

McClellan, George Brinton, 1826–1885.
The complete report on the organization and campaigns of the Army of the Potomac, by George B. McClellan, major-general United States army, with his last revision. [n. p., 1864?] cover-title. 142 p. 23½ cm.

Essential to any student of McClellan's campaigns; rich in documents and data, but defensive in tone.

McCormick, Robert Rutherford, 1880–
The war without Grant. Cartography by Axel Kellstrom. New York, B. Wheelwright, 1950.

245 p. fold. col. maps. 24 cm.

A disjointed, rambling account of the campaigns in which Grant did not participate; further marred by excessive value judgements.

McDowell, Irvin, 1818–1885.
Statement of Major Gen. Irvin McDowell, in review of the evidence before the court of inquiry, instituted at his request in special orders, no. 353, headquarters of the army. Washington, Printed by L. Towers & co., 1863.

cover-title, 64 p. 23 cm.

Gen. McDowell's vigorous, generally effective though not always convincing defense against charges brought against him.

McElroy, John, 1846–1929.
The struggle for Missouri, by John McElroy ... Washington, D. C., The National tribune co., 1909.

3 p. l., ix, 3–342 p. col. front., illus., col. pl., ports., maps. 21½ cm.

A detailed pro-Union account of the war in Missouri up through the battle of Pea Ridge.

McIntosh, David Gregg, 1836–1916.
Review of the Gettysburg campaign, by David Gregg McIntosh, col. of artillery, C. S. A. [n. p., 191–?]

83, [1] p. illus. (maps) 23½ cm.

A trenchant commentary on the whole Pennsylvania campaign, by a Confederate artillery battalion colonel.

McLaughlin, Jack.
Gettysburg: the long encampment. [1st ed.] New York, Appleton-Century [1963]

ix, 244 p. illus., ports., facsims., plans (on lining papers) 26 cm.

A rambling, popular story of incidents of the battle of Gettysburg; good illustrations.

Macartney, Clarence Edward Noble, 1879–
Highways and byways of the civil war, by Clarence Edward Macartney ... Pittsburgh, Pa., The Gibson press, 1938.

3 p. l., ix–xiii p., 1 l., 304 p. maps. 21 cm.

A travelogue-type description of the battlefields and campaigns of the war.

Maguire, Thomas Miller, 1849–1920.
The campaigns in Virginia, 1861–62, by T. Miller Maguire ... London, W. H. Allen & co., ltd., 1891.

70 p. 5 maps (incl. fold. front.) 25½ cm.

Brief and generally accurate; written by a British barrister of strong opinions.

Mahan, Asa, 1800–1889.
A critical history of the late American war; by A. Mahan. With an introductory letter by Lieut.-General M. W. Smith. New York, Chicago [etc.] A. S. Barnes & co., 1877.

viii, 461 p. 22 cm.

An undocumented though not uninformed analysis of the campaigns, East and West, by an author of strong views and implacable prejudice.

Marks, James J

The Peninsular campaign in Virginia, or Incidents and scenes on the battle-fields and in Richmond. By Rev. J. J. Marks, D. D. 5th ed. Philadelphia, J. B. Lippincott & co., 1864.

xx, 21–444 p. front., plates. 19ᶜᵐ.

A potpourri of eyewitness scenes and events by an observant though uncritical Pennsylvania chaplain.

Meredith, Roy, 1908–

Storm over Sumter; the opening engagement of the Civil War. New York, Simon and Schuster, 1957.

214 p. illus., ports., map. 22 cm.

An entertainingly written narrative of the Sumter affair.

Miers, Earl Schenck, 1910–   *ed.*

Gettysburg, ed. by Earl Schenck Miers and Richard A. Brown. Maps by Harold C. Detje. New Brunswick, Rutgers Univ. Press, 1948.

xviii, 308 p. illus., maps. 22 cm.

A hodgepodge collection of oftentimes-unrelated personal anecdotes.

Miers, Earl Schenck, 1910–

The web of victory; Grant at Vicksburg. ₁1st ed.₁ New York, Knopf, 1955.

xiv, 320, xii p. illus., ports., maps. 22 cm.

A thin but well-written (though at times overly lyrical) story; unfortunately lacking in maps.

Military historical society of Massachusetts, *Boston.*

... The Shenandoah campaigns of 1862 and 1864 and the Appomattox campaign, 1865 ... Boston, The Military historical society of Massachusetts, 1907.

6 p. l., ₁3₁–518 p., 1 l. 6 fold. maps. 24½ᶜᵐ. (*Half-title:* Papers of the Military historical society of Massachusetts ₁v. 6₁)

Articles of varying merit concentrating more on the Shenandoah Valley campaign of 1864.

Military historical society of Massachusetts, *Boston.*

The Virginia campaign of 1862 under General Pope, edited by Theodore F. Dwight. Boston and New York, Pub. for the Military historical society of Massachusetts by Houghton, Mifflin and co., 1895.

xxi, 541 p. 9 fold. maps. 24½ cm. (Military historical society of Massachusetts, Boston. Papers. Rev. and enl. ed. v. 2)

Although a valuable collection of articles on significant and controversial subjects, a number are written with such strong viewpoints as to amount almost to lawyer's briefs.

Military historical society of Massachusetts, *Boston.*

The Wilderness campaign, May–June, 1864 ... Boston, The Military historical society of Massachusetts, 1905.

vi p., 2 l., 471, ₁1₁ p. 6 fold. maps. 24½ᶜᵐ. (*Half-title:* Papers of the Military historical society of Massachusetts ... vol. IV)

These articles, of uneven merit, treat a number of critical phases and include several analyses of a general nature.

Military historical society of Massachusetts, *Boston.*

Operations on the Atlantic coast, 1861–1865, Virginia, 1862, 1864, Vicksburg ... Boston, The Military historical society of Massachusetts, 1912.

vi p., 2 l., 585. ₁1₁ p. 16 maps (13 fold.) 24½ᶜᵐ. (*Half-title:* Papers of the Military historical society of Massachusetts. ₁vol. IX₁)

Most of these critically written articles relate to the joint Army-Navy amphibious operations conducted by the Federals.

Military historical society of Massachusetts, *Boston.*

Campaigns in Kentucky and Tennessee including the battle of Chickamauga, 1862–1864 ... Boston, The Military historical society of Massachusetts, 1908.

vi p., 2 l., ₁3₁–557, ₁1₁ p. 9 fold. maps. 24½ᶜᵐ. (*Half-title:* Papers of the Military historical society of Massachusetts. ₁vol. VII₁)

A valuable collection of critical articles.

Military historical society of Massachusetts, *Boston.*

The Mississippi valley, Tennessee, Georgia, Alabama, 1861–1864, Papers of the Military historical society of Massachusetts ... Boston, The Military historical society of Massachusetts, 1910.

vi p., 3 l., ₁4₁–619, ₁1₁ p. 8 fold. maps. 24½ cm. (*Half-title:* Papers of the Military historical society of Massachusetts. ₁vol. VIII₁)

Articles of merit in this volume treat of operations in Missouri, at Port Hudson, the Red River expedition, and campaigns around Chattanooga.

Military historical society of Massachusetts, *Boston.*

Campaigns in Virginia, 1861–1862, ed. by Theodore F. Dwight. Boston and New York, Pub. for the Military historical society of Massachusetts by Houghton, Mifflin and company, 1895.

li, 369 p. 5 fold. maps. 24½ᶜᵐ. (*Half-title:* Papers of the Military historical society of Massachusetts, Boston. [Rev. and enl. ed. v. 1ª])

Articles of value on Patterson's and Jackson's Valley operations, as well as on McClellan's Peninsular campaign; includes an excellent summary by C. A. Whittier.

Military historical society of Massachusetts, *Boston.*

Campaigns in Virginia, Maryland and Pennsylvania, 1862–1863 ... Boston, Pub. for the Military historical society of Massachusetts, by Griffith-Stillings press, 1903.

2 p. l., 509 p. fold. map. 24ᶜᵐ. (Papers of the Military historical society of Massachusetts, vol. III)

A series of provocative articles on the Eastern campaigns through 1863.

Military historical society of Massachusetts, *Boston.*

Civil and Mexican wars, 1861, 1846 ... Boston, The Military historical society of Massachusetts, 1913.

vi p., 3 l., [3]–660 p., 1 l. 6 maps on 5 fold. sheets. 24½ cm. (Papers of the Military historical society of Massachusetts. vol. XIII)

Contains thoughtful articles on Civil War cavalry, artillery, field-works, medicine, the Negro as a soldier, Confederate numbers, Jefferson Davis, and Gettysburg.

Military historical society of Massachusetts, *Boston.*

Civil war and miscellaneous papers ... Boston, The Military historical society of Massachusetts, 1918.

vi p., 2 l., 474 p., 1 l. illus., 4 pl., ports., map, 2 plans. 24½ᶜᵐ. (Papers of the Military historical society of Massachusetts. Vol. XIV)

A useful collection of articles on such topics as Antietam, Gettysburg, Chattanooga, guerrilla operations in Tennessee, Cedar Creek, and military prisons.

Miller, Francis Trevelyan, 1877–   *ed.*

The photographic history of the Civil War. Francis Trevelyan Miller, editor in chief; Robert S. Lanier, managing editor. With a new introd. by Henry Steele Commager. New York, T. Yoseloff [1957]

10 v. in 5. illus., ports., maps. 28 cm.

A mammoth collection of Civil War pictures that has become the standard photographic compendium on most aspects of the conflict.

Mills, Lewis Este.

General Pope's Virginia campaign of 1862. Read before the Cincinnati literary club, February 5, 1870. By Lewis Este Mills. Detroit, Tribune book and job office, 1870.

32 p. 21ᶜᵐ.

This address amounts to a pro-Pope, anti-McClellan diatribe, and is unreliable as to its historical methodology.

Mitchell, Joseph Brady, 1915–

Decisive battles of the Civil War. With 35 maps designed by the author. New York, Putnam [1955]

226 p. illus. 22 cm.

The use of simple battlefield and operational maps, plotted on present-day road maps, augments a routine account of the major campaigns.

Monaghan, James, 1891–

Civil War on the western border, 1854–1865, by Jay Monaghan. [1st ed.] Boston, Little, Brown [1955]

x, 454 p. 23 cm.

An adequate, documented account of the pre-war strife in Kansas and the Civil War in Missouri, Kansas, and Arkansas.

Monnett, Howard N

Action before Westport, 1864, by Howard N. Monnett. Paintings and maps by George Barnett. Kansas City, Mo., Westport Historical Society, 1964.

xxi, 190 p. illus., plans, ports. 24 cm.

A competent narrative of the 1864 campaign; includes helpful maps and illustrations.

Montgomery, James Stuart.

The shaping of a battle: Gettysburg. With official maps published by the authority of the Secretary of War by the Office of the Chief of Engineers, U. S. Army. [1st ed.] Philadelphia, Chilton Co., Book Division [1959]

xxxi, 259 p. maps (3 fold. laid in) 25 cm.

An undocumented rehash, though generally accurate and entertainingly written; contains poor reprints of the Bachelder maps.

Mosby, John Singleton, 1833–1916.
Stuart's cavalry in the Gettysburg campaign, by John S. Mosby ... New York, Moffat, Yard & company, 1908.

5 p. l., v–xxxiii, 222 p. 2 port. (incl. front.) fold. map. 21½ cm.

A spirited defense of Stuart's role in the campaign, by a prominent Confederate cavalryman.

Murfin, James V
The gleam of bayonets; the battle of Antietam and the Maryland Campaign of 1862, by James V. Murfin. Maps by James D. Bowlby. Introd. by James I. Robertson, Jr. New York, T. Yoseloff [1965]

451 p. illus., facsims., maps, ports. 24 cm.

Although detailed and well-documented, this account is strongly anti-McClellan and otherwise opinionated.

Naisawald, L Van Loan.
Grape and canister; the story of the field artillery of the Army of the Potomac, 1861–1865. New York, Oxford University Press, 1960.

xiv, 593 p. illus., maps. 22 cm.

A thorough, standard though at times overwritten study of the role played in the Eastern campaigns by Federal field artillery.

National Geographic Society, *Washington, D. C. Cartographic Division.*
Battlefields of the Civil War, with descriptive notes. Compiled and drawn for the National geographic magazine. James M. Darley, chief cartographer. Washington, 1961.
col. map 78 x 103 cm.

A generally accurate and graphic map, in color, with notes that give the average student a good outline of the major operations.

Nelson, Alanson Henery, 1828–
The battles of Chancellorsville and Gettysburg. By Capt. A. H. Nelson, 57th Penna. vols. Minneapolis, Minn., 1899.

4 p. l., 183 p. illus. (incl. maps, plans) 18½ cm.

A mediocre survey of two famous campaigns; includes maps.

New York (*State*) *Monuments commission for the battlefields of Gettysburg, Chattanooga and Antietam.*
Dedication of the New York auxiliary state monument on the battlefield of Gettyburg authorized by chapter 181, Laws of 1925. Albany, J. B. Lyon company, printers, 1926.
xi, 226 p. front., plates, ports., maps. 27½ cm.

A potpourri of articles relating to Gettysburg and, more specifically, to forty-one New York officers listed on the state's auxiliary monument.

New York (*State*) *Monuments commission for the battlefields of Gettysburg and Chattanooga.*
... Final report on the battlefield of Gettysburg ... Albany, J. B. Lyon company, printers, 1900.
3 v. plates, ports., v fold. maps. 28 cm.

This compendium of material includes oftentimes valuable speeches delivered by participants.

Nicolay, John George, 1832–1901.
... The outbreak of rebellion, by John G. Nicolay ... Subscription ed. New York, C. Scribner's sons ['1885]

viii p., 1 l., 226 p. incl. maps. front. (port.) 20½ cm. (The army in the civil war. vol. i)

A weak survey, by Lincoln's private secretary, of the Sumter episode, the coming of the war, and the First Bull Run campaign.

Norton, Oliver Willcox.
The attack and defense of Little Round Top, Gettysburg, July 2, 1863, by Oliver Willcox Norton ... New York, The Neale publishing company, 1913.

350 p. front., 2 pl. (1 col.) ports. 21 cm.

An exhaustive evaluation of the fight for the key Union hill; includes excerpts from the accounts of other writers.

Nye, Wilbur Sturtevant, 1898–
Here come the Rebels! Maps by the author. Baton Rouge, Louisiana State University Press [1965]

xvi, 412 p. maps. 24 cm.

A lively, documented but episodic story of events leading up to the battle of Gettysburg, with emphasis on the march of Ewell's Confederate Corps.

O'Neill, Charles Kendall, 1909–
    Wild train; the story of the Andrews raiders. New York, Random House [1956]

       482 p. illus. 22 cm.

An undocumented but swiftly moving narrative of the famous Chattanooga Railroad Expedition.

Palfrey, Francis Winthrop, 1831–1889.
    ... The Antietam and Fredericksburg, by Francis Winthrop Palfrey ... New York, C. Scribner's sons, 1882.

       x p., 1 l., 228 p. maps. 19 cm. (Campaigns of the civil war. v)

Though brief and somewhat stilted in style, this is still a generally reliable story of the 1862 Maryland and Fredericksburg campaigns.

Paris, Louis Philippe Albert d'Orléans, *comte* de, 1838–1894.
    The battle of Gettysburg, from the History of the civil war in America, by the Comte de Paris ... New, rev. ed. Philadelphia, The John C. Winston co. [*c*1912]

       4 p. l., vii–ix, 315 p. incl. tables. 3 fold. maps. 23^{cm}. $1.50

Excellent, detailed chapters on the campaign, taken from the Count's massive four-volume work on war.

Paris, Louis Philippe Albert d'Orléans, *comte de*, 1838–1894.
    History of the civil war in America. By the Comte de Paris. Published by special arrangement with the author ... Philadelphia, Porter & Coates [*c*1875–88]

       4 v. front. (v. 3) fold. maps. 22 cm.

A massive and valuable narrative of operations up through Mine Run in the East and Chattanooga in the West, by a French nobleman on McClellan's staff.

Patch, Joseph Dorst, 1885–
    The battle of Ball's Bluff. Edited by Fitzhugh Turner, with an introd. by Virgil Carrington Jones. Photos. from the Library of Congress. Illus. and maps by Marjorie Keen. [Limited ed.] Leesburg, Va., Potomac Press [1958]

       123 p. illus., ports., maps (on lining papers) 23 cm.

This slender volume on a neglected engagement includes battle reports as well as Northern and Southern newspaper accounts.

Patrick, Rembert Wallace, 1909–
    The fall of Richmond. Baton Rouge, Louisiana State University Press [1960]

       144 p. illus. 23 cm. (The Walter Lynwood Fleming lectures in southern history)

An able series of analytical lectures on events occurring immediately before, during, and after the fall of Richmond.

Patterson, Robert, 1792–1881.
    A narrative of the campaign in the valley of the Shenandoah, in 1861. By Robert Patterson ... Philadelphia, Sherman & co., printers, 1865.

       128 p. incl. front. (map) 23½^{cm}.

Patterson's account is painfully defensive in tone, and unconvincing.

Peckham, James, 1828–1869.
    Gen. Nathaniel Lyon, and Missouri in 1861. A monograph of the great rebellion, by James Peckham ... New York, American news company, 1866.

       xvii, [18]–447 p. front. (port.) plates. 19 cm.

A detailed, opinionated narrative of the crucial events in the pivotal state of Missouri in 1861, and of the fiery, controversial Lyon's role therein.

Petersen, Frederick A
    Military review of the campaign in Virginia & Maryland, under Generals John C. Fremont, N. P. Banks, Irwin McDowell, Franz Sigel, John Pope, James S. Wadsworth, Wm. H. Halleck and George B. McClellan, in 1862, by Fred'k A. Petersen ... A contribution to the future history of the United States. New York, S. Tousey, H. Dexter [1862–63]

       2 pt. in 1 v. 22½^{cm}.

A passionate, one-sided defense of McClellan; of little use, except as a lawyer's brief reflecting the strong feelings of the times.

Peterson, Cyrus Asbury, *b.* 1848.
    Pilot Knob, the Thermopylae of the West, by Cyrus A. Peterson and Joseph Mills Hanson. New York, The Neale publishing company, 1914.

       324 p. 21 cm.

A comprehensive narrative and analysis of the repulse of Price's Confederate attack of Sept. 27, 1864, at Fort Davidson, Missouri.

Pierce, Francis Marshal 1847–

The battle of Gettysburg, the crest-wave of the American civil war, by Francis Marshal [pseud.] New York, The Neale publishing company, 1914.

337 p. front., pl., ports., maps. 21ᶜᵐ. $2.00

An all-embracing but undocumented story of the campaign, placed in its context with preceding and succeeding events; informed but not profound.

Pleasants, Henry, 1884–

Inferno at Petersburg, by Henry Pleasants, Jr., and George H. Straley. [1st ed.] Philadelphia, Chilton Co., Book Division [1961]

181 p. illus. 21 cm.

A brief, sympathetic story of the efforts of Col. Pleasants and his regiment to construct and detonate the famous "mine" at Petersburg; by the Colonel's cousin.

Pond, George Edward, 1837–1899.

... The Shenandoah valley in 1864, by George E. Pond ... New York, C. Scribner's sons, 1883.

ix p., 1 l., 287 p. incl. maps. fold. plans. 19 cm. (Campaigns of the civil war. XI)

A useful narrative of the 1864 operations of Early, Sheridan, and others in the Valley.

Porter, Fitz-John, 1822–1901.

Gen. Fitz John Porter's statement of the services of the Fifth army corps, in 1862, in northern Virginia. New York, Evening post steam presses, 1878.

1 p. l., viii, [3]–105 p. front. (plan) 23½ᶜᵐ.

Porter's overstated but on the whole convincing defense of his conduct and that of his troops during the Second Manassas campaign.

Rawle, William Brooke-, 1843–1915.

The right flank at Gettysburg. An account of the operations of General Gregg's cavalry command, showing their important bearing upon the results of the battle. By William Brooke-Rawle ... Philadelphia, 1878.

27 p. fold. plan. 26½ᶜᵐ.

A short but in the main accurate description and appreciation of the significant cavalry fight to the east of Gettysburg on the third day.

Redway, George William.

... Fredericksburg, a study in war, by Major G. W. Redway ... With five maps. London, S. Sonnenschein & co., ltd.; New York, The Macmillan company, 1906.

xvi, 297, [1] p. incl. map. 5 fold. maps. 19ᶜᵐ. (Special campaign series. no. 3)

A fairly satisfactory though unexciting study of Burnside's debacle; intended primarily for British Army officers.

Redway, George William.

... The war of secession, 1861–1862, Bull Run to Malvern Hill, by Major G. W. Redway ... London, S. Sonnenschein & co. lim., 1910.

viii, 392 p. 14 fold. maps (in pocket) 19½ᶜᵐ. (Special campaign series. no. 11)

Although written chiefly for British army officers, and not free from error, this is a useful operational study.

Reed, Samuel Rockwell, 1820?–1889.

The Vicksburg campaign, and the battles about Chattanooga under the command of General U. S. Grant, in 1862–63; an historical review. By Sam. Rockwell Reed ... Cincinnati, R. Clarke & co., 1882.

1 p. l., 201 p. 24 cm.

A mediocre, unbalanced tale of Grant and his campaigns against Vicksburg and at Chattanooga.

Rhodes, Charles Dudley, 1865–

History of the cavalry of the Army of the Potomac, including that of the Army of Virginia (Pope's), and also the history of the operations of the federal cavalry in West Virginia during the war. By Charles D. Rhodes ... Kansas City, Mo., Hudson-Kimberly pub. co., 1900.

200 p. 17½ x 14ᶜᵐ.

A lightly documented, gracelessly written but generally accurate account of the main Union cavalry operation in the East.

Rich, Joseph W 1838–

The battle of Shiloh, by Joseph W. Rich. Iowa City, Ia., State historical society of Iowa, 1911.

134 p. front. (port.) VIII maps on 4 l. 23½ᶜᵐ. $1.25

A brief, terse, documented study of Shiloh, by a participant; emphasizes Iowa's role in the battle.

Richardson, Charles.
The Chancellorsville campaign; Fredericksburg to Salem church, by Charles Richardson. New York and Washington, The Neale publishing company, 1907.

124 p. 19ᶜᵐ.

Short, sketchy, and at times overwritten; one half of this outline includes abstracts from official reports.

Ridley, Bromfield Lewis.
Battles and sketches of the Army of Tennessee, by Bromfield L. Ridley, Lieut-Gen. A. P. Stewart's staff, c. s. a. Mexico, Mo., Missouri printing & publishing co., 1906.

xvi, [17]–662, [10] p. front., illus., plates (1 col.) ports., maps. 24 cm.

Although rambling and poorly organized, this narrative does contain a wealth of detail (including documents) of the war in the West.

Rodick, Burleigh Cushing, 1889–
Appomattox: the last campaign. New York, Philosophical Library [1965]

220 p. illus., map (on lining paper) 22 cm.

A colorfully written story of the final major military operations waged between Lee's army and Federal forces under Grant and Meade.

Ropes, John Codman, 1836–1899.
... The Army under Pope, by John Codman Ropes ... New York, C. Scribner's sons, 1881.

xii p., 1 l., 229 p. illus. (plans) fold. map. 19 cm. (Campaigns of the civil war. ɪᴠ)

A brief but penetrating study that leans over backward to give Pope his due, but which nonetheless reveals that general's incapacity.

Ropes, John Codman, 1836–1899.
The story of the civil war; a concise account of the war in the United States of America between 1861 and 1865. By John Codman Ropes ... New York and London, G. P. Putnam's sons, 1894–1913.

3 pt. in 4 v. maps (part fold.) plans. 23 cm.

An incisive and masterly four-volume evaluation of the military strategy and operations of the war through Gettysburg and Vicksburg.

Schaff, Morris, 1840–1929.
The battle of the Wilderness, by Morris Schaff ... with maps and plans. Boston and New York, Houghton Mifflin company, 1910.

4 p. l., 345, [1] p. 5 maps (incl. front.) 21 cm.

Although the author is at times pompous, rambling, and lyrical, still this study remains a work of some merit.

Schaff, Morris, 1840–1929.
The sunset of the confederacy, by Morris Schaff ... with maps. Boston, J. W. Luce and company [ᶜ1912]

4 p. l., 302 p., 1 l. 3 maps (incl. fold. front.) 21 cm.

A somewhat sentimental treatment of the "Appomattox Chase," but of value in its interpretation of the actions of Grant and Lee.

Schalk, Emil, 1834–
Campaigns of 1862 and 1863, illustrating the principles of strategy. By Emil Schalk ... 2d ed. Philadelphia, J. B. Lippincott & co., 1863.

viii, 9–252 p. fold. maps, diagrs. 19ᶜᵐ.

Schalk delineated the "principles of strategy," described the geography of the arena of the Civil War, then discussed 1862 operations in the light of these principles.

Schenck, Martin, 1912–
Up came Hill; the story of the Light Division and its leaders. [1st ed.] Harrisburg, Pa., Stackpole Co. [1958]

344 p. illus. 23 cm. [Civil War campaigns]

A sprightly, narrative of A. P. Hill and his Light Division; hampered by the paucity of Hill manuscripts.

Scofield, Levi Tucker, 1842–
The retreat from Pulaski to Nashville, Tenn.; battle of Franklin, Tennessee, November 30th, 1864; with maps, sketches, portraits and photographic views, by Levi T. Scofield ... Cleveland, Press of the Caxton co., 1909.

1 p. l., 7–67 p. illus. 23½ᶜᵐ.

A short, popular narrative of the 1864 Franklin campaign; profusely illustrated with photographs and maps.

Scott, James Knox Polk, 1845–
     The story of the battles at Gettysburg, by James K. P. Scott ...   Harrisburg, Pa., The Telegraph press, 1927–

> v. front., illus. (maps) plates, ports. 22½ cm.

A rambling, poorly organized yet accurate story of the first day's fight at Gettysburg, with maps and terrain photographs.

Senour, Faunt Le Roy, 1824–1910.
     Major General William T. Sherman, and his campaigns. By Rev. F. Senour ...   Chicago, H. M. Sherwood, 1865.

> xiv, [15]–477 p. front. (port.) 19½ᶜᵐ.

An old, undocumented, sympathetic story, of little use except for colorful incidents and occasional newspaper quotations.

Seymour, Digby Gordon, 1923–
     Divided loyalties; Fort Sanders and the Civil War in East Tennessee. [1st ed.] Knoxville, University of Tennessee Press [1963]

> xii, 244 p. illus., ports., maps, facsims. 29 cm.

A popular, documented story of the war in eastern Tennessee, dwelling especially on the 1863 battle of Fort Sanders.

Sheppard, Eric William, 1890–
     The American civil war, 1864–1865, by Major E. W. Sheppard ...   Aldershot, London [etc.] Gale & Polden, ltd. [1938]

> xviii, 171 p. xii fold. maps (2 in pocket) 21½ᶜᵐ.

Though written in a lackluster, unimaginative style, this is nonetheless a knowledgeable outline of the last year of the war.

Sheppard, Eric William, 1890–
     ... The campaign in Virginia and Maryland, June 26th to Sept. 20th, 1862, Cedar Run, Manassas, and Sharpsburg, by Second-Lieut. E. W. Sheppard ...   London, G. Allen & company, ltd.; New York, The Macmillan company, 1911.

> xv, 306 p., 1 l. illus., 7 maps (in pocket) 19 cm. (Special campaign series, no. 14)

Written primarily for pre-World War I British officers, this is nevertheless a narrative of merit.

Sherman, William Tecumseh, 1820–1891.
     General Sherman's official account of his great march through Georgia and the Carolinas, from his departure from Chattanooga to the surrender of General Joseph E. Johnston and the Confederate forces under his command. To which is added, General Sherman's evidence before the Congressional committee on the conduct of the war; the animadversions of Secretary Stanton and General Halleck: with a defence of his proceedings, etc. New York, Bunce & Huntington, 1865.

> 214 p. 19 cm.

A useful bringing together of Sherman's reports, his testimony before a congressional committee, and his defense against Stanton's charges.

Smith, Gustavus Woodson, 1822–1896.
     The battle of Seven Pines. By Gustavus W. Smith ... New York, C. G. Crawford, printer, 1891.

> 202 p. incl. maps, facsim. 23½ cm.

A detailed but painfully defensive tract on the Confederate operations at Fair Oaks by the man who temporarily commanded the army.

Smith, William Farrar, 1824–1903.
     From Chattanooga to Petersburg under Generals Grant and Butler; a contribution to the history of the war, and a personal vindication, by William Farrar Smith ...   Boston and New York, Houghton, Mifflin and co., 1893.

> viii, 201 p. map, plans. 20ᶜᵐ.

"Baldy" Smith's generally convincing apologia concerning his campaigns and relations with Grant and Butler.

Smith, William Farrar 1824–1903.
     ... Military operations around Chattanooga, in October and November, 1863. [Wilmington, The James & Webb printing co., 1886]

> 12 numb. l. 37 x 21ᶜᵐ.

The brief, strongly worded personal interpretation of the Chattanooga campaign, by a prominent participant.

Snead, Thomas Lowndes, 1828–1890.
     The fight for Missouri from the election of Lincoln to the death of Lyon, by Thomas L. Snead ... New York, C. Scribner's sons, 1888.

> xiv, 322 p. front. (fold. map) pl. 19½ᶜᵐ.

One of the nearly-indispensable contributions by a participant in the early struggle for Missouri.

Stackpole, Edward James, 1894–
    Chancellorsville; Lee's greatest battle. ₁1st ed.₁ Harrisburg, Pa., Stackpole Co. ₁1958₁
    384 p. illus., maps, ports. 23 cm.

An undistinguished story of Hooker's campaign; contains excellent maps and illustrations.

Stackpole, Edward James, 1894–
    Drama on the Rappahannock: the Fredericksburg campaign. ₁1st ed.₁ Harrisburg, Pa., Military Service Pub. Co. ₁1957₁
    xx, 297 p. illus., ports., maps. 23 cm.

Although this book possesses good battle plans and pictures, the undocumented text is unscholarly and overly confident in tone.

Stackpole, Edward James, 1894–
    From Cedar Mountain to Antietam, August–September, 1862: Cedar Mountain, Second Manassas, Chantilly, Harpers Ferry, South Mountain, Antietam. Maps by Wilbur S. Nye. ₁1st ed.₁ Harrisburg, Pa., Stackpole Co. ₁1959₁
    466 p. illus., ports., maps. 23 cm. (Civil War campaigns)

A well-written but thin story, not sufficiently appreciative of McClellan's services.

Stackpole, Edward James, 1894–
    Sheridan in the Shenandoah; Jubal Early's nemesis. Maps by Wilbur S. Nye. Illus. from the Kean Archives. ₁1st ed.₁ Harrisburg, Pa., Stackpole Co. ₁1961₁
    413 p. illus. 23 cm. (Civil War centennial series)

A pro-Sheridan story which fails in appreciation of Jubal Early's problems, achievements, and inferior resources.

Stackpole, Edward James, 1894–
    They met at Gettysburg. ₁1st ed.₁ Harrisburg, Pa., Eagle Books ₁1956₁
    xxiv, 342 p. illus., ports., maps. 23 cm.

A glib, undocumented, thin account of the Pennsylvania campaign.

Steele, Matthew Forney, 1861–
    American campaigns, by Matthew Forney Steele ... Washington, United States infantry association, 1922.
    2 v. maps (part double) 24 cm.

Though the text is a bit dated, this long-standard analysis is superb for its battle maps; Civil War campaigns dominate.

Steere, Edward.
    The Wilderness Campaign. ₁1st ed.₁ Harrisburg, Pa., Stackpole Co. ₁1960₁
    522 p. maps. 23 cm. (Civil War campaigns)

An excellent study, though a bit too anti-Lee; contains a number of superior detailed maps.

Stern, Philip Van Doren, 1900–
    An end to valor; the last days of the Civil War. Boston, Houghton Mifflin, 1958.
    x, 418 p. illus., ports., maps. 22 cm.

A lightly documented story of the events of the final Appomattox campaign.

Stevenson, Alexander F
    The battle of Stone's river near Murfreesboro', Tenn. December 30, 1862, to January 3, 1863. By Alexander F. Stevenson. Boston, J. R. Osgood and company, 1884.
    vii p., 1 l., 197 p. fold. maps. 23½ᵐ.

An early, sometimes useful though occasionally unbalanced account of the battle.

Stewart, George Rippey, 1895–
    Pickett's charge; a microhistory of the final attack at Gettysburg, July 3, 1863. Boston, Houghton Mifflin, 1959.
    354 p. illus. 23 cm.

This is a detailed, documented narrative and analysis of the famous assault on the third day at Gettysburg; includes helpful maps and photographs.

Stickney, Albert, 1839–1908.

Warren court of inquiry. Argument of Mr. Albert Stickney, counsel for General Warren. ₍n. p., 188–₎

cover-title, 92 p. 24ᶜᵐ.

The generally convincing lawyer's brief in the defense of Gen. Warren against Sheridan's pertaining to the battle of Five Forks.

Stine, James Henry, d. 1906.

History of the Army of the Potomac. By J. H. Stine ... Philadelphia, J. B. Rodgers printing co., 1892.

xiii, 752 p. front., port. 24½ cm.

Although discursive, poorly organized, and pre-supposing advanced knowledge on the part of the reader, this large volume contains much useful information.

Storrick, William C

Gettysburg: the place, the battles, the outcome, by W. C. Storrick ... Harrisburg, Pa., J. Horace McFarland company ₍ᶜ1932₎

167 p. plates, maps. 20½ᶜᵐ.

A somewhat rambling, topically-organized treatment of Gettysburg by a former chief of the guides on the field.

Strait, Newton Allen, d. 1922, comp.

... An alphabetical list of the battles of the war of the rebellion with dates, from Fort Sumter, S. C., April 12 and 13, 1861, to Kirby Smith's surrender, May 26, 1865. Compiled from the official records of the offices of the adjutant-general and the surgeon-general, U. S. A. ... Also, the battles of the war of independence ... war with the North-West Indians, 1790 to 1795 ... and a chronological history of the late war, and of the war with Mexico, from 1845 to 1848; and a list of the presidents and vice-presidents of the United States, from Washington to Arthur. By Newton A. Strait ... Washington, D. C., N. A. Strait, 1883.

107 p. 24 cm.

A convenient listing of combats of the Civil War and other American conflicts.

Stribling, Robert Mackey, 1833–

Gettysburg campaign and campaigns of 1864 and 1865 in Virginia, by Robert M. Stribling ... Petersburg, Va., The Franklin press company, 1905.

x, ₍11₎–308 p. 19½ᶜᵐ.

This account by a Confederate artillery officer, though gracelessly written, is well organized and of some worth.

Strickler, Theodore D comp.

When and where we met each other on shore and afloat; battles, engagements, actions, skirmishes, and expeditions during the civil war, 1861–1866, to which is added concise data concerning the army corps and legends of the army corps badges; comp. from official and other authentic sources by Theodore D. Strickler. Washington, D. C., The National tribune ₍ᶜ1899₎

219, ₍1₎ p. 17½ᶜᵐ.

A listing, by states, of land and sea engagements of the Civil War.

Sturgis, Samuel Davis, 1822–1889.

The other side, as viewed by Generals Grant, Sherman, and other distinguished officers, being a defence of his campaign into N. E. Mississippi in the year 1864, by S. D. Sturgis ... Washington, D. C., 1882.

16 p. 23½ᶜᵐ.

A defense by Gen. Sturgis, including official reports and correspondence, of his failure against Forrest at Brice's Crossroads in 1864.

Surby, Richard W b. 1832.

Grierson raids, and Hatch's sixty-four days march, with biographical sketches, also the life and adventures of Chickasaw, the scout. By R. W. Surby. Chicago, Rounds and James, printers, 1865.

396 p. plates, ports. 19½ cm.

An early, sometimes colorful narrative by an Illinois sergeant; based largely on his own journal.

Swanberg, W A 1907–

First blood; the story of Fort Sumter. New York, Scribner ₍1957₎

viii, 373 p. illus., ports., maps, facsim. 24 cm.

This animated story is no substitute for Crawford's Genesis; nonetheless, a solid and useful study.

Swinton, William, 1833–1892.

Campaigns of the Army of the Potomac; a critical history of operations in Virginia, Maryland and Pennsylvania, from the commencement to the close of the war, 1861–1865, by William Swinton ... Revision and re-issue. New York, C. Scribner's sons, 1882.

2 p. l., 660 p. illus., 5 port. (incl. front.) 15 maps. 24 cm.

Originally published in 1866; an analysis by a New York Times war correspondent; perspicacious and wordy, but invaluable interpretation.

Swinton, William, 1833–1892.
The twelve decisive battles of the war; a history of the eastern and western campaigns, in relation to the actions that decided their issue. By William Swinton ... New York, Dick & Fitzgerald, 1867.

520 p. front., port., maps. 24 cm.

Pitched on a lower level than the author's book on the Army of the Potomac; the battle sketches are opinionated and uneven.

Todd, Albert, 1854–
The campaigns of the rebellion. By Albert Todd ... Manhattan, Kan., Printing department, State agricultural college, 1884.

vi p., 1 l., 130 p. 11 fold. maps. 21½ cm.

A condensed and dull outline of the principal campaigns of the war; written by an artillery officer.

Tomes, Robert, 1817–1882.
Battles of America by sea and land. With biographies of naval and military commanders ... By Robert Tomes ... New York, J. S. Virtue [1878]

3 v. fronts., plates, ports., maps. 28½ cm.

Vol. III, written by J. L. Wilson, compromises a mediocre, undocumented story of the main operations of the war.

Townsend, George Alfred, 1841–1914.
Rustics in rebellion; a Yankee reporter on the road to Richmond, 1861–65. With an introd. by Lida Mayo. Chapel Hill, University of North Carolina Press [1950]

xx, 292 p. 22 cm.

Vivid eyewitness vignettes by a Civil War reporter; first published in 1866 under the title, Campaigns of a Non-Combatant, though with some digressive material eliminated.

Tremain, Henry Edwin, 1841–1910.
Last hours of Sheridan's cavalry; a reprint of war memoranda, by Henry Edwin Tremain ... New York, Bonnell, Silver & Bowers, 1904.

563 p. front. (port.) pl., fold. map. 20 cm.

A modest personal narrative of the Appomattox campaign, by an officer on Sheridan's staff.

Tucker, Glenn.
Chickamauga: bloody battle in the West. Maps by Dorothy Thomas Tucker. [1st ed.] Indianapolis, Bobbs-Merrill [1961]

448 p. illus. 22 cm.

The ablest study of the greatest battle fought in the West; lightly documented and based solely on printed sources.

Tucker, Glenn.
High tide at Gettysburg; the campaign in Pennsylvania. [1st ed.] Indianapolis, Bobbs-Merrill [1958]

462 p. illus. 23 cm.

A competently documented story of the campaign, yet Tucker spends more time attempting to show not how the Federals won the battle but why the Confederates lost it.

Tucker, Samuel, 1872–
Price raid through Linn County, Kansas, October 24, 25, 1864. [n. p., 1958]

17 l. illus. 28 cm.

A folksy, prideful, article on the impact upon the countryside of Price's 1864 raid.

Turchin, John Basil, 1822–1901.
... Chickamauga; by John B. Turchin ... Chicago, Fergus printing company, 1888.

4 p. l., 295 p. front. (port.) 8 fold. maps. 25 cm. (*His* Noted battles for the union during the civil war in the United States of America, 1861–5, v. 1)

A detailed though far from impartial tract on the battle; poorly organized.

Turner, Edward Raymond, 1881–
The New Market campaign, May, 1864, by Edward Raymond Turner ... Richmond, Whittet & Shepperson, 1912.

xiv, 203 p. plates, ports. (incl. front.) maps. 23½ cm.

A thoroughly researched monograph on this Confederate victory in the Valley.

U. S. *General staff school, Fort Leavenworth, Kan.*
Source book of the Peninsula campaign in Virginia, April to July, 1862. The General service schools, the General staff school. Fort Leavenworth, Kan., The General service schools press [1921]
1 p. l., v–viii, 996 p. illus. (incl. maps, plans) 24cm.

A massive and convenient (though far from complete) compendium of primary source material.

U. S. *War Dept.*
Confederate victories in the Southwest; prelude to defeat. From the official records. Edited by the publishers. Albuquerque, Horn & Wallace, 1961.
2 v. ports., maps (1 fold.) 24 cm.

A helpful compilation of correspondence and reports from the <u>Official Records</u>; includes maps and illustrations.

Vanderslice, John Mitchell, 1846–1915.
Gettysburg then and now, the field of American valor; where and how the regiments fought and the troops they encountered; an account of the battle giving movements, positions, and losses of the commands engaged: by John M. Vanderslice ... Illustrated with one hundred and twenty-five full-page engravings from photographs by Tipton. New York, G. W. Dillingham co. [c1899]
492 p. incl. plates, ports. pl. 19 cm.

A terse, regiment-by-regiment description of the battle, by the chief of the old Battlefield Memorial Association.

Vandiver, Frank Everson, 1925–
Jubal's raid: General Early's famous attack on Washington in 1864. [1st ed.] New York, McGraw-Hill [1960]
198 p. illus. 22 cm.

A spirited, documented story of Early's 1864 campaign against Washington.

Van Horne, Thomas Budd, *d.* 1895.
History of the Army of the Cumberland; its organization, campaigns, and battles, written at the request of Major-General George H. Thomas chiefly from his private military journal and official and other documents furnished by him; by Thomas B. Van Horne ... Illustrated with campaign and battle maps, compiled by Edward Ruger. Cincinnati, R. Clarke & co., 1875.
2 v. diagr. *and* atlas. 23½ cm.

A large, compendium of information concerning Gen. Thomas and his Federal army; Vol. III is an atlas.

Van Noppen, Ina Woestemeyer, 1906–
Stoneman's last raid. [Boone? N. C., 1961]
112 p. illus. 26 cm.

A collection of articles describing adequately though ungracefully Stoneman's 1865 raid in the western North Carolina area.

Vaughan-Sawyer, George Henry, 1875–
... Grant's campaign in Virginia, 1864 (the Wilderness campaign) by Capt. Vaughan-Sawyer ... London, S. Sonnenschein & co., lim.; New York, The Macmillan company, 1908.
4 p. l., 3–197, [1] p. VIII fold. maps. 19cm. (Special campaign series. no. 8)

A generally accurate though unimaginatively written account by a British officer.

Victor, Orville James, 1827–1910.
Incidents and anecdotes of the war: with narratives of great battles, great marches, great events, and a record of heroic deeds and daring personal achievements, which characterized the great conflict for the union. Edited by Orville J. Victor ... New York, J. D. Torrey [1866]
2 p. l. [iii]–vi, [9]–495 p. front., plates. 22½cm.

An early, poorly organized hodgepodge of incidents and tales relating to selected campaigns and personalities of the war.

Vineyard, Thomas Elbert.
Battles of the civil war, by T. E. Vineyard. Spencer, W. Va. [Chicago, W. B. Conkey company] 1914.
154 p. plates, ports. 18½cm. $1.00

A popular, general story of the chief campaigns, West and East; unimaginatively written.

Warren, Gouverneur Kemble, 1830–1882.
Proceedings, findings, and opinions of the Court of inquiry convened by order of the President of the United States in special orders no. 277, headquarters of the army, Adjutant general's office, Washington, D. C., Dec. 9, 1879. In the case of Gouverneur K. Warren ... commanding the Fifth army corps in the campaign of Five Forks, Va., 1865. In three parts with maps. Washington, Govt. print. off., 1883.
3 v. incl. atlas of 6 fold. maps, diagrs. 23½cm (v. 3: 30½ x 24½cm)

A compendium of the massively detailed testimony and documents in the hearings which finally vindicated Gen. Warren.

Webb, Alexander Stewart, 1835–1911.
   ... The peninsula—McClellan's campaign of 1862, by
Alexander S. Webb ...   Subscription ed.   New York, C.
Scribner's sons [c1885]

   x p., 1 l., 219 p. incl. maps. 2 port. (incl. front.) fold. map. 20½ cm.
(The Army in the civil war. vol. III)

Although a bit digressive and uneven, this is
nonetheless a useful analysis by a Union general.

Weitzel, Godfrey, 1835–1884.
   Richmond occupied. Entry of the United States forces
into Richmond, Va., April 3, 1865; calling together of the
Virginia Legislature and revocation of the same. Edited
with an introd. by Louis H. Manarin. [Richmond, Richmond Civil War Centennial Committee, 1965]

   65 p. illus. (1 fold.) fold. map, ports. 23 cm. (Richmond. Civil
War Centennial Committee. Official publication no. 16)

A vain but somewhat sympathetic account by the
commander of the Federal forces that occupied
Richmond; first published in an 1861 issue of the
Philadelphia Weekly Times.

Werner, Edgar Albert.
   Historical sketch of the war of the rebellion, from 1861 to
1865. Movements of the Federal and Confederate armies:
chronological list of engagements: reconstruction proceedings:
proclamations, statistical tables, etc. Comp., and ed. by Edgar
A. Werner. Albany, N. Y., Weed, Parsons and company, 1890.

   viii, 270 p. front. 20½ x 15½ cm.

Though not well organized, and made up largely
of a collection of short sketches on selected
events, this book does contain useful statistical
tables.

Whan, Vorin E
   Fiasco at Fredericksburg. [University Park] Pennsylvania State University Press [1961]

   159 p. illus. 24 cm.

The most thorough study of the Union high command in the Fredericksburg campaign; documented and well-written, but unfortunately
lacks an index.

Williams, Kenneth Powers, 1887–1958.
   Lincoln finds a general; a military study of the Civil
War. With maps by Clark Ray. New York, Macmillan,
1949–59.

   5 v. ports., maps. 22 cm.

Though good in logistical analysis, these volumes are based too exclusively on the Official
Records, and show evidences of violent prejudices and poor historical methodology.

Williams, Thomas Harry, 1909–
   The military leadership of the North and the South.
Colorado, U. S. Air Force Academy, 1960.

   23 p. illus. 21 cm. (The Harmon memorial lectures in military
history, no. 2)

An informative, though free-wheeling analysis
of the Federal and Confederate high commands.

Wood, Walter Birkbeck, 1866–
   A history of the civil war in the United States, 1861–5, by
W. Birkbeck Wood ... and Major J. E. Edmonds ... With an
introduction by Spencer Wilkinson; with thirteen maps and
eleven plans. New York, G. P. Putnam's sons; London,
Methuen & co., 1905.

   xxii, 549, [1] p. XIII fold. maps (in pocket) 11 plans (1 fold.) 22½cm.

Written by two Britishers, this is one of the
ablest single-volume military accounts of the
war.

Wood, William Charles Henry, 1864–
   Captains of the civil war; a chronicle of the blue and the
gray, by William Wood. New Haven, Yale university press;
[etc., etc.] 1921.

   xiv, 424 p. front. (port.) maps (part fold.) 21 cm. (*Half-title:*
The Chronicles of America series, Allen Johnson, editor ... v. 31)

Although brief and undocumented, this is an entertainingly written introduction to the major
operations of the war.

Worthington, Glenn Howard, 1858–
   Fighting for time; or, The battle that saved Washington
and mayhap the Union; a story of the war between the states,
showing how Washington was saved from capture by Early's
army of invasion and how that achievement contributed to
the preservation of the Union, with many stories and incidents of the invasion hitherto untold. By Glenn H. Worthington ... [Baltimore, Press of Day printing company] 1932.
   ix, 306 p. front., plates, ports., map. 23½ cm.

An accurate but somewhat rambling study of
the 1864 battle of Monocacy; with maps and illustrations.

Young, Jesse Bowman, 1844–1914.
   The battle of Gettysburg; a comprehensive narrative, by
Jesse Bowman Young, an officer in the campaign; with
maps, plans and illustrations. New York and London,
Harper & brothers, 1913.

   ix, [1], 462, [1] p. plates, 2 port. (incl. front.) maps (part fold.)
21½ cm.

One of the ablest and clearest studies of this
pivotal campaign; includes valuable biographical
sketches of all officers above regimental command.

MILITARY ASPECTS
Soldier Life

James I. Robertson, Jr.

Abbott, Lemuel Abijah, 1842–
 Personal recollections and civil war diary, 1864; by Major Lemuel Abijah Abbott ... Burlington, Free press printing co., printers, 1908.

 x p., 2 l., 296 p. front. (port.) 12 pl. 21½ cm.

Abbott's diary of service in the 10th Vermont spans only the last seven months of 1864; much material was added to "correct false history" relative to Sheridan's Valley Campaign.

Abbott, Stephen G
 The First regiment New Hampshire volunteers in the great rebellion: containing the story of the campaign; an account of the "Great uprising of the people of state," and other articles upon subjects associated with the early war period ... By Rev. Stephen G. Abbott, A. M., chaplain ... Keene, Sentinel printing co., 1890.

 511 p. incl. illus., map. front., port. 24 cm.

Abbott relied too heavily on secondary sources; only one of the fourteen chapters treats of the regiment in battle.

Adams, John Gregory Bishop, 1841–
 ... Reminiscences of the Nineteenth Massachusetts regiment, by Captain John G. B. Adams. Boston, Wright & Potter printing company, 1899.

 viii, 186 p. incl. front. (port.) ports. 23 cm.

An empty personal narrative of action in the Eastern theater; after the author's capture at Cold Harbor, the work becomes a typical, prejudiced prison account.

Adams, John Ripley, 1802–1866.
 Memorial and letters of Rev. John R. Adams, D. D., chaplain of the Fifth Maine and the One hundred and twenty-first New York regiments during the war of the rebellion, serving from the beginning to its close ... [Cambridge] Priv. print. [University press, J. Wilson and son] 1890.

 viii p., 1 l., 242 p. front. (port.) 24 cm.

Chaplain Adams' many printed letters treat for the most part of military rather than spiritual matters in the Army of the Potomac.

Addey, Markinfield

"Old Jack" and his foot-cavalry; or, A Virginian boy's progress to renown. A story of the war in the Old Dominion. New-York, J. Bradburn, 1864.

300 p. illus. 18 cm.

One of the first biographies of the famed "Stonewall" Jackson, this eulogistic study also tells much about the caliber of men who served under the Confederate general.

Albert, Allen Diehl, 1844–1913.

A grandfather's oft told tales of the civil war, 1861–1865, by Allen D. Albert, private, Company D, Forty-fifth Pennsylvania veteran volunteer infantry. [Williamsport, Pa., Grit publishing company, 1913]

4 p. l., 30 p. front., pl., ports. 25½ cm.

A collection of anecdotes repeated so many times that teller and listener accepted them as pure truth.

Aldrich, Thomas M

The history of Battery A, First regiment Rhode Island light artillery in the war to preserve the union, 1861–1865, by Thomas M. Aldrich ... Providence, Snow & Farnham, printers, 1904.

vii, [1], 408 p. pl., 32 port. (incl. front.) plan. 24 cm.

Apparently based on a diary, but padded with excerpts from official sources; of limited use in studying the Eastern campaigns.

Alexander, Charles Wesley 1837–1927.

The volunteers' roll of honor. A collection of the noble and praiseworthy deeds performed in the cause of the Union by the heroes of the army and navy of the United States. By Wesley Bradshaw [pseud.] ... Philadelphia, Barclay & co. [1863]

2 p. l., 21–30, 39–52, 63–74, 85–100 p. pl. 24½ᶜᵐ.

A short-lived monthly magazine that contained both fictional and non-fictional accounts of battlefield valor; unfortunately, no distinction was made between the two.

Alexander, Edward Porter, 1835–1910.

Military memoirs of a Confederate; a critical narrative, by E. P. Alexander ... with sketch-maps by the author. New York, C. Scribner's sons, 1907.

xviii, 634 p. 2 port. (incl. front.) maps (1 fold.) 23 cm.

This incisive narrative has been acclaimed as "the best critique for operations of the Army of Northern Virginia"; Alexander was one of only three Confederate artillerists to attain the rank of general.

Alexander, Edward Porter, 1835–1910.

Military memoirs of a Confederate. With a new introd. and notes by T. Harry Williams. Bloomington, Indiana University Press [1962]

xii, 652 p. port., plans, tables. 21 cm.

In this new edition, Prof. Williams provides a lengthy introduction that throws much light on Alexander's skill in signaling as well as shooting.

Allen, George H   *corp. 4th R. I. infantry.*

Forty-six months with the Fourth R. I. volunteers, in the war of 1861 to 1865. Comprising a history of its marches, battles, and camp life. Comp. from journals kept while on duty in the field and camp, by Corp. Geo. H. Allen, of Company B ... Providence, R. I., J. A. & R. A. Reid, printers, 1887.

389 p. front. (port.) 22½ cm.

A full and revealing memoir of service in Burnside's IX Corps; Allen based his study on a meticulously kept journal.

Allen, John Fisk

Memorial of Pickering Dodge Allen. By his father. Boston, Printed by H. W. Dutton and son, 1867.

174 p. front. (port.) 19½ᶜᵐ.

Contains exceptionally fine soldiers' letters written from the Mississippi and Louisiana theaters.

Allen, Stanton P

Down in Dixie; life in a cavalry regiment in the war days, from the Wilderness to Appomattox, by Stanton P. Allen ... Illustrated by H. G. Laskey. Boston, D. Lothrop company [c1892]

2 p. l., [vii]–xiii p., 1 l., 13–494 p., 2 l. incl. illus., plates. front. 22 cm.

Completely unreliable; composed for the most part of manufactured conversation and unauthenticated stories.

Amann, William Frayne, *ed.*

Personnel of the Civil War. New York, T. Yoseloff [1961]

2 v. 22 cm.

A valuable set for any researcher of Federal or Confederate units; especially useful are the sections correlating nicknames and official designations of companies and regiments.

Ambler, Isaac W   *b.* 1825 *or* 6.
'Truth is stranger than fiction.' The life of Sergeant I. W. Ambler ... 12 illustrations. Boston, Lee and Shepard; New York, Lee, Shepard & Dillingham [c1873]

  xii, [13]–319 p. front. (port.) plates. 23ᶜᵐ.

The life of an English-born temperance leader who served briefly in the 6th Maine; only a brief section treats of Ambler's insignificant Civil War service.

Ambrose, Daniel Leib.
History of the Seventh regiment Illinois volunteer infantry, from its first muster into the U. S. service, April 25, 1861, to its final muster out, July 9, 1865. By D. Leib Ambrose. Springfield, Ill., Illinois journal co., 1868.

  xii, 391, [1] p. 19½ᶜᵐ.

A full, factual, diary-like account of the Western theater, with emphasis on Shiloh, Chickamauga, and Sherman's 1864–1865 campaigns.

Amory, Charles Bean, 1841–
A brief record of the army life of Charles B. Amory; written for his children. [Boston?] Priv. pub., 1902.

  2 p. l., [3]–43 p. front. (port.) 22½ᶜᵐ.

Privately printed for the author's children, this slim pamphlet gives a too brief account of the Carolina coastal campaigns.

Anderson, Ephraim McD
Memoirs: historical and personal; including the campaigns of the First Missouri Confederate brigade. By Ephraim McD. Anderson. Saint Louis, Times printing co., 1868.

  2 p. l., vi p., 1 l., [9]–436, [2] p. front. (port.) plates. 22 cm.

One of the better Confederate narratives; written by an upper-class Southerner and strongly revealing for social conditions in the Confederacy.

Anderson, John, 1841–
The Fifty-seventh regiment of Massachusetts volunteers in the war of the rebellion. Army of the Potomac. By Captain John Anderson, U. S. army. Boston, E. B. Stillings & co., printers, 1896.

  xiv p., 1 l., 212 p. front., port. 24ᶜᵐ.

In this detailed narrative, Anderson borrowed too much from other printed sources.

Anderson, John Q
A Texas surgeon in the C. S. A. [Limited ed.] Tuscaloosa, Ala., Confederate Pub. Co., 1957.

  123 p. 22 cm. (Confederate centennial studies, no. 6)

The abridged letters (1862–1865) of Dr. Edward W. Cade, whose service as a brigade surgeon was in the Trans-Mississippi department.

Anderson, Nicholas Longworth, 1838–1892.
The letters and journals of General Nicholas Longworth Anderson; Harvard, civil war, Washington, 1854–1892, edited by Isabel Anderson (Mrs. Larz Anderson) New York [etc.] Fleming H. Revell company [1942]

  320 p. incl. 1 illus., tables. front., ports. 22½ᶜᵐ.

Only a skimpy diary covers Anderson's war service with the 6th Ohio.

Andrew, Abram Piatt, 1843–
Some civil war letters of A. Piatt Andrew, III. Gloucester, Mass., Priv. print., 1925.

  x p., 2 l., 3–146 p., 1 l. front., plates, ports., facsims. 21ᶜᵐ.

Especially revealing for descriptions of places, people and society in wartime Kentucky and Tennessee; the author's only battle experience of note was at Chickamauga.

Andrews, Andrew Jackson, 1842–
A sketch of the boyhood days of Andrew J. Andrews, of Gloucester County, Virginia, and his experience as a soldier in the late war between the states. Written by himself. To which are added selected poems by the author. Richmond, Va., The Hermitage press, inc., 1905.

  163 p. front. (port.) 20ᶜᵐ.

Shallow reminiscences written too long after the war; the author was a member of the Richmond Howitzers.

Andrus, Onley, 1835–1881.
The Civil War letters of Sergeant Onley Andrus, ed. by Fred Albert Shannon. Urbana, 1947.

  147 p. map, facsims. 27 cm.

Descriptions of travel through the Deep South by a member of the 95th Illinois; included also are several letters to Andrus from his wife.

The **annals** of the Army of Tennessee and early western history, including a chronological summary of battles and engagements in the western armies of the confederacy. Ed. by Dr. Edwin L. Drake. v. 1, no. 1–9, Apr.–Dec., 1878. Nashville, Tenn., Printed by A. D. Haynes, 1878 [1879?]

vi, 432 p., 1 l., 99, [1] p. front. (fold. map) 21½ cm.

This collection of personal reminiscences and anecdotes is of varying value, mostly negative.

The **Annals** of the war written by leading participants north and south. Originally pub. in the Philadelphia weekly times. Philadelphia, The Times publishing company, 1879.

1 p. l., iv, ii p., 1 l., 17–800 p. illus. 23 cm.

Excellent commentaries on campaigns, written by officers on both sides; these articles are more reliable than similar monographs found in Battles and Leaders of the Civil War.

Applegate, John Stilwell, 1837–1916.
Reminiscences and letters of George Arrowsmith of New Jersey, late lieutenant-colonel of the One hundred and fifty-seventh regiment, New York state volunteers, by John S. Applegate. Red Bank, N. J., J. H. Cook, 1893.

3 p. l., [xiii]–xiv, [2], 254 p. front. (port.) 18½ cm.

A sentimental tribute to an officer killed at Gettysburg; contains excerpts from his letters, which are more personal than factual.

Armes, George Augustus, 1844–1919.
Ups and downs of an army officer. By Col. George A. Armes, U. S. A. Washington, D. C., 1900.

xix, 784 p. front. (port.) illus. (incl. ports., facsims.) 22½ cm.

Only three of thirty-three chapters of this embellished work treat of Armes's varied Civil War career.

Armstrong, Hallock, 1823–1904.
Letters from a Pennsylvania chaplain at the Siege of Petersburg, 1865. Edited by Hallock F. Raup. [Kent? Ohio, 1961]

47 p. map. 25 cm.

Most of the letters in this small collection were written after Lee's surrender.

Armstrong, Nelson.
Nuggets of experience; narratives of the sixties and other days, with graphic descriptions of thrilling personal adventures, by Dr. Nelson Armstrong ... [San Bernardino?] Times-mirror P. and B. house, 1906.

257 p. incl. front. (port.) 9 pl. 20½ cm.

These ramblings are practically useless as a personal narrative of wartime experience.

Ashburn, Joseph Nelson, 1838–
History of the Eighty-sixth regiment Ohio volunteer infantry, by Joseph Nelson Ashburn ... Cleveland, O. [A. S. Gilman printing co.] 1909.

149, [1] p. incl. illus., ports. 24 cm.

Disappointingly brief and empty.

Aten, Henry J 1841–   *comp.*
History of the Eighty-fifth regiment, Illinois volunteer infantry. Comp. and pub. under the auspices of the Regimental association, by Henry J. Aten ... Hiawatha, Kan., 1901.

xi, [1], [13]–506 p. incl. front., ports. ports. 20½ cm.

Largely a statistical record, based on failing memory and secondary sources; treats of the campaigns from Perryville to Bentonville.

Aubery, James Madison, 1843–
The Thirty-sixth Wisconsin volunteer infantry ... An authentic record of the regiment from its organization to its muster out. A complete roster of its officers and men with their record ... a copy of every official paper in the War department pertaining to the regiment ... With reminiscences from the author's private journal. [By] James M. Aubery ... [Milwaukee? 1900]

430 p. incl. front., illus. 25½ cm.

Aubery borrowed so heavily from printed sources that his study stands forth as a classic example of a scissors-and-paste compilation.

Austin, J **P**
The blue and the gray: sketches of a portion of the unwritten history of the great American civil war, a truthful narrative of adventure, with thrilling reminiscences of the great struggle on land and sea, by J. P. Austin ... Atlanta, Ga., The Franklin printing and publishing co., 1899.

xi, [1], 246 p. col. front. 21 cm.

A rambling but sometimes interesting recollection of service in Texas, Tennessee and Georgia; errors mar the narrative.

Austin, Victor, *ed.*
Der Amerikanische Bürgerkrieg in Augenzeugenberichten. Mit einem Vorwort von Wilhelm Treue. ₍Aus dem Amerikanischen von Tilla Schlenk. Düsseldorf₎ K. Rauch ₍1963₎

366 p. illus., maps (part fold.) ports. 21 cm.

A slanted history presented in the form of letters; printed in both German and French.

Avery, Phineas O   1838–
History of the Fourth Illinois cavalry regiment, by P. O. Avery ... Humboldt, Neb., The Enterprise: a print shop, 1903.

2 p. l., ₍3₎–194 p. ports. 23ᶜᵐ.

For the most part, Avery's descriptions of service in the West are too brief to be of great value.

Avirett, James Battle, 1837?–1912.
The memoirs of General Turner Ashby and his compeers. By Rev. James B. Avirett ... and other officers of the Army of northern Virginia, C. S. A. ... Baltimore, Selby & Dulany, 1867.

xi, 13–408 p. front. (port.) 19½ᶜᵐ.

This collection of personal reminiscences is the best source of material on the daring Confederate chief whose death in 1862 was a severe blow to the South.

Ayers, James T   1805–1865.
The diary of James T. Ayers, Civil War recruiter; ed., with an introd., by John Franklin. Springfield, Printed by authority of the State of Illinois, 1947.

xxv, 138 p. illus., port., facsims. 24 cm.

A rambling, disjointed diary by an elderly antislaveryite who served in the 129th Illinois and as a recruiter for Negro units; the narrative spans only the last eighteen months of the war in the West.

Babcock, Willoughby, 1832–1864.
Selections from the letters and diaries of Brevet-Brigadier General Willoughby Babcock of the Seventy-fifth New York volunteers: a study of camp life in the Union armies during the civil war, by Willoughby M. Babcock, jr. Issued by the Division of archives and history ... ₍Albany₎ The University of the state of New York, 1922.

cover-title, 3–110 p. illus., plates, ports. 23ᶜᵐ.

Very informative letters of army life in Florida and Louisiana; particularly valuable for data on camp scenes and soldier life.

Bacon, Edward, 1830–1901.
Among the cotton thieves. By Edward Bacon ... Detroit, The Free press steam book and job printing house, 1867.

299, ₍1₎ p. 22 cm.

A narrative on the war in Louisiana by a colonel of the 6th Michigan; the text is more balanced and concrete than its title.

Baker, Henry H.
A reminiscent story of the great civil war. First₍–second₎ paper, a personal experience, by Henry H. Baker. New Orleans, The Ruskin press, 1911.

2 v. in 1. plates, ports. 16½ᶜᵐ.

By a member of the famed Washington Artillery, this somewhat lengthy account rests too heavily on memory.

Baker, La Fayette Charles, 1826–1868.
History of the United States secret service, by General L. C. Baker ... Philadelphia, L. C. Baker, 1867.

704 p. front. (port.) plates. 24 cm.

Baker's actions as a secret service agent were sometimes helpful, sometimes despotic; his "history" is noted mainly for the constant use of the word "I."

Baker, Levi Wood.
History of the Ninth Mass. battery. Recruited July, 1862; mustered in Aug. 10, 1862; mustered out June 9, 1865, at the close of the rebellion. By Levi W. Baker ... South Framingham, Mass., Lakeview press, J. C. Clark printing co., 1888.

vi, ₍7₎–261 p., 1 l. front., illus., pl. port. 22½ᶜᵐ.

Baker utilized a host of reminiscences sent to him decades after the war; the contents must therefore be handled carefully.

Banes, Charles H
History of the Philadelphia brigade. Sixty-ninth, Seventy-first, Seventy-second, and One hundred and sixth Pennsylvania volunteers. By Charles H. Banes ... Philadelphia, J. B. Lippincott & co., 1876.

315 p. 20 cm.

An average chronicle of the Eastern campaigns through Cold Harbor; a few personal incidents break the battle narrative.

Baquet, Camille.

History of the First brigade, New Jersey volunteers, from 1861 to 1865, comp. under the authorization of Kearny's first New Jersey brigade society by Camille Baquet ... Published by the state of New Jersey, 1910. Trenton, N. J., MacCrellish & Quigley, state printers, 1910.

1 p. l., iii, [3]–515 p. front., plates (part col.) ports. 24cm.

Based on both manuscript and printed sources, this volume is a potpourri of useful material on six different New Jersey regiments.

Barber, Joseph *of New York.*

War letters of a disbanded volunteer. Embracing his experiences as honest old Abe's bosom friend and unofficial adviser ... New York, F. A. Brady, 1864.

312 p. front. 19 cm.

A series of letters to newspapers; heavy in philosophy and moral persuasions.

Barber, Lucius W   1839–1872.

Army memoirs of Lucius W. Barber, Company "D", 15th Illinois volunteer infantry. May 24, 1861, to Sept. 30, 1865. Chicago, The J. M. W. Jones stationery and printing co., 1894.

v p., 1 l., [9]–233 p. front. (port.) 23½cm.

Written in diary form; the author's extensive travels during the war, plus his discursive comments on all that he saw, make this one of the better personal narratives by a Federal soldier.

Bardeen, Charles William, 1847–1924.

A little fifer's war diary, with 17 maps, 60 portraits, and 246 other illustrations; by C. W. Bardeen ... with an introduction by Nicholas Murray Butler ... Syracuse, N.Y., C. W. Bardeen, 1910.

16 p., 1 l., 17–329 p. illus. (incl. ports., maps, facsims.) 24cm.

Of importance in this crowded category because Bardeen pointed out in detail both the good and the evil of army life.

Barnes, James A.

The Eighty-sixth regiment, Indiana volunteer infantry. A narrative of its services in the civil war of 1861–1865. Written by a committee consisting of James A. Barnes, James R. Carnahan and Thomas H. B. McCain. Crawfordsville, Ind., The Journal company, printers, 1895.

viii, 613, [1] p. front., port. 23¼ cm.

A voluminous study, with too many excerpts from the Official Records and too much comment on these excerpts.

Barr, James Michael, 1829–1864.

Confederate war correspondence of James Michael Barr and wife Rebecca Ann Dowling Barr [compiled by Ruth Barr McDaniel. n. p. ᶜ1963]

275 p. illus., ports., maps, facsims. 22 cm.

The 1863–1864 letters of a South Carolina soldier who died of complications following an amputation; Barr's letters (to his wife) treat more of personal than of military matters.

Barrett, Orvey S

Reminiscences, incidents, battles, marches and camp life of the old 4th Michigan infantry in war of rebellion, 1861 to 1864. By O. S. Barrett ... Dedicated to the survivors of the regiment ... Detroit, W. S. Ostler, 1888.

44 p., 1 l. 24 cm.

A highly personal memoir, marked by much humor and little attention to military campaigns.

Barron, Samuel Benton, 1834–1912.

The Lone Star defenders; a chronicle of the Third Texas cavalry, Ross' brigade, by S. B. Barron ... New York and Washington, The Neale publishing company, 1908.

3 p. l., 3–276 p. front., 10 port. 21 cm.

Even though based for the most part on memory, and occasionally drifting off on dramatic tangents, this narrative is a standard source for Texas in the Civil War.

Bartlett, Asa W   1839–

History of the Twelfth regiment, New Hampshire volunteers in the war of the rebellion, by Capt. A. W. Bartlett, historian Twelfth regiment association. Concord, I. C. Evans, printer, 1897.

x p., 1 l., 752, 87 p. front. (port.) illus. (incl. ports.) 8 pl. 27½cm.

In many respects the best regimental history for a Civil War unit; information is full, personal, and highly revealing for the Army of the Potomac.

Bartlett, Catherine (Thom) *ed.*

"My dear brother," a Confederate chronicle. Richmond, Dietz Press, 1952.

xiii, 224 p. illus., ports. 24 cm.

A large, rich collection of family letters, including the correspondence of Confederate Col. J. Pembroke Thom.

Bartlett, John Russell, 1805–1886.

Memoirs of Rhode Island officers who were engaged in the service of their country during the great rebellion of the South. Illustrated with thirty-four portraits. By John Russell Bartlett ... Providence, S. S. Rider & brother, 1867.

viii, [9]–452 p. pl., 34 port. 26½ x 22½ cm.

In this huge volume are 109 incomplete biographies, 34 portraits, and a short summary of the 1st Rhode Island.

Bartlett, Napier, 1836–1877.

Military record of Louisiana, including biographical and historical papers relating to the military organizations of the State. Baton Rouge, Louisiana State University Press [1964]

xv, 259 p. 23 cm.

An expansion of the author's memoirs, cited below; contains much data on the Washington Artillery and other Louisiana units.

Bartlett, Napier 1836–1877.

A soldier's story of the war; including the marches and battles of the Washington artillery, and of other Louisiana troops ... New Orleans, Clark & Hofeline, 1874.

1 p. l., 252 (i. e. 262) p. front., port. 22½ cm.

A highly reliable, even-tempered account of the war in Virginia by a member of the famed Washington Artillery; especially good for camp scenes.

Barton, Thomas H b. 1828.

Autobiography, including a history of the Fourth Regt. West Va. Vol. Inf'y with an account of Col. Lightburn's retreat down the Kanawha Valley, Gen. Grant's Vicksburg and Chattanooga campaigns together with the several battles in which the Fourth Regiment was engaged and its losses by disease, desertion and in battle. Charleston, West Virginia Print. Co., 1890.

viii, 340 p. port. 22 cm.

This rather empty narrative by a surgeon of the 4th West Virginia Infantry casts some light on medical affairs in the field.

Bates, Gilbert H

Sergeant Bates' march, carrying the stars and stripes unfurled, from Vicksburg to Washington: being a truthful narrative of the incidents which transpired during his journey on foot, without a cent, through the late rebellious states, and showing how the good old flag was received as the harbinger of peace and new hope to the distressed people of the South. By Gilbert H. Bates. New York, Cincinnati, B. W. Hitchcock [c1868]

35 p. 23cm.

A Wisconsin artillerist gives himself a hearty pat on the back, with an occasional hurrah for the Union.

Battle, *Mrs.* **Laura Elizabeth (Lee)**

Forget-me-nots of the civil war; a romance, containing reminiscences and original letters of two Confederate soldiers. By Laura Elizabeth Lee; illustrated by Bryan Burnes ... St. Louis, Mo., Press A. R. Fleming printing co. [c1909]

355 p. front. (port.) 10 pl. 20½cm.

This potpourri of sentimentality contains a few letters from the field by two soldiers in the 4th North Carolina.

Battle-fields of the South, from Bull Run to Fredericksburgh; with sketches of Confederate commanders, and gossip of the camps. By an English combatant, lieutenant of artillery on the field staff. With two maps. New-York, J. Bradburn, 1864.

xxvii, 517 p. 2 fold. maps. 23½ cm.

One of the most consulted of Southern sources for military operations; the author was an Englishman who served briefly in the Confederate army; his rancor and exaggerations offset in part his good observations.

Battles and leaders of the civil war ... being for the most part contributions by Union and Confederate officers. Based upon "The Century war series." Ed. by R. U. Johnson and C. C. Buel ... New-York, The Century co. [1887–88]

4 v. fronts., illus. (incl. ports., maps, facsims.) 28½ cm.

Opinionated and rationalizing memoirs by high-ranking officers on both sides make this work one of the most quoted in Civil War literature.

Battles and leaders of the Civil War. Being for the most part contributions by Union and Confederate officers. New introd. by Roy F. Nichols. New York, T. Yoseloff [1956]

4 v. illus., ports., maps, facsims., plans, tables. 25 cm.

A poor offset printing of the original edition, with an appropriate new introduction by Prof. Nichols.

Baylor, George, b. 1843.

Bull run to Bull run; or, Four years in the army of northern Virginia. Containing a detailed account of the career and adventures of the Baylor light horse, Company B, Twelfth Virginia cavalry, C. S. A., with leaves from my scrap-book. By George Baylor ... Richmond, B. F. Johnson publishing company, 1900.

412 p. incl. front., illus. (ports.) 23½cm.

A much-consulted memoir by a Virginia cavalryman; especially good for Baylor's discerning personal observations.

Beach, John N   *surgeon 40th Ohio infantry.*
    History of the Fortieth Ohio volunteer infantry; by John
N. Beach ...   London, O., Shepherd & Craig, printers, 1884.

    viii, ₍9₎–243, ₍1₎ p.   19 cm.

Written by the regimental surgeon, this work is
too polished and philosophical.

Beach, William Harrison, *b.* 1835.
    The first New York (Lincoln) cavalry from April 19, 1861
to July 7, 1865, by William H. Beach ...   New York, The Lincoln cavalry association, 1902.

    vii, 579 p.   plates, ports., facsims.   23½ᶜᵐ.

An exceptionally fine study by the regimental
adjutant;   all the basic information is here.

Beale, George William, 1842–
    A lieutenant of cavalry in Lee's army, by G. W. Beale.
Boston, The Gorham press, 1918.

    231 p.   19½ cm.

Totally concerned with the military movements
and engagements of Stuart's cavalry; written
with a somewhat impersonal detachment.

Beale, Richard Lee Tuberville, 1819–1893.
    History of the Ninth Virginia cavalry, in the war be-
tween the states.   By the late Brig. General R. L. T.
Beale.   Richmond, Va., B. F. Johnson publishing company, 1899.

    192 p.   front. (port.)   23ᶜᵐ.

An excellent personal and descriptive narrative
of cavalry operations in the East; the discerning
nature of the book makes it a valuable research
tool for all aspects of the war.

Beall, John Bramblett, 1833–1917.
    In barrack and field; poems and sketches of army life, by
Lieut. Col. John B. Beall ...   Nashville, Tenn., Dallas, Tex.,
Smith & Lamar, agents, Publishing house of the M. E. church,
South, 1906.

    420 p.   front. (port.)   19ᶜᵐ.

Less than one-third of this work covers the
author's service in the 19th Georgia.

Bean, William Gleason, 1891–
    The Liberty Hall Volunteers; Stonewall's college boys
₍by₎ W. G. Bean.   Charlottesville, University Press of Virginia ₍1964₎

    x, 227 p.   22 cm.

Although restricted to the exploits of one company, this study is based largely on heretofore
unused manuscripts.

Bear, Henry Clay, 1838–1927.
    The Civil War letters of Henry C. Bear, a soldier in the
116th Illinois Volunteer Infantry.   Edited by Wayne C.
Temple.   Harrogate, Tenn., Lincoln Memorial University
Press, 1961.

    54 p.   illus.   27 cm.

Letters to his wife from a member of the 116th
Illinois are confined largely to personal observations but contain traces of humor.

Beatty, John, 1828–1914.
    The citizen-soldier; or, Memoirs of a volunteer.   By John
Beatty.   Cincinnati, Wilstach, Baldwin & co., 1879.

    vii, ₍9₎–401 p.   20ᶜᵐ.

Highly readable observations on military affairs,
slavery, officers, and places in both major
theaters; the author attained postwar prominence
in literature and Ohio politics.

Beaudry, Louis Napoleon, 1833–1892.
    Historic records of the Fifth New York cavalry, First Ira
Harris guard: its organization, marches, raids, scouts, engagements and general services, during the rebellion of 1861–1865
...   Also interesting accounts of prison life and of the secret
service.   Complete lists of its officers and men.   By Rev. Louis
N. Beaudry, chaplain ...   3d ed., enl.   Albany, N. Y., J. Munsell, 1868.

    xv, ₍17₎–385 p. incl. plates, ports., tables.   front.   21ᶜᵐ.

Based on Beaudry's diary, the narrative mentions
all the important happenings of the regiment but
rarely goes into detail.

Beck, Stephen C   1842–
    A true sketch of his army life, by S. C. Beck.   ₍Edgar?
Neb., 1914₎

    cover-title, 51 p.   22ᶜᵐ.

Written by a member of the 124th Illinois; revealing for the 1863 campaigns in Mississippi.

Beecher, Harris H
Record of the 114th regiment, N. Y. S. V. Where it went, what it saw, and what it did ... By Dr. Harris H. Beecher ... Norwich, N. Y., J. F. Hubbard, jr., 1866.
2 p. l., x, [11]-582 p. front., port. 20 cm.

A more thorough study than the usual ones published right after the war, yet too padded with manufactured conversations.

Beecher, Herbert W
History of the First light battery Connecticut volunteers, 1861–1865. Personal records and reminiscences. The story of the battery from its organization to the present time. Comp. from official records, personal interviews, private diaries, war histories and individual experiences ... Historian, Herbert W. Beecher ... New York, A. T. De La Mare ptg. and pub. co., ltd. [pref. 1901]
2 v. illus., plates, ports., maps, facsims. 23½ cm.

One of the best of the Connecticut unit histories; contains many recollections by battery members.

Belknap, Charles Eugene 1846–1929.
History of the Michigan organizations at Chickamauga, Chattanooga and Missionary ridge, 1863. Lansing, Mich., R. Smith printing co., 1897.
2 p. l., 374 p., 1 l. front., pl., port. 25 cm.

A business-like account of Michigan units in three critical 1863 campaigns; based largely on data in the Official Records.

Belknap, William Worth 1829–1890, ed.
History of the Fifteenth regiment, Iowa veteran volunteer infantry, from October, 1861, to August, 1865, when disbanded at the end of the war ... Keokuk, R. B. Ogden & son, print., 1887.
644 p. front., pl., port., map, facsim. 23 cm.

This hodgepodge of company histories, rosters, official reports, biographical sketches, statistics, and tables lacks the one all-important ingredient-- personal touches.

Bell, John Thomas, 1842–
Tramps and triumphs of the Second Iowa infantry, briefly sketched, by John T. Bell, lieut. Co. "C." Omaha, Gibson, Miller & Richardson, printers, 1886.
32 p. 22½ cm.

A sketchy summary of the regiment's operations in the Western theater; particularly quotable in its account of Shiloh.

Benedict, George Grenville, 1826–1907.
Army life in Virginia. Letters from the Twelfth Vermont regiment and personal experiences of volunteer service in the war for the Union, 1862–63. By George Grenville Benedict ... Burlington, Free press association, 1895.
4 p. l., 194 p. pl., port. 21½ cm.

This series of personal and dramatic letters, originally published in the Burlington Free Press, is deserving of its longstanding high reputation.

Benedict, George Grenville, 1826–1907.
A short history of the 14th Vermont reg't. By Colonel G. G. Benedict ... An account of the reunion held July 4th, 1887. Also, a roster of the regiment, with present address of members. [Fair Haven?] Co. F., 14th Vermont regiment, 1887.
97 p., 1 l. incl. front., illus. (incl. ports.) 23 cm.

A disorganized potpourri of unrelated items; useless to all but the most patient researcher.

Benedict, George Grenville, 1826–1907.
Vermont in the civil war. A history of the part taken by the Vermont soldiers and sailors in the war for the Union, 1861–5. By G. G. Benedict. Burlington, The Free press association, 1886–88.
2 v. front., port., maps, plans. 24 cm.

An excellent source for statistical data and some personal material on Vermont soldiers; each chapter is a minature history of a regiment.

Bennett, Andrew J b. 1841 or 2.
The story of the First Massachusetts light battery, attached to the Sixth army corps. A glance at events in the armies of the Potomac and Shenandoah, from the summer of 1861 to the autumn of 1864. By A. J. Bennett ... Boston, Press of Deland and Barta, 1886.
200 p. pl., port., maps, facsim. 23½ cm.

This judicious account of a Federal battery's operations in the East also contains a sprinkling of comments on slavery and the countryside.

Bennett, Charles Wilkes, 1838–
Historical sketches of the Ninth Michigan infantry (General Thomas' headquarters guards) with an account of the battle of Murfreesboro, Tennessee, Sunday, July 13, 1862: four years campaigning in the Army of the Cumberland, by Charles W. Bennett ... regimental meetings since the war, by Henry C. Rankin ... regimental and company organizations, by Frank A. Lester, jr. ... Coldwater, Mich., Daily courier print, 1913.
75, [1] p. illus., plates (1 fold.) ports. 22½ cm.

Even though based on reminiscences and wartime letters, this narrative is too cursory to be more than a tribute to the regiment.

Bennett, Edwin Clark.
Musket and sword, or The camp, march, and firing line in the Army of the Potomac, by Edwin C. Bennett ... Boston, Coburn publishing co., 1900.

viii, 344 p. front. (2 port.) 18½ cm.

This account includes reminiscences of most of the major battles of the East through Early's Raid. It contains some detailed comments on individuals, events, and camp life.

Bennett, Lyman G
History of the Thirty-sixth regiment Illinois volunteers, during the war of the rebellion, by L. G. Bennett and Wm. M. Haigh. Aurora, Ill., Knickerbocker & Hodder, printers and binders, 1876.

viii, [9]–808 p. front., port. 22½ cm.

Treats too much of the larger aspects of battle; only occasionally does the author inject personal touches.

Bensell, Royal Augustus, 1838–1921.
All quiet on the Yamhill, the Civil War in Oregon; the journal of Corporal Royal A. Bensell ... Edited by Gunter Barth. Eugene, University of Oregon Books, 1959.

xx, 226 p. illus., port., fold. map. 24 cm.

Important only as a personal record of army life in Oregon during the war.

Benson, Berry.
Berry Benson's Civil War book: memoirs of a Confederate scout and sharpshooter. Edited by Susan Williams Benson. Athens, University of Georgia Press [1962]

203 p. illus. 23 cm.

Based in large part on the diaries and letters of two South Carolina brothers who fought with Jackson and Lee; a good human chronicle.

Bentley, William H
History of the 77th Illinois volunteer infantry, Sept. 2, 1862–July 10, 1865, by Lieut. W. H. Bentley, with an introduction by General D. P. Grier. Peoria, Ill., E. Hine, printer, 1883.

396 p. 20 cm.

Especially valuable for the author's personal observations in Louisiana and Texas; regimental data was obtained through correspondence with comrades.

Benton, Charles Edward, *b.* 1841.
As seen from the ranks; a boy in the Civil War, by Charles E. Benton. New York, Putnam, 1902.

xiii, 292 p. 20 cm.

This pretentious commentary by a New York soldier treats largely of Sherman's campaigns in Georgia and the Carolinas.

Bering, John A
History of the Forty-eighth Ohio vet. vol. inf. giving a complete account of the regiment from its organization at Camp Dennison, O., in October, 1861, to the close of the war, and its final muster-out, May 10, 1866 ... Embracing, also, an account of the escape and re-capture of Major J. A. Bering and Lieut. W. J. Srofe, and the closing events of the war in the trans-Mississippi dep't. By John A. Bering ... and Thomas Montgomery ... Hillsboro, O., Highland news office, 1880.

xv, 284 p. 17½ cm.

A good compilation, except for places where Bering's hand got heavy.

Berkeley, Henry Robinson, 1840–1918.
Four years in the Confederate artillery; the diary of Private Henry Robinson Berkeley. Edited by William H. Runge. Chapel Hill, Published for the Virginia Historical Society, by University of North Carolina Press, 1961.

xxv, 156 p. illus., ports., maps. 26 cm.

A day-by-day chronicle of artillery service, with some long, revealing passages; author was pointed, oftentimes critical, in his observations.

Bernard, George S   1837–1912.
War talks of Confederate veterans. Compiled and edited by Geo. S. Bernard ... Addresses delivered before A. P. Hill camp of Confederate veterans of Petersburg, Va., with addenda. Petersburg, Fenn & Owen, 1892.

xxiii, 335, [1] p., 1 l. front., pl., port., fold. maps, diagr. 23½ cm.

Addresses, short memoirs, and official reports on the Eastern campaigns, with heavy emphasis on the fighting around Petersburg.

Berry, Thomas Franklin, 1832–
Four years with Morgan and Forrest, by Col. Thomas F. Berry ... Oklahoma City, Okla., The Harlow-Ratliff company, 1914.

1 p. l., [vii]–xv, 476 p. front., plates, ports. 20½ cm.

Countless exaggerations, fabrications, and misspellings relegate these "reminiscences" to the category of the absurd.

Best, Isaac O   1841?–

History of the 121st New York state infantry, by Isaac O. Best. Chicago, Ill., J. H. Smith, 1921.

1 p. l., v–x, 254 p. pl., ports. 19½ᶜᵐ.

Best relied heavily on the widest variety of sources and testimony; a good study, but must be treated with caution.

Betts, Alexander Davis, 1832–

Experience of a Confederate chaplain, 1861–1864 [i. e. 1865] by Rev. A. D. Betts ... chaplain 30th N. C. troops. Ed. by W. A. Betts. [Greenville? S. C., 190–?]

103, [1] p. illus., ports. 18ᶜᵐ.

Full of sporadic events haphazardly thrown together, this volume is nevertheless of some use for information on the chaplaincy service.

Beverly, James M   1843–

A history of the Ninety-first regiment, Illinois volunteer infantry, 1862–1865, by James M. Beverly ... White Hall, Ill., Pearce printing co. [1913]

59 p. front., pl., ports. 23ᶜᵐ.

A work too short to be of significant value.

Bevier, Robert S

History of the First and Second Missouri Confederate brigades. 1861–1865. And, From Wakarusa to Appomattox, a military anagraph. By R. S. Bevier. St. Louis, Bryan, Brand & co., 1879.

480, 27 p. front., port. 22½ᶜᵐ.

A pontifical presentation notwithstanding, this work possesses much useful information on Confederate activities in the Trans-Mississippi.

Bickham, William Denison, 1827–1894.

Rosecrans' campaign with the fourteenth army corps, or the Army of the Cumberland: a narrative of personal observations with ... official reports of the battle of Stone River. By "W. D. B." ... Cincinnati, Moore, Wilstach, Keys & co., 1863.

viii, 9–476 p. front. (map) 19ᶜᵐ.

Personal and pointed observations by a correspondent of the Cincinnati Commercial who was there.

Bicknell, Rev. George W

History of the Fifth regiment Maine volunteers, comprising brief descriptions of its marches, engagements, and general services from the date of its muster in, June 24, 1861, to the time of its muster out, July 27, 1864. By Rev. Geo. W. Bicknell ... Portland, H. L. Davis, 1871.

xii, [13]–404 p. front. (port.) pl. 19ᶜᵐ.

A superior personal reminiscence of service in all major battles of the East save Chancellorsville; written with objectivity and insight.

Bidwell, Frederick David, comp.

History of the Forty-ninth New York volunteers. Comp. by Frederick David Bidwell ... Albany, J. B. Lyon company, printers, 1916.

1 p. l., 317 p. front. (port.) plates. 24ᶜᵐ.

This shallow history of a regiment from the Buffalo area contains little personal material; half of the text is a muster roll.

Bierce, Ambrose, 1842–1914?

Ambrose Bierce's Civil War. Edited and with an introd. by William McCann. Chicago, Gateway Editions; distributed by H. Regnery Co. [1956]

xi, 257 p. 18 cm.

Amid a collection of fictionalized war stories are seven well-written, eyewitness accounts by noted authors of such engagements as Shiloh and Chickamauga.

Bigger, David Dwight.

Ohio's silver-tongued orator: life and speeches of General William H. Gibson ... By David Dwight Bigger ... Dayton, O., United brethren publishing house, 1901.

xvii, 19–558 p. incl. illus., plates, ports., map, facsims. front., port. 23ᶜᵐ.

Important chiefly for the reminiscences and letters of Gibson while he served with the 49th Ohio.

Billings, John Davis, 1842–

Hardtack and coffee; or, The unwritten story of army life, including chapters on enlisting, life in tents and log huts, Jonahs and beats, offences and punishments, raw recruits, foraging, crops and crops badges, the wagon trains, the army mule, the engineer corps, the signal corps, etc. By John D. Billings ... Illustrated with six ... color plates; and over two hundred original sketches by Charles W. Reed ... Boston, G. M. Smith & co., 1887.

vi, 406 p. incl. illus., plates, ports. front. 6 col. pl. 23 cm.

The best source for the army life and feelings of a Federal soldier; this delightfully written and humorously illustrated work has rightfully become a classic.

Billings, John Davis, *b.* 1842.

Hardtack and coffee, the unwritten story of Army life. Edited by Richard Harwell. Chicago, R. R. Donnelley, 1960.

483 p. illus. 18 cm.

The best of several editions of this classic; the text, completely reset, profited also from skillful editing.

Billings, John Davis, 1842–

The history of the Tenth Massachusetts battery of light artillery in the war of the rebellion. Formerly of the Third corps, and afterwards of Hancock's Second corps. Army of the Potomac. 1862–1865. By John D. Billings ... Boston, Hall & Whiting, 1881.

xii p., 2 l., 400 p. incl. front., plates (1 col.) ports., 2 plans. 24cm.

Among the top dozen unit histories pertaining to the Civil War; Billings used his own diary, some 300 letters, and a comrade's manuscript as a basis for this book.

Bircher, William.

A drummer-boy's diary: comprising four years of service with the Second regiment Minnesota veteran volunteers, 1861 to 1865. By William Bircher. St. Paul, Minn., St. Paul book and stationery co., 1889.

199 p. front., pl. 12°.

This journal of a youth in the 2nd Minnesota concentrates mostly on weather and marches.

Bishop, Judson Wade, 1831–1917.

The story of a regiment; being a narrative of the service of the Second regiment, Minnesota veteran volunteer infantry, in the civil war of 1861–1865, by Judson W. Bishop ... written and published for, and by request of the surviving members of the regiment. St. Paul, 1890.

2 p. l., 256 p. front., port. 20½cm.

Written by the regiment's colonel, this work treats more of the major movements than of the regiment's actions.

Blackburn, James Knox Polk, 1837–1923.

Reminiscences of the Terry rangers. By J. K. P. Blackburn. ₍Austin₎ Published by the Littlefield fund for southern history, the University of Texas, 1919.

vii, 79 p. 27 cm.

Written fifty years after the war and based almost solely on failing memory.

Blackford, Charles Minor, 1865–

Annals of the Lynchburg Home guard ... Prepared by request by Charles M. Blackford, jr., M. D., chairman, assisted by the ... committee ... Pub. by the company. Lynchburg, Va., J. W. Rohr, printer, 1891.

185 p. front., pl., ports. 17½cm.

Included in this brief, choppy history of a company in the 11th Virginia are several letters written home by the soldiers.

Blackford, Susan Leigh (Colston) *b.* 1835, *comp.*

Letters from Lee's army; or, Memoirs of life in and out of the army in Virginia during the war between the states. Compiled by Susan Leigh Blackford from original and contemporaneous memoirs, correspondence and diaries, annotated by her husband, Charles Minor Blackford, edited and abridged for publication by Charles Minor Blackford III. New York, C. Scribner's sons; London, C. Scribner's sons, ltd., 1947.

vii p., 2 l., 312 p. 21½ cm.

A new edition, with short introduction and needed index, of Mrs. Blackford's Memoirs of Life.

Blackford, *Mrs.* **Susan Leigh (Colston)** 1835– *comp.*

Memoirs of life in and out of the army in Virginia during the war between the states. Comp. by Susan Leigh Blackford from original and cotemporaneous correspondence and diaries. Annotated and edited exclusively for the private use of their family by her husband, Charles Minor Blackford ... Lynchburg, Va., J. P. Bell company, printers, 1894–96.

2 v. 24cm.

Contains, among other rich material, the interchange of letters between an officer of the 2nd Virginia Cavalry and his wife.

Blackford, William Willis, 1831–1905.

War years with Jeb Stuart, by Lieut. Colonel W. W. Blackford, C. S. A. New York, C. Scribner's sons, 1945.

xiii p., 1 l., 322 p, incl. front. plates, ports., map. 21 cm.

Blackford was a Virginia socialite with many acquaintances; his narrative is therefore a mixture of military affairs in the East and social conditions in Virginia.

Blake, Henry Nichols, 1838–

Three years in the Army of the Potomac. By Henry N. Blake, late captain in the Eleventh regiment Massachusetts volunteers ... Boston, Lee and Shepard, 1865.

vi, 7–319 p. 18½ cm.

A caustic, carping narrative in which the author, a captain in the 11th Massachusetts, apparently did not see one thing on either side to praise during his term of service.

Blakeslee, Bernard F

History of the Sixteenth Connecticut volunteers. By B. F. Blakeslee ... Hartford, The Case, Lockwood & Brainard co., printers, 1875.

116 p. 19^{cm}.

More a personal narrative, and based on a diary the author kept; nevertheless, the text is too sketchy and is comparatively empty as a regimental history.

Blessington, Joseph P

The campaigns of Walker's Texas division. By a private soldier. Containing a complete record of the campaigns in Texas, Louisiana and Arkansas ... including the federal's report of the battles, names of the officers of the division, diary of marches, camp scenery, anecdotes ... &c., &c. ... New York, Pub. for the author, 1875.

314 p. 23 cm.

This above-average unit history touches on military operations in all sections, including the Trans-Mississippi, and contains many of the author's personal experiences.

Bloodgood, John D   d. 1915.

Personal reminiscences of the war, by Rev. J. D. Bloodgood ... New York, Hunt & Eaton; Cincinnati, Cranston & Curts, 1893.

342 p. 18^{cm}.

Highly dramatic memoirs by a sergeant of the 141st Pennsylvania; Bloodgood borrowed freely from David Craft's history of the same unit.

Boggs, William Robertson, 1829-1911.

... Military reminiscences of Gen. Wm. R. Boggs, c. s. a.; introduction and notes by William K. Boyd. Durham, N. C., The Seeman printery, 1913.

xxiii, 115 p. front. (port.) 20 cm.

A very confined autobiography-- quite in keeping with Bogg's few achievements.

Boies, Andrew J

Record of the Thirty-third Massachusetts volunteer infantry, from Aug. 1862 to Aug. 1865. By Andrew J. Boies. Fitchburg, Sentinel printing company, 1880.

168 p. front. (port.) 23½^{cm}.

An overrated volume by a soldier who saw action in both major theaters; the diary-like entries are short and coldly factual.

Bolton, Horace Wilbert, 1839-

Personal reminiscences of the late war, by H. W. Bolton. Introduced by F. A. Hardin, d. d. Ed. by H. G. Jackson, d. d. Chicago, Ill., H. W. Bolton, 1892.

viii, [9]-219 p. front., illus., port. 20^{cm}.

Antietam was the only major battle in which this member of the 16th Maine participated; the account continually slips from summaries of military matters to philosophical commentaries on life in general.

Booth, George Wilson 1844-1914.

Personal reminiscences of a Maryland soldier in the war between the states, 1861-1865. For private circulation only. Baltimore [Press of Fleet, McGinley & co.] 1898.

177 p. 24^{cm}.

Written by a young soldier who participated in many battles before his capture, this work contains so much on affairs both on and behind the lines that it is deserving of republication.

Borcke, Heros von, 1835-1895.

Memoirs of the Confederate war for independence, by Heros van Borcke ... Edinburgh and London, W. Blackwood and sons, 1866.

2 v. fold. map. 20 cm.

These personal, full, and highly revealing recollections by a Prussian officer who served with "Jeb" Stuart are a mandatory source for any study of Confederate cavalry.

Borton, Benjamin.

Awhile with the blue; or, Memories of war days. The true story of a private, by Benjamin Borton. Published by the author. Passaic, N. J., W. Taylor, printer, 1898.

2 p. l., [3]-168 p. front., plates, ports. 19½^{cm}.

Concerned for the most part with the Chancellorsville campaign; too manufactured and shallow to be of great significance.

Borton, Benjamin.

On the parallels; or, Chapters of inner history; a story of the Rappahannock, by Benjamin Borton ... Woodstown, N. J., Monitor-register print, 1903.

333 p. incl. front. (port.) plates. pl. 20^{cm}.

A more elaborate account of wartime by this New Jersey soldier, but Borton is still guilty of too much embellishment. This volume treats of the Fredericksburg campaign.

Bosbyshell, Oliver Christian, 1839–

The 48th in the war. Being a narrative of the campaigns of the 48th regiment, infantry, Pennsylvania veteran volunteers, during the war of the rebellion. By Oliver Christian Bosbyshell ... Philadelphia, Avil printing company, 1895.

4 p. l., 17–205 p. front., pl., port. 23½ᶜᵐ.

One of the better regimental histories; written with personal insight and obvious forethought; covers military and civilian topics in both Eastern and Western theaters.

Bosson, Charles Palfray.

History of the Forty-second regiment infantry, Massachusetts volunteers, 1862, 1863, 1864. By Sergeant-Major Charles P. Bosson. Boston, Mills, Knight & co., printers, 1886.

vi p., 1 l., 465 p. pl., port. 19½ᶜᵐ.

Valuable for the Louisiana campaigns, but disappointing as a unit history.

Bouton, Edward, 1834–

Events of the civil war, by General Edward Bouton; with sketch of the author. [Los Angeles, Kingsley, Moles & Collins co., printers, 1906]

114, [2] p. incl. illus., pl., 2 port. 26ᶜᵐ.

A self-testimonial to an artillery officer; contains some personal impressions of Grant.

Bowen, James Lorenzo.

History of the Thirty-seventh regiment, Mass., volunteers, in the civil war of 1861–1865, with a comprehensive sketch of the doings of Massachusetts as a state, and of the principal campaigns of the war. By James L. Bowen. Holyoke, Mass., and New York, C. W. Bryan & company, 1884.

2 p. l., [9]–431, [i] p. front., pl. 21ᶜᵐ.

The detailed history of a unit that campaigned from Fredericksburg to Appomattox; yet the work lacks personal incidents and too often encompasses the war as a whole.

Bowen, J[ames] R[iley] 1834–

Regimental history of the First New York dragoons (originally the 130th N. Y. vol. infantry) during three years of active service in the great civil war, by Rev. J. R. Bowen ... [Battle Creek, Mich.] The author, 1900.

x, [7]–464 p. incl. ports. front. 20½ᶜᵐ.

Too manufactured to be either revealing or trustworthy.

Boyce, Charles William, b. 1842.

A brief history of the Twenty-eighth regiment New York state volunteers, First brigade, First division, Twelfth corps, Army of the Potomac, from the author's diary and official reports. With the muster-roll of the regiment, and many pictures, articles and letters from surviving members and friends, with the report of proceedings of the thirty-fifth annual reunion held at Albion, New York, May 22, 1896. [By] C. W. Boyce. Buffalo, N. Y. [The Matthews-Northup co., 1896?]

190 p. incl. front. (port.) illus. (incl. maps) 25½ᶜᵐ.

The double-columned narrative is of average value; the latter half of the work contains reminiscences by various members of the regiment.

Boyle, John Richards.

Soldiers true; the story of the One hundred and eleventh regiment Pennsylvania veteran volunteers and of its campaigns in the war for the union, 1861–1865, by John Richards Boyle ... Published by authority of the regimental association. New York, Eaton & Mains; Cincinnati, Jennings & Pye, 1903.

368 p. incl. illus., plates, ports. 2 fold. maps. 23½ᶜᵐ.

More a history of the campaigns in which the regiment participated than a chronicle of the unit's activities and experiences.

Bradley, George S

The star corps; or, Notes of an army chaplain, during Sherman's famous "march to the sea." Rev. G. S. Bradley ... Milwaukee, Jermain & Brightman, printers, 1865.

xi, [13]–304 p. front. (port.) 20ᶜᵐ.

This narrative by the chaplain of the 22nd Wisconsin is a hodgepodge of diary quotation, extracts from letters, poetry, and observations both factual and philosophical. His descriptions of the victims of Sherman's march are particularly good.

Bradley, James, 1835–

The Confederate mail carrier; or, From Missouri to Arkansas, through Mississippi, Alabama, Georgia and Tennessee, An unwritten leaf of the "civil war". Being an account of the battles, marches and hardships of the First and Second brigades, Mo., C. S. A. Together with the thrilling adventures and narrow escapes of Captain Grimes and his fair accomplice, who carried the mail by the "underground route" from the brigade to Missouri. By James Bradley. Mexico, Mo., 1894.

2 p. l., 275 p. front., ports. 20ᶜᵐ.

Not as exciting as its lengthy title implies.

Bragg, Junius Newport, b. 1838.

Letters of a Confederate surgeon, 1861–65 [by] Mrs. T. J. Gaughan. [Camden? Ark., ᶜ1960]

276 p. illus., ports., facsim. 23 cm.

This fine collection of letters, written by the Surgeon of the 11th Arkansas, spans the entire war period in the Trans-Mississippi.

Brainard, Mary Genevie Green.

Campaigns of the One hundred and forty-sixth regiment, New York state volunteers, also known as Halleck's infantry, the Fifth Oneida, and Garrard's tigers; comp. by Mary Genevie Green Brainard, with 56 illustrations and maps. New York and London, G. P. Putnam's sons, 1915.

xiii, 542 p. front., plates, ports., fold. maps. 23½ cm.

Though the author had access to many letters and diaries, her unfamiliarity with either war or writing history is painfully apparent.

Brant, Jefferson E

History of the Eighty-fifth Indiana volunteer infantry, its organization, campaigns and battles. Written at the request of the members by Rev. J. E. Brant ... Bloomington, Ind., Cravens bros., printers, 1902.

1 p. l., 191, [5] p. incl. front., port. port. 21 cm.

Short day-by-day entries by the regiment's lieutenant colonel; based on his diary, letters and-- occasionally-- on his memory.

Brent, Joseph Lancaster, 1826-1905.

Memoirs of the war between the states, by Brigadier-general Joseph Lancaster Brent (C. S. A.) [New Orleans, La., Fontana printing company inc.] ©1940.

238 p., 1 l. port. 24 cm.

Written late in life, these recollections nevertheless are valuable for insights into Confederate actions during the Seven Days Campaign.

Briant, Charles C

History of the Sixth regiment Indiana volunteer infantry. Of both the three months' and three years' services ... by ... C. C. Briant ... Indianapolis, W. B. Burford, printer and binder, 1891.

iv p., 1 l., 423 p. front., ports. 19½ cm.

A rather full memoir on the war in the West; like a great many similar recollections, this one displays a constant bitterness toward Southern life.

Bright, Adam S _d._ 1888.

"Respects to all"; letters of two Pennsylvania boys [Adam S. and Michael S. Bright] in the War of the Rebellion. Edited by Aida Craig Truxall. [Pittsburgh] University of Pittsburgh Press [1962]

96 p. ports. 25 cm.

A small collection of personal letters by two orphaned brothers who served in different Pennsylvania regiments; valueless for historical facts.

Brinton, John Hill, 1832-1907.

Personal memoirs of John H. Brinton, major and surgeon U. S. V., 1861-1865 ... New York, The Neale publishing company, 1914.

361 p. front. (port.) 21 cm.

Brinton, a renowned surgeon and able scholar, provides intimate glimpses of both Federal hospitals in the West and the principal battlefields of the East.

Bristol, Frank Milton, _bp._, 1851-1932.

The life of Chaplain McCabe, bishop of the Methodist Episcopal church, by Frank Milton Bristol ... New York, Chicago [etc.] F. H. Revell company [©1908]

416 p. front., pl., ports., facsims. 21½ cm.

McCabe was Chaplain of the 122nd Ohio, but most of his war letters originated in Libby Prison.

Britton, Wiley.

Memoirs of the rebellion on the border, 1863, by Wiley Britton ... Chicago, Cushing, Thomas & co., 1882.

458 p. 19½ cm.

A basic source for civilian and military affairs in the Kansas-Missouri-Oklahoma area during that region's critical period; the author, a member of the 6th Kansas Cavalry, treats also of Indian and guerilla warfare.

Britton, Wiley.

The Union Indian brigade in the civil war, by Wiley Britton ... Kansas City, Mo., Franklin Hudson publishing co., 1922.

474 p. front., ports., maps. 20 cm.

A popularly written history of Indian soldiers and military events during the 1861-1864 campaigns in Missouri and Arkansas.

Brobst, John F 1838 or 9-1917.

Well, Mary; Civil War letters of a Wisconsin volunteer. Edited by Margaret Brobst Roth. Madison, University of Wisconsin Press, 1960.

165 p. illus. 23 cm.

The frank, literate, and humorous letters of a soldier who served with Sherman and who made no attempt to conceal his hatred of all things Southern.

Brooks, Ulysses Robert, 1846–1917.
  Butler and his cavalry in the war of secession, 1861–1865, by U. R. Brooks ... Columbia, S. C., The State company, 1909.
    591 p. incl. illus., ports. pl. 24 cm.

Eulogies, recollections, and testimonies from comrades form a hodgepodge of unbalanced information on a South Carolina cavalry regiment.

Brooks, Ulysses Robert, 1846–1917, *ed.*
  Stories of the confederacy, ed. by U. R. Brooks. Columbia, S. C., The State company, 1912.
    410 p. plates, ports. 24 cm.

A collection of minutae on a variety of subjects, mostly with South Carolina origins.

Brown, Alonzo Leighton, 1838–1904.
  History of the Fourth regiment of Minnesota infantry volunteers during the great rebellion, 1861–1865, by Alonzo L. Brown ... St. Paul, Minn., The Pioneer press company, 1892.
    594 p. front., 1 illus., plates, ports., maps, plans (1 fold.) 23ᶜᵐ.

Another work based too much on Official Records excerpts and hearsay evidence.

Brown, Augustus Cleveland, 1839–1915.
  The diary of a line officer, by Captain Augustus C. Brown ... ₍New York, 1906?₎
    1 p. l., 117 p. front. (port.) 19ᶜᵐ.

This short, strictly factual narrative treats only of Grant's campaign against Richmond in the May–December 1864, period.

Brown, Dee Alexander.
  The bold cavaliers; Morgan's 2nd Kentucky Cavalry Raiders. ₍1st ed.₎ Philadelphia, Lippincott ₍1959₎
    353 p. illus. 22 cm.

A popularly written history of Col. John Hunt Morgan and his 2nd Kentucky Cavalry (C. S. A.).

Brown, Edmund Randolph 1845–
  The Twenty-seventh Indiana volunteer infantry in the war of the rebellion, 1861 to 1865. First division, 12th and 20th corps. A history of its recruiting, organization, camp life, marches and battles, together with a roster of the men composing it ... By a member of Company C. ₍Monticello, Ind., 1899₎
    640, ₍2₎ p. incl. front., illus. (incl. ports.) 23ᶜᵐ.

One of the better regimental histories; letters, diaries, reports, and the author's own memory recount the exploits of a regiment that saw service in the principal battles of both theaters.

Brown, Henri Le Fevre.
  History of the third regiment, Excelsior brigade, 72d New York volunteer infantry, 1861–1865. Comp. by Henri Le Fevre Brown ... ₍Jamestown, N. Y., Journal printing co.₎ 1902.
    151, ₍7₎ p. front., pl., ports. 23 cm.

So shallow as to be all but worthless as a regimental study.

Brown, Leonard, 1837–1914.
  American patriotism : or, Memoirs of "common men." By Leonard Brown ... Des Moines, Redhead and Wellslager, 1869.
    vii, ₍1₎, 574 p. 19 cm.

A valuable collection of biographical sketches, as well as excerpts from wartime letters and diaries, of Iowa soldiers who died in service.

Brown, *Mrs.* **Maud (Morrow)**
  The University greys: Company A, Eleventh Mississippi regiment, Army of northern Virginia, 1861–1865, by Maud Morrow Brown. Richmond, Va., Garrett and Massie, incorporated ₍ᶜ1940₎
    xii p., 1 l., 80 p. front. (port.) 23½ᶜᵐ.

Included in this brief tribute to a famous college company are numerous letters and observations by its members.

Brown, Philip Francis, 1842–
  Reminiscences of the war of 1861–1865. By Philip F. Brown ... ₍Roanoke, Va., Printed by the Union printing co., ᶜ1912₎
    cover-title, 54 p. illus. (incl. port.) 22½ᶜᵐ.

The bulk of these recollections treat of the author's experiences while a clerk in a Richmond hotel; his prior service as a soldier ended with a wound at Antietam.

Brown, Spencer Kellogg, 1842–1863.

Spencer Kellogg Brown, his life in Kansas and his death as a spy, 1842–1863, as disclosed in his diary, ed. by George Gardner Smith.   New York, D. Appleton and company, 1903.

x, 380 p.   2 facsims. incl. front.   19½ cm.

The editor's sentimental trappings make even more suspect this fragmentary and rambling diary of a young secret service agent.

Brown, Varina Davis.

A colonel at Gettysburg and Spotsylvania, by Varina D. Brown ...   Columbia, S. C., The State company, 1931.

xvi, 333 p.   front., ports., maps (1 fold.)   24½ cm.

A military biography of Col. Joseph N. Brown, 14th South Carolina; the author made abundant use of letters, newspapers, addresses, and printed sources.

Bruce, George Anson.

The twentieth regiment of Massachusetts volunteer infantry, 1861–1865, by brevet Lt.-Col. George A. Bruce, at the request of the Officers' association of the regiment.   Boston and New York, Houghton, Mifflin and company, 1906.

viii p., 2 l., 519, [1] p.   1 illus., plates, 2 port. (incl. front.) maps. 22½ cm.

An underrated, comprehensive unit history containing an admirable blend of the personal, statistical, and factual; John C. Ropes began the study which Bruce completed.

Bruce, Philip Alexander, 1856–1933.

Brave deeds of Confederate soldiers, by Philip Alexander Bruce ...   Philadelphia, G. W. Jacobs & company [°1916]

351 p.   front., plates.   21½ cm.

Sixteen unreliable essays of Confederate heroism; written for popular consumption.

Bryant, Edwin Eustace, 1835–1903.

History of the Third regiment of Wisconsin veteran volunteer infantry 1861–1865.   By Edwin E. Bryant ...   With maps compiled by Wm. F. Goodhue, veteran of Company C, and a complete roster of all who were members of the regiment. Madison, Veteran association of the regiment, 1891.

xvii, 445 p., 1 l.   front., port., fold. maps.   23½ cm.

An excellent regimental history; maps and illustrations are above average, and the text is particularly revealing for battles.

Bryner, Byron Cloyd, 1849–

Bugle echoes; the story of Illinois 47th ...   By Cloyd Bryner ...   [Springfield, Ill., Phillips bros., printers, 1905]

ix p., 1 l., 11–262 p.   front., plates, ports.   23½ cm.

More a personal narrative than a unit history; the author appears to have spent more time traveling than fighting, and his view of the war was too broad to give his volume lasting value.

Buck, Irving, b. 1840.

Cleburne and his command, by Irving A. Buck ...   New York and Washington, The Neale publishing company, 1908.

xii p., 2 l., [17]–382 p.   front. (port.) pl., 5 maps.   22½ cm.

Unquestionably one of the best Confederate memoirs of the war in the West; the highly observant author was Gen. "Pat" Cleburne's adjutant.

Buck, Irving Ashby, 1840–1912.

Cleburne and his command, by Irving A. Buck, and Pat Cleburne, Stonewall Jackson of the West, by Thomas Robson Hay.   Foreword by Bell Irvin Wiley.   Jackson, Tenn., McCowat-Mercer Press, 1959.

378 p.   illus., ports., maps, facsim.   25 cm.

A 50-page editor's introduction, plus footnotes, appendices and index, make this a far superior edition to the above.

Buell, Augustus C   1847–1904.

"The cannoneer."   Recollections of service in the Army of the Potomac.   By "a detached volunteer" in the regular artillery.   Augustus Buell ...   Washington, D. C., The National tribune, 1890.

400 p.   front., illus., port., plans.   21 cm.

A wordy commentary on the experiences of a member of the 4th U. S. Artillery; the narrative is often spicy and highly critical of such officers as McClellan and Burnside.

Buffum, Francis Henry

A memorial of the great rebellion: being a history of the Fourteenth regiment New-Hampshire volunteers, covering its three years of service, with original sketches of army life. 1862–1865.   Issued by the committee of publication.   Boston, Rand, Avery, & company, 1882.

xii, 443 p.   front., pl., port., maps.   24 cm.

An exceptionally good regimental history for insights on camp life, equipment, personal experiences, and anecdotes; the 14th N. H. campaigned in both Mississippi and Virginia.

Burchard, Peter.
     One gallant rush; Robert Gould Shaw and his brave Black Regiment.   New York, St Martin's Press [1965]

x, 168 p.   illus., maps, port.   22 cm.

More readable than researched, this study nevertheless gives some details on the recruitment and organization of the 54th Massachusetts.

Burdette, Robert Jones, 1844–1914.
     The drums of the 47th, by Robert J. Burdette ...   Indianapolis, The Bobbs-Merrill company [c1914]

5 p. l., 211, [1] p.   19½ cm.

Although this is the best narrative pertaining to the 47th Illinois, it succumbs to the author's penchant for philosophical sermons and lack of real personal observations.

Burr, Frank A   1843–1894.
     Life and achievements of James Addams Beaver.   Early life, military services and public career.   By Frank A. Burr ...   Philadelphia, Ferguson bros. & co., printers, 1882.

224 p. incl. 2 facsim.   pl., 2 port. (incl. front.)   3 maps.   19 cm.

A comprehensive biography, with much primary material, of a man who rose from the colonelcy of the 148th Pennsylvania to the governorship of the Keystone State.

Burton, Elijah P
     Diary of E. P. Burton, surgeon, 7th reg. Ill., 3rd brig., 2nd div. 16 A. C.   Prepared by the Historical records survey, Division of professional and service projects, Work projects administration.   Des Moines, Iowa, The Historical records survey, 1939.

3 p. l., 92 numb. l.   28 cm.

A mimeographed project of the WPA, this document tells much of soldier life and of Sherman's march; written in a straightforward manner without prejudices.

Butler, Jay Caldwell, 1844–1885.
     Letters home [by] Jay Caldwell Butler, captain, 101st. Ohio volunteer infantry, arranged by his son Watson Hubbard Butler ...   [Binghamton, N. Y.] Priv. print., 1930.

x, 153 p.   21½ cm.

These letters by an officer of the 101st Ohio cover the Western campaigns from Perryville through Atlanta.   The epistles are short, oftentimes clipped, but they tell some facts not found elsewhere.

Butler, Marvin Benjamin, 1834–1914.
     My story of the civil war and the Under-ground railroad, by M. B. Butler ...   Huntington, Ind., The United brethren publishing establishment, 1914.

6 p. l., 5-390 p.   illus. (incl. ports.)   22½ cm.

Butler's service in the 44th Indiana was briefer than his postwar recollections.

Butterfield, *Mrs.* **Julia Lorrilard (Safford)** *ed.*
     A biographical memorial of General Daniel Butterfield, including many addresses and military writings, ed. by Julia Lorrilard Butterfield ...   New York, The Grafton press, 1904.

xii, 379 p.   front., plates, ports., facsims.   25 cm.

This voluminous tribute contains a large number of letters written by and to Butterfield, who is remembered primarily as the author of "Taps."

Cadwallader, Sylvanus, 1825 or 6–
     Three years with Grant, as recalled by war correspondent Sylvanus Cadwallader.   Edited, and with an introd. and notes, by Benjamin P. Thomas.   [1st ed.]   New York, Knopf, 1955.

xiv, 353, viii p.   maps (1 fold.)   22 cm.

The frank, controversial, and sometimes entertaining recollections of a Chicago newspaperman who, beginning in 1863, was almost constantly with Grant.

Cadwell, Charles K
     The old Sixth regiment, its war record, 1861-5, by Charles K. Cadwell ...   New Haven, Tuttle, Morehouse & Taylor, printers, 1875.

227, [1] p.   20½ cm.

A superior narrative of Federal campaigning along the Georgia and Florida coasts; the author was a member of the 6th New Hampshire.

Caldwell, James Fitz James.
     The history of a brigade of South Carolinians, known first as "Gregg's" and subsequently as "McGowan's brigade."   By J. F. J. Caldwell ...   Philadelphia, King & Baird, printers, 1866.

247 p.   20 cm.

The best unit history from the Palmetto State; the author describes all of the brigade's many engagements and adds enough personal material to make the account both personal and human in scope.

Calkins, William Wirt, 1842–

The history of the One hundred and fourth regiment of Illinois volunteer infantry. War of the great rebellion, 1862–1865, by William Wirt Calkins ... Historical committee: Frank M. Sapp, Milton B. Bushnell, John H. Widmer, William W. Calkins. Chicago, Donohue & Henneberry, printers, 1895.

7 p. l., 539 p. 3 pl., ports. 22½ cm.

A detailed chronicle of events rather than a compilation of personal material; but especially good for Sherman's 1864-1865 campaigns.

Calvert, Henry Murray.

Reminiscences of a boy in blue, 1862–1865, by Henry Murray Calvert. New York and London, G. P. Putnam's sons, 1920.

vii, 347 p. 20½ cm.

Another of those memoirs written years after the war and without benefit of mind-refreshing sources; reconstructed conversation and interpretation drown out the few facts presented.

Camper, Charles, comp.

Historical record of the First regiment Maryland infantry, with an appendix containing a register of the officers and enlisted men, biographies of deceased officers, etc. war of the rebellion, 1861–65. Comp. by Chas. Camper and J. W. Kirkley ... Washington, Gibson brothers, printers, 1871.

x, 312 p. 18½ cm.

Obviously based on a diary, but inferior to such companion volumes as that by Goldborough.

Canfield, Silas S

History of the 21st regiment Ohio volunteer infantry, in the war of the rebellion; by Captain S. S. Canfield. Toledo, Vrooman, Anderson & Bateman, printers, 1893.

192 p., 1 l., 47 p. front., port. 22½ cm.

Too dependent upon the Official Records and unsupported recollections rendered years after the war.

Cannon, J   P

Inside of rebeldom; the daily life of a private in the Confederate Army. Washington, National tribune, 1900.

288 p. illus., port. 22 cm.

An empty narrative, written for popular consumption, and containing only general information on the war in the West.

Cannon, Le Grand Bouton, 1815–1906.

Personal reminiscences of the rebellion, 1861–1866, by Le Grand B. Cannon ... New York [Burr printing house] 1895.

228 p. ports. (incl. front.) 19½ cm.

Garrulous recollections by an officer attached to Gen. John Wool's command at Norfolk, Va., during the first year of the war.

Carpenter, George N

History of the Eighth regiment Vermont volunteers. 1861–1865. By Geo. N. Carpenter. Issued by the committee of publication. Boston, Press of Deland & Barta, 1886.

x p., 1 l., 335 p. front., pl., port., plans, facsim. 23¼ cm.

A composite of reminiscences and wartime correspondence; this regiment served in Louisiana and took part also in the Second Valley Campaign.

Carter, Howell.

A cavalryman's reminiscences of the civil war. By Howell Carter. New Orleans, The American printing co., ltd. [19—]

2 p. l., [9]–212 p. incl. ports. ports. 18 cm.

Written some thirty years after the war, these recollections are sketchy, choppy, and oftentimes impersonal; the author was in the 1st Louisiana Cavalry.

Carter, Robert Goldthwaite, 1845–

Four brothers in blue; or, Sunshine and shadows of the war of the rebellion; a story of the great civil war from Bull Run to Appomattox, by Captain Robert Goldthwaite Carter ... Washington, Press of Gibson bros., inc., 1913.

xiii, 509 p. front. (group of ports.) 28 cm.

Singularly unique, for this volume is composed largely of the letters from the field of four Massachusetts brothers; all served in the Army of the Potomac.

Carter, William Randolph, 1843–

History of the First regiment of Tennessee volunteer cavalry in the great war of the rebellion, with the armies of the Ohio and Cumberland, under Generals Morgan, Rosecrans, Thomas, Stanley and Wilson. 1862-1865. By W. R. Carter ... Knoxville, Tenn., Gaut-Ogden co., printers, 1902.

335 p. front., pl., port., maps. 23 cm.

A unique and quite revealing unit study of a Unionist regiment from Tennessee; exceedingly scarce.

Casler, John Overton, 1838–

Four years in the Stonewall brigade. By John O. Casler. Private, Company A, 33d regiment Virginia infantry, Stonewall brigade, 1st division, 2d corps, Army of Northern Virginia, Gen. Robert E. Lee, commanding ... Guthrie, Okl., State capital printing company, 1893.

495 p. incl. illus., plates, ports., facsims. fold. facsim. 20½ cm.

This embellished memoir, as witty as it is informative, is in a class with volumes by Billings and McCarthy. The author occasionally stretches the truth for the sake of a good story.

Castle, Henry Anson, 1841–1916.

The army mule, and other war sketches, by Henry A. Castle ... With illustrations by J. W. Vawter. Indianapolis and Kansas City, The Bowen-Merrill company, 1898.

3 p. l., 269 p. front., illus., plates. 19 cm.

Tongue-in-cheek commentaries on such army items as mules and tents; Castle was an Illinois soldier.

Castleman, John Breckinridge, 1841–1918.

Active service. Louisville, Ky., Courier-Journal Job Print. Co., 1917.

269 p. plates, ports., facsims. 27 cm.

An overrated collection of reminiscences and excerpts from other works; written by a prominent Kentuckian in Confederate service.

Cate, Wirt Armistead, *ed.*

Two soldiers; the campaign diaries of Thomas J. Key, c. s. a., December 7, 1863–May 17, 1865, and Robert J. Campbell, u. s. a., January 1, 1864–July 21, 1864; edited, with an introduction, notes, and maps, by Wirt Armistead Cate. Chapel Hill, The University of North Carolina press, 1938.

xiii, 277 p. front., illus. (maps) 2 port. on 1 pl., facsims. 22 cm.

In this volume are the fragmentary diaries of one soldier from North Carolina and another from Iowa. Neither journal adds much beyond weather observations and strictly personal notes.

Cavanagh, Michael.

Memoirs of Gen. Thomas Francis Meagher, comprising the leading events of his career chronologically arranged, with selections from his speeches, lectures and miscellaneous writings, including personal reminiscences. By Michael Cavanagh ... Worcester, Mass., The Messenger press, 1892.

2 p. l., iv, [5]–496. 38 p. front., 3 pl., port. 23½ cm.

Less than a fourth of this volume treats of Gen. Meagher's Civil War career; yet many of the Irish Brigade commander's letters are included.

Chamberlain, Joshua Lawrence, 1828–1914.

The passing of the armies; an account of the final campaign of the Army of the Potomac, based upon personal reminiscences of the Fifth army corps, by Joshua Lawrence Chamberlain ... with portraits and maps. New York, and London, G. P. Putnam's sons, 1915.

xxi, 392 p. 2 port. (incl. front.) 3 plans (2 fold.) 22 cm.

The climax of Chamberlain's readable reminiscences is his moving description of the surrender ceremonies at Appomattox.

Chamberlaine, William W   1836?–

Memoirs of the civil war between the northern and southern sections of the United States of America, 1861–1865, by Captain William W. Chamberlaine ... Washington, D. C., Press of B. S. Adams, 1912.

138 p. front. (port.) 21 cm.

The author's reliance on an unreliable memory, plus his many factual inaccuracies, render this account of no tangible value.

Chamberlayne, John Hampden, 1838–1882.

Ham Chamberlayne—Virginian; letters and papers of an artillery officer in the war for southern independence, 1861–1865; with introduction, notes, and index, by his son, C. G. Chamberlayne. Richmond, Va., Press of the Dietz printing co., 1932.

xxx p., 1 l., 440 p. front., plates, ports., maps (2 fold.) facsims. 23½ cm.

An exceptionally revealing collection of papers by a young Virginia aristocrat who served long and faithfully in a Richmond artillery battery.

Chamberlin, Thomas, 1838–

History of the One hundred and fiftieth regiment, Pennsylvania volunteers, Second regiment, Bucktail brigade. By Lieutenant-Colonel Thomas Chamberlin ... Philadelphia, Printed by J. B. Lippincott company, 1895.

277 p. front., ports. 23½ cm.

A very readable narrative based on several diaries; the best section covers the 1864–1865 campaigns.

Chamberlin, William Henry, *b.* 1831 or 2.

History of the Eighty-first regiment Ohio infantry volunteers, during the war of the rebellion. By W. H. Chamberlin ... Cincinnati, Gazette steam printing house, 1865.

198 p., 1 l. front. (port.) 19 cm.

A highly revealing account, written soon after the war; particularly good for Sherman's campaigns.

Chapman, Robert D 1839–

A Georgia soldier in the civil war, 1861 to 1865, by R. D. Chapman ... [Little Rock, General T. J. Churchill chapter, United daughters of the confederacy, 1932]

2 p. l., 2–238 numb. l., 1 l. 22½ x 18cm.

This travelogue of a young soldier's wanderings through the war areas is too based on faulty recollection to be reliable.

Chase, John A b. 1831 or 2.

History of the Fourteenth Ohio regiment, O. V. V. I. From the beginning of the war in 1861 to its close in 1865. Comp. and written by Col. J. A. Chase. Toledo [St. John printing house] 1881.

130 p. front. (port.) 18cm.

A brief and sometimes boastful narrative of the regiment's activities in the Western theater.

Chattahoochee Valley Historical Society.

War was the place; a centennial collection of Confederate soldier letters. Old Oakbowery, Chambers County, Alabama. [n. p.] 1961.

198 p. illus., map. 23 cm.

In addition to many Confederate soldiers' letters, this paperback publication also contains eight monographs on life in wartime Alabama. The sum is a valuable pool of source material.

Cheek, Philip, 1841–

History of the Sauk County riflemen, known as Company "A," Sixth Wisconsin veteran volunteer infantry, 1861–1865; written and comp. by Philip Cheek, Mair Pointon. [Madison, Wis., Democrat printing company] 1909.

220 p., 1 l. front., pl., ports., plan. 21½cm.

One of the best company histories in Civil War literature; often quoted, and justifiably so.

Chenery, William H

The Fourteenth regiment Rhode Island heavy artillery (colored,) in the war to preserve the Union, 1861–1865. By William H. Chenery ... Providence, Snow & Farnham, 1898.

viii p., 2 l., 343 p. front., ports. 23½cm.

Half of this unique history of a Negro unit consists of muster rolls and short biographical sketches; the narrative is nothing more than quotations from other printed sources.

Cheney, Newel, 1836?–

History of the Ninth regiment, New York volunteer cavalry. War of 1861 to 1865. Compiled from letters, diaries, recollections and official records, by Newel Cheney ... Poland Center, N. Y., 1901.

423, [1] p. front., illus. 23½cm.

Despite its disorganization, this is a reasonably full account of the regiment's war service.

Child, William, 1834–

A history of the Fifth regiment, New Hampshire volunteers, in the American civil war, 1861–1865 ... By William Child ... Bristol, N. H., R. W. Musgrove, printer, 1893.

2 pt. in 1 v. front., pl., port. 23½cm.

One of the better regimental histories; composed for the most part of letters and diary excerpts by several members of the unit; covers fully the Eastern campaigns beginning with McClellan's advance up the Peninsula.

Civil War studies [by] John A. Carpenter [and others] Washington, Pa., Washington and Jefferson College, 1961.

71 p. 23 cm.

A series of monographs and lectures on a variety of topics, both military and political.

Claiborne, John Herbert, 1828–1905.

Seventy-five years in old Virginia; with some account of the life of the author and some history of the people amongst whom his lot was cast,—their character, their condition, and their conduct before the war, during the war and after the war, by John Herbert Claiborne ... New York and Washington, The Neale publishing company ... 1904.

xvi, [17], 360 p. 2 port. (incl. front.) 22½cm.

Important only for the author's comments on the Confederate retreat to Appomattox.

Clark, Charles M 1834–

The history of the Thirty-ninth regiment Illinois volunteer veteran infantry, (Yates phalanx,) in the war of the rebellion, 1861–1865. By Charles M. Clark, M. D. ... Published under the auspices of the veteran association of the regiment. Chicago, 1889.

xx p., 1 l., 554 p., 2 l. front., illus., pl., port. 22cm.

A good study, based on the accounts of several soldiers, and not too encumbered by dramatics.

Clark, Charles T   1845–
    Opdycke tigers, 125th O. V. I., a history of the regiment and the campaigns and battles of the Army of the Cumberland, by Charles T. Clark ... pub. by direction of the 125th O. V. I. association. Columbus, O., Spahr & Glenn, 1895.

    4 p. l., 472, ₍4₎ p. front., illus. (incl. maps) ports. 23 cm.

Short memoirs, diary extracts, etc. appear here and there in this profusely illustrated chronicle.

Clark, Emmons, 1827–1905.
    History of the Seventh regiment of New York. 1806–1889, by Colonel Emmons Clark ... New York, The Seventh regiment, 1890.

    2 v. fronts., illus., plates (part col.) ports. 25½ cm.

Five chapters of this two-volume work treat of the Civil War and give only general statistics and logistics.

Clark, George, 1841–
    A glance backward; or, Some events in the past history of my life, by George Clark. ₍Houston, Press of Rein & sons company, 1914?₎

    93 p. 22½ cm.

Clark fought with Lee's army in every major battle in the East, yet his recollections are cursory and confusing.

Clark, James H   1842–
    The iron hearted regiment: being an account of the battles, marches and gallant deeds performed by the 115th regiment N. Y. vols. ... By James H. Clark ... Albany, J. Munsell, 1865.

    xii, 337 p. 19 cm.

A reliable and revealing narrative based on the author's wartime journal; contains much on the Virginia and Carolina campaigns, as well as insights on Chicago's Camp Douglas.

Clark, James I
    The Civil War of Private Cooke; a Wisconsin boy in the Union Army. Madison, State Historical Society of Wisconsin, 1955.

    20 p. illus., port., maps. 23 cm.

A cursory narrative, interspersed with brief excerpts from the letters of a youth in the 25th Wisconsin.

Clark, James Samuel, 1841–
    Life in the Middle West; reminiscences of J. S. Clark. Chicago, The Advance publishing company ₍1916₎

    226 p. incl. front., ports. 20ᶜᵐ.

Clark served with the 1st Iowa at Wilson's Creek and later was captain of the 34th Iowa; his recollections of the Western theater are concise and trustworthy.

Clark, Orton S
    The One hundred and sixteenth regiment of New York state volunteers: being a complete history of its organization and of its nearly three years' active service in the great rebellion. To which is appended memorial sketches, and a muster roll of the regiment, containing the name of every man connected with it. By Orton S. Clark ... Buffalo, Printing house of Matthews & Warren, 1868.

    xii, ₍13₎–348 p. front. (port.) 20ᶜᵐ.

Apparently based on Clark's war journal; good for insights on the Louisiana and Second Valley campaigns.

Clark, Walter, 1846–   *ed.*
    Histories of the several regiments and battalions from North Carolina, in the great war 1861–'65. Written by members of the respective commands. Ed. by Walter Clark ... Pub. by the state. Raleigh, E. M. Uzzell, printer, 1901.

    5 v. front., illus., plates, ports., maps (part fold.) plans. 24ᶜᵐ.

Regimental sketches vary in quality, but the work fully merits Douglas S. Freeman's classification as one of the most indispensable works for the Army of Northern Virginia.

Clark, Walter Augustus.
    Under the stars and bars; or, Memories of four years service with the Oglethorpes, of Augusta, Georgia. By Walter A. Clark ... Augusta, Ga., Chronicle printing company, 1900.

    239, ₍3₎ p. 20½ cm.

A rather informal memoir by a soldier who saw duty in both theaters; the account is based on wartime letters and a diary.

Clark, William, *comp.*
    History of Hampton battery F, independent Pennsylvania light artillery, organized at Pittsburgh, Pa., October 8, 1861, mustered out in Pittsburgh, June 26, 1865. Comp. by William Clark ... ₍Akron, O. and Pittsburgh, The Werner company, ᶜ1909₎

    6 p., l., 11–179 p. front., illus., pl., ports., double map. 24½ᶜᵐ.

An empty, superficial account unworthy of publication in book form.

Clark, William H   *b.* 1840 *or* 41.

Poems and sketches with reminiscences of the "Old 34th." By William H. Clark ... South Framingham, Mass., Lakeview printing co., 1890.

55 p. 17^{cm}.

Sentimental, historically empty comments of 1864 army life in the Valley of Virginia.

Clark, William H   *b.* 1840 *or* 41.

Reminiscences of the Thirty-fourth regiment, Mass. vol. infantry. By William H. Clark ... Published for the author. Holliston, J. C. Clark & co., 1871.

31 p. 19^{cm}.

Little more than a footnote on the 1864 battle of New Market, Va.

Clark, William H   *b.* 1840 *or* 41.

The soldier's offering. By William H. Clark. Framingham [Mass., Press of the J. C. Clark printing company] 1875.

76 p. 19^{cm}.

A combination of the above two works, plus six romantic odes.

Clowes, Walter F

The Detroit light guard. A complete record of this organization from its foundation to the present day. By Walter F. Clowes. With full account of riot and complimentary duty, and the campaigns in the civil and Spanish-American wars. A complete roster of members at the time of muster-out of the United States service, as well as a roster of all classes of members. Detroit, Mich., J. F. Eby & company, 1900.

2 p. l., [3]–566 p. front. (ports.) plates. 24½^{cm}.

Brief references will be found here to the 1st Michigan (3 months) and such Wolverine officers as Alpheus Williams and H. M. Duffield.

Cluett, William W

History of the 57th regiment, Illinois volunteer infantry, from muster in, Dec. 26, 1861, to muster out, July 7, 1865, by William W. Cluett. Princeton [Ill.] T. P. Streeter, printer, 1886.

146 p. front., ports. 22^{cm}.

Too cursory to be of anything but minimal value.

Coffin, Charles Carleton, 1823–1896.

The boys of '61; or, Four years of fighting; personal observation with the Army and Navy, from the first battle of Bull Run to the fall of Richmond. By Charles Carleton Coffin ... Boston, Estes and Lauriat, 1896.

572 p. incl. front., illus., plates, ports., plans. 22 cm.

Coffin, a gifted writer and non-military observer, compiled this superior travelogue during his extensive travels in both theaters; very heavy on social scenes.

Cogley, Thomas Sydenham, 1840–

History of the Seventh Indiana cavalry volunteers, and the expeditions, campaigns, raids, marches, and battles of the armies with which it was connected, with biographical sketches of Brevet Major General John P. C. Shanks, and of Brevet Brig. Gen. Thomas M. Browne, and other officers of the regiment; with an account of the burning of the steamer Sultana on the Mississippi river, and of the capture, trial, conviction and execution of Dick Davis, the guerrilla. By Thomas S. Cogley ... Laporte, Ind., Herald company, printers, 1876.

2 p. l., v, [5]–267 p. front., illus., port. 19^{cm}.

An unbalanced, often empty history, written by a man who was absent from the regiment during several of its major expeditions in Arkansas and Missouri.

Cogswell, Leander Winslow, 1825–

A history of the Eleventh New Hampshire regiment, volunteer infantry in the rebellion war, 1861–1865 ... By Leander W. Gogswell ... Concord, Republican press association, 1891.

xi, [1], 784 p., 1 l. front., pl., port., fold. map, plan. 24 cm.

Padded with anecdotes and incidents-- many of questionable authenticity; this valorous regiment deserves a better history.

Cole, Jacob Henry, 1847–

Under five commanders; or, A boy's experience with the Army of the Potomac, by Jacob H. Cole ... Paterson, N. J., News printing company, 1906.

ix p., 1 l., 253 p. incl. illus., plates, ports. ports. 21 cm.

Another of those dramatic but totally unreliable accounts, this one was written forty years after the war and without benefit of wartime notes; the author was only a teenager when he enlisted in a New York unit.

Collier, Calvin L

"They'll do to tie to!" The story of the Third Regiment, Arkansas Infantry, C. S. A. [Little Rock? Ark.] J. D. Warren [°1959]

233 p. illus. 23 cm.

A poorly written, even more poorly produced unit history; has no documentation, bibliography, or index.

Collier, Calvin L

The War Child's children; the story of the Third Regiment, Arkansas Cavalry, Confederate States Army, by Calvin L. Collier. ₍Little Rock, Ark., Pioneer Press₎ 1965.

ix, 139 p. illus., maps, ports. 23 cm.

Similar to Collier's other studies; a summary history, lightly written, and based largely on data from the Official Records.

Collins, George K   1837?--

Memoirs of the 149th regt. N. Y. vol. inft., 3d brig., 2d div., 12th and 20th A. C. By Capt. Geo. K. Collins. Syracuse, N. Y., Pub. by the author, 1891.

viii, 426 p. front., illus., plates, ports. 22½ cm.

The highly interesting account of a regiment whose service extended from Virginia to Georgia; many personal insights.

Collins, R   M   *lieut. 15th Texas infantry.*

Chapters from the unwritten history of the war between the states; or, The incidents in the life of a Confederate soldier in camp, on the march, in the great battles, and in prison. By Lieut. R. M. Collins ... St. Louis, Nixon-Jones printing co., 1893.

335 p. front., illus. (incl. facsim.) port. 19¼ cm.

A very readable and reliable narrative by a member of the 15th Texas Cavalry who saw much service in the Western theater; the volume deserves more attention than it has heretofore re-received.

The **color-bearer:** Francis A. Clary. New York, The American tract society ₍ᶜ1864₎

106 p. 16 cm.

The letters of a devout and emotional young Massachusetts soldier who died in action at Port Hudson, La.

Complete history of the 46th Illinois veteran volunteer infantry, from the date of its organization in 1861, to its final discharge, February 1st, 1866, containing a full and authentic account of the participation of the regiment in the battles, sieges, skirmishes and expeditions in which it has been engaged, together with a complete roster of the regiment, showing the promotions, commissioned and non-commissioned, deaths, discharges and desertions. Freeport, Ill., Bailey & Ankeny, printers, 1866.

76 p. 23½ cm.

Too brief a sum for all the authors set out to include.

Confederate States of America. *Army. Dept. of northern Virginia.*

... Paroles of the Army of northern Virginia, R. E. Lee, gen., C. S. A., commanding, surrendered at Appomattox C. H., Va., April 9, 1865, to Lieutenant-General U. S. Grant, commanding armies of the U. S. Now first printed from the duplicate originals in the archives of the Southern historical society, ed. with introduction by R. A. Brock, secretary ... Richmond, Va., The Society, 1887.

xxvii, 508 p. 23½ cm.

Vol. XV of the Southern Historical Society Papers; an incomplete listing, preceded by an illuminating introduction by one of the first competent postwar compilers.

Confederate veteran. Published monthly in the interest of Confederate veterans and kindred topics. v. 1–40; Jan. 1893–Dec. 1932. Nashville, Tenn., 1893–1932.

40 v. illus. (incl. ports.) 27 cm.

The largest collection of personal experiences, anecdotes, battle footnotes, tall tales, and biographical sketches for the Confederate side; yet amid the minutae is a wealth of useful information.

Conn, Granville Priest, 1832–1916.

History of the New Hampshire surgeons in the war of rebellion, by Granville P. Conn ... Published by order of the New Hampshire association of military surgeons. Concord, N. H., I. C. Evans co., printers, 1906.

vii, 558 p. front. (port.) 24 cm.

Detailed biographical sketches of New Hampshire surgeons; arranged by regiments; some data on the regiments themselves.

Connecticut artillery. *1st regt., 1862–1865.*

History of the First Connecticut artillery and of the siege trains of the armies operating against Richmond, 1862–1865. Hartford, Conn., Press of the Case, Lockwood & Brainery company, 1893.

270, ₍2₎ p. front. (ports.) illus., plates, maps (part. fold.) 30¼ cm.

An extremely large volume with good maps; but the text by and large consists of material extracted from the Official Records.

Connecticut infantry. *21st regt., 1862–1865.*

The story of the Twenty-first regiment, Connecticut volunteer infantry, during the civil war. 1861–1865. By members of the regiment. Middletown, Conn., Press of the Stewart printing co., 1900.

xx, 448, 50 p. incl. illus., plates, ports., maps. front., 2 fold. maps. 21¼ cm.

Each chapter was written by a different member of the regiment. The 21st was in the XVIII Corps.

Connelly, Thomas W 1840–

History of the Seventieth Ohio regiment from its organization to its mustering out, by T. W. Connelly ... Cincinnati, O., Peak bros. [!] [1902]

182, v p. incl. ports. 22ᶜᵐ.

A good chronicle of service in the West, though Connelly's own feelings intrude often into the text.

Conner, James, 1829–1883.

Letters of General James Conner, C. S. A. [Columbia, S. C., The State co., 1933]

226 p. 24½ᶜᵐ.

In this scarce volume are the above-average letters of an officer who participated in many of the Eastern battles; two large gaps in the correspondence restrict the work's usefulness but do not deter the value of the letters included.

Connolly, James Austin, 1843–1914.

Three years in the Army of the Cumberland; the letters and diary of Major James A. Connolly. Edited by Paul M. Angle. Bloomington, Indiana University Press [1959]

399 p. illus. 21 cm.

These letters span the Aug., 1862-Mar., 1865, period and form a running narrative of army life in the West.

Conrad, Thomas Nelson.

The rebel scout; a thrilling history of scouting life in the southern army, by Capt. Thomas Nelson Conrad ... Washington City, The National publishing co., 1904.

220 p. 18½ᶜᵐ.

The slightly embellished memoirs of a Confederate cavalryman who made several solo expeditions to Washington.

Conyngham, David Power, 1840–1883.

The Irish brigade and its campaigns: with some account of the Corcoran legion, and sketches of the principal officers. By Capt. D. P. Conyngham ... Boston, P. Donahoe, 1869.

599 p. 19½ᶜᵐ.

One of the early brigade histories that concentrates on the unit's first campaigns; some recollections are included.

Conyngham, David Power, 1840–1883.

Sherman's march through the South. With sketches and incidents of the campaign. By Capt. David P. Conyngham. New York, Sheldon and co., 1865.

431 p. 19ᶜᵐ.

An indispensable volume for anyone studying Sherman's famous campaign; written by a New York Herald correspondent who observed much and recorded all that he saw.

Cook, Benjamin F 1833–1915.

History of the Twelfth Massachusetts volunteers (Webster regiment) By Lieutenant-Colonel Benjamin F. Cook. Boston, Twelfth (Webster) regiment association, 1882.

167 p. (incl. front., pl., 2 port.) fold. map (in pocket) 23½ cm.

Relying on diaries by other members of the regiment, Col. Cook compiled an uneven, almost day-by-day chronicle of the unit's action; the work contains a sprinkling of humor and only scant personal data.

Cook, Joel, 1842–1910.

The Siege of Richmond; a narrative of the military operations of Major-General George B. McClellan during the months of May and June, 1862. Philadelphia, G. W. Childs, 1862.

(American culture series, 137: 1)

Microfilm copy (positive) made in 1960 by University Microfilms, Ann Arbor, Mich.
Collation of the original, as determined from the film: viii, [7]–358 p.

Cook, a prolific writer, was a reporter for the Philadelphia Press during McClellan's spring, 1862 campaign; his account is excellent as a commentary on the country and its inhabitants.

Cook, Stephen Guernsey, 1831– ed.

The "Dutchess County regiment" (150th regiment of New York state volunteer infantry) in the civil war; its story as told by its members, based upon the writings of Rev. Edward O. Bartlett, D. D.; ed. by S. G. Cook, M. D. and Charles E. Benton. Danbury, Conn., The Danbury medical printing co., inc., 1907.

xv, [1], 512, [2] p. front. (port.) plates. 23ᶜᵐ.

The too-short narrative in this huge work concentrates on personal incidents within the regiment.

Cooke, Chauncey Herbert 1846–

Soldier boy's letters to his father and mother, 1861-5. [Independence, Wis., News-office, ᶜ1915]

cover-title, 97 p. 22ᶜᵐ.

Unedited, chatty letters by a Wisconsin soldier in the Western theater.

Cooke, John Esten, 1830–1886.
   Outlines from the outpost.   Edited by Richard Harwell.
Chicago, Lakeside Press, 1961.

   413 p.   illus.   18 cm.

Essays faithfully reproduced from originals in
The Southern Illustrated News; a stylistic and
often poetic narrative.

Cooke, John Esten, 1830–1886.
   Stonewall Jackson and the old Stonewall Brigade; edited
by Richard Barksdale Harwell.   Charlottesville, University
of Virginia Press for the Tracy W. McGregor Library [1954]

   76 p.   ports.   24 cm.

A eulogistic, highly quotable essay on Jackson
and his famous Valley fighters.

Cooke, John Esten, 1830–1886.
   Wearing of the gray; being personal portraits, scenes and
adventures of the war.   By John Esten Cooke ...   New York,
E. B. Treat & co.; Baltimore, J. S. Morrow; [etc., etc.] 1867.

   xvi, [17]–564, [585]–601 p.   front., plates, 7 port. on 1 pl.   22ᶜᵐ.

Cooke's most famous volume and the closest
thing to an autobiography of his war career;
much information on Jackson, Stuart, and other
Confederate leaders.

Cooke, John Esten, 1830–1886.
   Wearing of the gray; being personal portraits, scenes, and
adventures of the war.   Edited with an introd. and notes by
Philip Van Doren Stern.   Bloomington, Indiana University Press [1959]

   xxii, 572 p.   illus., ports.   21 cm.

An inadequately edited reprint of the above.

Cope, Alexis, 1841–1918.
   The Fifteenth Ohio volunteers and its campaigns, war of
1861–5, by Alexis Cope, captain, Fifteenth Ohio volunteer
infantry ...   Columbus, O., The author, 1916.

   796 p.   front., ports.   22¼ᶜᵐ.

Though the author had access to several diaries,
he relied more on such printed sources as Sherman's Memoirs.

Copeland, Willis R
   The Logan Guards of Lewistown, Pennsylvania; our first
defenders of 1861; a history.   Lewistown, Pa., Mifflin
County Historical Society, °1962.

   75 p.   illus.   23 cm.

Little more than an introduction to the unit; however, some excerpts from letters and diaries
are included.

Copp, Elbridge J   1844–
   Reminiscences of the war of the rebellion, 1861–1865, by
Col. Elbridge J. Copp, the youngest commissioned officer in
the Union army who rose from the ranks.   Published by the
author.   Nashua, N. H., Printed by the Telegraph publishing company, 1911.

   536, iv p. incl. illus., plates, ports.   front.   24 cm.

The author's memory failed him badly in the
half-century interval between the war and the
writing of this book; the volume is little more
than a diatribe against the South and slavery.

Corbin, Richard W
   Letters of a Confederate officer to his family in Europe during the last year of the war of secession.   Paris: Neal's English
library ...   New York, Reprinted, W. Abbatt, 1913.

   (*In* **The magazine of history with notes and queries. New York,
1913. 27 cm. Extra no. 24. 96 p.**)

Poignant observations by a staff officer of operations in Virginia from June, 1864, to Appomattox; an exceedingly rare work.

Corby, William, 1833–1897.
   Memoirs of chaplain life, by Very Rev. W. Corby ..
Three years chaplain in the famous Irish brigade
"Army of the Potomac."   Notre Dame, Ind., "Scholas
tic" press, 1894.

   391 p   front., plates, ports.   20ᶜᵐ.

Among the small group of chaplains' recollections, this is one of the better works.   Corby
served with the Irish Brigade and recorded many
human incidents in between his defenses of the
Catholic faith.

Corell, Philip, 1846?–   *ed.*
   History of the Naval brigade, 99th N. Y. volunteers,
Union coast guard. 1861[–]1865.   Historian, Philip Corell.   New York, Pub. under the auspices of the regimental veteran association, 1905.

   [251] p. incl. pl.   7 pl. (incl. front.)   2 port. on pl.   26ᶜᵐ.

Little more than a collection of official reports.

Corsan, W   C
Two months in the Confederate States; including a visit to New Orleans under the domination of General Butler. By an English merchant. London, R. Bentley, 1863.

2 p. l., 299 p. 19^{cm}.

These observations by an English merchant who visited the Confederacy in 1862 sympathetically reveal much of social and economic conditions in the wartime South.

Cort, Charles Edwin, 1841–1903.
"Dear friends"; the Civil War letters and diary of Charles Edwin Cort. Compiled and edited with commentaries by Helyn W. Tomlinson. ₁n. p., 1962₁

194 p. illus. 24 cm.

Factually reliable and personally revealing letters of service in the West by a member of the 92nd Illinois Mounted Infantry.

Cotton, John Weaver, 1831–1866.
Yours till death; Civil War letters of John W. Cotton, edited by Lucille Griffith. University, Ala., University of Alabama Press, 1951.

ix, 128 p. port. 24 cm.

The semi-literate letters of an Alabama farmer-turned-soldier to his wife; although a cavalryman, Cotton confined his remarks to personal matters and random references to army life.

Coulter, Ellis Merton, 1890–
Lost generation: the life and death of James Barrow, C. S. A. Tuscaloosa, Ala., Confederate Pub. Co., 1956.

118 p. 22 cm.

Fortified with the subject's cultured letters, this short biography recounts the brief life of a young officer from Georgia who was killed at the little-known battle of Olustee, Fla.

Cowden, Robert, 1833–
A brief sketch of the organization and services of the Fifty-ninth regiment of United States colored infantry, and biographical sketches. By Colonel Robert Cowden. Dayton, O., United Brethren publishing house, 1883.

3 p. l., ix–xxiii, ₁25₁–293 p. 19^{cm}.

Disorganized, but full of personal opinions and experiences.

Cowtan, Charles W
Services of the Tenth New York volunteers (National zouaves,) in the war of the rebellion. By Charles W. Cowtan ... New York, C. H. Ludwig, 1882.

1 p. l., 459, ₁1₁ p. front., maps (partly fold.) 19½^{cm}.

A typical unit history, but relatively weak on personal incidents and insights; the 10th New York campaigned almost entirely with the Army of the Potomac.

Craft, David, 1832–1908.
History of the One hundred forty-first regiment, Pennsylvania volunteers. 1862–1865. By David Craft, chaplain ... Published by the author. Towanda, Pa., Reporter-journal printing company, 1885.

ix, 270, ₁4₁ p. front., pl., port. 23^{cm}.

Though comparatively small in size, this regimental history contains several reminiscences of soldiers and is a reliable, highly personal chronicle of the unit's actions in the East.

Crary, Jerry, 1842–1936.
Jerry Crary, 1842–1936: teacher, soldier, industrialist. Warren, Pa., Newell Press, 1960.

142 p. illus. 29 cm.

Contains a brief diary and a few letters relative to service in the 143rd New York.

Crater, Lewis, 1843–
History of the Fiftieth regiment, Penna. vet. vols., 1861–65. By Lewis Crater ... Reading, Pa., Coleman printing house, 1884.

88, 1 p., 1 l. front., ports. 23½^{cm}.

An empty collection of statistics and excerpts from printed sources.

Crawford, J   Marshall.
Mosby and his men: a record of the adventures of that renowned partisan ranger, John S. Mosby, ⟨Colonel C. S. A.⟩ including the exploits of Smith, Chapman, Richards, Montjoy, Turner, Russell, Glasscock, and the men under them. By J. Marshall Crawford, of Company B. New York, G. W. Carleton & co.; ₁etc., etc.₁ 1867.

375 p. front., port. 18^{cm}.

Largely an impersonal narrative of the exploits of the Confederacy's famed "Gray Ghost"; few of the author's own experiences are included.

Crawford, Samuel Johnson, 1835–1913.
 Kansas in the sixties, by Samuel J. Crawford ... Chicago, A. C. McClurg & co., 1911.
   xvii, 441 p. front., ports. 21¼ cm.

Important chiefly for the author's recollections of service in the 2nd Kansas and 83rd U. S. Colored Infantry Regiments.

Crocker, James Francis, 1828–
 Gettysburg—Pickett's charge and other war addresses, by Judge James F. Crocker. Portsmouth, Va., W. A. Fiske, printer, 1915.
   132 p. front. (port.) illus. 21½ᶜᵐ.

Patriotic addresses by a survivor of the 9th Virginia and Pickett's Charge.

Cronin, David Edward 1839–
 The evolution of a life, described in the memoirs of Major Seth Eyland [*pseud.*] ... New York, S. W. Green's son, 1884.
   336 p. 19½ᶜᵐ.

The intelligent and discerning memoirs of a man who served simultaneously as a New York cavalryman and illustrator for Harper's Weekly; the book merits far greater attention and use.

Crooke, George, *comp.*
 The twenty-first regiment of Iowa volunteer infantry; a narrative of its experience in active service, including a military record of each officer, non-commissioned officer, and private soldier of the organization, comp. by George Crooke ... For private distribution only. Milwaukee, Wis., King, Fowle & co., 1891.
   232 p. illus., maps (part fold.) 23½ᶜᵐ.

Crooke, who was adjutant of the regiment, incorporated many statistical records into this work; personal accounts are scattered, but illustrations are many.

Croom, Wendell D
 The war-history of Company "C," (Beauregard volunteers) Sixth Georgia regiment, (infantry) with a graphic account of each member. Written by Wendell D. Croom ... and pub. by the survivors of the company. Fort Valley, Ga., Printed at the "Advertiser" office, 1879.
   2 p. l., 37 p. 22½ cm.

A badly organized, unilluminating pamphlet that reflects little more than the initial enthusiasm of Southern youths toward the war effort.

Crotty, Daniel G.
 Four years campaigning in the Army of the Potomac, by ... D. G. Crotty ... Grand Rapids, Mich., Dygert bros. & co., printers, 1874.
   207 p. 22ᶜᵐ.

An empty memoir by a member of the 3rd Michigan.

Crowell, Joseph Edgar, 1844–
 The young volunteer. A record of the experiences of a private soldier. By Joseph E. Crowell ... London, New York, F. T. Neely [1899]
   vi, [7]–490 p. 19½ cm.

Heavily padded, with an abundance of manufactured conversation; Crowell served in the 13th New Jersey.

Crowninshield, Benjamin William, *d.* 1892.
 A history of the First regiment of Massachusetts cavalry volunteers, by Benjamin W. Crowninshield ... With roster and statistics by D. H. L. Gleason ... For the First Massachusetts cavalry association. Boston and New York, Houghton, Mifflin and co., 1891.
   x, 490 p. front., plates, ports., maps (partly fold.) 24½ cm.

A better-than-average study of a cavalry unit whose services were mostly in Virginia.

Crummer, Wilbur Fisk, 1843–
 With Grant at Fort Donelson, Shiloh and Vicksburg, and an appreciation of General U. S. Grant, by Wilbur F. Crummer ... Oak Park, Ill., E. C. Crummer & Co., 1915.
   190 p. incl. port. plates, port. 20 cm.

Pretentious, sentimental, and empty; the author was an Illinois soldier.

Cudworth, Warren Handel, 1825–1883.
 History of the First regiment (Massachusetts infantry), from the 25th of May, 1861, to the 25th of May, 1864; including brief references to the operations of the Army of Potomac. By Warren H. Cudworth, chaplain of the regiment ... Boston, Walker, Fuller & co., 1866.
   528 p. pl. 20 cm.

A combination of regimental statistics and personal observations, this useful volume is a reservoir of data on the Eastern campaigns through the summer of 1864.

Cuffel, Charles A

History of Durell's battery in the civil war (Independent battery D. Pennsylvania volunteer artillery.) A narrative of the campaigns and battles of Berks and Bucks counties' artillerists in the war of the rebellion ... ₍Philadelphia, Craig, Finley & co., printers, 1903₎

265 p. incl. front. plates, ports. 24ᶜᵐ.

Good observations on camp life and army movements; Cuffel relied on printed sources for battle coverage.

Culp, Edward C

The 25ᵗʰ Ohio vet. vol. infantry in the war for the union, by Edward C. Culp ... Topeka, Kan., G. W. Crane & co., printers, 1885.

168 p., 1 l. 19½ cm.

Culp did nothing more than skim the surface.

Cummings, Charles L 1848– *comp.*

... The great war relic. Together with a sketch of my life, service in the army, and how I lost my feet since the war, also, many interesting incidents illustrative of the life of a soldier ... Comp. and sold by Chas. L. Cummings ... ₍n. p., 189–₎

cover-title, 48 p. illus. (ports.) 22½ᶜᵐ.

Though void of value, this memoir went through five editions; more than 35,000 copies were purchased by sympathetic readers.

Cunningham, John Lovell, 1840–

Three years with the Adirondack regiment, 118th New York volunteers infantry, from the diaries and other memoranda of John L. Cunningham, major 118th New York volunteers infantry, brevet lieutenant colonel United States volunteers. ₍Norwood, Mass., The Plimpton press₎ 1920.

v p., 1 l., 286 p. front., plates, ports. 21ᶜᵐ.

Based on the author's wartime diary, this work nevertheless is not blessed with chapter headings and thus appears endless at first sight; it is concerned solely with campaigns in the East.

Currie, George E

Warfare along the Mississippi; the letters of Lieutenant Colonel George E. Currie. Edited by Norman E. Clarke, Sr. Mount Pleasant, Clarke Historical Collection, Central Michigan University ₍1961₎

xvi, 153 p. illus., ports. 23 cm.

Twelve unusually long letters by a Marine officer who served for a period with Ellet's Mississippi River ram fleet.

Curry, William Leontes, 1839– *comp.*

Four years in the saddle. History of the First regiment, Ohio volunteer cavalry. War of the rebellion, 1861–1865. Comp. by W. L. Curry ... Columbus, O., Champlin printing co., 1898.

2 p. l., iv, iii, 13–401, ₍3₎, v p., 1 l., 50 p. front., illus., plates, ports., maps. 26ᶜᵐ.

One of the best regimental studies of Ohio troops; Curtis incorporated material from a wide variety of sources.

Curtis, Newton Martin, 1835–1910.

From Bull Run to Chancellorsville; the story of the Sixteenth New York infantry together with personal reminiscences, by Newton Martin Curtis ... New York & London, G. P. Putnam's sons, 1906.

xix, 384 p. 4 port. (incl. front.) 23½ cm.

A standard, authoritative source by an officer who later served three terms in the Congress; Curtis made much use of official and public documents.

Curtis, Orson Blair, 1841?–1901.

History of the Twenty-fourth Michigan of the Iron brigade, known as the Detroit and Wayne county regiment ... By O. B. Curtis ... Detroit, Mich., Winn & Hammond, 1891.

483 p. incl. illus. (incl. maps, plans) pl., ports. front., col. pl. 25½ᶜᵐ.

Curtis relied on soldiers' letters, official documents, and his own recollections in writing this fact-laden study; a necessary source for an understanding of the Iron Brigade.

Cutcheon, Byron Mac, 1836–1908, *comp.*

The story of the Twentieth Michigan infantry, July 15th, 1862, to May 30th, 1865; embracing official documents on file in the records of the state of Michigan and of the United States referring or relative to the regiment. Comp. by Byron M. Cutcheon ... Lansing, Mich., R. Smith printing co., 1904.

271, ₍1₎ p. front., pl., ports. 24ᶜᵐ.

A compilation, largely of official reports, relating to the 20th Michigan's activities.

Cutchins, John Abram, 1881–

A famous command, the Richmond light infantry blues, by John A. Cutchins. Richmond, Garrett & Massie ₍1934₎

xx p., 1 l., 399 p. incl. front. plates, ports., map. 27ᶜᵐ.

A detailed, 145-year history of a unit whose acme of service and sacrifice came in the Civil War years.

Cutter, Orlando Phelps.
Our battery; or, The journal of Company B, 1st O. V.
A., by O. P. Cutter. Cleveland, Nevins' book and job
printing establishment, 1864.

152 p. 17ᶜᵐ.

The author claimed that this small memoir was
"mostly written during the leisures of camp
life." Yet it shows distinct marks of much reworking and polishing.

Dahlgren, John Adolphus Bernard, 1809–1870.
Memoir of Ulric Dahlgren. By his father, Rear-Admiral
Dahlgren ... Philadelphia, J. B. Lippincott & co., 1872.

x, 11–308 p. front. (port.) 19ᶜᵐ.

Too eulogistic to be of value except for the basic
facts of the son's life.

Dalton, John Call, 1825–1889.
John Call Dalton, M. D., U. S. V. [Cambridge, Mass.] Priv.
print. [by H. O. Houghton and company] 1892.

3 p. l., 5–105 p. front. (port.) 20½ x 15½ᶜᵐ.

Dalton, a surgeon in the 7th New York, penned
these recollections from memory thirty-five
years after the war. The result is as negative
as one would expect.

Dalton, Kit, 1843–1920.
Under the black flag, by Captain Kit Dalton, a Confederate soldier, a guerilla captain under the fearless leader
Quantrell, and a border outlaw for seventeen years following
the surrender of the Confederacy. Associated with the most
noted band of free booters the world has ever known.
[Memphis, Tenn., Lockard publishing company, ᶜ1914]

252 p. front., illus. (ports.) pl. 19½ cm.

A blunt autobiography by one of Quantrill's ma-
rauders.

Daly, Louise Porter (Haskell)
Alexander Cheves Haskell; the portrait of a man, by
Louise Haskell Daly. Norwood, Mass., Priv. print. at the
Plimpton press, 1934.

viii p., 2 l., 224 p. front., ports. 24 cm.

Composed of letters and recollections by the
grandson of Langdon Cheves; this work casts
some light on the life of a Confederate soldier.

Dalzell, James McCormick, 1838–1924.
Private Dalzell, his autobiography, poems and comic war
papers, sketch of John Gray, Washington's last soldier, etc. ...
A centennial souvenir. Cincinnati, R. Clarke & co., 1888.

2 p. l., 3–242 p. front., plates, ports., facsims. 20ᶜᵐ.

This collection of humor, poetry, and other
minutae was designed for popular consumption;
historically speaking, it is valueless.

Dame, William Meade, 1844 *or* 5–
From the Rapidan to Richmond and the Spottsylvania campaign; a sketch in personal narration of the scenes a soldier
saw, by William Meade Dame ... Baltimore, Green-Lucas
company, 1920.

4 p. l., xi–xvi, 213 p. 3 port. (incl. front.) 23½ᶜᵐ.

These memoirs by a man who became an Episcopal rector contain a wealth of human interest
stories relative to the Army of Northern Virginia's last year.

Dana, Charles Anderson, 1819–1897.
Recollections of the civil war; with the leaders at Wash-
ington and in the field in the sixties, by Charles A. Dana ...
New York, D. Appleton and company, 1898.

xiii, 296 p. front. (port.) 21½ cm.

Reliable and oftentimes pointed observations by
a newspaperman and government official who
was with Grant during a major portion of the war.

Daniel, Ferdinand Eugene, 1839–1914.
Recollections of a Rebel surgeon (and other sketches); or, In
the doctor's sappy days. By F. E. Daniel ... Austin, Tex.,
Von Boeckmann, Schutze & co., 1899.

4 p. l., 264 p. illus., pl. 20ᶜᵐ.

Composed in the main of recorded conversations
long after the war with an army doctor; the text
is rambling, flippant, and strongly suspect.

Daniel, Frederick S
Richmond howitzers in the war. Four years campaigning
with the Army of northern Virginia. By a member of the
company. Richmond, 1891.

155 p. 19½ᶜᵐ.

A strictly military history of one of the Confederacy's most famous batteries; a few personal
insights appear amid the flood of facts.

Davenport, Alfred.

Camp and field life of the Fifth New York volunteer infantry. (Duryee zouaves.) By Alfred Davenport New York, Dick and Fitzgerald, 1879.

485 p. front. (port.) pl. 19½ cm.

This thoroughly useful narrative, based on diaries and letters, covers admirably the exploits of a regiment that saw valiant service through Chancellorsville.

Davidson, Henry M   *d.* 1900.

History of Battery A. First regiment of Ohio vol. light artillery. Milwaukee. Daily Wisconsin steam printing house, 1865.

vii, [9]–199 p. 19½ cm.

A cursory, early account, based largely on company records, alleged diaries, and the author's own recollections.

Davis, Charles E   *b.* 1842 *or* 1843–1915.

Three years in the army. The story of the Thirteenth Massachusetts volunteers from July 16, 1861, to August 1, 1864. By Charles E. Davis, jr. Boston, Estes and Lauriat, 1894.

xxxv, 476 p. maps. 23½ cm.

Five diaries and numerous official sources formed the basis for this highly regarded history of a unit that served in the Army of the Potomac until its disbandment in the summer of 1864.

Davis, Nicholas A

The campaign from Texas to Maryland. By Rev. Nicholas A. Davis ... Richmond. Printed at the office of the Presbyterian committee of publication of the Confederate States. 1863.

165, [1] p. 2 port. (incl. front.) 19½ cm.

One of the better narratives treating of Hood's Texas Brigade; contains personal comments on almost all aspects of the war.

Davis, Nicholas A

Chaplain Davis and Hood's Texas Brigade. Edited and with an introd. by Donald E. Everett. San Antonio, Principia Press of Trinity University, 1962.

234 p. 24 cm.

A vastly expanded version, with good editorial trappings added, of Davis's Campaign from Texas . . .

Davis, Oliver Wilson

Life of David Bell Birney, major-general United States volunteers. Philadelphia, King & Baird; New York, Sheldon & co., 1867.

xii, 418 p. front. (port.) 26 cm.

Its eulogistic passages notwithstanding, this military biography is a basic source for any study of the Army of the Potomac.

Davis, William Watts Hart, 1820–1910.

History of the 104th Pennsylvania regiment, from August 22nd, 1861, to September 30th, 1864. By W. W. H. Davis ... Philadelphia, J. B. Rogers, printer, 1866.

vii p., 1 l., 9–364 p. incl. front. pl., port. 23 cm.

Col. Davis entered the Civil War with the intention of writing his unit's history, and the resulting study is a highly reliable commentary on the Peninsular and Carolina coastal campaigns.

Dawes, Rufus R 1838–1899.

Service with the Sixth Wisconsin volunteers. By Rufus R. Dawes ... Marietta, O., E. R. Alderman & sons, 1890.

2 p. l., v, [5]–330 p. front., illus., port. 22½ cm.

The best narrative by a soldier from the Midwest; based on the author's letters and diary, the work is a standard source for the Eastern battles and the Iron Brigade.

Dawes, Rufus R 1838–1899.

Service with the Sixth Wisconsin Volunteers. Edited with an introd. by Alan T. Nolan. Madison, State Historical Society of Wisconsin for Wisconsin Civil War Centennial Commission, 1962.

xv, 330 (i. e. 336) p. illus., ports. 23 cm.

A needed reissue of the original, with a revealing introduction and critical bibliography.

Dawson, Francis W

Reminiscences of Confederate service, 1861–1865. By Capt. Francis W. Dawson ... Charleston, S. C., The News and courier book presses, 1882.

180 p. 23½ cm.

Dawson was an Englishman who served on Longstreet's staff and afterwards became the internationally known editor of the Charleston Courier; a penetrating commentary, deserving of republication.

Day, David L

My diary of rambles with the 25th Mass. volunteer infantry, with Burnside's coast division; 18th army corps, and Army of the James. By D. L. Day. ₍Milford, Mass., King & Billings, printers, 1884₎

153 p. 23ᶜᵐ.

A full and illuminating diary, with many insights and much philosophizing.

Day, Lewis W   *b.* 1839 *or* 40.

Story of the One hundred and first Ohio infantry. A memorial volume. By L. W. Day. Cleveland, W. M. Bayne printing co., 1894.

xiv, ₍15₎–463 p. incl. illus., port. front. 21ᶜᵐ.

Ordinary memoirs of army life by a non-commissioned officer who served briefly as a topographical engineer; the account spans the major Western campaigns.

Debray, Xavier Blanchard.

A sketch of the history of Debray's (26th) regiment of Texas cavalry. Austin, E. Von Boeckmann, printer, 1884.

28 p. 21ᶜᵐ.

A too-brief summary of a unit that merits more study; Debray's cavalry operated in the Trans-Mississippi.

De Fontaine, Felix Gregory 1832–1896.

Marginalia; or, Gleanings from an army note-book. By "Personne" ... Columbia, S. C., Steam power-press of F. G. DeFontaine & co., 1864.

2 p. l., iii, 248 p. 22 cm.

Brief essays and observations by an intellectual correspondent of the Charleston <u>Courier</u>.

De Forest, Bartholomew S

Random sketches and wandering thoughts; or, What I saw in camp, on the march, the bivouac, the battle field and hospital, while with the army in Virginia, North and South Carolina, during the late rebellion. With a historical sketch of the second Oswego regiment, Eighty-first New York state V. I.; a record of all its officers, and a roster of its enlisted men; also, an appendix. By B. S. De Forest ... Albany, A. Herrick, 1866.

324 p. pl. 19½ᶜᵐ.

Correctly entitled, this memoir by a member of the 81st New York rambles through a variety of topics pertaining to the author's service on the seaboard of Virginia and North Carolina.

De Forest, John William, 1826–1906.

A volunteer's adventures; a Union captain's record of the civil war, by John William De Forest. Edited, with notes, by James H. Croushore. With an introduction by Stanley T. Williams. New Haven, Yale university press; London, G. Cumberlege, Oxford university press, 1946.

xviii, 237 p. front. (port.) illus. (maps, facsims.) 24 cm.

The highly readable letters from Louisiana and Virginia by one of the most distinguished American novelists of that period; De Forest was an officer in the 12th Connecticut.

Demoret, Alfred.

A brief history of the Ninety-third regiment, Ohio volunteer infantry. Recollections of a private. By A. Demoret, private in Co. F. ₍Ross, O., Graphic print, pref., 1898₎

54 p. 19½ᶜᵐ.

Provides the basic information on the regiment's movements and little else.

Denison, Frederic, 1819–1901.

Sabres and spurs: the First regiment Rhode Island cavalry in the civil war, 1861–1865. Its origin, marches, scouts, skirmishes, raids, battles, sufferings, victories, and appropriate official papers; with the roll of honor and roll of the regiment ... By Rev. Frederic Denison, chaplain ... ₍Central Falls, R. I.₎ The First Rhode Island cavalry veteran association, 1876.

600 p. front., pl., port., fold. map. 20½ᶜᵐ.

A first-rate composite of diaries and letter excerpts; both reliable and useful for cavalry operations in the East.

Denison, Frederic, 1819–1901.

Shot and shell: the Third Rhode Island heavy artillery regiment in the rebellion, 1861–1865. Camps, forts, batteries, garrisons, marches, skirmishes, sieges, battles, and victories; also, the roll of honor and roll of the regiment ... By Rev. Frederic Denison ... Providence, For the Third R. I. H. art. vet. association, by J. A. & R. A. Reid, 1879.

368 p. front. (port.) illus., 3 pl., map. 23½ᶜᵐ.

Another full collection of primary materials; this battery saw much service along the Southern seaboard, and Denison's pen missed none of it.

Denny, Joseph Waldo, *b.* 1825 *or* 1826.

Wearing the blue in the Twenty-fifth Mass. volunteer infantry, with Burnside's coast division, 18th army corps, and Army of the James. By J. Waldo Denny. Worcester, Putnam & Davis, 1879.

xi, ₍1₎, 523 p. front., port. 23ᶜᵐ.

A conglomeration of personal accounts, largely arranged in chronological order; many of the reminiscences are suspect.

De Peyster, John Watts, 1821–1907.
Personal and military history of Philip Kearny, major-general United States volunteers ... By John Watts De Peyster. New York, Rice and Gage; Newark, N. J., Bliss & co., 1869.
3 p. l., xii, [13]–516 p. plates, ports., map. 23½ cm.

A voluminous, overly sympathetic biography of New Jersey's most famous soldier; the narrative must be treated with caution.

Derby, William P
Bearing arms in the Twenty-seventh Massachusetts regiment of volunteer infantry during the civil war, 1861–1865. By W. P. Derby. Boston, Wright & Potter printing co., 1883.
xvi, 607 p. front., port., maps. 24 cm.

Derby's account is a frank and honest appraisal of the North Carolina and Petersburg campaigns; he openly criticized Federal looting.

De Velling, Charles Theodore.
... History of the Seventeenth regiment, First brigade, Third division, Fourteenth corps, Army of the Cumberland, war of the rebellion, comp. by C. T. De Velling ... Zanesville, O., E. R. Sullivan, printer, 1889.
143, [1] p. incl. illus., pl. 26cm.

Nothing more than a beginning of the full history that the 17th Ohio merits.

The **diary** of an unknown soldier, September 5, 1862 to December 7, 1862, found on a battlefield. Edited by Elsa Vaught. [Van Buren, Ark., Press-Argus Print. Co., 1959]
45 p. maps, facsims. 23 cm.

This fragmentary diary by an unknown member of the 19th Iowa is a surprisingly good personal commentary on events leading up to the battle of Prairie Grove, Ark.

Dickert, D   Augustus.
History of Kershaw's brigade, with complete roll of companies, biographical sketches, incidents, anecdotes, etc., by D. Augustus Dickert. Introduction by Associate Justice Y. J. Pope. Newberry, S. C., E. H. Aull company, 1899.
583, 5, 2 p. front., ports. 22½cm.

A full, thick account of a famous South Carolina brigade; the author gives personal descriptions of campaigns in both East and West.

Dickey, Luther Samuel, 1846–
History of the Eighty-fifth regiment Pennsylvania volunteer infantry, 1861–1865, comprising an authentic narrative of Casey's division at the battle of Seven Pines, by Luther S. Dickey. New York [J. C. & W. E. Powers] 1915.
xiii, 467 p. front., plates, ports., map, plans. 26cm.

Dickey relied heavily on the Official Records and comrades' recollections; one-fourth of the study concentrates on the battle of Seven Pines.

Dickey, Luther Samuel, 1846–
History of the 103d regiment, Pennsylvania veteran volunteer infantry, 1861–1865, by Luther S. Dickey ... Chicago, L. S. Dickey, 1910.
xiv, 400 p. front., plates, ports., maps (1 fold.) plans. 26½cm.

Disorganized, but full of good material if one digs arduously enough.

Dickison, Mary Elizabeth.
Dickison and his men. Reminiscences of the war in Florida. By Mary Elizabeth Dickison ... Louisville, Ky., Courier-journal job printing company, 1890.
265, [1] p. front., illus., ports. 22cm.

Probably co-authored by the commander of the 2nd Florida Cavalry and his wife; a poorly organized but splendid picture of the almost unknown Florida campaigns.

Dickison, Mary Elizabeth.
Dickison and his men; reminiscences of the war in Florida. A facsimile reproduction of the 1890 ed., with introd. by Samuel Proctor. Gainesville, University of Florida Press, 1962.
xxiv p., facsim. (266 p. plates, ports.), 6 p. 22 cm.

A handsomely bound facsimile reproduction of the first edition, with an informative introduction added.

Dinkins, James, b. 1845.
1861 to 1865, by an old Johnnie. Personal recollections and experiences in the Confederate Army. By Captain James Dinkins. Illus. by L. T. Dickinson. Cincinnati, The Robert Clarke Co., 1897.
280 p. plates, ports. 20 cm.

Personal, oftentimes lightly written sketches by a North Carolina soldier; especially good for observations on the Peninsular Campaign.

Dodd, Ira Seymour, 1842–1922.

The song of the Rappahannock; sketches of the civil war, by Ira Seymour Dodd. New York, Dodd, Mead and company, 1898.

viii p., 1 l., 254 p.   17½ᶜᵐ.

Six dramatic and cursory essays on army life by a young member of the 26th New Jersey.

Dodge, William Sumner.

History of the old second division, Army of the Cumberland. Commanders: M'Cook, Sill, and Johnson. By Wm. Sumner Dodge. Chicago, Church & Goodman, 1864.

582, 51 p.   front., port., fold. maps.   23 cm.

A pleasant combination of statistical and personal data on service in the West; one of the few divisional histories in existence.

Dodge, William Sumner.

Robert Henry Hendershot; or, The brave drummer boy of the Rappahannock. By William Sumner Dodge ... Chicago, Church and Goodman, 1867.

vi. ₁7₁–202 p.   front. (port.)   22½ᶜᵐ.

This highly suspicious study purports to be a biography of a teenage drummer boy in the 8th Michigan.

Dodge, William Sumner.

A waif of the war; or, The history of the Seventy-fifth Illinois infantry, embracing the entire campaigns of the Army of the Cumberland. By Wm. Sumner Dodge ... Chicago, Church & Goodman, 1866.

vii, ₁17₁–241, ₁1₁ p.   22 cm.

Dodge was not even a member of the unit hereof he wrote; still, his personal experiences as a soldier in the Western theater have some merit.

Dodson, William Carey, 1846–   *ed.*

Campaigns of Wheeler and his cavalry, 1862–1865, from material furnished by Gen. Joseph Wheeler; to which is added his concise and graphic account of the Santiago campaign of 1898. Pub. under the auspices of Wheeler's Confederate cavalry association and ed. by W. C. Dodson, historian. Atlanta, Ga., Hudgins publishing company, 1899.

2 pt. in 1 v.   front., plates, ports.   24½ᶜᵐ.

Wheeler and close compatriots furnished most of the data for this study; as a result, Dodson's study possesses little objectivity.

Dollard, Robert.

Recollections of the civil war and going West to grow up with the country, by Robert Dollard. Scotland, S. Dak., The author, 1906.

5 p. l., ₁5₁–296 p.   front., ports.   23cm.

Less than half of this volume treats of Dollard's varied career in campaigns along the Virginia and North Carolina coasts.

Donaghy, John, 1837–

Army experience of Capt. John Donaghy, 103d Penn'a vols. 1861–1864. De Land, Fla., The E. O. Painter printing co. ₁1926₁

244 p.   front. (port.)   24ᶜᵐ.

This very confined memoir by a member of the 103rd Pennsylvania is good primarily for Donaghy's impressions of army life.

Dooley, John Edward, 1842–1873.

John Dooley, Confederate soldier, his war journal, edited by Joseph T. Durkin, s. J. ... Foreword by Douglas Southall Freeman ... ₁Washington₁ Georgetown university press, 1945.

xxiii p., 1 l., 244 p.   front. (port.)   facsims.   23½ cm.

The revealing and penetrating observations of August, 1862 - July, 1863, campaigning with the Army of Northern Virginia; the cultured Dooley was a member of the 8th Virginia.

Dornblaser, T   F.

Sabre strokes of the Pennsylvania dragoons, in the war of 1861–1865. Interspersed with personal reminiscences. By T. F. Dornblaser ... Published for the author. Philadelphia, Lutheran publication society, 1884.

viii, 9–264 p.   fold. map.   19ᶜᵐ.

Contrary to its flamboyant title, this narrative of cavalry operations in the Deep South is a factual, reliable account by an obviously fair-minded soldier.

Douglas, Henry Kyd, 1840–1903.

I rode with Stonewall, being chiefly the war experiences of the youngest member of Jackson's staff from the John Brown raid to the hanging of Mrs. Surratt ₁by₁ Henry Kyd Douglas ... Chapel Hill. The University of North Carolina press ₁ᶜ1940₁

vii p., 3 l., 401 p.   front., plates, ports., fold. map, facsim.   23½ cm.

Minor inaccuracies do not mar appreciably this delightful memoir by a young aid of "Stonewall" Jackson.

Downing, Alexander G 1842–

Downing's civil war diary, by Sergeant Alexander G. Downing, Company E, Eleventh Iowa infantry, Third brigade, "Crocker's brigade," Sixth division of the Seventeenth corps, Army of the Tennessee. August 15, 1861–July 31, 1865; ed. by Olynthus B. Clark ... Des Moines, The Historical department of Iowa, 1916.

1 p. l., vi p., 1 l., [3]–325 p. front., plates, ports. 23½ᶜᵐ.

Rewritten for publication, this journal is an unbroken narrative of Western service during four years of war; the author devoted many entries to descriptions of country through which he passed.

Downs, Edward C

Four years a scout and spy. "General Bunker," one of Lieut. General Grant's most daring and successful scouts. Being a narrative of the thrilling adventures, narrow escapes, noble daring, and amusing incidents in the experience of Corporal Ruggles during four years' service as a scout and spy for the Federal Army; embracing his services for twelve of the most distinguished generals in the U. S. Army. By E. C. Downs ... Zanesville, O., H. Dunne, 1866.

xii, 5–404 p. incl. plates. front. (port.) 22 cm.

Possibly the author was a spy and had many hair-raising experiences during the war; however, his recollections (which went through four editions) seem consistently exaggerated.

Drake, James Madison, 1837–

The history of the Ninth New Jersey veteran vols. A record of its service from Sept. 13th, 1861, to July 12th, 1865, with a complete official roster, and sketches of prominent members ... by Captain J. Madison Drake ... Elizabeth, Journal printing house, 1889.

501 p. front., illus. (incl. map) plates, ports. 23½ᶜᵐ.

This unbalanced study was based on a diary, official reports, newspaper articles, and minutae, yet it is superior to the Everts history of the same subject.

Drake, James Vaulx.

Life of General Robert Hatton, including his most important public speeches; together, with much of his Washington & army correspondence, by James Vaulx Drake ... Nashville, Tenn., Marshall & Bruce, 1867.

xi, 458 p. front. (port.) 22ᶜᵐ.

Contains many but relatively unrevealing letters of a general killed at Seven Pines.

Draper, William Franklin, 1842–1910.

Recollections of a varied career, by William F. Draper; with nine illustrations from photographs. Boston, Little, Brown, and company, 1908.

vii p., 2 l., 411 p. 5 pl., 4 port. (incl. front.) 23½ᶜᵐ.

Over a third of this autobiography recounts Draper's experiences as an officer in the 36th Massachusetts, IX Corps.

Driggs, George W

Opening of the Mississippi; or Two years' campaigning in the South-west. A record of the campaigns, sieges, actions and marches in which the 8th Wisconsin volunteers have participated. Together with correspondence, by a non-commissioned officer. Madison, Wis., W. J. Park & co., printers, 1864.

149, [1] p. 21 cm.

From letters written originally to his hometown newspaper, the author tells in light, sometimes witty fashion his experiences in the West with the 8th Wisconsin.

Dugan, James, *corporal 14th Ill. infantry.*

History of Hurlbut's fighting Fourth division: and especially the marches, toils, privations, adventures, skirmishes and battles of the Fourteenth Illinois infantry; together with camp-scenes, anecdotes, battle-incidents; also a description of the towns, cities, and countries through which their marches have extended since the commencement of the war; to which is added official reports of the battles in which they were engaged; with portraits of many distinguished officers; by James Dugan ... Cincinnati, E. Morgan & co., 1863.

viii, 9–265 p. front., port. 20ᶜᵐ.

A lightly written but thoroughly revealing study of the war in Missouri and Mississippi; both military and civilian matters receive ample attention.

Duganne, Augustine Joseph Hickey, 1823–1884.

The fighting Quakers; a true story of the war for our union. By A. J. H. Duganne. With letters from the brothers to their mother: and a funeral sermon by Rev. O. B. Frothingham. By authority of the Bureau of Military record. New York, J. P. Robens, 1866.

1 p. l., 116 p. front. 19ᶜᵐ.

At intervals in this extremely embellished work are excerpts from the soldier letters of two Pennsylvania brothers.

Duke, Basil Wilson, 1838–1916.

A history of Morgan's Cavalry. Edited with an introd. and notes by Cecil Fletcher Holland. Bloomington, Indiana University Press [1960]

595 p. illus. 21 cm.

A cursory introduction and three pages of notes make little improvement on the original edition.

Duke, Basil Wilson, 1838–1916.

Reminiscences of General Basil W. Duke ... Garden City, N. Y., Doubleday, Page & company, 1911.

xii, 512 p. front. (port.) 23½ cm.

Originally published as a series of newspaper articles, this exceptionally fine memoir of Confederate cavalry operations in the West is often consulted and widely quoted.

Duke, John K   1844–

History of the Fifty-third regiment Ohio volunteer infantry, during the war of the rebellion, 1861 to 1865. Together with more than thirty personal sketches of officers and men. By John K. Duke, company F, Fifty-third O. V. V. I. Portsmouth, O., The Blade printing company, 1900.

4 p. l., 303, ₁1₁ p. front., plates, ports. 22ᶜᵐ.

Too much reliance by the author on memory and a fragmentary diary; adds little to an understanding of the war in the West.

Dunaway, Wayland Fuller.

Reminiscences of a Rebel, by the Rev. Wayland Fuller Dunaway, formerly captain of Co. I, 40th Va. regt., Army of northern Virginia ... New York, The Neale publishing company, 1913.

133 p. 19½ᶜᵐ.

Unfortunately, these recollections of a quiet and unassuming soldier are too brief to make this work one of exceptional value.

Duncan, Thomas D

Recollections of Thomas D. Duncan, a Confederate soldier. Nashville, Tenn., McQuiddy printing company, 1922.

213 p. ports. 20ᶜᵐ.

The author, a member of Forrest's cavalry, waited until he was quite elderly before writing his memoirs; the result is a poor narrative lacking in both comprehension and insight.

Dunlop, William S

... Lee's sharpshooters; or, The forefront of battle. A story of southern valor that never has been told. Major W. S. Dunlop. Little Rock, Ark., Tunnah & Pittard, printers, 1899.

488 p. col. port. 20½ cm.

These reminiscences by a soldier who fought in both South Carolina and Mississippi units are lengthy but unbalanced.

Dupré, Louis J

Fagots from the camp fire. By "the newspaper man". Washington, D. C., E. T. Charles & co., 1881.

199 p. incl. front. (port.) 21½ᶜᵐ.

So journalistic and manufactured as to be worthless.

Dwight, Wilder, 1833–1862.

Life and letters of Wilder Dwight, lieut-col. Second Mass. inf. vols. ... Boston, Ticknor and Fields, 1868.

vii, 349, ₁1₁ p., 1 l. front. (port.) 24ᶜᵐ.

Voluminous, penetrating, and sometimes philosophical letters by a highly cultured officer who was killed at Antietam; one of the best sources for the 2nd Massachusetts.

Early, Jubal Anderson, 1816–1894.

A memoir of the last year of the war for independence, in the Confederate States of America, containing an account of the operations of his commands in the years 1864 and 1865, by Lieutenant-General Jubal A. Early ... ₁2d ed.₁ Lynchburg, C. W. Button, 1867.

xii, ₁13₁, 135, ₁1₁ p. 23ᶜᵐ.

The first memoir by a caustic Confederate general, this work was incorporated later -- with marked revisions-- in Early's Autobiographical Sketch.

Eddy, Richard, 1828–1906.

History of the Sixtieth regiment New York state volunteers, from the commencement of its organization in July, 1861, to its public reception at Ogdensburgh as a veteran command, January 7th, 1864. By Richard Eddy, chaplain. Philadelphia, Pub. by the author, 1864.

xii, 360 p. 19½ cm.

More a damnation of the South and slavery than a regimental history; Eddy's military service was confined to the Harpers Ferry region.

Eden, Robert C   *d*. 1907.

The sword and gun, a history of the 37th Wis. volunteer infantry. From its first organization to its final muster out. By Major R. C. Eden. Madison, Atwood & Rublee, printers, 1865.

120 p. 16½ᶜᵐ.

A reliable but shallow memoir, treating only of the last year of the war in Virginia.

Edmundson, Sarah Emma, 1841–1898.

Unsexed: or, The female soldier. The thrilling adventures, experiences and escapes of a woman, as nurse, spy and scout, in hospitals, camps and battle-fields, by S. Emma E. Edmonds ₁pseud.₁ Philadelphia, Philadelphia Pub. Co. ₁186–?₁

384 p. illus., port. 20 cm.

Published under several different and flamboyant titles, this highly personal account tells of the experiences of a woman who disguised herself, enlisted in the army, and for two years performed unusual duties.

Edwards, Frank *i. e.* **John Frank,** 1842–

Army life of Frank Edwards, Confederate veteran. Army of northern Virginia, 1861–1865. [n. p., 1911]

108 p. 2 port. (incl. front.) 19¾ᶜᵐ.

So embellished and self-praising that the work's brevity is its chief virtue.

Edwards, John Ellis, 1814–1891.

The Confederate soldier; being a memorial sketch of George N. and Bushrod W. Harris, privates in the Confederate army. By Rev. John E. Edwards ... New York, Blelock & co., 1868.

vi, 139 p. 18½ᶜᵐ.

An overly sentimental tribute to two brothers who died in the field during the war's first year.

Edwards, John Newman, 1839–1889.

Shelby and his men; or, The war in the West. By John N. Edwards. Cincinnati, Miami printing and publishing co., 1867.

ix, 10–551 p. front. (port.) fold. map. 23ᶜᵐ.

Through sentimentality and eulogy, Edwards elevated Shelby and his men to the ranks of the angels.

Eggleston, George Cary, 1839–1911.

A Rebel's recollections, by George Cary Eggleston ... New York, Hurd and Houghton; Cambridge, The Riverside press, 1875.

vi p., 1 l., 260 p. 18ᶜᵐ.

A charming, highly literate series of reminiscences by a young Confederate who obviously enjoyed his war experiences.

Eggleston, George Cary, 1839–1911.

A Rebel's recollections. Introd. by David Donald. Bloomington, Indiana University Press [ᶜ1959]

187 p. 22 cm.

An unannotated reprint, with a brief introduction by a distinguished scholar.

Elder, William Henry, *Abp.,* 1819–1904.

Civil War diary (1862–1865) of Bishop William Henry Elder, Bishop of Natchez. [Natchez? Miss.] R. O. Gerow, Bishop of Natchez-Jackson [1960?]

125 p. 24 cm.

The unique 1862–1865 diary of the Bishop of Natchez; particularly revealing for religious and homefront subjects.

Elderkin, James D   1820–

Biographical sketches and anecdotes of a soldier of three wars, as written by himself. The Florida, the Mexican war and the great rebellion, together with sketches of travel, also of service in a militia company and a member of the Detroit light guard band for over thirty years. By James D. Elderkin. Detroit, Mich. [Record printing company] 1899.

2 p. l., 202 p. front., pl., port. 17½ᶜᵐ.

Fifty pages of this biography skim over the subject's brief service as drum major in the 1st Michigan.

Eldredge, Daniel, *b.* 1840 or 1.

... The Third New Hampshire and all about it. By D. Eldredge ... Boston, Press of E. B. Stillings and co., 1893.

xxxi p., 1 l., 1054 p., 1 l. front., illus., port., maps (part fold.) 24ᶜᵐ.

This impressively thick but rather disjointed work contains recollections of service from South Carolina to Appomattox.

Elliott, James Carson, 1845–

The southern soldier boy; a thousand shots for the confederacy, by James Carson Elliott, Company F, 56 regiment N. C. T., C. S. A., 1861–'65 ... Historical incidents, reminiscences and personal experiences, covering the nine months siege of Petersburg and both prison pens, etc., etc. ... Raleigh, N. C., Edwards & Broughton printing company [ᶜ1907]

77, [1] p. front. (port.) 23ᶜᵐ.

Based on the faulty memory of a veteran of the 6th North Carolina; much of this work is little more than a series of anecdotes.

Ellis, Daniel, 1827–

Thrilling adventures of Daniel Ellis, the great union guide of east Tennessee, for a period of nearly four years during the great southern rebellion. Written by himself. Containing a short biography of the author ... New York, Harper & brothers, 1867.

1 p. l., [5]–430 p. incl. illus., ports., map. front. 19¼ᶜᵐ.

Too many of the Hollywood-like escapades of Ellis seem exaggerated, but this account throws light on divided sentiment in East Tennessee throughout the war.

Ellis, Thomas T

Leaves from the diary of an army surgeon; or, Incidents of field, camp, and hospital life. By Thomas T. Ellis ... New York, J. Bradburn, 1863.

312 p. facsim. 19ᶜᵐ.

Ellis, an English physician who volunteered his services to the Federal army, so admired military operations in general and McClellan in particular that his recollections add little to the field.

Elwood, John William, 1842–

Elwood's stories of the old Ringgold cavalry, 1847–1865; the first three year cavalry of the civil war, with introduction by the Rev. H. H. Ryland. Coal Center, Pa., The author, J. W. Elwood, 1914.

xvi, [17]–326 p. front., illus. (incl. ports.) 23ᶜᵐ.

A fairly reliable story of the 22nd Pennsylvania Cavalry with emphasis on its 1864 campaigns in Virginia.

Emerson, Edward Waldo, 1844–1930.

Life and letters of Charles Russell Lowell, captain Sixth United States cavalry, colonel Second Massachusetts cavalry, brigadier-general United States volunteers, by Edward W. Emerson. Boston and New York, Houghton, Mifflin and company, 1907.

viii p., 4 l., [3]–499, [1] p. front., pl., ports., fold. map. 20½ᶜᵐ.

The 1852-1864 letters of a distinguished Massachusetts citizen; Lowell commented pointedly on persons, places, and engagements.

Emilio, Luis Fenollosa, b. 1844.

History of the Fifty-fourth regiment of Massachusetts volunteer infantry, 1863–1865. By Luis F. Emilio. Boston, The Boston book co., 1891.

xvi, 410 p. front., port., maps (part fold.) 22ᶜᵐ.

This standard history of a famous Negro unit contains the usual statistics, facts, illustrations, and maps found in such compilations.

Emmerton, James Arthur, 1834–1888.

A record of the Twenty-third regiment Mass. vol. infantry in the war of the rebellion 1861–1865 with alphabetical roster; company rolls ... etc., by James A. Emmerton ... Boston, W. Ware & co., 1886.

xx, 352 p. front., pl., port., maps (part fold.) 23½ cm.

Full of diary and letter extracts, plus some reminiscences, by soldiers who campaigned along the North Carolina coast.

Estvàn, Bela, b. 1827.

War pictures from the South. By B. Estvàn ... London, Routledge, Warne and Routledge, 1863.

2 v. fronts., ports., 2 fold. plans. 19¼ᶜᵐ.

A purported history of the first campaigns in the East by a Hungarian soldier of fortune who allegedly joined the Southern forces.

Everts, Hermann.

A complete and comprehensive history of the Ninth regiment New Jersey vols. infantry. From its first organization to its final muster out. By Hermann Everts. Newark, A. S. Holbrook, printer, 1865.

197 p. 23ᶜᵐ.

A diary-like history too restricted in scope to qualify as a good unit history.

Ewell, Richard Stoddert, 1817–1872.

The making of a soldier; letters of General R. S. Ewell; arranged and edited by Captain Percy Gatling Hamlin ... Richmond, Va., Whittet & Shepperson, 1935.

161 p. 2 port. (incl. front.) pl. 21½ᶜᵐ.

Confederate Gen. Ewell's letters are few in number, skimpy in content, and, for the most part, bear pre-war dates.

Ewer, James Kendall, 1846–

The Third Massachusetts cavalry in the war for the union. By Rev. James K. Ewer ... Pub. by direction of the Historical committee of the Regimental association. [Maplewood, Mass., The Wᵐ G. J. Perry press] 1903.

452, cxiv, [2] p., 1 l. front., illus., 2 pl., ports., port. groups, plans (part fold.) 23½ cm.

In this thick history are good accounts of the battle of Sabine Crossroads and actions in western Louisiana; the author freely passes judgement.

Fairchild, Charles Bryant, 1842–   *comp.*

History of the 27th regiment N. Y. vols. ... Being a record of its more than two years of service in the war for the union, from May 21st, 1861, to May 31st, 1863. With a complete roster, and short sketches of commanding officers. Also, a record of experience and suffering of some of the comrades in Libby and other Rebel prisons. Compiled by C. B. Fairchild, of company "D". Published under the direction of the following committee: Gen. H. W. Slocum. Capt. C. A. Wells. Binghamton, N. Y., Carl & Matthews, printers [1888]

ix, 303 p., 1 l. incl. illus., ports., maps. front., 2 fold. maps, plan. 23ᶜᵐ.

An excellent source, based on Fairchild's wartime diary of service in the VI Corps; unfortunately, the text ends with the 1863 spring campaigns.

Fanning, Thomas W

The adventures of a volunteer, by a non-commissioned officer. Cincinnati, P. C. Browne, 1863.

94 p. 12°.

Unreliable and padded, this account was enlarged and reissued in 1865 under the title: The Hairbreath Escapes and Humorous Adventures.

Farrar, Samuel Clarke.

The Twenty-second Pennsylvania cavalry and the Ringgold battalion, 1861–1865; written and comp. by Samuel Clarke Farrar ... Pub. under the auspices of the Twenty-second Pennsylvania Ringgold cavalry association. ₍Akron, O. and Pittsburgh, The New Werner company₎ 1911.

xi, ₍3₎–538 p. front., illus., plates, ports., maps (1 fold.) 23½ᶜᵐ.

The narrative is too impersonal, and too much borrowed from other sources, to capture the true feelings of the men within the ranks.

Favill, Josiah Marshall.

The diary of a young officer serving with the armies of the United States during the war of the rebellion, by Josiah Marshall Favill, adjutant, captain, and brevet major 57th New York infantry, brevet lieutenant-colonel, and colonel U. S. volunteers. Chicago, R. R. Donnelley & sons company, 1909.

298 p. fronts., plates, ports. 21ᶜᵐ.

An almost complete day-by-day account by a young officer who campaigned from First Bull Run through Spotsylvania.

Fay, Edwin Hedge, 1832–1898.

This infernal war; the Confederate letters of Edwin H. Fay. Edited by Bell Irvin Wiley with the assistance of Lucy E. Fay. Austin, University of Texas Press ₍1958₎

viii, 474 p. ports., map (on lining papers) 24 cm.

An unusually full collection of letters by a Harvard-graduated schoolteacher who served in Louisiana cavalry; the correspondence is reflective of the intellectual and genteel Fay.

Fay, Franklin Brigham, 1821–1904.

War papers of Frank B. Fay, with reminiscences of service in the camps and hospitals of the Army of the Potomac, 1861–1865; ed. by William Howell Reed. ₍Boston₎ Priv. print. ₍press of Geo. H. Ellis co.₎ 1911.

vii, 161 p. front. (port.) illus., pl. 24½ᶜᵐ.

A very revealing memoir by a Chelsea (Mass.) mayor who served voluntarily and faithfully as a male nurse and member of the Sanitary Commission.

Feemster, Zenas E   1813–

The traveling refugee; or, The cause and cure of the rebellion in the United States; embracing a sketch of the state of society in the South, before, and at the commencement of the rebellion. Illustrated by facts and incidents. By Rev. Zenas E. Feemster, refugee, from Mississippi, in 1862. Springfield, Ills., Steam press of Baker & Phillips, 1865.

iv p., 2 l., ₍9₎–195, ₍1₎ p. 18 cm.

Self-pitying recollections of life in northern Mississippi by a minister under constant suspicion as a Unionist.

Fenner, Earl, 1841–

The history of Battery H, First regiment Rhode Island light artillery, in the war to preserve the union, 1861–1865, by Earl Fenner; illustrated with portraits. Providence, Snow & Farnham, printers, 1894.

viii p., 1 l., 216 p. front., ports. 23ᶜᵐ.

"Daily memoranda" comprise less than half of this work; biographical sketches and rosters make up the rest.

Ferris, Antoinette Barnum.

A soldier's souvenir: or, The terrible experiences of Lieut. L. L. Lancaster, of the Second Wisconsin cavalry ... by Antoinette Barnum Ferris ... Eau Claire, Wis., Pauly brothers, printers, 1896.

61 p. front. (port.) 16½ᶜᵐ.

A self-exoneration by an officer sentenced to death for petitioning for the removal of a superior officer.

Field, Charles D

Three years in the saddle from 1861 to 1865; memoirs of Charles D. Field; thrilling stories of the war in camp and on the field of battle ... By Charles D. Field ... ₍Goldfield? Ia., ᶜ1898₎

74 p. front. (port.) 21½ᶜᵐ.

A brief, rather empty narrative by an Illinois cavalryman whose service was in Arkansas and Missouri.

Field, Henry Martyn, 1822–1907.

Bright skies and dark shadows, by Henry M. Field ... New York, C. Scribner's sons, 1890.

3 p. l., ii p., 1 l., ₍9₎–316 p. front., illus. (plans) maps. 21 cm.

Recollections of a minister's travels through the wartime South, with a long chapter treating of the battle of Franklin, Tenn.

Figg, Royall W

"Where men only dare to go!" or, The story of a boy company (C. S. A.) By an ex-boy ... Richmond, Whittet & Shepperson, 1885.

viii, [17]-263 p. front., port. 20½ᶜᵐ.

Reinforced by imagination, these recollections by a member of the Parker Battery describe several major battles as well as life in Point Lookout prison.

Fisher, George Adams, 1835–

The Yankee conscript; or, Eighteen months in Dixie. By George Adams Fisher. With an introduction by Rev. William Dickson. Philadelphia, J. W. Daughaday, 1864.

251 p. front. (port.) plates. 18ᶜᵐ.

This travelogue of army life in the Trans-Mississippi was obviously designed as a political document for the 1864 election in the North; its strong Union undertones slant the narrative.

Fisher, Horace Cecil.

The personal experiences of Colonel Horace Newton Fisher in the Civil War; a staff officer's story. Boston, 1960.

134 p. ports., maps (part col.) facsims. 29 cm.

A discursive biography, reinforced by extracts from the letters of an inspector general in the Army of the Cumberland; particularly good for the battles of Perryville and Chickamauga.

Fisk, Joel C

A condensed history of the 56th regiment, New York veteran volunteer infantry, which was a part of the organization known as the "Tenth legion" in the civil war, 1861-1865, together with a register or roster of all the members of the regiment, and the war record of each member as recorded in the Adjutant general's office at Albany, New York. By Joel C. Fisk and William H. D. Blake. [Newburgh, N. Y., Newburgh journal printing house and book bindery, 1906]

424 p. front. (port.) pl. 26½ᶜᵐ.

Very little of this volume treats of the regiment's history; most of the pages contain statistics and a muster roll.

Fiske, George M   1842–

Civil War journal of Pvt. George M. Fiske, 42d Massachusetts Regiment of Volunteer Militia, U. S. Army. An account of the battle of Galveston and the subsequent fortunes of the enlisted men of the Federal garrison as compiled, arranged, and edited by Richard A. Atkins and Helen Fiske Atkins from the notes, letters and diaries of Pvt. George M. Fiske. Syracuse, R. A. Atkins, 1962.

59 l. illus. 28 cm.

The mimeographed letters of a Bay State soldier who campaigned with Banks in Texas; revealing for the oft-neglected battle of Galveston.

Fiske, Joseph Emery, 1839–1909.

War letters of Capt. Joseph E. Fiske ⟨Harvard, '61⟩ written to his parents during the war of the rebellion from Andover theological seminary and encampments in North Carolina and from southern prisons. Wellesley [Mass.] The Maugus press [19—?]

60 p. 21½ᶜᵐ.

Letters to his parents by an officer in the 2nd Massachusetts Heavy Artillery; somewhat useful for the North Carolina campaigns.

Fiske, Samuel Wheelock 1828–1864.

Mr. Dunn Browne's experiences in the army ... Boston, Nichols and Noyes; New York, O. S. Felt, 1866.

2 p. l., iii-xii, 11-390 p. front. (port.) 19 cm.

Above-average memoir by a minister who became a captain in the 14th Connecticut and died in action in the Wilderness.

Fitch, John *of Alton, Ill.*

Annals of the Army of the Cumberland: comprising biographies, descriptions of departments, accounts of expeditions, skirmishes, and battles; also its police record of spies, smugglers and prominent rebel emissaries. Together with anecdotes, incidents, poetry, reminiscences, etc. and official reports of the battle of Stone river. By an officer. Illustrated with steel portraits, wood engravings, and maps. Philadelphia, J. B. Lippincott & co., 1863.

1 p. l., 671 p. front., illus., plates, ports., fold. plan. 24 cm.

Little more than a bulky collection of military narratives, biographical sketches, anecdotes, and eulogies.

Fitch, Michael Hendrick, 1837–

Echoes of the civil war as I hear them, by Michael H. Fitch ... New York, R. F. Fenno & company, 1905.

368 p. plates, 2 port. (incl. front.) maps. 19½ cm.

An exceptionally good memoir of the Western campaigns by a Wisconsin officer.

Fleharty, Stephen F

Our regiment. A history of the 102d Illinois infantry volunteers, with sketches of the Atlanta campaign, the Georgia raid, and the campaign of the Carolinas. By S. F. Fleharty. Chicago, Brewster & Hanscom, printers, 1865.

192, xxiv p. 19½ cm.

Based on a diary, and written immediately after the events it describes, this work is excellent for Sherman's 1864-1865 campaign.

Fleming, Francis Philip, 1841–1908.

Memoir of Capt. C. Seton Fleming of the Second Florida infantry, c. s. a. Illustrative of the history of the Florida troops in Virginia during the war between the states. With appendix of the casualties. By Francis P. Fleming. Jacksonville, Fla., Times-Union publishing house, 1884.

2 p. l., [xi]–xiv p., 1 l., [17]–124 p., 1 l. incl. ports. port. 21½ᶜᵐ.

A little-known work, important chiefly for personal insights into action late in the war.

Fleming, George Thornton, 1855–

Life and letters of Alexander Hays, brevet colonel United States army, brigadier general and brevet major general United States volunteers. Ed. and arranged with notes and contemporary history by George Thornton Fleming from data compiled by Gilbert Adams Hays ... Pittsburgh, Pa., 1919.

viii, 708, [16] p. incl. front. (port.) plates, 2 port. on pl. 25 cm.

One of the largest collections of Civil War letters in print; this almost unknown book affords a splendid insight into the Army of the Potomac up to the Wilderness Campaign, where Hays was killed.

Fletcher, William Andrew, b. 1839.

Rebel private, front and rear. With a pref. by Bell Irvin Wiley. [New ed.] Austin, University of Texas Press, 1954.

162 p. illus. 24 cm.

An account put together forty years after the war by a member of Hood's Texas Brigade; what it omitted was more valuable that what it contains.

Floyd, David Bittle.

History of the Seventy-fifth regiment of Indiana infantry volunteers, its organization, campaigns, and battles (1862–65.) By Rev. David Bittle Floyd ... With an introduction by Major-General J. J. Reynolds ... Published for the author. Philadelphia, Lutheran publication society, 1893.

457 p. front., illus., port., maps. 22½ cm.

A compilation of soldiers' letters, diaries, and recollections; treats of the Western campaigns, beginning with Chickamauga; one of the better regimental histories.

Floyd, Frederick Clark, b. 1837.

History of the Fortieth (Mozart) regiment, New York volunteers, which was composed of four companies from New York, four companies from Massachusetts and two companies from Pennsylvania, by Sergeant Fred. C. Floyd ... Boston, F. H. Gilson company, 1909.

xvi, 469 p. front., illus. (facsims.) plates, ports. 24 cm.

A superior unit history, based on wartime letters and diaries; highly useful for personal insights into the Army of the Potomac.

Fonerden, Clarence Albert.

A brief history of the military career of Carpenter's battery, from its organization as a rifle company under the name of the Alleghany Roughs to the ending of the war between the states, by C. A. Fonerden. New Market, Va., Henkel & company, printers, 1911.

78 p. 3 pl. 20½ cm.

An adequate, impersonal summary of a unit that served for a time with the Stonewall Brigade.

Fontaine, Lamar, 1829–

My life and my lectures, by Lamar Fontaine, c. e., ph. d. New York and Washington, The Neale publishing company, 1908.

2 p. l., 3–361 p. front. (port.) 23ᶜᵐ.

Another of those accumulations of romanticism that have no value for the historian.

Foote, Corydon Edward, 1849–1944.

With Sherman to the sea; a drummer's story of the Civil War, as related by Corydon Edward Foote to Olive Deane Hormel. With a foreword by Elizabeth Yates. New York, John Day Co. [1960]

255 p. illus. 21 cm.

A totally unreliable account, reconstructed when the author was elderly and unconciously hazy on the events he attempted to describe.

Ford, Andrew Elmer.

The story of the Fifteenth regiment Massachusetts volunteer infantry in the civil war, 1861–1864. By Andrew E. Ford. Clinton [Mass.] Press of W. J. Coulter, 1898.

422 p. front., ports., maps (part fold.) 23½ᶜᵐ.

Ford, a non-member of the regiment, wrote this history from material supplied him by survivors; the result is a work both choppy and impersonal.

Ford, Arthur P[eronneau]

Life in the Confederate army; being personal experiences of a private soldier in the Confederate army, by Arthur P. Ford, and Some experiences and sketches of southern life, by Marion Johnstone Ford. New York and Washington, The Neale publishing company, 1905.

136 p. 2 port. (incl. front.) 19ᶜᵐ.

The untrustworthy memoir of a young lad whose military service was along the South Carolina coast.

Ford, Henry E   1839–

History of the 101st regiment, by Lieut. H. E. Ford. Syracuse, N. Y. [Press of Times publishing co.] 1898.

4 p. l., [7]–155 p. incl. ports. front. 22½ᶜᵐ.

Mostly biographical sketches; the narrative would make no more than average newspaper article.

Ford, Thomas J

With the rank and file. Incidents and anecdotes during the war of the rebellion, as remembered by one of the non-commissioned officers. By Thomas J. Ford ... Milwaukee, Press of the Evening Wisconsin co., 1898.

95 p. front. (port.) 14½ᶜᵐ.

A superficial memoir by a member of the 24th Wisconsin.

Forsyth, George Alexander, 1837–1915.

Thrilling days in army life, by General George A. Forsyth, U. S. A. With illustrations by Rufus F. Zogbaum. New York and London, Harper & brothers, 1900.

4 p. l., 3–196, [1] p. 16 pl. (incl. front.) 19½ᶜᵐ.

Treats largely of postwar Indian fighting; a small section recounts the author's participation in Sheridan's Second Valley Campaign.

Foster, Alonzo, 1841–

Reminiscences and record of the 6th New York V. V. cavalry. By Alonzo Foster, late sergeant Co. F. [Brooklyn, 1892]

148 p. 18ᶜᵐ.

Popularly written and originally published serially in a Long Island newspaper.

Foster, John Watson, 1836–1917.

War stories for my grandchildren, by John W. Foster. Washington, D. C., Printed for private circulation, the Riverside press, Cambridge, 1918.

4 p. l., 192 p. front. (2 port.) pl. 24½ᶜᵐ.

Written by the Indiana officer for whom John Foster Dulles was named; this slim narrative is made up for the most part of Foster's letters from the Western theaters.

Fowler, Andrew L   1840–1862.

Memoirs of the late Adjt. Andrew L. Fowler, of the 51st N. Y. V. who fell at the battle of Antietam bridge, September 17th, 1862. Comprising the funeral discourse ... by ... S. D. Burchard ... letters of condolence ... and abstracts of letters written by the Adjt. ... Comp. by a friend ... New York, Ferris & Pratt, printers, 1863.

67 p. 21½ᶜᵐ.

Some 35 pages of this slim volume contain excerpts from Fowler's wartime letters.

Fowler, Philemon Halsted 1814–1879.

Memorials of William Fowler. New York, A. D. F. Randolph & company, 1875.

172 p. front. (port.) 21ᶜᵐ.

Letters by a major in the 146th New York; especially good for the Red River and 1864–1865 Virginia campaigns.

Fox, Charles Barnard 1833–1895.

Record of the service of the Fifty-fifth regiment of Massachusetts volunteer infantry. Printed for the regimental association. Cambridge, Press of J. Wilson and son, 1868.

2 p. l., 144 p. 25ᶜᵐ.

This unit study is primarily Fox's wartime diary, published with little or no revisions.

Fox, Simeon M   1842–

Story of the Seventh Kansas. [Topeka? 1902?]

36, [1] p. 23ᶜᵐ.

A printed address which, as expected, merely summarizes and eulogizes.

Fradenburgh, Jason Nelson, 1843–

In memoriam Henry Harrison Cumings, Charlotte J. Cumings, by Rev. J. N. Fradenburgh ... Oil City, Pa., The Derrick publishing company, 1913.

236 p. incl. plates, ports. front. 24½ᶜᵐ.

Approximately 135 pages of this eulogy contain excerpts from the diary of Cumings, who served for three years in the 105th Ohio.

Francis, Charles Lewis.

Narrative of a private soldier in the volunteer army of the United States, during a portion of the period covered by the great war of the rebellion of 1861. By Charles Lewis Francis ... Brooklyn, W. Jenkins and co., 1879.

viii, [7]–185 p. 18½ cm.

The rich, witty, and oftentimes improbable recollections of a soldier who served the first two years of the war in both major theaters.

Frederick, Gilbert, *b.* **1841** *or* **1842.**

The story of a regiment: being a record of the military services of the Fifty-seventh New York state volunteer infantry in the war of the rebellion, 1861–1865. By Gilbert Frederick ... [Chicago] Pub. by the Fifty-seventh veteran association, 1895.

xii, 349 p. front., illus., pl., port. 21½ cm.

Allegedly based on wartime letters, and treating of personal matters in camp and field, this work adds little to a knowledge of the Eastern theater.

Freeman, Julia Susan (Wheelock) 1833–

The boys in white; the experience of a hospital agent in and around Washington. By Julia S. Wheelock ... New York, Printed by Lange & Hillman, 1870.

vii, [1] p., 1 l., [9]–274 p. 2 port. (incl. front.) 19 cm.

One of the better, straightforward accounts of life in Federal hospitals; Miss Wheelock was stationed throughout the last three years of the war at Alexandria, Va.

Freeman, Warren Hapgood 1844?–

Letters from two brothers serving in the war for the union to their family at home in West Cambridge, Mass. Cambridge, Printed for private circulation [by H. O. Houghton and company] 1871.

2 p. l., 164 p., 2 l. front. (port.) 17½ cm.

Unusually good collection of letters by two Massachusetts brothers who served in different theaters; the letters are intelligent, clear, and very revealing for the war in Virginia and along the Atlantic coast.

Fremantle, *Sir* **Arthur James Lyon, 1835–1901.**

Three months in the southern states: April–June, 1863. By Lieut.-Col. Fremantle ... New York, J. Bradburn (successor to M. Doolady) 1864.

309 p. front. (port.) 19 cm.

Fully deserving of its reputation as the best commentary on the wartime South by an English visitor.

Frémont, Jessie (Benton) 1824–1902.

The story of the guard: a chronicle of the war. By Jessie Benton Frémont ... Boston, Ticknor and Fields, 1863.

xiii, [15]–227, [2] p. 18½ cm.

Too feminine and prejudiced to be of value; treats of her husband's mounted bodyguard.

French, Samuel Bassett, 1820–1898.

Centennial tales; memoirs of Colonel "Chester" S. Bassett French, extra aide-de-camp to Generals Lee and Jackson, the Army of Northern Virginia, 1861–1865. Compiled by Glenn C. Oldaker. New York, Carlton Press, 1962.

150 p. illus. 21 cm.

Included in this unbalanced memoir by an "extra aide-de-camp" are descriptions of Lee, Jackson, and other Southern notables.

French, Samuel Gibbs, 1818–1910.

Two wars: an autobiography of General Samuel G. French ... Mexican war; war between the states, a diary; reconstruction period, his experience; incidents, reminiscences, etc. Nashville, Tenn., Confederate veteran, 1901.

xv, [1], 404 p. incl. illus., port. front. (port.) 24 cm.

The New Jersey born French became a Confederate general and used a diary for much of this military memoir of service in the West.

Fulfer, Richard J

A history of the trials and hardships of the Twenty-fourth Indiana Volunteer Infantry. [Indianapolis] Indianapolis Print. Co., 1913.

135 p. illus., ports. 23 cm.

A day-by-day but shallow account of marches, camp life, and battles.

Fuller, Charles Augustus, 1841?–

Personal recollections of the war of 1861, as private, sergeant and lieutenant in the Sixty-first regiment, New York volunteer infantry, by Charles A. Fuller, prepared from data found in letters, written at the time from the field to the people at home. Sherburne, N. Y., News job printing house, 1906.

108 p. incl. front. (port.) 23 cm.

Good observations on the Eastern campaigns by a literate New York infantryman.

Fuller, Richard Frederick, 1821–1869.

Chaplain Fuller: being a life sketch of a New England clergyman and army chaplain. By Richard F. Fuller ... Boston, Walker, Wise, and company, 1863.

vi, 342 p. front. (port.) 19½ᶜᵐ.

Only half of this work contains the illuminating letters written by the chaplain of the 16th Massachusetts; primarily important for behind-the-lines scenes.

Gage, Moses D

From Vicksburg to Raleigh; or, A complete history of the Twelfth regiment Indiana volunteer infantry, and the campaigns of Grant and Sherman, with an outline of the great rebellion, by M. D. Gage, chaplain. Chicago, Clarke & co., 1865.

xiv, [15]–356 p. 19ᶜᵐ.

Written by the regimental chaplain, this book pulls no punches in describing the widespread looting of Federal troops; the work is also sympathetic to Sherman.

Galloway, George Norton.

The Ninety-fifth Pennsylvania volunteers (Gosline's Pennsylvania zouaves") in the Sixth corps. An historical paper by G. Norton Galloway ... read at a reunion of the surviving members of the 95th Pennsylvania volunteers, held at Germantown, Pa., on the 12th of October 1883. To which is added a narrative of the Chancellorsville campaign, the Sixth corps' part in that campaign ... and the name of every commissioned officer killed or wounded ... Philadelphia [Collins, printer] 1884.

87 p. 25ᶜᵐ.

Little more than a chronicle of the regiment's movements and a roster of its officers.

Galwey, Thomas Francis, 1846–1913.

The valiant hours; narrative of "Captain Brevet," an Irish-American in the Army of the Potomac. [1st ed.] Edited by W. S. Nye. Harrisburg, Pa., Stackpole [1961]

262 p. maps. 23 cm.

A human and charming narrative by a teen-ager who campaigned in the East with the 8th Ohio.

Gammage, Washington Lafayette, 1827–1865.

The camp, the bivouac, and the battlefield; being a history of the Fourth Arkansas Regiment, from its first organization down to the present date: its campaigns and its battles, with an occasional reference to the current events of the times, including biographical sketches of its field officers and others of the "old brigade." The whole interspersed here and there with descriptions of scenery, incident[s] of camp life, etc. Selma, 1864. Introd. by Ted R. Worley. Little Rock, Arkansas Southern Press, 1958.

viii, 150 p. front., maps (1 fold.) facsim. 23 cm.

Fresh and reliable, Gammage's memoir treats of most of the major engagements in the West.

Gammons, John Gray, *comp.*

The Third Massachusetts regiment volunteer militia in the war of the rebellion, 1861–1863. By Rev. John G. Gammons, PH. D. Providence, Snow & Farnham co., printers, 1906.

x p., 1 l., 326 p. front., ports., fold. map. 19 cm.

A purely statistical summary with appeal only to genealogists.

Gardner, Ira B   1843?–

Recollections of a boy member of Co. I, Fourteenth Maine volunteers, 1861 to 1865. By Ira B. Gardner ... Lewiston, Me., Printed by Lewiston journal company, 1902.

55 p. front. (port.) 22½ᶜᵐ.

A highly personal, regrettably short account of service in Louisiana.

Garfield, James Abram, *Pres. U. S.,* 1831–1881.

The wild life of the Army: Civil War letters of James A. Garfield. Edited with an introd. by Frederick D. Williams. [East Lansing] Michigan State University Press, 1964.

xx, 325 p. illus., map (on lining papers) plans, group ports. 24 cm.

The extremely personal and revealing letters of future President Garfield to his wife while the former was campaigning in both major theaters.

Gaskill, Joseph W

Footprints through Dixie; everyday life of the man under a musket on the firing line and in the trenches, 1862–1865, by J. W. Gaskill. Alliance, O. [Bradshaw printing company] 1919.

186 p. illus., pl. 23½ᶜᵐ.

A reworked and highly embellished diary by a member of the 104th Ohio; his service was primarily in Tennessee.

Gaston, Robert H

Tyler to Sharpsburg [by] Robert H. and William H. Gaston, their war letters, 1861–62. Edited by Robert W. Glover. [1st ed.] Waco, Tex., W. M. Morrison, 1960.

22 p. illus. 23 cm.

These sixteen letters by two brothers contain some personal observations on army life; footnote material only.

Gates, Theodore B

The "Ulster guard" ⟨20th N. Y. state militia⟩ and the war of the rebellion. Embracing a history of the early organization of the regiment; its three months' service; its reorganization and subsequent service ... complete roster ... &c.; &c. Together with a brief treatise upon the origin and growth of secession; the militia system, and the dependence of the federal government upon it in the beginning of the war; with a critical history of the first battle of Bull run; campaign of Gen. Pope; McClellan's Maryland campaign; battle of Fredericksburg; Hooker's Chancellorsville campaign; Gettysburg campaign; and a glance at the campaign from the Rapidan to Appomattox court house. By Theodore B. Gates ... New York, B. H. Tyrrel, printer, 1879.

xxiii, 619 p. 24 cm.

An above-average personal narrative, not a unit history; Gates was colonel of the regiment.

Gause, Isaac, 1843–

Four years with five armies; Army of the frontier, Army of the Potomac, Army of the Missouri, Army of the Ohio, Army of the Shenandoah. By Isaac Gause, late of Co. E, Second Ohio cav. New York and Washington, The Neale publishing company, 1908.

2 p. l., ₃₁–384 p. pl., 11 port. (incl. front.) 21ᶜᵐ.

Even though written in matter-of-fact tones, this volume of service in both theaters rests on the shaky foundations of memory and secondary sources.

George, Henry, 1847–

History of the 3d, 7th, 8th and 12th Kentucky C. S. A. By Henry George, May, 1911. Louisville, Ky., C. T. Dearing printing co. ₁1911₁

193 p. pl., ports., maps, facsim. 24 cm.

Based almost entirely on excerpts from the Official Records; extremely weak as a brigade history.

Georgia cavalry. *Georgia hussars,* 1736–

Roll of officers and members of the Georgia hussars and of the cavalry companies, of which the hussars are a continuation, with historical sketch relating facts showing the origin and necessity of rangers or mounted men in the colony of Georgia from date of its founding. ₁Savannah, Ga., The Morning news, 1906?₁

560 p. incl. illus., plates (1 col.) ports. front. 24ᶜᵐ.

Descriptive muster rolls only.

Gerrish, Theodore, 1846–

Army life; a private's reminiscences of the civil war, by Rev. Theodore Gerrish ... With an introduction by Hon. Josiah H. Drummond. Portland ₁Me.₁ Hoyt, Fogg & Donham ₁1882₁

372 p. 19½ cm.

Often quoted, these memoirs of service in the Army of the Potomac are nevertheless fraught with errors and relatively limited observation.

Gibbon, John, 1827–1896.

Personal recollections of the civil war, by John Gibbon, brigadier-general, u. s. a. New York, London, G. P. Putnam's sons, 1928.

vii, 426 p. front. (port.) maps. 24ᶜᵐ.

Reliable, straightforward memoirs by an officer who for a time commanded the Iron Brigade; particularly good for the Gettysburg campaign.

Gibbons, Alfred Ringgold, 1846–

The recollections of an old Confederate soldier ₁by₁ A. R. Gibbons ... ₁Shelbyville, Mo., Herald print, 1914?₁

cover-title, 31, ₁1₁ p. illus. (incl. ports.) 21½ᶜᵐ.

Too short, and written from memory too long after the war.

Gibbs, James M   *comp.*

History of the First battalion Pennsylvania six months volunteers and 187th regiment Pennsylvania volunteer infantry; six months and three years service, civil war, 1863–1865; comp. by James M. Gibbs ... ₁Harrisburg, Pa., Central printing and publishing house₁ 1905.

4 p. l., ₁7₁–320 p. front., illus., plates, ports., map. 23½ cm.

This cursory summary is of value only for a few incidents relative to the siege of Petersburg.

Gilbert, Alfred West, 1816–1900.

Colonel A. W. Gilbert, citizen-soldier of Cincinnati; edited by William E. Smith and Ophia D. Smith. Cincinnati, Historical and philosophical society of Ohio, 1934.

122 p. front., ports., fold. map. 23½ᶜᵐ.

Little more than 60 pages of this volume recount the author's activities as an officer in the 39th Ohio.

Giles, Leonidas B   1841–

Terry's Texas rangers, by L. B. Giles. ₁Austin, Tex., Von Boeckmann-Jones co., printers, ᶜ1911₁

105 p. 18ᶜᵐ.

Unfortunately, another work based too much on a weak memory; only the subject matter gives the book value.

Giles, Valerius Cincinnatus, 1842–1915.

Rags and hope, the recollections of Val C. Giles, four years with Hood's Brigade, Fourth Texas Infantry, 1861–1865. Compiled and edited by Mary Lasswell. New York, Coward-McCann [1961]

280 p. 22 cm.

Convivial memoirs, written shortly after the war without apparent benefit of diary or letters; they afford some interesting pen-pictures of army life and Confederate generals.

Gill, John 1841–

Reminiscences of four years as a private soldier in the Confederate army, 1861–1865. Baltimore, Sun printing office, 1904.

xii, [13]–136 p., 1 l. front. (port.) 22 cm.

Highly personal recollections of a young soldier whose service was primarily in Virginia; Gill was a Marylander who enlisted in a cavalry unit.

Gilmor, Harry, 1838–1883.

Four years in the saddle. By Colonel Harry Gilmor ... New York, Harper & brothers, 1866.

xii, [13]–291 p. incl. front. 19½ᶜᵐ.

The author's career as a Confederate cavalryman was spent largely in the Valley of Virginia; his accounts of events are so embellished as to create doubts of authenticity.

Gilmore, James Roberts 1822–1903.

Among the pines: or, South in secession-time. By Edmund Kirke [pseud.] New York, J. R. Gilmore [etc.] 1862.

310 p. 18½ cm.

A propagandistic volume in support of the abolitionist cause; the author could not possibly have remembered all the conversations quoted.

Gilmore, James Roberts 1822–1903.

Down in Tennessee, and back by way of Richmond. By Edmund Kirke [pseud.] ... London, S. Low, son, & Marston, 1864.

2 p. l., [7]–282 p. 19½ᶜᵐ.

Another collection of lengthy conversations during the author's visit to the South in 1863; this work is as unreliable as the one cited above.

Girard, Charles Frédéric 1822–1895.

Les États Confédérés d'Amérique visités en 1863. Mémoire adressé à S. M. Napoléon III. Paris, E. Dentu, 1864.

viii, [9]–160 p. fold. map. 21½ᶜᵐ.

Recollections of a Frenchman who made a brief visit to the South in 1863; extremely sympathetic to the Confederate cause.

Girard, Charles Frédéric, 1822–1895.

A visit to the Confederate States of America in 1863; memoir addressed to His Majesty Napoleon III. Translated and edited with an introd. by Wm. Stanley Hoole. [Limited ed.] Tuscaloosa, Ala., Confederate Pub. Co., 1962.

126 p. port., map, facsims. 22 cm.

An accurate translation, with necessary editorial trappings, of the work previously cited.

Glazier, Willard, 1841–1905.

Battles for the union; comprising descriptions of many of the most stubbornly contested battles in the war of the great rebellion, together with incidents and reminiscences of the camp, the march, and the skirmish line. Embracing a record of the privations, heroic deeds, and glorious triumphs of the soldiers of the republic. By Willard Glazier. Hartford, Conn., Dustin, Gilman & co., 1875.

xix, [20]–407 p. incl. pl. front. (port.) pl. 19½ᶜᵐ.

An impersonal and embellished history of the Eastern campaigns by an overly prolific writer.

Glazier, Willard, 1841–1905.

Three years in the federal cavalry. By Captain Willard Glazier ... New York, R. H. Ferguson & company, 1874.

xvi, [2], [19]–347 p. incl. front., 8 pl. port. 19½ cm.

This well-known narrative, by an intelligent officer in the 2nd New York Cavalry, is especially good for camp scenes in Virginia.

Glover, Edwin A

Bucktailed Wildcats, a regiment of Civil War volunteers. New York, T. Yoseloff [1960]

328 p. illus. 22 cm.

A thoroughly researched study of a valorous band of Pennsylvania lumbermen in the Army of the Potomac.

Goldsborough, William Worthington, 1831–1901.
The Maryland line in the Confederate States army. By
W. W. Goldsborough ... Baltimore, Kelly, Piet & co., 1869.

357 p. front., port. 19½ cm.

The best study of a Maryland unit; Goldsborough
was one of the few Confederates who freely confessed to robbing dead soldiers.

Goodhart, Briscoe, 1845–1927.
History of the Independent Loudoun Virginia rangers.
U. S. vol. cav. (scouts) 1862–65. By Briscoe Goodhart,
co. A. Washington, D. C., Press of McGill & Wallace, 1896.

vi, 234 p. front., illus., plates, ports., maps. 22½ cm.

An almost totally factual account of a cavalry
unit's operations in northern Virginia; lacking
in color and personal incidents.

Goodloe, Albert Theodore.
Some Rebel relics from the seat of war. By Albert
Theodore Goodloe ... Nashville, Tenn., Printed for the
author, 1893.

315 p. front. (port.) 19 cm.

These valuable memoirs by an Alabama soldier
recount incidents of the war in the West; indispensable for any study of the Confederate
Army of Tennessee.

Gordon, Armistead Churchill, 1855–1931.
Memories and memorials of William Gordon McCabe, by
Armistead Churchill Gordon ... Richmond, Va., Old Do-
minion press, inc., 1925.

2 v. fronts., ports., facsim. 23½ cm.

Contains the sometimes revealing recollections
of an adjutant to, and close friend of, Col. W. J.
Pegram.

Gordon, George H[enry] 1825?–1886.
Brook Farm to Cedar Mountain; in the war of the great
rebellion 1861–62; a revision and enlargement (from the
latest and most authentic sources) of papers numbered I., II.
and III. entitled, "A history of the Second Massachusetts
regiment," and the "Second Massachusetts regiment and
Stonewall Jackson," by George H. Gordon ... Boston, J. R.
Osgood and company, 1883.

x p., 1 l., 376 p. front., pl., fold. maps. 21 cm.

Illuminating memoirs of the war's first year in
the East by the colonel of the 2nd Massachusetts.

Gordon, George Henry, 1825?–1886.
A war diary of events in the war of the great rebellion.
1863–1865. By George H. Gordon ... Boston, J. R. Osgood
and company, 1882.

vi p., 1 l., 437 p. illus., maps. 21 cm.

Relying heavily on his full diary, Gordon here
recounts his service along the coast from Yorktown to New Orleans; a more revealing work
than the one cited above.

Gordon, John Brown, 1832–1904.
Reminiscences of the civil war, by General John B. Gordon ... New York, C. Scribner's sons, 1903.

x p., 1 l., xi–xiii, 474 p. 3 port. (incl. front.) 22½ cm.

"Among the most entertaining of [generals']
memoirs," Freeman opined; however, possessed
of numerous exaggerations.

Gordon, Marquis Lafayette, 1843–1900.
M. L. Gordon's experiences in the civil war from his
narrative, letters and diary; edited by Donald Gordon ...
Boston, Priv. print., 1922.

7 p. l., 13–72 p. front., illus., plates, ports., facsims. (part fold.) 28½ cm.

A disorganized work containing a narrative and
then excerpts from letters and a diary; as a
member of the 85th Pennsylvania, Gordon took
part in the Peninsular Campaign.

Gorgas, Josiah, 1818–1883.
The Civil War diary of General Josiah Gorgas; ed. by
Frank E. Vandiver. University, Ala., Univ. of Alabama
Press, 1947.

xi, 208 p. ports. 23 cm.

The extremely valuable journal of the Confederacy's indefatigable Chief of Ordnance; treats
of practically all aspects of the Southern nation.

Goss, Warren Lee, 1835–1925.
Recollections of a private. A story of the Army of the
Potomac. By Warren Lee Goss ... New York, T. Y. Cro-
well & co. [c1890]

xi, 354 p. front., illus., plates. 23½ cm.

Very readable memoirs of a Massachusetts
soldier, its reconstructed conversation notwithstanding; many chapters first appeared in the
Century Magazine.

Gould, Edward K

Major-general Hiram G. Berry; his career as a contractor, bank president, politician, and major-general of volunteers in the civil war; together with his war correspondence, embracing the period from Bull Run to Chancellorsville, by Edward K. Gould. Rockland, Me., Press of the Courier-Gazette, 1899.

312 p. front., plates, ports. 23cm.

An unusually good biography of one of those un-assuming but devoted Federal generals; much of the book first appeared in newspaper serial form.

Gould, John Mead, *b.* 1839.

History of the First—Tenth—Twenty-ninth Maine regiment. In service of the United States from May 3, 1861, to June 21, 1866. By Maj. John M. Gould. With the History of the Tenth Me. battalion, by Rev. Leonard G. Jordan. Portland, S. Berry, 1871.

709, [1] p. front., illus., port., map. 23 cm.

The best regimental study of Maine troops; relied on a full diary to recount the experiences of a multi-named unit that campaigned from the Red River to the Shenandoah Valley.

Gould, Joseph, 1840–

The story of the Forty-eighth; a record of the campaigns of the Forty-eighth regiment Pennsylvania veteran volunteer infantry during the four eventful years of its service in the war for the preservation of the union. By Joseph Gould ... Pub. by authority of the regimental association. [Philadelphia, Arranged by F. H. Taylor; printed by Alfred M. Slocum co.] 1908.

471, [1] p. incl. illus., ports. port. 23cm.

More comprehensive than Bosbyshell's study of the same unit, but strikingly inferior in quality.

Gracey, Samuel Levis, 1835–1911.

Annals of the Sixth Pennsylvania cavalry. By Rev. S. L. Gracey, chaplain ... Published for the officers of the regiment. [Philadelphia] E. H. Butler & co., 1868.

4 p. l., 13–372 p. fold. map. 23cm.

A day-by-day chronicle of campaigning in Virginia; it would be a better book if the publisher had not used such weird type.

Graham, James Augustus, 1841–1908.

... The James A. Graham papers, 1861–1884, edited by H. M. Wagstaff ... Chapel Hill, The University of North Carolina press, 1928.

2 p. l., p. 91–324 p. 23 cm.

Personal letters of a member of the 27th North Carolina, followed by a descriptive roster of one company in that unit.

Graham, Matthew John.

The Ninth regiment, New York volunteers (Hawkins' zouaves); being a history of the regiment and veteran association from 1860 to 1900. By Lieut. Matthew J. Graham ... New York [E. P. Coby & co., printers] 1900.

xi, 634 p. front. 23½ cm.

A disappointing regimental history, based largely on material from printed sources.

Granger, Moses Moorhead, 1831–   *comp.*

The official war record of the 122nd regiment of Ohio volunteer infantry from October 8, 1862, to June 26, 1865. Copied from volumes 25, 27, 29, 33, 36, 37, 40, 42, 43 and 46, series I, U. S. war records, and from volumes 3 and 5 of series III. By Moses Moorhead Granger ... Zanesville, O., G. Lilienthal, printer, 1912.

146 p. 23cm.

Nothing more than what the title states.

Grant, Joseph W

The flying regiment. Journal of the campaign of the 12th regt. Rhode Island volunteers. By Capt. J. W. Grant. Providence. S. S. Rider & bro., 1865.

152 p. 15¾cm.

Initially published in 1863 under the title My First Campaign; far too restricted in content.

Graves, H   A

Andrew Jackson Potter, the fighting parson of the Texan frontier. Six years of Indian warfare in New Mexico and Arizona. Many wonderful events in his ministerial life ... By the Rev. H. A. Graves ... Nashville, Tenn., Southern Methodist publishing house, 1881.

471 p. front. (port.) 19cm.

Only a portion of this dramatic study pertains to Graves's service in the 26th and 32nd Texas Cavalry.

Graves, Henry Lea, 1842–1892.

A Confederate marine; a sketch of Henry Lea Graves with excerpts from the Graves family correspondence, 1861–1865. Edited by Richard Harwell. Tuscaloosa, Ala., Confederate Pub. Co., 1963.

140 p. illus. 22 cm.

Extremely useful, for this is one of the very few sources on the C. S. Marines; in addition, the letters have charm and a high degree of literacy.

Gray, John Chipman, 1839–1915.
War letters, 1862–1865, of John Chipman Gray ... and John Codman Ropes ... with portraits. Boston and New York, Houghton Mifflin company, 1927.

3 p. l., 532 p. 2 port. (incl. front.) 24½ cm.

The unique correspondence of two prominent Bostonians who wrote of the war with deep insight; Gray was an officer, and Ropes gained eminence as an historian.

The **grayjackets:** and how they lived, fought and died, for Dixie. With incidents & sketches of life in the confederacy. Comprising narratives of personal adventure, army life, naval adventure, home liee [!], partisan daring, life in camp, field and hospital: together with the songs, ballads, anecdotes and humorous incidents of the war for southern independence ... By a Confederate. Richmond [etc.] Jones brothers & co. [°1867]

574 p. front., port., maps. 22½ cm.

A collection of anecdotes and sketches, many of which have humor and doubtful authenticity.

Grayson, Andrew J *sergeant.*
"The spirit of 1861." History of the Sixth Indiana regiment in the three months' campaign in western Virginia ... With the names of every officer and private in the Sixth regiment. By A. J. Grayson. [Madison, Ind., Courier print. 1875?]

52 p. 23 cm.

A short, informally written summary of a regiment's movements in the first three months of the war.

Grecian, Joseph.
History of the Eighty-third regiment, Indiana volunteer infantry. For three years with Sherman. Compiled from the regimental and company books, and other sources, as well as from the writer's own observations and experience ... By J. Grecian, of company A. Cincinnati, J. F. Uhlhorn, printer, 1865.

iv, 5–163 p. 19 cm.

Written during the war, this is a fresh though brief work-- more the author's recollections than a unit history.

Green, Charles Ransley, 1845–
Volunteer service in Army of Cumberland. Pt. first. History of the volunteers from Clarksfield, Huron Co., Ohio, in the 101st O. V. I. ... Pt. second. List of the volunteers from Wakeman, O., the whole war. And their history since ... Pt. third. Sergeant Benj. T. Strong's biography, and history of the Chickamauga campaign ... Pt. fourth. Descendants of Justus Minor, who moved from Conn. in 1821 to Wakeman, O. All these several pieces written up and published by C. R. Green ... 1913–14. Ed. 200. [Olathe? Kan., 1914]

[48] p. illus., pl., ports. 21 cm.

Includes two very brief memoirs of service in the 101st Ohio.

Green, John Williams, 1841–1920.
Johnny Green of the Orphan Brigade; the journal of a Confederate soldier. Edited by A. D. Kirwan. [Lexington] University of Kentucky Press [°1956]

xxviii, 217 p. ports., maps. 24 cm.

Highly descriptive, this diary is the best personal commentary known for life in Kentucky's most famous brigade.

Gregg, John Chandler.
Life in the army, in the departments of Virginia, and the Gulf, including observations in New Orleans, with an account of the author's life and experience in the ministry. By Rev. J. Chandler Gregg ... Philadelphia, Perkinpine & Higgins, 1866.

271 p. 4 pl. (incl. front.) 19 cm.

These observations by a Pennsylvania chaplain are full of hearsay stories and errors of fact.

Gresham, Matilda (McGrain) b. 1839.
Life of Walter Quintin Gresham, 1832–1895, by Matilda Gresham ... Chicago, Rand, McNally & company, 1919.

2 v. fronts. (ports.) 23½ cm.

About 150 pages of this work treat of Gresham's service with the 53rd Indiana; included are extracts from his wartime letters.

Grimes, Absalom Carlisle, 1834–1911.
Absalom Grimes, Confederate mail runner, edited from Captain Grimes' own story by M. M. Quaife ... New Haven, Yale university press; London, H. Milford, Oxford university press, 1926.

xii, 216 p. front. (port.) plates, facsim. 23½ cm.

Significant primarily for information on the Mississippi Valley; editor's notes are far more scholarly than the author's narrative.

Grimes, Bryan, 1828–1880.
Extracts of letters of Major-Gen'l Bryan Grimes to his wife, written while in active service in the Army of northern Virginia. Together with some personal recollections of the war, written by him after its close, etc. Compiled from original manuscripts by Pulaski Cowper ... of Raleigh, N. C. Raleigh, N. C., Edwards, Broughton & co., printers, 1883.

137, [1] p. 22½ cm.

One of the few extant collections of letters by a Confederate general; somewhat colorless, the letters nevertheless throw light on the war in the East.

Grose, William 1812–1900.
The story of the marches, battles and incidents of the **36th regiment Indiana volunteer infantry. By a member of the regiment.** New Castle, Ind., The Courier company press, 1891.

256 p. front., ports. 23½ᶜᵐ.

A purely military and statistical chronicle of the marches and Western campaigns; the narrative stops with the fall of Atlanta.

Gunn, Jane Augusta (Terry)
Memorial sketches of Doctor Moses Gunn, by his wife. With extracts from his letters and eulogistic tributes from his colleagues and friends. Chicago, W. T. Keener, 1889.

xx, 380 p. illus., ports. 20 cm.

The subject of this work was Surgeon of the 5th Michigan; in letters to his wife, he described 1861–1862 scenes in and around Washington.

Hackley, Woodford B
The Little Fork rangers; a sketch of Company "D", Fourth Virginia cavalry, by Woodford B. Hackley ... Richmond, Va., Press of the Dietz printing co., 1927.

3 p. l., 11–117 p. illus., plates. 23½ᶜᵐ.

Compiled years after the war by the grandson of the Rangers, this work is little more than a scissors-and-paste narrative of known or unsupported data.

Hadley, Amos.
Life of Walter Harriman, with selections from his speeches and writings, by Amos Hadley. Boston and New York, Houghton, Mifflin and company, 1888.

vii p., 1 l., 385 p. front., pl., ports. 22½ᶜᵐ.

A work concentrating more on Harriman's leadership in state politics than on his service as colonel of the 11th New Hampshire.

Hagan, John W   1836–1918.
Confederate letters; edited by Bell Irvin Wiley. Athens, University of Georgia Press [1954]

55 p. port. 23 cm.

Hagan joined the 29th Georgia and saw service along the Atlantic coast and in the battles for Atlanta; his letters are a classic illustration of phonetic spelling.

Hagood, Johnson, 1829–1898.
Memoirs of the war of secession, from the original manuscripts of Johnson Hagood, brigadier-general, C. S. A. I. Hagood's 1st 12 months S. C. V. II. Hagood's brigade. Columbia, S. C., The State company, 1910.

5 p. l., 9–496 p. front. (port.) illus., maps (1 fold.) 24 cm.

As much a biography as an autobiography; Gen. Hagood's account of service in South Carolina and Virginia is heavily padded with official and relatively unimportant correspondence.

Haines, Alanson Austin.
History of the Fifteenth regiment New Jersey volunteers. By Alanson A. Haines, chaplain ... New York, Jenkins & Thomas, printers, 1883.

388 p. incl. illus., maps. front. (port.) 23½ᶜᵐ.

Relying on a diary and data supplied by comrades, Chaplain Haines relates the regiment's history as it began with the Fredericksburg service in Louisiana and Virginia.

Haines, Zenas T
Letters from the Forty-fourth regiment M. V. M.: a record of the experience of a nine months' regiment in the Department of North Carolina in 1862–3. By "Corporal" [pseud.] Boston, Printed at the Herald job office, 1863.

121 p. 24 cm.

The most comprehensive account by a private soldier of the 1862–1863 campaigns in North Carolina.

Hale, Edward Everett, 1822–1909.
Stories of war told by soldiers. Collected and ed. by Edward E. Hale. Boston, Roberts brothers, 1879.

2 p. l., 264 p. incl. map. 17½ᶜᵐ.

Battles rather than personal observations are the major subject of this early anthology.

Hall, Harry H
A Johnny Reb band from Salem: the pride of Tarheelia. Raleigh, the North Carolina Confederate Centennial Commission, 1963.

118 p. illus. 23 cm.

An unusual and unusually revealing story of the famous band of the 26th North Carolina; based in large part on the war diary of one of the musicians.

Hall, Henry, 1845–
Cayuga in the field. A record of the 19th N. Y. volunteers, all the batteries of the 3d New York artillery, and 75th New York volunteers ... By Henry Hall and James Hall. Auburn, N. Y. ₁Truair, Smith & co., printers, Syracuse₁ 1873.
2 v. in 1. 21½ᶜᵐ.

Treats of coastal campaigns from North Carolina to Louisiana, yet the narrative is too general and lacking in facts.

Hall, Hillman Allyn, 1835–1914.
History of the Sixth New York cavalry (Second Ira Harris guard) Second brigade — first division — Cavalry corps, Army of the Potomac, 1861–1865; compiled from letters, diaries, recollections and official records by Committee on regimental history, Major Hillman A. Hall, chairman, Regt. Qr. Mr. Sgt. W. B. Besley, treasurer, Sgt. Gilbert G. Wood, historian. 1908. Worcester, Mass., The Blanchard press, 1908.
575 p. front., plates, ports., maps. 23½ cm.

Hall's diary forms the base of a work heavily padded with excerpts from the Official Records; the sum leaves much to be desired.

Hall, Isaac, b. 1818 or 1819.
History of the Ninety-seventh regiment, New York volunteers ("Conkling rifles,") in the war for the Union. By Isaac Hall. Utica, Press of L. C. Childs & son, 1890.
vii, ₁3₁–477 p. front., pl., port., maps. 23½ cm.

More a history of a division in the Army of the Potomac, with regimental data inserted at the end of battles and chapters.

Hall, James Edmond, 1841–1915.
The diary of a Confederate soldier: James E. Hall. Edited by Ruth Woods Dayton. ₁Lewisburg? W. Va., 1961₁
141 p. port. 20 cm.

While this journal spans all four years of the war, the daily entries are short and, for the most part, non-revealing.

Hall, Winchester, 1819–
The story of the 26th Louisiana infantry, in the service of the Confederate States. By Winchester Hall. ₁n. p., 1890?₁
4 p. l. 228, ₁2₁ p. plan. 24ᶜᵐ.

A fairly reliable narrative of the war in Mississippi and Louisiana, although it was written without benefit of wartime letters or diary.

Haller, Granville Owen, 1820–1897.
The dismissal of Major Granville O. Haller, of the regular army, of the United States by order of the secretary of war, in special orders, no. 331, of July 25th, 1863. Also, a brief memoir of his military services, and a few observations ... Paterson, N. J., Printed at the Daily guardian office, 1863.
1 p. l., 84 p. 22½ᶜᵐ.

A self-exoneration of no particular value.

Hallum, John, 1833–
Reminiscences of the civil war, by John Hallum ... volume I. Little Rock ₁Ark.₁ Tunnah & Pittard, printers, 1903.
400 p. 20ᶜᵐ.

A series of monographs on people, places, and events; highly embellished and strongly suspect.

Hamilton, William Douglas, 1832–
Recollections of a cavalryman of the civil war after fifty years, 1861–1865, by William Douglas Hamilton ... Columbus, O., The F. J. Heer printing co., 1915.
xvi, 309 p. front., ports. 19½ᶜᵐ.

Contains many sidelights on army life, but the narrative as a whole is far too embellished to be acceptable at face value.

Hammock, John C
With honor untarnished; the story of the First Arkansas Infantry Regiment, Confederate States Army. With an introd. by John L. Ferguson. ₁Little Rock, Ark., Pioneer Press, 1961₁
164 p. illus. 23 cm.

The best account of the Arkansas (C. S. A.), but weakened by poor organization.

Hanaburgh, David Henry, 1839–1907.
History of the One hundred and twenty-eighth regiment, New York volunteers (U. S. infantry) in the late civil war. By D. H. Hanaburgh ... Pokeepsie, N. Y. ₁Press of Enterprise publishing company₁ 1894.
xv, 280 p. incl. illus., ports. fold. front. 23½ cm.

Based on the re-worked journal of Lt. B. T. Benson; an above-average study of the regiment's service in Louisiana and Virginia.

Hanaford, Phebe Ann (Coffin) 1829–1921.
Field, gunboat, hospital, and prison; or, Thrilling records of the heroism, edurance, and patriotism displayed in the Union army and navy during the great rebellion. By Mrs. P. A. Hanaford ... Boston, C. M. Dinsmoor and company, 1866.

379 p. front. (port.) 19½ᶜᵐ.

A narrative of many dramatic and emotional incidents in both camp and field, written by an overly sentimental woman.

Hancock, Richard Ramsey, 1840–1906.
Hancock's diary: or, A history of the Second Tennessee Confederate cavalry, with sketches of First and Seventh battalions; also, portraits and biographical sketches. Two volumes in one. Nashville, Tenn., Brandon printing co., 1887.

644 p. front., port. 23½ᶜᵐ.

A voluminous record that includes much material from printed sources and the author's comrades; Hancock took part in the alleged "Fort Pillow Massacre."

Handerson, Henry Ebenezer, 1837–1918.
Yankee in gray: the Civil War memoirs of Henry E. Handerson, with a selection of his wartime letters. A biographical introd. by Clyde Lottridge Cummer. ₁Cleveland₁ Press of Western Reserve University ₁ᶜ1962₁

132 p. illus. 27 cm.

The unique memoir and letters of an Ohio-born schoolteacher who saw service in the East with the 9th Louisiana; after the war Handerson became an eminent medical historian.

Hanifen, Michael, 1841–
History of Battery B, First New Jersey artillery, by Michael Hanifen ... ₁Ottawa, Ill., Republican-times, printers, ᶜ1905₁

4 p., 1 l., ₁5₁–174 p. front., plates, ports. 23½ᶜᵐ.

A too-brief account, based largely on memory; some personal accounts are included, as well as much official correspondence.

Hannaford, Ebenezer, 1840–
The story of a regiment: a history of the campaigns, and associations in the field, of the Sixth regiment Ohio volunteer infantry. By E. Hannaford ... Cincinnati, The author, 1868.

xvi, 17–622 p. 22 cm.

An unusually full history of a unit that campaigned from western Virginia through Atlanta; written shortly after the war, it has freshness and authenticity.

Hanson, G   A
Minor incidents of the late war, as seen and chronicled by an eye-witness. Actual occurrences, truly related just as they transpired ... By one of the participants. Bartow ₁Fla.₁ Sessions, Barker & Kilpatrick, 1887.

97 p. 20½ᶜᵐ.

The restricted observations of one who rode with Bedford Forrest.

Hanson, John Wesley, 1823–1901.
Historical sketch of the old Sixth regiment of Massachusetts volunteers, during its three campaigns in 1861, 1862, 1863, and 1864. Containing the history of the several companies previous to 1861, and the name and military record of each man connected with the regiment during the war. By John W. Hanson, chaplain ... Boston, Lee and Shepard, 1866.
352 p. front., port. 19½ cm.

A factual history of a unit whose sixteen months of active duty included involvement in a Baltimore riot.

Hard, Abner.
History of the Eighth cavalry regiment, Illinois volunteers, during the great rebellion; by Abner Hard ... Aurora, Ill., 1868.

4 p. l., ₁33₁–368 p. 22½ᶜᵐ.

Written by the regimental surgeon, this study contains both facts and personal incidents; some humor also enriches the narrative.

Hardin, Martin D   1837–1923.
History of the Twelfth regiment, Pennsylvania reserve volunteer corps (41st regiment of the line), from its muster into the United States service, August 10th, 1861, to its muster out, June 11th, 1864, together with biographical sketches of officers and men and a complete muster-out roll. Compiled from official reports, letters, and other documents. By M. D. Hardin ... New York, Pub. by the author, 1890.

4 p. l., 224, ₁24₁ p. front., port., map, plans. 23½ᶜᵐ.

Too impersonal; further weakened by too much reliance on excerpts from the <u>Official Records</u>.

Harris, Nathaniel Edwin, 1846–
Autobiography; the story of an old man's life, with reminiscences of seventy-five years, by Nathaniel E. Harris ... Macon, Ga., The J. W. Burke company, 1925.

550 p. front., illus. (incl. ports.) 20ᶜᵐ.

Only a small portion of this memoir treats of the author's Confederate experiences on the fringes of the Eastern theater.

Harris, Samuel, 1836–
Personal reminiscences of Samuel Harris. Chicago, The Rogerson press, 1897.

1 p. l., 172 p. plates, 2 port. (incl. front.) 20 cm.

Harris dramatizes camp life and service with the 5th Michigan Cavalry; heavy on the battle of Gettysburg and Harris's capture and confinement.

Harrison, Mary Douglass (Waring) *b.* 1845.
Miss Waring's journal: 1863 and 1865, being the diary of Miss Mary Waring of Mobile, during the final days of the War Between the States. Edited by Thad Holt, Jr. Chicago, Wyvern Press of S. F. E. [ᶜ1964]

17 p. illus. 25 cm.

A short but somewhat revealing diary of tribulations in war-torn Mobile during the war's final weeks.

Harrison, Walter.
Pickett's men: a fragment of war history. By Walter Harrison ... New York, D. Van Nostrand, 1870.

202 p. front. (port.) pl. 19 cm.

Too confined to b⁻ a good division history, but possessed of some stimulating passages on such commanders as Pickett and Richard B. Garnett.

Hart, Ephraim J
History of the Fortieth Illinois inf., (volunteers.) By Sergeant E. J. Hart ... Cincinnati, H. S. Bosworth, 1864.

198 p. 19½ᶜᵐ.

A drab, disappointing chronicle of military service in the Mississippi Valley.

Hartpence, William Ross.
History of the Fifty-first Indiana veteran volunteer infantry. A narrative of its organization, marches, battles and other experiences in camp and prison; from 1861 to 1866. With revised roster. By Wm. R. Hartpence ... Harrison, O., Pub. by the author; Cincinnati, The Robert Clarke company, printers, 1894.

viii, 405 p. pl., 7 port. (incl. front.) 24 cm.

Although this is one of the better organized and more revealing regimental histories, the unit's comparative inactivity gives the study little value.

Haskell, John Cheves, 1841–1906.
The Haskell memoirs. Edited by Gilbert E. Govan and James W. Livingood. New York, Putnam [1960]

176 p. illus. 22 cm.

Written by an audacious fighter who freely passed judgement on almost all high-ranking commanders in Lee's army; especially critical of Jackson.

Haupt, Herman, 1817–1905.
Reminiscences of General Herman Haupt ... giving hitherto unpublished official orders, personal narratives of important military operations, and interviews with President Lincoln, Secretary Stanton, General-in-chief Halleck, and with Generals McDowell, McClellan, Meade, Hancock, Burnside, and others in command of the armies in the field, and his impressions of these men. ⟨Written by himself⟩ With notes and a personal sketch by Frank Abial Flower. Illustrated from photographs of actual operations in the field. [Milwaukee, Wis., Wright & Joys co., printers] 1901.

xl, 331 p. incl. 31 pl. 2 port. (incl. front.) 25 cm.

An extremely valuable source on Union transportational problems; Haupt headed the Bureau of Military Railroads.

Hawley, Joseph Roswell, 1826–1905.
Major General Joseph R. Hawley, soldier and editor (1826–1905) Civil War military letters. Gen. William T. Sherman's letter concerning the responsibility of the decision of the March to the Sea. Edited by Albert D. Putnam. [Hartford? Connecticut Civil War Centennial Commission] 1964.

84 p. port. 23 cm.

This undocumented pamphlet contains excerpts from the letters of a Connecticut general who campaigned from First Bull Run to the Georgia coast; quite stimulating for comments on Sherman's famous march.

Hayes, Rutherford Birchard, *pres. U. S.,* 1822–1893.
Diary and letters of Rutherford Birchard Hayes, nineteenth president of the United States, edited by Charles Richard Williams ... [Columbus, O.] The Ohio state archæological and historical society, 1922–26.

5 v. fronts., plates, ports. 24½ cm.

Vol. II of this set contains the major writings of Hayes, who was colonel of the 23rd Ohio.

Haynes, Draughton Stith, 1837–1879.
The field diary of a Confederate soldier, while serving with the Army of Northern Virginia, C. S. A. Darien, Ga., Ashantilly Press, 1963.

xv, 44 p. illus., mounted port., maps. 21 cm.

Fragmentary diary by a lieutenant in the 49th Georgia; unfortunately, the volume is far more attractive than its contents are useful.

Haynes, Edwin Mortimer, 1836–

A history of the Tenth regiment, Vermont volunteers, with biographical sketches of the officers who fell in battle. And a complete roster of all the officers and men connected with it—showing all changes by promotion, death or resignation, during the military existence of the regiment. By Chaplain E. M. Haynes. ₁Lewiston, Me., printed₁ Pub. by the Tenth Vermont regimental association, 1870.

viii, ₁9₁–249 p. 22 cm.

A dry and oftentimes statistical study of a regiment on active duty in Virginia in the 1862-1865 period.

Haynes, Edwin Mortimer, 1836–

A history of the Tenth regiment, Vt. vols., with biographical sketches of nearly every officer who ever belonged to the regiment, and many of the non-commissioned officers and men, and a complete roster of all the officers and men connected with it—showing all changes by promotion, death or resignation, during the military existence of the regiment. 2d ed., rev., enlarged and embellished by over sixty engravings and ... maps and charts of battlefields. By the chaplain, E. M. Haynes, D. D. Rutland, The Tuttle company, printers, 1894.

v, ₁1₁ p., 1 l., 504 p. front., plates, ports., maps (part fold.) plans. 24cm.

As the subtitle states, the 1870 edition was enlarged by additional biographical sketches and enhanced with five dozen illustrations; only minor revisions were made in the text.

Haynes, Martin A   1845–

A history of the Second regiment, New Hampshire volunteer infantry, in the war of the rebellion. By Martin A. Haynes ... Lakeport, N. H., 1896.

xv, 350, ₁2₁, 125 p., 1 l. front., illus., pl., port., plans. 23cm.

A greatly enlarged and superior history to the one Haynes penned thirty-five years earlier.

Haynes, Martin A   1845–

History of the Second regiment New Hampshire volunteers: its camps, marches and battles. By Martin A. Haynes ... Manchester, N. H., C. F. Livingston, printer, 1865.

viii, ₁9₁–223, ₁1₁ p. 19½ cm.

One of the better-written personal narratives; Haynes had a keen sense of observation and included many personal experiences in this unit history.

Haynie, Henry *i. e.* **James Henry,** 1841–1912.

The Nineteenth Illinois; a memoir of a regiment of volunteer infantry famous in the civil war of fifty years ago for its drill, bravery, and distinguished services. Ed. by J. Henry Haynie, of company D ... ₁Chicago, M. A. Donohue & co., ᶜ1912₁

396 p. front., plates, ports. 23cm.

Full of manufactured conversation and endless statistics; void in all else.

Hays, Gilbert Adams, *comp.*

Under the red patch; story of the Sixty third regiment, Pennsylvania volunteers, 1861–1864 ... comp. by Gilbert Adams Hays, with personal narrative by William H. Morrow, Company A. Pittsburgh, Pa., Sixty-third Pennsylvania volunteers regimental association, 1908.

476, ₁3₁ p. front., plates, ports. 23cm.

A rather good compilation of soldiers' letters, memoirs and articles-- all bound together by a strong narrative.

Hazen, William Babcock, 1830–1887.

A narrative of military service, by General W. B. Hazen. Boston, Ticknor and company, 1885.

x, 450 p. front., plates, ports., fold. maps, plans. 22½ cm.

Gen. Hazen served with Federal forces in every major battle of the Western theater; his memoir is a mixture of garrulous recollections and correspondence with comrades.

Head, Thomas A

Campaigns and battles of the Sixteenth regiment Tennessee volunteers, in the war between the states, with incidental sketches of the part performed by other Tennessee troops in the same war. 1861–1865. By Thomas A. Head. Nashville, Tenn., Cumberland Presbyterian pub. house, 1885.

488 p. incl. illus., port. front. 20cm.

Heavily statistical study; the author, who attained the rank of major before his capture at Kennesaw Mountain, spent the last year of the war at Camp Douglas.

Heartsill, William Williston, 1839–

Fourteen hundred and 91 days in the Confederate army. A journal kept by W. W. Heartsill, for four years, one month, and one day: or, Camp life; day-by-day, of the W. P. Lane rangers, from April 19th 1861, to May 20th 1865. ₁Marshall, Tex., W. W. Heartsill, 1876₁

4 p. l., 264 p., 1 l. 61 phot. on 19 pl. 20½cm.

A product of homemade printing, this work recounts not only the experiences of a soldier in the Trans-Mississippi, but also his travels through the North as a war prisoner.

Heartsill, William Williston, 1839–1916.

Fourteen hundred and 91 days in the Confederate Army. A journal kept by W. W. Heartsill for four years, one month, and one day. Or, Camp life, day by day, of the W. P. Lane Rangers from April 19, 1861, to May 20, 1865. Edited by Bell Irvin Wiley. Jackson, Tenn., McCowat-Mercer Press ₁ᶜ1953₁

xxiv p., facsim. (4 l., 264 p., 1 l. ports.), ₁267₁–332 p. illus., port. 23 cm.

In this edition, full introduction and index compensate in part for the offset printing of the faded original text.

Hedley, Fenwick Y

Marching through Georgia. Pen-pictures of every-day life in General Sherman's army, from the beginning of the Atlanta campaign until the close of the war, by F. Y. Hedley ... Illustrated by F. L. Stoddard. Chicago, Donohue, Henneberry & co., 1890.

490 p. incl. illus., plates, facsims. front., pl. 20 cm.

A well-known and oft-quoted narrative, in spite of a discernible air of non-authenticity.

Heg, Hans Christian, 1829-1863.

The civil war letters of Colonel Hans Christian Heg; edited by Theodore C. Blegen. Northfield, Minn., Norwegian-American historical association, 1936.

ix p., 1 l., 260 p. front., plates, ports., facsims. (1 fold.) 23½ cm.

For the most part, these letters are commentaries on slaves and Southern life by a Norwegian-born officer stationed in Tennessee, Alabama, and Mississippi.

Henderson, Edward Prioleau.

Autobiography of Arab. By E. Prioleau Henderson. [Columbia, S. C., The R. L. Bryan company, 1901]

170 p. 19½ cm.

A South Carolina cavalryman's padded memoir; of some value for the Peninsular Campaign.

Henderson, George Francis Robert, 1854-1903.

The Civil War: a soldier's view; a collection of Civil War writings. Edited by Jay Luvaas. [Chicago] University of Chicago Press [1958]

xi, 322 p. maps (1 fold.) plans. 25 cm.

In this study, by an English officer and biographer of "Stonewall" Jackson, are essays on Fredericksburg and Jackson, plus several chapters from another of the author's works, The Science of War.

Henderson, Lindsey P 1922-

The Oglethorpe Light Infantry, a military history. [1st ed. Savannah] Civil War Centennial Commission of Savannah and Chatham County [1961]

57 p. illus. 22 cm.

Muster rolls and a slim, factual text comprise this tribute to a famous Georgia infantry company.

Henry, Robert Selph, 1889– *ed.*

As they saw Forrest; some recollections and comments of contemporaries. Jackson, Tenn., McCowat-Mercer Press, 1956.

xvi, 306 p. illus., ports., 2 maps (on fold. leaf) facsims. 24 cm.

A useful collection of short memoirs by men who fought with and against "Old Bedford."

Hepworth, George Hughes, 1833-1902.

The whip, hoe, and sword; or, The Gulf-department in '63. By George H. Hepworth. Boston, Walker, Wise and co., 1864.

vi, [7]-298 p. 18 cm.

Six somewhat embellished commentaries by a Federal chaplain on duty in Louisiana; illuminating for criticisms of corruption in the Union army of occupation.

Hermann, Isaac, 1838–

Memoirs of a veteran who served as a private in the 60's in the war between the states; personal incidents, experiences and observations, written by Capt. I. Hermann ... Atlanta, Ga., Byrd printing company, 1911.

285 p. incl. front. (port.) plates. 21 cm.

These memoirs of a Georgia soldier touch on the western Virginia campaign, the defenses of Savannah, Ga., and hospital service; much of the material is of questionable accuracy.

Herr, George Washington, 1844–

Episodes of the Civil war, nine campaigns in nine states; Fremont in Missouri—Curtis in Missouri and Arkansas—Halleck's siege of Corinth—Buell in Kentucky—Rosecrans in Kentucky and Tennessee—Grant at the battle of Chattanooga—Sherman from Chattanooga to Atlanta—Thomas in Tennessee and North Carolina—Stanley in Texas. In which is comprised the history of the Fifty-ninth regiment Illinois veteran volunteer infantry—Together with special mention of the various regiments with which it was brigaded from 1861 to 1865. By Corporal Geo. W. Herr ... San Francisco, The Bancroft company, 1890.

xiv p., 1 l., 461, xxx p. incl. front., port. pl. 25½ cm.

A wordy narrative, with but occasional references to the war service of the 59th Illinois, in which the author was a corporal.

Heverly, Clement Ferdinand.

Our boys in blue. Heroic deeds, sketches and reminiscences of Bradford County soldiers in the civil war. By C. F. Heverly ... Towanda, Pa., The Bradford star print, 1898-1908.

2 v. fronts., illus. (incl. ports.) 20½ cm.

The outgrowth of a series of newspaper articles, this collection is both unbalanced and disorganized.

Higginson, Thomas Wentworth, 1823–1911.
Army life in a black regiment. A new ed. with notes and a supplementary chapter. Boston, Houghton, Mifflin, 1900.

413 p   port.

Unrivaled for a picture of the first Negro unit organized; campaigns include forays along the Georgia and Florida coasts.

High, Edwin W   1841–
History of the Sixty-eighth regiment, Indiana volunteer infantry, 1862–1865, with a sketch of E. A. King's brigade, Reynolds' division, Thomas' corps, in the battle of Chickamauga; by Edwin W. High ... Published by request of the Sixty-eighth Indiana infantry association, 1902. ₁Metamora? Ind.₁ 1902.

xii p., 1 l., 416 p. front., pl., port. 23½ cm.

A straight regimental narrative, void of color and personal incidents; the author did use several diaries and collections of letters by comrades.

Hight, John J   1834–1886.
History of the Fifty-eighth regiment of Indiana volunteer infantry. Its organization, campaigns and battles from 1861 to 1865. From the manuscript prepared by the late chaplain John J. Hight, during his service with the regiment in the field. Comp. by his friend and comrade, Gilbert R. Stormont ... Illustrated with maps of campaigns and marches, and portraits of a number of officers and enlisted men of the regiment. Princeton, Press of the Clarion, 1895.

577 p. front., illus. (incl. maps) ports. 23½ cm.

Based in large part on the chaplain's diary, this work is marred by the author's bitterness toward slavery.

Hill, Alonzo F
Our boys. The personal experiences of a soldier in the Army of the Potomac. By A. F. Hill ... Philadelphia, J. E. Potter, 1864.

xii, 13–412 p. incl. front. 18½ cm.

Treats of the Eastern campaigns through Antietam; much conversation and unsupported statements make this work highly suspect as a reliable source.

Hill, Isaac J   1826–
A sketch of the 29th regiment of Connecticut colored troops, by J. ₁!₁ J. Hill, giving a full account of its formation; of all the battles through which it passed, and its final disbandment. Baltimore, Printed by Daugherty, Maguire & co., 1867.

42 p. 22½ cm.

Hill was one of the very few Negro soldiers who wrote recollections of the war; unfortunately, this is but a slim travelogue.

Hinkley, Julian Wisner, 1838–1916.
... A narrative of service with the Third Wisconsin infantry, by Julian Wisner Hinkley ... ₁Madison₁ Wisconsin history commission, 1912.

xi, 197 p. front. (port.) 23 cm.

A thoroughly organized and completely reliable memoir, based on letters, diary, and postwar manuscript; Hinkeley saw much service in both major battle areas.

Hinman, Wilbur F   *comp.*
Camp and field. Sketches of army life written by those who followed the flag. '61–'65. Compiled by W. F. Hinman ... Cleveland, The N. G. Hamilton publishing co. ₁°1892₁

704 p. front., illus., plates, ports. 23½ᶜᵐ.

A hodgepodge of anecdotes and alleged personal experiences; too much hearsay is said here.

Hinman, Wilbur F
The story of the Sherman brigade. The camp, the march, the bivouac, the battle; and how "the boys" lived and died during four years of active field service ... With 368 illustrations ... By Wilbur F. Hinman ... ₁Alliance, O.₁ The author, 1897.
xxxii, 33–1104 p. illus., ports. (incl. front.) 23½ cm.

In scope alone, this volume must rank as one of the top ten narratives by a Federal soldier; a necessity for any study of the Western theater.

Hitchcock, Ethan Allen, 1798–1870.
Fifty years in camp and field, diary of Major-General Ethan Allen Hitchcock, U. S. A.; ed. by W. A. Croffut, PH. D. New York and London, G. P. Putnam's sons, 1909.

xv, 514 p. front. (port.) 25 cm.

Unfortunately, less than fifty pages of Gen. Hitchcock's diary treat of his service as a military adviser to Pres. Lincoln and Sec. Stanton.

Hitchcock, Frederick Lyman, 1837–
War from the inside; or, Personal experiences, impressions, and reminiscences of one of the "boys" in the war of the rebellion, by Col. Frederick L. Hitchcock. Philadelphia, Press of J. B. Lippincott company, 1904.

308 p. front., plates, ports. 21½ cm.

Hitchcock, colonel of the 132nd Pennsylvania, revised his recollections twice prior to publication in book form; his observations from Antietam through Chancellorsville are eventempered and judicious.

Hitchcock, Henry, 1829–1902.

Marching with Sherman; passages from the letters and campaign diaries of Henry Hitchcock, major and assistant adjutant general of volunteers. November 1864–May 1865, edited, with an introduction, by M. A. De Wolfe Howe. New Haven, Yale university press; London, H. Milford, Oxford university press, 1927.

6 p. l., 332 p.   plates, 2 port. (incl. front.) fold. map, facsim.   23½ cm.

A basic and valuable source on Sherman's 1864-1865 campaigns; the highly educated Hitchcock rarely failed to note incidents and scenes of interest.

Hoadley, John Chipman, 1818–1886, *ed.*

Memorial of Henry Sanford Gansevoort, captain Fifth artillery ... colonel Thirteenth New York state volunteer cavalry ... Ed. by J. C. Hoadley, A. M.   Printed for private distribution.   Boston, Rand, Avery, & co., 1875.

2 p. l., [3]–335 p.   12 pl., 7 port. (incl. front.) map, fold. facsim.   21 x 16 cm.

The personal and official correspondence of a New York officer who rose to the rank of brevet brigadier general.

Hobart-Hampden, *Hon.* **Augustus Charles,** 1822–1886.

Sketches from my life.   By the late Admiral Hobart Pasha ... New York, D. Appleton and company, 1887.

viii, 282 p.   front. (port.)   18½ cm.

The author was a notorious blockade-runner; yet only two small sections of this autobiography touch on life in the wartime South.

Hoffman, Wickham, 1821–1900.

Camp, court and siege; a narrative of personal adventure and observation during two wars: 1861–1865; 1870–1871. By Wickham Hoffman ... New York, Harper & brothers, 1877.

285 p.   19½ cm.

Only a third of this work treats of the author's inconsequential services in the Western theater.

Hogan, Wilber Fisk

The story of sixty years, by Ino [*pseud.*]   Birmingham, Ala., 1902 [°1908]

112 p.   22½ cm.

A philosophical, pretentious, and useless story of war.

Hoge, Jane Currie (Blaikie) "*Mrs.* **A. H. Hoge.**"

The boys in blue; or, Heroes of the "rank and file." Comprising incidents and reminiscences from camp, battle-field, and hospital, with narratives of the sacrifice, suffering, and triumphs of the soldiers of the republic.   By Mrs. A. H. Hoge ... With an introduction by Thomas M. Eddy, D. D.   With illustrations from original drawings of the most striking scenes of the war of the rebellion.   New York, E. B. Treat & co.; Chicago, Ill., C. W. Lilley, 1867.

4 p. l., [13]–477 p.   front., plates.   23 cm.

Another of those emotional presentations by a volunteer female nurse in the field.

Holbrook, William C

A narrative of the services of the officers and enlisted men of the 7th regiment of Vermont volunteers (veterans), from 1862 to 1866.   By Wm. C. Holbrook ...   New York, American bank note co., 1882.

viii, [1]–219 p.   front. (port.)   21½ cm.

A bad history, written by a man who had little idea of the organization and presentation of material.

Holland, Mary A   Gardner, *comp.*

Our army nurses. Interesting sketches, addresses, and photographs of nearly one hundred of the noble women who served in hospitals and on battlefields during our civil war.   Comp. by Mary A. Gardner Holland ...   Boston, Mass., B. Wilkins & co., 1895.

548 p. incl. front., illus., pl., port.   23 cm.

Biographical tributes to a host of women who served and sacrificed as volunteer nurses in the Union armies.

Hollister, Ovando James, 1834–1892.

Boldly they rode; a history of the First Colorado Regiment of Volunteers.   With an introd. by William Macleod Raine.   Lakewood, Colo., Golden Press, 1949.

190 p.   22 cm.

An empty reprint of the original 1863 edition of this solitary study of the 1st Colorado.

Hollister, Ovando James, 1834–1892.

Colorado volunteers in New Mexico, 1862.   Edited by Richard Harwell.   Chicago, R. R. Donnelley, 1962.

xxxii, 309 p.   illus., port., facsim.   18 cm.

Harwell's introductory essay and occasional footnotes enhance the study; the narrative is faithfully reproduced without abridgement.

Holmes, Mead.

A soldier of the Cumberland: memoir of Mead Holmes jr., sergeant of company K, 21st regiment Wisconsin volunteers. By his father. With an introduction by John S. Hart ... Boston, American tract society [1864]

xiv, 15-240 p. incl. front. (port.) plates. 17^{cm}.

A worthless eulogy by a grief-stricken father.

Holmes, Oliver Wendell, 1841–1935.

Touched with fire; civil war letters and diary of Oliver Wendell Holmes, jr., 1861–1864, edited by Mark De Wolfe Howe. Cambridge, Mass., Harvard university press, 1946.

x p., 3 l., 3-158 p. front., illus. (incl. plans, facsims.) ports. 21$\frac{1}{2}$^{cm}.

Written by one of the most distinguished of Americans, these observations of service with the 20th Massachusetts fall regrettably short of expectations.

Hoole, William Stanley, 1903–

Alabama Tories; the First Alabama Cavalry, U. S. A., 1862–1865. Tuscaloosa, Ala., Confederate Pub. Co., 1960.

141 p. 22 cm.

A cursory sketch of the only unit from Alabama that served in the Federal armies.

Hoole, William Stanley, 1903–

Lawley covers the Confederacy. Tuscaloosa, Ala., Confederate Pub. Co., 1964.

132 p. facsim., port. 22 cm.

The best available study on the noted London Times correspondent; yet too few passages were extracted from Lawley's more than 100 long dispatches.

Hoole, William Stanley, 1903–

Vizetelly covers the Confederacy. Tuscaloosa, Ala., Confederate Pub. Co., 1957.

173 p. illus., port. 22 cm.

More important than the wordy and homely biographical text are thirty of Vizetelly's drawings on Confederate army life, which are included.

Hopkins, Luther W   1843–

From Bull run to Appomattox; a boy's view, by L. W. Hopkins of Genl. J. E. B. Stuart's cavalry, 6th Virginia regiment. C. S. A. Baltimore, Press of Fleet-McGinley co. [c1908]

219, [1] p. front., plates, ports., fold. map. 20^{cm}.

A member of the 6th Virginia Cavalry, Hopkins composed this overly dramatic memoir late in life and primarily for young readers.

Hopkins, Owen Johnston, 1844–1902.

Under the flag of the Nation; diaries and letters of a Yankee volunteer in the Civil War. Edited by Otto F. Bond. Columbus, Ohio State University Press for the Ohio Historical Society [1961]

xi, 308 p. ports. 22 cm.

Interesting letters by an exuberant and youthful member of the 42nd Ohio who participated in the Cumberland and Vicksburg campaigns; weakly edited.

Hopkins, William Palmer, 1845–

The Seventh regiment Rhode Island volunteers in the civil war, 1862–1865, by William P. Hopkins. Providence, R. I., Snow & Farnham, printers; Boston, Mass., Hub engraving co., engravers, 1903.

xxiv, 543, [1] p. front., pl., port., fold. maps, plan. 23$\frac{1}{2}$^{cm}.

Presented in diary form, this work is a composite of written and recalled events of service from Fredericksburg to Appomattox; half of the volume consists of biographical sketches and muster rolls.

Horrall, Spillard F   1829–

History of the Forty-second Indiana volunteer infantry. Comp. and written ... by S. F. Horrall, late captain of Company G, 42d Indiana regiment. [Chicago, Donohue & Henneberry, printers] 1892.

x, 11-283 p. front., ports. 20 cm.

Easy readability notwithstanding, this study adds little to a history of the Western campaigns.

Horton, Joshua H

A history of the Eleventh regiment, (Ohio volunteer infantry,) containing the military record ... of each officer and enlisted man of the command—a list of deaths—an account of the veterans—incidents of the field and camp—names of the three months' volunteers, etc., etc. Compiled from the official records by Horton & Teverbaugh ... Dayton, W. J. Shuey, 1866.

xv, 17-287 p. 22 cm.

Two writers failed to do anything more than compile an elaborate timetable of a regiment's travels.

Hosmer, James Kendall, 1834–1927.
The color-guard: being a corporal's notes of military service in the Nineteenth army corps. By James K. Hosmer ... Boston, Walker, Wise, and co., 1864.

xii, 9–244 p. 18 cm.

An excellent and even-tempered memoir of army life in Louisiana.

Hotze, Henry, 1834–1887.
Three months in the Confederate Army; printed in facsimile from the London Index, 1862. With an introd. and notes by Richard Barksdale Harwell. University, Ala., University of Alabama Press, 1952.

38 p. (p. 13–33 facsim.) 28 cm.

Hotze, the Confederacy's leading propagandist in Europe, served initially in the 3rd Alabama; his field letters appeared in a newspaper and are here reproduced as printed.

Hough, Alfred Lacey, 1826–1908.
Soldier in the West; the Civil War letters of Alfred Lacey Hough. Edited by Robert G. Athearn; with an introd. by John Newbold Hough. Philadelphia, University of Pennsylvania Press [1957]

250 p. illus. 22 cm.

Hough was in his late thirties when he joined the 17th Pennsylvania; he became Commissary of Musters for the Army of the Cumberland; his letters are therefore mature and unique commentaries.

Hough, Franklin Benjamin, 1822–1885.
History of Duryée's brigade, during the campaign in Virginia under Gen. Pope, and in Maryland under Gen. McClellan, in the summer and autumn of 1862. By Franklin B. Hough. Albany, J. Munsell, 1864.

vi, [9]–200 p. front. (port.) 25 cm.

Published in a limited edition of 300 copies, the study recounts superficially the actions of a Northern brigade in two campaigns.

Houghton, Edwin B
The campaigns of the Seventeenth Maine. By Edwin B. Houghton ... Portland, Short & Loring, 1866.

x p., 1 l., 333 p. 19½ cm.

Published soon after the war, and based on a diary, this narrative affords a clear view of life in the Army of the Potomac in the latter stages of the conflict.

Houston, Henry Clarence, b. 1847.
The Thirty-second Maine regiment of infantry volunteers; an historical sketch by Henry C. Houston ... Portland, Press of Southworth brothers, 1903.

xii p., 1 l., 537 p. 25 port. (incl. front.) 24 cm.

A history of the 1864–1865 campaigns in Virginia, with an occasional reference to the actions of the 32nd Maine.

Howard, McHenry.
Recollections of a Maryland Confederate soldier and staff officer under Johnston, Jackson and Lee, by McHenry Howard. Baltimore, Williams & Wilkins company, 1914.

1 p. l., 423 p. front., illus., pl., ports., fold. map, facsim. 23 cm.

Possessed of both insight and interest, these reminiscences by a Confederate aide are particularly worthwhile for Jackson's campaigns.

Howard, Oliver Otis, 1830–1909.
Autobiography of Oliver Otis Howard, major general, United States army. New York, The Baker & Taylor company, 1907.

2 v. fronts., plates, ports., facsims. 23½ cm.

Embellished, and at times wordy, these recollections by the ill-fated commander of the XI Corps are nevertheless above the average in style and content.

Howard, Richard L
History of the 124th regiment Illinois infantry volunteers, otherwise known as the "Hundred and two dozen," from August, 1862, to August, 1865. By R. L. Howard ... Springfield, Ill., Printed and bound by H. W. Rokker, 1880.

ix, 519 p. 20½ cm.

A solid study, based on diaries, letters, and conversations with other members of the regiment; the 124th Illinois campaigned mostly in the Gulf region.

Howard, Robert Milton, 1834–
Reminiscences, by Robert M. Howard. Columbus, Ga., Gilbert printing co., 1912.

3 p. l., 346 p. front. (port. group) 20½ cm.

Untrustworthy reminiscences; Howard was outspoken in his belief that the fall of the Confederacy spelled the doom of the Union.

Howe, Daniel Wait, 1839–1920.
   Civil war times, 1861–1865, by Daniel Wait Howe ... Indianapolis, The Bowen-Merrill company ₁1902₎

   x, 421 p. 20½ cm.

A narrative, sometimes in diary form, of service in the Army of the Cumberland; Howe was an Indiana soldier.

Howe, Henry Warren, 1841–
   Passages from the life of Henry Warren Howe, consisting of diary and letters written during the civil war, 1816–1865. A condensed history of the Thirtieth Massachusetts regiment and its flags, together with the genealogies of the different branches of the family ... Lowell, Mass., Courier-citizen co., printers, 1899.

   211 p. front, ports. 21½ cm.

Good wartime letters and short diary entries make this a most revealing work on the 30th Massachusetts.

Howell, Helena Adelaide, *comp.*
   Chronicles of the One hundred fifty-first regiment New York state volunteer infantry, 1862–1865; contributed by its surviving members; comp. by Helena Adelaide Howell. ₁Albion, N. Y., A. M. Eddy, printer, 1911₎

   301, ₍1₎ p. incl. front., illus., pl., ports. pl. 22½ cm.

This work is divided almost equally between a descriptive roster of the regiment and a narrative based on diary and letter excerpts, fading memory, and war tales; the text must be handled with care.

Hubbard, Charles Eustis 1842–
   The campaign of the Forty-fifth regiment, Massachusetts volunteer militia. "The cadet regiment." Boston, Printed by J. S. Adams, 1882.

   xiv p., 1 l., 126 p. front., plates. 25½ cm.

Reliable but rather shallow reminiscences of nine months' service along the North Carolina seaboard.

Hubbard, John Milton.
   Notes of a private, by John Milton Hubbard, Company E, 7th Tennessee regiment, Forrest's cavalry corps, C. S. A. ... Memphis, Tenn., E. H. Clarke & brother, 1909.

   3 p. l., 189 p. front. (port.) pl. 20ᶜᵐ.

The author's service as a member of Forrest's cavalry gives this work great appeal-- in spite of the fact that it was written a half century after the war and without refreshing materials.

Hubert, Charles F   1843–
   History of the Fiftieth regiment, Illinois volunteer infantry in the war for the union. By Charles F. Hubert, assisted by members of the regiment. Kansas City, Mo., Western veteran publishing company, 1894.

   630 p. incl. front., illus. pl., 11 port., double map. 23ᶜᵐ.

Many excerpts from soldiers' letters and diaries make this among the best of the Illinois unit studies.

Hudson, Joshua Hilary, 1832–
   Sketches and reminiscences, by Joshua Hilary Hudson, LL. D. Columbia, S. C., The State company, 1903.

   190 p. front. (port.) plates, facsim. 23 cm.

This somewhat disjointed account by an officer of the 26th South Carolina is most useful for Confederate operations around Petersburg.

Huffman, James, 1840–1922.
   Ups and downs of a Confederate soldier, by James Huffman ... New York, W. E. Rudge's sons, 1940.

   4 p. l., 175 p. mounted illus. (incl. ports., facsim.) 21ᶜᵐ.

Relying on printed sources and personal interviews, Huffman re-created his experiences with the 10th Virginia and as a prisoner of war at Point Lookout.

Hughes, William Edgar 1840–
   The journal of a grandfather. ₁St. Louis, Priv. print., Nixon-Jones ptg. co., ᶜ1912₎

   239 p. front., plates, ports. 22½ᶜᵐ.

Only a few pages of this journal treat of the subject's service in the 1st Texas Artillery (C. S. A.).

Hull, *Mrs.* **Susan Rebecca (Thompson)**₁ 1833–
   Boy soldiers of the confederacy, collated by Susan R. Hull ... New York and Washington, The Neale publishing company, 1905.

   256 p. front., plates, ports. 21½ᶜᵐ.

Short essays and eulogies on a handful of Confederate soldiers; of small concrete value.

Humphreys, Charles Alfred, 1838–
Field, camp, hospital and prison in the civil war. 1863–1865; Charles A. Humphreys, chaplain, Second Massachusetts cavalry volunteers. Boston, Press of Geo. H. Ellis co., 1918.

xi p., 1 l., 428 p. front., plates, ports. 20½cm.

The warped and vindictive memoirs of a Massachusetts soldier who spent much of his time as a prisoner of war.

Humphreys, David, 1832–
Heroes and spies of the civil war, by David Humphreys ... New York and Washington, The Neale publishing company, 1903.

223 p. front. (port.) 20 cm.

Short, sometimes shallow sketches of Confederate espionage agents.

Hunter, Alexander, 1843–
Johnny Reb and Billy Yank, by Alexander Hunter; illustrated by Harold Macdonald and R. O. Tolman. New York and Washington, The Neale publishing company, 1905.

720 p. front., plates, ports. 23 cm.

A "veracious account of the life of a soldier in Lee's army"; highly quoted and highly in demand.

Hunter, Alfred G
History of the Eighty-second Indiana volunteer infantry, its organization, campaigns and battles. Written at the request of the members by Alf. G. Hunter ... Indianapolis, W. B. Burford, printer, 1893.

255 p. incl. front., port. 19 cm.

Another volume in which the author spent more time "waving the bloody shirt" than in amassing useful facts.

Hunton, Eppa, 1822–1908.
Autobiography of Eppa Hunton. Richmond, Va., The William Byrd press, inc., 1933.

xx, 268 p. front., ports. 22½cm.

Although written by a Confederate general, these reminiscences contain many insights into the life of the Southern "GI."

Hurst, Samuel H
Journal-history of the Seventy-third Ohio volunteer infantry; by Samuel H. Hurst ... Chillicothe, O., 1866.

viii, [9]–253, [1] p. 20cm.

Hurst left the service as a brigadier general and immediately expanded his diary with remembrances to compile this useful journal of service in both theaters.

Hutchins, Edward Ridgeway, 1841–   *comp.*
The war of the 'sixties, comp. by E. R. Hutchins ... New York, The Neale publishing company, 1912.

490 p. 22½cm.

A series of articles by soldiers on both sides; subject material ranges from battles to prison life.

Hutchinson, Gustavus B   *comp.*
A narrative of the formation and services of the Eleventh Massachusetts volunteers, from April 15, 1861, to July 14, 1865. Being a brief account of their experiences in the camp and in the field, to which is added a roster, containing the names of all surviving members known to the Veteran association ... Published by Gustavus B. Hutchinson ... Boston, A. Mudge & son, printers, 1893.
96 p. 19cm.

An all-too-brief summary of a regiment that served in the II Corps of the Army of the Potomac; contains no personal material save statistical data.

Hutchinson, Nelson V
History of the Seventh Massachusetts volunteer infantry in the war of the rebellion of the southern states against constitutional authority. 1861–1865. With description of battles, army movements, hospital life, and incidents of the camp, by officers and privates; and a comprehensive introduction of the moral and political forces which precipitated the war of secession upon the people of the United States. By the author, Nelson V. Hutchinson. Taunton, Mass., Pub. by authority of the regimental association, 1890.
vii, 320 p. pl., port. 23 cm.

A typical unit history, filled with a variety of recollections, correspondence, personal incidents, and factual summaries; the regiment served in the East with the VI Corps.

Hyde, Thomas Worcester, 1841–1899.
Following the Greek cross; or, Memories of the Sixth army corps, by Thomas W. Hyde ... Boston and New York, Houghton, Mifflin and company, 1894.

1 p. l., xi p., 1 l., 269 p. front., pl., port. 18½ cm.

An excellent memoir by a Maine officer whose valor in Eastern campaigns brought him brevet promotion to brigadier general.

Hyde, William Lyman, 1819–1896.

History of the One hundred and twelfth regiment N. Y. volunteers. By Wm. L. Hyde, chaplain of the regiment. Fredonia, N. Y., W. McKinstry & co., 1866.

viii, [9]-214 p. front., port. 20^{cm}.

Written when the facts were still fresh; somewhat weak in comprehensiveness and personal touches.

Hyndman, William, b. 1842 or 43.

History of a cavalry company. A complete record of Company "A," 4th Penn'a cavalry, as identified with that regiment ... in all the campaigns of the Army of the Potomac, during the late civil war. By Capt. William Hyndman. Philadelphia, J. B. Rodgers co., printers, 1870.

2 p. l., ix–xxiv, 25–343 p. 19^{cm}.

Disguised as a unit history; nevertheless, a good personal memoir by a very observant soldier.

Ickis, Alonzo Ferdinand, 1836–1917.

Bloody trails along the Rio Grande: a day-by-day diary of Alonzo Ferdinand Ickis, 1836–1917, a soldier and his activities with Company B, the first volunteer regiment to leave the territory of Colorado for the Civil War, their participation in the Battle of Valverde, New Mexico, by Nolie Mumey. Denver, Old West Pub. Co., 1958.

123 p. port., fold. map (mounted on end leaf) 26 cm.

This limited edition is important more for where Ickis served than for what he said.

Illinois. *Shiloh battlefield commission.*

Illinois at Shiloh; report of the Shiloh battlefield commission and ceremonies at the dedication of the monuments erected to mark the positions of the Illinois commands engaged in the battle; the story of the battle, by Stanley Waterloo. Compiled by Marjor George Mason, secretary of the commission. [Chicago, M. A. Donohue & co., printers, 1905?]

187 p. plates, ports., 2 fold. maps. 23½^{cm}.

Disorganized but occasionally useful for the role of Illinois troops at Shiloh.

Illinois artillery. *1st regt., 1862–1865. Battery M.*

History of the organization, marches, campings, general services and final muster out of Battery M, First regiment Illinois light artillery, together with detailed accounts of incidents both grave and facetious connected therewith; comp. from the official records and from the diaries of the different members. By members of the battery. Princeton, Ill., Mercer & Dean, 1892.

viii p., 1 l., [11]–301 p. 24½^{cm}.

A full summary of the battery's three years' service, with emphasis on the Atlanta campaign.

Illinois cavalry. *9th regt., 1861–1865.*

History of the Ninth regiment Illinois cavalry volunteers. Pub. under the auspices of the Historical committee of the regiment ... Ed. by Edward A. Davenport ... [Chicago, Donohue & Henneberry, printers] 1888.

xii, 13–450 p., 1 l. ports. 23¼ cm.

This shallow history skims over the regiment's career with a disappointing rapidity.

Illinois infantry. *13th regt., 1861–1864.*

Military history and reminiscences of the Thirteenth regiment of Illinois volunteer infantry in the civil war in the United States, 1861–65. Prepared by a committee of the regiment, 1891. Publication committee: H. T. Noble, S. C. Plummer, H. D. Dement, C. E. Bolles. Historians: A. B. Munn, A. H. Miller, W. O. Newton. Chicago, Woman's temperance publishing association, 1892.

viii, 672 p. front., plates, ports., maps, facsim. 23¼^{cm}.

An ordinary unit compilation of service in the trans-Mississippi theater.

Illinois infantry. *55th regt., 1861–1865.*

The story of the Fifty-fifth regiment Illinois volunteer infantry in the civil war, 1861–1865. By a committee of the regiment. [Clinton, Mass., Printed by W. J. Coulter] 1887.

519 p. 23¼^{cm}.

Each of the four sections of this history was the work of a different veteran; hence, the total narrative of Western service fluctuates in quality.

Illinois infantry. *73d regt., 1862–1865.*

A history of the Seventy-third regiment of Illinois infantry volunteers: its services and experiences in camp, on the march, on the picket and skirmish lines, and in many battles of the war, 1861–65 ... Embracing an account of the movement from Columbia to Nashville, and the battles of Spring hill and Franklin ... Published by authority of the Regimental reunion association of survivors of the 73d Illinois infantry volunteers. [Springfield, Ill., °1890]

682 p. incl. illus., port. front., port. 22¼ cm.

Written jointly by three veterans; the narrative, presented in diary form, gives a good account of campaigning in Tennessee.

Illinois infantry. *92d regt., 1862–1865.*

Ninety-second Illinois volunteers. Freeport, Ill., Journal steam publishing house and bookbindery, 1875.

390 p. 19½^{cm}.

A penetrating history, based on diaries and letters, and full of personal experiences.

Illinois infantry. *103d regt., 1862–1865.*

Reminiscences of the civil war from diaries of members of the 103d Illinois volunteer infantry. 1904. Comp. by the following committee: H. H. Orendorff, G. M. Armstrong, Newton Ellis, M. V. D. Voorhees, S. R. Quigley, C. F. Matteson, A. J. Stutes. Chicago, Press of J. F. Leaming & co. [1904]

293 p. front., ports. 20½cm.

Good for marches and battle dispositions, but lacking in personal data.

Imler, George R

1864 pocket diary of Pvt. George R. Imler, Co. E, 138th Regiment, Pennsylvania Volunteers; personal account of the campaign of the Army of the Potomac from the Wilderness to Petersburg. Edited by Richard A. Gray, Jr. [n. p.] 1963.

102 l. 28 cm.

An empty, mimeographed diary of service in the last months of the war; Imler's is the poorest of the extant sources on the 138th Pennsylvania.

Indiana. *Antietam monument commission.*

Indiana at Antietam. Report of the Indiana Antietam monument commission and ceremonies at the dedication of the monument ... Together with history of events leading up to the battle of Antietam; the report of General George B. McClellan, of the battle; the formation of the Army of the Potomac, at the battle; and the histories of the five Indiana regiments engaged. Indianapolis, Ind. [The Aetna press] 1911.

153 p. front., plates, ports. 23½cm.

One of many similar volumes on a state's role in a certain battle; a typical collection of data of variable usefulness.

Indiana. *Commissioners for the Chickamauga and Chattanooga national park.*

Indiana at Chickamauga, 1863–1900. Report of Indiana commissioners Chickamauga national military park. Indianapolis, Sentinel printing co., printers, 1900.

318 p. front., plates, ports., fold. plan in pocket. 25 cm.

Similar to the preceding volume, except that the setting is in the West.

Indiana. *Vicksburg national military park commission.*

Indiana at Vicksburg. Pub. pursuant to an act of the Sixtysixth General assembly ... by the Indiana-Vicksburg military park commission. Comp. by Henry C. Adams, jr. ... 1910. Indianapolis, W. B. Burford, contractor for state printing and binding, 1911.

476 p. incl. front., illus., plates, ports. fold. map. 23½cm.

Amid a series of eulogies, testimonials and dedications are short but useful histories of a Hoosier unit involved in the Vicksburg campaign.

Indiana legion.

Operations of the Indiana legion and minute men, 1863–4. Documents presented to the General assembly, with the governor's message, January 6, 1865. Indianapolis, W. R. Holloway, state printer, 1865.

iv, 104 p. 22cm.

An unbalanced chronicle, heavily spiced with anecdotes and/or "recollections."

Indiana infantry. *46th regt., 1861–1865.*

History of the Forty-sixth regiment Indiana volunteer infantry, September, 1861–September, 1865: compiled by order of the Regimental association. [Logansport, Ind., Press of Wilson, Humphreys & co.] 1888.

vi, [7]–220 p. 23½cm.

Official reports treating almost entirely of events connected with Morgan's Indiana Raid.

Indiana infantry. *79th regt., 1862–1865.*

History of the Seventy-ninth regiment Indiana volunteer infantry in the civil war of eighteen sixty-one in the United States. Indianapolis, The Hollenbeck press, 1899.

v, 221 p. 23½cm.

This diary-like narrative has too many short and empty daily entries.

Ingersoll, Chalmers 1838–1908.

The unknown friends, a Civil War romance; letters of my father and my mother. Comp. by Charlotte Ingersoll Morse. Chicago, A. Kroch, 1948.

110 p. ports., facsim. 24 cm.

A fragment of the 1861-1863 interchange of correspondence between an Illinois cavalryman and his beloved; the letters abound in sentimentality and little else.

Ingersoll, Lurton Dunham.

Iowa and the rebellion. A history of the troops furnished by the state of Iowa to the volunteer armies of the Union, which conquered the great southern rebellion of 1861–5. By Lurton Dunham Ingersoll. 3d ed. Philadelphia, J. B. Lippincott and co.; Dubuque, B. M. Harger; [etc., etc.] 1867.

743 p. incl. maps. 23½cm.

The first attempt at a summary of each Iowa regiment's composition and contributions to the war; filled with the unbalance and disorganization one might expect.

Ingraham, Charles Anson, 1852–

Elmer E. Ellsworth and the zouaves of '61, by Charles A. Ingraham ... Chicago, Pub. for Chicago historical society by the University of Chicago press [c1925]

xi, 167 p. front., plates, ports., facsim. 23½ᶜᵐ.

A short, overly eulogistic biography of one of the Union's first fatalities.

Iobst, Richard W

The Bloody Sixth; the Sixth North Carolina Regiment, Confederate States of America. History by Richard W. Iobst; roster by Louis H. Manarin. With a narrative on the reactivated regiment by Wade Lucas. [Durham? N. C., 1965]

xv, 493 p. illus., ports. 23 cm.

The first half of this study is a tedious narrative of events; the latter half is a descriptive roster of the regiment's members.

Irby, Richard.

Historical sketch of the Nottoway grays, afterwards Company G, Eighteenth Virginia regiment, Army of northern Virginia; prepared at the request of the surviving members of the company at their first reunion at Bellefont church, July 21, 1877. By Richard Irby ... Richmond, J. W. Fergusson & son, 1878.

48 p., 1 l. 24 cm.

Another of those cursory works in great demand more because of the scarcity of extant copies than for the value of its contents.

Irwin, Richard Biddle, 1839–1892.

History of the Nineteenth army corps, by Richard B. Irwin ... New York, London, G. P. Putnam's sons, 1892.

vi p., 1 l., 528 p. maps, plans. 24½ᶜᵐ.

A straightforward, factual history of the Corps from New Orleans to Cedar Creek; no personal incidents and only a few observations give life to an otherwise dry account.

Irving, Theodore 1809–1880.

"More than conqueror," or Memorials of Col. J. Howard Kitching, Sixth New York artillery, Army of the Potomac. By the author of "The conquest of Florida" ... New York, Hurd and Houghton, 1873.

viii p., 2 l., [3]–239 p. front. (port.) 18ᶜᵐ.

Contains many quotations from the personal, highly readable letters of an officer whose promising career ended at Cedar Creek.

Isham, Asa Brainerd, 1844–

An historical sketch of the Seventh regiment Michigan volunteer cavalry from its organization, in 1862, to its muster out, in 1865. By Asa B. Isham ... New York, Town topics publishing company [1893]

118 p. front., illus. (ports.) facsim. 20½ᶜᵐ.

Even with the author's padding, this work is too short to be of value.

Isham, Frederic Stewart, 1866–1922, *comp.*

History of the Detroit light guard: its records and achievements. Comp. by Frederic S. Isham and Purcell & Hogan, Detroit. Detroit. Detroit light guard, 1896.

104 p., 1 l. incl. port. 28ᶜᵐ.

An empty collection of dramatic presentations that reads more like a series of newspaper articles.

Izlar, William Valmore.

A sketch of the war record of the Edisto rifles, 1861–1865, by William Valmore Izlar; Company "A," 1st regiment S. C. V. infantry ... Provisional army of the Confederate States 1861–1862; Company "G," 25th regiment S. C. V. infantry ... Confederate States army 1862–1865. Pub. by August Kohn. Columbia, S. C., The State company, 1914.

168 p. 2 pl., 16 port. (incl. front.) 19½ᶜᵐ.

These brief reminiscences include an account of the fall of Fort Fisher, as well as the author's experiences while a prisoner at Point Lookout.

Jackman, Lyman.

History of the Sixth New Hampshire regiment in the war for the union. Captain Lyman Jackman, historian; Amos Hadley, PH. D., editor. Concord, Republican press association, 1891.

vi p., 1 l., 630 p. front., port. 23ᶜᵐ.

Although the author laid claim to using his wartime diary as a base for this study, comrades' stories and recollections predominate; this regiment saw service in three different theaters.

Jackson, Edgar Allan, 1845–1863.

Letters of Edgar Allan Jackson, September 7, 1860–April 15, 1863. [Franklin? Va., 193–]

cover-title, 22 p. 27½ x 12ᶜᵐ.

The personal and moving correspondence (1860–1863) of a teenage Confederate who lost his life at Chancellorsville; good for descriptions of camp life.

Jackson, Harry F

Back home in Oneida; Hermon Clarke and his letters ₍by₎ Harry F. Jackson and Thomas F. O'Donnell. ₍Syracuse, N. Y.₎ Syracuse University Press, 1965.

ix, 212 p. 22 cm.

A narrative history based on the seventy-two letters of Herman Clarke of the 117th New York; the co-authors contribute more than do Clarke's letters.

Jackson, Isaac, 1842–1903.

"Some of the boys ..." The Civil War letters of Isaac Jackson, 1862–1865. Edited by Joseph Orville Jackson. With a foreword by Bell Irvin Wiley. Carbondale, Southern Illinois University Press ₍1960₎

264 p. illus. 22 cm.

Written by a pious and seemingly contented soldier in the 83rd Ohio, these letters are even-tempered commentaries on army life in the Arkansas-Mississippi theater.

Jackson, Oscar Lawrence, 1840–1920.

The colonel's diary; journals kept before and during the civil war by the late Colonel Oscar L. Jackson ... sometime commander of the 63rd regiment O. V. I. ₍Sharon?₎ Pa., 1922₎

3 p. l., 232 p., 1 l., 233–262 p. front., ports. 22½ᶜᵐ.

Very readable and revealing memoirs by a school teacher who commanded a regiment during much of the fighting in the West.

James, Henry B   1841–

Memories of the civil war. By Henry B. James. Co. B 32nd Mass. volunteers ... New Bedford, Mass., F. E. James, 1898.

3 p. l., 133 p., 2 l. fronts., pl., ports. 18ᶜᵐ.

A memoir written for self-satisfaction; that is as much as it contributes.

Jamison, Matthew H   1840–

Recollections of pioneer and army life, by Matthew H. Jamison, lieutenant E company, Tenth regiment, Illinois veteran volunteer infantry ... Kansas City, Hudson press ₍1911₎

2 p. l., iv, 7–363 p. front. (port.) illus. 23ᶜᵐ.

Jamison's diary of life with an Illinois regiment is the major content of note in this rambling work.

Jaques, John Wesley.

Three years' campaign of the Ninth, N. Y. S. M., during the southern rebellion, by John W. Jaques ... New York, Hilton & co., 1865.

199, ₍2₎, 47, ₍1₎ p. 19ᶜᵐ.

An above-average diary, filled with personal opinions and observations.

Jeffries, C   **C**

Terry's Rangers. ₍1st ed.₎ New York, Vantage Press ₍1962₎

139 p. 21 cm.

An example of how not to write a unit history.

Jewett, Albert Henry Clay, 1841–1898.

A boy goes to war, by Albert Henry Clay Jewett. War memories of 1860 to 1864 ... Poem-preface by his daughter Grace Jewett Austin. Bloomington, Ill., 1944.

x, 73 p. front. (port.) 20ᶜᵐ.

Written from memory thirty years after the war, these reminiscences of a New Hampshire soldier are shallow, error-laden, and sometimes intangible.

Johns, Henry T   *b.* 1827 *or* 8.

Life with the Forty-ninth Massachusetts volunteers. By Henry T. Johns ... Pittsfield, For the author, 1864.

391 p. front., pl., port. 19½ cm.

Because of Johns' descriptive powers, it is unfortunate that his military service was confined solely to the Louisiana theater.

Johnson, Adam Rankin   1834–

The Partisan rangers of the Conferedate States army; ed. by William J. Davis. Louisville, Ky., G. G. Fetter company, 1904.

xii p., 1 l., 476 p. front., plates, ports. 23 cm.

A somewhat embellished account of cavalry operations in Kentucky and Tennessee by a Confederate who attained the rank of brigadier general.

Johnson, Benjamin C   1840–1888.

A soldier's life; the Civil War experiences of Ben C. Johnson. Originally entitled: Sketches of the Sixth Regiment, Michigan Infantry. Edited, with an introd., by Alan S. Brown. Kalamazoo, School of Graduate Studies, Western Michigan University Press, 1962.

122 p. port. 23 cm.

Johnson participated in no battles, but his slim recollections are useful for a personal view of the neglected Department of the Gulf.

Johnson, Charles Beneulyn, 1843–

Muskets and medicine; or, Army life in the sixties, by Charles Beneulyn Johnson ... Philadelphia, F. A. Davis company; [etc., etc.,] 1917.

276 p. front., plates, ports. 21cm.

Interesting memoirs of hospital service from Memphis to Texas; Johnson's is the only printed record of note for the 130th Illinois.

Johnson, Charles F   1843–

The long roll; being a journal of the civil war, as set down during the years 1861–1863 by Charles F. Johnson, sometime of Hawkins zouaves. Illustrated with many sketches & photographs. Duluth ed. East Aurora, N. Y., The Roycrofters, 1911.

5 p. l., 5–241, [1] p. front., plates, ports. 20cm.

Vivid recollections of service in North Carolina by a Swedish-born youth who served in the 9th New York.

Johnson, John Lipscomb, *ed.*

The University memorial; biographical sketches of alumni of the University of Virginia who fell in the Confederate war; five volumes in one, by Rev. John Lipscomb Johnson, B. A. Baltimore, Turnbull brothers, 1871.

765 p. front., ports. 23½cm.

Many of these biographical sketches contain letters from the field of Confederate soldiers; a valuable work for the Old Dominion's contributions to the war.

Johnson, Richard W   1827–1897.

A soldier's reminiscences in peace and war. By Brig.-Gen. R. W. Johnson ... Philadelphia, Press of J. R. Lippincott company, 1886.

428 p. front. (port.) pl. 23 cm.

A disappointing memoir by a Federal general; treats solely of military matters from Kentucky to Atlanta.

Johnson, William Benjamin, 1846–1908.

Union to the hub and twice around the tire; reminiscences of the Civil War. [n. p., 1950]

vi, 119 l. 28 cm.

A typescript collection of humorous-- and oftentimes unbelievable-- tales by a Midwestern soldier who followed Sherman to the sea.

Johnston, Adam S

The soldier boy's diary book; or, Memorandums of the alphabetical first lessons of military tactics. Kept by Adam S. Johnston, from September 14, 1861, to October 2, 1864. Pittsburg, 1866.

v, [6]–139 p. 17cm.

The first half of this journal treats of marches and camp life with the 79th Pennsylvania; the second half recounts Johnston's experiences as a prisoner of war.

Johnston, David Emmons, 1845–

The story of a Confederate boy in the civil war, by David E. Johnston ... with introduction by Rev. C. E. Cline ... [Portland, Or., Glass & Prudhomme company, c1914]

xiv, 379 p. front., ports. 19½cm.

A garrulous, overly sentimental narrative of service with a Virginia unit.

Joinville, François Ferdinand Philippe Louis Marie d'Orléans, *prince* de, 1818–1900.

... The Army of the Potomac: its organization, its commander, and its campaign. By the Prince de Joinville. Tr. from the French, with notes, by William Henry Hurlbert. New York, A. D. F. Randolph, 1862.

118 p. front. (fold. map) 23 cm.

A French nobleman's unique and personal account of McClellan's ill-fated Peninsular Campaign; observations are many, and sentiments are decidedly pro-Federal.

Jones, Benjamin Washington 1841–

Under the stars and bars; a history of the Surry light artillery; recollections of a private soldier in the war between the states ... Richmond, E. Waddey co., 1909.

xiii, 297 p. 20½cm.

Jones's letters while a member of a Confederate artillery unit offer many insights into the life of wartime Richmond.

Jones, Charles Colcock, 1831–1893.

Historical sketch of the Chatham artillery during the Confederate struggle for independence. By Charles C. Jones, jr. ... Albany, J. Munsell, 1867.

240 p. maps. 24ᶜᵐ.

In an impersonal narrative, the author recounts military service in the various Carolina campaigns.

Jones, Evan Rowland, 1840–1920.

Fours years in the Army of the Potomac: a soldier's recollections. By Major Jones ... London, The Tyne publishing company, limited [1881]

8 p. l., [9]–246 p. front. (port.) double map. 22 cm.

A sentimental and sharply anti-Southern memoir by an officer in the 5th Wisconsin; Jones spent more time philosophizing than describing.

Jones, Jenkins Lloyd, 1843–1918.

... An artilleryman's diary, by Jenkin Lloyd Jones ... [Madison] Wisconsin history commission, 1914.

xviii, 395 p. front., ports., facsim. 23½ cm.

Jones participated only in the Atlanta campaign, but his diary contains a wealth of insights and information on army life.

Jones, John Beauchamp, 1810–1866.

A Rebel war clerk's diary at the Confederate States capital. By J. B. Jones ... Philadelphia, J. B. Lippincott & co., 1866.

2 v. 20ᶜᵐ.

The most consulted journal for wartime Richmond and the Confederate government; Jones, who reworked the diary shortly after the war, had an exaggerated opinion of his military judgments.

Jones, John Beauchamp, 1810–1866.

A rebel war clerk's diary at the Confederate States capital, by J. B. Jones ... A new and enl. ed., edited with an introduction and historical notes by Howard Swiggett ... New York, Old hickory bookshop, 1935.

2 v. 23½ cm.

A more qualitative edition of the above, but marred too much by inaccurate notes.

Jones, John William, 1836–1909.

Army of northern Virginia memorial volume. Compiled by Rev. J. William Jones ... at the request of the Virginia division of the Army of northern Virginia association. Richmond, J. W. Randolph & English, 1880.

347 p. 24½ cm.

A series of useful addresses made at annual reunions of Confederate veterans; all of the material treats of battles and other, purely military matters.

Jones, John William, 1836–1909.

Christ in the camp: or, Religion in Lee's army; by Rev. J. Wm. Jones ... With an introduction by Rev. J. C. Granberry ... bishop of the Methodist Episcopal church, South ... Richmond, Va., B. F. Johnson & co., 1887.

528 p. front. (port.) illus., plates. 21½ cm.

The best source for aspects and incidents of religion in the Confederate armies; however, the material is loosely organized and poorly presented.

Jones, Samuel Calvin, 1838–

Reminiscences of the Twenty-second Iowa volunteer infantry, giving its organization, marches, skirmishes, battles, and sieges, as taken from the diary of Lieutenant S. C. Jones of Company A. Iowa City, Ia., 1907.

164, [2] p. 2 double pl., ports. 23½ᶜᵐ.

Among the best reminiscences of Iowa soldiers; Jones recounted in diary form his travels through the Gulf region and his experiences as a war prisoner.

Jones, Thomas B 1841–

Complete history of the 46th regiment, Illinois volunteer infantry, a full and authentic account of the participation of the regiment in the battles, sieges, skirmishes and expeditions in which it was engaged. Also a complete roster of the regiment, together with biographical sketches ... Sketch of the organization of the Grand army of the republic ... Giving a complete record of the reunions of the 46th regiment up to the present time ... [Freeport, Ill., W. H. Wagner & sons, printers, 1907?]

379, [5] p. ports., fold. map. 23½ᶜᵐ.

The best study of the 46th Illinois, though possessed of vices as well as virtues.

Joyce, John Alexander, 1842–1915.

A checkered life. By Col. John A. Joyce ... Chicago, S. P. Rounds, jr., 1883.

2 p. l., [7]–9 p., 3 l., 17–318, [1] p. incl. front. (port.) illus., facsims. 20½ cm.

The first sections of this weak memoir recount the author's experiences in the 24th Kentucky (U. S.).

Judd, David Wright, 1838–1888.
The story of the Thirty-third N. Y. S. vols: or Two years campaigning in Virginia and Maryland. By David W. Judd ... Illustrations from drawings by Lieut. L. C. Mix. Rochester, Benton & Andrews, 1864.
iv, 349, 76 p. incl. illus., pl. front. 19½ᶜᵐ.

More a memoir than a unit study; well-balanced and without undue prejudice, even though published during the war.

Judson, Amos M
History of the Eighty-third regiment Pennsylvania volunteers. By A. M. Judson ... Erie, Pa., B. F. H. Lynn [1865]
2 p. l., xiii–xv, 17–139, [1] p. 24ᶜᵐ.

Its slimness notwithstanding, this is one of the better regimental histories that appeared immediately after the war; author recounts many experiences of regimental members during the campaigns in the East.

Katz, Irving I
The Jewish soldier from Michigan in the Civil War. Detroit, Wayne State University Press, 1962.
62 p. illus. 22 cm.

A valuable reference guide, not only for individuals, but also for Michigan homefront activities and units noted for Jewish members.

Kaufmann, Wilhelm, 1858–
Die Deutschen im amerikanischen bürgerkriege ⟨sezessionskrieg 1861–1865⟩ von Wilhelm Kaufmann; mit 36 karten und plänen. München und Berlin, R. Oldenbourg, 1911.
xii p., 1 l., 588 p. illus. (maps, plans) 23½ cm.

This statistical compilation of Germans who served in the armies deserves updating, translation, and republication.

Keener, Lawson Jefferson, 1840–1888.
Letters from Lawson Jefferson Keener written during his Confederate service to Alcesta (Allie) Benson Carter. Compiled by Lawson Keener Lacy (Mrs. Rogers Lacy) Longview, Tex., Mrs. Rogers Lacy, ᶜ1963.
1 v. (unpaged) facsims. 29 cm.

A typescript, with photostats of the original letters, of the wartime correspondence of a private in the W. P. Lane Rangers.

Keesy, William Allen, 1843–
War as viewed from the ranks. By Rev. W. A. Keesy. Personal recollections of the war of the Rebellion, by a private soldier ... Norwalk, O., The Experiment and news co.. ᶜ1898.
xvi, 240 p. illus.. 2 port. (incl. front.) 25ᶜᵐ.

This conglomeration of tales and incidents is too manufactured to be accepted without reservation.

Keil, Frederick W
Thirty-fifth Ohio. A narrative of service from August, 1861 to 1864. By F. W. Keil ... With an introductory by General H. V. Boynton. The original Persimmon regiment. Fort Wayne, Ind., Archer, Housh & co., printers, 1894.
xii, 272 p. front., illus., pl., port., maps. 19½ cm.

Disorganized and opinionated; a horrible example as a regimental study.

Kellogg, John Jackson, 1837–1916.
War experiences and the story of the Vicksburg campaign from "Milliken's Bend" to July 4, 1863; being an accurate and graphic account of campaign events taken from the diary of Capt. J. J. Kellogg, of Co. B, 113th Illinois volunteer infantry. [Washington, Ia., Evening journal, ᶜ1913]
64 p. front. (port.) 17½ cm.

The author's recollections of war along the Mississippi are too short and discursive to be of value.

Kelsey, Charles C
To the knife; the biography of Major Peter Keenan, 8th Pennsylvania Cavalry, by Charles C. Kelsey. [Ann Arbor? 1964]
vi, 56 p. illus., maps, ports. 23 cm.

More Kelsey than Keenan, though excerpts from the latter's wartime letters are occasionally inserted.

Kelsey, D   M.
Deeds of daring by both blue and gray; thrilling narratives of personal adventure ... on each side the line during the great civil war. By D. M. Kelsey ... Philadelphia and St. Louis, Scammell & company; [etc., etc.] 1883.
xxi, [1], 23–608 p. incl. front., illus. 22½ᶜᵐ.

A collection of highly dramatic, lavishly embellished, and totally unreliable escapades by various Civil War participants.

Kemper, General William Harrison, 1839–1927.

The Seventh regiment Indiana volunteers, three months enlistment: By G. W. H. Kemper ... Muncie, Ind., Press of R. H. Cowan printing co., 1903.

16 p. illus. 24ᶜᵐ.

Little more than a personal summary of the movements of one of the Hoosier State's most distinguished units.

Kennedy, Elijah Robinson, 1844–

John B. Woodward, a biographical memoir, by Elijah R. Kennedy. For private distribution. New York, Printed at the De Vinne press, 1897.

3 p. l., 222 p. front. (port.) 23ᶜᵐ.

Two-thirds of this study comprise the wartime letters of an officer in the 13th New York Militia; Woodward's letters are unusually revealing for life in the Army of the Potomac during the 1862-1863 campaigns.

Kent, Charles Nelson, 1843–1906.

History of the Seventeenth regiment, New Hampshire volunteer infantry. 1862–1863. By Lieut. Charles N. Kent ... Concord, N. H., By order of the Seventeenth New Hampshire veteran association, 1898.

325 p. front., illus., plates, ports., plan. 23ᶜᵐ.

A padded history of a regiment that never left New Hampshire's borders.

Kepler, William, b. 1841 or 1842.

History of the three months' and three years' service from April 16th, 1861, to June 22d, 1864, of the Fourth regiment Ohio volunteer infantry in the war for the Union. By Wm. Kepler ... Cleveland, Leader printing co., 1886.

287 p. front., pl., port., maps. 23ᶜᵐ.

This is an exceptionally good source for the trials and tribulations of life in the Army of the Potomac.

Kerbey, Joseph Orton, d. 1913.

The boy spy; a substantially true record of events during the war of the rebellion. The only practical history of war telegraphers in the field ... thrilling scenes of battles, captures and escapes, by Major J. O. Kerbey. Chicago, New York [etc.] Belford, Clarke & co., 1889.

vii, 8–556 p. front., plates. 20½ᶜᵐ.

A thoroughly unreliable account of one thrilling escapade after another, written by a soldier with an unlimited imagination; providentially, the book was designed for young readers.

Kerwood, Asbury L

Annals of the Fifty-seventh regiment Indiana volunteers. Marches, battles, and incidents of army life, by a member of the regiment. Dayton, O., W. J. Shuey, 1868.

374 p. 19½ᶜᵐ.

Another little-known but very reliable account of the war in the West; more a personal narrative than a regimental study.

Keyes, Charles M   *ed.*

The military history of the 123d regiment of Ohio volunteer infantry. Edited by C. M. Keyes ... Sandusky, Register steam press, 1874.

196 p. 20ᶜᵐ.

Although based in part on memory, this narrative of service in East and West, as well as a short tenure in a military prison, is worthwhile and valuable.

Kidd, James Harvey, 1840–1913.

Personal recollections of a cavalryman with Custer's Michigan cavalry brigade in the civil war, by J. H. Kidd, formerly colonel, Sixth Michigan cavalry ... Ionia, Mich., Sentinel printing company, 1908.

xiv p., 1 l., 476 p. front., ports., 3 maps. 23ᶜᵐ.

The author penned his "recollections" near the turn of the century and relied on a large variety of sources; nevertheless, this remains a basic source for Federal cavalry operations in the East.

Kiefer, William R

History of the One hundred and fifty-third regiment Pennsylvania volunteers infantry which was recruited in Northampton county, Pa. 1862–1863. Written by Rev. W. R. Kiefer ... assisted by Newton H. Mack ... Easton, The Chemical publishing co. [1909]

4 p. l., 352 p. front., illus., plates, ports., fold. map. 23½ cm.

A useful collection of personal observations, marred by Kiefer's penchant for wandering off into tangents.

Kieffer, Henry Martyn, b. 1845.

The recollections of a drummer-boy, by Harry M. Kieffer ... Boston, J. R. Osgood and company, 1883.

2 p. l., [3]–332 p. front., illus., plates. 17½ᶜᵐ.

Using articles first written for young readers and borrowing sketches by noted war-artist A. C. Redwood, the author issued this semi-fictionalized account of a soldier's life.

Kimball, Orville Samuel 1842–
History and personal sketches of Company I, 103 N. Y. S. V., 1862–1864. Elmira, N. Y., The Facts printing co., 1900.

1 p. l., 161, [1] p. front., ports. 21ᶜᵐ.

Worthless as a war narrative; only the biographical sketches have potential usefulness.

Kimbell, Charles Bill, *b.* 1839.
History of Battery "A," First Illinois light artillery volunteers [by] Charles B. Kimbell. Chicago, Cushing printing company, 1899.

viii, [9]–320 p. incl. col. front., illus. (incl. ports.) plates. 23½ cm.

A compilation based on scrimpy notes and fading memory; 114 photographs embellish this summary of prison life and service in the West.

Kimberly, Robert L
The Forty-first Ohio veteran volunteer infantry in the war of the rebellion. 1861–1865. By Robert L. Kimberly and Ephraim S. Holloway, with the co-operation of the committee of the Regimental association. Cleveland, W. R. Smellie, 1897.

292, [2] p. front., pl., ports. 23½ᶜᵐ.

A good introduction to the war history of the regiment, and nothing more.

King, David H   1835–   *comp.*
History of the Ninety-third regiment, New York volunteer infantry, 1861–1865. Comp. by David H. King, A. Judson Gibbs and Jay H. Northrup, pub. by the Association of the 93d N. Y. S. V. vols. Milwaukee, Wis., Swain & Tate co., printers, 1895.

xii, [13]–639 p. front., plates (1 col.) ports., maps. 23½ᶜᵐ.

Some confusion of material exists, but generally a revealing story of the regiment's war career.

Kingsbury, Allen Alonzo, 1840–1862.
The hero of Medfield; containing the journals and letters of Allen Alonzo Kingsbury, of Medfield, member of Co. H, Chelsea volunteers, Mass. 1st reg., who was killed by the rebels near Yorktown, April 26, 1862 … Boston, J. M. Hewes, printer, 1862.

144 p. front. (port.) 18ᶜᵐ.

The personal reminiscences of a young bugler killed early in the war; Kingsbury's writings are more full than one might expect.

Kinnear, John R
History of the Eighty-sixth regiment, Illinois volunteer infantry, during its term of service. By J. R. Kinnear … Chicago, Tribune company's book and job printing office, 1866.

viii, [9]–139 p. 19ᶜᵐ.

Begun during the war, this exceptionally good personal narrative treats of the major western battles from Perryville to Bentonville.

Kirk, Charles H   *ed. and comp.*
History of the Fifteenth Pennsylvania volunteer cavalry which was recruited and known as the Anderson cavalry in the rebellion of 1861–1865; ed. and comp. by Charles H. Kirk … assisted by the Historical committee of the Society of the Fifteenth Pennsylvania cavalry. Philadelphia, 1906.

784 p. front., plates, ports., fold. map. 25½ cm.

Composed in the main of personal recollections, official correspondence, and some material from wartime writings, this is an unbalanced compilation of limited usefulness.

Kirk, Hyland Clare, 1846–1917.
Heavy guns and light: a history of the 4th New York heavy artillery. By Hyland C. Kirk … New York, C. T. Dillingham [1890]

iv, viii, [9]–661 p. incl. illus., pl., port., maps. front., port. 23½ᶜᵐ.

The work of a popular postwar writer, this volume is heavily embellished with conversations and anecdotes; where fact ends and fiction begins is never quite clear.

Kirwan, Thomas, 1829–1911.
Memorial history of the Seventeenth regiment, Massachusetts volunteer infantry (old and new organizations) in the civil war from 1861–1865, issued by the authority of the supervisors, authorized to write and publish the history. Written and comp. in part by Thomas Kirwan, ed. and completed by Henry Splaine … Salem, Mass., Pub. for the Committee on history by the Salem press co., ᶜ1911.

8 p. l., 402 p., 1 l. front., 1 col. illus., pl., ports., plans. 24ᶜᵐ.

A suspicious compilation in which the author accepted at face value every tale related to him by members of the regiment.

Kirwan, Thomas 1829–1911.
Soldiering in North Carolina: being the experiences of a 'typo' in the pines, swamps, fields, sandy roads, towns, cities, and among the fleas, wood-ticks, 'gray-backs,' mosquitoes, bluetail flies, moccasin snakes, lizards, scorpions, rebels, and other reptiles, pests and vermin of the 'Old north state.' Embracing an account of the three-years and nine-months Massachusetts regiments in the department, the freedmen, etc., etc., etc. By "one of the Seventeenth." Boston, T. Kirwan, 1864.

126 p. illus. 18 x 14ᶜᵐ.

Commentaries and observations while campaigning in the Carolinas; inferior to Kirwan's history of the 17th Massachusetts.

Kniffin, Gilbert Crawford, 1832–1917.
... "The cavalry of the Army of the Cumberland in 1863." Prepared by Companion Lieutenant-Colonel Gilbert C. Kniffin ... and read at the stated meeting of December 2, 1896. [Washington, 1896]

15 p. 23ᶜᵐ. (Military history of the loyal legion of the United States. Commandery of the District of Columbia. War papers. 24)

Too brief to be of great value, but a lucid evaluation nevertheless.

Knox, Thomas Wallace, 1835–1896.
Camp-fire and cotton-field: southern adventure in time of war. Life with the Union armies, and residence on a Louisiana plantation. By Thomas W. Knox ... New York, Blelock and company, 1865.

524 p. front., plates. 22 cm.

A superb documentary on the Mississippi theater by a newspaper correspondent who seemed to stay "in hot water" with most Federal commanders.

Kreutzer, William.
Notes and observations made during four years of service with the Ninety-eighth N. Y. volunteers, in the war of 1861. By William Kreutzer, colonel. Philadelphia, Grant, Faires & Rodgers, printers, 1878.

1 p. l., 368 p. front., illus., pl., port., maps. 22½ᶜᵐ.

A pretentious collection of observations too lofty to be of importance; Kreutzer relied too much on high-sounding words and phrases.

La Bree, Benjamin, *ed.*
Camp fires of the Confederacy; a volume of humorous anecdotes, reminiscences, deeds of heroism, thrilling narratives, campaigns, hand-to-hand fights, bold dashes, terrible hardships endured, imprisonments ... etc. Confederate poems and selected songs ... Ed. by Ben La Bree ... Louisville, Ky., Courier-journal job printing company, 1898.

2 p. l., 560 p. illus. 24½ cm.

An almost endless collection of miscellany, most of it gleaned from other sources cited in this section.

The **Land** we love, a monthly magazine devoted to literature, military history, and agriculture. v. 1-6; May 1866–Mar. 1869. Charlotte, N. C., J. P. Irwin & D. H. Hill [etc.] 1866–69.

6 v. pl., ports., maps. 23ᶜᵐ.

Founded and edited by caustic Gen. D. Harvey Hill, this monthly magazine often served as an outlet for reminiscences, official reports, and chauvinistic poetry.

Lane, David
A soldier's diary; the story of a volunteer, 1862–1865 ... [Jackson? Mich., ᶜ1905]

270 p. 20ᶜᵐ.

A day-by-day account of three years' service with the 17th Michigan.

Lane, Walter Paye, 1817–1892.
The adventures and recollections of General Walter P. Lane, a San Jacinto veteran; containing sketches of the Texan, Mexican and late wars, with several Indian fights thrown in. Marshall, Tex., News messenger pub. co. [ᶜ1928]

180 p. front. (port.) pl. 19½ᶜᵐ.

Less than a third of this slanted work centers on Lane's Civil War experiences as a cavalry officer.

Lapham, William Berry, 1828–1894.
My recollections of the war of the rebellion; by William B. Lapham ... Privately printed. Augusta, Me., Burleigh & Flynt, printers, 1892.

240 p. port. 19½ cm.

In spite of the fact that the author achieved postwar fame as a physician and writer, his memoirs of service in two Maine units is an empty chronicle of the Eastern campaigns.

Larson, James, 1841–1921.
Sergeant Larson, 4th cav., by James Larson. San Antonio, Southern literary institute, 1935.

6 p. l., 326 p. incl. plates. front. (port.) 24 cm.

These reminiscences by a Federal cavalryman in the West abound with errors and suffer from the memory on which they were based.

Lathrop, David.
The history of the Fifty-ninth regiment Illinois volunteers, or A three years' campaign through Missouri, Arkansas, Mississippi, Tennessee and Kentucky, with a description of the country, towns, skirmishes and battles ... embellished with twenty-four lithographed portraits of the officers of the regiment. By Dr. D. Lathrop. Indianapolis, Hall & Hutchinson, printers, 1865.

243 p. front., port. 19½ cm.

An above-average recollection, based on a diary and written while the events were still fresh in the mind; the 59th Illinois campaigned from Pea Ridge through Stone's River.

Lavender, John W   1837–1921.
   The war memoirs of Captain John W. Lavender, C. S. A.
[They never came back; the story of Co. F. Fourth Arks.
Infantry, C. S. A., originally known as. the Montgomery
Hunters, as told by their commanding officer] Edited by
Ted R. Worley. Pine Bluff, Ark., W. M. Hackett and
D. R. Perdue [1956]
      158 p. 22 cm.

The unusual recollections of a semi-literate
carpenter who commanded a battle-shattered
company and ended the war as a prisoner on
Johnson's Island.

Lawrence, George Alfred 1827–1876.
   Border and bastille. By the author of "Guy Livingstone".
2d ed. rev. London, Tinsley brothers, 1863.
      xii, 277 p. 23ᶜᵐ.

The slanted recollections of an Englishman who
was imprisoned by Federals and then ordered
from the country for attempting to enter the
Confederacy.

LeConte, Joseph, 1823–1901.
   'Ware Sherman, a journal of three months' personal ex-
perience in the last days of the Confederacy, by Joseph Le-
Conte; with an introductory reminiscence by his daughter
Caroline LeConte. Berkeley, University of California press,
1937.
      xxxi, 146 p. incl. front. (port.) illus. 19½ cm.

The best account by a Southerner of Sherman's
march through the Carolinas; the author was a
noted scientist.

Ledford, Preston Lafayette, 1837–
   Reminiscences of the civil war, 1861–1865, by P. L. Ledford ... Thomasville, N. C., News printing house, 1909.
      104 p. 19 x 11ᶜᵐ.

In spite of its brevity, this work casts some
light on the trying life of a Confederate soldier.

Le Duc, William Gates, 1823–1917.
   Recollections of a Civil War quartermaster; the autobiog-
raphy of William G. Le Duc. St. Paul, Minn., North
Central Pub. Co. [c1963]
      xii, 167 p. port. 23 cm.

Le Duc wrote his memoirs of service in the XI
Corps at the age of eighty-four; he relied
heavily on a fragmentary diary; the recollections suffer also from unbelievably bad publishing.

Lee, Robert Edward, 1843–1914.
   My father, General Lee. A new ed. of Recollections and
letters of General Robert E. Lee, by his son Robert E. Lee,
Jr. With a new introd. and Lee chronology by Philip Van
Doren Stern. Garden City, N. Y., Doubleday, 1960.
      xxv, 453 p. illus., ports., facsims. 22 cm.

A reissue of the next title, replete with all its
errors; a cursory introduction and gallery of
Lee photographs were added.

Lee, Robert Edward, 1843–1914.
   Recollections and letters of General Robert E. Lee, by his
son, Captain Robert E. Lee ... New York, Doubleday, Page
& company, 1904.
      xii p., 1 l., 461 p. 4 port. (incl. front.) 23½ cm.

The closest thing to an autobiography that Gen.
Lee ever wrote; his letters to his family from
the front reveal a different side to the man than
is generally pictured.

Lee, Susan (Pendleton)
   Memoirs of William Nelson Pendleton, D. D., rector of Lati-
mer parish, Lexington, Virginia; brigadier-general C. S. A.;
chief of artillery, army of northern Virginia. By his daughter,
Susan P. Lee ... Philadelphia, J. B. Lippincott company, 1893.
      490 p. front. (port.) 24ᶜᵐ.

A valuable work; contains a large number of
letters by the controversial bishop-general who
commanded Lee's artillery.

Lee, William O   1844–   *comp.*
   Personal and historical sketches and facial history of
and by members of the Seventh regiment Michigan volunteer cavalry, 1862–1865. Comp. by William O. Lee ...
Detroit, 7th Michigan cavalry association [1902?]
      1 p. l., ix, 10–313 p. illus. (incl. ports.) 20½ᶜᵐ.

Short reminiscences by sixty veterans, plus
biographical sketches and a roll of honor.

Leib, Charles.
   Nine months in the quartermaster's department; or, The
chances for making a million. By Charles Leib ... Cincinnati, Moore, Wilstach, Keys & co., printers, 1862.
      vi, 7–200 p. front., pl., port. 19ᶜᵐ.

An informally written work that alternates between criticism and humor; Leib's service was
confined to duty in West Virginia.

Letterman, Jonathan, 1824–1872.

Medical recollections of the Army of the Potomac. By Jonathan Letterman, M. D., late surgeon United States army, and medical director of the Army of the Potomac. New York, D. Appleton and company, 1866.

194 p. 23ᶜᵐ.

Because of Letterman's position and incisive observations, this volume is of far greater importance than its slimness would indicate.

Lewis, George, 1831–

The history of Battery E, First regiment Rhode Island light artillery, in the war of 1861 and 1865, to preserve the Union. By George Lewis. Illustrated with portraits and map. Providence, Snow & Farnham, printers, 1892.

xi, [1], 540 p. front., pl., ports., fold. map. 25½ᶜᵐ.

Relying heavily on official reports and some diaries of comrades, Lewis put together a work whose fatal weakness is verbosity.

Lewis, G[eorge] W 1837–

The campaigns of the 124th regiment, Ohio volunteer infantry, with roster and roll of honor. By G. W. Lewis ... Akron, O., The Werner company [1894]

285 p. front., ports. 23ᶜᵐ.

Lewis's autobiography, heavily embellished; the presence of so many "I's" is distracting.

Lewis, John Henry, 1834–

Recollections from 1860 to 1865. With incidents of camp life, descriptions of battles, the life of the southern soldier, his hardships and sufferings, and the life of a prisoner of war in the northern prisons. By John H. Lewis ... Washington, D. C., Peake & company, 1895.

1 p. l., 92 p. port. 15ᶜᵐ.

The bulk of this narrative by a Virginia officer who was captured at Gettysburg treats of his experiences at Fort Delaware and Johnson's Island prison camps.

Lewis, Osceola

History of the One hundred and thirty-eighth regiment, Pennsylvania volunteer infantry. By Osceola Lewis. Norristown, [Pa.] Wills, Iredell & Jenkins, 1866.

198 p. front. (port.) 18 cm.

This unit history was written hastily and without needed reflection; the result is a work expectedly slim and shallow.

Lewis, *Lieut.* **Richard.**

Camp life of a Confederate boy, of Bratton's brigade, Longstreet's corps, C. S. A. Letters written by Lieut. Richard Lewis, of Walker's regiment, to his mother, during the war. Facts and inspirations of camp life, marches, &c. Charleston, S. C., The News and courier book presses, 1883.

113 p. 23½ᶜᵐ.

Graphic letters by a South Carolina soldier; the letters stop with his 1864 wounding.

Lincoln, William Sever, 1811–1889.

Life with the Thirty-fourth Mass. infantry in the war of the rebellion. By William S. Lincoln ... Worcester, Press of Noyes, Snow & company, 1879.

3 p. l., [5]–459, 18 p. front. (ports.) 24ᶜᵐ.

An excellent source for life in the Washington defenses and the 1864 action in the Shenandoah Valley; based on the author's diary and letters, as well as similar documents by comrades.

Little, Henry F W 1842–

... The Seventh regiment New Hampshire volunteers in the war of the rebellion, by Henry F. W. Little ... regimental historian ... Pub. by the Seventh New Hampshire veteran association. Concord, N. H., I. C. Evans, printer, 1896.

xviii, 567, 110, xxi p. front., illus., plates, ports., plans (part fold.) 23½ᶜᵐ.

One of the better sources on the X Corps and the campaigns in Florida and along the Atlantic coast; the author made good use of all known manuscript material.

Livermore, Thomas Leonard, 1844–1918.

Days and events, 1860–1866, by Thomas L. Livermore ... Boston and New York, Houghton Mifflin company, 1920.

x p., 2 l., [3]–485, [1] p. front. (port.) illus., fold. pl. 24½ cm.

The highly literate recollections by the colonel of the 18th New Hampshire; Livermore participated in all of the major campaigns in the East.

Livermore, Thomas Leonard, 1844–1918.

History of the Eighteenth New Hampshire volunteers, 1864–5, by Thomas L. Livermore ... Boston, The Fort Hill press, 1904.

124 p. front., plates, ports. 24ᶜᵐ.

Col. Livermore used the diaries of six men in preparing this brief summary, but the bulk of the text came from the Official Records; this work is markedly inferior to the Colonel's Days and Events.

Lloyd, William Penn 1837–1911.
History of the First reg't. Pennsylvania reserve cavalry, from its organization, August, 1861, to September, 1864, with list of names of all officers and enlisted men who have ever belonged to the regiment ... Philadelphia, King & Baird, printers, 1864.

216 p. 19¼ᶜᵐ.

A compilation of the basic information about a cavalry regiment that saw only minor action in Virginia.

Locke, David Ross, 1833–1888.
Civil War letters of Petroleum V. Nasby ₜpseud.₎ Compiled with an introd. by Harvey S. Ford. ₜColumbus₎ Ohio State University Press for the Ohio Historical Society ₜ°1962₎

34 p. 24 cm.

A selection of seventeen "letters" by Lincoln's favorite humorist; written in the dialect for which newspaperman Locke won renown, this work whets the appetite for more.

Locke, David Ross, 1833–1888.
The struggles of Petroleum V. Nasby ₜpseud.₎ Original illus. by Thomas Nast. Abridged ed. selected, edited, and with an introd. by Joseph Jones. Notes to the chapters by Gunther Barth. Boston, Beacon Press ₜ1963₎

246 p. illus. 21 cm.

An abridgement of a classic 1872 work; contains a third of Nasby's 189 essays on as many wartime subjects, as well as eight illustrations by famous cartoonist Thomas Nast.

Locke, E   W
Three years in camp and hospital. By E. W. Locke ... Boston, G. D. Russell & co. ₜ°1870₎

ix, ₜ10₎–408 p. 19½ᶜᵐ.

Locke has a varied career extending from temperance lecturer to song-writer; this "memoir" is light on what he actually saw but heavy on constructed conversation and self-esteem.

Locke, William Henry.
The story of the regiment. By William Henry Locke, ᴀ. ᴍ., chaplain. Philadelphia, J. B. Lippincott & co., 1868.

xii, 401 p. front. 19½ᶜᵐ.

An embellished history of the 11th Pennsylvania, but good on movements and battles.

Lockwood, James D
Life and adventures of a drummer-boy: or, Seven years a soldier. By James D. Lockwood ... A true story ... Albany, N. Y., J. Skinner, 1893.

191 p. front. 20ᵐ.

Too shallow and superficial; another work written for self-satisfaction.

Loehr, Charles T
War history of the old First Virginia infantry regiment, Army of Northern Virginia, by Charles T. Loehr. Published by request of the Old First Virginia infantry association. Richmond, W. E. Jones, printer, 1884.

87 p. 22½ cm.

Only fifty pages of this slim volume comprise Loehr's diary-based reminiscences, but they are an above-average personal narrative on service in Lee's army.

Logan, Indiana Washington (Peddicord) 1835–
Kelion Franklin Peddicord of Quirk's scouts, Morgan's Kentucky cavalry, C. S. A.; biographical and autobiographical, together with a general biographical outline of the Peddicord family, by Mrs. India W. P. Logan. New York and Washington, The Neale publishing company, 1908.

170 p. 4 port. (incl. front.) 21 cm.

The best portion of this conglomeration of material is the war and prison narrative of Col. Peddicord of the 1st Kentucky Cavalry.

Logan, John Alexander, 1826–1886.
The volunteer soldier of America. By John A. Logan. With Memoir of the author and Military reminiscences from General Logan's private journal. Chicago and New York, R. S. Peale & company, 1887.

xxiii, 25–706 p. col. front., plates, ports. 24½ cm.

Less than half of this tome contains Gen. Logan's embellished, somewhat self-centered recollections.

Longstreet, James, 1821–1904.
From Manassas to Appomattox; memoirs of the civil war in America, by James Longstreet ... Philadelphia, J. B. Lippincott company, 1896.

xx, ₜ2₎, 13–690 p. front., illus., plates, ports., facsim. 23½ cm.

A combination of reminiscences and rebuttals by a gallant soldier ostracized by his comrades in the Reconstruction period; a necessary source for any study of Lee's army.

Longstreet, James, 1821–1904.
  From Manassas to Appomattox, memoirs of the Civil War in America. Edited with an introd. and notes by James I. Robertson, Jr. Bloomington, Indiana University Press ₁1960₁

  692 p. illus. 22 cm.

A provocative introduction and voluminous notes for a text reproduced in its entirely make "Old Pete's" recollections even more useful.

Lord, Edward Oliver, 1856–   *ed.*
  History of the Ninth regiment, New Hampshire volunteers in the war of the rebellion. Ed. by Edward O. Lord, A. M. Concord, Republican press association, 1895.

  xii, 761, ₁3₁, 171 p. front., pl., port. 23½ cm.

Another composite history of diary extracts and personal recollections - but in this instance excessively embellished by the author; two chapters treat of prisoner experiences; this regiment campaigned in the East.

Lothrop, Charles Henry, 1831–1890.
  A history of the First regiment Iowa cavalry veteran volunteers, from its organization in 1861 to its muster out of the United States service in 1866. Also, a complete roster of the regiment. By Charles H. Lothrop ... Lyons, Ia., Beers & Eaton, printers, 1890.

  x p., 1 l., ₁13₁–422, v p., 1 l. front., illus., pl., port. 23 cm.

A jumbled regimental study broken too often by the insertion of official correspondence readily available elsewhere.

Lucas, Daniel R
  History of the 99th Indiana infantry, containing a diary of marches, incidents, biography of officers and complete rolls. By Chaplain D. R. Lucas. Lafayette, Ind., Rosser & Spring, printers, 1865.

  iv, ₁5₁–179, ₁1₁ p. 20½ cm.

Written by the regimental chaplain, this study is a cursory commentary on some of the minor campaigns in the West.

Lufkin, Edwin B   *b.* 1841.
  History of the Thirteenth Maine regiment from its organization in 1861 to its muster-out in 1865. By Edwin B. Lufkin ... With a sketch of the Thirteenth Maine battalion attached to the Thirtieth Maine; and an appendix containing a complete roster of the regiment. Bridgton, Me., H. A. Shorey & son, 1898.

  xiii, 140, 67 p., 1 l. 4 port. 21½ cm.

A shallow summary of the regiment's movements, with the usual muster roll affixed.

Lusk, William Thompson, 1838–1897.
  War letters of William Thompson Lusk, captain, assistant adjutant-general, United States volunteers 1861–1863, afterward M. D., LL. D. New York, Priv. print., 1911.

  x p., 1 l., 304 p. front., pl., ports., maps. 24½ᶜᵐ.

One of the better collections of Federal soldiers' letters; especially good for operations around Beaufort, S. C.

Lyle, William W   *b.* 1825.
  Lights and shadows of army life: or, Pen pictures from the battlefield, the camp, and the hospital. By Rev. W. W. Lyle ... 2d ed. Cincinnati, R. W. Carroll & co., 1865.

  xii, 9–403 p. 19ᶜᵐ.

Virtually a sermon on army hospitals and religious life in the field.

Lyman, Theodore, 1833–1897.
  Meade's headquarters, 1863–1865; letters of Colonel Theodore Lyman from the Wilderness to Appomattox, selected and ed. by George R. Agassiz. Boston, The Atlantic monthly press, 1922.

  x p., 3 l., 371 p. front., ports., maps. 25 cm.

The poignant and constantly quoted letters of a volunteer aide' necessary for any study of the Army of the Potomac in the last eighteen months of the war.

Lynch, Charles H
  The civil war diary, 1862–1865, of Charles H. Lynch, 18th Conn. vol's. ₁Hartford, Conn., Priv. print. by the Case, Lockwood & Brainard co., 1915₁

  1 p. l., 5–163 p. 2 port. (incl. front.) 23½ᶜᵐ.

An above-average diary of a soldier's experiences and observations; very good for pictures of camp life.

Lyon, William Penn, 1822–1913.
  Reminiscences of the civil war; comp. from the war correspondence of Colonel William P. Lyon and from personal letters and diary by Mrs. Adelia C. Lyon. Published by William P. Lyon, jr. ₁San Jose, Cal., Press of Muirson & Wright₁ 1907.

  3 p. l., 274 p. front., ports. 24ᶜᵐ.

These letters by a Wisconsin officer are unusually good accounts of occupational service in the West; included in the volume are several letters from his wife, who spent the war in the South.

McAdams, Francis Marion.
Every-day soldier life, or A history of the One hundred and thirteenth Ohio volunteer infantry. By F. M. McAdams ... Columbus, C. M. Cott & co., printers, 1884.

400 p. front. (port.) 23^{cm}.

This underrated work is a detailed, reliable, and very revealing account of the Western campaigns.

McAllister, Robert, 1813–1891.
The Civil War letters of General Robert McAllister. Edited by James I. Robertson, Jr. New Brunswick, N. J., Published for the New Jersey Civil War Centennial Commission by Rutgers University Press [1965]

x, 638 p. illus., map, ports. 24 cm.

This collection of 637 letters by a New Jersey officer is a valuable, almost unbroken chronicle of events from First Bull Run to Appomattox.

McBride, John Randolph, 1842–
History of thirty-third Indiana veteran volunteer infantry during the four years of civil war, from Sept. 16, 1861, to July 21, 1865; and incidentally of Col. John Coburn's second brigade, third division, twentieth army corps, including incidents of the great rebellion; by John R. McBride. Indianapolis, W. B. Burford, printer, 1900.

280 p. front., port. 23 cm.

Based in part on the Official Records and a few diaries; a flowery presentation wilts many of the facts concerning the regiment's career.

M'Bride, Robert Ekin, 1846–
In the ranks: from the Wilderness to Appomattox Courthouse. The war, as seen and experienced by a private soldier in the Army of the Potomac. By Rev. R. E. M'Bride ... Cincinnati, Walden & Stowe, 1881.

246 p. front. (port.) 17½ cm.

When a old man attempts to recall the complex experiences of youth, the result is a semi-fabricated, semi-empty work such as this.

McCalmont, Alfred B
Extracts from letters from the front during the War of the Rebellion. [Franklin? Pa.] Printed for private circulation by R. McCalmont [1908?]

134 p. plates, ports. 24 cm.

A good collection of letters by a Pennsylvania officer; very revealing for the Virginia campaigns in the last two years of the war.

McCarthy, Carlton, 1847–
Detailed minutiæ of soldier life in the Army of northern Virginia, 1861–1865, by Carlton McCarthy ... With illustrations by Wm. L. Sheppard ... Richmond, C. McCarthy and company, 1882.

vi, 224 p. front., illus., plates. 18 cm.

This Confederate narrative is deserving of its reputation as "the most interesting and the most informative of all memoirs written by privates"; McCarthy served with the Richmond Howitzers.

McClellan, George Brinton, 1826–1885.
McClellan's own story: the war for the Union, the soldiers who fought it, the civilians who directed it and his relations to it and to them; by George B. McClellan ... New York, C. L. Webster & company, 1887 [1886]

xiv, 678 p. incl. illus., pl., maps, facsim. front. (port.) 23½ cm.

A classic rationalization by one of the war's most controversial figures.

McClellan, Henry Brainerd, 1840–1904.
I rode with Jeb Stuart; the life and campaigns of Major General J. E. B. Stuart. With an introd. and notes by Burke Davis. Bloomington, Indiana University Press [1958]

xv, 455 p. port., maps. 21 cm.

An offset reprinting of the title below, with some editorial work added.

McClellan, Henry Brainerd, 1840–
The life and campaigns of Major-General J. E. B. Stuart, commander of the cavalry of the Army of northern Virginia. By H. B. McClellan ... Boston [etc.] Houghton, Mifflin and company; Richmond, Va., J. W. Randolph and English, 1885.

xv p., 1 l., 468 p. front. (port.) 7 fold. maps. 23½ cm.

Primarily a military biography of the idolized Stuart, yet McClellan, who was chief of staff of Confederate cavalry, inadvertently added many personal observations.

McClendon, William Augustus 1844–
Recollections of war times, by an old veteran, while under Stonewall Jackson and Lieutenant General James Longstreet; how I got in, and how I got out. Montgomery, Ala., The Paragon press, 1909.

238 p. front. (port.) 23^{cm}.

Vivid memoirs by a soldier in the ranks who admitted freely that he was writing from memory.

McCorkle, John, 1838–

Three years with Quantrell; a true story, told by his scout John McCorkle, written by O. S. Barton. Armstrong, Mo., Armstrong herald print [c1914]

157 p. front., ports. 24½ cm.

One of the best sources on Quantrell, though McCorkle sometimes described too vividly events to which he was not a witness.

McCrea, Tully, 1838–1918.

Dear Belle; letters from a cadet & officer to his sweetheart, 1858–1865. Narrative and editing by Catherine S. Crary. Foreword by Bruce Catton. With drawings by Cecile Johnson. [1st ed.] Middletown, Conn., Wesleyan University Press [1965]

xviii, 256 p. illus., ports. 22 cm.

A too-eulogistic story developed around the letters of an Ohio orphan who roomed at West Point with Custer and served in the Army of the Potomac as an artillery officer.

McDermott, Anthony W

A brief history of the 69th regiment Pennsylvania veteran volunteers, from its formation until final muster out of the United States service, by Adjutant Anthony W. McDermott. Also an account of the reunion of the survivors of the Philadelphia brigade and Pickett's division of Confederate soldiers, and the dedication of the monument of the 69th regiment Pennsylvania infantry, at Gettysburg, July 2d and 3d, 1887, and of the rededication, September 11th, 1889, by Captain John E. Reilly. [Philadelphia, D. J. Gallagher & co., 1889]   1 p. l., 106 p. front., plates (incl. ports.) 21½ cm.

Based too much on a shaky memory, and too brief to be of great value.

McDonald, William Naylor, 1834–1898.

A history of the Laurel brigade, originally the Ashby cavalry of the Army of northern Virginia and Chew's battery, by the late Captain William N. McDonald, ordnance officer of the brigade; ed. by Bushrod C. Washington. Published by Mrs. Kate S. McDonald. [Baltimore, Sun job printing office] 1907.

499 p. front., plates, ports. 24 cm.

One of the most noted of early brigade histories; the author adroitly weaves his story from the 1861 formation of the 7th Virginia Cavalry to the 1865 disbandment of this mounted brigade.

McGavock, Randal William, 1826–1863.

Pen and sword; the life and journals of Randal W. McGavock. The biography [by] Herschel Gower. The early journals, 1848–1851; Herschel Gower, editor. The political and Civil War journals, 1853–1862; Jack Allen, editor. Nashville, Tennessee Historical Commission, 1959.

695 p. illus., ports., map. 25 cm.

Contains the diaries of the colonel of the 10th Tennessee; McGavock spent some time in a Federal prison and then was killed at the battle of Raymond, Miss.

McGee, Benjamin F   1834–

History of the 72d Indiana volunteer infantry of the mounted lightning brigade ... Especially devoted to giving the reader a definite knowledge of the service of the common soldier. With an appendix containing a complete roster of officers and men. Written and comp. by B. F. McGee ... Ed. by Wm. R. Jewell ... LaFayette, Ind., S. Vater & co., printers, 1882.

xviii p., 1 l., 698, 21, [1] p. front., port. 24 cm.

Wordy and somewhat disorganized, yet possessed of many personal incidents relative to Western campaigns.

McGrath, Franklin, *ed.*

The history of the 127th New York volunteers, "Monitors," in the war for the preservation of the union—September 8th, 1862, June 30th, 1865. Material collected and arranged by Franklin McGrath ... [n. p., 1898?]

3 p. l., 5–222, [8] p. illus. (incl. maps) ports. 22½ cm.

A detailed account of the regiment's movements, with personal illnesses, deaths, promotions, etc., inserted in chronological order.

McGregor, Charles.

History of the Fifteenth regiment, New Hampshire volunteers, 1862–1863, by Charles McGregor. [Concord, N. H., I. C. Evans] 1900.

xiv, 624 p. incl. illus., ports. front., plates, ports. 24 cm.

A photograph-laden study that is half statistical and half narrative; several primary sources were used in the diary-like presentation; the 15th New Hampshire spent its one year of service in Louisiana.

McGuire, Hunter Holmes, 1835–1900.

The Conferedate cause and conduct in the war between the states, as set forth in the reports of the History committee of the grand camp, C. V., of Virginia, and other Confederate papers, by Hunter McGuire ... and Hon. George L. Christian ... With an introduction by Rev. James Power Smith ... Richmond, Va., L. H. Jenkins [c1907]
xi, 229 p. 2 port. (incl. front.) 22 cm.

Perhaps the most important source for the wounding and death of "Stonewall" Jackson.

McIlwaine, Richard, 1834–

Memories of three score years and ten, by Richard McIlwaine ... New York and Washington, The Neale publishing company, 1908.

4 p. l., vii–xiv, [11]–383 p. front., ports. 23 cm.

Only a small portion of this even-tempered autobiography recounts Rev. McIlwaine's service in the 44th Virginia.

McIntyre, Benjamin Franklin, *b.* 1827.
    Federals on the frontier; the diary of Benjamin F. Mc-
Intyre, 1862–1864. Edited by Nannie M. Tilley. Austin,
University of Texas Press [1963]

    429 p. illus. 24 cm.

The day-by-day experiences in the Trans-Mississippi by a highly observant soldier in the 19th
Iowa; especially good for descriptions of life
and scenes in Texas.

McKay, Charlotte Elizabeth (Johnson)
    Stories of hospital and camp. By Mrs. C. E. McKay.
Philadelphia. Claxton. Remsen & Haffelfinger, 1876.

    2 p. l., vii–xii, 13–230 p. 19½ cm.

A collection of eulogies and sentimentalities,
interspersed with sometimes useful insights on
Union nurses and field hospitals.

McKee, James Cooper.
    Narrative of the surrender of a command of U. S. forces at
Fort Fillmore, N. M., in July, 1861, at the breaking out of the
civil war ... By James Cooper McKee ... 2d ed., rev. and
cor. New York, 1881.

    30 p. 19 cm.

Important only because it recounts a singular
and unknown event in a relatively isolated region.

McKee, James Harvey, 1840–1918.
    Back "in war times". History of the 144th regiment, New
York volunteer infantry, with itinerary, showing contempo-
raneous date of the important battles of the civil war, by
James Harvey McKee ... [New York] H. E. Bailey, 1903.

    378 p. front., plates, ports., maps. 23 cm.

This account is too non-original to be a primary
source; yet it throws some light on campaigns
in South Carolina.

McKim, Randolph Harrison, 1842–1920.
    A soldier's recollections; leaves from the diary of a young
Confederate, with an oration on the motives and aims of the
soldiers of the South, by Randolph H. McKim ... New York
[etc.] Longmans, Green, and co., 1910.

    xvii, 362 p. front., 5 port. 22 cm.

The author re-wrote and embellished his diary
to produce an authentic and valuable narrative
on soldier life in the Army of Northern Virginia.

McKinney, Edward Pascal.
    Life in tent and field, 1861–1865, by E. P. McKinney ...
Boston, R. G. Badger [°1922]

    8 p., 2 l., 11–161 p. front., ports. 21 cm.

Based on memory and supported by hearsay
evidence, this volume is still too general to be
of significance.

McLeod, Martha Norris, *ed.*
    Brother warriors; the reminisences [!] of Union and Confed-
erate veterans, edited, with an introduction, notes, and maps,
by Martha Norris McLeod. Washington, D. C., The Darling
printing company, 1940.

    A–P, 358 p. ports., maps. 23 cm.

A collection of legends, tales, and sentimental
dribblings recounted by veterans at the last
Gettysburg reunion.

McMorries, Edward Young.
    History of the first regiment, Alabama volunteer infantry,
C. S. A., by Edward Young McMorries ... Montgomery, Ala.,
The Brown co., 1904.

    142 p. front., plates. ports., maps (1 fold.) plan. facsim. 23½ cm.

A factual summary of a regiment's actions in
the East, with personal touches here and there.

McMurray, William Josiah, 1842–1905.
    History of the Twentieth Tennessee regiment volunteer in-
fantry, C. S. A. By W. J. McMurray, M. D. Nashville, Tenn.,
The Publication committee, consisting of W. J. McMurray,
D. J. Roberts, and R. J. Neal, 1904.

    520 p. front., ports. 24 cm.

A full and reasonably reliable account of a Western unit, but too often weakened by the author's
impassioned commentaries.

McNeil, Samuel A
    Personal recollections of service in the Army of the
Cumberland and Sherman's army, from August 17, 1861
to July 20, 1865. By S. A. McNeil, company F. 31st Ohio
veteran volunteer infantry. [Richwood, O., 1910?]

    2 p. l., 76 p. 21 cm.

What little data is here is so embellished as to
render the whole pamphlet of untrustworthy
status.

Macnamara, Daniel George.

The history of the Ninth regiment, Massachusetts volunteer infantry, Second brigade, First division, Fifth army corps, Army of the Potomac, June, 1861–June, 1864. By Daniel George Macnamara ... Boston, E. B. Stillings & co., printers, 1899.

xii p., 1 l., 543 p. 24ᶜᵐ.

An even more embellished history than the one conceived thirty-five years earlier by the same author.

Macnamara, Michael H

The Irish Ninth in bivouac and battle; or, Virginia and Maryland campaigns. By M. H. Macnamara ... Boston, Lee and Shepard, 1867.

1 p. l., 306 p. front., pl. 19½ᶜᵐ.

Covering the author's three years' service in the East, these memoirs are too garrulous and opinionated to be of value.

Maddocks, Elden B   1843–

History of the Twenty-sixth Maine regiment ... comp. by Comrade Elden B. Maddocks. Bangor [Me.] C. H. Glass & co., printers, 1899.

viii, [3]–374 p. incl. ports. 23½ᶜᵐ.

Another collection of statistics and unimportant details.

Maddox, George T

Hard trials and tribulations of an old Confederate soldier. By Geo. T. Maddox. Van Buren, Ark., Printed at the Argus office, 1897.

82 p. front. (port.) 19ᶜᵐ.

Highly manufactured, but of possible use in a study of the early campaigns in Missouri.

Main, Edwin M   1837–

The story of the marches, battles and incidents of the Third United States colored cavalry, a fighting regiment in the war of the rebellion, 1861–5. With official orders and reports relating thereto, compiled from the Rebellion records. By Ed. M. Main, late major, New Orleans, Louisiana. Louisville, Ky., The Globe printing company, 1908.

1 p. l., iii, [3]–321 p. front., ports. 23½ᶜᵐ.

Among the better Negro unit histories, but padded with much previously printed material.

Maine. *Gettysburg commission.*

Maine at Gettysburg; report of Maine commissioners prepared by the executive committee ... [Portland; The Lakeside press] 1898.

viii p., 1 l., 602 p. incl. diagr. front., plates. 25ᶜᵐ.

Another of those volumes highlighting the role of a state's troops in a specific campaign.

Maine artillery. *4th battery, 1861–1865.*

History of the Fourth Maine battery, light artillery, in the civil war, 1861–65; containing a brief account of its services compiled from diaries of its members and other sources. Also personal sketches of many of its members and an account of its reunions from 1882 to 1905. Augusta, Me., Burleigh & Flynt, printers, 1905.

vi, [7]–183 p. front. (port.) 23½ᶜᵐ.

A very shallow narrative of events; personal touches are almost non-existent.

Maine infantry. *11th regt., 1861–1866.*

The story of one regiment; the Eleventh Maine infantry volunteers in the war of the rebellion. Comp. by a committee of the regimental association. New York [Press of J. J. Little & co.] 1896.

xv, 435, lxx p. front. (port.) 23ᶜᵐ.

Probably the best of the Maine regimental histories; highly detailed and highly personal; revealing for the Atlanta and Petersburg campaigns.

Malone, Bartlett Yancey, 1838–

The diary of Bartlett Yancey Malone, ed. by William Whatley Pierson, jr.

(*In* The James Sprunt historical publications; pub. under the direction of the North Carolina historical society. Chapel Hill, 1919. 23ᶜᵐ. v. 16, p. [3]–59)

Because of the daily weather observations contained herein, Malone has been called "the unofficial meteorologist for the Army of Northern Virginia;" the author served with the 6th North Carolina.

Malone, Bartlett Yancey, 1838–

Whipt 'em everytime; the diary of Bartlett Yancey Malone. Edited by William Whatley Pierson, Jr. Jackson, Tenn., McCowat-Mercer Press, 1960.

131 p. illus. 21 cm.

An authentic reprint of the above, with a needed introduction and some notes.

Mann, Albert William, 1841–   *comp.*
History of the Forty-fifth regiment, Massachusetts volunteer militia ... comp. by Albert W. Mann ... ₍Boston, Mass., Printed by W. Spooner, ᶜ1908₎

vi p., 1 l., 562, ₍3₎ p. front., plates, ports., maps. 23½ cm.

A contributory work with a natural imbalance of material; as part of the XVII Corps, this regiment campaigned principally in North Carolina.

Marbaker, Thomas D   1846–
History of the Eleventh New Jersey volunteers, from its organization to Appomattox; to which is added experiences of prison life and sketches of individual members, by Thos. D. Marbaker ... Trenton, MacCrellish & Quigley, printers, 1898.

viii, 364 p. front., illus., port. **23**ᶜᵐ.

Based for the most part on the author's diary and the then-unpublished letters of Gen. Robert McAllister (q. v.); a useful volume for the later campaigns in Virginia.

Mark, Penrose G
Red: white: and blue badge, Pennsylvania veteran volunteers. A history of the 93rd regiment, known as the "Lebanon infantry" and "One of the 300 fighting regiments" from September 12th, 1861, to June 27th, 1865. By Penrose G. Mark ... Authorized by the executive committee of the 93rd Pennsylvania veteran volunteer association. ₍Harrisburg, Pa., The Aughinbaugh press, 1911₎

577 p. front., plates, ports. **22**½ᶜᵐ.

Written by a staff officer with a strong penchant for detail, this work embodies everything from newspaper extractions and personal recollections to anecdotes and official dispatches; for the most part, the history is reliable.

Marshall, Albert O
Army life. From a soldier's journal. (Copyrighted.) By Albert O. Marshall. Incidents, sketches and record of a Union soldier's army life, in camp and field; 1861–64. Special ed. Joliet, Ill., Printed for the author, 1886.

₍100₎ p. 20ᶜᵐ.

A heavily embossed account by a soldier whose principal service was in Missouri; interesting passages must be handled with caution.

Marshall, Charles, 1830–1902.
An aide-de-camp of Lee, being the papers of Colonel Charles Marshall, sometime aid-de-camp, military secretary, and assistant adjutant general on the staff of Robert E. Lee, 1862–1865, edited by Major General Sir Frederick Maurice ... Boston, Little, Brown, and company, 1927.

xxix, 287 p. front., illus. (facsim.) plates, ports., maps (part fold.) 22 cm.

Fragmentary and somewhat disjointed, this reminiscence nevertheless is a valuable source for the hierarchy of the Army of Northern Virginia.

Marshall, John Wesley, 1834–1922.
Civil War journal of John Wesley Marshall, recorded on a daily basis and sent, when practicable, to his fiancee, Rachel Ann Tanner. ₍n. p.₎ ᶜ1958.

373 l. 28 cm.

This typescript contains a daily, unusually detailed account by an ever-observing member of the 97th Ohio; and almost unprecedented narrative of army life in the Tennessee-Alabama-Georgia theaters.

Marshall, Thomas B
History of the Eighty-third Ohio volunteer infantry, the Greyhound regiment, by T. B. Marshall ... first sergeant, Co. K. Cincinnati, O., The Eighty-third Ohio volunteer infantry association, 1912.

227 p. front., ports. 23½ cm.

A sometimes revealing story of campaigning in Louisiana; full of many little incidents.

Marvin, Edwin E
The Fifth regiment, Connecticut volunteers. A history compiled from diaries and official reports, by Edwin E. Marvin ... Published for the Reunion association of the regiment. Hartford, Press of Wiley, Waterman & Eaton, 1889.

ix, 394, ₍63₎ p. maps. 24 cm.

Marvin confessed to using state and Federal sources for this history, but the work also possesses a surprising amount of diary excerpts by members of the regiment.

Mason, Frank Holcomb, 1840–1916.
The Forty-second Ohio infantry: a history of the organization and services of that regiment in the war of the rebellion; with biographical sketches of its field officers and a full roster of the regiment. Comp. and written for the Veteran's association of the Forty-second Ohio, by F. H. Mason ... Cleveland, Cobb, Andrews & co., 1876.

306 p., 1 l. front., port. 22ᶜᵐ.

A company captain, Mason worked carefully on this compilation and produced an above-average study; the 42nd Ohio campaigned from West Virginia to Texas.

Massachusetts. *Adjutant-general's office.*
Record of the Massachusetts volunteers, 1861–1865. Published by the adjutant-general, under a resolve of the General court. Boston, Wright & Potter, 1868–70.

2 v. 30ᶜᵐ.

The first serious attempt at assimilating a reference guide on Bay State units; superceded by at least two other, fuller compilations.

Massachusetts artillery. *5th battery*, 1861–1865.

History of the Fifth Massachusetts battery. Organized October 3, 1861, mustered out June 12, 1865. Boston, L. E. Cowles, 1902.

xiv, 991 p. col. front., plates. ports., maps. 25 cm.

A full and useful history, containing excerpts from letters, diaries, and recollections; a good source for the Army of the Potomac.

Massachusetts infantry. *19th regt.*, 1861–1865.

History of the Nineteenth regiment, Massachusetts volunteer infantry, 1861–1865; issued by the History committee. Salem, Mass., The Salem press co., 1906.

vi p., 1 l., 446 p. front., plates, facsim. 22cm.

An unusually detailed history of a regiment in the Army of the Potomac; personal incidents abound, though many are of doubtful authenticity.

Massachusetts infantry. *35th regt.*, 1862–1865.

History of the Thirty-fifth regiment Massachusetts volunteers, 1862–1865. With a roster. By a committee of the regimental association. Boston, Mills, Knight & co., 1884.

viii, 409, 66 p. 19cm.

In this reliable study are a host of personal accounts ranging from the battles of Antietam and Chickamauga to life in Southern prisons.

Massachusetts infantry. *36th regt.*, 1862–1865.

History of the Thirty-sixth regiment Massachusetts volunteers. 1862–1865. By a committee of the regiment. Boston, Rockwell and Churchill, 1884.

xiii, 405 p. 23cm.

Seven different veterans wrote the chapters of this history, which in essence is a human chronicle of a regiment in the IX Corps.

Massachusetts infantry. *44th regt.*, 1862–1863.

Record of the service of the Forty-fourth Massachusetts volunteer militia in North Carolina, August 1862 to May 1863. Boston, Priv. print., 1887.

xvi, 364 p. illus., pl., port., maps, facsim. 26½cm.

A huge book, but too often padded in an attempt to create interest and drama; the authors strove too hard for humor.

Mathews, Alfred Edward, 1831–1874.

Interesting narrative; being a journal of the flight of Alfred E. Mathews, of Stark Co., Ohio, from the State of Texas, on the 20th of April, and his arrival at Chicago on the 28th of May, after traversing on foot and alone a distance of over 800 miles across the States of Louisiana, Arkansas and Missouri, by the most unfrequented routes; together with interesting descriptions of men and things; of what he saw and heard; appearance of the country, habits of the people, &c., &c., &c. [n. p.] 1861. [Denver, N. Mumey, 1961]

34 p. 22 cm.

The unusual travelogue of a Northern-born teacher caught in the South at the outbreak of war. Mathews made his way home in an interesting though roundabout fashion.

Matson, Daniel, 1842–1920.

Life experiences of Daniel Matson. [Fowler, Col., Tribune print, ©1924]

2 p. l., 9–144 p., 1 l. front. (port.) 24cm.

These rambling recollections by a transplanted Englishman throw only minimum light on campaigns in Tennessee.

Maury, Dabney Herndon, 1822–1900.

Recollections of a Virginian in the Mexican, Indian, and Civil wars; by General Dabney Herndon Maury ... New York, C. Scribner's sons, 1894.

xi, 279, [1] p. front. (port.) 20½ cm.

The product of a professional soldier and scholar, these reminiscences pertain to the war along the Gulf and in the Trans-Mississippi.

Mauzy, James H   *b. 1842, comp.*

Historical sketch of the Sixty-eighth regiment Indiana volunteers. Its commanders, officers and men. With short biographies of corps, division and brigade commanders. Rushville, Ind., The Republican co., printers, 1887.

3 p. l., 98 p. port., fold. map. 19 cm.

More statistical than personal; superceded completely by High's study of the same unit.

Meade, George Gordon, 1815–1872.

The life and letters of George Gordon Meade, major-general United States Army, by George Meade ... ed. by George Gordon Meade. New York, C. Scribner's sons, 1913.

2 v. fronts. (v. 1, port.) fold. maps. 23½ cm.

Meade's many blunt and opinionated letters to his wife make this work a rich source for any study of the high command of the Army of the Potomac.

Merrill, Catharine 1824–1900.
The soldier of Indiana in the war for the union ... Indianapolis, Merrill and company, 1866–69.

2 v. fronts., ports., maps. 23cm.

A disorganized collection of essays, reminiscences, biographical sketches, etc. ; unfortunately, it lacks a table of contents and index.

Merrill, Julian Whedon.
Records of the 24th independent battery, N. Y. light artillery, U. S. V. Comp. by J. W. Merrill. [New York] Pub. for the Ladies' cemetery association of Perry, N. Y., 1870.

280, 22 p. plates (incl. plans) 20½cm.

Too impersonal to be more than a chronicle of the battery's activities.

Merrill, Samuel, 1831–1924.
The Seventieth Indiana volunteer infantry in the war of the rebellion, by Samuel Merrill. Indianapolis, The Bowen-Merrill company [1900]

4 p. l., 372 p. front., pl., port. 23½ cm.

Composed in the main of excerpts from diaries and letters, this unit history is a choppy chronicle of 1862-1865 events in the Western theater.

Merrill, Samuel Hill, 1805–1873.
The campaigns of the First Maine and First District of Columbia cavalry. By Samuel H. Merrill ... Portland, Bailey & Noyes, 1866.

xv, [17]–436 p. port. 20 cm.

Written soon after the war, Merrill's study is a reliable account, particularly good for the 1864 operations in Virginia.

Meyer, Henry Coddington, 1844–
Civil war experiences under Bayard, Gregg, Kilpatrick, Custer, Raulston, and Newberry, 1862, 1863, 1864, by Henry C. Meyer ... Priv. print. New York [G. P. Putnam's sons] 1911.

ix, 119 p. front. (port.) 22½cm.

Though moving and human, this account shows signs of having been greatly embellished; Meyer served in two New York cavalry regiments.

Meyers, Augustus, 1841–
Ten years in the ranks, U. S. Army, by Augustus Meyers. New York, The Stirling press, 1914.

3 p. l., 356 p. 22 cm.

Though written largely from memory, this is an unexpectedly good narrative of army ways and life.

Michie, Peter Smith, 1839–1901.
The life and letters of Emory Upton, colonel of the Fourth regiment of artillery, and brevet major-general, U. S. Army. By Peter S. Michie ... With an introduction by James Harrison Wilson ... New York, D. Appleton and company, 1885.

xviii, 511 p. front. (port.) 19½ cm.

Only 135 pages of this work treat of Upton's Civil War career; unfortunately, the author quotes more from the Official Records than from Upton's personal correspondence.

Michigan. *Michigan-Vicksburg military park commission.*
Michigan at Vicksburg; pub. pursuant to a concurrent resolution of the Michigan Legislature, April 11th, 1917, by the Michigan-Vicksburg military park commission; comp. by Captain Charles G. Hampton ... Detroit, Printed by Moore printing company, 1917.

1 p. l., [9]–116 p. front. (port.) illus., pl. 22cm.

An inadequate collection of unrelated material on Wolverine troops at Vicksburg.

Miles, Nelson Appleton, 1839–1925.
Personal recollections and observations of General Nelson A. Miles, embracing a brief view of the civil war; or, From New England to the Golden gate, and the story of his Indian campaigns, with comments on the exploration, development and progress of our great western empire; copiously illustrated with graphic pictures by Frederic Remington and other eminent artists. Chicago, New York, The Werner company, 1896.

vii, 590 p. incl. front., illus., plates, ports. 25 x 21 cm.

In both of his memoirs, Miles treated his Civil War service as but a prelude to his successes against the hapless Indians of the West.

Miles, Nelson Appleton, 1839–1925.
Serving the Republic; memoirs of the civil and military life of Nelson A. Miles ... New York and London, Harper & brothers, 1911.

vii, [1] p., 1 l., 339, [1] p. front., illus. (plans) plates, ports., map. 21½ cm.

Little more than a condensation of the above work.

Military order of the loyal legion of the United States.
District of Columbia commandery.

War papers. ₍nos.₎ 1–25, 25½–
Washington, 1887–19

v. in   23ᶜᵐ.

Military order of the loyal legion of the United States.
Illinois commandery.

Military essays and recollections; papers read before the commandery of the state of Illinois, Military order of the loyal legion of the United States ... Pub. by order of the commandery. Chicago, 1891–

v. fronts., ports., maps. 23½ cm.

Military order of the loyal legion of the United States.
Indiana commandery.

War papers, read before the Indiana commandery, Military order of the loyal legion of the United States. ₍v. 1–   Indianapolis, Published by the Commandery, 1898–

v. front., illus., ports., fold. map. 25ᶜᵐ.

Military order of the loyal legion of the United States.
Iowa commandery.

War sketches and incidents as related by companions of the Iowa commandery, Military order of the loyal legion of the United States. v. 1–   Des Moines, 1893–

v. 23½ᶜᵐ.

Military order of the loyal legion of the United States.
Kansas commandery.

War talks in Kansas; a series of papers read before the Kansas commandery of the Military order of the loyal legion of the United States. ₍v. 1–
Kansas City, Mo., Press of the F. Hudson publishing company, 1906–

v. 22½ᶜᵐ.

Military order of the loyal legion of the United States.
Maine commandery.

War papers, read before the commandery of the state of Maine, Military order of the loyal legion of the United States. v. 1–
Portland, Lefavor-Tower Company, 1898–19

v. plates, ports., maps, plans. 24½ cm.

Military order of the loyal legion of the United States.
Massachusetts commandery.

Civil war papers read before the commandery of the state of Massachusetts, Military order of the loyal legion of the United States ... Boston, For the commandery, 1900.

2 v. 2 plans (1 double) 24½ cm.

Military order of the loyal legion of the United States.
Michigan commandery.

War papers read before the Michigan commandery of the Military order of the loyal legion of the United States ...
v. 1–   ; 1886–   Detroit, Ostler printing company ₍etc.₎ 1888–

v. illus., maps. 22½–23ᶜᵐ.

Military order of the loyal legion of the United States.
Minnesota commandery.

Glimpses of the nation's struggle. ₍1st₎–6th series. Papers read before the Minnesota commandery of the Military order of the loyal legion of the United States ₍1887₎–1903/08. Published for the commandery ... St. Paul, Minn. ₍etc.₎ 1887–1909.

6 v. illus., maps (1 fold.) 23 cm.

Military order of the loyal legion of the United States.
Missouri commandery.

War papers and personal reminiscences. 1861–1865. Read before the Commandery of the state of Missouri, Military order of the loyal legion of the United States. Published by the Commandery. Volume I. St. Louis, Becktold & co., 1892.

vi, 451 p. fold. map. 24ᶜᵐ.

Military order of the loyal legion of the United States. *New York commandery.*

Personal recollections of the war of the rebellion; addresses delivered before the New York commandery of the loyal legion of the United States. 1883–
₍First₎–   series ... New York, Pub. by the commandery ₍etc.₎ 1891–

v. fronts. (ports.) pl. 25ᶜᵐ.

Military order of the loyal legion of the United States.
Ohio commandery.

Sketches of war history, 1861–1865; papers read before the Ohio commandery of the Military order of the loyal legion of the United States, 1883–19   Published by the commandery; v. 1–   Cincinnati, R. Clarke & co., 1888–19
v. illus., plates, ports., maps (part fold.) 24½ cm.

Military order of the loyal legion of the United States.
Oregon commandery.

War paper₍s₎ no. 1–   Oregon commandery, M. O. L. L. U. S. ₍Portland, Or., 1890–

v. 23ᶜᵐ.

Military order of the loyal legion of the United States.
Wisconsin commandery.

War papers read before the commandery of the state of Wisconsin, Military order of the loyal legion of the United States. Pub. under direction of the commandery, vol. 1–   Milwaukee, Burdick, Armitage & Allen ₍etc.₎ 1891–19

v. fronts. (ports.) maps. 23ᶜᵐ.

The more active of the various state commanderies of this organization published volumes containing personal reminiscences of life in camp, battle, and prison. The accounts vary widely in accuracy and quality; generally speaking, however, these volumes can, with considerable digging, yield useful nuggets.

Miller, Delavan S
Drum taps in Dixie; memories of a drummer boy, 1861–1865, by Delavan S. Miller. Watertown, N. Y., Hungerford-Holbrook co., 1905.

vii, 9–256 p. front., plates, ports. 20ᶜᵐ.

Miller was only twelve when war began, and teenage exuberance colored his later remembrances of service in Virginia.

Mills, John Harrison.
Chronicles of the Twenty-first regiment, New York state volunteers. Embracing a full history of the regiment from the enrolling of the first volunteer in Buffalo, April 15, 1861, to the final mustering out, May 18, 1863. Including a copy of muster out rolls of field and staff, and each company ... By J. Harrison Mills ... Buffalo, J. M. Layton, 1867.

v p., 1 l., [9]–294 p., 1 l. front., ports., fold. tables. 30½ x 25ᶜᵐ.

An ornate volume of tributes, disorganizingly arranged and valueless as a unit history.

Mississippi infantry. *11th regt., 1861–1865. Co. G.*
Lamar rifles, a history of Company G, Eleventh Mississippi regiment, C. S. A., with the official roll, giving each man's record from time of enlistment to twenty-ninth of March, eighteen hundred and sixty-five; individual and company sketches ... May, 1861, to April, 1865. [Roanoke, Va., The Stone printing compy., 1802?]

93, [1] p. incl. front., illus. 23½ᶜᵐ.

This useless collection of tributes and biographical sketches has value only for genealogists.

Mixson, Frank M   1846–
Reminiscences of a private, by Frank M. Mixson, Company "E" 1st S. C. Vols. (Hagood's) ... Columbia, S. C., The State company, 1910.

130 p. 3 port. (incl. front.) 20 cm.

Mixson waited too late in life to pen his memoirs of service with Longstreet's First Corps.

Monteiro, Aristides
War reminiscences by the surgeon of Mosby's command. Richmond, Va., E. Waddey, 1890.

viii, [9]–208 p. front. (port.) 18½ᶜᵐ.

An excellent, unexaggerated narrative of life with the Confederacy's foremost partisan ranger; Dr. Monteiro penned his recollections in the decade immediately following the war.

Montgomery, Franklin Alexander, *b.* 1830.
Reminiscences of a Mississippian in peace and war, by Frank A. Montgomery ... Cincinnati, The Robert Clarke company press, 1901.

xv p., 1 l., 305 p. front., ports. 23 cm.

Montgomery's service as a Confederate was confined to Mississippi; a few preserved letters aided his memory in the writing of his below-average narrative.

Montgomery, Horace, 1906–
Johnny Cobb, Confederate aristocrat. Athens, University of Georgia Press, 1964.

viii, 104 p. 22 cm.

Especially worthwhile, for this study contains an interchange of correspondence between a Georgia soldier-planter and his socially prominent family.

Moore, Alison.
The Louisiana Tigers; or, The two Louisiana brigades of the Army of Northern Virginia, 1861–1865. Baton Rouge, La., Ortlieb Press, 1961.

183 p. illus. 24 cm.

A rather flippant sketch, void of scholarly perception, and based solely on well-known and well-used printed sources.

Moore, Edward Alexander, 1842–
The story of a cannoneer under Stonewall Jackson, in which is told the part taken by the Rockbridge artillery in the Army of northern Virginia, by Edward A. Moore ... with introductions by Capt. Robert E. Lee, jr., and Hon. Henry St. George Tucker. Fully illustrated by portraits. Lynchburg, Va., J. P. Bell company, inc., 1910.

331 p. incl. front. plates, ports., facsim. 22 cm.

The favorite Civil War book of Gen. George C. Marshall; a human, moving narrative by a young member of one of the Confederacy's most celebrated units.

Moore, James, *surgeon 9th Pa. cavalry.*
Kilpatrick and our cavalry: comprising a sketch of the life of General Kilpatrick, with an account of the cavalry raids, engagements, and operations under his command, from the beginning of the rebellion to the surrender of Johnston. By James Moore, M. D. ... With 12 illustrations from original designs by Waud. New York, W. J. Widdleton, 1865.

14, [25]–245 p. incl. front. (port.) pl. 19ᶜᵐ.

Basically a factual account, but weakened by the amateur's use of adornment and sentimentality.

Moore, Robert Augustus, 1838–1863.

A life for the Confederacy, as recorded in the pocket diaries of Pvt. Robert A. Moore, Co. G, 17th Mississippi Regiment, Confederate Guards, Holly Springs, Mississippi. Edited by James W. Silver. Foreword by Bell Irvin Wiley. Jackson, Tenn., McCowat-Mercer Press, 1959.

182 p. illus., ports., facsim. 25 cm.

Daily jottings by an educated and mature Mississippian whose candid observations ended abruptly with his death at Chickamauga.

Moors, John Farwell.

History of the Fifty-second regiment, Massachusetts volunteers, by the chaplain, J. F. Moors. Boston, Press of G. H. Ellis, 1893.

220, lxiii p. incl. map. front., port. 24cm

A superior collection of diary entries, letters from the field to newspapers, and extracts from personal correspondence -- all relating to the regiment's brief service in Louisiana.

Morford, Henry 1823–1881.

Red-tape and pigeon-hole generals: as seen from the ranks during a campaign in the Army of the Potomac. By a citizen-soldier ... New York, Carleton, 1864.

318 p. 19 cm.

A delightful denunciation of Federal commanders by a Federal private in the East; much of the book borders on satire.

Morgan, William Henry, 1836–

Personal reminiscences of the war of 1861–5; in camp—en bivouac—on the march—on picket—on the skirmish line—on the battlefield—and in prison, by W. H. Morgan, Lynchburg, Va., J. P. Bell company, inc., 1911.

4 p. l., 7–286 p. front. (port.) 20½ cm.

Written years after the war by a soldier in the 11th Virginia, this work adds little of interest or value to the story of Lee's army.

Morgan, William Henry, 1843–

A narrative of the service of Company D, First Massachusetts heavy artillery, in the war of the rebellion, 1861 to 1865. From the organization of the company to its final discharge; with a list of members, and individual history of each, as far as obtainable. Comp. by Sergeant Wm. H. Morgan. Adopted as the company history, at the annual reunion, February 22, 1905. Boston, Mass., Press of S. Woodberry & co., 1907.

79 p. 19cm.

Too cursory even to be quotable.

Morris, George W

History of the Eighty-first regiment of Indiana volunteer infantry in the great war of the rebellion, 1861 to 1865 ... A regimental roster. Prison life, adventures, etc., by Corporal Geo. W. Morris. [Louisville, Ky., The Franklin printing company, 1901]

202 p. 21½ cm.

A loosely connected compilation of facts and singular incidents pertaining to another regiment in the Western theater.

Morris, Gouverneur, U. S. V., fl. 1860–1890.

The history of a volunteer regiment. Being a succinct account of the organization, services and adventures of the Sixth regiment New York volunteers infantry known as Wilson zouaves. Where they went—what they did—and what they saw in the war of the rebellion, 1861 to 1865. Prepared from official data, by Gouverneur Morris, late U. S. V., illustrated by James E. Taylor. New York, Veteran volunteer publishing company, 1891.

160 p. incl. front., pl., port., maps. 22cm.

The 6th New York campaigned from Pensacola to the Red River. Morris captured all of the drama and most of the color in this narrative of the regiment's unique activities.

Morrison, Marion, 1821–

A history of the Ninth regiment, Illinois volunteer infantry. By the chaplain, Marion Morrison. Monmouth, Ill., J. S. Clark, printer, 1864.

95 p. 22cm.

A personal narrative that treats too much of the unit's organization and first days in camp.

Morse, Bliss, 1837–1923.

Civil War diaries. Compiled, edited, and published by Loren J. Morse. 1st ed. Pittsburg, Kan., Pittcraft, 1964 [c1963]

92 p. illus., facsims, port. 24 cm.

The empty, cryptic jottings of a soldier in the 105th Ohio; of no value to a better understanding of the campaigns of which he was a part.

Morse, Charles Fessenden 1839–

Letters written during the civil war, 1861–1865. [Boston, Mass.] Priv. print., 1898.

3 p. l., [5]–222 p. front. (port.) 23½ cm.

A colonel in the 2nd Massachusetts, Morse wrote almost entirely of military matters during his unit's service first in Virginia and then in the West.

Morse, Francis W

Personal experiences in the war of the great rebellion, from December, 1862, to July, 1865. By F. W. Morse... Albany, Printed, but not published [Munsell, printer] 1866.

iv, [5]–152 p.   23 cm.

Morse's recollections are cursory and seem possessed of much hearsay data; yet his account of Wilson's 1865 raid through Alabama is exceptionally good.

Morton, John Watson.

The artillery of Nathan Bedford Forrest's cavalry, "the wizard of the saddle," by John Watson Morton... Nashville, Tenn., Dallas, Tex., Publishing house of the M. E. church, South, Smith & Lamar, agents, 1909.

374 p.   front., plates (1 fold.) ports., facsims.   24cm.

Morton, chief of artillery in Forrest's cavalry, refreshed his memory by checking painstakingly all available sources.

Mosgrove, George Dallas.

... Kentucky cavaliers in Dixie; or, The reminiscences of a Confederate cavalryman. By Geo. Dallas Mosgrove... Louisville, Ky., Courier-journal job printing co., 1895.

265 p.   front., illus., plates, ports.   22½ cm.

"A strange conglomerate of romanticism and realism, " and possessed of "some of the choicest stories ever to be written about the Civil War.

Mosgrove, George Dallas.

Kentucky cavaliers in Dixie; reminiscences of a Confederate cavalryman. Edited by Bell Irvin Wiley. Jackson, Tenn., McCowat-Mercer Press, 1957.

xxvi p., facsim. (265 p. illus., ports.), [266]–281 p. illus., ports. 22 cm.

A facsimile reprinting of the above, to which have been added incisive introduction, a gallery of useful photographs, and a full index.

Moss, A   Hugh, *b.* 1843 *or* 4.

The diary of A. Hugh Moss, Coulie Croche, St. Landry Parish, Louisiana, stationed at Vicksburg, Miss., April 25, 1863, mustered in the service of Lieutenant Millett, Washington, Louisiana, March 22, 1862; a diary or cursory sketch of events transpiring to my knowledge during the war between the Confederate and United States of America. A daily account ... of the last siege of Vicksburg, beginning May 18 and ending July 4, 1863. [Lake Charles? La., 1948]

56 p.   21 cm.

Of importance only for Moss's recollections while his regiment was besieged at Vicksburg.

Mowris, James A

A history of the One hundred and seventeenth regiment, N. Y. volunteers, (Fourth Oneida,) from the date of its organization, August, 1862, till that of its muster out, June, 1865. By J. A. Mowris, M. D., regimental surgeon. Hartford, Case, Lockwood and co., printers, 1866.

xi, [13]–315 p.   21½ᶜᵐ.

Straightforward, fresh recollections of a soldier whose service was primarily along the Atlantic coast.

Muffly, Joseph Wendel, 1840–   *ed.*

The story of our regiment: a history of the 148th Pennsylvania vols., written by the comrades. Adjt. J. W. Muffly, editor. Des Moines, Ia., The Kenyon printing & mfg. co., 1904.

1096 p.   front., plates, ports.   24½cm.

Teeming with personal incidents and commentaries, this thick study is an extraordinary source for the Chancellorsville - Appomattox campaigns; one of the best regimental histories ever compiled.

Mulholland, St. Clair Augustin, 1839–

The story of the 116th regiment, Pennsylvania infantry. War of secession, 1862–1865. By Brevet Major General St. Clair A. Mulholland. [Philadelphia, F. McManus, jr., & co., printers, 1899]

422 p.   front. (fold. map) plates, ports.   23cm.

Obviously based on Gen. Mulholland's voluminous journal, this well-written and even-tempered account is one of the better narratives of 1863 - 1865 operations in the East.

Munson, John William, 1854–

Reminiscences of a Mosby guerrilla, by John W. Munson ... New York, Moffat, Yard and company, 1906.

x p., 2 l., 277 p.   front., plates, ports., facsims.   21 cm.

Too much manufactured drama, and too much reliance on non-original material.

Murphey, Thomas G

Four years in the war. The history of the First regiment of Delaware veteran volunteers, (infantry,) containing an account of marches, battles, incidents, promotions. The names of all the officers and men who have been connected with the regiment from its organization in 1861, to the close of the war in 1865. By the Rev. Thomas G. Murphey, chaplain ... Philadelphia, J. S. Claxton, 1866.

viii, [9]–315 p.   fold. maps.   19 cm.

A very shallow narrative with limited usefulness.

Murphy, Ignatius Ingoldsby.

Life of Colonel Daniel E. Hungerford, by I. I. Murphy. Hartford, Conn., Press of the Case, Lockwood & Brainard company, 1891.

2 p. l., 319 p. front. (port.) facsims. 23½ cm.

Part of this biography narrates the subject's two-year service with the 36th New York.

Murray, John Ogden, 1840–1921.

Three stories in one: The statesman: The Confederate soldier, the ideal soldier of the world: The South's peerless women of the world; by Major J. Ogden Murray ... [Richmond, Whittet & Shepperson, printers] 1915.

65, [1] p. ports. (incl. front.) 23½ cm.

Composed of three separate addresses, of which the second gives general comments on life in Confederate armies.

Murray, Thomas Hamilton, 1857–

History of the Ninth regiment, Connecticut volunteer infantry, "The Irish regiment," in the war of the rebellion, 1861–65. The record of a gallant command on the march, in battle and in bivouac. By Thomas Hamilton Murray ... New Haven, Conn., The Price, Lee & Adkins co., 1903.

446 p. col. front., plates, ports. 23½ cm.

A disappointing compilation more statistical than personal.

Myers, Frank M *captain 35th Va. cavalry.*

The Comanches: a history of White's battalion, Virginia cavalry, Laurel brig., Hampton div., A. N. V., C. S. A. Written by Frank M. Myers. Late capt. Co. A, 35th Va. cav. Approved by all the officers of the battalion. Baltimore, Kelly, Piet & co., 1871.

400 p. 18½ cm.

A light, witty study of a cavalry unit; comparable in spirit and charm to John Casler's narrative (q. v.).

Myers, John C

A daily journal of the 192d reg't Penn'a volunteers, commanded by Col. William B. Thomas, in the service of the United States for one hundred days. By John C. Myers. Philadelphia, Crissy & Markley, printers, 1864.

203 p. front. (port.) 19¼ cm.

A reworked journal of three months' service behind the lines.

Nagle, Theodore M 1840–

Reminiscences of the civil war, by Theodore M. Nagle, formerly sergeant Company "C", 21st regiment, N. Y. S. vol. inf. [Erie, Pa., Dispatch ptg. & eng. co., 1923]

2 p. l., [9]–84 p., 1 l. ports. 21 cm.

A brief and superficial memoir of two years' service in the 21st New York.

Nash, Eugene Arus, 1837–1911.

A history of the Forty-fourth regiment, New York volunteer infantry, in the civil war, 1861–1865, by Captain Eugene Arus Nash. Chicago, R. R. Donnelley & sons company, 1911.

xiv, 484 p. front., plates, ports., 4 maps. 24 cm.

A disappointing, shallow history of the "Ellsworth Avengers;" too often Nash's prejudices obliterate facts.

Nason, George Warren, 1834–1913.

History and complete roster of the Massachusetts regiments, minute men of '61 who responded to the first call of President Abraham Lincoln, April 15, 1861, to defend the flag and Constitution of the United States ... and biographical sketches of minute men of Massachusetts, by George W. Nason. Boston, Mass., Smith & McCance, 1910.

413, [1], iv, iv p., 1 l. incl. illus., plates. front. 23½ cm.

A laudatory narrative on seven of the first Bay State units to answer Lincoln's call.

The **National** tribune scrap book; stories of the camp, march, battle, hospital and prison told by comrades ... [no. 1– Washington, D. C., The National tribune [1909?]

v. 22 cm.

Another potpourri of minutae by and about Federal soldiers.

Neal, William A *ed. and comp.*

An illustrated history of the Missouri engineer and the 25th infantry regiments; together with a roster of both regiments and the last known address of all that could be obtained ... Ed. and comp. by Dr. W. A. Neal ... Chicago, Donohue and Henneberry, printers, 1889.

vii, [9]–305, [ix]–xvi p. incl. front., illus. 28 port. on 11 pl. 24½ cm.

A hodgepodge of recollections, presented in day-by-day form; very good for how engineers functioned during the Civil War.

Neese, George Michael, 1839–

Three years in the Confederate horse artillery, by George M. Neese ... New York and Washington, The Neale publishing company, 1911.

4 p. l., 3–362 p. 21 cm.

One of the better pen-pictures of Confederate soldier life; Neese's army service was confined to the Shenandoah Valley and surrounding country.

New Jersey infantry. *12th regt., 1862–1865. Co. F.*

History of the men of Co. F, with description of the marches and battles of the 12th New Jersey vols. ... Dedicated to "our dead." By Wm. P. Haines, private, Co. F. Mickleton, N. J. [Camden, C. S. Magrath, printer] 1897.

1 p. l., [v]–vii, 293 p. 22½ cm.

Some diary extracts and recollections were used for a brief narrative, but for the most part this volume is a series of biographical sketches.

New York (*State*) *Monuments commission for the battlefields of Gettysburg, Chattanooga and Antietam.*

In memoriam, Alexander Stewart Webb, 1835–1911; pub. by authority of the state of New York, under the supervision of the New York Monuments commission. Albany, J. B. Lyon company, printers, 1916.

6 p. l., 11–123 p. front., plates, ports., facsim. 27½ᶜᵐ.

A profusely illustrated tribute to Webb, his brigade, and their participation in the battle of Gettysburg.

New York (*State*) *Monuments commission for the battlefields of Gettysburg and Chattanooga.*

In memoriam: George Sears Greene, brevet major-general, United States volunteers, 1801–1899; pub. by authority of the state of New York, under the supervision of the New York Monuments commission. Albany, J. B. Lyon company, state printers, 1909.

106, [2] p. front., plates, ports., maps (part fold.) 28 cm.

Same format as above, except that another general and his troops are the principal subjects.

New York (*State*) *Monuments commission for the battlefields of Gettysburg and Chattanooga.*

In memoriam: Henry Warner Slocum, 1826–1894; pub. by authority of the state of New York, under the supervision of the New York Monuments commission. Albany, J. B. Lyon company, printers, 1904.

4 p. l., 5–325 p. front. (port.) 26 pl., 4 fold. map. 27½ x 22ᶜᵐ.

The best volume in the series; the lengthy biographical sketches of principals in each volume were written by noted historian William F. Fox.

New York infantry. *83d reg't, 1861–1864.*

History of the Ninth regiment N. Y. S. M.—N. G. S. N. Y. (Eighty-third N. Y. volunteers.) 1845–1888. Historian, George A. Hussey. Editor, William Todd. New York, Pub. under the auspices of veterans of the regiment, 1889.

xvi p., 1 l., 737, [1] p. incl. front. plates, ports., maps, plans. 25ᶜᵐ.

A disappointing unit history; too much space is devoted to quotations from other printed sources.

New York infantry. *165th regt., 1862–1865.*

History of the Second battalion Duryee Zouaves, One hundred and sixty-fifth regt. New York volunteer infantry, mustered in the United States service at Camp Washington, Staten Island, N. Y.... [New York?] 1905.

330 p., 1 l. 24ᶜᵐ.

A useless compilation of statistics.

Newcomb, Mary A   "*Mrs.* **H. A. W. Newcomb**"
1817–1893?

Four years of personal reminiscences of the war. Chicago, H. S. Mills & co., 1893.

vii, [9]–131 p. front. (port.) 19½ᶜᵐ.

A volunteer nurse for the Federal armies in the West, Mrs. Newcomb was so blinded by her hatred of slavery that her memoirs are slanted to the point of uselessness.

Newcomer, Christopher Armour.

Cole's cavalry; or, Three years in the saddle in the Shenandoah valley, by C. Armour Newcomer ... Baltimore, Cushing and co., booksellers and stationers, 1895.

x, [9]–165, [1] p. front., port. 23½ᶜᵐ.

Equally divided between Cole's service in the Shenandoah Valley and his experiences as a prisoner of war.

Newell, Joseph Keith, *ed.*

"Ours." Annals of 10th regiment, Massachusetts volunteers, in the rebellion. Ed. by Captain Joseph Keith Newell ... Springfield, C. A. Nichols & co., 1875.

609 p. front., port. 23½ cm.

The first half of this work is a diary-like narrative of the regiment's career -- and it is good for personal incidents in field and camp; biographical sketches comprise the remainder.

Newsome, Edmund
Experience in the war of the great rebellion. By a soldier of the Eighty-first regiment Illinois volunteer infantry. From August 1862, to August 1865. Including nearly nine months of life in southern prisons, at Macon, Savannah, Charleston, Columbia and other places. Carbondale, Ill., E. E. Newsome, 1879.

1 p. l., 137, [4] p. 14½ᶜᵐ.

A cheaply printed but authentic account of Western service, the Red River campaign, and prison life in various locales of the South.

Newton, Alexander Herritage, 1837–
Out of the briars; an autobiography and sketch of the Twenty-ninth regiment, Connecticut volunteers, by A. H. Newton ... with introduction by Rev. J. P. Sampson ... [Philadelphia, The A. M. E. book concern, ᶜ1910]

xv p., 1 l., 19–269 p. front., plates, ports. 21ᶜᵐ.

Though this memoir of service in the 29th Connecticut is slim, it is extremely valuable as one of the few narratives written by a Negro soldier.

Newton, James King, d. 1892.
A Wisconsin boy in Dixie, the selected letters of James K. Newton. Edited by Stephen E. Ambrose. Madison, University of Wisconsin Press, 1961.

188 p. illus. 23 cm.

Youthful exuberance toward war is reflected throughout these letters from a schoolteacher-turned-soldier to his parents.

Nichols, G   W   of Jesup, Ga.
A soldier's story of his regiment (61st Georgia) and incidentally of the Lawton-Gordon-Evans Brigade, Army Northern Virginia. Kennesaw, Ga., Continental Book Co., 1961 [ᶜ1898]

291 p. illus. 21 cm.

Based on a newspaper article written shortly after the war, Nichols' reminiscences are a witty, fast-moving summary of life in Lee's army.

Nichols, George Ward, 1837–1885.
The story of the great march. From the diary of a staff officer. By Brevet Major George Ward Nichols ... With a map and illustrations. New York, Harper & brothers, 1865.

xii, [13]–394 p. incl. front. (ports.) illus., plates. fold. map. 19½ cm.

Better known as a prolific postwar novelist, Nichols first gained fame with this dramatic but opinionated memoir.

Nichols, James Moses, 1835–1886.
Perry's saints; or, The fighting parson's regiment in the war of the rebellion; by James M. Nichols. Boston, D. Lothrop and company [1886]

299 p. incl. illus., plates, map, plans. fold. map, plan. 19ᶜᵐ.

Contains diaries and reminiscences of several members of the 48th New York; the regiment took part in the major operations along the South Carolina and Florida coasts.

Nichols, Samuel Edmund, 1842–1898.
"Your soldier boy Samuel"; civil war letters of Lieut. Samuel Edmund Nichols, Amherst, '65, of the 37th regiment Massachusetts volunteers, arranged by Charles Sterling Underhill. [Buffalo] Priv. print., 1929.

133 p. front., plates, ports., facsims. 20ᶜᵐ.

This limited edition contains some of the letters written by a Massachusetts officer whose service was mostly in Virginia.

Nickerson, Ansel D   d. 1896.
A raw recruit's war experiences. By Ansel D. Nickerson ... Providence, Printed by the Press company, 1888.

viii, 64 p. front. 17½ x 14ᶜᵐ.

The too-personal narrative of nine months' service in the 11th Rhode Island.

Nisbet, James Cooper.
Four years on the firing line, by Col. James Cooper Nisbet. Chattanooga, The Imperial press [ᶜ1914]

2 p. l., 445 p. front. (port.) 20½ᶜᵐ.

Excellent memoirs by a Georgia farmer who rose to command of a regiment; much personal information on major battles in both theaters.

Nisbet, James Cooper.
4 years on the firing line. Edited by Bell Irvin Wiley. [Jackson, Tenn.] McCowat-Mercer Press, 1963.

267 p. illus. 22 cm.

An improved, annotated edition prepared by the leading authority on Civil War soldiers.

Noel, Theophilus, 1840–

Autobiography and reminiscences of Theophilus Noel. Chicago, Theo. Noel company print, 1904.

348 p., 1 l. front. (port.) plates. 23½ᶜᵐ.

Important because of the light it throws on Sibley's campaign in the Southwest.

Noel, Theophilus, *b.* 1840.

A campaign from Santa Fe to the Mississippi; being a history of the old Sibley Brigade. With an introd. by Neal Austin. Raleigh, C. R. Sanders, Jr., 1961.

[17] p., facsim. (152 p. facsims.), [2] p. 26 cm.

A beautifully printed and bound reissue of Noel's original text; editorial trappings are absent.

Noel, Theophilus, *b.* 1840.

A campaign from Santa Fe to the Mississippi, being a history of the old Sibley Brigade from its first organization to the present time; its campaigns in New Mexico, Arizona, Texas, Louisiana, and Arkansas in the years 1861–2–3–4. Newly edited and with an introd. by Martin Hardwick Hall and Edwin Adams Davis. Houston, Tex., Stagecoach Press, 1961.

xxvii, 183 p. maps. 24 cm.

A reset text, a 14-page introduction, and some explanatory notes make this the best edition of Noel's recollections; however, it too lacks an index.

Nolan, Alan T

The Iron Brigade; a military history. With maps by Wilson K. Hoyt III. New York, Macmillan, 1961.

412 p. illus. 22 cm.

A painstakingly researched history of a fighting unit from the Old Northwest; no known facts have been omitted.

Norman, William M   1833–

A portion of my life; being of short & imperfect history written while a prisoner of war on Johnson's Island, 1864. Winston-Salem, N. C., J. F. Blair, 1959.

242 p. illus. 22 cm.

Written while the author was a prisoner of war at Johnson's Island, these slim reminiscences contain an unusual number of observations on the battles of Fredericksburg, Chancellorsville, and Gettysburg.

North, Thomas.

Five years in Texas; or, What you did not hear during the war from January 1861 to January 1866. A narrative of his travels, experiences, and observations, in Texas and Mexico. By Thomas North. Cincinnati, Elm street printing co., 1871.

viii, [9]–231 p. 18ᶜᵐ.

Written by a Northerner who became a preacher in order to avoid conscription, this is a barbed commentary on the Lone Star State during the war years.

Norton, Chauncey S

"The red neck ties," or, History of the Fifteenth New York volunteer cavalry, containing a record of the battles, skirmishes, marches, etc., that the regiment participated in from its organization in August, 1863, to the time of its discharge in August, 1865. Compiled and edited by Chauncey S. Norton. Ithaca, Journal book and job printing house, 1891.

vii, [9]–152 p. front. (port.) 20ᶜᵐ.

Brevity is the major weakness here, although an occasional related incident does enrich the story.

Norton, Henry, *of Co. H, 8th N. Y. cavalry.*

Deeds of daring, or, History of the Eighth N. Y. volunteer cavalry, containing a complete record of the battles, skirmishes, marches, etc., that the gallant Eighth New York cavalry participated in, from its organization in November, 1861, to the close of the rebellion in 1865. Compiled and edited by Henry Norton. Norwich, N. Y., Chenango telegraph printing house, 1889.

vii, [9]–184 p., 1 l. front. (port.) 20ᶜᵐ.

Composed for the most part of the author's diary-- which has very little value.

Norton, Oliver Willcox.

Army letters, 1861–1865. Being extracts from private letters to relatives and friends from a soldier in the field during the late civil war, with an appendix containing copies of some official documents, papers and addresses of later date. By Oliver Willcox Norton, private Eighty-third regiment Pennsylvania volunteers, first lieutenant Eighth United States colored troops ... [Chicago, Printed by O. L. Deming, 1903]

355 p. incl. front., plates (1 col.) ports. 23½ᶜᵐ.

Although Norton's letters reveal much on civilian scenes and army life in the Eastern theater, their usefulness is limited by his narrow vision.

Nott, Charles Cooper, 1827–1916.

Sketches of the war: a series of letters to the North Moore street school of New York. By Charles C. Nott ... New York, C. T. Evans, 1863.

174 p. 19½ cm.

Exceptionally good account of the first battles in the West by a captain in the 5th Iowa Cavalry; his prison life, which began in the summer of 1863, is vividly described in another volume, Sketches in Prison Camps.

Noyes, George Freeman, 1824–1868.
The bivouac and the battlefield; or, Campaign sketches in Virginia and Maryland. By George F. Noyes ... New York, Harper & brothers, 1863.

xi, [13]–339 p. 20 cm.

Capt. Noyes served for a year in the Army of the Potomac; his narrative adds nothing to the campaigns of which he was a part.

Oates, William Calvin, 1835–1910.
The war between the union and the confederacy and its lost opportunities, with a history of the 15th Alabama regiment and the forty-eight battles in which it was engaged ... the war between the United States and Spain, by Williams C. Oates ... 5th thousand. New York and Washington, The Neale publishing company, 1905.

xxiv, [25]–808 p. front., plates, ports. 23 cm.

An opinionated but generally reliable commentary on life in the Army of Northern Virginia; written by the Colonel of the 15th Alabama.

O'Connor, Henry.
History of the First regiment of Iowa volunteers. By Henry O'Connor, a private in company "A". Originally prepared for the Iowa state historical society. Muscatine, Printed at the Faust first premium printing house, 1862.

24 p. 22 cm.

Extremely brief report of the regiment's formation and later participation in the battle of Wilson's Creek; some personal insights.

O'Ferrall, Charles Triplett, 1840–1905.
Forty years of active service; being some history of the war between the confederacy and the union and of the events leading up to it, with reminiscences of the struggle and accounts of the author's experiences of four years from private to lieutenant-colonel and acting colonel in the cavalry of the Army of northern Virginia ... by Charles T. O'Ferrall. (3d thousand) New York and Washington, The Neale publishing company, 1904.
367 p. front. (port.) 22½ cm.

Half of this very personal narrative recounts the author's service in the Shenandoah Valley as an officer in the 12th Virginia Cavalry; O'Ferrall later served as a congressman and as governor of Virginia.

Ohio. *Shiloh battlefield commission.*
Ohio at Shiloh: report of the commission, by T. J. Lindsey [Cincinnati. Printed by C. J. Krehbiel & co., 1903]

iv, 226 p. front., plates, fold. map. 24 cm.

Important principally for thirty-four sketches of Buckeye units that fought in the battle.

Ohio. *Vicksburg battlefield commission.*
Ohio at Vicksburg; report of the Ohio Vicksburg battlefield commission, by W. P. Gault ... secretary of the commission. [Columbus? O., °1906]

3 p. l., 3–374 p. front. (6 port.) illus. (map) plates, double map. 23½ cm.

Similar to the preceding volume except that here Vicksburg is the setting.

Ohio artillery. *16th battery,* 1861–1865.
History of the Sixteenth battery of Ohio volunteer light artillery, U. S. A., from enlistment, August 20, 1861, to muster out, August 2, 1865. Compiled from the diaries of comrades, the best recollections of survivors, and official records. [n. p.] 1906.

xiv, 202 (i. e. 220) p. illus. (incl. ports., maps, facsim.) 19 cm.

A brief but entertaining narrative that elaborates on individual acts of battery members.

Ohio cavalry. *3d regt.,* 1861–1865.
History of the service of the Third Ohio veteran volunteer cavalry in the war for the preservation of the Union from 1861–1865. Compiled from the official records and from diaries of members of the regiment by Serg't Thos. Crofts, Company C, regimental historian ... Toledo, O., Columbus, O., The Stoneman press, 1910.

296, [4] p. front., plates, ports. 25 cm.

Presented in diary form; though padded with material from the Official Records, it is still a useful and informative source.

Ohio infantry. *9th regt.,* 1861–1864.
"Die Neuner." Eine schilderung der kriegsjahre des 9ten regiments Ohio vol. infanterie, vom 17. april 1861 bis 7. juni 1864. Mit einer einleitung von oberst Gustav Tafel. Cincinnati, O., Druck von S. Rosenthal & co., 1897.

ix, 11–290 p. incl. front. (5 port.) illus. 20 cm.

Above-average memoirs of service in the West by an officer of the all-German 9th Ohio.

Ohio infantry. *32d regt.,* 1861–1865.
History of the Thirty-second regiment Ohio veteran volunteer infantry. Ed. by E. Z. Hays ... Columbus, O., Cott & Evans, printers, 1896.

viii, [9]–270 p. front., pl., ports. 23½ cm.

Inadequate as a unit history.

Ohio infantry. *94th regt., 1862–1865.*

Record of the Ninety-fourth regiment, Ohio volunteer infantry, in the war of the rebellion. Cincinnati, The Ohio Valley press [189–?]

166 p. 24ᶜᵐ.

A day-by-day tribute, with an occasional fact inserted.

Olmstead, Charles H

Reminiscences of service with the First volunteer regiment of Georgia, Charleston harbor, in 1863. An address delivered before the Georgia historical society, March 3, 1879, by Colonel Charles H. Olmstead. Savannah, Ga., Printed and presented by J. H. Estill, 1879.

15 p. 23½ᶜᵐ.

A cursory description of Charleston and its 1863 defenses.

Opie, John Newton.

A rebel cavalryman with Lee, Stuart, and Jackson, by John N. Opie. Chicago, W. B. Conkey company, 1899.

336 p. front., illus., plates, ports., facsim. 20ᶜᵐ.

Opie left the Stonewall Brigade and campaigned as a cavalryman until 1864 capture; the remainder of the narrative recounts his experiences at Elmira.

Orwig, Joseph Ray, *b.* 1838.

History of the 131st Penna. volunteers, war of 1861–5. By Capt. Joseph R. Orwig ... Williamsport, Pa., Sun book and job printing house, 1902.

269, [1] p. front., ports. 23ᶜᵐ.

Much on the war in the East, but little on the regiment's part in it.

Osborn, Hartwell.

Trials and triumphs; the record of the Fifty-fifth Ohio volunteer infantry, by Captain Hartwell Osborn and others; with eighty portraits, four views, and ten maps. Chicago, A. C. McClurg & co., 1904.

364 p. front., plates, ports., maps. 23ᶜᵐ.

A strictly military history of a unit that served in the East through Gettysburg and then participated in the 1864–1865 engagements in the West.

Osborne, William H

The history of the Twenty-ninth regiment of Massachusetts volunteer infantry, in the late war of the rebellion. By William H. Osborne ... Boston, A. J. Wright, printer, 1877.

393 p. 23½ᶜᵐ.

The detailed, sometimes personal travelogue of a unit that saw action from the Peninsula to Vicksburg.

Otto, John.

History of the 11th Indiana battery, connected with an outline history of the Army of the Cumberland during the war of the rebellion. 1861–1865. By John Otto ... [Fort Wayne, Ind., W. D. Page, 1894]

109, [2] p. 22½ᶜᵐ.

Without benefit of any wartime notes, Otto recalled his four years of fighting in the major Western battles.

Our living and our dead; devoted to North Carolina—her past, her present and her future. v. 1–4, no. 1; Sept. 1874–Mar. 1876. Raleigh, N. C. [1874–76]

4 v. illus., plates, port. 23½ᶜᵐ. monthly.

A short-lived periodical that contained much chauvinistic writings; however, some personal accounts of value are interspersed amid the not-so-useful.

Owen, William Miller, 1832–

In camp and battle with the Washington artillery of New Orleans. A narrative of events during the late civil war from Bull run to Appomattox and Spanish fort ... By William Miller Owen ... Boston, Ticknor & co., 1885.

1 p. l., xv p., 1 l., 467 p. front., pl., maps. 22½ cm.

The unchallenged champion of Louisiana soldiers' narratives; packed with color, drama, personal incidents, and battle descriptions, this volume is a Confederate classic.

Owens, Ira S

Greene County in the war. Being a history of the Seventy-fourth regiment, with sketches of the Twelfth, Ninety-fourth, One hundred and tenth, Forty-fourth, and One hundred and fifty-fourth regiments and the Tenth Ohio battery, embracing anecdotes, incidents and narratives of the camp, march and battlefield, and the author's experience while in the army. By Ira S. Owens. Xenia, O., Torchlight job rooms, 1872.

2 p. l., [ix]–xii, [13]–196 p. 18ᶜᵐ.

This work is little more than a series of short sketches on several Buckeye units.

Owens, John Algernon.

Sword and pen; or, Ventures and adventures of Willard Glazier ... in war and literature ... By John Algernon Owens ... Philadelphia, P. W. Ziegler & company, 1881.

xvi p., 1 l., 21–436 p. front. (port.) plates. 19¼ cm.

Nothing more than a combination of two of the narratives written by Capt. Glazier and previously cited.

Page, Charles A

Letters of a war correspondent. By Charles A. Page ... Edited, with notes, by James R. Gilmore ... Boston, L. C. Page and company, 1899 ₁pub. 1898₁

xii p., 1 l., 397 p. front., port., maps. 23 cm.

Page was chief reporter in the field for Greeley's New York Tribune, and his vivid commentaries on the Eastern campaigns beginning with Gaines's Mill explain why.

Page, Charles Davis, 1839–

History of the Fourteenth regiment, Connecticut vol. infantry. By Charles D. Page ... Meriden, Conn., The Horton printing co., 1906.

509 p. incl. illus., plates, ports. front. 23½ cm.

Largely statistical, with an occasional reminiscences by a member of the regiment.

Page, Richard Channing Moore 1841–

Sketch of Page's battery, or Morris artillery, 2d corps, Army northern Virginia, by one of the company. New York, T. Smeltzer, stationer and printer, 1885.

82 p., 1 l. 18½ cm.

An overly expensive booklet, owing more to the scarcity of copies than to the contents of its text.

Palfrey, Francis Winthrop, 1831–1889.

Memoir of William Francis Bartlett. By Francis Winthrop Palfrey. Boston, Houghton, Osgood and company, 1878.

1 p. l., 309 p. front. (port.) facsim. 18½ cm.

The first half of this volume is an intimate account of Bartlett's service as a member of the 20th Massachusetts; Palfrey had access to numerous letters and wartime manuscripts.

Palmer, Abraham John, 1847–1922.

The history of the Forty-eighth regiment New York state volunteers, in the war for the union. 1861–1865. By Abraham J. Palmer ... Brooklyn, Pub. by the Veteran association of the regiment, 1885.

xvi, 314, ₁2₁ p. front., illus., pl., port., maps. 21½ᶜᵐ.

A dry, drab account when compared to James M. Nichols' history of the same unit.

Palmer, Donald McN

Four weeks in the Rebel army. By Don Mc. N. Palmer. New London ₁Conn.₁ D. S. Ruddock, 1865.

40 p. 22ᶜᵐ.

Somewhat of a tongue-in-cheek account of Price's 1864 raid, by a Connecticut man "impressed" into service with Price.

Palmer, Edwin Franklin 1836–1914.

The second brigade; or, Camp life. By a volunteer ... Montpelier, Printed by E. P. Walton, 1864.

224 p. 19½ᶜᵐ.

A rather weak memoir of service in the 13th Vermont.

Palmer, John McAuley, 1817–1900.

Personal recollections of John M. Palmer; the story of an earnest life. Cincinnati, The R. Clarke company, 1901.

xv p., 1 l., 631 p. front., ports., facsims. 24 cm.

Written by a distinguished Illinois statesman and soldier; most of the chapters on the war period are composed largely of his official dispatches and reports.

Palmer, Sarah A

The story of Aunt Becky's army-life. By S. A. Palmer. New York, J. F. Trow & co., 1867.

xix, 215 p. front. (port.) plates. 19½ᶜᵐ.

An embellished tale of woe and grief by a sentimentalist who served as a nurse for the wounded of the Army of the Potomac.

Park, Robert Emory, 1868–

Sketch of the Twelfth Alabama infantry of Battle's brigade, Rode's division, Early's corps, of the Army of northern Virginia, by Robert Emory Park ... Richmond, W. E. Jones, book and job printer, 1906.

106 p. 23ᶜᵐ.

Much of this unit history consists of the author's own and many experiences, which appeared originally in serial form in the <u>Southern Historical Society Papers</u>.

Parker, David Bigelow, 1842–1910.

A Chautauqua boy in '61 and afterward; reminiscences by David B. Parker, second lieutenant, Seventy-second New York, detailed superintendent of the mails of the Army of the Potomac, United States marshal, district of Virginia, chief post office inspector; ed. by Torrance Parker; introduction by Albert Bushnell Hart ... Boston, Small, Maynard and company [c1912]

xxvi, 388 p. front., plates, ports., facsims. 21½ cm.

Capt. Parker served briefly in the 72nd New York before becoming an army marshal and post office inspector; his memoirs neglect battles but reveal much on the outstanding Federal figures.

Parker, Francis Jewett, 1825–1909.

The story of the Thirty-second regiment, Massachusetts infantry. Whence it came; where it went; what it saw, and what it did. By Francis J. Parker, colonel. Boston, C. W. Calkins & co., 1880.

xi, 260 p. 20 cm.

Parker's service ended in 1862; but he continued his account through the course of the war; a typical unit history.

Parker, John Lord.

Henry Wilson's regiment. History of the Twenty-second Massachusetts infantry, the Second company sharpshooters, and the Third light battery, in the war of the rebellion. By John L. Parker ... assisted by Robert G. Carter ... and the historical committee. Boston, Pub. by the regimental association, Press of Rand Avery co., 1887.

xxii p., 1 l., 591 p. front., pl., port. 23ᶜᵐ.

A full and useful history; many men in the 22nd Massachusetts re-enlisted in 1864 in the 32nd Massachusetts.

Parker, Thomas H   *capt. 51st Pa. infantry.*

History of the 51st regiment of P. V. and V. V., from its organization, at Camp Curtin, Harrisburg, Pa., in 1861, to its being mustered out of the United States service at Alexandria, Va., July 27th, 1865. By Thomas H. Parker ... Philadelphia, King & Baird, printers, 1869.

xx, [9]–703 p. front., ports. 21½ cm.

A narrative of exceptional quality and based on the author's extensive daily notes; the regiment saw action in both major theaters.

Partridge, Charles Addison, 1843–   *ed.*

History of the Ninety-sixth regiment, Illinois volunteer infantry, pub. under the auspices of the Historical society of the regiment ... Ed. by Charles A. Partridge. Chicago [Brown, Pettibone & co., printers] 1887.

xv, 17–938, [2] p. front., plates, ports., maps. 24ᶜᵐ.

This would be a much more revealing narrative except for the fact that Partridge departs from the regiment in 1864 to recount his prison life.

Patrick, Marsena Rudolph, 1811–1888.

Inside Lincoln's Army; the diary of Marsena Rudolph Patrick, Provost Marshal General, Army of the Potomac. Edited by David S. Sparks. New York, T. Yoseloff [1964]

536 p. illus., ports. 22 cm.

One of the better diaries to appear in recent years; Patrick, who saw much and had opinions on everything, filled his journal with provocative observations.

Patrick, Robert, 1835–1866.

Reluctant rebel; the secret diary of Robert Patrick, 1861–1865. Edited by F. Jay Taylor. [Baton Rouge] Louisiana State University Press [1959]

271 p. illus. 24 cm.

A basic, authoritative source on operations behind the front lines of the West; Patrick, an articulate member of the 4th Louisiana, throws light on such little-known subjects as army logistics and civilian conditions.

Paver, John M   , 1839–

What I saw from 1861 to 1864; personal recollections of John M. Paver, 1st lieutenant Company C, and R. Q. M. 5th Ohio vol. infantry. [Indianapolis, Scott-Miller company, 1906?]

100 p. ports. 23ᶜᵐ.

An empty memoir that contains nothing not found in other sources.

Paxton, Elisha Franklin, 1828–1863.

Memoir and memorials: Elisha Franklin Paxton, brigadier-general, c. s. a., composed of his letters from camp and field while an officer in the Confederate army, with an introductory and connecting narrative, collected and arranged by his son, John Gallatin Paxton ... Printed, not published, 1905.

vi, 114 p. 24½ᶜᵐ.

This volume, privately printed for the family, is highly important for the warmly human comments of one of the commanders of the Stonewall Brigade.

Payne, Edwin Waters, 1837–

History of the Thirty-fourth regiment of Illinois volunteer infantry. September 7, 1861, July 12, 1865. [By] Edwin W. Payne ... [Clinton, Ia., Allen printing company, printers, 1903]

viii, 370 p. front., illus., ports., maps. 23½ᶜᵐ.

A badly organized composite of comrades' reminiscences and testimonials; the 34th served in the Western theater.

Peck, Rufus H 1839?–

Reminiscences of a Confederate soldier of Co. C., 2nd Va. cavalry. By R. H. Peck ... [Fincastle? Va., 1913]

cover-title, 73 p. 2 port. 21ᶜᵐ.

Another unreliable tract written from memory a half-century after the war.

Pellet, Elias Porter, 1837–

History of the 114th regiment, New York state volunteers. Containing a perfect record of its services, embracing all its marches, campaigns, battles, sieges and sea-voyages, with a biographical sketch of each officer, and a complete register of the regiment ... By Brevet-Major Elias P. Pellet. Norwich, N. Y., Telegraph & chronicle power press print, 1866.

1 p. l., viii, ii p., 1 l., 406 p. front. (port.) 20½ᶜᵐ.

Based for the most part on Pellet's wartime journals; a fresh memoir of Federal service in Louisiana and the Valley of Virginia.

Pender, William Dorsey, 1834–1863.

The general to his lady; the Civil War letters of William Dorsey Pender to Fanny Pender. Edited by William W. Hassler. Chapel Hill, University of North Carolina Press [1965]

xiii, 271 p. illus., facsims., ports. 24 cm.

Based on four fragmentary diaries, and memory thirty years after the war; the text centers on Fredericksburg and Chancellorsville and adds little to each.

Pennsylvania. *Chickamauga-Chattanooga battlefields commission.*

Pennsylvania at Chickamauga and Chattanooga. Ceremonies at the dedication of the monuments erected by the commonwealth of Pennsylvania to mark the positions of the Pennsylvania commands engaged in the battles ... 1897. [Harrisburg, Pa., W. S. Ray, state printer, 1901]

499 p. front., plates, ports. 24½ cm.

A full though at times unbalanced compendium of Keystone troops in action at two Western battles.

Pennsylvania. *Gettysburg battlefield commission.*

Pennsylvania at Gettysburg. Ceremonies at the dedication of the monuments erected by the commonwealth of Pennsylvania to Major-General George G. Meade, Major-General Winfield S. Hancock, Major-General John F. Reynolds, and to mark the positions of the Pennsylvania commands engaged in the battle ... [Harrisburg, W. S. Ray, state printer] 1914–

v. fronts., plates (part fold., 1 col.) ports., maps (part fold.) 24½ cm.

This four-volume work is the last word on the contribution of Pennsylvania troops at the most noted battle fought on their soil.

Pennsylvania cavalry. *3d regt.,* 1861–1865.

History of the Third Pennsylvania cavalry, Sixtieth regiment Pennsylvania volunteers, in the American civil war, 1861–1865. Comp. by the Regimental history committee, in accordance with a resolution of the Third Pennsylvania cavalry association. Philadelphia, Franklin printing company, 1905.

xxxvi, 614 p. front., plates, ports., fold. maps. 25½ cm.

An exceptionally full, day-by-day chronicle of the regiment first commanded by William W. Averell; indispensable for an insight into Eastern cavalry operations throughout the four years of war.

Pennsylvania cavalry. *11th regt.,* 1861–1865.

History of the Eleventh Pennsylvania volunteer cavalry, together with a complete roster of the regiment and regimental officers. Philadelphia, Franklin printing company, 1902.

289 p. front., ports. 24ᶜᵐ.

A below-average compilation with little of concrete value.

Pennsylvania cavalry. *17th regt.,* 1862–1865.

History of the Seventeenth regiment Pennsylvania volunteer cavalry, or one hundred and sixty-second in the line of Pennsylvania volunteer regiments, war to suppress the rebellion, 1861–1865; comp. from records of the rebellion, official reports, recollections, reminiscences, incidents, diaries and company rosters, with an appendix, by H. P. Moyer, formerly bugler Co. E, 17th regt., Pa. vol. cavalry. [Lebanon, Pa., Sowers printing company, 1911]

472 p. front., plates, ports. 24 cm.

Much statistical and biographical data, but lacking in factual and personal matters.

Pennsylvania cavalry. *18th regt.,* 1862–1865.

History of the Eighteenth regiment of cavalry, Pennsylvania volunteers (163d regiment of the line) 1862–1865 ... comp. & ed. by the Publication committee of the regimental association. New York [Wynkoop Hallenbeck Crawford co.] 1909.

299 p. col. front., plates, ports., maps. 23 cm.

A series of shallow essays that together still leave a history of the regiment wanting.

Pennsylvania infantry. *23d regt.*, 1861–1864.

History of the Twenty-third Pennsylvania volunteer infantry. Birneys zouaves: three months and three years service, civil war … Comp. by the secretary by order of the Survivors association, Twenty third regiment … 1903–1904. [Philadelphia? 1904?]

432 p. front. (group of ports.) illus. (incl. ports) 25½ cm.

A melange of reports, reminiscences, and anecdotes, but important because this was the regiment with which David Birney got his start on the rise to general.

Pennsylvania infantry. *45th regt.*, 1861–1865.

History of the Forty-fifth regiment Pennsylvania veteran volunteer infantry, 1861–1865, written by the comrades. Ed. and arranged by Allen D. Albert … Williamsport, Pa., Grit publishing company, 1912.

530 p. plates, ports. 24cm.

A brief narrative, company sketches, and a series of personal recollections form a disorganized summary of the unit's Western service.

Pennsylvania infantry. *52d regt.*, 1861–1865.

The campaigns of the Fifty-second regiment, Pennsylvania volunteer infantry, first known as "The Luzerne regiment"; being the record of nearly four years' continuous service, from October 7, 1861, to July 12, 1865, in the war for the suppression of the rebellion, comp. under the authority of the Regimental association by Smith B. Mott, late quartermaster of the regiment. Philadelphia, Press of J. B. Lippincott company, 1911.

266 p. plates, ports., maps. 21½cm.

Too much reliance on other sources, but some diary excerpts throw personal light on the Eastern campaigns.

Pennsylvania infantry. *57th regt.*, 1861–1865.

History of the Fifty-seventh regiment, Pennsylvania veteran volunteer infantry … Comp. by James M. Martin, E. C. Strouss, R. G. Madge, R. I. Campbell, M. C. Zahniser. [Meadville, Pa., McCoy & Calvin, printers, 19—?]

196 p. front., pl., ports. 20cm.

This vivid memoir of war service is not deep enough to be regarded as a unit history.

Pennsylvania infantry. *61st regt.*, 1861–1865.

History Sixty-first regiment Pennsylvania volunteers, 1861–1865, under authority of the regimental association … A. T. Brewer, historian. [Pittsburgh, Art engraving & printing co., 1911]

234 p. ports. 25½cm.

One of the poorer regimental histories, made so by too much reliance on printed sources and sentimentality.

Pennsylvania infantry. *78th regt.*

History of the Seventy-eighth Pennsylvania volunteer infantry; ed. by J. T. Gibson under the direction of the Historical committee of the regimental association, 1905. [Pittsburgh, Pa., Press of the Pittsburgh printing co., c1905]

267 p. incl. illus. (maps) plates, ports. 23½ cm.

A below-average study of Western campaigning.

Pennsylvania infantry. *118th regt.*, 1862–1865.

History of the Corn exchange regiment, 118th Pennsylvania volunteers, from their first engagement at Antietam to Appomattox. To which is added a record of its organization and a complete roster. Fully illustrated with maps, portraits, and over one hundred illustrations. By the Survivors' association, 118th (Corn exchange) reg't P. V. Philadelphia, Pa., J. L. Smith, 1888.

xvi, 746 p. illus., plates, ports., maps (1 fold.) 24cm.

This voluminous study contains everything from a lengthy personal narrative and photographs to biographical sketches and maps; deservingly quoted by many modern writers.

Pennsylvania infantry. *121st regt.*, 1862–1865.

History of the 121st regiment Pennsylvania volunteers. By the Survivors' association. "An account from the ranks." Philadelphia, Pa., Press of Burk & McFetridge co., 1893.

292 p. front., illus., plates, ports., fold. maps. 25 cm.

Amid this mass of unimportant trivia, an occasional nugget of value will be found.

Pennsylvania infantry. *124th regt.*, 1862–1863.

History of the One hundred and twenty-fourth regiment, Pennsylvania volunteers in the war of the rebellion—1862–1863: regimental re-unions, 1885–1906; history of monument; compiled by Robert M. Green; approved by the regimental committee. Philadelphia, Ware bros. company, printers, 1907.

2 p. l., 9–396, [4] p. incl. illus., plates, ports. front. 24½cm.

A disjointed collection of rosters, personal reminiscences, and sketches of a regiment whose nine-month service had its climax at Antietam.

Pennsylvania infantry. *125th regt.*, 1862–1863.

History of the One hundred and twenty-fifth regiment, Pennsylvania volunteers, 1862–1863, by the regimental committee. Philadelphia, Printed by J. B. Lippincott company, 1906.

342 p. incl. front., illus., plates, ports. 24cm.

Another potpourri of statistics and short narratives about a nine-month regiment; treats almost entirely of Antietam.

Pennsylvania infantry. *127th regt.*, 1862–1863.

History of the 127th regiment, Pennsylvania volunteers, familiarly known as the "Dauphin County regiment". Authorized by the regimental association and prepared by its committee. [Lebanon, Pa., Press of Report publishing company, 1902?]

2 p. l., 335 p. pl., 32 port. (incl. front.) 20ᶜᵐ.

Based on four fragmentary diaries, and memory thirty years after the war; the text centers on Fredericksburg and Chancellorsville and adds little to each.

Pennsylvania infantry. *155th regt.*, 1862–1865.

Under the Maltese cross, Antietam to Appomattox, the loyal uprising in western Pennsylvania, 1861–1865; campaigns 155th Pennsylvania regiment, narrated by the rank and file. Pittsburg, Pa., The 155th regimental association, 1910.

1 p. l., xiii, [3], 817 p. col. front., illus. (incl. ports.) plates (part col., 1 fold.) fold. map. 26½ᶜᵐ.

A full, heavily illustrated history, but lacking in human touches.

Pepper, George Whitfield, 1833–1899.

Personal recollections of Sherman's campaigns, in Georgia and the Carolinas. By Capt. George W. Pepper. Zanesville, O., H. Dunne, 1866.

522 p. 21 cm.

The highly revealing and reliable recollections of a journalist who served simultaneously as an officer in the 80th Ohio and a newspaper field correspondent.

Perkins, George, 1844?–

A summer in Maryland and Virginia; or, Campaigning with the 149th Ohio volunteer infantry, a sketch of events connected with the service of the regiment in Maryland and the Shenandoah Valley, Virginia; written by George Perkins, a member of Company A, at the earnest request of his comrades of the regiment. Chillicothe, O. [The Scholl printing company, 1911]

5 p. l., 13–106 p. incl. 2 port. 19½ᶜᵐ.

Too restricted and too based on nothing more than memory.

Perry, Henry Fales, 1834–

History of the Thirty-eighth regiment Indiana volunteer infantry, one of the three hundred fighting regiments of the Union army in the war of the rebellion, 1861–1865, by Henry Fales Perry. Palo Alto, Cal., F. A. Stuart, printer, 1906.

2 p. l., [9]–385 p. front., plates, ports. 23½ᶜᵐ.

Possesses some personal features, but the narrative at times is too dramatic.

Perry, John Gardner 1840–1926.

Letters from a surgeon of the civil war; comp. by Martha Derby Perry; illustrated from photographs. Boston, Little, Brown, and company, 1906.

xii p., 1 l., 225 p. 6 pl., 2 port. (incl. front.) 21ᶜᵐ.

Especially valuable for revelations on hospital service and personal observations in Virginia.

Pettengill, Samuel B

The college cavaliers. A sketch of the service of a company of college students in the Union army in 1862. By S. B. Pettengill ... Chicago, H. McAllaster & co., printers, 1883.

94 p., 1 l. front. (port.) 18½ cm.

A too-brief account of Dartmouth College students who fought in the 1862 Valley Campaign as members of the 7th Rhode Island Cavalry Squadron.

Petty, A   W   M

A history of the Third Missouri cavalry from its organization at Palmyra, Missouri, 1861, up to November sixth, 1864: with an appendix and recapitulation. By A. W. M. Petty ... Little Rock, J. W. Demby, 1865.

111 p. 23ᶜᵐ.

Published immediately after the war, this thin work is basically a chronicle of the regiment's movements.

Pickerill, William N

History of the Third Indiana cavalry, by W. N. Pickerill. Indianapolis, Ind. [Aetna printing co.] 1906.

201 p. front., ports. 23½ᶜᵐ.

A chronicle of movements and events; the author relied principally on the Official Records.

Pickett, George Edward, 1825–1875.

The heart of a soldier as revealed in the intimate letters of Genl. George E. Pickett, c. s. a. New York, Seth Moyle (incorporated) ᶜ1913.

5 p. l., 215 p. illus., plates. 23 cm.

Forty-eight highly edited-- and probably highly abridged-- letters of one of Lee's infantry commanders; Mrs. Pickett prepared the text.

Pickett, George Edward, 1825–1875.
Soldier of the South; General Pickett's war letters to his wife, edited by Arthur Crew Inman ... Boston and New York, Houghton Mifflin company, 1928.

xii p., 2 l., 157, [1] p. col. front., ports., facsim. 21 cm.

A reissue of the preceding, with two letters and a new title added; in neither work does a clear picture emerge of Pickett the general.

Pickett, La Salle (Corbell) "Mrs. G. E. Pickett," 1848–1931.
Pickett and his men, by La Salle Corbell Pickett (Mrs. G. E. Pickett) with sixteen illustrations. Philadelphia & London, J. B. Lippincott company, 1913.

xi, 313 p. front., plates, ports. 21½ cm.

Too sympathetic toward the subjects to be of intrinsic value; like Mrs. James Longstreet, Mrs. Pickett never moderated her defense of her husband.

Pierce, Charles F   *of Worcester, Mass.*
History and camp life of Company C, Fifty-first regiment, Massachusetts volunteer militia, 1862–1863. By C. F. Pierce. Worcester, Printed by C. Hamilton, 1886.

ix p., 1 l., [9]–130 p., 1 l. pl., port., maps (part fold.) 24 cm.

A series of revealing letters treating largely of the 1862-1863 campaigns in North Carolina.

Pierce, Lyman B
History of the Second Iowa cavalry; containing a detailed account of its organization, marches, and the battles in which it has participated; also, a complete roster of each company. By Sergeant Lyman B. Pierce ... Burlington, Iowa, Hawkeye steam book and job printing establishment, 1865.

viii, [9]–237 p. 22 cm.

Statistical at a cost of personal touches; apparently intended as a reference work.

Pierce, Thomas Jefferson, 1836–1864.
Letters home, by Thomas Jefferson Pierce. Also a roster of descendants of Charles and Catharine Pierce. Compiled by Ellen K. Korbitz. [Burlington? Iowa, 1957]

33 p. illus. 22 cm.

These letters by an Illinois soldier are too brief, too empty, and too few to make any appreciable contribution to an understanding of Billy Yanks.

Pierrepont, Alice V   D   1866–
Reuben Vaughan Kidd, soldier of the Confederacy. Petersburg, Va. [1947]

xii, 462 p. illus., ports., map. 24 cm.

This work is so disorganized as to be unwieldly; but with effort one can find among the family minutae many good letters by soldiers in the 4th Alabama.

Pike, James, 1834–
The scout and ranger: being the personal adventures of Corporal Pike, of the Fourth Ohio cavalry. As a Texan ranger, in the Indian wars, delineating western adventure; afterward a scout and spy, in Tennessee, Alabama, Georgia, and the Carolinas, under Generals Mitchell, Rosecrans, Stanley, Sheridan, Lytle, Thomas, Crook, and Sherman. Fully illustrating the secret service. Twenty-five full-page engravings. Cincinnati & New York, J. R. Hawley & co., 1865.

xi, 19–394 p. incl. 24 pl. front. (port.) 22 cm.

Although obviously ornamented, this account of a Federal soldier's varied and unusual experiences contains many authenticated facts and much color.

Pinney, Nelson A   1844–
History of the 104th regimental Ohio volunteer infantry from 1862 to 1865, by N. A. Pinney ... Akron, O., Printed by Werner & Lohmann, 1886.

148 p. incl. ports. front. 23½ cm.

More Pinney's recollections than a regimental history, yet a primary reference for this unit.

Pittenger, William, 1840–1905.
Capturing a locomotive: a history of secret service in the late war. By Rev. William Pittenger. Philadelphia, J. B. Lippincott & co., 1882.

354 p. front., pl., port., map. 19 cm.

One of eleven subsequent editions of the next title; the basic story became progressively embellished with each re-telling.

Pittenger, William, 1840–1904.
Daring and suffering; a history of the great railroad adventure. With an introd. by Alexander Clark. Philadelphia, J. W. Daughaday, 1863.

288 p. illus. 19 cm.

The starting point for any study of the "Great Locomotive Chase," though Pittenger's statements at times are suspect.

Pleasants, Henry, 1884–
The tragedy of the Crater, by Henry Pleasants, jr. Boston, The Christopher publishing house [c1938]
110 p. front. (port.) 20½ᶜᵐ.

Written by the cousin of the 48th Pennsylvania's commander; based on the Colonel's notes and letters; use of the first person weakens the overall presentation.

Plummer, Albert
History of the Forty-eight regiment, M. V. M. during the civil war. [Boston, Mass., Press of the New England druggist publishing company] 1907.
2 p. l., [7]–133 p. front., plates, ports. 23½ᶜᵐ.

A short narrative of the regiment's brief tour in Louisiana; most of the text is a roster of the companies.

Poague, William Thomas, 1835–1914.
Gunner with Stonewall; reminiscences of William Thomas Poague, a memoir, written for his children in 1903. Edited by Monroe F. Cockrell; with an introd. by Bell Irvin Wiley. Jackson, Tenn., McCowat-Mercer Press, 1957.
181 p. illus. 24 cm.

One of the few good recollections by a Confederate artilleryman; Col. Poague relied on several published works to refresh his memory.

Poe, Clarence Hamilton, 1881– *ed.*
True tales of the South at war; how soldiers fought and families lived, 1861–1865. Collected and edited by Clarence Poe. Betsy Seymour, assistant editor. Chapel Hill, University of North Carolina Press [1961]
208 p. 21 cm.

A collection of reminiscences and other primary material-- none of it annotated and some of it painfully condensed; this is a good introduction to extant sources, but little else.

Polk, J M 1838–
The Confederate soldier; and Ten years in South America. By J. M. Polk ... Austin, Tex., Press of Von Boeckmann-Jones company [1910]
57 p. front. (port.) illus. 22½ᶜᵐ.

After a cursory summary of life in the 4th Texas, the author devoted the majority of this slim work to his travels south of the border.

Polk, J M 1838–
Memories of the lost cause; stories and adventures of a Confederate soldier in General R. E. Lee's army, 1861 to 1865; and Ten years in South America, its resources, trade and commerce, and business intercourse with other countries, by J. M. Polk. Austin, Tex., 1905.
46 p. front. (port.) 23ᶜᵐ.

First edition of the above title; reprinted in 1907.

Polk, J M 1838–
The North and South American review, by J. M. Polk ... Austin, Tex., Press of Von Boeckmann-Jones co., printers, 1912.
61 p. incl. front. (port.) illus. 22½ᶜᵐ.

The third title employed for the same work.

Polley, Joseph Benjamin, 1840–1918.
Hood's Texas brigade, its marches, its battles, its achievements, by J. B. Polley ... New York and Washington, The Neale publishing company, 1910.
347 p. front., pl., ports. 22½ cm.

A composite of personal reminiscences of service in one of the most famous Confederate units; more reliable than the next title.

Polley, Joseph Benjamin, 1840–
A soldier's letters to charming Nellie, by J. B. Polley, of Hood's Texas brigade ... New York and Washington, The Neale publishing company, 1908.
vj p., 1 l., [9]–317 p. front., ports. 21ᶜᵐ.

Doubts exist as to the authenticity of these letters; Polley may well have composed them after the war.

Porter, Burton B 1832–
One of the people; his own story, by Burton B. Porter. [Colton, Calif.] The author [c1907]
v p., 1 l., 382 p. front. (port.) 19½ᶜᵐ.

Only three chapters treat of the author's service in the 10th New York Cavalry.

Porter, David Dixon, 1813–1891.

Incidents and anecdotes of the civil war. By Admiral Porter ... New York, D. Appleton and co., 1885.

357 p. front. (port.) 22½ᶜᵐ.

A reliable collection of wartime details, in spite of an abundance of reconstructed conversation.

Porter, Horace, 1837–1921.

Campaigning with Grant. By General Horace Porter, LL.D. New York, The Century co., 1897.

xviii p., 1 l., 546 p. front., illus., plates, ports., maps, fold. facsim. 23½ cm.

Penetrating pictures of Grant in action by an educated officer who served as his aide and later assisted Grant in the writing of his memoirs; Porter's narrative first appeared serially in The Century Magazine.

Porter, Horace, 1837–1921.

Campaigning with Grant. Edited with introd. and notes by Wayne C. Temple. Bloomington, Indiana University Press [1961]

xxvii, 558 p. 21 cm.

An offset reprinting of the above, with two prefaces and ten pages of notes added.

Post, *Mrs.* **Lydia (Minturn)** *ed.*

Soldiers' letters, from camp, battle-field and prison ... Ed. by Lydia Minturn Post. Published for the U. S. sanitary commission. New York, Bunce & Huntington, 1865.

472 p. 19½ᶜᵐ.

Some 200 letters on diverse topics by Federal soldiers in all theaters; most of the contents are chauvinistic, dramatic, and/or religious in tone.

Potter, *Rev.* **John,** *of the 101st Illinois infantry.*

Reminiscences of the civil war in the United States, by Rev. John Potter ... including also an account of a visit to the battle grounds of Tennessee and Georgia in 1895, and a memorial sermon, preached at Montezuma, Iowa, May 26th, 1895. [Oskaloosa, Ia., The Globe presses, 1897]

196 p. incl. front. (port.) 19½ᶜᵐ.

Potter had a penchant for describing in detail small, isolated incidents which he beheld; his memoir as a whole is a disappointment.

Potts, Frank, 1835–1890.

The death of the Confederacy: the last week of the Army of northern Virginia as set forth in a letter of April, 1865, by Frank Potts, captain, Confederate States army ... Edited, with a foreword, by Douglas Southall Freeman. Richmond, Va., Priv. print. for A. Potts, 1928.

15 p. 23ᶜᵐ.

A little-known eyewitness account of the Confederate retreat from Richmond to Appomattox; throws some light on Lee during surrender proceedings.

Powell, William Henry, 1838–1901.

The Fifth army corps (Army of the Potomac) A record of operations during the civil war in the United States of America, 1861–1865, by William H. Powell ... London, G. P. Putnam's sons, 1896.

1 p. l., xi, 900 p. front., port., maps (part fold.) plans. 25ᶜᵐ.

The most comprehensive corps history of the Civil War, though entirely void of personal recollections and human interest stories.

Powers, Elvira J

Hospital pencillings: being a diary while in Jefferson general hospital, Jeffersonville, Ind., and others at Nashville, Tennessee, as matron and visitor. By Elvira J. Powers ... Boston, E. L. Mitchell, 1866.

viii, 211 p. front. 19½ᶜᵐ.

A seven-month journal of wanderings and incidents by a nurse attached to Federal hospitals in Kentucky and Tennessee.

Powers, George Whitefield, 1834–1903.

The story of the Thirty eighth regiment of Massachusetts volunteers. By George W. Powers. Cambridge, Dakin and Metcalf, 1866.

x p., 1 l., 308 p. 19½ cm.

Powers used his own diary and correspondence of other members to compile this history of a unit that traveled much but fought little.

Preston, Noble D

History of the Tenth regiment of cavalry New York state volunteers, August, 1861, to August, 1865, by N. D. Preston, with an introduction by Gen. D. McM. Gregg; published by the Tenth New York cavalry association. New York, D. Appleton and co., 1892.

xix, 710 p. front., illus., pl. ports., fold. maps. 24½ cm.

An almost full story of regimental service in Virginia; at a cost of organization, Preston incorporated many soldier's writings and recollections.

Price, Isaiah, *b.* 1822.

History of the Ninety-seventh regiment, Pennsylvania volunteer infantry, during the war of the rebellion, 1861–65, with biographical sketches ... Prepared at the request of the regiment, by Isaiah Price ... Philadelphia, By the author for the subscribers, 1875.

viii, [3]–608 p., 1 l. front., illus., port. 28 cm.

A useful reservoir of personal narratives for the campaigns along the Atlantic coast.

Price, William Newton, 1831–1905.

One year in the civil war; a diary of the events from April 1st, 1864, to April 1st, 1865, by William N. Price, a private soldier in company D, 6th Tennessee, United States volunteer infantry. [n. p., 190–?]

59 p. 23½ cm.

A paperback diary containing for the most part weather observations and daily summaries of marches through Georgia and Tennessee.

Prowell, George Reeser, 1849–1928.

History of the Eighty-seventh regiment, Pennsylvania volunteers, prepared from official records, diaries, and other authentic sources of information. By George R. Prowell ... Pub. under the auspices of the regimental association ... York, Pa., Press of the York daily, 1903.

vii, [1], 306, xxv p. illus., plates, ports. 23 cm.

An unbalanced regimental history, containing everything from official reports to tales told at reunions; the use of much quoted conversation tends to make the whole narrative suspect.

Pullen, John J

The Twentieth Maine; a volunteer regiment in the Civil War. [1st ed.] Philadelphia, Lippincott [1957]

338 p. illus. 22 cm.

A model regimental history; the author drew largely from primary sources and presented his material in a style both dramatic and realistic.

Putnam, George Haven, 1844–1930.

Memories of my youth, 1844–1865, by George Haven Putnam ... New York and London, G. P. Putnam's sons, 1914.

vi p., 1 l., 447 p. 2 port. (incl. front.) 23½ cm.

The judicious recollections of service in Virginia by a distinguished veteran of the 176th New York.

Putnam, George Haven, 1844–1930.

Some memories of the civil war, together with an appreciation of the career and character of Major General Israel Putnam, leader in the colonial wars and in the American revolution, by George Haven Putnam ... New York and London, G. P. Putnam's sons, 1924.

v, 301 p. front. (port.) pl. 23½ cm.

Nine essays on the war and its leaders, together with some of Putnam's letters written while a prisoner of war.

Putnam, Samuel Henry.

The story of Company A, Twenty-fifth regiment, Mass. vols. in war of the rebellion. By Samuel H. Putnam. Worcester, Putnam, Davis and co., 1886.

1 p. l., 324 p. front. (port.) maps. 24½ cm.

This valuable chronicle of service in North Carolina contains many personal incidents of color and drama.

Pyne, Henry R

The history of the First New Jersey cavalry. (Sixteenth regiment, New Jersey volunteers.) By Henry R. Pyne, chaplain. Trenton, J. A. Beecher, 1871.

350 p. incl. front. (port.) col. pl. 19 cm.

More the chaplain's wartime autobiography than a regimental history; the narrative is both vivid and humorous, and treats largely of campaigning against Mosby.

Pyne, Henry R

Ride to war, the history of the First New Jersey Cavalry. Edited with an introd. and notes by Earl Schenck Miers. New Brunswick, Rutgers University Press [1961]

340 p. illus. 22 cm.

A completely new edition of the above, with editor's introduction, new text, copious notes, but no needed index.

Quint, Alonzo Hall, 1828–1896.

The Potomac and the Rapidan. Army notes from the failure at Winchester to the reënforcement of Rosecrans. 1861–3. By Alonzo H. Quint ... Boston, Crosby and Nichols; New York, O. S. Felt, 1864.

407 p. front. (fold. map) 20 cm.

This account by a Massachusetts chaplain is basically a vindictive indictment of the South; part of the narrative first appeared serially in religious publications.

Quint, Alonzo Hall, 1828–1896.
    The record of the Second Massachusetts infantry, 1861–65. By Alonzo H. Quint, its chaplain. Boston, J. P. Walker, 1867.

    viii p., 1 l., 528 p. front., port. 20½cm.

Slightly more even-tempered than the above, this work traces the regiment's movements and actions first in Virginia and later with Sherman.

Quintard, Charles Todd, *bp.,* 1824–1898.
    Doctor Quintard, chaplain c. s. a. and second bishop of Tennessee; being his story of the war (1861–1865) ed. and extended by the Rev. Arthur Howard Noll ... Sewanee, Tenn., The University press, 1905.

    5 p. l., 183 p., 1 l., vi p. front. (port.) 20½ cm.

Using his wartime diary as a base, this memoir by the chaplain of the 1st Tennessee is most revealing for religion in the army.

Ramey, Emily G   *comp.*
    The years of anguish, Fauquier County, Virginia, 1861–1865. Collected and compiled for the Fauquier County Civil War Centennial Committee, by Emily G. Ramey ₍and₎ John K. Gott. With the editorial assistance of Gertrude Trumbo and John Eisenhard. ₍Warrenton? Va., 1965₎

    233 p. illus. 24 cm.

A small taste of practically every type of source material is in this tribute to embattled soldiers and civilians.

Rauscher, Frank.
    Music on the march, 1862–'65, with the Army of the Potomac. 114th regt. P. V., Collis' Zouaves. By Frank Rauscher. Philadelphia, Press of W. F. Fell & co., 1892.

    vii, 9–270 p. illus. (music) pl., ports. (incl. front.) 19½cm.

An above-average personal account, based on a diary and letters; the best part of the narrative treats of the 1864 campaign in Virginia.

Rawling, Charles J
    History of the First regiment Virginia infantry. Being a narrative of the military movements in the mountains of Virginia, in the Shenandoah Valley and east of the Blue Ridge during the war of the rebellion, of the First regiment Virginia infantry volunteers — three months' and three years' service. By C. J. Rawling. Philadelphia, Printed by J. B. Lippincott co., 1887.

    284 p. 19½ cm.

Mostly the author's personal observations of service in western Virginia; the narrative is choppy.

Reader, Francis Smith, 1842–
    History of the Fifth West Virginia cavalry, formerly the Second Virginia infantry, and of Battery G, First West Va. light artillery, by Frank S. Reader ... New Brighton, Pa., F. S. Reader, 1890.

    304 p. pl., ports. 24 cm.

A melange of material, with some personal recollections buried in the rambling narrative.

The **Rebellion** record; a diary of American events, with documents, narratives, illustrative incidents, poetry, etc. Ed. by Frank Moore ... With an introductory address on the causes of the struggle, and the great issues before the country, by Edward Everett ... New York, G. P. Putnam, 1861–63; D. Van Nostrand, 1864–68.

    11 v. fronts., ports., maps (part fold.) plans (part fold.) diagrs. 25 cm.

The valuable in this conglomeration of newspaper extracts and printed minutae would not make one sizable, useful volume.

Reed, David Wilson, 1841–
    Campaigns and battles of the Twelfth regiment Iowa veteran volunteer infantry, from organization, September, 1861, to muster-out, January 20, 1866. By Major David W. Reed. ₍Evanston, Ill., 1903₎

    2 p. l., 319, ₍1₎ p., 1 l., 28 p. 4 pl. (incl. front., 2 fold. maps) 21cm.

A loose collection of personal reminiscences on the war in the West; the best section treats of Shiloh.

Reed, John A   1845–
    History of the 101st regiment, Pennsylvania veteran volunteer infantry 1861–1865, by John A. Reed ... with Luther S. Dickey as collaborator. Chicago, L. S. Dickey & co., 1910.

    5 p. l., 285 p. front., plates, ports., maps (part fold.) plan. 26½cm.

A hodgepodge of useful and useless information; similar in format to Dickey's study of the 103rd Pennsylvania.

Reed, William Howell, 1837–
    Hospital life in the Army of the Potomac. By William Howell Reed. Boston, W. V. Spencer, 1866.

    199 p. 18½ cm.

The product of a highly literate mind, this work is superior for insights on army life in Virginia, with particular emphasis on sickness and hospitals.

Reeves, James J

History of the Twenty-fourth regiment, New Jersey volunteers. By James J. Reeves. Printed by direction of the Society at their reunion in Woodbury, N. J., December 13, 1888. Camden, N. J., S. Chew, printer, 1889.

45 p. 22^{cm}.

Little more than a brief travelogue, with un-important material added.

Reichardt, Theodore.

Diary of Battery A, First regiment Rhode Island light artillery. By Theodore Reichardt. Written in the field. Providence, N. B. Williams, 1865.

v, [6]–153 p. 19½^{cm}.

This choppy diary treats mostly of army movements.

Reid, Jesse Walton, b. 1824.

History of the Fourth regiment of S. C. volunteers, from the commencement of the war until Lee's surrender. Giving a full account of all its movements, fights and hardships of all kinds. Also a very correct account of the travels and fights of the Army of northern Virginia ... This book is a copy of letters written in Virginia at the time by the author and sent home to his family ... With a short sketch of the life of the author. By J. W. Reid ... Greenville, S. C., Shannon & co., printers, 1892.

143 p. incl. front. (port.) 22½ cm.

Deserving of republication, these letters by a soldier who fought with Lee are frank, some-times witty, and almost always revealing.

Reminisco, Don Pedro Quærendo, *pseud.*

Life in the union army; or, Notings and reminiscences of a two years' volunteer. A rhythmical history of the Fifteenth N. Y. volunteer engineers, Colonel John McLeod Murphy, during its recent two years' campaign in and about Washington, and in the state of Virginia. By Don Pedro Quærendo Reminisco. New York, S. Tousey, 1864.

147 p. 23^{cm}.

Essays and poems, written in satirical form, of aspects of army life.

Rennolds, Edwin Hansford, 1839–

A history of the Henry county commands which served in the Confederate States army, including rosters of the various companies enlisted in Henry county, Tenn. ... By Lieut. Edwin H. Rennolds ... Jacksonville, Fla., Sun publishing company, 1904.

301 p. front. (port.) illus. (ports.) pl. 19½^{cm}.

Contains some company sketches and partial muster rolls, plus a rather full history of the author's unit, the 5th Tennessee.

Rerick, John H   1830–

The Forty-fourth Indiana volunteer infantry, history of its services in the war of the rebellion and a personal record of its members. By John H. Rerick ... Lagrange, Ind., The author, 1880.

293 p. front., fold. pl., ports., fold. map. 19½^{cm}.

Little more than a collection of impersonal statistics relative to the regiment.

Rhode Island artillery. *5th regt.,* 1861–1865.

History of the Fifth regiment of Rhode Island heavy artillery, during three years and a half of service in North Carolina. January 1862–June 1865. Comp. under the supervision of John K. Burlingame. Providence, Snow & Farnham, 1892.

xv, 382 p. front., illus., ports., maps (partly fold.) plan. 23½^{cm}.

A full history, based on wartime jottings, word-of-mouth stories, and printed sources.

Rhode Island infantry. *12th regt.,* 1862–1863.

History of the Twelfth regiment, Rhode Island volunteers, in the civil war, 1862–1863. Prepared by a committee of the survivors, in 1901–4. [Providence, Snow & Farnham, 1904]

xiv, 394 p. 11 pl. 39 port. (incl. front.) map. 23½^{cm}.

Contains some personal reminiscences, statistics, and previously published material relative to the regiment's ten-month service in Virginia and Kentucky.

Rhode Island soldiers and sailors historical society.

Personal narratives of events in the war of the rebellion, being papers read before the Rhode Island soldiers and sailors historical society ... [1st]–7th ser. Providence, The Society [etc.] 1878–1915.

100 v. in 10. fronts., plates, ports., maps, fold. facsim. 20½ x 16^{cm}.

The finest collection of monographs and short personal sketches in the field of Civil War memoirs; some of the more outstanding items are cited separately in this listing.

Rhodes, John H

The history of Battery B, First regiment Rhode Island light artillery, in the war to preserve the union, 1861–1865. By John H. Rhodes ... Providence, Snow & Farnham, printers, 1894.

xi, 406 p., 1 l. front., illus., port., maps (part fold.) 23½^{cm}.

Sgt. Rhodes used a diary and official documents to write this full and descriptive history; the battery campaigned from Ball's Bluff to Appomattox.

Riley, James Wesley.
Civil War diary of James Wesley Riley who served with the Union Army in the War Between the States, April 22, 1861–June 18, 1865. ₁Washington? Stamped: C. W. Denslinger, ᶜ1960₁

108 l. 28 cm.

A mimeographed copy of the sketchy journal kept by an enlistee in the 42nd Illinois; covers four years of service in the West but is too restricted to personal and company details.

Ripley, Edward Hastings, 1839–1915.
Vermont general: the unusual war experiences of Edward Hastings Ripley, 1862–1865. Edited by Otto Eisenschiml. New York, Devin-Adair, 1960.

viii, 340 p. illus., ports., maps. 21 cm.

A superb collection of 500 letters; especially useful for the 1862 fall of Harpers Ferry and the 1865 fall of Richmond.

Roback, Henry.
The veteran volunteers of Herkimer and Otsego counties in the war of the rebellion; being a history of the 152d N. Y. V. With scenes, incidents, etc., which occurred in the ranks, of the 34th N. Y., 97th N. Y., 121st N. Y., 2d N. Y. heavy artillery, and 1st and 2d N. Y. mounted rifles; also the active part performed by the boys in blue who were associated with the 152d N. Y. V. in Gen. Hancock's Second army corps during Grant's campaign, from the Wilderness to the surrender of Gen. Lee at Appomattox Court House, Va. Compiled and ed. by Henry Roback ... ₁Utica, N. Y., Press of L. C. Childs & son, 1888₁
196 p. 23ᶜᵐ.

A cursory, thoroughly inadequate summary.

Robbins, Walter Raleigh, 1843–1923.
War record and personal experiences of Walter Raleigh Robbins, from April 22, 1861, to August 4, 1865, edited by Lilian Rea. ₁Chicago?₁ Priv. print., 1923.

vii, 220 p. 3 port. (incl. front.) 19 cm.

This memoir suffers not only from an over-embellishment with manufactured conversation but also from erratic editing.

Robertson, George F   1853–
A small boy's recollections of the civil war (war between the states) by George F. Robertson ... Clover, S. C., G. F. Robertson, 1932.

116 p. 20ᶜᵐ.

The author was only seven when war began, and he freely confessed three quarters of a century later that he was writing from memory; no evaluation is therefore needed.

Robertson, James I
The Stonewall Brigade. Baton Rouge, Louisiana State University Press ₁1963₁

271 p. illus. 24 cm.

The only full and scholarly study of a famous Confederate brigade; based in large part on soldiers' letters, diaries, and reminiscences.

Robertson, Jerome Bonaparte, 1815–1890.
Touched with valor; Civil War papers and casualty reports of Hood's Texas Brigade. Written and collected by Jerome B. Robertson. Edited and with a biography of General Robertson by Harold B. Simpson. ₁1st ed.₁ Hillsboro, Tex., Hill Junior College Press ₁1964₁

xv, 126 p. illus., ports. 24 cm.

A composite work that includes a biography of Gen. Robertson, some of his wartime correspondence, and casualty lists for Hood's Texas Brigade.

Robertson, Robert Stoddart, 1839–
Personal recollections of the war. A record of service with the Ninety-third New York vol. infantry, and the First brigade, first division, second corps, Army of the Potomac, by Robert Stoddart Robertson ... Milwaukee, Wis., Swain & Tate co., 1895.

126 p. front. (port.) 23ᶜᵐ.

A brief diary, valuable only for the author's observations during the siege of Vicksburg.

Robinson, Frank Torrey, 1845–1898.
History of the Fifth regiment, M. V. M. By Frank T. Robinson ... Boston, W. F. Brown & co., printers, 1879.

vi p., 1 l., 237, ₁1₁ p. front., port. 22½ᶜᵐ.

A totally statistical compilation of the regiment; a much better work on the same unit is that by A. S. Roe (q. v.).

Robson, John S   1844–
How a one legged Rebel lives, or, A history of the 52nd Virginia regiment. Incidents in the life of the writer, during and since the close of the war. Concluding with a biographical sketch of John ₁i. e. William₁ Randolph Barbee, the distinguished Virginia sculptor. By John S. Robson. Richmond, W. H. Wade & co., printers, 1876.

vi, 138 p. 18½ᶜᵐ.

Only a portion of this prejudiced memoir treats of the author's service in the 52nd Virginia.

Rodenbough, Theophilus Francis, 1838–1912, *ed.*
Uncle Sam's medal of honor; some of the noble deeds for which the medal has been awarded, described by those who have won it. 1861–1866. Collected and edited by Theo. F. Rodenbough ... New York & London, G. P. Putnam's sons [c1886]

xiv, [2], 424 p. incl. illus., port., facsim. front. 21½ cm.

These short accounts of heroic acts for which Federal soldiers received the nation's highest award are marred by the author's embellishments, particularly his penchant for the over-dramatic.

Roe, Alfred Seelye, 1844–1917.
The Fifth regiment Massachusetts volunteer infantry in its three tours of duty 1861, 1862–'63, 1864, by Alfred S. Roe ... Boston, Mass., Fifth regiment veteran association, 1911.

510 p. incl. front., illus., maps, ports. 23½ cm.

One of the most popular historians of his day, employing all the tools at his command, has recaptured the humaneness and exploits of a unit composed of different companies in each of its three tours of duty.

Roe, Alfred Seelye, 1844–1917.
History of the First regiment of heavy artillery, Massachusetts volunteers, formerly the Fourteenth regiment of infantry, 1861–1865, by Alfred Seelye Roe ... and Charles Nutt ... [Worcester & Boston] The Regimental association, 1917. xi, 507 p. front., 32 pl. (incl. ports.) 23½ cm.

This was the fifth regimental study written by Roe; here he utilized both primary and secondary sources; especially good for life in the Virginia defenses of Washington.

Roe, Alfred Seelye 1844–1917, *ed.*
The Melvin memorial. Sleepy Hollow cemetery, Concord, Massachusetts, a brother's tribute; exercises at dedication, June 16, 1909. Cambridge, Priv. print. at the Riverside press, 1910.

xii p., 2 l., 148 p. front., plates (1 double) ports. (1 double) fold. facsim. 24½ cm.

A composite of tributes to three brothers who died in the field; included also is the slim diary of one of the soldiers.

Roe, Alfred Seelye, 1844–1917.
The Ninth New York heavy artillery. A history of its organization, services in the defenses of Washington, marches, camps, battles, and muster-out ... and a complete roster of the regiment. By Alfred Seelye Roe ... Worcester, Mass., The author, 1899.

615 p. front., illus. (incl. plans) plates, ports. 24 cm.

Another regimental history by the indefatigable Roe; this one reflects painstaking research and skillful presentation.

Roe, Alfred Seelye, 1844–
The Tenth regiment, Massachusetts volunteer infantry, 1861–1864, a western Massachusetts regiment, by Alfred S. Roe, a veteran of the civil war. Regimental committee on history; John W. Hersey, chairman, Joel H. Hendrick, secretary [and others] ... Springfield, Mass., Tenth regiment veteran association, 1909.

535 p. incl. illus., ports. front. 24 cm.

Using as a base the earlier unit history by J. K. Newell (q. v.), Roe added extracts from three soldiers' diaries and produced a highly readable and useful study.

Roe, Alfred Seelye, 1844–1917.
The Thirty-ninth regiment Massachusetts volunteers, 1862–1865, by Alfred S. Roe ... Worcester, Mass., Regimental veteran association, 1914.

1 p. l., 493 p. front., ports., facsim. 21½ cm.

Roe was forced to rely more on printed sources for this history of a unit in the Army of the Potomac, and the result is not as personal and as comprehensive as his other volumes.

Roe, Alfred Seelye, 1844–1917.
The Twenty-fourth regiment, Massachusetts volunteers, 1861–1866, "New England guard regiment," by Alfred S. Roe ... Regimental committee on history: Charles B. Amory, John C. Cook, George Hill. Worcester, Mass., Twenty-fourth veteran association, 1907.

573 p. front. (port.) illus. 23½ cm.

For this work Roe leaned heavily on the writings of Cols. Thomas G. Stevenson (q. v.) and Francis A. Osborn; other memoirs were also employed in describing the regiment's several campaigns along the South Atlantic coast.

Roehrenbeck, William Joseph, 1913–
The regiment that saved the Capital. Introd. by Allan Nevins. New York, T. Yoseloff [1961]

244 p. illus. 22 cm.

The latest detailed history of the 7th New York, relying primarily on printed sources, the author incorporates many excerpts from statements of soldiers.

Roemer, Jacob, 1818–1896.
Reminiscences of the war of the rebellion 1861–1865, by Bvt.-Maj. Jacob Roemer ... Ed. by L. A. Furney ... Flushing, N. Y., Pub. by the estate of J. Roemer, 1897.

316 p., 1 l. front. (port.) 21 cm.

An even-tempered memoir by a New York artillery officer; however, Roemer relied too much on memory thirty years after the events he described.

Rogers, Edward H.

Reminiscences of military service in the Forty-third regiment, Massachusetts infantry, during the great Civil war, 1862–63. By Edward H. Rogers, Company H, Chelsea, Mass. Boston, Franklin press, Rand, Avery, & co., 1883.

210 p. front.. illus., plates. 23½ cm.

These recollections first appeared serially in Massachusetts newspapers; they give a personal record of nine months' service in the North Carolina theater.

Rogers, James B.

War pictures. Experiences and observations of a chaplain in the U. S. Army, in the war of the southern rebellion. By Rev. J. B. Rogers ... Chicago, Church & Goodman, 1863.

xi, [12]–258 p. incl. front. (port.) pl. 19 cm.

An extremely good commentary on the 1862 campaigns for Shiloh and Corinth; some religious thoughts were naturally inserted.

Rogers, William H.

History of the One hundred and eighty-ninth regiment of New-York volunteers. By Rev. Wm. H. Rogers, A. M., chaplain. New-York, J. A. Gray & Green, printers, 1865.

113 p. front. (port.) 19 cm.

Nothing more than inadequate sketches of companies and officers.

Rood, Hosea W   1845–

Story of the service of Company E, and of the Twelfth Wisconsin regiment of veteran volunteer infantry, in the war of the rebellion. Beginning with September 7, 1861, and ending July 21, 1865. Written by one of the boys. [n. p., 1898?]

547 p., 2 l., 14, 10, 13, 7, 44, [4] p. illus., 1 pl., 27 port. (incl. front.) 23½ cm.

A full and sometimes useful history, but one obviously embellished.

Rose, Victor M   *d.* 1893.

Ross' Texas brigade. Being a narrative of events connected with its service in the late war between the states. By Victor M. Rose ... Louisville, Courier-Journal, 1881.

185 p. front., port. 20½ cm.

An average account based in part on available sources and in part on memory fifteen years after the war.

Ross, Fitzgerald.

Cities and camps of the Confederate States. Edited by Richard Barksdale Harwell. Urbana, University of Illinois Press, 1958.

262 p. illus. 21 cm.

A completely new edition of the below work, with a highly revealing introduction, notes, and full index.

Ross, Fitzgerald.

A visit to the cities and camps of the Confederate states, by Fitzgerald Ross ... Edinburgh and London, W. Blackwood and sons, 1865.

x, 300 p. front. (fold. map) 19 cm.

Apparently a Scotsman who served in the Austrian army, Ross visited the South in 1863-1864 and penned observations in many respects equal in quality to those of A. J. L. Fremantle.

Royall, William Lawrence, 1844–

Some reminiscences, by William L. Royall. New York and Washington, The Neale publishing company, 1909.

210 p. 19 cm.

The best section of this volume is an account of the Wilderness fighting by A. P. Hill's chief of staff.

Royse, Isaac Henry Clay.

History of the 115th regiment, Illinois volunteer infantry, by Isaac Henry Clay Royse ... Terre Haute, Ind., The author, 1900.

vi p., 1 l., 404, [1] p. front., illus. (incl. plans) ports. 24 cm.

A history of the war in the West, with regimental minutae frequently inserted.

Runyan, Morris C

Eight days with the Confederates and capture of their archives, flags, &c. by Company "G" Ninth New Jersey vol. Written by Captain Morris C. Runyan. Princeton, N. J., W. C. C. Zapf, printer, 1896.

44 p. front. (port.) 22½ cm.

A brief narrative of a Federal expedition from Raleigh to Charlotte, N. C., immediately after Johnston's surrender.

Rusling, James Fowler, 1834–1918.

Men and things I saw in civil war days. New ed., by James Fowler Rusling ... New York, Cincinnati, The Methodist book concern, 1914.

2 p. l., 3–420 p. front., ports. 19½ᶜᵐ.

The author rose during the war from a line officer in the 5th New Jersey to a brevet brigadier and quartermaster; his useful study contains recollections, excerpts from printed sources, and a small collection of letters.

Russell, *Sir* **William Howard,** 1820–1907.

My diary North and South. By William Howard Russell. In two volumes. London, Bradbury and Evans, 1863.

2 v. fold. map. 19½ᶜᵐ.

The garrulous and embellished memoirs of an egotistical English reporter; treats only of the first nine months of the war in the East.

Ryder, Richard H 1843–

The village color-bearer. Together with a story of a U. S. life-saving service keeper. By Capt. Richard H. Ryder ... Brooklyn, N. Y., G. S. Patton, 1891.

200 p. incl. front. (port.) illus., pl. 21ᶜᵐ.

A popularly written, very dramatic account by a member of the 40th New York; inferior to all other sources on that particular regiment.

Sala, George Augustus Henry, 1828–1895.

My diary in America in the midst of war. By George Augustus Sala ... London, Tinsley brothers, 1865.

2 v. 22ᶜᵐ.

A small part of this well-traveled Britisher's memoir recounts one visit to the winter quarters of the Army of the Potomac.

Sallada, William Henry, 1846–

Silver sheaves: gathered through clouds and sunshine. In two parts. Part 1st: Civil and military life of the author. Part 2d: Miscellaneous collection of prose and poetry. By William H. Sallada. 2d ed. Des Moines, The author, 1879.

2 p. l., ₍9₎–360 p. front. (port.) illus. 19½ᶜᵐ.

Only the first half of this work contains Sallada's untrustworthy account of service with the 57th Pennsylvania.

Sanford, Washington L 1825– *comp.*

History of Fourteenth Illinois cavalry and the brigades to which it belonged; compiled from manuscript history by Sanford, West, and Featherson, and from notes of comrades ... Compiled and published by W. L. Sanford ... Chicago, R. R. Donnelley & sons company, 1898.

2 p. l., 347, ₍1₎ p. front., ports. 19ᶜᵐ.

Presented in diary form, this history gives a very revealing account of army life and campaigns.

Saunier, Joseph A *ed.*

A history of the Forty-seventh regiment, Ohio veteran volunteer infantry, Second brigade, Second division, Fifteenth army corps. Army of the Tennessee. Ed. by Joseph A. Saunier, regimental historian, assisted by diaries and manuscripts furnished by Samuel J. Johnston ... and many others, and official reports of War department. From June 15th, 1861, to August 24th. 1865. ₍Hillsboro, O., Press the Lyle printing company, 1903?₎

576 p. 22ᶜᵐ.

Another war diary heavily embellished with excerpts from the Official Records.

Sawyer, Franklin.

A military history of the 8th regiment Ohio vol. inf'y: its battles, marches and army movements. By Franklin Sawyer ... Ed. by Geo. A. Groot ... Cleveland, O., Fairbanks & co., printers, 1881.

260 p. front. (port.) 23½ᶜᵐ.

Written by the regiment's lieutenant colonel; the narrative is too shallow and too concerned with the larger aspects of the war.

Scheibert, Justus, 1831–1903.

Seven months in the Rebel States during the North American war, 1863. Translated from the German by Joseph C. Hayes. Edited, with an introd., by Wm. Stanley Hoole. ₍Limited ed.₎ Tuscaloosa, Ala., Confederate Pub. Co., 1958.

166 p. port., plans. 22 cm.

An American translation of the title below; the editing is not as full as one would have desired.

Scheibert, Justus, 1831–1903.

Sieben monate in den rebellen-staaten während des nordamerikanischen krieges 1863, von Scheibert. Hierzu vier gefechts- und situationspläne. Stettin, T. von der Nahmer, 1868.

v, 126 p., 1 l. 4 fold. plans. 22 cm.

A Prussian army engineer sent to study the American war, Scheibert penned a sometimes revealing narrative of his 1863 observations with Confederate forces.

Schmutz, George S   1846?–
History of the 102d regiment, O. V. I. Pub. and comp. by Geo. S. Schmutz ... ₁Wooster, O., G. S. Schmutz₁ 1907.

285 p. front., plates, ports. 22½ᶜᵐ.

Muster rolls, biographical sketches, and an occasional anecdote only.

Schofield, John McAllister, 1831–1906.
Forty-six years in the army, by Lieutenant-General John M. Schofield. New York, The Century co., 1897.

xvi p., 1 l., 577 p. front. (port.) 23½ᶜᵐ.

What could have been an enlightening and valuable memoir is little more than a critique of published official reports on the engagements of which Gen. Schofield was a part.

Schurz, Carl, 1829–1906.
... Intimate letters of Carl Schurz, 1841–1869, translated and edited by Joseph Schafer ... Madison, State historical society of Wisconsin, 1928.

xx p., 2 l., 491 p. front., pl., ports. 22½ cm.

The pointed but sometimes rambling correspondence of a fiery figure who left the ambassadorial ranks to become a field commander.

Schurz, Carl, 1829–1906.
The reminiscences of Carl Schurz ... illustrated with portraits and original drawings. New York, The McClure company, 1907–08.

3 v. fronts., plates, ports., maps. 23½ cm.

Verbose and highly opinionated memoir of the German-American; Frederic Bancroft and W. A. Dunning added a long biographical sketch.

Scott, John, 1820–1907.
Partisan life with Col. John S. Mosby. By Major John Scott ... With portraits and engravings on wood ... New York, Harper & brothers, 1867.

1 p. l., ₁vii₁–xvi p., 1 l., ₁19₁–492 p. front., illus., ports., fold. map, facsim. 24 cm.

Although presented as a series of letters, this narrative was written after the war from memory and a few sources; gives many personal insights of Mosby and his rangers.

Scott, John, 1824–   *comp.*
Story of the Thirty-second Iowa infantry volunteers, comp. and pub. by John Scott. Nevada, Ia., J. Scott, 1896.

4 p. l., ₁13₁–526 p. front., ports., fold. plan. 24ᶜᵐ.

A poor effort toward a history; the author borrowed heavily from official sources and some letters published in newspapers; there is no evidence that Scott relied on any manuscript sources.

Scott, Kate M
History of the One hundred and fifth regiment of Pennsylvania volunteers. A complete history of the organization, marches, battles, toils, and dangers participated in by the regiment from the beginning to the close of the war, 1861–1865. By Kate M. Scott. Philadelphia, New-world publishing company, 1877.

xv, 17–329 p. front., ports. 23½ᶜᵐ.

Though designed as a narrative history, the text is nothing more than a long tribute by one who was not with the regiment.

Scott, Samuel W
History of the Thirteenth regiment, Tennessee volunteer cavalry, U. S. A., including a narrative of the bridge burning; the Carter county rebellion, and the loyalty, heroism and suffering of the Union men and women of Carter and Johnson counties, Tennessee, during the civil war ... written by Samuel W. Scott ... and Samuel P. Angel ... Knoxville, Tenn. ₁1903₁

510 p. front., port. 22½ᶜᵐ.

This somewhat padded narrative of a Union regiment is inferior to a similar study by William R. Carter.

Scott, William Forse, 1843–1933.
The story of a cavalry regiment. The career of the Fourth Iowa veteran volunteers from Kansas to Georgia, 1861–1865, by Wm. Forse Scott ... New York ₁etc.₁ G. P. Putnam's sons, 1893.

xxii p., 1 l., 602 p. front. (port.) illus., maps (part fold.) 23½ cm.

The best history of a Hawkeye cavalry unit; a detailed narrative, maps, and full index recount the regiment's campaigns in the Western theater.

Scribner, Benjamin Franklin, 1825–1900.
How soldiers were made; or, The war as I saw it under Buell, Rosecrans, Thomas, Grant and Sherman. By B. F. Scribner, late colonel Thirty-eighth Indiana veteran volunteers, and brevet brigadier-general, commanding brigade, First division, Fourteenth army corps, Army of the Cumberland. New Albany, Ind. ₁Chicago, Donohue & Henneberry₁ 1887.

2 p. l., iii–iv, 5–316 p. 20ᶜᵐ.

Little more than a colorless chronicle of battles and military movements in the Western theater.

Scrymser, James Alexander, 1839–1918.

Personal reminiscences of James A. Scrymser, in times of peace and war. [Easton, Pa., Eschenbach printing company, c1915]

5 p. l., 9–151, [1] p. plates, ports., double map, facsim. 23½ cm.

The opening section of this autobiography contains random comments on service with the 12th New York.

Se Cheverell, John Hamilton.

Journal history of the Twenty-ninth Ohio veteran volunteers, 1861–1865. Its victories and its reverses. And the campaigns and battles of Winchester, Port Republic, Cedar mountain, Chancellorsville, Gettysburg, Lookout mountain, Atlanta, the march to the sea, and the campaign of the Carolinas, in which it bore an honorable part. By J. Hamp Se Cheverell ... Cleveland, 1883.

2 p. l., [9]–284 p. front. (port.) 19 cm.

This choppy and discursive study, written by the regiment's commander, is more a memorial than a solid history of the regiment.

Sedgwick, John, 1813–1864.

Correspondence of John Sedgwick, major-general. [New York] Printed for C. and E. B. Stoeckel [by the De Vinne press] 1902–03.

2 v. fronts. (ports.) 23½ cm.

Volume II contains the only known papers of the beloved commander of the VI Corps who was killed at Spotsylvania.

Senour, Faunt Le Roy, 1824–1910.

Morgan and his captors. By Rev. F. Senour. Cincinnati, Chicago, C. F. Vent & co., 1865.

x, 11–389 p. front. (port.) 19 cm.

An unbalanced, scissors-and-paste account, largely of Morgan's 1863 raid; the author was a better minister than historian.

Shaver, Lewellyn Adolphus, 1842–

A history of the Sixtieth Alabama regiment, Gracie's Alabama brigade; by Lewellyn A. Shaver. Montgomery, Barrett & Brown, 1867.

111 p. 21 cm.

A weak travelogue of the author's service in West and East; it was apparently written entirely from memory.

Shaw, Horace H 1842?–

The First Maine heavy artillery, 1862–1865; a history of its part and place in the war for the union, with an outline of causes of war and its results to our country, by Horace H. Shaw; with organization, company, and individual records, by Charles J. House. Portland, Me., 1903.

xiii, [1], 516, ii, [a]–x p., 1 l. incl. front., illus., ports. plates (partly double) 22 cm.

Although the author's writing tends to become overly dramatic, this history possesses much personal and statistical data on a unit that suffered heavy losses in Virginia.

Sheeran, James B 1819–1881.

Confederate chaplain, a war journal. Edited by Joseph T. Durkin. With a pref. by Bruce Catton. Milwaukee, Bruce Pub. Co. [1960]

168 p. illus. 23 cm.

Outspoken comments on events in the Army of Northern Virginia by the chaplain of the 14th Louisiana; the editorial work is choppy.

Sheldon, Winthrop Dudley, 1839–1931.

The "Twenty-seventh." A regimental history. By Winthrop D. Sheldon ... New-Haven, Morris & Benham, 1866

144 p. front., port. 19 cm.

The author, a member of the 27th Connecticut, took part in the battles of Fredericksburg and Chancellorsville only; his extreme bitterness toward the South mars the whole narrative.

Sherlock, Eli J

Memorabilia of the marches and battles in which the One hundredth regiment of Indiana infantry volunteers took an active part. War of the rebellion, 1861–5. By Captain E. J. Sherlock. [Kansas City, Mo., Press of Gerard-Woody printing co., 1896]

432 p. incl. plates, ports. 20 cm.

Some confusion exists because of the disorganization of material, but with patience much useful data can be found between the covers.

Sherman, Sylvester M

History of the 133d regiment, O. V. I. and incidents connected with its service during the "war of the rebellion." By the historian of the association of its survivors, S. M. Sherman, M. D. Columbus, O., Champlin printing co., 1896.

163 p., 1 l. 20 cm.

Though heavily padded with Official Records extracts, the pretentious narrative is lacking in information.

Sherwood, Isaac R   1835–1925.
   Memories of the war, by Gen. Isaac R. Sherwood. Toledo, O., The H. J. Chittenden co., 1923.

   4 p. l., 238 p. pl. ports. 20½ᶜᵐ.

When Sherwood was not borrowing from other sources, he tended to be overly dramatic.

Shorey, Henry Augustus.
   The story of the Maine Fifteenth; being a brief narrative of the more important events in the history of the Fifteenth Maine regiment; together with a complete roster of the regiment ... and illustrations and brief biographical sketches of nearly all the commissioned officers ... By Henry A. Shorey ... Bridgton, Me., Press of the Bridgton news, 1890.

   2 p. l., 178, 26 p. ports. 26½ᶜᵐ.

An opinionated account of campaigns and leaders in the Trans-Mississippi.

Shotwell, Randolph Abbott, 1844–1885.
   Papers. Edited by J. G. de Roulhac Hamilton, with the collaboration of Rebecca Cameron. Raleigh, North Carolina Historical Commission, 1929–31.

   2 v. port. 24 cm.

Included in these two volumes is the rather full diary of a dedicated and emotional youth who fought with Lee until his capture in the summer of 1864.

Shreve, William Price, 1835–   *comp.*
   The story of the Third army corps union, comp. from the original records by William P. Shreve ... Boston, Mass., Priv. print., 1910.

   2 p. l., 96 p. front. (port.) 22½ cm.

A dry summary of the activities of a group organized to promote religious spirit in the Army of the Potomac.

Simmons, Louis A
   The history of the 84th reg't Ill. vols. By L. A. Simmons. Macomb, Ill., Hampton brothers, 1866.

   345 p., 1 l. 19½ cm.

One of the better personal histories to appear immediately after the war; like its sisters, this Illinois regiment served in the West.

Simons, Ezra De Freest.
   A regimental history. The One hundred and twenty-fifth New York state volunteers. By Chaplain Ezra D. Simons ... New York, E. D. Simons, 1888.

   xxi, 352, xxix, [2] p., 1 l. front., illus., port. 24½ cm.

Less than half of the text is a narrative-- and too much of it appeared originally in other works.

Simpson, Harold B
   Gaines' Mill to Appomattox; Waco & McLennan County in Hood's Texas Brigade. Introd. by Roger N. Conger. Waco, Tex., Texian Press, 1963.

   294 p. illus. 24 cm.

A concentrated study of Co. E, 4th Texas, a unit whose service in the East was so costly that at Appomattox a sergeant was its highest officer.

Sipes, William B   *d.* 1905.
   The Seventh Pennsylvania veteran volunteer cavalry; its record, reminiscences and roster; with an appendix; by William B. Sipes. [Pottsville, Pa., Miners' journal print, 1905?]

   1 p. l., iv, 6, 169, [1], 60, 143 p., 3 l. pl., ports. 24ᶜᵐ.

Written by the regimental colonel, this history is too much based on printed sources to be of primary value.

Slaughter, Philip, 1808–1890.
   A sketch of the life of Randolph Fairfax, a private in the ranks of the Rockbridge artillery, attached to the "Stonewall brigade," and afterwards to the First regiment Virginia light artillery, second corps, Army of northern Virginia. Including a brief account of Jackson's celebrated Valley campaign. 3d ed. By Rev. Philip Slaughter ... [Baltimore, Innes and company, printers] 1878.

   x, 72 p. front. (port.) 19ᶜᵐ.

Amid eulogies and sermons are many revealing letters of a young Confederate gunner who died at Fredericksburg.

Sligh, Charles R
   History of the services of the First regiment Michigan engineers and mechanics, during the civil war, 1861–1865, by Charles R. Sligh ... Grand Rapids, Mich. [White printing company] 1921.

   112 p. incl. front. illus. (incl. map) ports. 26½ᶜᵐ.

Included in this loosely constructed history are letter excerpts, contemporary photographs, rosters, and much minutae.

Sloan, John Alexander.

Reminiscences of the Guilford grays, Co. B, 27th N. C. regiment, by John A. Sloan. Washington, R. O. Polkinhorn, printer, 1883.

1 p. l., iv, 129, [1] p. 20½ᶜᵐ.

Important for data on a valorous regiment first commanded by John R. Cooke.

Small, Abner Ralph, 1836–1910.

The road to Richmond; the civil war memoirs of Major Abner R. Small of the Sixteenth Maine volunteers. Together with the diary which he kept when he was a prisoner of war. Edited by Harold Adams Small. Berkeley, Calif., University of California press, 1939.

xiii, 314 p. front. (port.) plates, map. 22½ᶜᵐ.

Using wartime notes as a buttress for memory, the author wrote this narrative at the turn of the century; it is an exceptionally good personal account of soldier and prison life.

Small, Abner Ralph, 1836–1910.

The Sixteenth Maine regiment in the war of the rebellion, 1861–1865, by Major A. R. Small; with an introduction written by Gen. James A. Hall ... Portland, Me., Pub. for the regimental association, by B. Thurston & company, 1886.

iv, 323 p. front., plates, ports. 22½ᶜᵐ.

More an autobiography than a regimental study; Small followed this work with his more valuable Road to Richmond.

Smith, Abram P *1st lieut., 76th N. Y. infantry.*

History of the Seventy-sixth regiment New York volunteers; what it endured and accomplished; containing descriptions of its twenty-five battles; its marches; its camp and bivouac scenes; with biographical sketches of fifty-three officers, and a complete record of the enlisted men. By A. P. Smith ... Cortland, N. Y. [Truair, Smith and Miles, printers, Syracuse] 1867.

429 p. incl. port. front., pl. 22 cm.

An accurate account of the regiment's role in the Eastern campaign; Quartermaster Smith had access to much correspondence; 48 pen-and-ink sketches enhance the study.

Smith, Adelaide W 1831–

Reminiscenses of an Army nurse during the Civil war [by] Adelaide W. Smith, independent volunteer. New York, Greaves publishing company, 1911.

1 p. l., [7]–263 p. illus., 2 port. (incl. front.) 19½ cm.

A glaring example why one should not wait forty years before writing wartime memoirs.

Smith, Benjamin T 1844–1908.

Private Smith's journal; recollections of the late war, edited by Clyde C. Walton. Chicago, R. R. Donnelley, 1963.

lxii, 253 p. illus., port., maps. 18 cm.

Smith enlisted in the 51st Illinois, served in the ranks, and finished his duty as an aide at division headquarters; his well-edited diary spans four years of war in the Tennessee area.

Smith, Charles H 1837–

The history of Fuller's Ohio brigade, 1861–1865; its great march, with roster, portraits, battle maps and biographies. By Charles H. Smith ... Cleveland [Press of A. J. Watt] 1909.

14, [4], [21]–623 p. illus. (incl. ports.) 25½ᶜᵐ.

A dependable brigade history, though too much was borrowed from the Official Records; Smith was the creator of the legendary "Bill Arp."

Smith, Daniel Elliott Huger, *ed.*

Mason Smith family letters, 1860–1868; edited by Daniel E. Huger Smith, Alice R. Huger Smith [and] Arney R. Childs. Columbia, University of South Carolina Press, 1950.

xxiv, 292 p. ports. 24 cm.

A valuable collection of letters by members of prominent Charleston families; contains the correspondence of William Mason, a young Confederate soldier mortally wounded at Cold Harbor.

Smith, Daniel P

Company K, First Alabama regiment, or Three years in the Confederate service, by Daniel P. Smith. Prattville, Ala., The Survivors, 1885.

135 p., 5 l. 20ᶜᵐ.

A good but brief narrative, far above the usual, statistical monologue normally found for company histories.

Smith, Donald L 1913–

The Twenty-fourth Michigan of the Iron Brigade. [1st ed.] Harrisburg, Pa., Stackpole Co. [1962]

312 p. illus. 23 cm.

A twenty-five-year labor of love, this thoroughly complete history recounts the exploits and experiences of a vital unit in the Army of the Potomac.

Smith, George Gilbert, 1825–
Leaves from a soldier's diary; the personal record of Lieutenant George G. Smith, Co. C., 1st Louisiana regiment infantry volunteers ⟨white⟩ during the war of the rebellion; also a partial history of the operations of the army and navy in the Department of the Gulf from the capture of New Orleans to the close of the war. Putnam, Conn., G. G. Smith, 1906.

5, 151 p. front. (port.) pl. 18 cm.

In spite of its diary-like presentation, Smith's account may not be contemporary; in any event, it contributes little to the history of the war.

Smith, Gustavus Woodson, 1822–1896.
Confederate war papers. Fairfax Court House, New Orleans, Seven Pines, Richmond and North Carolina. By Gustavus W. Smith ... New York, Atlantic pub. and engraving co., 1884.

381 p. front. (port.) fold. maps. 19 cm.

Smith was a failure as a general; this work is largely his rationalization for shortcomings at Seven Pines.

Smith, Henry I.
History of the Seventh Iowa veteran volunteer infantry during the civil war, by H. I. Smith, four years a member ... Mason City, Iowa, E. Hitchcock, printer, 1903.

313 p. plates. ports. 22 cm.

One of the best of the Iowa regimental histories; a charming mixture of the heroic and the humorous.

Smith, Jacob, 1840?–
Camps and campaigns of the 107th regiment Ohio volunteer infantry, from August, 1862, to July, 1865; comp. and written by Jacob Smith, Company D, 107th Ohio volunteer infantry ... [n. p., 1910?]

314 p. plates, ports., map. 19 cm.

A diary, obviously reworked after the war, with muster rolls appended.

Smith, James E   b. 1831 *or* 1832.
A famous battery and its campaigns, 1861–'64. The career of Corporal James Tanner in war and in peace. Early days in the Black Hills with some account of Capt. Jack Crawford, the poet scout; by Captain James E. Smith, 4th N. Y. independent battery. Washington, W. H. Lowdermilk & co., 1892.

vii, 237 p. front., illus., port., plan. 19 cm.

An empty chronicle of three years' service in the East; Smith apparently used no wartime diary or letters in compiling this study.

Smith, John Day, 1845–
The history of the Nineteenth regiment of Maine volunteer infantry, 1862–1865, by John Day Smith ... Prepared at the request of the Nineteenth Maine regimental association, with an introduction written by Brevet Major-General Alexander S. Webb. Minneapolis, Great Western printing company, 1909.

xv, 356 p. plates, ports., maps. 24 cm.

Balanced material, including many personal contributions, makes this study a fine unit history.

Smith, John Thomas, *col. 31st Ind. infantry.*
A history of the Thirty-first regiment of Indiana volunteer infantry in the war of the rebellion, by John Thomas Smith ... Cincinnati, Western Methodist book concern, 1900.

226 p. incl. front., ports. 24 cm.

All in all, among the best of the few Hoosier unit histories available.

Smith, Sydney Kerr, 1850–
Life, army record, and public services of D. Howard Smith. By Sydney K. Smith. Louisville, Ky., The Bradley & Gilbert company, 1890.

211 p. front. (port.) 24 cm.

Too brief a biography of the colonel of the 5th Kentucky Cavalry (CSA); the section on his Civil War career is proportionally briefer.

Smith, Thomas West, *b.* 1844 *or* 5.
The story of a cavalry regiment: "Scott's 900" Eleventh New York cavalry, from the St. Lawrence River to the Gulf of Mexico, 1861–1865; by Thomas West Smith ... [Chicago] Veteran association of the regiment [1897]

viii, 344, [33] p. front., illus., plates, ports. 27 cm.

The narrative treats of operations in Louisiana, but the author's attempts at humor make much of the text suspect.

Smith, Tunstall, *ed.*
Richard Snowden Andrews, lieutenant-colonel commanding the First Maryland artillery (Andrews' battalion) Confederate States army; a memoir, ed. by Tunstall Smith ... [Baltimore] Press of the Sun job printing office, 1910.

151 p. col. front., plates, ports., facsims. 23½ cm.

A loose collection of postwar correspondence and recollections of an able but autocratic artillery commander.

Smith, Walter George, 1854-1924.
Life and letters of Thomas Kilby Smith, brevet major-general, United States volunteers, 1820-1887; by his son, Walter George Smith ... New York and London, G. P. Putnam's sons, 1898.

ix, 487 p. front., ports. 23½ᶜᵐ.

This above-average collection consists of a memoir and letters to his wife by an Ohio officer in the Trans-Mississippi theater.

Smith, William Farrar, 1824-1903.
From Chattanooga to Petersburg under Generals Grant and Butler; a contribution to the history of the war, and a personal vindication, by William Farrar Smith ... Boston and New York, Houghton, Mifflin and co., 1893.

viii, 201 p. map, plans. 20ᶜᵐ.

Smith primarily used the Official Records to defend his military conduct and to attack his two chief persecutors: U. S. Grant and Ben Butler.

Snyder, *Mrs.* **Ann E**
The civil war from a southern standpoint. By Mrs. Ann E. Snyder ... Nashville, Tenn., Publishing house of the M. E. church, South, 1890.

308 p. front., plates. 19ᶜᵐ.

Of value only for an appendix that contains the memoir of a Presbyterian minister who served as a Confederate Chaplain.

The **Soldiers'** and sailors' half-dime tales: of the late rebellion. v. 1. New York, Philadelphia [etc.] Soldiers' and sailors' publishing co., 1868.

120, 360, ii p. illus. 20ᶜᵐ.

A series of sixteen weeklies that contributed more fiction and legend to the story of the war.

The **Soldier's** casket. v. 1; Jan.–Dec. 1865. Philadelphia, C. W. Alexander, 1865.

768, ii p. illus., plates (part col.) 24ᶜᵐ.

A collection of personal exploits, sentimentalities, and daring deeds comprised the bulk of this periodical; the lead illustration was usually a heart-wrencher.

Sorrel, Gilbert Moxley, 1838-1901.
Recollections of a Confederate staff officer, by Gen. G. Moxley Sorrel ... with introduction by Senator John W. Daniel. New York and Washington, The Neale publishing company, 1905.

315 p. front. (port.) 21½ cm.

Incisive memoirs by the cultured, mild-mannered chief of staff for Gen. James Longstreet; contains much on the high command of the Army of Northern Virginia.

Sorrel, Gilbert Moxley, 1838-1901.
Recollections of a Confederate staff officer. Edited by Bell Irvin Wiley. Jackson, Tenn., McCowat-Mercer Press, 1958.

322 p. illus. 23 cm.

Editor Wiley reorganized the original text, made it more readable, and added necessary introduction, notes and index.

Southern historical society.
Southern historical society papers. v. 1-38, 1876-1910; new ser., no. 1– (whole no. 39–) 1914–
Richmond, Va. [1876]-19

v. illus., plates, ports. 23½ cm.

These fifty-two volumes, containing everything from congressional minutes to personal reminiscences, are indispensable for any study in depth of the Confederacy.

Southwick, Thomas Paine, 1837-1892.
A Duryee zouave, by Thomas P. Southwick of the Fifth New York volunteers; journal and reminiscences of camp life and the personal experiences on the march and in the field, of an ordinary, common soldier of the civil war. [Washington, D. C., Acme printing co., ᶜ1930]

119 p. incl. front. (mounted port.) 2 illus. (1 mounted) 23½ᶜᵐ.

An opinionated memoir of service in Virginia; the book has limited usefulness.

Spangler, Edward Webster, 1846–
My little war experience. With historical sketches and memorabilia, by Edward W. Spangler ... [York, Pa., Printed by the York daily publishing company, 1904]

xv, 202, [3] p. front., plates, ports., facsims. 23½ᶜᵐ.

In spite of its disorganization, this narrative by a soldier of the 130th Pennsylvania gives moving descriptions of the carnage at Antietam and Fredericksburg.

Sperry, Andrew F

History of the 33d Iowa infantry volunteer regiment. 1863-6. By A. F. Sperry. Des Moines, Mills & co., 1866.

viii, 237 p. front. (port.) 23^{cm}.

Based on a diary, and written without pretense or exaggeration, this is an excellent source for the campaigns in Arkansas.

Spicer, William Arnold 1845–1913.

History of the Ninth and Tenth regiments Rhode Island volunteers, and the Tenth Rhode Island battery, in the Union army in 1862. Providence, Snow & Farnham, printers, 1892.

3 p. l., 5–415 p. front., illus. 23^{cm}.

Revealing for army life around Washington and in Virginia.

Sprague, Homer Baxter, 1829–

History of the 13th infantry regiment of Connecticut volunteers, during the great rebellion. By Homer B. Sprague ... Hartford, Case, Lockwood & co., 1867.

viii, [9]–353 p. 19 cm.

A member of that small group of superb unit histories; excellent for events in the Trans-Mississippi theater.

Sprenger, George F

Concise history of the camp and field life of the 122d regiment, Penn'a volunteers. Compiled from notes, sketches, facts and incidents, as recorded in the diary of George F. Sprenger ... Lancaster, Pa., The New era steam book print, 1885.

vii, [1], 9–372 p. incl. illus., maps. front., pl., port. 19$\frac{1}{4}$^{cm}.

A diary-like history, excellent for personal feelings and insights.

Stanard, Beverly, 1845–1864.

Letters of a New Market cadet. Edited by John G. Barrett and Robert K. Turner, Jr. Chapel Hill, University of North Carolina Press [1961]

70 p. illus. 24 cm.

Nineteen-year-old Beverly Stanard died in the charge of the VMI cadets at New Market; this volume contains seventeen letters written in the months prior to his death.

Stanley, David Sloane, 1828–1902.

Personal memoirs of Major-General D. S. Stanley, U. S. A. Cambridge, Mass., Harvard university press, 1917.

1 p. l., 271 p. 23^{cm}.

An average memoir by a Union officer; its greatest weakness are several errors of fact.

Stanyan, John M

A history of the Eighth regiment of New Hampshire volunteers, including its service as infantry, Second N. H. cavalry, and Veteran battalion in the civil war of 1861–1865, covering a period of three years, ten months, and nineteen days. By John M. Stanyan ... Concord, I. C. Evans, printer, 1892.

583 p. front., illus., port. 23$\frac{1}{2}$^{cm}.

Badly arranged excerpts from diaries and letters nevertheless manage to throw some light on the regiment's activities in Louisiana.

Stern, Philip Van Doren, 1900–   *ed.*

Soldier life in the Union and Confederate Armies. Edited with an introd. and notes, from Hardtack and coffee by John D. Billings, and Detailed minutiae of soldier life in the Army of Northern Virginia by Carlton McCarthy. Original sketches by Charles W. Reed and William L. Sheppard. Greenwich, Conn., Fawcett Publications [1961]

400 p. illus. 18 cm.

In combining the splendid narratives of Billings and McCarthy, the editor did a great disservice to both; annotations are non-existent; pagination is erratic; and the introduction is meaningless.

Stevens, Charles Augustus, b. 1835.

Berdan's United States sharpshooters in the Army of the Potomac, 1861–1865. By Capt. C. A. Stevens ... St. Paul, Minn. [Printed by the Price-McGill company] 1892.

xxiii, 555 p. front., illus., pl., port. 24 cm.

A superb regimental history of one of the North's most famous commands; a professional journalist, Stevens captured drama, color, and excitement.

Stevens, George Thomas, 1832–1921.

Three years in the Sixth corps. A concise narrative of events in the Army of the Potomac from 1861 to the close of the rebellion, April, 1865. By George T. Stevens ... 2d ed., rev. and cor., with seven steel portraits and numerous wood engravings. New York, D. Van Nostrand, 1870.

4 p. l., [v]–xvi, 449 p. front., illus., plates, ports., plan. 20$\frac{1}{4}$^{cm}.

One of the justifiably basic sources for any study of the Army of the Potomac; fresh, reliable, accurate account that spans the entire war years.

Stevens, Hazard, 1842–1918.
The life of Isaac Ingalls Stevens, by his son, Hazard Stevens ... Boston and New York, Houghton, Mifflin and company, 1900.

2 v. front., illus., plates, ports., maps (part fold.) plans, fold. facsim. 23½ cm.

Gen. Stevens met his death in 1862 at Chantilly, Va.; most of this work treats of his prewar career in Mexico and the West.

Stevens, William Burnham, 1843–
History of the Fiftieth regiment of infantry, Massachusetts volunteer militia, in the late war of the rebellion, by William B. Stevens ... Boston, Griffith-Stillings press, 1907.

xii, 399 p. front., pl., ports., plan. 23½ cm.

An excellent source for 1862-1863 campaigns in Louisiana; composed in the main of several soldiers' diaries.

Stevenson, Benjamin Franklin.
Letters from the army, by B. F. Stevenson, surgeon to the Twenty-second Kentucky infantry. Cincinnati, W. E. Dibble & co., 1884.

vi, [7]–311 p. 20 cm.

The revealing letters of a surgeon stationed for most of the war in Louisiana and Mississippi; many personal observations.

Stevenson, James Hunter, 1833–
"Boots and saddles." A history of the first volunteer cavalry of the war, known as the First New York (Lincoln) cavalry, and also as the Sabre regiment. Its organization, campaigns and battles. By Jas. H. Stevenson ... Harrisburg, Patriot publishing company, 1879.

xviii, 388 p. front. (port.) pl. 20 cm.

Capt. Stevenson relied on his voluminous diary for this exceptionally revealing story of cavalry life in northern Virginia and the Shenandoah Valley.

Stevenson, Thomas M   b. 1825 or 26.
History of the 78th regiment O. V. V. I., from its "muster-in" to its "muster-out"; comprising its organization, marches, campaigns, battles and skirmishes. By Rev. Thomas M. Stevenson, chaplain ... Zanesville, O., H. Dunne, 1865.

vii, [9]–349, [2] p. 22½ cm.

More a personal narrative by the regimental chaplain than a regimental history; organization of the material suffered from the author's haste to get the work into print.

Stevenson, William G
Thirteen months in the Rebel army: being a narrative of personal adventures in the infantry, ordnance, cavalry, courier, and hospital services ... By an impressed New Yorker. New York, A. S. Barnes & Burr, 1862.

232 p. front. 17 cm.

A highly excitable author's account of his almost bizarre adventures in trying to re-gain the Union lines; the study was probably written primarily for propagandistic purposes.

Stewart, Alexander Morrison, 1814–1875.
Camp, march and battle-field; or, Three years and a half with the Army of the Potomac. By Rev. A. M. Stewart ... Philadelphia, J. B. Rodgers, 1865.

x, 413 p. front. (port.) 19½ cm.

A composite of individual studies that originally appeared in a Pittsburgh newspaper; the author was chaplain of the 13th Pennsylvania and served in Virginia.

Stewart, Nixon B
Dan McCook's regiment, 52nd O. V. I. A history of the regiment, its campaigns and battles. From 1862 to 1865. By Rev. Nixon B. Stewart ... [Claysville, O.] The author, 1900.

255 p. incl. illus., port. front. 20½ cm.

A good, highly personal memoir loaded with Stewart's incisive observations of war.

Stewart, Robert Laird, 1840–1919.
History of the One hundred and fortieth regiment Pennsylvania volunteers, by Professor Robert Laird Stewart ... Pub. by authority of the Regimental association. [Philadelphia, Printed by the Franklin bindery] 1912.

3 p. l., 504 p. front. (fold. map) illus. (incl. plans) plates, ports. 23 cm.

Another instance of too much reliance on printed sources; the final sections contain personal reminiscences of some importance.

Stewart, William Henry, 1838–
A pair of blankets; war-time history in letters to the young people of the South, by William H. Stewart. New York, Broadway publishing co. [c1911]

8 p., 1 l., 9–217 p. incl. front. (port.) port. 19½ cm.

Its disorganization notwithstanding, these recollections by a colonel of the 61st Virginia possess some usefulness in analyzing Lee's 1864-1865 campaigns.

Stiles, Robert, 1836–
Four years under Marse Robert, by Robert Stiles ... **New York & Washington,** The Neale publishing company, 1903.

xvi, ₁17₁–368 p.   front.   22½ᵐ.

An informative and entertaining memoir by a very intelligent member of Lee's army; particularly good for the 1864-1865 campaigns.

Stillwell, Leander, 1843–
The story of a common soldier of army life in the civil war, 1861-1865. 2d ed. By Leander Stillwell ... ₁Erie? Kan.₁ Franklin Hudson publishing co., 1920.

278 p.   front., ports.   20ᵐ.

A comprehensive and solid memoir by an observant soldier; based on letters and a diary; indispensable for any understanding of a Federal "GI."

Stockwell, Elisha, 1846–1935.
Private Elisha Stockwell, Jr., sees the Civil War. Edited by Byron R. Abernethy. ₁1st ed.₁ Norman, University of Oklahoma Press ₁1958₁

210 p.   illus.   21 cm.

Stockwell joined the 14th Wisconsin at the age of fifteen and took part in most of the major battles of the West; it is regrettable that he waited over sixty years to pen his memoirs without benefit of any wartime writings.

Stone, Edwin Winchester.
Rhode Island in the rebellion. By Edwin W. Stone ... Providence, G. H. Whitney, 1864.

xxxviii, 398 p.   20ᶜᵐ.

This mis-titled memoir of service in Virginia during the first year of war is even-tempered, reliable, and one of the best of the early publications of life in the army.

Stone, James Madison, 1840–
Personal recollections of the civil war, by one who took part in it as a private soldier in the 21st volunteer regiment of infantry from Massachusetts, by James Madison Stone. Boston, Mass., The author, 1918.

193 p.   front. (port.)   19ᶜᵐ.

A fairly reliable account of duty with the 21st Massachusetts; of particular value for insights into the Antietam and Fredericksburg campaigns.

Stonebraker, Joseph R
... A rebel of '61. By Jos. R. Stonebraker ... New York and Albany, Wynkoop, Hallenbeck, Crawford co., printers, 1899.

116 p.   front., illus. (facsims.) plates, ports., fold. geneal. tab.   23½ᶜᵐ.

Of cautious use only for the Second Valley Campaigns.

Storrs, John Whiting.
The "Twentieth Connecticut"; a regimental history. By John W. Storrs ... Ansonia, Conn., Press of the "Naugatuck Valley sentinel," 1886.

288, xviii p.   front., phot., fold. map.   19½ᶜᵐ.

This regiment fought in the Chancellorsville, Gettysburg, Atlanta, and Carolina campaigns; short diary entries are interspersed among a too-general narrative.

The **Story** of American heroism: thrilling narratives of personal adventures during the great civil war as told by the medal winners and roll of honor men ... Chicago, New York, The Werner co., 1896.

1 p. l., xxvi, 21–798 p. incl. illus., pl., port. front.   25½ᶜᵐ.

A massive collection of tributes and essays of self-praise; contributors include such generals as O. O. Howard and Fitzhugh Lee.

Stowits, George H   1822–
History of the One hundredth regiment of New York state volunteers: being a record of its services from its muster in to its muster out: its muster in roll, roll of commissions, recruits furnished through the Board of trade of the city of Buffalo, and short sketches of deceased and surviving offiers. By Geo. H. Stowits ... Buffalo, Printing house of Matthews & Warren, 1870.

xxiv, ₁25₁–424 p.   front., pl., port.   19½ᶜᵐ.

An impersonal chronicle of the regiment's war activities, with biographical sketches affixed.

Strong, Robert Hale.
A Yankee private's Civil War. Edited by Ashley Halsey. Chicago, H. Regnery Co., 1961.

218 p.   illus.   21 cm.

A typical Civil War memoir; as a private in the 105th Illinois, Strong campaigned with Sherman and in later years used some wartime letters as a partial memory-refresher.

Strother, David Hunter, 1816–1888.
A Virginia Yankee in the Civil War; the diaries of David Hunter Strother. Edited with an introd. by Cecil D. Eby, Jr. Chapel Hill, University of North Carolina Press [1961]

xx, 294 p. illus. 24 cm.

The celebrated "Porte Crayon's" Civil War diaries are a rich source for data on the Eastern theater in general and the Shenandoah Valley in particular.

Stuart, Addison A
Iowa colonels and regiments: being a history of Iowa regiments in the war of the rebellion; and containing a description of the battles in which they have fought. By Captain A. A. Stuart ... Des Moines, Mills & co., 1865.

656 p. 23 cm.

Through biographical sketches of eighty-four Iowa officers, Capt. Stuart produced one of the first accurate compilations of his state's military contributions.

Stuart, James Ewell Brown, 1833–1864.
Letters of General J. E. B. Stuart to his wife, 1861, edited by Bingham Duncan ... Atlanta, Ga., The Library, Emory university, 1943.

2 p. l., 7–30 p. incl. front. (facsim.) 24ᶜᵐ.

Interesting letters by the Confederacy's Beau Ideal, but of limited historical value.

Stuber, Johann, 1838?–1895?
Mein tagebuch über die erlebnisse im revolutions-kriege von 1861 bis 1865. Von Johann Stuber. In ehrender und liebevoller erinnerung herausgegeben von seiner wittwe, frau Rosa Stuber. Cincinnati, O., Druck von S. Rosenthal & co., 1896.

206 p. illus. 24 cm.

The only published account by a member of the 58th Ohio; author concentrates on his military experiences from Fort Henry to Fort Morgan.

Sturtevant, Ralph Orson, 1838–1910.
Pictorial history Thirteenth regiment Vermont volunteers, war of 1861–1865 [by] Ralph Orson Sturtevant, historian. [n. p., 1910]

861, [1] p., 1 l. incl. illus., plates (part fold.) ports. 27ᶜᵐ.

The most voluminous of the Vermont unit studies; however, only the first half is a narrative of the regiment's activities.

Sullivan County (N. Y.) Historical Society. *Sullivan County Civil War Centennial Commission.*
Brass buttons and leather boots; Sullivan County and the Civil War. [South Fallsburg, N. Y., Printed by Steingart Associates, 1963]

84 p. illus., maps, facsims. 23 cm.

Contains some material, including letters, relative to the 56th and 143rd New York.

Sumner, George C
Battery D, First Rhode Island light artillery, in the civil war, 1861–1865. By Dr. George C. Sumner ... Providence, Rhode Island printing company, 1897.

3 p. l., 192 p. front., illus. (incl. ports.) 21½ᶜᵐ.

Particularly good for little personal incidents that took place within the battery; Sumner is also noted for several published monographs of war experiences.

Surby, Richard W   *b.* 1832.
Grierson raids, and Hatch's sixty-four days march, with biographical sketches, also the life and adventures of Chickasaw, the scout. By R. W. Surby. Chicago, Rounds and James, printers, 1865.

396 p. plates, ports. 19¼ cm.

A revealing and accurate narrative of Grierson's raid through Louisiana; author spent some time as a prisoner of war; two enlarged editions of the work appeared later.

Sutton, Joseph J
History of the Second regiment West Virginia cavalry volunteers, during the war of the rebellion. By J. J. Sutton ... Portsmouth, O., 1892.

262 p. front., illus., pl., port. 23½ᶜᵐ.

One of those weak works where the author concerned himself more with army movements than with the activities of his regiment.

Swinton, William, 1833–1892.
History of the Seventh regiment, National guard, state of New York, during the war of the rebellion: with a preliminary chapter on the origin and early history of the regiment, a summary of its history since the war, and a roll of honor, comprising brief sketches of the services rendered by members of the regiment in the army and navy of the United States. By William Swinton ... Illustrated by Thomas Nast. New York and Boston, Fields, Osgood & co., 1870.

iv, 501 p. front., illus., pl., port. 22½ cm.

Much official correspondence and statistical material on this three-year regiment make the study impersonal and of limited value.

Sykes, Edward Turner, 1839–
 Walthall's brigade: a cursory sketch, with personal experiences of Walthall's brigade, Army of Tennessee, C. S. A., 1862–1865. By E. T. Sykes, late adjutant-general. Walthall's brigade.
 (*In* Mississippi historical society. **Publications. Centenary series.** 1916. 24ᶜᵐ. v. 1. p. [477]–623. port.)

The subtitle accurately describes this rather shallow summary that apparently was written with little reliance on personal documents.

Symonds, Henry Clay, *d.* 1900.
 Report of a commissary of subsistence, 1861–65, by H. C. Symonds ... Sing Sing, N. Y., The author [ᶜ1888]
 207 p. 17½ᶜᵐ.

Symonds's unique position makes this little-known work a necessary source for any study of Federal supply and administration.

Sypher, Josiah Rhinehart, 1832–
 History of the Pennsylvania reserve corps: a complete record of the organization; and of the different companies, regiments and brigades; containing descriptions of expeditions, marches, skirmishes, and battles; together with biographical sketches of officers and personal records of each man during his term of service. Compiled from official reports and other documents. By J. R. Sypher, esq. Lancaster, Pa., Published by E. Barr & co., 1865.
 723 p. 4 port. (incl. front.) 22½ᶜᵐ.

The author's flair for the overdramatic, and a lack of abundant primary sources, are the chief weaknesses of this history of the Keystone State's first thirteen infantry regiments.

Talbot, Edith (Armstrong)
 Samuel Chapman Armstrong; a biographical study, by Edith Armstrong Talbot. New York, Doubleday, Page & company, 1904.
 vi p., 3 l., 3–301 p. front., plates, ports. 20½ cm.

Included in this memoir are many excerpts from letters written while Armstrong was serving the 125th New York.

Tarbox, Increase Niles, 1815–1888.
 Missionary patriots. Memoirs of James H. Schneider and Edward M. Schneider. By Increase N. Tarbox ... Boston, Massachusetts Sabbath school society, 1867.
 iv, 7–357 p. 2 port. (incl. front.) 17½ᶜᵐ.

A eulogy to a father and son, one of whom was a chaplain of colored troops and the other a member of the 57th Massachusetts; more sentimental than factual.

Tarrant, Eastham.
 The wild riders of the First Kentucky cavalry. A history of the regiment in the great war of the rebellion, 1861–1865, telling of its origin and organization; a description of the material of which it was composed; its rapid and severe marches, hard service, and fierce conflicts ... A regimental roster. Prison life, adventures and escapes. By Sergeant E. Tarrant ... Published by a committee of the regiment. [Louisville, Press of R. H. Carothers, ᶜ1894]
 x, 503 p. front., port. 22 cm.

Tarrant's narrative, based on wartime documents, clear memory, and good judgement, is the best account by a member of a Kentucky unit in Federal service.

Taylor, Benjamin Franklin, 1819–1887.
 Mission ridge and Lookout mountain, with pictures of life in camp and field. By Benj. F. Taylor. New York, D. Appleton & company; Chicago, S. C. Griggs & co., 1872.
 vi, [7]–272 p. 21 cm.

Written by a Chicago Evening Journal correspondent, this collection of monographs gives an exceptionally revealing picture of the 1863 campaigns around Chattanooga.

Taylor, Frank Hamilton, *b.* 1846.
 Philadelphia in the civil war 1861–1865 [by] Frank H. Taylor. Illustrated from contemporary prints and photographs and from drawings by the author. [Philadelphia] The city, 1913.
 360 p. front., illus., plates, port., fold. map. 23 cm.

That this is a large collection of small summaries is borne out by the table of contents, which contains no less than 101 headings.

Taylor, Richard, 1826–1879.
 Destruction and reconstruction: personal experiences of the late war. By Richard Taylor ... New York, D. Appleton and company, 1879.
 274 p. 23 cm.

A constantly quoted commentary by a distinguished Confederate general and son of Zachary Taylor; particularly good for the author's observations on "Stonewall" Jackson.

Taylor, Richard, 1826–1879.
 Destruction and reconstruction; personal experiences of the late war. Edited by Richard B. Harwell. [1st ed.] New York, Longmans, Green, 1955.
 xxxii, 380 p. 24 cm.

Editor's introduction, explanatory notes, and index enhance a superb narrative, which was reproduced in unabridged form.

Taylor, Susie King, *b.* 1848.
    Reminiscences of my life in camp with the 33d United States colored troops, late 1st S. C. volunteers, by Susie King Taylor ... Boston, The author, 1902.

    xii p., 1 l., 82 p.   front., pl., ports.   19½ cm.

Sketchy but unique recollections by a Negress who served as a nurse for one of the first all-colored units; her war experiences were confined to the South Carolina and Georgia coasts.

Taylor, Walter Herron, 1838–1916.
    Four years with General Lee; being a summary of the more important events touching the career of General Robert E. Lee, in the war between the states; together with an authoritative statement of the strength of the army which he commanded in the field. By Walter H. Taylor ... New York, D. Appleton and company, 1877.

    199 p.   front. (port.)   24 cm.

A basic, valuable source on the character of Lee and the strength of the Army of Northern Virginia.

Taylor, Walter Herron, 1838–1916.
    Four years with General Lee. With a new introd., index, and notes by James I. Robertson, Jr. Bloomington, Indiana University Press ₁1962₎

    xi, ₁7₎–218 p.   ports.   21 cm.

Added to this offset printing of the first edition are introduction, notes, index, and some excerpts from Taylor's more lengthy memoirs, cited below.

Taylor, Walter Herron, 1838–1916.
    General Lee, his campaigns in Virginia, 1861–1865, with personal reminiscences, by Walter H. Taylor ... Norfolk, Va., For sale by the Nusbaum book and news company ₁Brooklyn, N. Y., Press of Braunworth & co., ᶜ1906₎

    x, 314 p.   fold. maps.   23½ᶜᵐ.

The better of Col. Taylor's two volumes of reminiscences because this work contains more personal observations and remembrances.

Tennessee. *Civil War Centennial Commission.*
    Tennesseans in the Civil War; a military history of Confederate and Union units with available rosters of personnel. Nashville, 1964–

    v.   28 cm.

This uncompleted compilation contains useful sketches on various Volunteer State regiments.

Tenney, Luman Harris, 1841–1880.
    War diary, 1861–1865. Printed for private circulation by Frances Andrews Tenney, Oberlin, Ohio. Cleveland, Evangelical Pub. House, 1914.

    xix, 195 p.   illus., ports., fold. map.   25 cm.

This full four-year diary of campaigning in Tennessee and Virginia contains short entries but much personal data on army life.

Terrill, John Newton, *d.* 1916.
    Campaign of the Fourteenth regiment New Jersey volunteers, by Sergeant J. Newton Terrill ... 2d ed. New Brunswick, Daily home news press, 1884.

    132 p.   19½ᶜᵐ.

Written in the months immediately after the war, this slim volume is a day-by-day chronicle of service; it is especially revealing for the 1864–1865 campaigns of the VI Corps.

Tevis, C   V
    ... The history of the fighting Fourteenth, published in commemoration of the fiftieth anniversary of the muster of the regiment into the United States service, May 23, 1861. ₁Brooklyn, Brooklyn eagle press, 1911?₎

    366, ₁2₎ p.   illus. (incl. ports.) col. pl.   27½ cm.

Some short diary entries are incorporated into an otherwise useless narrative.

Thatcher, Marshall P
    A hundred battles in the West, St. Louis to Atlanta, 1861–65. The Second Michigan cavalry, with the armies of the Mississippi, Ohio, Kentucky and Cumberland ... with mention of a few of the famous regiments and brigades of the West. By Captain Marshall P. Thatcher ... Detroit, The author, 1884.

    xiv, ₁15₎–416, 15, ₁63₎ p. incl. front., illus., port., maps. pl., port. 23 cm.

The reliable and readable memoirs of participation in most of the principal cavalry campaigns of the West; based on the author's voluminous journal.

Thoburn, Thomas Crawford, 1829–1911.
    My experiences during the Civil War. ₁Compiled and edited by Lyle Thoburn. Cleveland? 1963₎

    197 p.   illus.   29 cm.

This typescript contains a much more detailed account than is found in the usual journal. Thoburn was Colonel of the 50th Ohio.

Thomas, Henry Walter, 1842–

History of the Doles-Cook brigade, army of northern Virginia, C. S. A.; containing muster roles of each company of the Fourth, Twelfth, Twenty-first and Forty-fourth Georgia regiments, with a short sketch of the services of each member, and a complete history of each regiment, by one of its own members ... By Henry W. Thomas ... Atlanta, Ga., The Franklin printing and publishing company, 1903.

x, 629 p., 1 l., 631–632 p. front., plates, ports. 23 cm.

Two-thirds of this history consists of rosters and biographical sketches; the comparatively short narrative has some quotable data.

Thomas, Howard, 1898–

Boys in Blue from the Adirondack foothills. Maps by John D. Mahaffy. [1st ed.] Prospect, N. Y., Prospect Books, 1960.

297 p. illus. 22 cm.

Thomas relied heavily on manuscript sources for this composite history of eight New York regiments; much discussion also exists on home-front activities.

Thompson, Edwin Porter, 1834–

History of the Orphan brigade. By Ed Porter Thompson ... Louisville, Ky., L. N. Thompson, 1898.

1104 p. col. front., plates (1 col.) ports. 24 cm.

Possessing everything from rosters to tall tales, Thompson's thick study is a standard source for any study of the Western theater, especially the 1862 fighting in Louisiana.

Thompson, Heber Samuel, 1840–

The first defenders; by Heber S. Thompson, president of the First defenders' association. [n. p., 1910]

1 p. l., vii–xiii p., 1 l., 179 p. pl., ports., facsims. 23½ cm.

A praising account of the Pennsylvania units that allegedly were the first troops to reach Washington after Lincoln's call.

Thompson, John C   *corp. 11th R. I. infantry.*

History of the Eleventh regiment, Rhode Island volunteers, in the war of the rebellion. By R. W. Rock [pseud.] Published by a committee of the Eleventh regiment veteran association. Providence, Providence press company, printers, 1881.

vii, 217 p. 20 cm.

Short on military matters but long on personal incidents, this history is one of the better sources for 1862–1863 campaigning around Washington and Norfolk, Va.

Thompson, Joseph Parrish, 1819–1879.

Bryant Gray: the student, the Christian, the soldier. By Joseph P. Thompson ... New York, A. D. F. Randolph, 1864.

148 p. front. (port.) 15½ cm.

Another of those non-revealing eulogies to a dead Union soldier.

Thompson, Joseph Parrish 1819–1879.

The sergeant's memorial. By his father. New York, A. D. F. Randolph, 1863.

242 p. front. (port.) 16 cm.

This lengthy eulogy to a Union soldier who died in 1863 contains nothing of historical value.

Thompson, S   Millett, 1838–1911.

Thirteenth regiment of New Hampshire volunteer infantry in the war of the rebellion, 1861–1865. A diary covering three years and a day. By S. Millett Thompson ... Boston and New York, Houghton, Mifflin and co., 1888.

xi, [1] p., 1 l., 717 p. incl. pl., maps. front. 24 cm.

A superb diary-like narrative of service in the Virginia Tidewater; Thompson meticulously amassed a wealth of information on the regiment and its members.

Thompson, Seymour Dwight, 1842–1904.

Recollections with the Third Iowa regiment: by Lieut. S. D. Thompson. Cincinnati, Pub. for the author, 1864.

xi, [13]–396 p. 19 cm.

A patriotic and verbose account of the 3rd Iowa's first two years of service in the West; the author elaborated greatly on a diary he kept while in the field.

Thomson, Osmund Rhodes Howard, 1873–

History of the "Bucktails," Kane rifle regiment of the Pennsylvania reserve corps (13th Pennsylvania reserves, 42nd of the line) Pub. by William H. Rauch, historian, for the regimental association. By O. R. Howard Thomson ... and William H. Rauch ... with a dedicatory note by the Hon. Edward A. Irvin ... Philadelphia, Electric printing company, 1906.

x p., 1 l., 466 p., 1 l. front., plates, ports., facsim. 24 cm.

Thomson presents much on Confederates and the countryside, but very little on his regiment.

Thorpe, Sheldon Brainerd, 1838–1924.
The history of the Fifteenth Connecticut volunteers in the war for the defense of the Union, 1861–1865. By Sheldon B. Thorpe ... New Haven, The Price, Lee & Adkins co., 1893.

3 p. l., [5]–362 p. front., illus., plates, ports., plan. 24ᶜᵐ.

A typical regimental history, based in great part on soldiers' diaries and letters; the 15th Connecticut spent its four-year career with the IX Corps.

Tiemann, William Francis.
The 159th regiment infantry, New York state volunteers, in the war of the rebellion, 1862–1865. Comp. and published by William F. Tiemann ... Brooklyn, 1891.

135, [1]ll p. front., pl., maps. 23¼ᶜᵐ.

Too often the author appears to have relied solely on data from muster rolls; but the study has occasional merits.

Tilney, Robert.
My life in the Army, three years and a half with the Fifth Army corps, Army of the Potomac 1862–1865, by Robert Tilney ... Philadelphia, Ferris & Leach, 1912.

247 p. front. (port.) 21½ cm.

The best part of this highly polished narrative treats of Grant's campaigns in Virginia; the author was an Englishman attached to V Corps headquarters.

Tobie, Edward Parsons, 1838–
History of the First Maine cavalry, 1861–1865. By Edward P. Tobie. Published by the First Maine cavalry association. Boston, Press of Emery & Hughes, 1887.

xix, 735, [1] p. front., plates, port. 23¼ᶜᵐ.

Among the better of the unit histories; this regiment consisted of companies from Maine and the District of Columbia.

Todd, William, b. 1839 or 1840.
The Seventy-ninth Highlanders, New York volunteers in the war of rebellion, 1861–1865; by William Todd ... Albany, Press of Brandow, Barton & co., 1886.

xv, 513 p. incl. front., illus. pl., maps. 25 cm.

An excellent regimental history based on numerous letters, diaries, and similar records; the unit's principal campaigns were in Virginia.

Toney, Marcus Breckenridge, 1840–1929.
The privations of a private. The campaign under Gen. R. E. Lee; the campaign under Gen. Stonewall Jackson; Bragg's invasion of Kentucky; the Chickamauga campaign; the Wilderness campaign; prison life in the North; the privations of a citizen; the Ku-Klux klan; a united citizenship. By Marcus B. Toney. Nashville, Tenn., Printed for the author, 1905.

133 p. incl. front. (port.) illus. 20½ᶜᵐ.

A light, chatty memoir of service in both major theaters; unique illustrations enhance the slim volume.

Toombs, Samuel, 1844–1889.
New Jersey troops in the Gettysburg campaign, from June 5 to July 31, 1863. By Samuel Toombs ... Illustrated by specially drawn maps of the battle-field, the monuments erected by the state of New Jersey, and portraits of brigade and regimental commanders. Orange, N. J., The Evening mail publishing house, 1888.

xvi, 406 p. incl. illus., pl., ports., plans. front., fold. plan. 19 cm.

Sgt. Toombs relied completely on printed sources for this tribute to Jerseyans at Gettysburg; over sixty illustrations are included.

Toombs, Samuel, 1844–1889.
Reminiscences of the war, comprising a detailed account of the experiences of the Thirteenth regiment New Jersey volunteers in camp, on the march, and in battle. By Samuel Toombs. With the personal recollections of the author. Orange, Printed at the Journal office, 1878.

4 p. l., 232, 47 p. 17½ cm.

This reliable narrative of service in both theaters was produced from letters, published documents, and official sources.

Torrey, Rodney Webster, b. 1836.
War diary of Rodney W. Torrey, 1862–1863. [n. p., 19—]

93 p. incl. port. front. 20ᶜᵐ.

These short recollections of the war in Louisiana are basically weather reports by a member of the 49th Massachusetts.

Tourgée, Albion Winegar, 1838–1905.
The story of a thousand. Being a history of the service of the 105th Ohio volunteer infantry, in the war for the union from August 21, 1862 to June 6, 1865. By Albion W. Tourgée, LL. D. Buffalo, S. McGerald & son, 1896.

8 p. l., 409 p., 1 l., xiv p. incl. illus., port. map. 23 cm.

Tourgée, who became a notorious Carpetbagger, served with the regiment until 1863 and gives much personal material; the unit's history after that date is treated only lightly.

Tourtellotte, Jerome 1837–

A history of company K of the Seventh Connecticut volunteer infantry in the civil war, compiled by a member who was second in rank in the company when the regiment left the state for the front, and second in rank in the regiment when it returned to the state for final discharge. [n. p.] 1910.

2 p. l., 217, [1] p. 24ᶜᵐ.

A diary-like history, with many personal incidents and individual acts recorded.

Townsend, Edward Davis, 1817–1893.

Anecdotes of the civil war in the United States. By Brevet Major-General E. D. Townsend ... New York, D. Appleton and co., 1884 [1883]

xii, 287 p. illus. 19½ᶜᵐ.

A hodgepodge of personal incidents, with no attempt made to differentiate between the factual and the fictional; the bulk of the material lies in the latter category.

Townsend, Luther Tracy, 1838–1922.

History of the Sixteenth regiment, New Hampshire volunteers. By Adjutant, Luther Tracy Townsend. Published by Henry L. Johnson and Luther T. Townsend. Washington, N. T. Elliott, 1897.

574 p. incl. pl., port., maps. front. 23½ᶜᵐ.

Written from the adjutant's viewpoint, this full history of a year's duty in Louisiana also contains over twoscore sketches and drawings.

Tracie, Theodore C 1836?–

Annals of the Nineteenth Ohio battery, volunteer artillery; including an outline of the operations of the Second division, Twenty-third army corps; lights and shadows of army life, as seen on the march, bivouac and battlefield. By Theodore C. Tracie. Cleveland, O., Pub. for the Battery committee by J. B. Savage, 1878.

xvi, [17]–470 p. 19ᶜᵐ.

Though interesting and sometimes enlightening, the narrative is too embellished to be trustworthy. This is more a memoir than a unit history.

Travis, Benjamin F

The story of the Twenty-fifth Michigan. By B. F. Travis ... Kalamazoo, Kalamazoo publishing co., 1897.

400 p. incl. front., illus., port. map. 23½ᶜᵐ.

Relying on his own recollections and diary, Travis created a monthly chronicle of events; to this he added biographical sketches and the usual roster.

Tremain, Henry Edwin, 1841–1910.

Two days of war, a Gettysburg narrative, and other excursions, by Henry Edwin Tremain ... New York, Bonnell, Silver and Bowers, 1905.

xi p., 2 l., 513 p. front., plates, ports., fold. maps, facsims. 20 cm.

Among numerous unrelated essays are discussions on Gettysburg and Gen. Joseph Hooker.

Trimble, Harvey Marion, 1842–   *ed.*

History of the Ninety-third regiment, Illinois volunteer infantry, from organization to muster out; statistics comp. by Aaron Dunbar ... rev. and ed. by Harvey M. Trimble ... Chicago, The Blakeley printing co., 1898.

441 p. incl. front., illus., ports. fold map. 22½ cm.

Written by the regimental adjutant; highly statistical and at times overly dramatic.

Trobriand, Philippe Régis Denis de Keredern, comte de, 1816–1897.

Four years with the Army of the Potomac. By Régis de Trobriand ... Translated by George K. Dauchy ... Boston, Ticknor and company, 1889.

1 p. l., xix p., 1 l., 757 p. front. (port.) maps (part fold.) 22 cm.

A primary source for any study of high command in the Army of the Potomac; author was a French nobleman and socialite who rose to major general in the II Corps.

Trumbull, Henry Clay, 1830–1903.

The captured scout of the Army of the James. A sketch of the life of Sergeant Henry H. Manning, of the Twenty-fourth Mass. regiment. By Chaplain H. Clay Trumbull. Boston, Nichols and Noyes, 1869.

60 p. 17½ᶜᵐ.

A tribute to a Massachusetts soldier who succumbed to the ordeal of Andersonville.

Trumbull, Henry Clay, 1830–1903.

... The knightly soldier: a biography of Major Henry Ward Camp, Tenth Conn. vols. By Chaplain H. Clay Trumbull. Boston, Nichols and Noyes; New York, O. S. Felt, 1865.

xii, 13–331 p. front. (port.) plates. 18½ cm.

Composed in the main of letters and diary excerpts, this is a straightforward, unprejudiced narrative of service in North Carolina and Virginia; subject was killed in action late in 1864.

Trumbull, Henry Clay, 1830–1903.

War memories of an army chaplain, by H. Clay Trumbull ... New York, C. Scribner's sons, 1898.

x, 421 p. front. (port.) plates. 20½ cm.

A basic source on the labors of army chaplains; yet the author relies too heavily on reconstructed conversation, spiritual matters and suppositions in recounting his services as chaplain of the 10th Connecticut.

Tunnard, William H.

A southern record. The history of the Third regiment Louisiana infantry. By W. H. Tunnard ... Baton Rougle, La., Printed for the author, 1866.

[xx], [21]–393, [1] p. 2 port. (incl. front.) 19½ cm.

An excellent composite of personal accounts of battles and army life in the Arkansas-Missouri region.

Twitchell, Albert Sobieski, 1840–

History of the Seventh Maine light battery, volunteers in the great rebellion ... also, personal sketches of a large number of members, portraits, illustrations and poems. Written and compiled by Quartermaster-Sergeant A. S. Twitchell ... Boston, Mass., E. B. Stillings & co., printers and lithographers, 1892.

1 p. l., vi, 9–248 p. front., illus. (ports.) pl. 24 cm.

Biographical sketches comprise the bulk of this work.

Tyler, Elnathan B

"Wooden nutmegs" at Bull Run. A humorous account of some of the exploits and experiences of the three months Connecticut brigade, and the part they bore in the national stampede. By Frinkle Fry [pseud.] Hartford, G. L. Coburn, 1872.

viii, [9]–86 p. illus. 22 cm.

In his attempts to be witty, Tyler too often strays far from the truth.

Tyler, Mason Whiting, 1840–1907.

Recollections of the civil war; with many original diary entries and letters written from the seat of war, and with annotated references, by Mason Whiting Tyler, late lieut.-colonel and brevet-colonel, 37th reg't Mass. vols. Ed. by William S. Tyler. With maps and illustrations. New York and London, G. P. Putnam's sons, 1912.

xvii, 379 p. front., ports., fold. maps. 22½ cm.

A valuable personal account of the war in Virginia by an officer of the 37th Massachusetts; includes letters, diary excerpts, and a long narrative by the editor.

Underwood, Adin Ballou.

The three years' service of the Thirty-third Mass. infantry regiment 1862–1865. And the campaigns and battles of Chancellorsville, Beverley's ford, Gettysburg, Wauhatchie, Chattanooga, Atlanta, the march to the sea and through the Carolinas, in which it took part. By Adin B. Underwood ... Boston, A. Williams & co., 1881 [1880]

xiv, 299, [35] p. 23½ cm.

This dramatic account is concerned more with large movements than with the regiment's actions; it is also based too much on hearsay testimony.

Underwood, George C

History of the Twenty-sixth regiment of the North Carolina troops, in the great war, 1861–'65. By George C. Underwood ... Goldsboro, N. C., Nash brothers, printers [1901?]

2 p. l., 122, 6 p. front., ports. 23 cm.

A reprinted chapter from Vol. II of Walter Clark's history of North Carolina units (q. v.).

Upson, Theodore Frelinghuysen, 1845–1919.

With Sherman to the sea; the civil war letters, diaries & reminiscences of Theodore F. Upson, edited with an introduction by Oscar Osburn Winther ... University Station, Baton Rouge, La., Louisiana state university press, 1943.

xxii, 181 p. front., plates, port. 21 cm.

One of the more important, personal accounts of Sherman's march; Upson was a pious member of the 100th Indiana.

Upson, Theodore Frelinghuysen, 1845–1919.

With Sherman to the sea; the Civil War letters, diaries & reminiscences of Theodore F. Upson. Edited with an introd. by Oscar Osburn Winther. Bloomington, Indiana University Press [1958]

xxviii, 181 p. illus., port., map. 22 cm.

An offset reprinting of the above, with an enlarged introduction and still no index.

Vail, Enos Ballard, 1843–

Reminiscences of a boy in the civil war, by Enos B. Vail. [Brooklyn] Printed by the author for private distribution, 1915.

159 p. incl. front. (port.) 23½ cm.

Some good material exists in this dramatic and very polished narrative.

Vaill, Dudley Landon.

The county regiment; a sketch of the Second regiment of Connecticut volunteer heavy artillery, originally the Nineteenth volunteer infantry, in the civil war, by Dudley Landon Vaill. [Winsted? Conn.] Litchfield county university club, 1908.

xii, 108 p., 1 l. front., plates, ports. 21ᶜᵐ.

Compiled from printed sources; too brief to be of value.

Vaill, Theodore Frelinghuysen, 1832–1875.

History of the Second Connecticut volunteer heavy artillery. Originally the Nineteenth Connecticut vols. By Theodore F. Vaill, first lieutenant and adjutant ... Winsted, Conn., Winsted printing company, 1868.

366 p. ports. 20 cm.

Written immediately after the war and largely a product of Vaill's memory; in spite of some disorganization, a revealing study of the VI Corps in action.

Vale, Joseph G

Minty and the cavalry. A history of cavalry campaigns in the western armies. By Joseph G. Vale ... Harrisburg, Pa., E. K. Meyers, printer, 1886.

xxxi, 550 p. front., plates, ports., maps. 24ᶜᵐ.

Written by the commander of the XX Corps to his daughter, this long run of letters presents an undiluted picture of war; especially valuable for Sherman's campaigns.

Valentine, Herbert Eugene, 1841–

Story of Co. F, 23d Massachusetts volunteers, in the war for the union, 1861–1865, by Herbert E. Valentine (Guidon) Boston, W. B. Clarke & co., 1896.

vii, [1] p., 1 l., ix–xii, [9]–166 p. front., plates, ports. 23½ᶜᵐ.

A revealing account of army life in North Carolina; contains much personal data.

Van Alstyne, Lawrence, *b.* 1839.

Diary of an enlisted man, by Lawrence Van Alstyne ... New Haven, Conn., The Tuttle, Morehouse & Taylor company, 1910.

x, 348 p. front. (port.) 21 cm.

An excellent example of how a soldier's writing and style improved as he progressed in the preparation of this memoir; Van Alstyne saw service late in war as a member of the 90th U. S. Colored Infantry.

Van Santvoord, Cornelius, 1816–1901.

The One hundred and twentieth regiment New York state volunteers. A narrative of its services in the war for the Union. By C. Van Santvoord ... Pub. by the One hundred and twentieth N. Y. regimental union. Rondout, N. Y., Press of the Kingston freeman, 1894.

2 p. l., 327 p. front. (ports.) 2 pl. 23½ᶜᵐ.

A disappointingly thin unit history, comparatively void of personal material.

Vaughan, Alfred J   1830–

Personal record of the Thirteenth regiment, Tennessee infantry. By its old commander ... [Memphis, Press of S. C. Toof & co., 1897]

95 p. incl. front., port. 21ᶜᵐ.

Primarily a muster roll; the short narrative does not even qualify as a foreword to the roll itself.

Vautier, John D

History of the 88th Pennsylvania volunteers in the war for the union, 1861–1865. By John D. Vautier ... Philadelphia, Printed by J. B. Lippincott company, 1894.

280 p. front., plates, ports., maps. 23ᶜᵐ.

A very personal and extremely revealing study; especially good for the regiment's history and individual acts by its members.

Velazquez, Loreta Janeta, 1842–

The woman in battle: a narrative of the exploits, adventures, and travels of Madame Loreta Janeta Velazquez, otherwise known as Lieutenant Harry T. Buford, Confederate States army ... Edited by C. J. Worthington ... Hartford, T. Belknap, 1876.

606 p. front., illus., plates, ports., maps, plans. 22½ᶜᵐ.

The unbelievable story of a woman who masqueraded as a Confederate officer and received a wound at Shiloh.

Vickers, George Morley 1841–   *ed.*

Under both flags ... a panorama of the great civil war as represented in story, anecdote, adventure, and the romance of reality, written by celebrities of both sides ... Philadelphia, St. Louis, People's publishing company, ᶜ1896.

8 p. l., 592 p. incl. illus., port. front. 29½ cm.

Another outlet for the recollections and rationalizations of leading Civil War participants.

Virginia artillery. *Richmond howitzers,* 1859–
Contributions to a history of the Richmond howitzer battalion. Pamphlet no. 1–4. Richmond, Va., C. McCarthy & co., 1883–86.

4 v. 25ᶜᵐ.

Among the unbalanced material are several diary excerpts by members of this renowned artillery unit.

Virginia. State library, *Richmond.*
... Two Confederate items, ed. by W. W. Scott, law librarian. Richmond, D. Bottom, superintendent of public printing, 1927.

76 p. 23 cm.

Reprinted from the 1927 Bulletin of the Virginia State Library; contains the diary of Capt. Henry Wingfield and the brief recollections of Judge Eustace Moncure.

Vredenburgh, Peter, 1837–1864.
... Letters of Major Peter Vredenburgh ... [relating to] the battles and marches of the old Fourteenth regiment, N. J. vols. ... [n. p., Printed for private circulation, 18—]

37, [1] p. 24ᶜᵐ.

An unfortunately small collection of letters by a discerning officer killed at Winchester, Va., in 1864.

Waddle, Angus L 1826?–
Three years with the armies of the Ohio, and the Cumberland. By Angus L. Waddle ... Chillicothe [O.] Scioto gazette book and job office, 1889.

iv p., 1 l., [7]–81 p. 21½ᶜᵐ.

Waddle, an adjutant in the 33rd Ohio, relied chiefly on memory in producing this general account of the war in the West.

Wainwright, Charles Shiels, 1826–1907.
A diary of battle; the personal journals of Colonel Charles S. Wainwright, 1861–1865. Edited by Allan Nevins. [1st ed.] New York, Harcourt, Brace & World [1962]

549 p. illus. 24 cm.

One of the best primary sources uncovered and published in recent years; contains a reservoir of data on almost every aspect of the Army of the Potomac.

Walcott, Charles Folsom.
History of the Twenty-first regiment, Massachusetts volunteers, in the war for the preservation of the union, 1861–1865. With statistics of the war and of Rebel prisons. By Charles F. Walcott ... Boston, Houghton, Mifflin and co., 1882.

xlii p., 1 l., 502 p. front., port., maps. 22½ cm.

An impassive, oftentimes impersonal, narrative of military campaigns in North Carolina, Virginia, and Tennessee.

Walker, Aldace Freeman, 1842–1901.
The Vermont Brigade in the Shenandoah Valley, 1864. Burlington, Free Press Association, 1869.

191 p. map, plans. 20 cm.

A standard and reliable source for Sheridan's campaign in the Valley of Virginia.

Walker, Cornelius Irvine, 1842–
Rolls and historical sketch of the Tenth regiment, So. Ca. volunteers, in the army of the Confederate states, by C. I. Walker ... Charleston, Walker, Evans & Cogswell, printers, 1881.

138 p. front. 18½ᶜᵐ.

Noted for its accuracy, this study passed under the scrutiny of several of the regiment's members before it was published.

Walker, Francis Amasa, 1840–1897.
History of the Second army corps in the Army of the Potomac, by Francis A. Walker ... 2d ed. New York, C. Scribner's sons, 1891.

xx, 737 p. front., ports., maps (part fold.) 21ᶜᵐ.

A voluminous compilation, heavily padded with official reports and correspondence; readers should beware of the author's sudden injections of personal opinion.

Walker, William Carey.
History of the Eighteenth regiment Conn. volunteers in the war for the Union. By Chaplain Wm. C. Walker. Norwich, Conn., Published by the committee, 1885.

5 p. l., 444 p. pl., port., map. 24½ᶜᵐ.

Chaplain Walker drew on diary excerpts, personal reminiscences, and some sentimentality to recount the campaigns of a regiment that was stationed for the most part in the Shenandoah Valley.

Walkley, Stephen W   *jr.*
    History of the Seventh Connecticut volunteer infantry,
Hawley's brigade, Terry's division, Tenth army corps, 1861–
1865; comp. by Stephen Walkley ... ₍Hartford, 1905₎

    226, 22, lxix, 9 p. incl. illus., plates, port., maps, facsims. front.,
    pl., ports., maps (partly fold.) 21 cm.

A highly personal history, in diary-like organization; much better than Tourtellot's study of
the same unit.

Wallace, Lewis, 1827–1905.
    Lew Wallace; an autobiography ... New York and London,
Harper & brothers, 1906.

    2 v. fronts., illus., plates, ports., facsims. 21½ cm.

The sometimes manufactured and overly dramatic memoirs of the author of Ben Hur.

Walton, William Martin, 1832–1915.
    An epitome of my life; Civil War reminiscences ₍by₎
Buck Walton. ₍1st ed.₎ Austin, Tex., Waterloo Press
₍1965₎

    99 p. port. 24 cm.

A short, very human memoir of service in the
21st Texas Cavalry; throws some light on army
life in the Trans-Mississippi theater.

Ward, George Washington, *b.* 1845.
    History of the Second Pennsylvania veteran heavy ar-
tillery (112th regiment Pennsylvania volunteers) from 1861
to 1866, including the Provisional second Penn'a heavy artillery, by George W. Ward ... Revised. Philadelphia, Pa.,
G. W. Ward, printer, 1904.

    xii, 311 p. front., illus., ports. 24 cm.

A very weak history, but of some value for
Washington defenses late in the war.

Ward, Joseph Ripley Chandler, 1845–
    History of the One hundred and sixth regiment, Pennsyl-
vania volunteers, 2d brigade, 2d division, 2d corps, 1861–1865,
by Joseph R. C. Ward ... Philadelphia, F. McManus, jr. & co.,
1906.

    xii, 457 p. front., plates, ports. 23ᶜᵐ.

Another good compilation of personal accounts;
the 106th saw much service with the Army of
the Potomac.

Ware, Eugene Fitch, 1841–1911.
    The Indian War of 1864. With an introd. and notes by
Clyde C. Walton. New York, St. Martin's Press ₍1960₎

    483 p. illus. 25 cm.

This unique and picturesque narrative recounts
the role played by the 7th Iowa Cavalry in operations against the Indians during the war.

Ware, Eugene Fitch, 1841–1911.
    The Lyon campaign in Missouri. Being a history of the
First Iowa infantry and of the causes which led up to its or-
ganization, and how it earned the thanks of Congress, which
it got. Together with a birdseye view of the conditions in
Iowa preceding the great civil war of 1861. By E. F. Ware
... Topeka, Kan., Printed by Crane & company, 1907.

    xi, 377 p. front. (facsim.) maps, ports. 20 cm.

Too much manufactured information restricts
fatally the usefulness of these "recollections."

Warfield, Edgar, 1842–1934.
    A Confederate soldier's memoirs, by Edgar Warfield ...
Richmond, Masonic home press, inc., 1936.

    238 p. front. (port.) 24½ᶜᵐ.

The excellent memoirs, in spite of embellishments, of a member of the 17th Virginia.

Washburn, George H   1843–1905.
    A complete military history and record of the 108th regi-
ment N. Y. vols., from 1862 to 1894. Together with roster,
letters, Rebel oaths of allegience, Rebel passes, reminiscences,
life sketches, photographs, etc., etc. By Private Geo. H. Washburn, Co. D. Rochester, N. Y. ₍Press of E. R. Andrews₎ 1849.

    521 p. front., illus., plates, ports. 28½ᶜᵐ.

The Civil War chapters are of value only for
various soldiers' reminiscences and letters
that were excerpted.

Watkins, Samuel R
    ... "Co. Aytch", Maury Grays, First Tennessee regiment; or,
A side show of the big show. By Sam. R. Watkins ... Chattanooga, Tenn., Times printing company, 1900.

    viii, ₍9₎–223 p. illus. 22ᶜᵐ.

Much like John Casler's narrative, this one
suffers at times from a tall tale inserted for
the sale of humor; Watkins was with the Confederate Army of Tennessee.

Watkins, Samuel R
"Co. Aytch," Maury Grays, First Tennessee Regiment; or, A side show of the big show. With an introd. by Bell Irvin Wiley. Jackson, Tenn., McCowat-Mercer Press, 1952.
231 p. illus., ports., facsims. 24 cm.

A facsimile reprint, with index and biographical notes on Watkins added.

Watson, Benjamin Frank, 1826–1905.
Addresses, reviews and episodes, chiefly concerning the "Old Sixth" Massachusetts regiment, by B. F. Watson ... New York, 1901.
1 p. l., 142 p. 23cm.

Seven essays on various topics loosely related to the 6th Massachusetts; the first recounts sketchily its involvement in the April 19, 1861, riot in Baltimore.

Watson, William, *of Skelmorlie, Scotland.*
Life in the Confederate army, being the observations and experiences of an alien in the South during the American civil war. By William Watson. New York, Scribner & Welford, 1888.
xvi, [17]–456 p. 19 cm.

Sketchy memoirs of a British subject who served in the Confederate army until 1863, then engaged in blockade-running; an excellent commentary on Southern military life.

Watson, William, 1837 *or* 8–1879.
Letters of a Civil War surgeon, edited by Paul Fatout. [West Lafayette, Ind., 1961]
110 p. illus. 22 cm.

Contains only excerpts from the letters of the surgeon of the 105th Pennsylvania; Watson was more concerned in his letters with men and military events than with medical affairs.

Way, Virgil Gilman, 1847–　　*comp.*
History of the Thirty-third regiment Illinois veteran volunteer infantry in the civil war, 22nd August, 1861, to 7th December, 1865, by General Isaac H. Elliott, with company and personal sketches by other comrades, also complete historical rosters comp. by Virgil G. Way ... by whom the work has been prepared for publication ... Gibson City, Ill., The [Regimental] association, 1902.
288 p. incl. ports., plan. 27½cm.

Muster rolls and biographical sketches comprise most of this study; the narrative is too cursory to be of value.

Welch, Spencer Glasgow.
A Confederate surgeon's letters to his wife, by Spencer Glasgow Welch ... New York and Washington, The Neale publishing company, 1911.
121 p. 19cm.

Extremely revealing letters of army health and field medicine on the Southern side; Welch was surgeon of the 13th South Carolina.

Weld, Stephen Minot, 1842–
War diary and letters of Stephen Minot Weld, 1861–1865. [Cambridge, Mass.] Priv. print., The Riverside press, 1912.
xiii, 428 p. front., illus., plates (part fold.) ports., fold. map, facsims. (part fold.) 25cm.

This exceptionally fine collection of letters and diary excerpts came from the pen of a Massachusetts officer who for a time served on the staff of Gen. FitzJohn Porter.

Wellman, Manly Wade, 1905–
Rebel boast: first at Bethel—last at Appomattox. [1st ed.] New York, H. Holt [1956]
317 p. illus. 22 cm.

A dramatic narrative built around the personal writings of five kinsmen who served together in the 1st and 43rd North Carolina.

Wells, Edward Laight, 1839–
Hampton and his cavalry in '64. By Edward L. Wells ... Richmond, Va., B. F. Johnson pub. company, 1899.
2 p. l., 429, xiv p. incl. front., plates, ports., maps. 21 cm.

A sympathetic and inadequate study by a New Yorker-turned-South Carolinian; several of Wells' wartime letters are in the Daniel E. H. Smith volume (q. v.).

Wells, James Monroe, 1838–
"With touch of elbow;" or, Death before dishonor; a thrilling narrative of adventure on land and sea, by Captain James M. Wells. Philadelphia, Chicago [etc.] The J. C. Winston co., 1909.
1 p. l., iii, [2] p., 1 l., 362 p. front., plates, ports., facsims. 19½ cm.

The exciting title notwithstanding, this work is too general and too padded to be of significant value.

West, John Camden, 1834–
    A Texan in search of a fight.   Being the diary and letters of
a private soldier in Hood's Texas brigade. By John C. West
... Waco, Tex., Press of J. S. Hill & co., 1901.

    189, 8 p., 1 l. incl. port.   19½ᶜᵐ.

Among the best personal accounts of life in Hood's
famous brigade; West relied on letters and a
diary to recount his wide travels and service in
both theaters.

Westbrook, Robert S.
    History of the 49th Pennsylvania volunteers. By
Robert S. Westbrook, late sergeant of Company "B".
A correctly compiled roll of the members of the regiment
and its marches from 1861 to 1865. Altoona, Pa. ₍Altoona
Times print₎ 1898.

    272, ₍2₎ p. front., illus., plates (1 col.) ports. 28½ᶜᵐ.

A better-than-average, daily account of the life
and campaigns of a unit in the VI Corps; Westbrook used a number of rich sources, including
the diaries of eight of his comrades.

Weygant, Charles H   1839–1909.
    History of the One hundred and twenty-fourth regiment,
N. Y. S. V. By Charles H. Weygant. Newburgh, N. Y.,
Journal printing house, 1877.

    2 p. l., vi, ₍7₎–460 p. front. (port.) fold. tab. 24½ cm.

A typical and fairly reliable composite of personal accounts of army life from Antietam to
Appomattox.

Wheeler, William, 1836–1864.
    ... Letters of William Wheeler of the class of 1855, Y. C. ...
₍Cambridge, Mass., Printed by H. O. Houghton and company₎
1875.

    2 p. l., ₍iii₎–v, 468 p. 22½ᶜᵐ.

The personal letters home from a Yale graduate
who served first in Virginia, then campaigned
with Sherman, and ultimately died on the march
to Atlanta.

Whitcomb, Caroline Elizabeth, 1862–
    History of the Second Massachusetts battery (Nims' bat-
tery) of light artillery, 1861–1865, comp. from records of
the rebellion, official reports, diaries and rosters, by Caroline
E. Whitcomb. Concord, N. H., The Rumford press ₍ᶜ1912₎

    111 p. front., plates, ports. 22 cm.

The 70-page narrative is based on newspapers
and printed sources; the sum total is an empty
work.

White, *Mrs*. Betsey Ann.
    Richmond and way stations. '61 and '64. By Didama
(Mrs. B. A. White) ... ₍Milford, Mass., Commercial printing house₎ 1889.

    54 p., 1 l. 19½ᶜᵐ.

A small collection of letters allegedly written
by a soldier in the 16th Massachusetts.

White, Oliver.
    Pencil sketches of service in the Marine artillery.
With some incidental reflections on the use and abuse
of "shoulder-straps, and things." By Oliver White.
Toulon, Ill., Printed at the office of the "Stark County
news," 1863.

    2 p. l., ₍7₎–86 p. incl. pl. 22½ᶜᵐ.

One of the few sources, and a good one at that,
of service in the U. S. Marines.

White, William Spottswood 1800–1873.
    Sketches of the life of Captain Hugh A. White, of the
Stonewall brigade. By his father. Columbia, S. C.,
South Carolinian steam press, 1864.

    124 p. 21ᶜᵐ.

Amid the author's eulogies to his slain son are
many of Capt. White's letters from the field;
the Confederate officer was killed at Second
Manassas.

Whitford, William Clarke, 1828–1902.
    Colorado volunteers in the Civil War; the New Mexico
campaign in 1862. Denver, State Historical and Natural
History Society, 1906. Boulder, Colo., Republished by
Pruett Press, 1963.

    159, ₍16₎ p. illus., ports., maps. 23 cm.

Popularly written and thin in content, this work
is at most of very limited value.

Whitman, Walt, 1819–1892.
    Memoranda during the war. By Walt Whitman. Camden,
N. J., Author's publication, 1875–76.

    2 p. l., ₍3₎–68 p. 2 front. (ports.) 20½ᶜᵐ.

One of the most penetrating pictures of life and
suffering in army hospitals; the famous Whitman wrote with powerful apolmb.

Whitman, Walt, 1819–1892.

Memoranda during the war & Death of Abraham Lincoln. Reproduced in facsimile. Edited with an introd. by Roy P. Basler. Bloomington, Indiana University Press, 1962.

1 v. (various pagings) ports., facsims. 21 cm.

An offset reprinting of the previous, to which editor Basler has added an informative introduction and Whitman's famous eulogy to Abraham Lincoln.

Whitman, Walt, 1819–1892.

Specimen days in America, by Walt Whitman. London, H. Milford, Oxford university press [1932]

xiv, 317, [1] p. 15¼ cm.

The most basic of several volumes on the war by the Union's dedicated poet and volunteer nurse.

Whitman, Walt, 1819–1892.

Walt Whitman's Civil War. Compiled & edited from published & unpublished sources by Walter Lowenfels, with the assistance of Nan Braymer. [1st ed.] New York, Knopf, 1960.

xvi, 333 p. illus. 22 cm.

The only one-volume collection of Whitman's prose and poetry on the war; as such, it is an inestimable source for behind-the-lines support in the North for the war effort.

Whitman, Walt, 1819–1892.

The wound dresser; a series of letters written from the hospitals in Washington during the war of the rebellion, by Walt Whitman, ed. by Richard Maurice Bucke ... Boston, Small, Maynard & company, 1898.

viii p., 1 l., 201 p., 1 l. front., port. 19¼ cm.

A collection of letters that Whitman wrote while serving as a nurse in Union hospitals.

Whitman, William Edward Seaver, 1832–

Maine in the war for the union: a history of the part borne by Maine troops in the suppression of the American rebellion. By William E. S. Whitman, and Charles H. True. Lewiston, N. Dingley jr. & co., 1865.

viii, 637 p. front., port. 22¼ cm.

Little more than a reference guide for the thirty-six regiments Maine sent into the war; chapters are impersonal and were written without adequate reflection.

Whitney, J   H   E

The Hawkins zouaves: (Ninth N. Y. V.) their battles and marches. By J. H. E. Whitney ... New-York, The author, 1866.

x p., 1 l., [13]–216 p. 19 cm.

A bitter account, principally of the Roanoke Island campaign; the author relied primarily on memory.

Whittemore, Henry.

History of the Seventy-first regiment N. G. S. N. Y., including the history of the Veteran association with biographical sketches of members. By Henry Whittemore ... New York, W. McDonald & co., 1886.

viii, 302 p. ports. (incl. front.) 26 cm.

The Civil War sections concentrate mainly on regimental organization and command decisions.

Whittlesey, Charles, 1808–1886.

War memoranda. Cheat river to the Tennessee, 1861–1862, by Colonel Charles Whittlesey ... Cleveland, O., W. W. Williams, 1884.

1 p. l., 89 p. maps. 23 cm.

Unimportant sketches on campaigns in western Virginia and eastern Tennessee.

Wild, Frederick William, 1841–

Memoirs and history of Capt. F. W. Alexander's Baltimore battery of light artillery, U. S. V., by Frederick W. Wild ... Baltimore [Loch Raven, Md., Press of the Maryland school for boys] 1912.

8 p. l., [9]–232 p. plates, ports. 22½ cm.

Wild spends half of this narrative describing his life as a prisoner of war.

Wilder, Theodore.

The history of Company C, Seventh regiment, O. V. I., by Theodore Wilder. Oberlin, J. B. T. Marsh, printer, 1866.

2 p. l., 83 p. 18 cm.

A too-brief, too-empty narrative, plus the usual biographical sketches.

Wildes, Thomas Francis, 1834–1883.
Record of the One hundred and sixteenth regiment, Ohio infantry volunteers in the war of the rebellion, by Thos. F. Wildes ... Sandusky, O., I. F. Mack & bro., printers, 1884.

xxiv, 364 p. 24cm.

Another example of a regimental study written by its colonel, who was too concerned with the larger picture of the war.

Wiley, Bell Irvin, 1906–
The life of Billy Yank, the common soldier of the Union. [1st ed.] Indianapolis, Bobbs-Merrill [1952]

454 p. illus., ports. 24 cm.

Included in this category because of the wealth of excellent quotations from soldiers' letters, diaries, and recollections (many heretofore unpublished) which it contains; the encyclopedia for army life of the men in blue.

Wiley, Bell Irvin, 1906–
The life of Johnny Reb, the common soldier of the Confederacy, by Bell Irvin Wiley. Indianapolis, New York, The Bobbs-Merrill company [1943]

444 p. front., plates, ports., facsims. 24½ cm.

An equally authoritative work for the men in gray.

Wiley, Bell Irvin, 1906–
They who fought here. Text by Bell Irvin Wiley; illus. selected by Hirst D. Milhollen. New York, Macmillan, 1959.

vii, 273 p. illus., ports. 29 cm.

An admirable companion volume for David Donald's popular Divided We Fought; pictures and text recapture vividly all the attributes of Civil War GI's.

Wilkeson, Frank, 1848–
Recollections of a private soldier in the Army of the Potomac, by Frank Wilkeson. New York & London, G. P. Putnam's sons, 1887 [1886]

ix, 246 p. 17½ cm.

Refreshing and charming memoirs, abounding in wit and sarcasm; among Wilkeson's varied assignments was guard duty at Elmira Prison.

Wilkie, Franc Bangs, 1832–1892.
Pen and powder, by Franc B. Wilkie (Poliuto) ... Boston, Ticknor and company, 1888.

383 p. 19½cm.

A newspaper correspondent, Wilkie traveled with the Federal forces from Wilson's Creek through Vicksburg; his various sketches are penetrating and personal observations on a wide variety of military subjects.

Williams, Alpheus Starkey, 1810–1878.
From the cannon's mouth; the Civil War letters of General Alpheus S. Williams. Edited with an introd. by Milo M. Quaife. Detroit, Wayne State University Press, 1959.

x, 405 p. illus., port., maps on lining papers, plan. 24 cm.

Written by the commander of the XX Corps to his daughter, this long run of letters presents an undiluted picture of war; especially valuable for Sherman's campaigns.

Williams, Edward Peet.
Extracts from letters to A. B. T. from Edward P. Williams, during his service in the civil war, 1862–1864. New York, For private distribution, 1903.

122 p. 21cm.

These letters by a cultured and even-tempered officer are as valuable for insights into the early history of the 100th Indiana as Theodore Upson's memoir is for that unit's 1864-1865 operations.

Williams, Ellen.
Three years and a half in the army; or, History of the Second Colorado. By Mrs. Ellen Williams. New York, Pub. for the author by Fowler & Wells co. [c1885]

2 p. l., 178 p. front. (port.) 19½cm.

A shallow memoir by the wife of a bugler in the 2nd Colorado; gives a few sidelights on the little-known Southwestern campaigns.

Williams, Frederick D
Michigan soldiers in the Civil War. Lansing, Michigan Historical Commission, 1960.

43 p. illus. 22 cm.

A very brief survey of the organization and battle careers of Michigan units.

Williams, John A   **B**   *d.* 1893.
Leaves from a trooper's diary. Philadelphia, The author, 1869.

    103 p.   17½^{cm}.

A cursory narrative of service in the 15th Pennsylvania Cavalry; contains an interesting account of an 1862 soldier mutiny.

Williams, John C   1843–
Life in camp: a history of the nine months' service of the Fourteenth Vermont regiment, from October 21, 1862, when it was mustered into the U. S. service, to July 21, 1863, including the battle of Gettysburg. By J. C. Williams ... Claremont, N. H., For the author, by the Claremont manufacturing company, 1864.

    viii, [9]–167, [1] p.   17½ cm.

A hastily reworked diary that gives a shallow account of army life; Williams saw service in the Washington defenses and at Gettysburg.

Williams, John Melvin
The "Eagle regiment," 8th Wis. inf'ty vols. A sketch of its marches, battles and campaigns. From 1861 to 1865. With a complete regimental and company roster, and a few portraits and sketches of its officers and commanders, by a "non-vet." of Co. "H." Belleville, Wis., "Recorder" print, 1890.

    3 p. l., 166 p. illus. 23½^{cm}.

In spite of a diary-like presentation, Williams's narrative is disjointed and empty; double-columned pages only add to the confusion.

Williams, Thomas Harry, 1909–
Hayes of the twenty-third; the Civil War volunteer officer, by T. Harry Williams. [1st ed.] New York, Knopf, 1965.

    xii, 324 p. vi p. illus., maps, ports. 22 cm.

A superb study that brings to bear all of Hayes's voluminous wartime writings.

Williamson, James Joseph, 1834–1915.
Mosby's rangers: a record of the operations of the Forty-third battalion Virginia cavalry, from its organization to the surrender, from the diary of a private, supplemented and verified with official reports of federal officers and also of Mosby; with personal reminiscences, sketches of skirmishes, battles and bivouacs, dashing raids and daring adventures, scenes and incidents in the history of Mosby's command ... Muster rolls, occupation and present whereabouts of surviving members. By James J. Williamson ... New York, R. B. Kenyon, 1896.

    1 p. l., [vii]–xii, 13–510 p., 1 l. incl. illus., port., maps, front. 23 cm.

Heavily embellished and padded with excerpts from the Official Records, Williamson's account nevertheless contains personal observations and unique illustrations.

Willis, Edward, 1840–1864.
... Memorials of Gen. Edward Willis, C. S. army, commandant of the 12th Georgia infantry who fell at the head of his regiment in the battle of Mechanicsville, May 31, 1864 ... Richmond, W. E. Jones, steam book and job printer, 1890.

    31 p. 24½^{cm}.

Extracts from many official and some personal letters comprise this monograph, which originally appeared in Vol. XVII of the Southern Historical Society Papers.

Willis, Henry Augustus, 1830–1918.
The Fifty-third regiment Massachusetts volunteers. Comprising also a history of the siege of Port Hudson. By Henry A. Willis. Fitchburg, Press of Blanchard & Brown, 1889.

    247 p. front. (port.) 24^{cm}.

A somewhat impersonal history of the regiment's movements, battles, and losses.

Willison, Charles A   1846?–
Reminiscences of a boy's service with the 76th Ohio, in the Fifteenth army corps, under General Sherman, during the civil war, by that "boy" at three score. Charles A. Willison ... [Menasha, Wis., Press of The George Banta publishing company, 1908]

    127 p. 20^{cm}.

This untrustworthy recollection was written years after the events recalled.

Wills, Charles Wright, 1840–1883.
Army life of an Illinois soldier, including a day by day record of Sherman's march to the sea; letters and diary of the late Charles W. Wills, private and sergeant 8th Illinois infantry; lieutenant and battalion adjutant 7th Illinois cavalry; captain, major and lieutenant colonel 103rd Illinois infantry. Compiled and published by his sister [Mary E. Kellogg] ... Washington, D. C., Globe printing company, 1906.

    383 p. incl. front. (port.) 23½ cm.

A participant in the Western campaigns, Wills relied on lengthy letters for the events through the fall of Atlanta, then reproduced a sketchy diary for Sherman's march; undertones of humor mark the whole narrative.

Willson, Arabella M   **(Stuart)**
Disaster, struggle, triumph. The adventures of 1000 "boys in blue," from August, 1862, to June, 1865. By Mrs. Arabella M. Willson ... Dedicated to the 126th regiment of New York state volunteers. With an appendix, containing a chronological record of the principal events in the history of the regiment, and the personal history of its officers and enlisted men. Prepared by the historical committee of the regiment. Albany, Argus co., printers, 1870.

    593 p. front., pl., port., maps. 23½ cm.

This potpourri of inadequate and sometimes erratic material substantiates anew that women do not make good military historians.

Wilson, Ephraim A   1837–
Memoirs of the war, by Captain Ephraim A. Wilson, of
Co. "G," 10th Illinois veteran volunteer infantry ... Cleveland,
O., W. M. Bayne printing co., 1893.

xxi, [23]–435 p. front., illus., 4 pl. (ports.) 18½ᶜᵐ.

In spite of faulty grammar, Wilson's reminiscences are reliable for the major campaigns in
the West.

Wilson, James Harrison, 1837–1925.
Under the old flag; recollections of military operations in
the war for the Union, the Spanish war, the Boxer rebellion,
etc., by James Harrison Wilson ... New York and London,
D. Appleton and company, 1912.

2 v. fronts. (ports.) 21½ cm.

Wilson too often relied on memory and the
Official Records for this overly dramatic memoir; but it is still valuable for the story of cavalry operations.

Wilson, John Alfred, 1832–
Adventures of Alf. Wilson; a thrilling episode of the dark
days of the rebellion, by John A. Wilson ... Toledo, Blade
printing & paper company, 1880.

xiv, 15–237 p. front. (port.) plates. 20 cm.

The chief value of this grossly embellished
account is the author's "recollections" of the
1862 Andrews Raid.

Wilson, Lawrence, 1842–1922, *comp. and ed.*
Itinerary of the Seventh Ohio volunteer infantry, 1861–
1864, with roster, portraits and biographies. Ed. and comp.
by Lawrence Wilson, first sergeant, Company D, assisted
by the Historical committee of the Regimental association.
New York and Washington, The Neale publishing company,
1907.

652 p. front., plates, ports., plans. 22½ cm.

One of the largest volumes the Neale Company
ever published—and one of the worst.

Wilson, Suzanne (Colton) 1895–
Column south: with the Fifteenth Pennsylvania Cavalry
from Antietam to the capture of Jefferson Davis. Compiled
by Suzanne Colton Wilson. Edited by J. Ferrell Colton
and Antoinette G. Smith. Drawings by Barton A. Wright.
Flagstaff [Ariz.] J. F. Colton, 1960.
xxi, 389, 25 p. illus., ports., maps (part fold.) 27 cm.

A unique and valuable unit history, based for the
most part on the recollections of two brothers
in the regiment; this study is too often underrated.

Wilson, William Lyne, 1843–1900.
A borderland Confederate. Edited by Festus P. Summers. [Pittsburgh] University of Pittsburgh Press [1962]
138 p. illus. 25 cm.

The memoirs of a youthful but intelligent member of the 12th Virginia Cavalry; Wilson occasionally broke his short, daily entries to comment at length on persons and events.

Winthrop, Theodore, 1828–1861.
Life in the open air, and other papers. By Theodore Winthrop ... Boston, Ticknor and Fields, 1863.

iv p., 2 l., [3]–374 p. front. (port.) pl. 19ᶜᵐ.

Beautiful prose by a New Englander who fell at
Big Bethel.

Wisconsin. *Shiloh monument commission.*
Wisconsin at Shiloh, report of the commission, comp. by
Capt. F. H. Magdeburg. [Madison, Wis.] Issued by Wisconsin
Shiloh monument commission, 1909.
257 p. incl front., illus., plates, ports., 4 fold. maps, diagrs. 23½ᶜᵐ.

In spite of much trivia, this work does recount
the part played by Wisconsin soldiers in the
first great battle in the West.

Wisconsin artillery. *3d battery,* 1861–1865.
History of the services of the Third battery, Wisconsin
light artillery, in the civil war of the United States, 1861–
65. Comp. ... principally from members themselves.
Berlin [Wis.] Courant press [1902]

102, [2] p. illus. 15½ᶜᵐ.

This brief work contains some personal incidents relative to the battery's war service.

Wise, George *d.* 1923.
History of the Seventeenth Virginia infantry, C. S. A.
Baltimore, Kelly, Piet & company, 1870.

312 p. 19½ cm.

A human chronicle, with many insights, of a
little-known but valorous unit in Lee's army.

Wise, Jennings Cropper, 1881–

The long arm of Lee; the history of the artillery of the Army of Northern Virginia. With a foreword by L. Van Loan Naisawald. New York, Oxford University Press, 1959.

995 p. 22 cm.

An exhaustive, valuable study, often consulted and widely quoted; included a summary of the Confederate Ordnance Bureau.

Wise, John Sergeant, 1846–1913.

The end of an era, by John S. Wise. [10th impression] Boston and New York, Houghton, Mifflin and company, 1902.

iv p., 1 l., 474 p., 1 l. 21cm.

These memoirs by an aristocratic and well-educated soldier are often quoted for the events surrounding the fall of the Confederacy.

Wistar, Isaac Jones, 1827–1905.

Autobiography of Isaac Jones Wistar, 1827–1905; half a century in war and peace. Philadelphia, The Wistar institute of anatomy and biology, 1937.

vii, 528 p. front., 2 illus. (incl. coat of arms) 2 pl., ports., fold. map. 26½ cm.

Only a brief section of this memoir treats of the author's service in the 71st Pennsylvania; however, Wistar's account of Ball's Bluff is intriguing.

Wister, Sarah (Butler) "*Mrs.* **O. J. Wister**" 1835–1908.

Walter S. Newhall. A memoir ... Philadelphia, Pub. for the benefit of the Sanitary commission, 1864.

2 p. l., [iii]–iv, [2], [9]–140 p. front. (port.) 21 cm.

A memorial to a young Pennsylvania cavalry officer who died in action late in 1863; contains many excerpts from his own writings.

Wood, George L *b.* 1837 *or* 8.

The Seventh regiment: a record. By Major George L. Wood. New York, J. Miller, 1865.

304 p. 19½ cm.

A trustworthy memoir of life in the 7th Ohio; the author participated in several major battles in both theaters.

Wood, James H

The war; "Stonewall" Jackson, his campaigns and battles, the regiment as I saw them, by James H. Wood, captain Co. "D," 37th Va. infty. regiment. Cumberland, Md., The Eddy press corporation [1910]

4 p. l., 181 p. front., pl., ports. 18½cm.

Wood relied for the most part on memory in writing this account, which is revealing only for the 1861 campaigns in western Virginia.

Wood, Wales W

A history of the Ninety-fifth regiment, Illinois infantry volunteers, from its organization in the fall of 1862, until its final discharge from the United States service, in 1865. By Wales W. Wood ... Chicago, Tribune company's book and job printing office, 1865.

xii, [13]–240 p. 18½cm.

As the author confessed in the preface to this story of life with the XVI Corps, the work contains "nothing of particular interest."

Wood, William Nathaniel, 1839–1909.

Reminiscences of Big I; edited by Bell Irvin Wiley. Jackson, Tenn., McCowat-Mercer Press, 1956.

138 p. illus. 24 cm.

The direct and poignant recollections of a yeoman who worked up through the ranks and became an officer in the 19th Virginia; introduction, illustrations and index enhance the generally accurate text.

Woodbury, Augustus, 1825–1895.

Major General Ambrose E. Burnside and the Ninth army corps: a narrative of campaigns in North Carolina, Maryland, Virginia, Ohio, Kentucky, Mississippi and Tennessee, during the war for the preservation of the Republic. By Augustus Woodbury ... Providence, S. S. Rider & brother, 1867.

viii, 554 p. front., pl., port., maps. 23cm.

A hastily compiled study that suffers additionally from the author's uncontained admiration for the pathetic Burnside.

Woodbury, Augustus, 1825–1895.

A narrative of the campaign of the First Rhode Island regiment, in the spring and summer of 1861 ... By Augustus Woodbury ... Providence, S. S. Rider, 1862.

4 p. l., 260 p. front. (port.) map. 19½ cm.

Written by the highly observant regimental chaplain, this work suffers only from the short space of time which it treats.

Woodbury, Augustus, 1825–1895.

The Second Rhode Island regiment: a narrative of military operations in which the regiment was engaged from the beginning to the end of the war for the union. By Augustus Woodbury ...   Providence, Valpey, Angell and company, 1875.

633 p. front. (port.) fold. map. 25½ᶜᵐ.

Written by a non-member of the regiment, this study lacks the insights and understanding necessary for a good unit history.

Woodruff, George H   *b.* 1814.

Fifteen years ago: or, The patriotism of Will County, designed to preserve the names and memory of Will County soldiers, both officers and privates—both living and dead: to tell something of what they did, and of what they suffered, in the great struggle to preserve our nationality. By George H. Woodruff ... Joliet, Pub. for the author by J. Goodspeed, 1876.

xiv, [15]–515, 82 p. front. (port.) 24ᶜᵐ.

A wordy tribute to many soldiers, some of whom were doubtless undeserving of the honor.

Woodruff, William Edward, 1831–

With the light guns in '61–'65; reminiscences of eleven Arkansas, Missouri and Texas light batteries. in the civil war ... By W. E. Woodruff, late major art., C. S. A.   Little Rock, Ark., Central printing company, 1903.

8 p., 1 l., 9–115 p. front. (port.) plans. 20½ᶜᵐ.

Woodruff's forgetfulness twenty years after the war weakens this potentially good study of Confederate artillery in the Trans-Mississippi.

Woodward, Evan Morrison.

History of the One hundred and ninety-eighth Pennsylvania volunteers, being a complete record of the regiment, with its camps, marches and battles; together with the personal record of every officer and man during his term of service. By Major E. M. Woodward ...   Trenton, N. J., MacCrellish & Quigley, printers, 1884.

xiv, 136 p. front., pl., port. 23½ cm.

The most shallow of Woodward's Civil War volumes; this one even lacks some of the basic facts.

Woodward, E[van] M[orrison]

History of the Third Pennsylvania reserve: being a complete record of the regiment, with incidents of the camp, marches ... and battles; together with the personal record of every officer and man during his term of service. By Major E. M. Woodward ...   Trenton, N. J., MacCrellish & Quigley, printers, 1883.

256, 60, 11 p. front., pl., port. 24ᶜᵐ.

Though Woodward treats campaigns in much too general terms, this volume is far superior to his Our Campaigns.

Woodward, Evan Morrison.

Our campaigns; or, The marches, bivouacs, battles, incidents of camp life and history of our regiment during its three years term of service. Together with a sketch of the Army of the Potomac ... By E. M. Woodward, adjutant, Second Pa. reserves. Philadelphia, J. E. Potter, 1865.

vii, 9–362 p. 18 cm.

Designed as propaganda for Federal recruiting, this embittered memoir adds nothing factually to the Eastern campaigns it purports to describe.

Woodward, Joseph T   1838–

Historic record and complete biographic roster, 21st Me. vols. with reunion records of the 21st Maine regimental association, by Adj't Jos. T. Woodward, sec'y and historian of the Association ... Augusta, Me., Press of C. E. Nash and son, 1907.

4 p. l., 251, [5] p. front. (map) ports. 23½ᶜᵐ.

A potpourri of just about everything pertaining to the regiment except its war history.

Woolworth, Solomon.

Experiences in the civil war, by Solomon Woolworth. Newark, N. J., 1903.

79, [1] p. front. (port.) 17ᶜᵐ.

A crudely written memoir by a blunt grocer-turned-soldier in the 113th Illinois.

Wormeley, Katharine Prescott, 1830–1908.

The other side of war; with the Army of the Potomac. Letters from the headquarters of the United States sanitary commission during the peninsular campaign in Virginia in 1862. By Katharine Prescott Wormeley. Boston, Ticknor and company, 1889 [1888]

ix p., 1 l., 210 p. front., port. 23 cm.

In letters to her mother, Miss Wormeley described horrors she beheld as a nurse in the Peninsular Campaign.

Worsham, John H

One of Jackson's foot cavalry; his experience and what he saw during the war 1861–1865, including a history of "F company," Richmond, Va., 21st regiment Virginia infantry, Second brigade, Jackson's division, Second corps, A. N. Va., by John H. Worsham ... New York, The Neale publishing company, 1912.

353 p. front., plates, ports. 21ᶜᵐ.

One of the most valuable personal narratives by a Confederate soldier; of primary importance are its revelations on army life, equipment, and commanding officers.

Worsham, John H

One of Jackson's Foot Cavalry, by John H. Worsham. Edited by James I. Robertson, Jr. General editor, Bell Irvin Wiley. Jackson, Tenn., McCowat-Mercer Press, 1964.

xxix, 215 p. illus., map (on lining papers) ports. 24 cm.

A new edition of the preceding; the text has been editorially polished; introduction, voluminous footnotes, and index have been added.

Worsham, William Johnson, 1840–

Old Nineteenth Tennessee regiment, C. S. A. June, 1861. April, 1865. By Dr. W. J. Worsham ... Supplementary chapter by Col. C. W. Heiskell ... Knoxville, Tenn., Press of Paragon printing company, 1902.

2 p. l. [7]–235 p. incl. plans. ports., plan. 23½ cm.

A rather empty memoir of service in the Army of Tennessee.

Wright, Charles, b. 1833 or 1834.

A corporal's story. Experiences in the ranks of Company C, 81st Ohio vol. infantry, during the war for the maintenance of the Union, 1861–1864. By Charles Wright ... With an introduction by Major W. H. Chamberlin. Philadelphia [J. Beale, printer] 1887.

iv, [5]–143, viii p. pl. 24 cm.

On par with Chamberlin's account of service in the same unit.

Wright, Henry H   1840–1905.

A history of the Sixth Iowa infantry, by Henry H. Wright. Iowa City, Ia., The State historical society of Iowa, 1923.

xii, 539 p. 23 cm.

Sgt. Wright began his narrative in 1898 and relied for the most part on the <u>Official Records</u>, which he quoted extensively; the study is far more factual than personal.

Wright, Marcus Joseph, 1831–1922.

Diary of Brigadier-General Marcus J. Wright, C. S. A., April 23, 1861–February 26, 1863. [n. p., 193–?]

8 p. front. (port.) 23½ cm.

The disappointingly short journal of one of the Confederacy's remarkable generals and postwar statisticians.

Wright, Thomas J   *captain 8th Ky. infantry.*

History of the Eighth regiment Kentucky vol. inf., during its three years campaigns, embracing organization, marches, skirmishes, and battles of the command, with much of the history of the old reliable Third brigade, commanded by Hon. Stanley Matthews, and containing many interesting and amusing incidents of army life. By Capt. T. J. Wright. St. Joseph, Mo., St. Joseph steam printing co., 1880.

286 p., 1 l. 17½ cm.

A rich memoir of service in the West; author was a Federal officer who compiled his account shortly after the war and made constant reference to his wartime diary.

Wyeth, John Allan, 1845–1922.

With sabre and scalpel; the autobiography of a soldier and surgeon, by John Allan Wyeth ... New York and London, Harper & brothers, 1914.

xix, [1] p., 1 l., 534, [1] p. front., plates, ports., map. 22 cm.

An exceptionally interesting and reliable memoir by a surgeon who served in the cavalry of Bedford Forrest.

Young, Bennett Henderson, 1843–1919.

Confederate wizards of the saddle; being reminiscences and observations of one who rode with Morgan, by Bennett H. Young ... Boston, Chapple publishing company, ltd., 1914.

xxii, 633 p. front., plates, ports., maps. 24½ cm.

A necessary source for any study of Confederate cavalry operations in Kentucky and Tennessee.

Young, Jesse Bowman, 1844–1914.

What a boy saw in the Army; a story of sight-seeing and adventure in the war for the union. By Jesse Bowman Young. 100 original drawings by Frank Beard. New York, Hunt & Eaton [c1894]

398 p. incl. illus., plates, ports. pl. 25 cm.

A manufactured narrative of "experiences" abounding with reconstructed conversation; the book's major asset is the series of sketches done by noted postwar artist Frank Beard.

Young, John Preston, 1847–

The Seventh Tennessee cavalry. (Confederate.) A history. By J. P. Young, of company A. Nashville, Tenn., Printed for the author, Publishing house of the M. E. church, South, Barbee & Smith, agents, 1890.

227 p. front., ports. 23½ cm.

A chronicle of marches and maneuvers, with a muster roll appended.

Young, Lot D   *b.* 1842.
  Reminiscences of a soldier of the Orphan brigade, by Lieut. L. D. Young ... ₍Louisville, Courier-journal job printing company, 1918?₎

   99, ₍1₎ p. 22½ cm.

Too full of manufactured drama to be of either significance or value.

Young, William H
  Journal of an excursion, from Troy, N. Y., to Gen. Carr's head quarters at Wilson's landing, ⟨Fort Pocahontas,⟩ on the James river, Va., during the month of May, 1865. By one of the party. Troy, N. Y., Priv. print., 1871.

   59 p. 26ᶜᵐ.

A particularly revealing picture of destruction on the Virginia peninsula written by a member of a civilian group that visited the area in May, 1865.

Zettler, Berrien McPherson, *b.* 1842.
  War stories and school-day incidents for the children, by B. M. Zettler ... New York, The Neale publishing company, 1912.

   168 p. 19 cm.

An important, reasonably reliable narrative, written by a man who was first a Confederate soldier and then a wartime tax collector in Georgia.

PRISONS
AND PRISONERS OF WAR

Frank Byrne

Abbott, Allen O

Prison life in the South: at Richmond, Macon, Savannah, Charleston, Columbia, Charlotte, Raleigh, Goldsborough, and Andersonville, during the years 1864 and 1865. By A. O. Abbott ... New York, Harper & brothers, 1865.

x p., 1 l., [13]–374 p. incl. front., illus., plates. 18½ᶜᵐ.

Based on a manuscript written while in prison; anti-Southern but generally factual.

Bacon, Alvan Q   *d.* 1863.

Adventures of a pioneer boy, while a prisoner of war. Alvan Q. Bacon, his capture at the battle of Shilo and escape from Macon, Ga., going sixty miles in canoes by night, got to a Union gunboat, and sailed by sea to New York. Written by himself. [n. p., 18—]

32 p. 21ᶜᵐ.

Contains brief description of prisons at Montgomery and Macon; plus a detailed, perhaps exaggerated, account of an escape.

Barbiere, Joseph, *d.* 1895.

Scraps from the prison table, at Camp Chase and Johnson's island. By Joe Barbiere ... Doylestown, Pa., W. W. H. Davis, printer, 1868.

vi p., 1 l., [9]–397 p. front. (plan) plates. 22½ᶜᵐ.

Bitter, disorganized account by a Southerner, yet contains much on daily life, mainly at Johnson's Island.

Bartleson, Frederick A   1833–1864.

Letters from Libby Prison; being the authentic letters written while in Confederate captivity in the notorious Libby Prison, at Richmond; as preserved and edited by Margaret W. Peelle. [1st ed.] New York, Greenwich Book Publishers, 1956.

95 p. facsim. 21 cm.

Main content is actually a journal for early 1864, with one long letter; valuable facts on Libby life, including escapes.

Bartlett, John Russell 1805–1886, *comp.*
The barbarities of the Rebels, as shown in their cruelty to the federal wounded and prisoners; in their outrages upon Union men; in the murder of Negroes, and in their unmanly conduct throughout the rebellion. By Colonel Percy Howard, late of the Royal horse guards [*pseud.*] Providence, R. I., Printed for the author, 1863.

40 p. 24½ᶜᵐ.

Noted bibliographer's unscholarly compilation of atrocity stories; illustrative of hysterical wartime propaganda.

Barziza, Decimus et Ultimus, 1838–1882.
The adventures of a prisoner of war, 1863–1864. Edited by R. Henderson Shuffler. Austin, University of Texas Press [1964]
xiv, 140 p. illus., facsim., ports. 23 cm.

Reprinted from the rare original edition; a highly literate account of life at Johnson's Island, with hearsay on other Federal prisons.

Bates, Ralph Orr, 1847–1909.
Billy and Dick from Andersonville prison to the White House, by Ralph O. Bates (Billy) ... Santa Cruz, Cal., Press Sentinel pub. co. 1910.
99, [3] p. front., illus., ports. 19¼ᶜᵐ.

Bad fiction masquerading as fact; author claimed that Wirz shot him three times.

Benson, Berry.
Berry Benson's Civil War book : memoirs of a Confederate scout and sharpshooter. Edited by Susan Williams Benson. Athens, University of Georgia Press [1962]
203 p. illus. 23 cm.

Brief descriptions of Point Lookout and Old Capitol; a fine account of Elmira prison life.

Berry, Chester D   1844–
Loss of the Sultana and reminiscences of survivors. History of a disaster where over one thousand five hundred human beings were lost, most of them being exchanged prisoners of war on their way home after privation and suffering from one to twenty-three months in Cahaba and Andersonville prisons. By Rev. Chester D. Berry. Lansing, Mich., D. D. Thorp, printer, 1892.
426 p. incl. front., ports. port. 19ᶜᵐ.

A useful collection of recollections treating somewhat of prison conditions and mainly with this steamboat explosion.

Bixby, O   H
Incidents in Dixie; being ten months' experience of a Union soldier in the military prisons of Richmond, N. Orleans and Salisbury. Published for the benefit of Maryland state fair for the Christian and Sanitary commissions. Baltimore, Printed by J. Young, 1864.
89 p. 15 cm.

Temperate, interesting pamphlet based on a diary; has one of the few descriptions of New Orleans Parish Prison.

Boggs, Samuel S
Achtzehn monate ein gefangener unter der rebellenflagge. Eine kurze federzeichnung der gefängnisse von Belle Isle, Danville, Andersonville, Charleston, Florence und Libby, aus eigener erfahrung. Lovington, Ill., S. S. Boggs, 1889.
76 p. front., pl. 8°.

A German edition of Boggs' work below; appended materials differ slightly from both English editions.

Boggs, Samuel S
Eighteen months a prisoner under the Rebel flag; a condensed pen-picture of Belle Isle, Danville, Andersonville, Charleston, Florence and Libby Prisons, from actual experience. Lovington, Ill., 1887.
96 p. illus. 21 cm.

A melange of memories and borrowings from other sources; many atrocity stories. A fine example of prison propaganda.

Booth, Benjamin F   1837?–
Dark days of the rebellion, or, Life in southern military prisons, giving a correct and thrilling history of unparalled [!] suffering ... Written from a diary kept while in Libby and Salisbury prisons in 1864–5, and now in possession of the author. By B. F. Booth ... Indianola, Ia., Booth publishing company, 1897.
375 p. front., illus. (incl. ports.) 19¼ᶜᵐ.

This much-rewritten, enlisted man's diary gives the most detailed published account of Salisbury.

Braun, Herman A
Andersonville, an object lesson on protection. A critical sketch, by Herman A. Braun ... Milwaukee, Wis., C. D. Fahsel publishing co., 1892.
2 p. l., [iii]–xi, [13]–164, [2] p. 2 plans. 17½ᶜᵐ.

An all-out defender of Wirz uses legal and practical arguments, sometimes convincing, sometimes farfetched, to justify the Andersonville commandant.

Brewer, John M
 Prison life ... by J. M. Brewer, late reading clerk of the Maryland Senate, of 1860 and 1861 and still later of forts Lafayette and Warren. [Baltimore, S. S. Mills, 1862?]
 31 p. 22½ cm.

Better account by a political prisoner; adds little to the parallel works of Howard and Sangston (q. v.).

Bross, William, 1813–1890.
 Biographical sketch of the late Gen. B. J. Sweet. History of Camp Douglas. A paper read before the Chicago historical society ... June 18th, 1878, by William Bross ... Chicago, Jansen, McClurg & co., 1878.
 28 p. illus. (plan) 22½ cm.

Useful data on Camp Douglas and one of its commanders.

Brown, Dee Alexander.
 The Galvanized Yankees. [Urbana, University of Illinois Press, 1963]
 243 p. illus., ports., map (on lining papers) 23 cm.

The only history of Confederate prisoners who enlisted in the U. S. Army.

Browne, Junius Henri, 1833–1902.
 Four years in Secessia: adventures within and beyond the Union lines: embracing a great variety of facts, incidents, and romance of the war ... By Junius Henri Browne ... Hartford, O. D. Case and company; [etc., etc.] 1865.
 vi, 450 p. 8 pl. (incl. front.) 21½ cm.

A N. Y. Tribune correspondent's bitter story of imprisonment and escape, 1863-1865; adds little to parallel account of Richardson (q. v.), and is replete with poetic exaggeration.

Bullard, K   C   comp.
 Over the dead-line; or, Who killed "Poll Parrot," comp. by K. C. Bullard. New York and Washington, The Neale publishing company, 1909.
 33 p. 19 cm.

Contains two letters from ex-guards at Andersonville with useful facts on the shooting of a prisoner dubbed "Chickamauga."

Burson, William, 1833–
 A race for liberty; or, My capture, imprisonment, and escape. By William Burson, of Company A, 32d reg't. O. V. I. With an introduction by W. B. Derrick ... Wellsville, O., W. G. Foster, printer, 1867.
 xii, [5]–135 p. 16½ cm.

Author stresses and exciting escape from Florence, S. C., in 1864; gives excellent details on aid by Negroes and others.

Byers, Samuel Hawkins Marshall, 1838–1933.
 What I saw in Dixie; or, Sixteen months in Rebel prisons. By Adjutant S. H. M. Byers. Dansville, N. Y., Robbins & Poore, printers, 1868.
 3 p. l., 126 p. 18 cm.

A reworked diary of 1863-1865 confinements at Libby, Macon, Charleston, and Columbia; bitterly anti-Confederate.

Byers, Samuel Hawkins Marshall, 1838–1933.
 With fire and sword, by Major S. H. M. Byers ... New York, The Neale publishing company, 1911.
 203 p. 2 port. (incl. front.) 19 cm.

The rewritten version of an earlier account; much mellowed toward captors.

Carnahan, James Richards, 1840–
 Camp Morton; reply to Dr. John A. Wyeth by James R. Carnahan. Indiana commandery, M. O. L. L. A. February 22, 1892. [Indianapolis] Baker-Randolph L. & E. co. [1892?]
 79 p. 22½ cm.

An often effective reply to ex-prisoners; charges of mistreatment.

Cavada, Frederic Fernandez, 1832–1871.
 Libby life: experiences of a prisoner of war in Richmond, Va., 1863–64, by Lieut. Colonel F. F. Cavada, U. S. V. Philadelphia, King & Baird, 1864.
 221 p. illus., plates. 19 cm.

The best source for the human interest side of Libby during its period of heaviest use.

Cesnola, Luigi Palma di, 1832–1904.

Ten months in Libby prison. By Louis Palma di Cesnola ... ₍Philadelphia? 1865₎

7 p. 23ᶜᵐ.

A moderately exaggerated account of hardships by a Sardinian U.S. officer.

Cherry, Peterson H

Prisoner in blue; memories of the civil war after 70 years, by Peterson H. Cherry. Los Angeles, Calif., Wetzel publishing co., inc. ₍ᶜ1931₎

70 p. incl. front., illus. 20ᶜᵐ.

An old man's general recollections of Andersonville; of slight value only.

Chipman, Norton Parker, 1836–

The horrors of Andersonville rebel prison; trial of Henry Wirz, the Andersonville jailer; Jefferson Davis' defense of Andersonville prison fully refuted by General N. P. Chipman ... San Francisco, The Bancroft company, 1891.

89 p. 17ᶜᵐ.

The very partisan account of atrocities, written by the Judge Advocate at the Wirz Trial.

Chipman, Norton Parker, 1836–1924.

The tragedy of Andersonville; trial of Captain Henry Wirz, the prison keeper, by General N. P. Chipman ... ₍Sacramento? Calif.₎ The author, 1911.

511 p. incl. front. (port.) illus. 23½ᶜᵐ.

This work greatly expands, and largely supercedes, Chipman's pamphlet (above).

Civil War history. v. 1–
Mar. 1955–
₍Iowa City₎
v. illus., maps, facsims. 24 cm. quarterly.

The June, 1962, issue, was devoted completely to prisons. The best collection of modern scholarship on Andersonville, Ft. Warren, Rock Island, Cahaba, Macon, Savannah, and Charleston.

Confederate States of America. *Bureau of exchange.*

Report of the agent of exchange. ₍Richmond, 1864₎

3 p. 22½ᶜᵐ.

Several wartime pamphlets published at Richmond contain correspondence and reports of these offices.

Confederate States of America. *Army. Dept. of Henrico.*

₍Report of Brigadier General John H. Winder, headquarters, Department Henrico, listing the civilians in custody, under authority of the War department, in the city of Richmond. Richmond, 1863₎

8 p. 23½ᶜᵐ.

Personal data, including vague causes of arrest, on 171 Southern political prisoners and Northern civilians captured in the field.

Confederate States of America. *War dept.*

₍Communication from the secretary of war, enclosing a list of the civilian prisoners in custody at Salisbury, North Carolina, under military authority. Richmond, 1863₎

7 p. 21½ᶜᵐ.

Personal data, including vague charges, about 131 political captives.

Connecticut. *Andersonville monument commission.*

Dedication of the monument at Andersonville, Georgia, October 23, 1907, in memory of the men of Connecticut who suffered in southern military prisons, 1861–1865. Hartford, Pub. by the state, 1908.

2 p. l., 73 p. front., plates, ports. 25½ᶜᵐ.

Includes insignificant reminiscences and a list of Connecticut soldiers buried there.

Cooper, Alonzo.

In and out of rebel prisons, by Lieut. A. Cooper ... Oswego, N. Y., R. J. Oliphant, printer, 1888.

vii, ₍8₎–335 p. incl. 10 pl. front. (port.) 23ᶜᵐ

A fairly objective, above-average account of Macon, Savannah, Charleston, Columbia, escape, recapture, and Danville.

Corcoran, Michael, 1827–1863.

The captivity of General Corcoran. The only authentic and reliable narrative of the trials and sufferings endured, during his twelve months' imprisonment in Richmond and other southern cities, by Brig.-General Michael Corcoran ... Philadelphia, Barclay & co., 1862.

1 p. l., [21]–100 (i. e. 54) p. 3 pl. 24^{cm}.

While complaining of some abuses, this prominent prisoner indicated generally mild treatment prevalent early in the war.

Craven, John J

Prison life of Jefferson Davis. Embracing details and incidents in his captivity, particulars concerning his health and habits, together with many conversations on topics of great public interest. By Bvt. Lieut. Col. John J. Craven ... New York, Carleton; [etc., etc.] 1866.

x, [11]–377 p. incl. front. 19 cm.

Very sympathetic daily record of Davis's imprisonment at Ft. Monroe, by a U. S. Army doctor who cared for him.

Creelman, Samuel.

... Collections of a coffee cooler, consisting of daily prison scenes in Andersonville, Ga., and Florence, S. C., with poetic effusions on foraging ... [Pittsburg, Photoengraving co., 1890]

74 p. illus., pl. 20^{cm}.

Brief, superficial, sometimes confused reminiscences of an enlisted man.

Dahl, Ole Rasmussen, 1817–1882.

Key to southern prisons of United States officers ... New-York, J. A. Gray & Green, 1865.

23 p. 12°.

These sketches by Dahl, a captive officer, were reprinted without credit in Abbott (q. v.) and elsewhere.

Darby, George W.

Incidents and adventures in rebeldom; Libby, Belle-Isle, Salisbury. By Geo. W. Darby. Pittsburg, Pa., Press of Rawsthorne engraving & printing company, 1899.

1 p. l., [7]–228 p. front. (port.) illus., pl. 23½^{cm}.

Good descriptions of Belle Isle and of Richmond prison hospital, 1864, but very embittered.

Davidson, Henry M   *d.* 1900.

Fourteen months in southern prisons; being a narrative of the treatment of federal prisoners of war in the rebel military prisons of Richmond, Danville, Andersonville, Savannah and Millen ... By H. M. Davidson ... Milwaukee, Daily Wisconsin printing house, 1865.

viii, [9]–393 p. front. (fold. plan) 20^{cm}.

Very vivid, bitter, often exaggerated descriptions of horrors which Davidson believed were the result of a Confederate plot to destroy captives.

Davis, Jefferson, 1808–1889.

Andersonville and other war-prisons, by Jefferson Davis. New York, Belford company [°1890]

[37] p. 22^{cm}.

Reprinted from Belford's Magazine, this is a defense of the Confederacy against charges of deliberate mistreatment of prisoners.

Davis, Samuel Boyer

Escape of a Confederate officer from prison. What he saw at Andersonville. How he was sentenced to death and saved by the interposition of President Abraham Lincoln. Norfolk, Va., The Landmark publishing company, 1892.

72 p. 21^{cm}.

One of few public defenses by an ex-prison official; contains very valuable data on charges against Gen. Winder.

Day, William W

Fifteen months in Dixie; or, My personal experience in rebel prisons. A story of the hardships, privations and sufferings of the "boys in blue" during the late war of the rebellion. By W. W. Day ... Owatonna, Minn., The People's press print, 1889.

2 p. l., 80 p. 22^{cm}.

Reminiscences, with slight errors, of Eastern enlisted men's prisons, 1863-1864; some useful facts on Danville, Andersonville, and Florence.

Dickinson, Henry Clay, 1830–1871.

Diary of Capt. Henry C. Dickinson, C. S. A. Morris island, 1864–1865. [Denver, Press of Williamson-Haffner co., 191–]

6 p. l., 15–189 p. plates, ports., facsims. 22½^{cm}.

A long summary of earlier imprisonment at Point Lookout and Ft. Delaware; unusually bitter.

Domschcke, Bernhard.

Zwanzig monate in kriegs-gefangenschaft. Erinnerungen von Bernhard Domschcke. Nebst einem anhang. Milwaukee, W. W. Coleman, 1865.

247 pp. 12°.

Memoir of a German who made the customary officers' circuit through Libby, Danville, Macon, Savannah, Charleston and Columbia; opposed Sanderson (q. v.) in the Libby controversy.

Dougherty, Michael.

Prison diary, of Michael Dougherty, late Co. B, 13th., Pa., cavalry. While confined in Pemberton, Barrett's, Libby, Andersonville and other southern prisons. Sole survivor of 127 of his regiment captured the same time, 122 dying in Andersonville. Bristol, Pa., C. A. Dougherty, printer, 1908.

2 p. l., 75, [1] p. front. (port.) 19½ᶜᵐ.

Gives data on rations and illness; but the work is rendered dubious by postwar reworking, including extensive plagiarism from Boggs (q. v.).

Dowling, Morgan E.

Southern prisons; or, Josie the heroine of Florence. Four years of battle and imprisonment. Richmond, Atlanta, Belle Isle, Andersonville and Florence, a complete history of all southern prisons ... By Morgan E. Dowling ... Detroit, W. Graham, 1870.

xii, [13]–506 p. 16 pl., 2 port. (incl. front.) 22ᶜᵐ.

Has many unlikely, probably fictionalized, episodes; also padded with quotations and paraphrases from other sources.

Drake, James Madison, 1837–

Fast and loose in Dixie. An unprejudiced narrative of personal experience as a prisoner of war at Libby, Macon, Savannah, and Charleston, with an account of a desperate leap from a moving train of cars, a weary tramp of forty-five days through swamps and mountains, places and people visited, etc., etc. By J. Madison Drake ... New York, The Authors' publishing company, 1880.

x, [11]–310 p. incl. front., plates, ports. 20 cm.

A rewritten version of an earlier work (q. v.); adds a few useful details, also some improbable embellishments.

Drake, James Madison, 1837–

Narrative of the capture, imprisonment and escape of J. Madison Drake, captain Ninth New Jersey veteran volunteers ... 1868. [n. p., 1868]

cover-title, 93 p. 21ᶜᵐ.

A brief, bitter account of Eastern prisons in 1864; Drake relied on a diary, but exaggerated his adventures.

Duff, William Hiram, 1844–

Terrors and horrors of prison life; or, Six months a prisoner at Camp Chase, Ohio, by W. H. Duff. [Lake Charles, La., Orphan helper print, ᶜ1907]

5 p. l., 37, 51 p., 1 l. front., plates., ports. 20½ᶜᵐ.

Despite the title, this is a relatively calm account; yet very poorly written.

Dufur, Simon Miltimore, 1843–

Over the dead line; or, Tracked by blood-hounds; giving the author's personal experience during eleven months that he was confined in Pemberton, Libby, Belle Island, Andersonville, Ga., and Florence, S. C., as a prisoner of war ... By S. M. Dufur ... [Burlington, Vt., Printed by Free press association, 1902]

viii, 283 p. front. (port.) 22 cm.

A general, often fanciful enlisted man's reminiscences, with evident errors.

Duganne, Augustine Joseph Hickey, 1823–1884.

Camps and prisons. Twenty months in the department of the Gulf. By A. J. H. Duganne ... New York, 1865.

424 p. front., pl. 19 cm.

One of the rare published accounts of Camps Groce and Ford by a prolific writer; unimpassioned and well written.

Dunkle, John J

Prison life during the rebellion. Being a brief narrative of the miseries and sufferings of six hundred Confederate prisoners sent from Fort Delaware to Morris' Island to be punished. Written by Fritz Fuzzlebug [pseud.] one of their number. Pub. by the author. Singer's Glen, Va., J. Funk's sons, printers, 1869.

48 p. 22½ᶜᵐ.

An early example of Southern-style prison propaganda; basically a diatribe against Union officers and Negro guards.

Eby, Henry Harrison, 1841–

Observations of an Illinois boy in battle, camp and prisons— 1861 to 1865, by Henry H. Eby. Mendota, Ill., The author, 1910.

284 p. incl. front., illus., port., map. 20ᶜᵐ.

An enlisted man tells of Richmond, Danville, and of an escape attempt; the best feature of the book is his description of life on Belle Isle.

Elliott, James Walter, 1927–

Transport to disaster. [1st ed.] New York, Holt, Rinehart and Winston [1962]

247 p. illus. 22 cm.

A popularly written, but adequate history of the "Sultana" steamboat disaster involving paroled prisoners.

Elliott, William 1838–1908, *comp.*

List showing inscriptions on headstones for the Confederate soldiers and sailors who, while prisoners of war, died at Columbus and camp Denison, Ohio, and were buried in camp Chase Confederate cemetery, those dying at camp Denison having been thence removed. Washington, Govt. print. off., 1907.

cover-title, 54 numb. l. 28½ x 21½ᶜᵐ.

Provides names, units, and grave numbers.

Ely, Alfred, 1815–1892.

Journal of Alfred Ely, a prisoner of war in Richmond. Edited by Charles Lanman. New York, D. Appleton and company, 1862.

359 p. front. (port.) pl. 20½ᶜᵐ.

By a Republican congressman captured at Bull Run; quite temperate toward jailors.

Ennis, John W

Adventures in rebeldom; or, Ten months experience of prison life. New York, "Business Mirror" Print, 1863.

60 p. 20 cm.

More bitter than most accounts of Richmond, Charleston, and Columbia.

Estabrooks, Henry L

Adrift in Dixie; or, A Yankee officer among the Rebels. With an introduction by Edmund Kirke [pseud.] New York, Carleton, 1866.

224 p. 19 cm.

A well-written account of an escape and a trip across Virginia with the aid of Negroes.

Famous adventures and prison escapes of the civil war. New York, The Century co., 1893.

x p., 1 l., 338 p. incl. front., illus. 21 cm.

Popular accounts by participants of escape of Morgan's group from Ohio Penitentiary and of Union Officers from Libby and Columbia.

Ferguson, Joseph.

Life-struggles in Rebel prisons: a record of the sufferings, escapes, adventures and starvation of the Union prisoners. By Joseph Ferguson ... Containing an appendix with the names, regiments, and date of death of Pennsylvania soldiers who died at Andersonville. With an introduction by Rev. Joseph T. Cooper, D. D. ... Philadelphia, J. M. Ferguson, 1865.

206, xxiv p. incl. front. (port.) pl. 17½ᶜᵐ.

Ferguson's extreme bitterness and frequent use of hearsay evidence lessens the reliability of the whole book.

Forbes, Eugene, *d.* 1865.

Diary of a soldier, and prisoner of war in the Rebel prisons. Written by Eugene Forbes ... Trenton [N. J.] Murphy & Bechtel, printers. 1865.

iv, 68 p. 22½ᶜᵐ.

Less bitter against prison officials than many accounts-- even though the diarist died; seemingly his account was little altered.

Fosdick, Charles.

Five hundred days in Rebel prisons, by Charles Fosdick, formerly of Co. K, 5th Iowa vols. ... Bethany, Mo., Printed at the Clipper book and job office, 1887.

132 p. incl. port. 20ᶜᵐ.

Bitter recollections of an enlisted man's captivity at Belle Isle, Andersonville, and Florence; contains obvious Republican propaganda.

Fox, James D

A true history of the reign of terror in southern Illinois, a part of the campaign in western Virginia, and fourteen months of prison life at Richmond ... Macon ... Charleston ... and Columbia. By James D. Fox ... Aurora, Ill., J. D. Fox, 1884.

vi p., 1 l., [7]–60 p. incl. front., pl. 21½ᶜᵐ.

Tries hard to be fair to captors; yet so general and brief as to be nearly worthless.

Fraser, John, 1827–1878.
A petition regarding the conditions in the C. S. M. Prison at Columbia, S. C., addressed to the Confederate authorities. Edited by George L. Anderson. Lawrence, University of Kansas Libraries, 1962.
57 p. illus., port. 24 cm.

This colonel's complaint gives considerable data on conditions at "Camp Sorghum."

Frost, Griffin.
Camp and prison journal, embracing scenes in camp, on the march, and in prisons ... Also, scenes and incidents during a trip for exchange, from St. Louis, Mo., via. Philadelphia, Pa., to City Point, Va. By Griffin Frost. Quincy, Ill. ₍Printed at the Quincy herald book and job office₎ 1867.
vi p., 1 l., 303 p. incl. front. 20½ᶜᵐ.

The slightly edited diary of a Confederate officer; one of the few accounts of Gratiot St., and Alton prisons; includes reminiscences of others.

Geer, John James, 1833–
Beyond the lines: or, A Yankee prisoner loose in Dixie. By Captain J. J. Geer ... With an introduction by Rev. Alexander Clark ... Philadelphia, J. W. Daughaday, 1863.
285 p. front. (port.) pl. 18 cm.

Propaganda for abolition, the Union, and Northern Methodism; very unreliable.

Glazier, Willard, 1841–1905.
The capture, the prison pen, and the escape; giving a complete history of prison life in the South, principally at Richmond, Danville, Macon, Savannah, Charleston, Columbia, Belle Isle, Millin, Salisbury, and Andersonville ... embracing, also, the adventures of the author's escape from Columbia, South Carolina, his recapture, subsequent escape, recapture, trial as a spy, and final escape from Sylvania, Georgia ... By Captain Willard W. Glazier ... To which is added an appendix, containing the name, rank, regiment, and post-office address of prisoners ... New York, United States publishing company, 1868.
xiv p., 2 l., ₍19₎–422 p. incl. plates. front. (port.) 18½ cm.

A work of many editions; is based on a reworked, romanticized diary; some utility for Eastern officers' prisons.

Godfrey, Carlos Emmor.
Sketch of Major Henry Washington Sawyer, First regiment, cavalry, New Jersey volunteers; a Union soldier and prisoner of war in Libby prison under sentence of death. By Dr. C. E. Godfrey ... Trenton, N. J., Mac-Crellish & Quigley, printers, 1907.
11 p. front. (port.) 23ᶜᵐ.

Very brief but supplies facts on the pre- and post-war careers of Sawyer; adequately describes the incident of proposed retaliations involving him.

Goss, Warren Lee, 1835–1925.
The soldier's story of his captivity at Andersonville, Belle Isle, and other rebel prisons. With an appendix containing the names of the Union soldiers who died at Andersonville ... Illustrations by Thomas Nast. Boston, Lee and Shepard ₍1866₎
(American culture series, 170: 7)
Microfilm copy (positive) made in 1961 by University Microfilms, Ann Arbor, Mich.
Collation of the original, as determined from the film: 357 p. illus., port., map.

Much useful data on daily life and officials at such prisons as Charleston and Florence; very bitter against Confederates.

Greenhow, Rose (O'Neal) 1814–1864.
My imprisonment and the first year of abolition rule at Washington. By Mrs. Greenhow. London, R. Bentley, 1863.
x, 352 p. front. (port.) 19½ cm.

With much anti-Republican vituperation, this socially prominent spy tells of imprisonment in her own house and in Old Capitol Prison.

Grigsby, Melvin, 1845–
The smoked Yank, by Melvin Grigsby. Sioux Falls, Dakota bell publishing co., 1888.
ix, ₍10₎–227 p. 24 cm.

Useful data on Southern woman's kindness to captives at Cahaba, 1864; and of huckstering at Andersonville.

Hadley, John Vestal, 1840–
Seven months a prisoner, by J. V. Hadley. New York, Charles Scribner's sons, 1898.
3 p. l., 258 p. 16½ cm.

A slightly abridged and rewritten version of his earlier work (q. v.); contains a few additional facts, but the original edition is preferable.

Hadley, John Vestal 1840–
Seven months a prisoner; or, Thirty-six days in the woods. Giving the personal experience of prison life in Gordonsville ₍and other places₎ ... and two escapes, the last successful, from Columbia to Knoxville, over a distance of four hundred miles ... By an Indiana soldier. Indianapolis, J. M. & F. J. Meikel, printers, 1868.
2, iii, 180 p. 22 cm.

One of better officers' accounts; well written and temperate.

Hamilton, Andrew G

Story of the famous tunnel escape from Libby prison, as told by Maj. A. G. Hamilton, one of the projectors. ₍Chicago? 1893?₎

11 p. illus. (incl. port.) 23½ cm.

A good pamphlet account clearly indicating Col. Rose's leadership in the project.

Hamlin, Augustus Choate, 1829–1905.

Martyria; or, Andersonville prison. By Augustus C. Hamlin ... Boston, Lee and Shepard, 1866.

256 p. front., illus., plates, plans (part fold.) map. 19½ᶜᵐ.

A secondary account of prison horrors, stressing medical aspects, by a physician who believed Southern whites to be racially degenerate.

Handy, Isaac William Ker, 1815–1878.

United States bonds; or Duress by federal authority: a journal of current events during an imprisonment of fifteen months, at Fort Delaware, by Isaac W. K. Handy, D. D., of Augusta county, Va. Baltimore, Turnbull brothers, 1874.

xxviii, 670 p. front., plates, ports. 22½ᶜᵐ.

A Virginia minister's diary of 1863-1864 political captivity; an embittered but fine source.

Harris, William C

Prison-life in the tobacco warehouse at Richmond. By a Ball's Bluff prisoner, Lieut. Wm. C. Harris ... Philadelphia, G. W. Childs, 1862.

2 p. l., 9-175 p. incl. front. 18½ᶜᵐ.

Reflects lax, fairly comfortable conditions in early officers' prison; good descriptions of Winder, Wirz, and other officials.

Harrold, John.

Libby, Andersonville, Florence. The capture, imprisonment, escape and rescue of John Harrold, a Union soldier in the war of the rebellion ... Philadelphia, W. B. Selheimer, 1870.

132 p. 18½ᶜᵐ.

A brief general description of enlisted men's prisons; Harrold relates the unusual story of escaping and becoming a neighborhood shoemaker.

Hasson, Benjamin F

Escape from the confederacy; overpowering the guards—midnight leap from a moving train—through swamps and forest—blood hounds—thrilling events. ₍By₎ B. F. Hasson ... ₍Bryan? O., ᶜ1900₎

3 p. l., ₍9₎-59, ₍1₎ p. illus. 20 cm.

Plausible reminiscences of an escape to the North Carolina coast in 1864.

Hawes, Jesse, 1843–1901.

Cahaba. A story of captive boys in blue, by Jesse Hawes ... New York, Burr printing house ₍ᶜ1888₎

xviii, 480 p. incl. front. pl., ports., plan. 23½ cm.

A fine account of a little-known prison; objective, allowing for prisoner's bias and desire to equal Andersonville's horrors.

Hemmerlein, Richard F

Prisons and prisoners of the civil war, by Richard F. Hemmerlein. Boston, The Christopher publishing house ₍ᶜ1934₎

116 p. 21 cm.

A secondary account based on limited printed sources.

Hernbaker, Henry, *jr.*

True history. Jefferson Davis answered. The horrors of Andersonville prison pen. The personal experience of Henry Hernbaker and John Lynch, late of the United States volunteer army, and formerly prisoners of war. Philadelphia, Merrihew & son, 1876.

14 p. 22ᶜᵐ.

Hernbaker's reminiscences are very confused; both are general, bitter, and factually worthless.

Hesseltine, William Best, 1902–

Civil war prisons; a study in war psychology ₍by₎ William Best Hesseltine ... Columbus, O., The Ohio state university press, 1930.

xi, 290 p. 23 cm.

The best secondary account of military prisons, exhausting most published sources; especially adequate on exchange controversy and war psychosis.

Hinds, Thomas.
Tales of war times; being the adventures of Thomas Hinds during the American Civil War. Watertown, N. Y., Herald, 1904.

Microfilm copy (positive) made in 1962 by New York Public Library.

Collation of the original, as determined from the film: 208 p. illus., port.

A colloquial, sometimes confused reminiscence plausible and interesting.

Hockersmith, Lorenzo Dow, 1833–
Morgan's escape. A thrilling story of war times. A true history of the raid of General Morgan and his men through Kentucky, Indiana and Ohio ... By Capt. L. D. Hockersmith ... Madisonville, Ky., Glenn's graphic print, 1903.

iv, [5]–54 p. incl. port., plan. 22cm.

Reminiscences originally written in 1885; tries to reclaim credit taken by T. H. Hines for planning the escape from Ohio Penitentiary.

Holmes, Clayton Wood, 1848–
The Elmira prison camp; a history of the military prison at Elmira, N. Y., July 6, 1864, to July 10, 1865, by Clay W. Holmes, A. M.; with an appendix, containing names of the Confederate prisoners buried in Woodlawn national cemetery; with 62 illustrations. New York and London, G. P. Putnam's sons, 1912.

xvii, 465 p. front., 1 illus. (plan) plates, ports. 25 cm.

A reply to Southern complaints of mistreatment at Elmira; tries unsuccessfully to blame climate and homesickness for prisoners' suffering.

Howard, Frank Key 1826–1872.
Fourteen months in American bastiles ... [3d ed.] Baltimore, Kelly, Hedian & Piet, 1863.

89 p. 23cm.

A Marylander's bitter complaint against his political arrest; tells something about prison conditions at Fts. Lafayette and Warren.

Howe, Thomas H
Adventures of an escaped Union prisoner from Andersonville. San Francisco, H. S. Crocker & co., printers, 1886.

48 p. 22½ cm.

Useful only as another example of great aid given fugitives by slaves.

Hundley, Daniel Robinson, 1832–1899.
Prison echoes of the great rebellion. By Col. D. R. Hundley ... New-York, S. W. Green, printer, 1874.

235 p. 19½cm.

A Confederate's excellent, relatively objective account of Johnson's Island; includes a rewritten diary about capture, a verbatim diary on the island, and an account written later of an attempted escape.

Hyde, Solon.
A captive of war, by Solon Hyde, hospital steward Seventeenth regiment Ohio volunteer infantry. New York, McClure, Phillips & co., 1900.

389 p. 19½cm.

These occasionally confused recollections give important details on prison hospitals and personnel; bitter against Confederate leaders.

Indiana. *Andersonville monument commission.*
Report of the unveiling and dedication of Indiana monument at Andersonville, Georgia (National cemetery) Thursday, November 26, 1908 ... Indianapolis, W. B. Burford, contractor for state printing, 1909.

128 p. incl. front., illus., ports., plans. 25½cm.

Report contains memorial speeches on prison, copies of wartime pictures, and a list of Indianans buried there.

Isham, Asa Brainerd, 1844–
Prisoners of war and military prisons; personal narratives of experience in the prisons of Richmond, Danville, Macon, Andersonville, Savannah, Millen, Charleston, and Columbia ... with list of officers who were prisoners of war from January 1, 1864. By Asa B. Isham ... Henry M. Davidson ... and Henry B. Furness ... Cincinnati, Lyman & Cushing, 1890.

xii, 571 p. front., illus., pl., port., diagr. 24cm.

Isham's account adds little to the narratives of other U. S. officers in Eastern prisons. Davidson repeated his earlier work (q. v.); Furness wrote a polemic based largely on a congressional report.

Jeffrey, William Hartley, 1867–
Richmond prisons 1861–1862, compiled from the original records kept by the Confederate government; journals kept by Union prisoners of war, together with the name, rank, company, regiment and state of the four thousand who were confined there. By William H. Jeffrey ... St. Johnsbury [Vt.] The Republican press [c1893]

271 p. incl. illus., plates, ports. facsims. 21½cm.

Contains a disconnected history of Richmond prisons, reminiscences (including one by an official of Liggon's Prison), and one describing New Orleans and Salisbury prisons.

Johnson, Hannibal Augustus, 1841–

The sword of honor; a story of the civil war by Lieut. H. A. Johnson, Third Maine regiment, N. V. M. ... Hallowell, Me., Register printing house, 1906.

96 p., 1 l. incl. front. ports. 18cm.

This work includes brief reminiscences of Eastern Confederate prisons; most valuable part is a diary of escape over mountains.

Johnston, Adam S

The soldier boy's diary book; or, Memorandums of the alphabetical first lessons of military tactics. Kept by Adam S. Johnston, from September 14, 1861, to October 2, 1864. Pittsburg, 1866.

v, [6]–139 p. 17cm.

Much on imprisonment at Richmond and Danville; a simple, very bitter account, mainly stressing rations; heavily rewritten.

Johnston, Isaac N

Four months in Libby, and the campaign against Atlanta. By Capt. I. N. Johnston, Co. H., Sixth Kentucky volunteer infantry. Cincinnati, Printed at the Methodist book concern, for the author, 1864.

191 p. 17½cm.

An excellent early account of a tunnel escape from Libby.

Keiley, Anthony M   1835–1905.

In vinculis; or, The prisoner of war. Being, the experience of a rebel in two federal pens, interspersed with reminiscences of the late war; anecdotes of southern generals, etc. By a Virginia Confederate. Petersburg, Va., "Daily index" office, 1866.

2 p. l., [3]–216 p. 19 cm.

A revision of Keiley's Prisoner of War (q. v.), adding new preface and references to postwar events, subtracting some of wartime comments.

Keiley, Anthony M

Prisoner of war, or Five months among the Yankees. Being a narrative of the crosses, calamities, and consolations of a Petersburg militiaman during an enforced summer residence north. By A. Rifleman, esq., gent. Richmond, Va., West & Johnson [1865]
120 p. 22½cm.

A well-written wartime account based on a diary; good description of Point Lookout and Elmira; bitter but relatively objective.

Kelley, Daniel George.

What I saw and suffered in Rebel prisons. By Daniel G. Kelley ... With an introduction by Major Anson G. Chester ... Buffalo, Printing house of Matthews & Warren, 1866.
86 p. 18cm.

Contains moderate bitterness, considering the fact that the author left Andersonville a paralytic.

Kellogg, John Azor, 1828–1883.

... Capture and escape; a narrative of army and prison life, by John Azor Kellogg ... [Madison] Wisconsin history commission, 1908.

xvi, 201 p. front. (port.) 23½cm.

An officer's reminiscence, with fictionalized conversations; treats mainly of Macon and Charleston.

Kellogg, Robert H

Life and death in rebel prisons: giving a complete history of the inhuman and barbarous treatment of our brave soldiers by rebel authorities, inflicting terrible suffering and frightful mortality, principally at Andersonville, Ga., and Florence, S. C., describing plans of escape, arrival of prisoners, with numerous and varied incidents and anecdotes of prison life. By Robert H. Kellogg ... Prepared from his daily journal. To which is added as full sketches of other prisons as can be given without repetition of the above, by parties who have been confined therein ... Hartford, Conn., L. Stebbins, 1865.
viii, [11]–400 p. incl.   front., pl., plan. 19cm.

A sergeant's journal of captivity, reworked by the editor; very bitter over deliberate cruelty to prisoners, but also gives facts tending to show the opposite.

Kent, Will Parmiter.

The story of Libby prison, also some perils and sufferings of certain of its inmates. By Will Parmiter Kent. Compiled from personal narratives and various authentic sources. 2d ed. Chicago, Ill., The Libby prison war museum association [189–?]

1 p. l., [5]–60 p. illus. 25cm.

Largely a series of quotations from prisoners' accounts— including that of Ely (q. v.), who was in Libby.

King, John Henry, 1843–

Three hundred days in a Yankee prison; reminiscences of war life, captivity, imprisonment at Camp Chase, Ohio, by John H. King ... Atlanta, Ga. [J. P. Daves] 1904.
114 p. port. 19½ cm.

Brief recollections of a bitter old man; some general facts are made less reliable by the effort to compete with complaints of imprisoned Yankees.

King, John Rufus, 1842–
My experience in the Confederate army and in northern prisons, written from memory by John R. King. Clarksburg, W. Va., Stonewall Jackson chapter no. 1333, United daughters of confederacy, ᶜ1917.

52 p. incl. front. (port.) 22½ᶜᵐ.

The short, general reminiscence of an enlisted man; contains a few human interest stories about Point Lookout and Elmira.

Knauss, William H.
The story of Camp Chase; a history of the prison and its cemetery, together with other cemeteries where Confederate prisoners are buried, etc. By William H. Knauss. Nashville, Tenn. and Dallas, Tex., Publishing house of the Methodist Episcopal church, South, Smith & Lamar, agents, 1906.

xx, 407 p. incl. front., illus., plates, ports. fold. tab. 24ᶜᵐ.

Mainly a secondary account of Camp Chase and Johnson's Island; a very extensive reprinting of letters, articles, and pictures.

Lane, James Henry, 1814–1866.
Speech of Hon. James H. Lane, in the Cooper institute, New York, and General Neal Dow, in the New city hall, Portland, Thursday evening, March 24, 1861 [!] on his return from captivity in a rebel prison. Washington, W. H. Moore, printer, 1864.

16 p. 22ᶜᵐ.

Republican campaign literature; Dow gives an exaggerated account of prisoners' suffering in Libby and Belle Isle.

Langworthy, Daniel Avery, 1832–
Reminiscences of a prisoner of war and his escape, by Daniel Avery Langworthy, late captain 85th N. Y. vol. infantry ... Minneapolis, Minn., Byron printing company, 1915.

4 p. l., [13]–74 p. front., plates, ports. 21½ᶜᵐ.

An old man's unaided recollections of Macon, Charleston, Columbia, and escape; of little value except for photos of escaped officers.

Lawrence, F   Lee, 1926–
Camp Ford C. S. A.; the story of Union prisoners in Texas, by F. Lee Lawrence and Robert W. Glover. Austin, Texas Civil War Centennial Advisory Committee [1964]

xi, 99 p. illus., facsims., map (on lining paper) ports. 24 cm.

A sound, secondary work based on primary sources; good but slightly apologetic for the Confederates.

Leonard, Albert Charles, 1845–
The boys in blue of 1861–1865; a condensed history worth preserving ... Lancaster, Pa., A. C. Leonard [1904]

79 p. incl. front. (port.) illus., plates. 23ᶜᵐ.

A superficial, worthless reminiscence of Andersonville and Belle Island.

The **Libby** chronicle. Devoted to facts and fun. A true copy of the Libby chronicle as written by the prisoners of Libby in 1863. v. 1, no. 1–7; Aug. 21–Oct. 2, 1863. Albany, N. Y., L. N. Beaudry [1889]

2 p. l., 51 p. front. (port.) illus. 26½ cm.

Beaudry was the editor; contains enlightening essays and poems on prison life. Despite the title, there is one obvious addition to the original.

Libby prison chronicle. v. 1, no. 8–12, v. 2, Feb. 1894–
Chicago [J. L. Ransom] 1894–

v. illus. 51ᶜᵐ. monthly.

Published by Ransom (q. v.) and Libby Museum until 1895 as a revival of the wartime <u>Chronicle</u>; many brief reminiscences.

Lightcap, William Henry.
The horrors of southern prisons during the war of the rebellion, from 1861 to 1865, by W. H. Lightcap ... [Platteville, Wis., Journal job rooms, 1902]

95 p. incl. front. (port.) 22ᶜᵐ.

Fine pictures of Andersonville, Millen and other Georgia prisons, and of confusion in the last year of the war; suffers from flaws of memory.

Lomax, Virginia *b.* 1831.
The Old capitol and its inmates. By a lady, who enjoyed the hospitalities of the government for a "season." New York, E. J. Hale & son, 1867.

226 p. 19ᶜᵐ.

Gives flavor of political prison during the excitement over Lincoln's murder; value diminished by use of pseudonyms and confusion in time sequence.

Long, Lessel.

Twelve months in Andersonville. On the march—in the battle—in the Rebel prison pens, and at last in God's country. By Lessel Long ... Huntington, Ind., T. and M. Butler, 1886.

199 p., 1 l., ɪ p. incl. pl. 23ᶜᵐ.

Simply written and reliable when not repeating hearsay; most valuable for descriptions of Millen, Blackshear, and Andersonville.

Lyon, William Franklin, 1842–

In and out of Andersonville prison, by W. F. Lyon ... Detroit, Mich., G. Harland co., 1905.

3 p. l., [11]–121 p. illus., plates, ports. 18 cm.

This book has vagueness and small errors stemming from faulty memory; offers no significant new facts.

McCowan, Archibald.

The prisoners of war; a reminiscence of the rebellion, by Archibald McCowan ... New York, London [etc.] The Abbey press [ᶜ1901]

187 p. front. (port.) 20ᶜᵐ.

Improbable contents, and conflict with author's published service record, indicate that this work is largely or wholly fictitious.

McElroy, John, 1846–1929.

Andersonville: a story of Rebel military prisons, fifteen months a guest of the so-called southern confederacy. A private soldier's experience in Richmond, Andersonville, Savannah, Millen, Blackshear and Florence. By John McElroy ... Toledo, D. R. Locke, 1879.

xxx p., 1 l., [33]–654 p., 1 l. incl. front., illus., plates, maps. 23 cm.

Well-written, gripping, and very detailed; but reliance on memory and bitterness often distort the facts. This very popular narrative influenced many other prisoners' accounts.

McElroy, John, 1846–1929.

This was Andersonville; the true story of Andersonville Military Prison as told in the personal-recollections of John McElroy, sometime private, Co. L, 16th Illinois Cavalry. Edited with an introd. by Roy Meredith; illustrated by Arthur C. Butts, ɪv. New York, McDowell, Obolensky, 1957.

xii, 355 p. illus., ports., map. 28 cm.

The introduction shares McElroy's bias; this edition is abridged, and includes dubious editorial statements.

Mahony, Dennis A

The prisoner of state. By D. A. Mahony. New-York, Carleton, 1863.

viii, [9]–414 p. 18 cm.

An Iowa Democratic editor's sore objections to his political imprisonment.

Maile, John Levi, 1844–

"Prison life in Andersonville" with special reference to the opening of Providence spring, by John L. Maile ... Los Angeles, Grafton publishing company [ᶜ1912]

152 p. incl. illus., port. plates, port. 18ᶜᵐ.

These rambling recollections are an example of the use of prison experience for evangelization.

Maine. *Andersonville monument commission.*

Report of the Maine Andersonville monument commissioners ... 1904. Augusta, Kennebec journal print, 1904.

31 p. 4 pl. (incl. front.) 23½ᶜᵐ.

Memorial speeches containing few historical facts.

Maine. *Salisbury monument commission.*

Report of the Maine commissioners on the monument erected at Salisbury, N. C., 1908 ... Waterville, Sentinel publishing company, 1908.

27, [5] p. front., plates. 23½ᶜᵐ.

Includes a list of Maine men buried at Salisbury as well as a good picture of it.

Marshall, John A

American bastile. A history of the illegal arrests and imprisonment of American citizens during the late civil war ... Philadelphia, T. W. Hartley, 1869.

lxix, [71]–728 p. illus., 7 pl. (incl. front.) 23½ cm.

This book, reprinted in at least 34 editions, is the most important contemporary secondary account of political arrests; yet it is very hostile to the Lincoln administration.

Massachusetts. *Commission on Andersonville monument.*
... Report of the Commission on Andersonville monument ...
₍Boston, Wright & Potter printing co., state printers, 1902₎

75 p. front. 23ᶜᵐ.

Includes rather lurid, reminiscent speech by an ex-prisoner, plus a list of Massachusetts soldiers buried there.

Merrell, William Howard, *d.* 1897.
Five months in rebeldom; or, Notes from the diary of a Bull Run prisoner, at Richmond. By Corporal W. H. Merrell ... Rochester, N. Y., Adams and Dabney, 1862.

iv, ₍5₎–64 p. front. 21½ᶜᵐ.

A very early prisoner's account; moderate toward captors but unfavorable comments on several; much on hospitals and daily life.

Miller, James Newton.
The story of Andersonville and Florence, by James N. Miller ... Des Moines, Ia., Welch, the printer, 1900.

47 p. incl. front. (port.) 22ᶜᵐ.

Temperate reminiscences, based on a brief diary from which excerpts are included; regards Florence as the worst of the two prisons.

Minnich, J   W
Inside of Rock Island prison, from December, 1863, to June, 1865. By J. W. Minnich ... Nashville, Tenn., Dallas, Tex., Publishing house of the M. E. church, South, 1908.

59, ₍1₎ p. front. (port.) illus. 18½ᶜᵐ.

An ill-organized, polemical little pamphlet designed to show the horrors of Northern prison; but full of specific details on daily life, guards, and atrocities.

Moran, Frank E
Bastiles of the confederacy, a reply to Jefferson Davis, being a narrative of the treatment of Union prisoners in the military prisons of the South during the war of the rebellion ... By Frank E. Moran, late captain of company "H," 73d New York volunteers ... Baltimore, Md., Printed for the family of the author ₍1890?₎

vi p., 1 l., 201 p. front. (port.) plates. 20ᶜᵐ.

A violent, ex parte summary of evidence (some false) concerning mistreatment of prisoners.

Murray, George W
A history of George W. Murray, and his long confinement at Andersonville, Georgia. Also the starvation and death of his three brothers at the same place. By himself. ₍Hartford, Press of Case, Lockwood and company, 186–?₎

iv, ₍5₎–30 p. 18½ᶜᵐ.

A worthless, undetailed little work by an author who gives no evidence of ever having been in Andersonville.

Murray, John Ogden, 1840–1921.
The immortal six hundred; a story of cruelty to Confederate prisoners of war, by Major J. Ogden Murray, one of the six hundred. Winchester, Va., The Eddy press corporation, 1905.

274 p. incl. front. ports. 19ᶜᵐ.

An angry reminiscence of retaliation involving Confederate officers imprisoned on Morris Island, S. C.; also data on Hilton Head and Fts. Delaware and Pulaski.

New York (*State*) *Andersonville monument dedication commission.*
A pilgrimage to the shrines of patriotism, being the report of the commission to dedicate the monument erected by the state of New York, in Andersonville, Georgia, to commemorate the heroism, sacrifices and patriotism of more than nine thousand of her sons who were confined in that prison ... with an account of services of the New York resident surviving Andersonville veterans held thereat and also enroute at Richmond and Danville, Va., Salisbury, N. C., and Lookout mountain, Tenn., April 26–30, 1914. Pub. by authority of the state of New York, under the supervision of the Andersonville monument dedication commission. Albany, J. B. Lyon company, printers, 1916.

241, ₍16₎ p. front., plates (1 fold.) ports., plan, forms. 27ᶜᵐ.

Contains memorial speeches of slight historical value, and Clara Barton's report on marking the cemetery.

Newlin, William Henry.
An account of the escape of six federal soldiers from prison at Danville, Va.: their travels by night through the enemy's country to the Union pickets at Gauley Bridge, West Virginia, in the winter of 1863–64. By W. H. Newlin ... Cincinnati, Western Methodist book concern print, 1888.

136 p. plates. 23 cm.

Undistinguished in content or style.

Nineteen months a prisoner of war in the hands of the Rebels: experience at Belle Isle, Richmond, Danville, and Andersonville: some items with reference to Capt. **Wirz,** with a map of Andersonville prison camp, called **Camp Sumter.** Milwaukee, Starr & son, printers, 1865.

67 p. front. (fold. plan) 22 cm.

James S. Anderson, as enlisted man, hastily wrote this hostile narrative, evidently to exploit interest in the Wirz Trial.

Northrop, John Worrell.

Chronicles from the diary of a war prisoner in Andersonville and other military prisons of the South in 1864 ... An appendix containing statement of a Confederate physician and officer relative to prison condition and management. By John Worrell Northrop ... Wichita, Kan., The author, 1904.

228 p. 17½ᶜᵐ.

With literary aspirations, Northrup wrote an extensive diary and poems, then reworked them after the war. Useful facts on Andersonville and Florence.

Nott, Charles Cooper, 1827–1916.

Sketches in prison camps: a continuation of Sketches of the war. By Charles C. Nott, late colonel of the 176th New York vols. ... 3d ed. New-York, A. D. F. Randolph, 1865.

204 p. 19½ᶜᵐ.

Parallels Duganne (q. v.) on Camps Groce and Ford, but is less specific. Nott conciously wrote of the brighter side.

O'Dea, Thomas.

History of O'Dea's famous picture of Andersonville prison, as it appeared August 1st, 1864, when it contained 35,000 prisoners of war . . . Cohoes, N. Y., Clark & Foster, 1887.

20 pp. 8°.

An ex-prisoner's embittered explanation of his primitive picture, which does not appear here but is found in many prisoners' accounts.

O'Hara, M

Reminiscences of Andersonville and other Rebel prisons. A story of suffering, starvation and death . . . Lyons, Ia., J. C. Hopkins, 1880.

74 pp. 8°.

Simply written, but caustic and sometimes confused.

The **Old** flag, 1864; fiftieth anniversary, 1914. First published by Union prisoners at Camp Ford, Tyler, Texas, 1864. Respectfully dedicated to "The old 72." Entered according to act of Congress, in the year of 1864, by Wm. H. May, in the clerk's office of the District court of the United States, for the Southern district of New York. Reproduced by his comrades, Captain Alfred B. Beers, Major Thomas Boudren, Comrade Frank Miller, under the auspices of Elias Howe, jr., post, number three, Department of Connecticut, G. A. R. Decoration day, 1914. [Bridgeport, Conn., "The Old flag" publishing company, 1914]

[64] p. incl. illus., ports., facsims. 32ᶜᵐ.

A reproduction similar to the original edition (following). Among other new matter are several wartime essays on Camp Ford and a sketch of the life of the editor, William H. May.

The **Old** flag. First pub. by Union prisoners at Camp Ford, Tyler, Texas ... v. 1, no. 1–3; Feb. 17–Mar. 13, 1864. New York, W. H. May [c1864]

cover-title, 1 p. l., 4, 4, 4, [3] p. 29½ᶜᵐ.

Includes much on the lighter side of prison life, a map of the stockade, and a list of officers imprisoned there.

Opium eating. An autobiographical sketch. By an habituate. Philadelphia, Claxton, Remsen & Haffelfinger, 1876.

2 p. l., vii–xii, 13–150 p. 19ᶜᵐ.

Very vivid descriptions of the diseases and hardships of Andersonville and Florence. The anonymous author blamed later medical treatment of prison-derived ailments for his drug addiction.

Page, James Madison, 1839–

The true story of Andersonville prison; a defense of Major Henry Wirz, by James Madison Page, late 2d lieut. Company A, Sixth Michigan cavalry, in collaboration with M. J. Haley. With portraits. New York and Washington, The Neale publishing company, 1908.

248 p. front., ports. 21½ cm.

The attempt by an ex-prisoner who was very accommodating toward Confederate captors to rebut other accounts of Wirz. Vehement, detailed, sometimes convincing.

Peirson, Charles Lawrence, 1834–

... Ball's Bluff; an episode and its consequences to some of us. A paper written for the Military historical society of Massachusetts. By Charles Lawrence Peirson ... Salem, Mass., Priv. print. by the Salem press company, 1913.

1 p. l., 54 p. front. 22½ᶜᵐ.

A superficial, sometimes confused, reminiscence; much inferior to such parallel accounts as that of Ely (q. v.).

Pennsylvania. *Andersonville memorial commission.*

Pennsylvania at Andersonville, Georgia; ceremonies at the dedication of the memorial erected by the commonwealth of Pennsylvania in the National cemetery at Andersonville, Georgia, in memory of the 1849 soldiers of Pennsylvania who perished in the Confederate prison at Andersonville, Georgia, 1864 and 1865. 1905. [n. p., C. E. Aughinbaugh, printer to the state of Pennsylvania, 1909]

94 p. front., plates, ports., facsims. 22½ cm.

Memorial speeches of minimal historical value.

Pennsylvania. *Salisbury memorial commission.*
Pennsylvania at Salisbury, North Carolina: ceremonies at the dedication of the memorial erected by the commonweath of Pennsylvania in the national cemetery at Salisbury, North Carolina, in memory of the soldiers of Pennsylvania who perished in the Confederate prison at Salisbury, North Carolina, 1864 and 1865. 1910. [Harrisburg, C. E. Aughinbaugh, printer to the state of Pennsylvania, 1912]

70 p. front., plates, ports, plan. 22 cm.

Includes plan and pictures of the prison plus unimportant reminiscence.

Pennsylvania. *Surgeon general's office.*
List of soldiers, (prisoners of war,) belonging to Pennsylvania regiments, who died at the military prison, at Andersonville, Georgia, from February 26, 1864, to March 24, 1865. [Harrisburg] Singerly & Myers, state printers [1865]

2 p. l., 24 p. 26½cm.

List copied from prison record by Charles Lang, a hospital steward in the 103d Pennsylvania.

Pollard, Edward Alfred, 1831–1872.
Observations in the North: eight months in prison and on parole. By Edward A. Pollard. Richmond, E. W. Ayres, 1865.

vii, [9]–142 p. 20½ᵐ.

A Richmond editor compares his prison treatment specifically and unfavorably with that given of Southern prisons.

Prutsman, Christian Miller.
A soldier's experience in southern prisons, by C. M. Prutsman ... a graphic description of the author's experiences in various southern prisons. New York, A. H. Kellogg, 1901.

80 p. front. (port.) 18½cm.

A brief and often confused reminiscence of very little value.

Putnam, George Haven, 1844–1930.
A prisoner of war in Virginia 1864–5, by George Haven Putnam, adjt. and bvt.-major 176th N. Y. S. vols. Reprinted, with additions, from the report of an address presented to the N. Y. commandery of the U. S. loyal legion, December 7, 1910 ... New York and London, G. P. Putnam's sons, 1912.

v, 104 p. incl. plates. front. (port.) plates. 21½ cm.

Relatively mild account of Libby and officers' prison at Danville.

Quincy, Samuel Miller, 1833–1887.
History of the Second Massachusetts regiment of infantry. A prisoner's diary. A paper read at the officers' reunion in Boston, May 11, 1877, by Samuel M. Quincy ... Boston, G. H. Ellis, printer, 1882.

24 p. 24ᵐ.

A few brief entries on hospitals at Staunton and Libby; of small worth.

Ransom, John L.
Andersonville diary, escape, and list of the dead, with name, co., regiment, date of death and no. of grave in cemetery. John L. Ransom ... author and publisher. Auburn, N. Y., 1881.

304 p. incl. illus., ports. 19ᶜᵐ.

A superior, gripping account; the author admits making several changes in the original edition; Ransom has a strong interest in securing pensions for prisoners.

Rich, Edward Robins, 1841–
Comrades! By Edward R. Rich ... during the civil war a member of Company E, First Maryland cavalry, Confederate States' army. [Easton, Md., S. E. Whitman, 1898]

vi, 168 p. front., plates. 17½ᶜᵐ.

Significant recollections of Ft. Delaware, including excerpts from manuscript prison newspaper.

Richardson, Albert Deane, 1833–1869.
The secret service, the field, the dungeon, and the escape ... by Albert D. Richardson ... Hartford, Conn., American publishing company; Philadelphia, Jones bros. & co.; [etc., etc.] 1865.

512 p. incl. facsim. front., plates, ports. 22 cm.

A N. Y. Tribune correspondent's account; parallels Browne's narrative (q. v.), but has greater detail and accuracy.

Roach, Alva C
The prisoner of war, and how treated. Containing a history of Colonel Streight's expedition to the rear of Bragg's army, in the spring of 1863, and a correct account of the treatment and condition of the Union prisoners of war ... and history of Andersonville prison pen ... Indianapolis, Railroad city pub. house, 1865.

244 p. 20ᵐ.

Often distorted because of Roach's great hostility to the Confederacy and to U. S. prisoners with whom Streight, his colonel, quarreled.

Rose, Thomas Ellwood, 1830–1907.

Col. Rose's story of the famous tunnel escape from Libby prison ... A thrilling account of the daring escape of 109 Union officers from Libby prison through the famous Yankee tunnel. [n. p., 189–?]

7 l. illus. 8°.

Not written by Rose; reprinted from Kent (q. v.); includes list of escapees.

Rouse, J   H

Horrible massacre at Guyandotte, Va., and a journey to the Rebel capital, with a description of prison life in a tobacco warehouse at Richmond. By Dr. J. H. Rouse ... [n. p.] 1862.

56 p. 21 cm.

Mostly a lurid account of the arrest and trip to Richmond of the author and other Unionist civilians from western Virginia.

Roy, Andrew.

Recollections of a prisoner of war. 2d ed., rev. Columbus, Ohio, J. L. Trauger Print. Co., 1909.

216 p. ports. 20 cm.

Includes temperate, sometimes vague reminiscences of brief imprisonment at Richmond; much on the specific treatment of a wound during captivity and parole.

Russell, David E

Seven months in prison; or, Life in rebeldom ... Details of real prison life in Richmond and Danville, with a list of Wisconsin men who died in the Andersonville prison, in perfect order, by regiments. Milwaukee, Godfrey & Crandall, 1866.

104 p. 19 cm.

Value lessened by extreme bitterness, use of hearsay, vagueness on dates and names, and pretentious style.

Rutherford, Mildred Lewis, 1852–

Facts and figures vs. myths and misrepresentations, Henry Wirz and the Andersonville prison [by] Mildred Lewis Rutherford ... [Athens? Ga., 1921]

52, [3] p. 23½ cm.

A hodgepodge of evidence, favorable to Wirz; useful but very biased.

Sabre, Gilbert E

Nineteen months a prisoner of war. Narrative of Lieutenant G. E. Sabre, Second Rhode Island cavalry, of his experience in the war prisons and stockades of Morton, Mobile, Atlanta, Libby, Belle island, Andersonville, Macon, Charleston, and Columbia, and his escape ... list of officers confined at Columbia, during the winter of 1864 and 1865. New York, The American news company, 1865.

207 p. front., pl. 19 cm.

Vivid descriptions of prison life, but possessed also of confusion and bias. Ferguson (q. v.) alleged that Sabre collaborated with his captors.

Sanderson, James M

My record in rebeldom, as written by friend and foe. Comprising the official charges [!] and evidence before the military commission in Washington, Brig. Gen'l J. C. Caldwell, pres't, together with the report and finding of the court. Printed for private circulation and future reference, by James M. Sanderson ... New-York, W. E. Sibell, 1865.

160, liv p. 22½ cm.

The author's defense against charges that he collaborated with the enemy at Libby.

Sangston, Lawrence

The bastiles of the North. By a member of the Maryland legislature ... Baltimore, Kelly, Hedian & Piet, 1863.

136 p. 22½ cm.

A sophisticated journal of political imprisonment at Fts. McHenry, Monroe, Lafayette, and Warren.

Schwartz, Stephan

Twenty-two months a prisoner of war. A narrative of twenty-two months' imprisonment by the Confederates, in Texas, through General Twigg's treachery, dating from April, 1861, to February, 1863. By Stephan Schwartz ... St. Louis, Mo., A. F. Nelson publishing co., 1892.

5 p. l., 17–221 p. front. (port.) plates. 20 cm.

A rare account by a German soldier of the Regular Army; colloquial, much human interest, and occasional confusion.

Shanks, J[ohn] P   C

Speech of Gen. J. P. C. Shanks, of Indiana, on treatment of prisoners of war, delivered before the Grand army of the republic, Washington, D. C., March 19, 1870 . . . Washington, Judd & Detweiler [n. d.]

16 pp. 24½ cm.

A partisan, heavily statistical critique by the head of the House of Representatives' committee to investigate the subject.

Shepherd, Henry Elliot, 1844–1929.
Narrative of prison life at Baltimore and Johnson's island, Ohio, by Henry E. Shepherd ... Baltimore, Commercial ptg. & sta. co., 1917.

1 p. l., ₍5₎–22 p. front., port. 17½ᶜᵐ.

Very brief and superficial.

Sherrill, Miles O
A soldier's story: prison life and other incidents in the war of 1861–'65. By Miles O. Sherrill ... ₍n. p., 1904?₎

20 p. 23ᶜᵐ.

These reminiscences as a whole are inconsequential, except for a bit on Elmira hospitals.

Shriver, Philip Raymond, 1922–
Ohio's military prisons in the Civil War ₍by₎ Phillip R. Shriver ₍and₎ Donald J. Breen. ₍Columbus₎ Ohio State University Press for the Ohio Historical Society ₍ᶜ1964₎

62 p. 24 cm.

A scholarly though brief secondary account; the most recent treatment of Camp Chase and Johnson's Island.

Simpson, T   J
Pictorial history of the prison life of Union soldiers in the South ... Washington, McGill & Witherow, printers and stereotypers, 1867–

pts. illus., ports. 28 cm.

At least two parts of this serial work were issued. Contain secondary accounts of two men's captivities and four insignificant pictures.

Smedley, Charles, 1836–1864.
Life in southern prisons; from the diary of Corporal Charles Smedley, of Company G, 90th regiment Penn'a volunteers, commencing a few days before the "battle of the Wilderness," in which he was taken prisoner, in the evening of the fifth month fifth, 1864: also, a short description of the march to and battle of Gettysburg, together with a biographical sketch of the author ... ₍Lancaster? Pa.₎ Ladies' and gentlemen's Fulton aid society, 1865.

60 p. front. (port.) 19 cm.

A seemingly unaltered diary of Andersonville and Florence, 1864; very valuable.

Smith, William B
On wheels and how I came there; a real story for real boys and girls, giving the personal experiences and observations of a fifteen-year-old Yankee boy as soldier and prisoner in the American civil war, by Private W. B. Smith, of company K, 14th Illinois voluntary infantry. Ed. by Rev. Joseph Gatch Bonnell ... New York, Hunt & Eaton; Cincinnati, Cranston & Curts, 1893.

2 p. l., ₍7₎–338 p. front. (port.) pl., plan. 19 cm.

Reminiscence written on an adult level, despite the title; less detailed than Long (q. v.) on same prisons.

Snow, Edward Rowe.
Historic Fort Warren, by Edward Rowe Snow. Boston, Mass., The Yankee publishing company ₍ᶜ1941₎

1 p. l., 5–87 p. illus. (incl. ports.) fold. map. 22½ᶜᵐ.

Half of this popularly written account is on the Fort's use as a prison. Based on wide, slightly uncritical research into wartime sources.

The southern bazaar, held in St. George's hall, Liverpool, October, 1864. Report of proceedings. London, R. Bentley; Liverpool, Webb and Hunt ₍1864₎

51 p. 20 cm.

A detailed account of an effort to raise funds for the relief of imprisoned Confederates.

Southern historical society.
Confederate view of the treatment of prisoners. Compiled from official records and other documents. By Rev. J. William Jones, D. D., secretary Southern historical society. Richmond, Southern historical society, 1876.

2 p. l., ₍113₎–330 p. 23ᶜᵐ.

An outstanding polemic on this side of question. Contains a great mass of evidence, of varying reliability, on prisons and exchange on both sides.

Spencer, Ambrose.
A narrative of Andersonville, drawn from the evidence elicited on the trial of Henry Wirz, the jailer. With the argument of Col. N. P. Chipman, judge advocate. By Ambrose Spencer. New York, Harper & brothers, 1866.

xiii, ₍15₎–272 p. incl. front. 19½ cm.

A history by a Unionist who lived near the prison; rabidly hostile to Confederates and often careless with facts.

Sprague, Homer Baxter, 1829–1918.
... Lights and shadows in Confederate prisons; a personal experience, 1864–5, by Homer B. Sprague ... with portraits. New York and London, G. P. Putnam's sons, 1915.

viii p., 1 l., 163 p. front. (7 port.) 19 cm.

A deliberately moderate account of life at Libby, Salisbury, and Danville; partly parallel to the work by Putnam (q. v.).

Stafford, David W
In defense of the flag. A true war story. (Illustrated.) A pen picture of scenes and incidents during the great rebellion.—Thrilling experiences during escape from southern prisons, etc. By David W. Stafford ... of Company D, Eighty-third Pennsylvania volunteers. Kalamazoo, Mich., Ihling bros. & Everard, printers, 1904.

88 p. incl. front., 4 pl., port. 22½ cm.

Vague, confused reminiscences of Andersonville, Florence and an escape; so poorly written as to be amusing.

The **Stars** and stripes in rebeldom. A series of papers written by federal prisoners (privates) in Richmond, Tuscaloosa, New Orleans, and Salisbury, N. C. With an appendix. [v. 1, no. 1–6, v. 2, no. 1–2; Nov. 28, 1861–Jan. 15, 1862] Boston, T. O. H. P. Burnham, 1862.

iv, [5]–137 p. 19 cm.

Useful, but relatively few details on New Orleans, where it was edited by William C. Bates.

Stearns, Amos Edward, 1833–
Narrative of Amos E. Stearns, member Co. A., 25th regt., Mass. vols., a prisoner at Andersonville. With an introduction by Samuel H. Putnam. Worcester, Mass., F. P. Rice, 1887.

57 p. front. (port.) 23½ cm.

A nicely written reminiscence of Andersonville, Charleston, and Florence; unembittered.

Stephens, Alexander Hamilton, 1812–1883.
Recollections of Alexander H. Stephens; his diary kept when a prisoner at Fort Warren, Boston harbour, 1865; giving incidents and reflections of his prison life and some letters and reminiscences. Ed., with a biographical study, by Myrta Lockett Avary. New York, Doubleday, Page & company, 1910.

xiii, 572 p. front. (port.) 23 cm.

A mainly mild and warmly human diary; omissions by editor are not clearly indicated.

Stevenson, R   Randolph.
The southern side; or, Andersonville prison. Compiled from official documents by R. Randolph Stevenson, M. D. ... Together with an examination of the Wirz trial; a comparison of the mortality in northern and southern prisons; remarks on the exchange bureau, etc. ... Baltimore, Turnbull brothers, 1876.

488 p. front. (fold. diagr.) plates, fold. facsim. 23 cm.

Some helpful medical data exists in this polemic by Andersonville's chief surgeon. Similar to Jones' book (q. v.), but less thorough and convincing.

Sturgis, Thomas, 1846–
Prisoners of war, 1861–65; a record of personal experiences, and a study of the condition and treatment of prisoners on both sides during the war of the rebellion, by Thomas Sturgis, late 1st lieut. 57th regt., Mass. vet. vols., and aide-de-camp 3rd brig., 1st div. 9th A. C. Reprinted from the report of an address delivered before the N. Y. commandery of the Military order of the loyal legion, Feb. 1, 1911 ... New York and London, G. P. Putnam's sons, 1912.

iv, [1], 266–328 p. front., 7 pl., 2 facsim. 25 cm.

The recollections of a guard officer at Camp Morton who was later a prisoner at Libby; gives evidence to indict Confederates.

Sumner, Charles, 1811–1874.
Treatment of prisoners of war. Speech of Hon. Charles Sumner, in the Senate of the United States, January 29th, 1865, on the resolution of the Committee on military affairs, advising retaliation in kind for Rebel cruelties to prisoners. New York, Young men's Republican union, 1865.

8 p. 23 cm.

Argued against retaliation in kind as being uncivilized and futile.

Turley, Thomas Battle, 1845–1910.
A narrative of his capture and imprisonment during the War Between the States, by Thomas Battle Turley. With an introd. by John H. Davis. [Memphis] Southwestern at Memphis, 1961.

4 p. illus. 23 cm.

Written during or shortly after author's imprisonment, but nearly valueless because of its brevity.

Two months in Fort Lafayette. By a prisoner ... New York, Printed for the author, 1862.

53 p. 14 cm.

Attributed to William Gilchrist, this work adds little to more detailed descriptions such as that of Sangston (q. v.).

United Confederate veterans. *Illinois. Ex-Confederate association of Chicago camp, no. 8.*

Register of Confederate soldiers who died in Camp Douglas, 1862–65 and lie buried in Oakwoods cemetery, Chicago, Ills., 1892. Cincinnati, Cohen & co. [1892]

58 p. 18½ᶜᵐ.

Includes names and units.

U. S. *Congress. Joint committee on the conduct of the war.*
... [Fort Pillow massacre; inquiry and testimony] In the Senate of the United States. May 5, 1864.—Ordered to be printed ... [Washington, 1864]

128 p. 23 cm. (38th Cong., 1st sess. Senate. Rept. com. 63)

Hurriedly written and hate-filled, yet contains a mass of evidence essential to any study of this alleged massacre.

U. S. *Congress. Joint committee on the conduct of the war.*
... Fort Pillow massacre. [Washington, 1864]

128 p. 23 cm. (38th Cong., 1st sess. House. Rept. 65)

An incorrect title, for this work concerns prisoners returned from Richmond in May, 1864. Some useful facts, but distorted by war psychosis.

U. S. *Congress. House. Committee on war claims.*

Claim of certain Confederate officers. Statement of Maj. J. Ogden Murray before the Committee on war claims, House of representatives. Sixty-third Congress, second session, in support of H. R. 14170, a bill for the relief of certain officers of the Confederate States army in the war between the states. March 28, 1914. Washington, Govt. print. off., 1914.

43 p. 23½ᶜᵐ.

Murray's request for compensation for prisoners kept on Morris Island adds no facts to his book (q. v.). But two diaries, and several statements from other prisoners, are useful.

U. S. *Congress. House. Committee on war claims.*

Pay of federal soldiers confined in confederate military prisons. Committee on war claims, House of representatives ... February 26, 1910 ... [Washington, Govt. print. off., 1910]

6 p. 23ᶜᵐ.

Remarks by Cong. Edward L. Taylor, Jr., supporting bounty to ex-prisoners, with estimates of numbers of dead and of survivors.

U. S. *Congress. House. Special Committee on the Treatment of Prisoners of War and Union Citizens.*

Report on the treatment of prisoners of war by the rebel authorities during the War of the Rebellion: to which are appended the testimony taken by the committee, and official documents and statistics, etc. Washington, Govt. Print. Off., 1869.

1205 p. 23 cm.

A virulently anti-Confederate report; much valuable testimony requiring cautious use.

U. S. *Quartermaster's dept.*

... The martyrs who, for our country, gave up their lives in the prison pens in Andersonville, Ga. Washington, Govt. print. off., 1866.

225 p. 23½ᶜᵐ.

The official account of marking the cemetery, plus a grave list.

United States Christian commission.

Record of the federal dead buried from Libby, Belle isle, Danville & Camp Lawton prisons, and at City Point, and in the field before Petersburg and Richmond. Pub. by the U. S. Christian commission, from reports of its agents. Philadelphia, J. B. Rodgers, printer, 1865.

3 p. l., [5]–168 p. 23ᶜᵐ.

Covers only some of prisoners' graves, giving contemporary locations.

United States sanitary commission.

Narrative of privations and sufferings of United States officers and soldiers while prisoners of war in the hands of the Rebel authorities. Being the report of a commission of inquiry, appointed by the United States sanitary commission. With an appendix, containing the testimony. Philadelphia, Printed for the U. S. sanitary commission by King and Baird, 1864.

283 p. incl. plan. 4 pl. 22½ cm.

A highly partisan work that exaggerates the horrors of Richmond prisons and the comforts of Northern ones.

United States sanitary commission.

... Preliminary report of the operations of the U. S. sanitary commission in North Carolina, March, 1865, and upon the physical condition of exchanged prisoners lately received at Wilmington, N. C. New York, Sanford, Harroun & co., steam printing house, 1865.

18 p. 22ᶜᵐ.

A useful, detailed account of measures for the relief of ex-prisoners.

United States sanitary commission.

Sanitary memoirs of the war of the rebellion. Collected and published by the United States sanitary commission. [New York, U. S. sanitary commission; Cambridge, Riverside press, 1867–69]

2 v. 24½ᶜᵐ.

Contains a slightly-abridged copy of a significant report on prisoners by a Confederate surgeon; a volume often used by polemicists.

Urban, John W

Battle field and prison pen; or, Through the war, and thrice a prisoner in rebel dungeons. A graphic recital of personal experiences throughout the whole period of the late war for the Union ... Philadelphia, Hubbard Bros. [°1882]

486 p. illus., ports. 20 cm.

Reprinted under many titles; contains some useful facts but often in error on details.

Vaughter, John B

Prison life in Dixie. Giving a short history of the inhuman and barbarous treatment of our soldiers by Rebel authorities, by Sergeant Oats [pseud.] ... To which is added the speech of Gen. J. A. Garfield, delivered at the Andersonville reunion, at Toledo, Ohio, Oct. 3, 1879. Chicago, Central book concern, 1880.

209 p. incl. front., illus., plan. 17½ᶜᵐ.

Grim reminiscence of Andersonville, Millen, Blackshear, and an unsuccessful escape. Vagueness and lack of significant new facts make it of small utility.

A voice from Rebel prisons; giving an account of some of the horrors of the stockades at Andersonville, Milan and other prisons. By a returned prisoner of war. Boston, Press of G. C. Rand & Avery, 1865.

16 p. 23½ᶜᵐ.

Useful for descriptions of the author's capture at Olustee and of the killing of Negro soldiers; a caustic account of prisons that contains errors.

Walker, John Lowry, 1841–1910.

Cahaba prison and the Sultana disaster, by John L. Walker. Hamilton, O. [Press of Brown & Whitaker] 1910.

[33] p. front. (port.) 17½ᶜᵐ.

Brief and general, but possessed of some facts about Cahaba; slightly edited after the author's death.

Walls that talk: a transcript of the names, initials and sentiments written and graven on the walls, doors and windows of the Libby prison at Richmond, by the prisoners of 1861–'65 ... Richmond: pub. by R. E. Lee camp, no. 1, C. V., 1884. [Richmond] Republished by J. W. Randolph & English, 1889.

19 p. 17½ᶜᵐ.

A collection of Libby's graffiti.

Wash, W   A

Camp, field and prison life; containing sketches of service in the South, and the experience, incidents and observations connected with almost two years' imprisonment at Johnson's Island, Ohio ... With an introd. by L. M. Lewis and a Medical history of Johnson's Island by I. G. W. Steedman. Saint Louis, Southwestern Book and Pub. Co., 1870.

382 p. 19 cm.

An outstanding account based on a diary; temperate and well written.

Weiser, George.

Nine months in Rebel prisons ... Philadelphia, J. N. Reeve & co., 1890.

53, [1] p. incl. front. port. 20¼ cm.

The badly written, often erroneous, reminiscence of life at Andersonville and Florence.

West, Beckwith

Experience of a Confederate States prisoner, being an ephemeris regularly kept by an officer of the Confederate States army. Richmond, West & Johnston, 1862.

64 p. 21½ᶜᵐ.

Valuable details on conditions and officials at Old Capitol and Ft. Delaware. Too much space is devoted to quotes from the Northern press and patriotic effusions.

Williamson, James Joseph, 1834–1915.

Prison life in the Old capitol and reminiscences of the civil war, by James J. Williamson ... illustrations by B. F. Williamson. West Orange, N. J., 1911.

x, 11–162 p. front., illus. 19½ cm.

The 1863 diary of a civilian, with much on treatment and fellow prisoners.

Wilson, John, *of Truro, Mass.*
    Seven months in a rebel prison. [n. p., n. d.]
    28 p. port. 22 cm.

A brief, general reminiscence of prison life at Danville.

Wilson, Thomas L   *of Tennessee.*
    A brief history of the cruelties and atrocities of the rebellion. Compiled from the most authentic sources, by Thos. L. Wilson ... [Washington, Printed by McGill & Witherow for the Union congressional committee, 1864]
    8 p. 24^{cm}.

A short, political, campaign version of the author's major work (below).

Wilson, Thomas L   *of Tennessee.*
    Sufferings endured for a free government; or, A history of the cruelties and atrocities of the rebellion ... By Thos. J. Wilson. Washington, The author, 1864.
    x p., 1 l., 13–300 p. 19^{cm}.

A Southern Unionist's compilation of atrocity stories, many involving military and political prisoners.

Wilson, W   Emerson.
    Fort Delaware. Newark, **University of Delaware Press,** 1957.
    32 p. illus. 22 cm.

A popularly written, accurate history based on published sources.

Wiltse, Henry Martin, 1852–
    The centennial liar, by Henry M. Wiltse. Chattanooga, Tenn., Press printing company, 1897.
    160 p. illus. (incl. ports.) 19^{cm}.

Includes reminiscences of Northern and Southern prisons gathered through interviews;   much error and confusion.

Winder, William H
    Secrets of the American bastile ... Philadelphia, J. Campbell, 1863.
    viii, 47 p. 22^{cm}.

A pamphlet by the brother of the Confederate prison chief; treats more of the causes of his imprisonment by Federals than with prison conditions.

Winship, Albert Edward, 1845–
    A fastidious prisoner, by Albert E. Winship. A reply to "Cold cheer at Camp Morton." A work of fiction in the April Century ... Boston [1891]
    19 p. 18½^{cm}.

A sarcastically polemical, sometimes successful rebuttal to articles complaining about Camp Morton by John A. Wyeth.

Winslow, *Mrs.* **Hattie Lou.**
    Camp Morton, 1861–1865, Indianapolis prison camp, by Hattie Lou Winslow and Joseph R. H. Moore. Indianapolis, Indiana historical society, 1940.
    2 p. l., p. 229–383. illus. (plans) plates, port. 23½^{cm}.

A scholarly, thorough history based on extensive research in published and manuscript sources.

Wirz, Henry, 1823?–1865, *defendant.*
    The demon of Andersonville; or, The trial of Wirz, for the cruel treatment and brutal murder of helpless Union prisoners in his hands ... His life and execution. Containing also a history of Andersonville ... Philadelphia, Barclay & co. [c1865]
    1 p. l., 29–120 p. incl. plates. front. (plan) 23½^{cm}.

A sensational summary of trial testimony, with an account of Wirz's execution.

Wirz, Henry, 1823?–1865, *defendant.*
    ... Trial of Henry Wirz. Letter from the secretary of war ad interim, in answer to a resolution of the House of April 16, 1866, transmitting a summary of the trial of Henry Wirz. [Washington, Govt. print. off., 1868]
    xxxviii, 850 p. 23½ cm.

Testimony on Andersonville; sometimes quoted directly, usually summarized; much variation in reliability; often a source for ex-prisoners' narratives.

THE NEGRO

Dudley T. Cornish

Addeman, J[oshua] M[elancthon] 1840–

Reminiscences of two years with the colored troops. By J. M. Addeman ... Providence, N. B. Williams & co., 1880.

38 p. 21 x 16½ cm.

A valuable record by an officer of the 14th Rhode Island Heavy Artillery (Colored) from 1863 to war's end.

Alexander, William T

History of the colored race in America. Containing also their ancient and modern life in Africa ... the origin and development of slavery in the Old World, and its introduction on the American continent; the slave trade; slavery, and its abolition in Europe and America. The civil war, emancipation, education and advancement of the colored race, their civil and political rights. Prepared and arranged by Wm. T. Alexander ... Kansas City, Mo., Palmetto publishing co., 1887.

2 p. l., 600 p. 11 pl., ports. (incl. front.) 23 cm.

Of slight value; only 7 of 30 chapters deal with the Civil War, and only one treats of Negroes as soldiers; curious organization.

Aptheker, Herbert, 1915–   *ed.*

A documentary history of the Negro people in the United States. Pref. by W. E. B. Du Bois. [1st ed.] New York, Citadel Press [1951]

xvi, 942 p. 22 cm.

Section IV contains forty Civil War documents on Negro education, civil rights, land-holding, military activities, and political opportunities.

Aptheker, Herbert, 1915–

The Negro in the civil war [by] Herbert Aptheker. New York, International publishers [c1938]

48 p. 19½ cm.

A militant, stimulating, pioneer attack on the myth of the docile, happy slave; emphasizes Negro activists' participation in the war.

Baird, Henry Carey 1825–1912.
Washington and Jackson on negro soldiers. Gen. Banks on the bravery of negro troops. Poem--the Second Louisiana, by George H. Boker. Philadelphia, Printed for gratuitous distribution [1863]

cover-title, 15 p. 21½ᶜᵐ.

Urges Union use of the Negro; shows how he served in the Revolution and War of 1812; also includes Banks' report to Halleck on Port Hudson assualts; Boker's poem memorializes same action.

Banks, Nathaniel Prentice 1816–1894.
Emancipated labor in Louisiana. [New York? 1864]

45 p. 22½ᶜᵐ.

A hasty, shallow, self-serving, anti-British survey of the subject; includes details on labor and wages.

Beard, Augustus Field, 1833–1934.
A crusade of brotherhood, a history of the American missionary association, by Augustus Field Beard ... Boston, New York [etc.] The Pilgrim press [ᶜ1909]

xii, 334 p. front., plates, ports. 21½ᶜᵐ.

Old and eulogistic, but contains valuable details essential to understanding AMA's extensive wartime work with freedmen.

Bentley, George R
A history of the Freedmen's Bureau. Philadelphia, University of Pennsylvania, 1955.

x, 298 p. 24 cm.

The standard comprehensive work on the subject.

Biddle, Charles John, 1819–1873.
The alliance with the Negro. Speech of Hon. Charles J. Biddle of Pennsylvania; delivered in the House of representatives of the United States, March 6, 1862. [Washington, L. Towers & co., printers, 1862]

8 p. 24ᶜᵐ.

Opposes using Negro soldiers (Sumner's "natural alliance") as leading to "new Santo Domingo" on Pennsylvania border.

Botume, Elizabeth Hyde.
First days amongst the contrabands, by Elizabeth Hyde Botume. Boston, Lee and Shepard, 1893.

iii, 286 p. 19ᶜᵐ.

A valuable collection of detailed, first-hand accounts of Port Royal experiences by an outstanding Northern teacher.

Briggs, Walter De Blois, 1901–
Civil War surgeon in a colored regiment. [Berkeley, Calif., 1960]

166 p. illus. 25 cm.

Fresh, intelligent observations (combat, freedmen, hospitals, Southern civilians, Yankee teachers) on war in South Carolina, Florida; by a surgeon with the 54th Massachusetts.

Brown, William Wells, *b.* 1815.
The black man, his antecedents, his genius, and his achievements. By William Wells Brown ... 4th ed. Boston, R. F. Wallcut, 1865.

312 p. 19ᶜᵐ.

Brown eloquently argues against popular notions of Negro inferiority; designed to mobilize support for the Emancipation Proclamation.

Brown, William Wells, *b.* 1815.
The Negro in the American rebellion, his heroism and his fidelity, by William Wells Brown ... Boston, Lee & Shepard, 1867.

xvi, 380 p. 19 cm.

A Negro abolitionist traces the Negro soldier from the Revolution to John Brown; and anecdotal, episodic, pioneer work with many letters and orders.

Browne, Frederick W
My service in the U. S. colored cavalry, a paper read before the Ohio commandery of the Loyal legion, March 4, 1908, by Frederick W. Browne ... [Cincinnati? 1908]

cover-title, 14 p. 22½ᶜᵐ.

Valuable detailed descriptions of Negro cavalry on border service in Texas and in combat in Virginia; includes as attempted mutiny after Appomattox.

Califf, Joseph Mark 1843–1914.

Record of the services of the Seventh regiment, U. S. colored troops, from September, 1863, to November, 1866, by an officer of the regiment. Providence, E. L. Freeman & co., printers to the state, 1878.

v p., 1 l., 138, 8 p.   front. (port.)   23½ᶜᵐ.

A detailed and valuable account of a unit raised in Maryland that compiled a long and distinguished combat service in Virginia, South Carolina, and on the Mexican border.

Child, David Lee, 1794–1874.

Rights and duties of the United States relative to slavery under the laws of war. No military power to return any slave. "Contraband of war" inapplicable between the United States and their insurgent enemies. By David Lee Child. ⟨Republished, with notes, from "The Liberator."⟩ ... Boston, R. F. Wallcut, 1861.

48 p.   18½ᶜᵐ.

An important exposition of the right of the Federal government to free slaves under war powers and by right of conquest.

Child, Lydia Maria (Francis) 1802–1880.

The right way the safe way, proved by emancipation in the British West Indies, and elsewhere. By L. Maria Child ... New York, 1862.

108 p.   19ᵐ.

An abolitionist argument for emancipation based in part on a study of the British experience in the West Indies.

Cobbe, Frances Power, 1822–1904.

The red flag in John Bull's eyes. By Frances Power Cobbe ... London, E. Faithfull, 1863.

24 p.   18ᶜᵐ.   (Ladies' London emancipation society. Tracts. no. 1)

Attacks the argument that emancipation will lead to a "carnival of crime"; designed to reassure the British on Negro behavior.

Coffin, Levi, 1798–1877.

Reminiscences of Levi Coffin, the reputed president of the Underground railroad; being a brief history of the labors of a lifetime in behalf of the slave, with the stories of numerous fugitives, who gained their freedom through his instrumentality ... 2d ed.—with appendix. Cincinnati, R. Clarke & co., 1880.

1 p. l., viii, 3–732 p.   2 port. (incl. front.)   20½ᶜᵐ.

An important personal narrative of an Ohio abolitionist, central figure in the Underground Railroad, organizer and general agent of the Western Freedmen's Aid Commission.

Colyer, Vincent, 1825–1888.

Report of the services rendered by the freed people to the United States Army, in North Carolina, in the spring of 1862, after the battle of Newbern, by Vincent Colyer ... New York, V. Colyer, 1864.

63, [1] p. incl. front., illus., plates.   22½ cm.

A full and illustrated report of the various work done by, and activities organized for, North Carolina Negroes; highly critical of Military Governor Stanly.

Conway, Moncure Daniel 1832–1907.

The rejected stone; or, Insurrection vs. resurrection in America. By a native of Virginia. 3d ed. Boston, Walker, Wise, and company, 1862.

131 p.   20ᶜᵐ.

An early, popular, moving plea for emancipation as a moral as well as a military necessity.

Cornish, Dudley Taylor.

The sable arm; Negro troops in the Union Army, 1861–1865. [1st ed.] New York, Longmans, Green, 1956.

337 p.   22 cm.

This standard work traces the development of Union military policy and analyzes the problem of application and Negro utilization; good bibliography.

Crummell, Alexander, 1819–1898.

The relations and duties of free colored men in America to Africa. A letter to Charles B. Dunbar ... by the Rev. Alex. Crummell ... Hartford, Press of Case, Lockwood and company, 1861.

54 p.   23ᶜᵐ.

The eloquent African argument for participation by American Negroes in the commercial, educational, religious development of Africa, particularly Liberia.

Dennett, George M   *lieut-col. 9th. U. S. C. T.*

History of the Ninth U. S. C. troops, from its organization till muster out, with list of names of all officers and enlisted men, who have ever belonged to the regiment ... Lieut. Col. Geo. M. Dennett, commanding. Philadelphia, King & Baird, printers, 1866.

148 p. incl. front. (port.)   16ᶜᵐ.

An excellent record of the regiment's service, which began in Maryland and extended to the Carolinas, Florida, Virginia (Petersburg and Richmond), and the Mexican border after Appomattox.

Douglas, William Orville, 1898–
Mr. Lincoln & the Negroes; the long road to equality. [1st ed.] New York, Atheneum, 1963.
xi, 237 p. 22 cm.

An ambitious project with poetic design, but disappointing, sketchy, and thin.

Douglass, Frederick, 1817?–1895.
Life and times of Frederick Douglass: his early life as a slave, his escape from bondage, and his complete history, written by himself. With a new introd. by Rayford W. Logan. New York, Collier Books [1962]
640 p. 18 cm. (Collier books, BS74)

Two invaluable chapters cover the war years and Douglass's activities in them.

Douglass, Frederick, 1817–1895.
Men of color, to arms! A call by Frederick Douglass. [Rochester, N. Y., 1863]
1 l. 22ᶜᵐ.

An editorial persuasively urging Negroes to enlist for the Union, specifically in the 54th Massachusetts; "this is our golden opportunity."

Douglass, Frederick, 1817–1895.
Negroes and the national war effort, an address by Frederick Douglass, with a foreword by James W. Ford ... [New York, Workers library publishers, inc., 1942]
14, [1] p. illus. (port.) 19ᶜᵐ.

Eloquently urges Negroes to support the Federal government by enlisting and "burying rebellion and slavery in a common grave."

Eaton, John, 1829–1906.
Grant, Lincoln and the freedmen; reminiscences of the civil war with special reference to the work for the contrabands and freedmen of the Mississippi valley, by John Eaton ... in collaboration with Ethel Osgood Mason ... New York [etc.], Longmans, Green, and co., 1907.
xxxvii, 331 p. front. (port.) pl., facsims. (1 fold.) 22 cm.

Subjective reminiscences of a chaplain deeply involved with contrabands in the Mississippi Valley from November, 1862, to December, 1865.

Emancipation league.
Facts concerning the freedmen. Their capacity and their destiny. Collected and pub. by the Emancipation league. Boston, Press of Commercial printing house, 1863.
12 p. 23½ cm.

An important detailed summary of replies to a League questionnaire on the condition and needs of freedmen within the Union lines.

Fleetwood, Christian Abraham, 1840–1914.
The Negro as a soldier; written by Christian A. Fleetwood, late sergeant-major 4th U. S. colored troops, for the Negro congress, at the Cotton states and international exposition, Atlanta, Ga., November 11 to November 23, 1895. Pub. by Prof. Geo. Wm. Cook. Washington, D. C., Howard university print, 1895.
1 p. l., 19 p. 23 cm.

This brief but comprehensive review points to Confederate use of the Negro, especially in Louisiana; includes some statistics.

Forten, Charlotte L
Journal; with an introd. and notes by Ray Allen Billington. New York, Dryden Press [1953]
248 p. maps. 25 cm.

Provides worthwhile insights and details of Sea Islands activities, from the point of view of an educated, free, Northern Negro teacher.

French, *Mrs.* **A   M**
Slavery in South Carolina and the ex-slaves; or, The Port Royal mission. By Mrs. A. M. French ... New York, W. M. French, 1862.
xii, 13–312 p. illus. 19ᶜᵐ.

Saccharine details on the first months of Union occupation of Sea Islands, by the wife of a New York chaplain.

Garnet, Henry Highland, 1815–1882.
A memorial discourse; by Rev. Henry Highland Garnet, delivered in the hall of the House of representatives, Washington city, D. C., on Sabbath, February 12, 1865. With an introduction by James McCune Smith, M. D. Philadelphia, J. M. Wilson, 1865.
1 p. l., [15]–91 p. front. (port.) 23ᶜᵐ.

A New York Negro minister in an eloquent plea for equality of opportunity, fair treatment, and equal justice under national, state, and local laws.

Guthrie, James M

Camp-fires of the Afro-American; or, The colored man as a patriot, soldier, sailor, and hero, in the cause of free America: displayed in colonial struggles, in the revolution, the war of 1812, and in later wars, particularly the great civil war—1861–5, and the Spanish-American war—1898: concluding with an account of the war with the Filipinos—1899 ... By Chaplain Jas. M. Guthrie ... Philadelphia, Afro-American pub. co., 1899.

710 p. incl. illus., plates, ports. front. 23ᶜᵐ.

The panegyric history of American Negro heroes from Jamestown to San Juan Hill; hardly to be trusted implicitly.

Hallowell, Norwood Penrose, 1839–1914.

Selected letters and papers. Peterborough, N. H., R. R. Smith Co. ₁1963₁

148 p. 21 cm.

Includes his The Negro as Soldier plus letters in which, until his 1914 death, Hallowell argued for justice for the Negro soldier and criticized Civil War historiography.

Haven, Gilbert, *bp.,* 1821–1880.

National sermons. Sermons, speeches and letters on slavery and its war: from the passage of the Fugitive slave bill to the election of President Grant. By Gilbert Haven. Boston, Lee and Shepard, 1869.

xxiv, 656 p. 21ᶜᵐ.

Contains many important outspoken statements by a New England Methodist leader for equality of treatment and total desegration of American life.

Howe, Samuel Gridley, 1801–1876.

The refugees from slavery in Canada West. Report to the Freedmen's inquiry commission, by S. G. Howe. Boston, Wright & Potter, printers, 1864.

iv, 110 p. 23½ᶜᵐ.

An excellent contemporary analysis of Negroes in Canadian communities, with prescient recommendations for the future.

Hutchins, John, 1812–1891.

Remarks of Mr. Hutchins, of Ohio, & Mr. Kelley, of Pa., in the House of representatives, January 29, 1863, on the bill to organize regiments of persons of African descent. ₁Washington, 1863₁

8 p. 24ᶜᵐ.

Hutchins argued the Union's legal right to take slaves from masters as either persons or property; Kelley, supporting Stevens' substitute bill, argued the practical manpower necessities.

Jay, John, 1817–1894.

₁Slavery & the war: speeches, letters, &c. by John Jay. New York, etc., 1859–68₁

21 v. in 1. 23ᶜᵐ.

A collection of letters, pamphlets, and speeches, by the president of the New York League, favoring emancipation and the creation of a freedmen's bureau.

Keckley, Elizabeth (Hobbs) 1824–1907.

Behind the scenes; or, Thirty years a slave, and four years in the White House. Buffalo, Stansil and Lee ₁ᶜ1931₁

370 p. port. 21 cm.

Probably a ghost-written account of the White House experiences of Mrs. Lincoln's mulatto dressmaker; illuminating detail, fairly reliable.

Kelley, William Darrah, 1814–1890.

Addresses of the Hon. W. D. Kelley, Miss Anna E. Dickinson, and Mr. Frederick Douglass, at a mass meeting ... Philadelphia, July 6, 1863, for the promotion of colored enlistments. ₁Philadelphia, 1863₁

8 p. 22ᶜᵐ.

Kelley hails the Negro as the "coming man" and the key to Union victory; Dickinson argues that the Negro must fight to help the Union and himself.

Kelley, William Darrah, 1814–1890.

The equality of all men before the law claimed and defended; in speeches by Hon. William D. Kelley, Wendell Phillips, and Frederick Douglass, and letters from Elizur Wright and Wm. Heighton. Boston, Press of G. C. Rand & Avery, 1865.

43 p. 23 cm.

Speeches favoring Negro suffrage and legal equality by Kelley, Frederick Douglass, and Wendell Phillips.

Langston, John Mercer, 1829–1897.

From the Virginia plantation to the national capitol; or, The first and only Negro representative in Congress from the Old Dominion. John Mercer Langston ... Hartford, Conn., American publishing company, 1894.

x, 11–534 p. front., plates, ports. 23ᶜᵐ.

Three valuable chapters by a Oberlin graduate and army recruiter.

McKim, James Miller, 1810–1874.

The freedmen of South Carolina. An address delivered by J. Miller M'Kim, in Sansom hall, July 9th, 1862. Together with a letter from the same to Stephen Colwell, esq., chairman of the Port Royal relief committee. Philadelphia, W. P. Hazard, 1862.

cover-title, 32 p. 22ᶜᵐ.

One of the earliest encouraging reports on the Port Royal Experiment; widely circulated in the North to counteract hypercritical rumors.

McPherson, James M

The Negro's Civil War; how American Negroes felt and acted during the war for the Union [by] James M. McPherson. New York, Pantheon Books [1965]

xii, 358 p. illus., ports. 22 cm.

An impressive, valuable collection of contemporary or eyewitness accounts, descriptions, and discussions of all phases of Negro concern and participation in the struggle.

McPherson, James M

The struggle for equality; abolitionists and the Negro in the Civil War and Reconstruction, by James M. McPherson. Princeton, N. J., Princeton University Press, 1964.

ix, 474 p. illus. 25 cm.

A revealing examination of all aspects of the subject: emancipation, education, freedmen's bureau, land and votes, Negro soldiers, reconstruction; has a superb bibliography.

Morgan, Thomas Jefferson, 1839–1902.

Reminiscences of service with colored troops in the Army of the Cumberland, 1863–65. By Thomas J. Morgan ... Providence, The Society, 1885.

52 p. 21ᶜᵐ. (*Added t.-p.:* Personal narratives of events in the war of the rebellion, being papers read before the Rhode Island soldiers and sailors historical society. 3d ser.—no. 13)

An excellent account of the recruiting and service of 14th U. S. C. T., including actions in Georgia, Alabama, Tennessee; details the battle of Nashville, in which Morgan commanded the First Colored Brigade.

National freedman's relief association of the District of Columbia.

... Annual report. 1st–
[1862/63–
Washington, D. C., 1863–

v. 22ᶜᵐ.

Details operations "to relieve the immediate wants of contrabands": clothing, shelter, employment, education, etc.

New York. Union league club.

... Report of the Committee on volunteering; presented October 13th, 1864. New York, Club house, 1864.

55 p. 23ᶜᵐ.

A richly detailed treatment of the formation of the 20th, 26th, and 31st U. S. C. T.

New York association for colored volunteers.

First organization of colored troops in the state of New York, to aid in suppressing the slave-holders' rebellion. Statements concerning the origin, difficulties and success of the movement: including official documents, military testimonials, proceedings of the "Union league club," etc.:—collated for the "New York association for colored volunteers," by Henry O'Rielly, secretary ... New York, Baker & Godwin, printers, 1864.

cover-title, 24 p. 23 cm.

Valuable details on the activities of prominent New Yorkers who recruited the 20th, 26th, and 31st U. S. C. T. in the months immediately following the draft riots.

New York. Committee of merchants for the relief of colored people suffering from the late riots, 1863.

Report of the Committee of merchants for the relief of colored people, suffering from the late riots in the city of New York. New York, G. A. Whitehorne, printer, 1863.

48 p. 22½ᶜᵐ.

A detailed compilation of preambles, resolutions, newspaper extracts, individual incidents, and treasurer's report ($41,000 in contributions). Vincent Coyler was secretary.

Nordhoff, Charles, 1830–1901.

... The freedmen of South-Carolina: some account of their appearance, character, condition, and peculiar customs. By Charles Nordhoff. New-York, C. T. Evans, 1863.

cover-title, 27 p. 24ᶜᵐ. (Papers of the day; collected and arranged by Frank Moore. no. 1)

Detailed descriptions of Negroes' activities as laborers and in school rooms, with acute observations on accomplishments and potential for the future.

Notes on colored troops and military colonies on southern soil. By an officer of the 9th army corps. New-York, 1863.

16 p. 22½ᶜᵐ.

Curious speculations on the use of Negro troops during and after the war; proposes an agricultural and industrial organization of the South under military regime.

Owen, Robert Dale, 1801–1877.
The wrong of slavery, the right of emancipation, and the future of the African race in the United States. By Robert Dale Owen ... Philadelphia, J. B. Lippincott & co., 1864.

246 p. 18cm.

A modified version of the final report of the Freedmen's Inquiry Commission ("blueprint for radical reconstruction"), submitted to the War Department in May, 1864.

Pearson, Elizabeth Ware, *ed.*
Letters from Port Royal written at the time of the civil war, ed. by Elizabeth Ware Pearson. Boston, W. B. Clarke company, 1906.

ix, 345, [1] p. double map. 20½ cm.

This superb collection includes letters from Edward S. Philbrick; life and problems on Sea Islands are disclosed in intimate detail.

Pease. William Henry, 1924–
Black Utopia; Negro communal experiments in America, by William H. Pease and Jane H. Pease. Madison, State Historical Society of Wisconsin, 1963.

ix, 204 p. 21 cm.

A pioneer study; the final chapters provide valuable, intimate, illuminating analyses of the major aspects of the Port Royal experiments.

Philadelphia. Supervisory committee for recruiting colored regiments.
Free military school for applicants for command of colored troops, no. 1210 Chestnut street, Philadelphia, established by the Supervisory committee for recruiting colored regiments, John H. Taggart ... chief preceptor. 2d ed. Philadelphia, King & Baird, printers, 1864.

43 p. incl. tables. 20cm

Detailed instructions to applicants: methods of examination, qualifications, rosters, rules, schedules, tables; brief history of school.

Philadelphia. Supervisory committee for recruiting colored regiments.
Report of the Supervisory committee for recruiting colored regiments. Philadelphia, King & Baird, printers, 1864.

8 p. 23½cm.

This valuable report touches all aspects of recruiting, officering, supplying and training Pennsylvania regiments of U. S. C. T.

Pierce, Edward Lillie, 1829–1897.
Enfranchisement and citizenship: Addresses and papers, by Edward L. Pierce. Ed. by A. W. Stevens. Boston, Roberts brothers, 1896.

vii p., 1 l., 397 p. 23 cm.

An excellent account of the educational program, with valuable observations on recruitment, performance, and the gradual acceptance of Negro soldiers.

Quarles, Benjamin.
Frederick Douglass. Washington, Associated Publishers [1948]

xi, 378 p. illus., ports. 21 cm.

This definitive biography devotes two valuable chapters to the war years and the subject's multiple activities in them.

Quarles, Benjamin.
Lincoln and the Negro. New York, Oxford University Press, 1962.

275 p. illus. 21 cm.

An illuminating, valuable exploration of maturation of Lincoln's attitudes; based on a thorough examination of contemporary materials.

Quarles, Benjamin.
The Negro in the Civil War. [1st ed.] Boston, Little, Brown [1953]

xvi, 379 p. illus. 21 cm.

A readable, thorough narrative of the activities and changing fortunes of American Negroes, North and South, during the war.

Rickard, James H
Services with colored troops in Burnside's corps. By James H. Rickard, ⟨late captain 19th U. S. colored troops.⟩ Providence, The Society, 1894.

43 p. 21cm. (*Added t.-p.:* Personal narratives of events in the war of the rebellion, being papers read before the Rhode Island soldiers and sailors historical society. 5th ser.—no. 1)

A spirited, detailed account of the combat use of Negro soldiers in the Virginia theater.

Rollin, Frank A

Life and public services of Martin R. Delany, sub-assistant commissioner, Bureau relief of refugees, freedmen, and of abandoned lands, and late major 104th U. S. colored troops. By Frank A. Rollin ... Boston, Lee and Shepard, 1868.

367 p. 20^{cm}.

Eulogistic, but ten chapters contain valuable material on the role of a prominent Negro leader during the war years.

Romeyn, Henry.

... With colored troops in the Army of the Cumberland. Prepared by Companion Brevet Major Henry Romeyn ... and read at the stated meeting of January 6, 1904. [Washington, 1904]

26 p. 23^{cm}. (Military order of the loyal legion of the United States. Commandery of the District of Columbia. War papers. 51)

The brief but useful account of the employment of Negro troops in Tennessee.

Rose, Willie Lee Nichols, 1927–

Rehearsal for Reconstruction; the Port Royal experiment [by] Willie Lee Rose. With an introd. by C. Vann Woodward. Indianapolis, Bobbs-Merrill [1964]

xviii, 442 p. illus., fold. map, ports. 24 cm.

A comprehensive, judicious analysis of all aspects of the subject, including Negroes, Northern missionaries, teachers, soldiers and plantation superintendents.

Sears, Cyrus.

Paper of Cyrus Sears, late lieut. col. of the 49th U. S. colored infantry vols. of African descent—originally 11th La. vol. infantry—A. D. of Harpster, Ohio ... Columbus, The F. J. Heer printing co., 1909.

29 p. front. (port.) 23^{cm}.

An illuminating eyewitness description of the early combat use of Negro troops; written by the colonel of the 49th U. S. C. T.

Shaw, James, 1830–

Our last campaign and subsequent service in Texas. By James Shaw, ⟨late colonel of Seventh United States colored troops ...⟩ Providence, The Society, 1905.

52 p. front., port. 21^{cm}. (*Added t.-p.:* Personal narratives of events in the war of the rebellion, being papers read before the Rhode Island soldiers and sailors historical society. 6th ser.—no. 9)

Recollections of the colonel of the 7th U. S. C. T. raised in Maryland under William Birney's direction.

Sherman, George R

The Negro as a soldier. By George R. Sherman, ⟨captain Seventh United States colored infantry and brevet-lieut.-colonel United States volunteers.⟩ Providence, The Society, 1913.

34 p. 2 port. (incl. front.) 21 cm. (*Added t.-p.:* Personal narratives of events in the war of the rebellion, being papers read before the Rhode Island soldiers and sailors historical society. 7th ser.—no. 7)

Surveys the past military use of Negroes and the organization of the 1st U. S. C. T.; details the assault on Ft. Gilmer, September 29, 1864.

Sherman, John, 1823–1900.

Speech by Hon. John Sherman, of Ohio, on emancipation as a compensation for military service rendered by slaves. Delivered in the Senate of the United States, February 2, 1864. Washington, D. C., McGill & Witherow, printers, 1864.

16 p. 24½^{cm}.

An exhaustive (2-hour) discussion, rich in historic, legal precedents; asks more specific guarantees, a "reasonable compensation" to loyal masters, and an end to slavery.

Slaughter, Linda Warfel.

The freedmen of the South. By Linda Warfel Slaughter ... Cincinnati, Elm street printing company, 1869.

201 p. 19^{cm}.

A typical report by an Ohio abolitionist and AMA teacher in the South; polemical and zealous, but useful because of intimate details.

Stearns, Frank Preston, 1846–1917.

The life and public services of George Luther Stearns, by Frank Preston Stearns ... Philadelphia & London, J. B. Lippincott company, 1907.

vii, [1] p., 2 l., 13–401, [1] p. 3 pl., 11 port. (incl. front.) 21½ cm.

Uncritical but rich with valuable data (including much unpublished correspondence) on an important Boston abolitionist.

Swint, Henry Lee.

The northern teacher in the South, 1862–1870, by Henry Lee Swint ... Nashville, Tenn., Vanderbilt university press, 1941.

ix, 221 p. illus. (map) 23½ cm.

The definitive pioneer survey of the subject; "required reading" for all students in the field, despite its brevity and somewhat Southern bias.

Taylor, Joseph Henry, 1898–
The American Negro soldier in the Civil War; a pictorial documentary. With 10 engravings suitable for framing, from rare Civil War drawings. Centennial issue. [Durham, N. C., J. S. C. & A. Publishers] c1960.

[2] p., 10 plates. port. 26 x 36 cm.

An interesting collection, adequately footnoted, ranging from Milliken's Bend and Fort Wagner, to the Alabama sinking and Lincoln's entrance into Richmond.

Taylor, Susie King, b. 1848.
Reminiscences of my life in camp with the 33d United States colored troops, late 1st S. C. volunteers, by Susie King Taylor ... Boston, The author, 1902.

xii p., 1 l., 82 p. front., pl., ports. 19½ cm.

Written by an ex-slave, teacher, laundress, nurse, and wife of a sergeant in the first Negro regiment raised in the war.

Tilton, Theodore, 1835–1907.
The negro: a speech by Theodore Tilton, at Cooper institute, New York, May 12, 1863, at the anniversary of the American anti-slavery society. Phonographically reported. 2d ed. New York & Boston, Anti-slavery offices [etc.] 1863.

16 p. 14 cm.

A moving speech to the 1863 meeting of the American Anti-Slavery Society argues the lack of scientific proof of alleged Negro inferiority.

Towne, Laura Matilda, 1825–1901.
Letters and diary of Laura M. Towne; written from the Sea islands of South Carolina, 1862–1884; ed. by Rupert Sargent Holland. Cambridge, Printed at the Riverside press, 1912.

xviii, 310 p. front. (port.) plates, map. 20½ cm.

An unsentimental, perceptive and critical account by the most successful of all Yankee teachers; half the book treats of the war years.

Ullmann, Daniel, 1810–1892.
Address by Daniel Ullmann, LL. D., before the Soldier's and sailor's union of the state of New York, on the organization of colored troops and the regeneration of the South, delivered at Albany, February 5, 1868. Washington, Printed at the Great republic office, 1868.

cover-title, 16 p. 22 cm.

A perceptive, valuable (if egocentric) account of the organization of a Negro brigade in Louisiana, 1863-1865; details anti-Negro sentiment, North and South, and urges Federal support of education.

U. S. *American freedmen's inquiry commission.*
Preliminary report touching the condition and management of emancipated refugees; made to the Secretary of war, by the American freedmen's inquiry commission, June 30, 1863. ⟨Publication authorized by the Secretary of war.⟩ New York, J. F. Trow, printer, 1863.

40 p. 22½ cm.

A valuable detailed report by R. D. Owen, S. G. Howe, and James McKaye; recommends the establishment of a freedmen's bureau to bring order out of a chaotic situation.

U. S. *Army. Dept. of the Gulf. Bureau of free labor.*
The freedmen of Louisiana. Final report of the Bureau of free labor, Department of the Gulf, to Major General E. R. S. Canby, commanding: by Thomas W. Conway, general superintendent of freedmen. [New Orleans] Printed at the New Orleans times book and job office, 1865.

37, [1] p. 23 cm.

Richly detailed reports on all aspects of the subject from police persecution to poll taxes; condems carpetbaggers and state officials.

U. S. *Army. Dept. of the Gulf. Bureau of free labor.*
Report on the condition of the freedmen, of the Department of the Gulf, to Major General N. P. Banks, commanding, by Chaplain T. W. Conway, U. S. A., superintendent Bureau of free labor. New Orleans, H. P. Lathrop, printer, 1864.

11 p. 21½ cm.

A detailed endorsement of Banks's labor regulations, with comments on justice, education, management and treatment of labor, and the recruitment of Negro soldiers.

U. S. *Commission for United States colored troops.*
Orders relating to colored men and colored troops. [Nashville, 1863]

23 p. 22 cm.

Valuable details on the recruitment and organization of Negro troops; Mussey, later colonel of the 100th U. S. C. T., was mustering officer for colored troops under George L. Stearns.

U. S. *Congress. Joint committee on the conduct of the war.*
... Fort Pillow massacre. [Washington, 1864]

128 p. 23 cm. (38th Cong., 1st sess. House. Rept. 65)

Details collected by D. W. Gooch and B. F. Wade including testimony by military personnel, white and Negro survivors, and civilian witnesses.

Wagandt, Charles Lewis.
The mighty revolution: Negro emancipation in Maryland, 1862–1864. Baltimore, Johns Hopkins Press [1964]

xii, 299 p. illus., maps. 24 cm.

A solid examination of the movement, with good material on Lincoln's colonizing and compensated emancipation plans.

Wesley, Charles Harris, 1891–
Ohio Negroes in the Civil War. [Columbus] Ohio State University Press for the Ohio Historical Society [1962]

46 p. 24 cm. (Publications of the Ohio Civil War Centennial Commission, no. 6)

A brief but comprehensive survey of Negro Buckeyes' contributions to the Union.

Whiting, William, 1813–1873.
The war powers of the President, Military arrests, and Reconstruction of the Union. By William Whiting. 8th ed. Boston, J. L. Shorey, 1864.

1 p. l., vi, 263, [1] p. 24 cm.

The most extensive and valuable development of war-powers argument (by a War Department solicitor); ran through over forty subsequent editions with additions, revisions, and title changes.

Wiley, Bell Irvin, 1906–
Southern Negroes, 1861–1865. [2d ed.] New York, Rinehart [1953, c1938]

366 p. illus. 21 cm. (Yale historical publications. Miscellany, 31)

This important pioneer work treats of every aspect of Negro life, North and South, during the war; well-researched, carefully documented, and marred only by a Confederate bias.

Williams, George Washington, 1849–1891.
A history of the Negro troops in the war of the rebellion, 1861–1865, preceded by a review of the military services of Negroes in ancient and modern times, by George W. Williams ... New York, Harper & brothers, 1888.

2 p. l., [ix]–xvi, 353 p. front. (port.) 1 illus., pl. 20½ cm.

The best of the first three full-length studies of the subject; anecdotal, detailed, heavy with official reports and correspondence, but over-written to a point of tediousness.

Wilson, Henry, 1812–1875.
History of the antislavery measures of the Thirty-seventh and Thirty-eighth United States Congresses, 1861–64. By Henry Wilson. Boston, Walker, Wise, and company, 1864.

xv, 384 p. 19½ cm.

A valuable guide to debates and legislation on abolition in D. C., compensated emancipation, contrabands, education, freedmen, Negro troops, reconstruction, and repeal of fugitive slave acts.

Wilson, Joseph Thomas, 1836–1891.
The black phalanx; a history of the Negro soldiers of the United States in the wars of 1775–1812, 1861–'65. By Joseph T. Wilson ... 56 illustrations. Hartford, Conn., American publishing company, 1892.

8 p. l., 21–528 p. incl. illus., plates, ports. front. 23 cm.

A significant work by a former Negro soldier; full of official dispatches and lengthy essays; uneven and poorly documented, but valuable for a discussion of anti-Negro prejudice in the army.

Wilson, Joseph Thomas, 1836–1891.
Voice of a new race. Original selections of poems, with a trilogy and oration, by Joseph T. Wilson. Hampton, Va., Normal school steam press, 1882.

iv, [5]–43 p. 14½ cm.

Tributes in poetry and prose to Charles Sumner, Andre Cailloux (a Negro captain mortally wounded at Port Hudson), and to Negro bravery in various actions.

Yeatman, James E   1818–1901.
Report to the Western sanitary commission, in regard to leasing abandoned plantations, with rules and regulations governing the same, by James E. Yeatman ... St. Louis, Western sanitary commission rooms, 1864.

16 p. 22 cm.

Rich in detail on crop reports, plantation protection, recruiting officers, rules and regulations, schools, and wages.

Yeatman, James E   1818–1901.
Suggestions of a plan of organization for freed labor, and the leasing of plantations along the Mississippi River, under a bureau or commission to be appointed by the government. Accompanying a report presented to the Western sanitary commission by James E. Yeatman, president of the commission, Dec. 17, 1863. St. Louis, Mo., Western sanitary commission, 1864.

8 p. 22 cm.

Detailed and critical comments on the living and working conditions in contraband camps and on captured and leased plantations.

THE NAVIES

Thomas Wells

Abbot, Willis John, 1863–
Blue jackets of '61. A history of the navy in the war of secession, by Willis J. Abbot. With illustrations principally by W. C. Jackson. New York, Dodd, Mead & co., 1866.

viii, 318 p. incl. illus., pl. ' front. 23½ x 20 cm.

A general history from the Union viewpoint; includes quotations of unidentified participants, but has neither bibliography nor index.

Alden, Carroll Storrs, 1876–
George Hamilton Perkins, commodore, U. S. N.; his life and letters, by Carroll Storrs Alden ... with portraits and other illustrations. Boston and New York, Houghton Mifflin company, 1914.

xii p., 1 l., 302 p., 1 l. front., plates, ports. 20½ cm.

A satisfactory but pedestrian biography of the executive officer of U. S. S. Cayuga at New Orleans and the commander of the Chickasaw at Mobile Bay; includes numerous contemporary letters.

Almy, John Jay, 1815–1895.
... Incidents of the blockade. Prepared by Companion Rear Admiral John J. Almy ... and read at the stated meeting of February 3, 1892. [Washington, 1892]

10 p. 23cm. (Military order of the loyal legion of the United States. Commandery of the District of Columbia. War papers. 9)

Service aboard the Connecticut off Wilmington, North Carolina.

Ammen, Daniel, 1820–1898.
The old navy and the new, by Rear-Admiral Daniel Ammen ... With an appendix of personal letters from General Grant. Philadelphia, J. B. Lippincott company, 1891.

xvi, [15]–553 p. front., port., facsims. 23cm.

The colorful and gossipy autobiography of an officer aboard the U. S. S. Roanoke, Seneca, Sebago, Patapsco, Mohican; also includes an account of mutiny aboard S. S. Ocean Queen.

Anderson, Bern.
By sea and by river; the naval history of the Civil War. ₁1st ed.₁ New York, Knopf, 1962.

303 p. illus. 22 cm.

The best broad strategic view of the Civil War from a naval point of view; has several minor inaccuracies.

Barnes, James, 1866–1936.
David G. Farragut. London, K. Paul, Trench, Trübner ₁1899₁

xviii, 132 p. port. 15 cm. (The Beacon biographies of eminent Americans. London)

Brief and not very informative.

Barnes, John Sanford, 1836–1911.
Submarine warfare, offensive and defensive, including a discussion of the offensive torpedo system, its effects upon iron-clad ship systems, and influence upon future naval wars. New York, Van Nostrand, 1869.

233 p. illus. 24 cm.

A naval officer analyzes the construction and operations of submarine and surface mines and make proposals for future uses.

Barrett, Edward, 1828–1880.
Gunnery instructions, simplified for the volunteer officers of the U. S. navy; with hints to executive and other officers. By Lieut. Edward Barrett ... New York, D. Van Nostrand, 1862.

88 p. diagrs. 19½ᶜᵐ.

A brief manual which gives some rudimentary facts on the operation of naval guns.

Bartol, Barnabas H
A treatise on the marine boilers of the United States. By B. H. Bartol ... Philadelphia, R. W. Barnard & sons, printers, 1851.

4 p. l., 143 p. fold. pl., diagrs. 23ᶜᵐ.

Contains detailed characteristics of the U. S. S. Susquehanna, Powhatten, Mississippi, Saranac, Princeton, San Jacinto, Michigan, and a number of merchant vessels.

Batten, John Mullin, 1837–1916.
Reminiscences of two years in the United States navy. By John M. Batten ... Printed for the author. Lancaster, Pa., Inquirer printing and publishing co., 1881.

125 p. 19ᶜᵐ.

Batten was a surgeon on the gunboat Vallet City in North Carolina waters from April, 1864, to the end of war; mostly reprints of newspaper clippings.

Baxter, James Phinney, 1893–
The introduction of the ironclad warship, by James Phinney Baxter, 3rd ... Cambridge, Harvard university press, 1933.

x p., 4 l., ₁3₁-398 p. front. plates. 24 cm.

A first-rate piece of scholarship which crosses national lines to show the interchange of ideas leading up to, and following, the armored ships of the Civil War.

Bennett, Frank Marion, 1857–1924.
The steam navy of the United States. A history of the growth of the steam vessel of war in the U. S. navy, and of the naval engineer corps ... By Frank M. Bennett ... 2d ed. Pittsburgh, Pa., Warren & company, 1897.

2 v. illus., plates (part col.) ports., facsim., diagrs. (part fold.) 24ᶜᵐ.

Contains much technical data on engineering plants and personal data on engineering officers.

Besse, Sumner Bradford, 1902–
C. S. ironclad Virginia, with data and references for a scale model, by S. B. Besse ... Newport News, Va., The Mariners' museum, 1937.

47 p. incl. front., illus. 19½ cm.

Reliable information on the configuration, characteristics, and dimensions of the vessel.

Besse, Sumner Bradford, 1902–
U. S. ironclad Monitor, with data and references for a scale model, by S. B. Besse ... Newport News, Va., The Mariners' museum, 1936.

24 p. incl. front., illus. 2 fold. mounted plans.

Identical in format to Besse's volume on the Virginia.

Bigelow, John, 1817–1911.

France and the Confederate navy, 1862–1868; an international episode, by John Bigelow. New York, Harper & brothers, 1888.

x p., 1 l., 247 p. 19½ᶜᵐ.

Essentially a reply to Bullock; concentrates on the Armand Contract for Ironclads.

Blanding, Stephen F

Recollections of a sailor boy; or, The cruise of the gunboat Louisiana. By Stephen F. Blanding ... Providence, E. A. Johnson & co., 1886.

vi, [7]–330 p. 19½ᶜᵐ.

Excellent material on the enlistment and subsequent daily life as a sailor on a blockading vessel.

Blatchford, Samuel, 1820–1893, *comp.*

Reports of cases in prize, argued and determined in the Circuit and District courts of the United States, for the Southern district of New York. 1861–'65. By Samuel Blatchford. New York, Baker, Voorhis & co., 1866.

viii, 729 p. 23½ᶜᵐ.

Contains summaries, rulings, and notices of appeal, but no verbatim testimony or other details.

Boyer, Samuel Pellman, 1839–1875.

Naval surgeon; the diary of Dr. Samuel Pellman Boyer. Edited by Elinor Barnes and James A. Barnes. Introd. by Allan Nevins. Bloomington, Indiana University Press [1963]

2 v. illus., ports., maps, facsims. 24 cm.

The diary of a medical officer aboard the Fernandina, September, 1862-February, 1864, and the Mattabasset, April, 1864-May, 1865; good information on medical problems.

Boykin, Edward Carrington, 1889–

Ghost ship of the Confederacy; the story of the Alabama and her captain. Raphael Semmes. New York, Funk & Wagnalls [1957]

404 p. illus. 22 cm.

A biography of Semmes with emphasis on his service on the Alabama.

Boykin, Edward Carrington, 1889–

Sea devil of the Confederacy; the story of the Florida and her captain, John Newland Maffitt. New York, Funk & Wagnalls [1959]

306 p. illus. 22 cm.

A detailed but documented account of the career of John Newland Maffitt, the Florida, the blockade runners Owl and Lillian, and the bark Tacony.

Boynton, Charles Brandon, 1806–1883.

The history of the navy during the rebellion. By Charles B. Boynton ... New York, D. Appleton & co., 1867–68.

2 v. front., illus., plates (part col.) port., maps. 23½ᶜᵐ.

A full, generally accurate, but strongly pro-Union and pro-Welles account.

Bradlee, Francis Boardman Crowninshield, 1881–1928.

Blockade running during the civil war and the effect of land and water transportation on the Confederacy, by Francis B. C. Bradlee ... Salem, Mass., The Essex institute, 1925.

xii, 340 p. front., plates, ports., maps, facsims. 24 cm.

A good but brief study; the volume also includes chapters on Confederate railroads, post office, telegraph, and express company.

Bradlee, Francis Boardman Crowninshield, 1881–

A forgotten chapter in our naval history. A sketch of the career of Duncan Nathaniel Ingraham, commander U. S. N. and commodore C. S. N. By Francis B. C. Bradlee ... Salem, Mass., The Essex institute, 1923.

25 p. front., plates, ports. 25½ cm.

A brief and favorable biography of Duncan Ingraham; superficial and scanty.

Bradlow, Edna.

Here comes the Alabama; the career of a Confederate raider, by Edna and Frank Bradlow. Cape Town, A. A. Balkema, 1958.

128 p. illus., ports., maps, music. 21 cm.

This source includes some contemporary South African newspapers not usually available.

Brandt, John D.
Gunnery catechism, as applied to the service of naval ordnance. Adapted to the latest official regulations, and approved by the Bureau of ordnance, Navy department. By J. D. Brandt ... New York, D. Van Nostrand, 1864.

197 p. plates, diagrs. 16^{cm}.

A concise, easily understood collection of practical facts concerning large guns and ammunitions; very useful for establishing basic data.

Brown, Claude.
The ram Switzerland. [n. p., 1958]

1 v. illus. 29 cm.

An account of a ship in Ellet's fleet; contains a number of undocumented sidelights gathered from local newspapers and tradition.

Browne, A   K
The story of the Kearsarge and Alabama. San Francisco, H. Payot & co., 1868.

27 numb. l. 22½^{cm}.

A brief, uninformative, early report of the action.

Buckner, William P   *d.* 1869.
Calculated tables of ranges for navy and army guns. With a method of finding the distance of an object at sea. By Lieut. W. P. Buckner, u. s. n. Approved by the Ordnance bureau, Navy department. New York, D. Van Nostrand, 1865.

79 p. incl. tables, 2 diagr. 23½^{cm}.

Erroneous calculations based upon the primitive science of exterior ballistics.

Bulloch, James Dunwody, 1823–1901.
The secret service of the Confederate States in Europe; or, How the Confederate cruisers were equipped. With a new introd. by Philip Van Doren Stern. New York, T. Yoseloff [1959]

2 v. illus., ports., maps. 22 cm.

The most comprehensive and interesting source concerning C. S. N. purchasing operations abroad.

Butts, Francis Banister.
The Monitor and the Merrimac. By Frank B. Butts ... Providence, The Society, 1890.

51 p. 21^{cm}. (*Added t.-p.:* Personal narratives of events in the war of the rebellion, being papers read before the Rhode Island soldiers and sailors historical society. 4th ser.—no. 6)

A good deal of personal observations by the paymaster's clerk of the Monitor.

Canfield, Eugene B
Notes on naval ordnance of the American Civil War, 1861–1865. Washington, American Ordnance Association, 1960.

24 p. illus. 26 cm.

A highly detailed, technical, and important tract on a subject rarely treated.

Carse, Robert, 1903–
Blockade; the Civil War at sea. New York, Rinehart [1958]

279 p. illus. 22 cm.

An interestingly written but somewhat disjointed account of the experiences of some of the blockade runners.

Castlen, Harriet (Gift)
Hope bids me onward, by Harriet Gift Castlen ... Biography of George Gift arranged by his daughter, from letters George Gift wrote to her mother before they were married. [Savannah, Chatham printing company, 1945]

2 p. l., 7–198 p. 23½^{cm}.

Concerns the C. S. S. Arkansas, Chattahoochee, and commando operations.

Church, William Conant, 1836–1917.
The life of John Ericsson, by William Conant Church ... New York, C. Scribner's sons, 1890.

2 v. fronts., ilus., plates, ports., facsims. 23 cm.

Strongly biased in favor of Ericsson but contains extensive material on the Monitor.

Clark, Charles Edgar, 1843–

My fifty years in the navy, by Charles E. Clark, rear admiral, U. S. navy ... Boston, Little, Brown, and company, 1917.

5 p. l., 346 p. front., plates, ports., diagrs. 21½ᶜᵐ.

Clark served on the U. S. S. Ossipee and was at the battle of Mobile Bay.

Clark, George Edward.

Seven years of a sailor's life. By George Edward Clark. "Yankee Ned" ... Boston, Adams & company [1867]

6 p. l., [11]–358 p. ix pl. (incl. front.) 19½ᶜᵐ.

A merchant sailor joins the Union navy; colorful in minor details of shipboard life.

Cochran, Hamilton, 1898–

Blockade runners of the Confederacy. [1st ed.] Indianapolis, Bobbs-Merrill [1958]

350 p. illus. 23 cm.

A superficial and sometimes inaccurate treatment.

Coleman, Silas Bunker, 1843–

A July morning with the rebel ram "Arkansas." A paper prepared and read before the Michigan commandery of the Military order of the loyal legion of the U. S. By S. B. Coleman ... March 6th, 1889. Detroit, Winn & Hammond, printers, 1890.

13 p. 23ᶜᵐ.

A brief account of the battle by a participant aboard the U. S. S. Tyler.

Confederate States of America. *Congress. Joint special committee to investigate the Navy department.*

Report of evidence taken before a joint special committee of both houses of the Confederate Congress, to investigate the affairs of the Navy department. P. Kean, reporter. Richmond, Va., G. P. Evans & co., printers [1863]

472 p. 22½ᶜᵐ.

The report, less copies of shipbuilding contracts, is reprinted in Navy OR, Sect. II, Vol. I.

Confederate States of America. *Navy dept.*

Ordnance instructions for the Confederate States navy relating to the preparation of vessels of war for battle, to the duties of officers and others when at quarters, to ordnance and ordnance stores, and to gunnery. 3d ed. Pub. by order of the Navy department. London, Saunders, Otley, & co. [Printed by Spottiswoode and co.] 1864.

xix, 171, cix p. 21 pl. 24ᶜᵐ.

Treats not only of ordnance subjects, but also gives much information concerning preparation for battle.

Confederate States of America. *Navy dept.*

Register of the commissioned and warrant officers of the navy of the Confederate States, to January 1, 1863. Richmond, Macfarlane & Fergusson, 1862.

2 p. l., 38 p. 23½ᶜᵐ.

Consists of published extracts from the register maintained by the Office of Orders and Detail.

Corbin, *Mrs.* **Diana Fontaine (Maury)**

A life of Matthew Fontaine Maury ... Comp. by his daughter, Diana Fontaine Maury Corbin. London, S. Low, Marston, Searle, & Rivington, limited, 1888.

vi, 326 p. front. (port.) 22½ᶜᵐ.

A partisan and poorly written book by the oceanographer's daughter, but it reproduces Civil War correspondence not published elsewhere.

Costi, Angelo Michele.

Memoir of the Trent affair. By An: Michele Costi ... Washington, D. C., McGill & Witherow, printers and stereotypers, 1865.

23 p. 22½ᶜᵐ.

Contains an introduction by Charles Wilkes in vindication of his conduct.

Cowley, Charles, 1832–1908.

Leaves from a lawyer's life, afloat and ashore. By Charles Cowley ... Lowell, Mass., Penhallow printing company; Boston, Lee & Shepard, 1879.

1 p. l., [5]–245 p. 20ᶜᵐ.

A disappointing account by Dahlgren's judge advocate; contains little first-hand information and only fragments concerning naval legal matters.

Cranwell, John Philips, 1904–
    Spoilers of the sea, wartime raiders in the age of steam [by] John Philips Cranwell. New York, W. W. Norton & company, inc. [°1941]
        308 p. plates, ports., fold. maps. 22 cm.

A dramatically written, popularized account of cruiser warfare.

Currie, George E
    Warfare along the Mississippi; the letters of Lieutenant Colonel George E. Currie. Edited by Norman E. Clarke, Sr. Mount Pleasant, Clarke Historical Collection, Central Michigan University [1961]
        xvi, 153 p. illus., ports. 23 cm.

A history of the Marine Brigade, principally consisting of the letters and post-war writings of Col. George E. Currie, a regimental commander, 1862-1864.

Dahlgren, Madeleine (Vinton) 1835–1898.
    Memoir of John A. Dahlgren, rear-admiral United States navy, by his widow. Madeleine Vinton Dahlgren ... Boston, J. R. Osgood & company, 1882.
        xi, 660 p. illus. (plans) double pl., 2 port. (incl. front.) fold. map. 23½ cm.

A poorly edited and imperfectly assimilated collection of the unusually informative journals and letters of Adm. Dahlgren.

Daly, Robert Welter, 1916–
    How the Merrimac won; the strategic story of the C. S. S. Virginia. New York, Crowell [1957]
        211 p. illus. 21 cm.

Views the Merrimac's career from its effect on McClellan's Peninsular Campaign; contains an extensive list of articles from contemporary periodicals.

Dalzell, George Walton, 1877–
    The flight from the flag; the continuing effect of the civil war upon the American carrying trade, by George W. Dalzell. Chapel Hill, The University of North Carolina press, 1940.
        xviii, [2], 292 p. front., plates, port., facsims. 24 cm.

Emphasizes the long-range effect of Confederate cruiser warfare; contains a very useful glossary of terms used in blockade warfare.

Davenport, Charles Benedict, 1866–1944.
    Naval officers, their heredity and development, by Charles Benedict Davenport ... assisted by Mary Theresa Scudder ... Washington, Carnegie institution of Washington, 1919.
        iv p., 1 l., 236 p. diagrs. 25½ cm. (*On verso of t.-p.:* Carnegie institution of Washington. Publication no. 259)

An odd book which combines geneaology with an effort to psychoanalyze men from their biographies; has useful thumbnail sketches of many officers.

Davis, Charles Henry, 1845–1921.
    Life of Charles Henry Davis, rear admiral, 1807–1877; by his son, Captain Charles H. Davis, U. S. N. Boston and New York, Houghton, Mifflin and company, 1899.
        2 p. l., 349, [1] p. front. (port.) 1 illus. 22½ cm.

A thorough and thoughtful biography by the son of a great planner and administrator, with emphasis on these two phases of Davis's career.

Davis, Robert Stewart 1839–
    History of the Rebel steam ram "Atlanta", now on exhibition at foot of Washington street, for the benefit of the Union volunteer refreshment saloon, Philadelphia, with an interesting account of the engagement which resulted in her capture. November, 1863. [Philadelphia] Printed by G. H. Ives [1863]
        cover-title, 10 p., 1 l. illus. 15ᶜᵐ.

A leaflet for distribution to visitors aboard the ship at Philadelphia; contains a diagram of her interior and a brief description of her capture.

Dawson, Francis W
    Reminiscences of Confederate service, 1861–1865. By Capt. Francis W. Dawson ... Charleston, S. C., The News and courier book presses, 1882.
        180 p. 23½ᶜᵐ.

The light and gracefully written manuscript of a young Englishman who served on the <u>Nashville</u>, <u>Beaufort</u>, and <u>Drewry</u>.

Dewey, George, 1837–1917.
    Autobiography of George Dewey, admiral of the Navy ... New York, C. Scribner's sons, 1913.
        xii, 337 p. front., plates, ports., map, facsims. 23½ cm.

Contains accounts of Dewey's service as executive officer of the U. S. S. <u>Mississippi</u> at New Orleans and Port Hudson and <u>Colorado</u> at Fort Fisher; light and personal.

Drayton, Percival, 1812–1865.

Naval letters from Captain Percival Drayton, 1861–1865; printed from the original manuscripts presented to the New York Public library by Miss Gertrude L. Hoyt. New York, 1906.

1 p. l., 81 p. 26ᶜᵐ.

Poorly edited, unannotated copies of Drayton's frank and discursive letters to friends.

Du Pont, Henry Algernon, 1838–1926.

Rear-Admiral Samuel Francis Du Pont, United States navy: a biography, by H. A. Du Pont ... New York, National Americana society, 1926.

5 p. l., 3–320 p. plates, 2 port. (incl. front.) maps. 23ᶜᵐ.

A satisfactory but not penetrating biography, based largely on DuPont's correspondence.

Du Pont, Samuel Francis, 1803–1865.

Official dispatches and letters of Rear Admiral Du Pont, U. S. navy. 1846–48. 1861–63. Wilmington, Del., Press of Ferris bros., printers, 1883.

2 p. l., 531 p. 23½ᶜᵐ.

Unannotated, outgoing naval correspondence; lacks index.

Durkin, Joseph Thomas, 1903–

Stephen R. Mallory: Confederate Navy chief. Chapel Hill, University of North Carolina Press, 1954.

xi, 446 p. 25 cm.

A sympathetic and uncritical biography; disappointing, but the best there is on the subject.

Edge, Frederick Milnes.

An Englishman's view of the battle between the Alabama and the Kearsarge; an account of the naval engagement in the British Channel on Sunday, June 19th, 1864. From information personally obtained in the town of Cherbourg, as well as from the officers and crew of the United States sloop of war Kearsarge, and the wounded and prisoners of the confederate privateer. By Frederick Milnes Edge. New York, A. D. F. Randolph, 1864. Reprinted, New York, W. Abbatt, 1908.

36 p. 26½ᶜᵐ.

An excellent report written shortly after the action; based on personal interviews and inspections by the author.

Edwards, E   M   H

Commander William Barker Cushing, of the United States navy. By E. M. H. Edwards. Genealogy, reminiscences of childhood, boyhood, and manhood; incidents of his naval career ... original letters ... London, New York, F. T. Neely [ᶜ1898]

1 p. l., [v]–vii, 202 p. front., plates, ports. 19½ᶜᵐ.

An incomplete and unsatisfactory biography, yet it contains numerous personal letters written during the war.

Ellicott, John Morris, 1859–

The life of John Ancrum Winslow, rear-admiral, United States navy, who commanded the U. S. steamer "Kearsarge" in her action with the Confederate cruiser "Alabama"; by John M. Ellicott ... New York and London, G. P. Putnam's sons, 1902.

x p., 1 l., 281 p. front. (port.) 3 pl., 2 maps, diagr. 23½ᶜᵐ.

Based on Winslow's letters to his wife and others; presents a fair picture of a rather dull man on dull duty.

Evans, Robley Dunglison, 1846–1912.

A sailor's log; recollections of forty years of naval life, by Robley D. Evans ... New York, D. Appleton and company, 1901.

1 p. l., ix, 467 p. front. (ports.) plates. 21½ cm.

Memoir of a midshipman wounded at Fort Fisher; a graphic description of the landing force in that campaign.

Farenholt, Oscar Walter, 1845–

The monitor "Catskill"; a year's reminiscences! 1863–1864, by ex-Commander Oscar Walter Farenholt, rear admiral U. S. navy (retired), read before the California commandery of the Military order of the loyal legion of the United States, at a banquet at San Francisco, California, Wednesday, January seventeenth, one thousand nine hundred and twelve. S[an] F[rancisco] Shannon-Conmy printing co., 1912.

13 p. 22ᶜᵐ. (On cover: War paper no. 23, Commandery of the state of California, Military order the loyal legion of the United States)

Recounts service as helmsman of the Catskill during its 1863 attacks on Charleston; brief but vivid.

Farragut, Loyall, 1844–

The life of David Glasgow Farragut, first admiral of the United States navy, embodying his journal and letters. By his son, Loyall Farragut. With portraits, maps, and illustrations. New York, D. Appleton and company [ᶜ1907]

vi, 586 p. illus., plates, 2 port. (incl. front.) maps (1 fold.) double facsim. 24ᶜᵐ.

An uncritical but accurate biography by the admiral's son; a source for letters frequently quoted elsewhere.

Fiveash, Joseph Gardner, 1846–
  Virginia-(Merrimac) Monitor engagement, and a complete history of the operations of these two historic vessels in Hampton Roads and adjacent waters. C. S. S. Virginia, March 8–May 11, 1862, U. S. S. Monitor, March 9 [1862]–January 2d, 1863. By Joseph G. Fiveash. Norfolk, Va., Fiveash publishing corporation [c1907]

  29 p. front., plates, ports. map. 27¼cm.

Brief, sketchy, uninformative.

Foltz, Charles Steinman, 1859–1941.
  Surgeon of the seas; the adventurous life of Surgeon General Jonathan M. Foltz in the days of wooden ships, told from his notes of the moment, by Charles S. Foltz ... Indianapolis, The Bobbs-Merrill company [c1931]

  8 p. l., 15–351 p. front., plates (1 double) ports., maps, facsims. 23cm.

Written by the son of Farragut's surgeon from the latter's journal and letters; too much tactics and not enough medical information.

Fox, Gustavus Vasa, 1821–1883.
  Confidential correspondence of Gustavus Vasa Fox, assistant secretary of the navy, 1861–1865, edited by Robert Means Thompson and Richard Wainwright ... New York, Printed for the Naval history society by the De Vinne press, 1918–19 [c1920]

  2 v. front. (port.) 24 cm.

An excellent source for information on the strategic and administrative operations of the Union navy and on the principal commanders.

Franklin, Samuel Rhoades, 1825–1909.
  Memories of a rear-admiral who has served for more than half a century in the Navy of the United States. By S. R. Franklin ... New York and London, Harper & brothers, 1898.

  xiii, [1] p., 1 l., 397, [1] p. front. (port.) plates. 21½ cm.

A colorless autobiography of a name-dropper who treats very superficially of his duties as fleet captain to Farragut.

Fullam, George Townley
  The cruise of the "Alabama," from her departure from Liverpool until her arrival at the cape of Good Hope. By an officer on board. Liverpool, Lee and Nightingale, W. H. Peat, 1863.
  48 p. front. (port.) pl. 18cm.

An officer's journal from the time of the ship's commissioning to January 20, 1864.

Gleaves, Albert, 1858–1937.
  Life and letters of Rear Admiral Stephen B. Luce, U. S. Navy, founder of the Naval war college, by Rear Admiral Albert Gleaves ... with 16 illustrations. New York & London, G. P. Putnam's sons, 1925.

  xii, 381 p. front., plates, ports., map. 23½ cm.

Most of Luce's service was at the Naval Academy, but he commanded the ironclad Nantucket off Charleston.

Gosnell, Harpur Allen, 1890–
  Guns on the western waters; the story of river gunboats in the Civil War. Baton Rouge, Louisiana State University Press [1949]

  xii, 273 p. illus., maps, ports. 24 cm.

An excellent, vivid, and thorough account, yet lacking in documentation and index.

Graves, Henry Lea, 1842–1892.
  A Confederate marine; a sketch of Henry Lea Graves with excerpts from the Graves family correspondence, 1861–1865. Edited by Richard Harwell. Tuscaloosa, Ala., Confederate Pub. Co., 1963.

  140 p. illus. 22 cm. (Confederate centennial studies, no. 24)

Letters of a young marine officer stationed mostly around Savannah and Drewry's Bluff; includes some letters from Henry Graves's brother Iverson, who was a master's mate.

Grimes, James Wilson, 1816–1872.
  Achievements of the western naval flotilla. Remarks of Hon. James W. Grimes, of Iowa. Delivered in the Senate of the United States, March 13, 1862. [Washington, Printed by L. Towers & co., 1862]

  8 p. 24½cm.

Especially laudatory of Foote.

Hackett, Frank Warren, 1841–1926.
  Deck and field; addresses before the United States Naval war college and on commemorative occasions, by Frank Warren Hackett ... Washington, W. H. Lowdermilk & company, 1909.
  xi, 222 p., 1 l. 20cm.

Contains first-hand descriptions of Farragut and Flusser.

Halle, Ernst von 1868–1909.

Die blockade der nordamerikanischen südstaaten. Die baumwollenhungersnoth in Lancashire. Berlin, E. S. Mittler und sohn, 1900.

cover-title, 46 p. 21ᶜᵐ.

A superficial consideration of the blockade; written by a distinguished German military historian.

Hamersly, Lewis Randolph, 1847–1910.

The records of living officers of the U. S. Navy and Marine corps; with a history of naval operations during the rebellion of 1861–5, and a list of the ships and officers participating in the great battles, comp. from official sources by Lewis R. Hamersly ... Philadelphia, J. B. Lippincott & co., 1870.

350 p. 24ᶜᵐ.

Contains brief biographical sketches, a short naval history of the Civil War, and rosters of officers for participating vessels in the principal campaigns.

Hamilton, *Sir* **Richard Vesey,** 1829–

... Facts connected with the naval operations during the civil war in the United States. By Rear-Admiral R. V. Hamilton, c. b.

(*In* Royal united service institution, London. Journal. London, 1878. 22ᶜᵐ. v. 22, no. 96, p. ₁612₁–640. fold. map)

A lecture on the problems of coast artillery and navy, based mainly on Boynton.

Harris, Thomas Le Grand, 1863–

The Trent affair, including a review of English and American relations at the beginning of the civil war, by Thomas L. Harris, a. m. With an introduction by James A. Woodburn ... Indianapolis and Kansas City, The Bowen-Merrill co., 1896.

288 p. 21 cm.

Mostly concerned with diplomatic maneuvering.

Harwood, Andrew Allen, 1802–1884.

The law and practice of United States naval courts-martial. By A. A. Harwood, u. s. n. New York, D. Van Nostrand, 1867.

325 p. illus. (plan) 24ᶜᵐ.

A technical manual which includes a copy of the Articles for the Government of the Navy, as well as directives and laws concerning the navy.

Haywood, P   D

The cruise of the Alabama, by one of the crew; with notes from historical authorities. Boston and New York, Houghton, Mifflin and company, 1886.

150 p. pl., 2 maps (incl. fold. front.) 18½ᶜᵐ.

An interesting account purportedly written by a sailor, but regarded as spurious by officers who served on the Alabama.

Headley, Joel Tyler, 1813–1897.

Farragut, and our naval commanders. By Hon. J. T. Headley ... A companion volume to Headley's "Grant and Sherman." Comprising the early life and public services of the prominent naval commanders who, with Grant and Sherman and their generals, brought to a triumphant close the great rebellion of 1861–1865 ... New York, E. B. Treat & co.; Chicago, Ill., C. W. Lilley; ₁etc., etc.₁ 1867.

ix p., 1 l., ₁13₁–609 p. front., plates, ports. 23 cm.

Contains biographies of from a half-page to fifty pages in length of Union officers only; somewhat anti-Welles.

Headley, Joel Tyler, 1813–1897.

Our navy in the great rebellion. Heroes and battles of the war 1861–65. By Hon. J. T. Headley ... Comprising an authentic account of battles and sieges ... New York, E. B. Treat, 1891.

ix, ₁11₁–616 p. incl. front., illus., ports. plates, ports. 22½ᶜᵐ.

A strongly pro-Union but generally accurate account; includes biographical sketches of principal Union officers.

Headley, John William, *b.* 1841.

Confederate operations in Canada and New York, by John W. Headley; illustrated with portraits. New York and Washington, The Neale publishing company, 1906.

xv p., 1 l., ₁19₁–480 p. front., ports. 23 cm.

Contains chapters on the activities of John Y. Beall.

Headley, Phineas Camp, 1819–1903.

Life and naval career of Vice-admiral David Glascoe ₁!₁ Farragut, by Rev. P. C. Headley ... New York, William H. Appleton, 1865.

342 p. 18ᶜᵐ.

Faulty and inaccurate, yet the first biography of Farragut.

Henderson, Daniel MacIntyre, 1880–
    The hidden coasts; a biography of Admiral Charles
Wilkes. New York, Sloane, 1953.

    306 p. port., map (on lining papers) 22 cm.

Strongly pro-Wilkes; very skimpy on the Civil
War period.

Hero tales of the American soldier and sailor as told by the
heroes themselves and their comrades; the unwritten history
of American chivalry. Philadelphia, Pa., Century manufacturing company [c1899]

    x, 33–503 p. double col. front., illus., plates, ports., maps. 24½ x 19ᶜᵐ.

Short narratives by participants.

Hill, Frederic Stanhope, 1829–1913.
    Twenty years at sea; or, Leaves from my old log-books.
By Frederic Stanhope Hill. Boston and New York, Houghton, Mifflin and company, 1893.

    vii p., 1 l., 273 p. 18ᶜᵐ.

An account by a master's mate on the Richmond
at New Orleans and a lieutenant commanding a
blockader off the Texas coast.

Hill, Jim Dan, 1897–
    Sea dogs of the sixties; Farragut and seven contempo-
raries, by Jim Dan Hill. Minneapolis, Minn., The University of Minnesota press, 1935.

    xiv, 265 p. front., illus. (maps) plates, ports. 23½ cm.

Accurate short biographies based on thorough
scholarship and understanding.

Hobart-Hampden, *Hon.* **Augustus Charles,** 1822–1886.
    Sketches from my life. By the late Admiral Hobart Pasha
... New York, D. Appleton and company, 1887.

    viii, 282 p. front. (port.) 18½ᶜᵐ.

A highly interesting, frank, and authoritative
personal account by a successful blockade-
runner.

Holley, Alexander Lyman, 1832–1882.
    A treatise on ordnance and armor: embracing descriptions,
discussions, and professional opinions concerning the material,
fabrication, requirements, capabilities, and endurance of European and American guns for naval, sea-coast, and iron-clad
warfare, and their rifling, projectiles and breech-loading.
Also, results of experiments against armor, from official records. With an appendix, referring to gun-cotton, hooped
guns, etc., etc. By Alexander L. Holley ... With 493 illustrations. New York, D. Van Nostrand; London, Trübner &
company, 1865.

    xliv p., 2 l., 900 p. incl. illus., tables. pl. 23ᶜᵐ.

Excellent technical comparisons of American
and British guns, armor, and ammunition.

Hoole, William Stanley, 1903–
    Four years in the Confederate Navy; the career of Cap-
tain John Low on the C. S. S. Fingal, Florida, Alabama,
Tuscaloosa, and Ajax. Athens, University of Georgia Press
[1964]

    xiv, 147 p. illus., ports., chart, facsims. 25 cm.

Written from Low's long-sought journal; disappointingly sterile.

Hoppin, James Mason, 1820–1906.
    Life of Andrew Hull Foote, rear-admiral United States
navy. By James Mason Hoppin ... With a portrait and
illustrations. New York, Harper & brothers, 1874.

    x p., 1 l., [13]–411 p. front. (port.) illus., 8 pl., map. 22ᶜᵐ.

A first-rate biography; includes numerous
letters not usually found.

Horn, Stanley Fitzgerald, 1889–
    Gallant rebel, the fabulous cruise of the C. S. S. Shenan-
doah. New Brunswick [N. J.] Rutgers Univ. Press, 1947.

    viii, 292 p. map (on lining-papers) 21 cm.

The story of the Shenandoah, embellished with
reconstructed conversations and scenes.

Hunt, Cornelius E.
    The Shenandoah; or, The last Confederate cruiser. By
Cornelius E. Hunt ... New York, G. W. Carleton & co.; [etc.,
etc.] 1867.

    273 p. front. 19ᶜᵐ.

A very readable and intimate story by one of
the officers.

Johnson, John, 1829–1907.
The defense of Charleston harbor, including Fort Sumter and the adjacent islands. 1863–1865. By John Johnson ... With original papers in appendix, full official reports, maps, and illustrations. Charleston, S. C., Walker, Evans & Cogswell co., 1890.

276, clxxxvi p. illus., plates (part fold.) ports., maps (part fold.) plans (part fold.) 24 cm.

Principally concerned with military matters; relies very heavily on Scharf for naval data.

Jones, Charles Colcock, 1831–1893.
The life and services of Commodore Josiah Tattnall; by Charles C. Jones, jr. ... Savannah, Morning news steam printing house, 1878.

ix, 255, 4 p. front. (port.) 23½ cm.

An over-romantic but reliable work which includes some of Tattnall's wartime correspondence not published elsewhere.

Jones, Virgil Carrington, 1906–
The Civil War at sea. Foreword by E. M. Eller. [1st ed.] New York, Holt, Rinehart, Winston [1960–62]

3 v. illus. 22 cm.

A comprehensive but undistinguished history of both navies; poorly indexed.

Jones, Wilbur Devereux.
The Confederate rams at Birkenhead; a chapter in Anglo-American relations. Tuscaloosa, Ala., Confederate Pub. Co., 1961.

124 p. illus. 22 cm. (Confederate centennial studies, no. 19)

Concerned principally with international and British civil law.

Keeler, William Frederick, 1821–1886.
Aboard the USS Monitor: 1862; the letters of Acting Paymaster William Frederick Keeler, U. S. Navy, to his wife, Anna. Edited by Robert W. Daly. Annapolis, U. S. Naval Institute [1964]

xvii, 278 p. illus., port., maps. 24 cm. (Naval letters series, v. 1)

Detailed observations by the Monitor's paymaster; excellent for atmosphere and shipboard life.

Kell, John McIntosh, 1823–1900.
Recollections of a naval life, including the cruises of the Confederate States steamers "Sumter" and "Alabama." By John McIntosh Kell ... Washington, The Neale company, 1900.

307 p. front. (port.) 23 cm.

A modest but good autobiography by Semmes's executive officer; Kell's account of brief service with the James River Squadron in 1865 is one of the best.

Kendricken, Paul Henry, 1834–
Memoirs of Paul Henry Kendricken. Boston, Priv. print., 1910.

2 p. l., 355 p. front., plates, ports. 24 cm.

Service as an engineer on the Conemaugh, at Port Royal, Mobile Bay, and Charleston; some interesting details on the ship's organization.

Lepotier, Adolphe Auguste Marie, 1898–
... Les corsaires du Sud et le pavillon étoilé de l'Alabama à l'Emden; préface du vice-amiral Castex. Paris, Société d'éditions géographiques, maritimes et coloniales, 1936.

202 p., 2 l. illus. (incl. maps) 25½ cm.

A thoughtful assessment of cruiser warfare; contains useful track charts of the cruisers.

Lepotier, Adolphe Auguste Marie, 1898–
... Mer contre terre. Paris, Éditions Mirambeau [1945]

357, [1] p. illus. (incl. maps) 24½ cm.

Mainly interested in proving the importance of cruiser warfare.

Lewis, Charles Lee, 1886–
David Glasgow Farragut ... by Charles Lee Lewis ... Annapolis, United States naval institute [1941–43]

2 v. fronts., illus. (facsim.) plates, ports., map. 24 cm.

A carefully written, thoughtful, and comprehensive biography.

Lewis, Charles Lee, 1886–
Matthew Fontaine Maury, the pathfinder of the seas, by Charles Lee Lewis ... Annapolis, The United States naval institute, 1927.

xvii, 264 p. plates, ports. 24½ cm.

Brief, unannotated biography; highly sympathetic to Maury.

Low, Alfred Maurice, 1860–
Blockade and contraband, by A. Maurice Low ... Washington, Columbian printing company, inc. [1916?]

16 p. 24½ᶜᵐ.

Treats of the long-range impact upon international law of prize cases in the Civil War.

Lucas, Daniel Bedinger 1836–1909.
Memoir of John Yates Beall: his life, trial; correspondence; diary; and private manuscript found among his papers, including his own account of the raid on lake Erie. Montreal, Printed by J. Lovell, 1865.

vi p., 1 l., 297 p. front. (port., mounted photo.) 22ᶜᵐ.

The special pleadings of an erratic Confederate irregular.

Luce, Stephen Bleecker, 1827–1917.
Seamanship: comp. from various authorities, and illustrated with numerous original and select designs, for the use of the United States Naval academy, by S. B. Luce ... 3d ed.—rev. and enl. New York, D. Van Nostrand, 1866.

3 p. l., [v]–xv, 663 p. illus., 89 pl. (part fold.) 25ᶜᵐ.

A highly technical textbook written for the naval academy but widely used in the merchant marines as well as the navy.

Macartney, Clarence Edward Noble, 1879–
Mr. Lincoln's admirals. With a foreword by George Fielding Eliot. New York, Funk & Wagnalls Co., 1956.

xiii, 335 p. illus., ports., map. 22 cm.

Brief, incisive biographies of Welles, Fox, Farragut, Foote, DuPont, Dahlgren, Worden, Cushing, Winslow, Collins, and Porter.

MacBride, Robert.
Civil War ironclads; the dawn of naval armor. [1st ed.] Philadelphia, Chilton Books [1962]

185 p. illus. 25 cm.

Contains outline sketches of most of the ironclads; brief and lacking in depth, it still helps a student to understand and sort out the tools of the naval war.

Maclay, Edgar Stanton, 1863–1919.
Reminiscences of the old navy, from the journals and private papers of Captain Edward Trenchard, and Rear-Admiral Stephen Decatur Trenchard, by Edgar Stanton Maclay ... New York and London, G. P. Putnam's sons, 1898.

3 p. l., v–x p., 1 l., 362 p. 22ᶜᵐ.

A dull narrative of the dull life of the Rhode Island as a supply ship and gunboat; written from Trenchard's journal.

McCarten, Francis.
In peace and in war; or, Seven years in the U. S. navy, by Francis McCarten. [Printed on board the U. S. flagship Tennessee, 1876–78]

cover-title, 1 p. l., 32, [1], 3–69 p. 22½ᶜᵐ.

A summary of the cruises of the Augusta and the Metacomet.

McCordock, Robert Stanley, 1897–
The Yankee cheese box, by Robert Stanley McCordock ... Philadelphia, Dorrance and company [c1938]

470 p. illus. (map) 22 cm.

A comprehensive history of both the Merrimack and the Monitor; includes widespread newspaper research.

Maffitt, *Mrs.* **Emma (Martin)**
The life and services of John Newland Maffitt, by Emma Martin Maffitt (his widow) ... New York and Washington, The Neale publishing company, 1906.

436 p. pl., 6 port. (incl. front.) 23½ᶜᵐ.

A poor biography; largely a compilation of Maffitt's official and personal correspondence.

Mahan, Alfred Thayer, 1840–1914.

... Admiral Farragut, by Captain A. T. Mahan ... New York, D. Appleton and company, 1892.

4 p. l., 333 p. front. (port.) fold. map, plans (1 fold.) 19½ᶜᵐ.

A masterful and thought-provoking analysis; still the best biography of Farragut.

Mahan, Alfred Thayer, 1840–1914.

... The gulf and inland waters, by A. T. Mahan ... New York, C. Scribner's sons, 1883.

viii p., 1 l., 267 p. illus., maps (part fold.) 19 cm. (The Navy in the civil war. III)

Mahan's first book; clear and thoughtful, but written from limited sources.

Mannix, D   Pratt.

The extent and value of the co-operation of the navy during our late civil war. Essay by Lieut. Mannix ... [n. p.] 1878.

31 p. 23ᶜᵐ.

A short history of the Union Navy written soon after the war.

Markens, Isaac.

President Lincoln and the case of John Y. Beall, by Isaac Markens. New York, Printed for the author, 1911.

cover-title, 11 p. port. 25 cm.

An account of the futile efforts to persuade Lincoln to commute Beall's death sentence for sabotage.

Marshall, Edward Chauncey, 1824–

History of the United States Naval academy, with biographical sketches, and the names of all the superintendents, professors and graduates, to which is added a record of some of the earliest votes by Congress, of thanks, medals, and swords to naval officers. By Edward Chauncey Marshall ... New York, D. Van Nostrand, 1862.

156 p. front., pl. 18½ᶜᵐ.

Contains details on regulations, routine, and course of instruction for the early Civil War years.

Maury, Richard Lancelot, 1840–1907.

A brief sketch of the work of Matthew Fontaine Maury during the war, 1861–1865, by his son, Richard L. Maury ... Richmond, Whittet & Shepperson, 1915.

36 p. 19½ cm.

A pamphlet discussion of mine warfare; satisfactory, but not outstanding.

Meade, *Mrs.* **Rebecca (Paulding)**

Life of Hiram Paulding, rear-admiral, U. S. N., by Rebecca Paulding Meade. New York, The Baker & Taylor company, 1910.

ix p., 1 l., 321 p. 7 port. (incl. front.) pl. 19ᶜᵐ.

Emphasizes Paulding's early career, but has some material about his service during the early part of the Civil War at Washington, Norfolk, and the New York Navy Yard.

Meriwether, Colyer, *d.* 1920.

... Raphael Semmes, by Colyer Meriwether ... Philadelphia, G. W. Jacobs & company [1913]

367 p. front. (port.) 19 cm.

A satisfactory biography in some respects, but outdated and overly favorable.

Merrill, James M

The rebel shore; the story of Union sea power in the Civil War. [1st ed.] Boston, Little, Brown [1957]

246 p. illus. 21 cm.

Rather breezy, and often revisionist without the support of new evidence.

Military historical society of Massachusetts, *Boston.*

Naval actions and history, 1799–1898. Boston, Pub. for the Military historical society of Massachusetts, by Griffith-Stillings press, 1902.

4 p. l., 3–398 p. 24 cm.

Several useful articles in this volume treat of the Cumberland and Monitor, the siege of Charleston, and the battle of Mobile Bay.

Morgan, James Morris, *b*. 1845.
    Recollections of a Rebel reefer, by James Morris Morgan ... Boston and New York, Houghton Mifflin company, 1917.

    xix p., 1 l., 491, [1] p. front., plates, ports. 22 cm.

A colorful autobiography of an ubiquitous and observant youngster; much useful information on the Confederate Naval School.

Nelson, Thomas.
    ... Echoes and incidents from a gunboat flotilla. Prepared by Companion Captain Thomas Nelson ... and read at the stated meeting of December 1, 1909. [Washington, 1909]

    19 p. 23ᶜᵐ. (Military order of the loyal legion of the United States. Commandery of the District of Columbia. War papers. 78)

Discusses small unit operations on the rivers of Virginia.

Olañeta, José Antonio de.
    Guerra de los Estados-Unidos. Estudios sobre artilleria, fortificacion y marina militar. Madrid, Impr. del Memorial de Ingenieros, 1868.

    203 p. fold. map, diagrs. 22 cm.

A report for the Spanish army on coast artillery; good technical discussions on Dahlgren's attacks on Charleston.

Orvin, Maxwell Clayton.
    In South Carolina waters, 1861–1865. [Charleston? S. C., 1961]

    196 p. illus. 24 cm.

Contains much material from contemporary newspapers and local tradition not usually available.

Osbon, Bradley Sillick, 1827–1912.
    Hand book of the United States navy: being a compilation of all the principal events in the history of every vessel of the United States navy. From April, 1861, to May, 1864. Comp. and arranged by B. S. Osbon. New York, D. Van Nostrand; [etc., etc.] 1864.

    iv, [5]–277 p. 19½ᶜᵐ.

A dictionary of material about the navy to 1864; contains interesting descriptions of technical books in use during the Civil War.

Osbon, Bradley Sillick, 1827–1912.
    A sailor of fortune; personal memoirs of Captain B. S. Osbon, by Albert Bigelow Paine. New York, McClure, Phillips & co., 1906.

    ix, 332 p. 20ᶜᵐ.

Osbon was a journalist, volunteer clerk and signal officer to Farragut. Hero of his own dispatches, he was a combination of public information officer and war correspondent.

Owsley, Frank Lawrence, 1923–
    The C. S. S. Florida: her building and operations. Philadelphia, University of Pennsylvania Press [1965]

    208 p. plates, ports. 22 cm.

A short, but comprehensive and very thoughtful account; the best by far on any Confederate cruiser.

Parker, Foxhall Alexander, 1821–1879.
    The battle of Mobile Bay, and the capture of forts Powell, Gaines and Morgan, by the combined sea and land forces of the United States under the command of Rear-Admiral David Glasgow Farragut, and Major-General Gordon Granger, August, 1864. By Commodore Foxhall A. Parker, U. S. N. ... Boston, A. Williams & co., 1878.

    136 p. front. (port.) fold maps. 25ᶜᵐ.

A straightforward account written mostly from official records and papers.

Parker, Foxhall Alexander, 1821–1879.
    The naval howitzer afloat. By Foxhall A. Parker ... New-York, D. Van Nostrand, 1866.

    34 p. front., 31 pl. (part fold.) 23½ᶜᵐ.

A technical manual for employment of the weapon.

Parker, Foxhall Alexander, 1821–1879.
    The naval howitzer ashore. By Foxhall A. Parker ... New-York, D. Van Nostrand, 1865.

    64 p. front., 27 pl. (part fold.) 23½ᶜᵐ.

This technical book treats principally of the evolution and duties of the gun crew; a Naval Academy text.

Parker, Foxhall Alexander, 1821–1879.
... Squadron tactics under steam. By Foxhall A. Parker ... New York. D. Van Nostrand, 1864.

172 p. fold. front., 78 pl. (2 fold.) 23½ᶜᵐ.

Maneuvering instructions for eight-ship squadrons (four-ship divisions); hair-raising for those unfamiliar with naval tactics.

Parker, William Harwar, 1826–1896.
Recollections of a naval officer, 1841–1865, by Capt. William Harwar Parker ... New York, C. Scribners' [!] sons, 1883.

xv, 372 p. 19½ cm.

An excellent, straightforward account by the Superintendent of the Confederate Naval School.

Perkins, George Hamilton, 1835–1899.
Letters of Captain Geo. Hamilton Perkins, U. S. N. Ed. and arranged. Also, a sketch of his life, by Commodore George E. Belknap, U. S. N. 2d ed. Concord, N. H., The Rumford press, 1901.

293 p. front., illus., plates, ports., maps. 24ᶜᵐ.

A poorly edited collection of letters from, and clippings concerning, the executive officer of the Cayuga during its attack on New Orleans and the captain of ironclad Chickasaw at Mobile.

Perry, Milton F
Infernal machines; the story of Confederate submarine and mine warfare [by] Milton F. Perry. [Baton Rouge] Louisiana State University Press [1965]

xi, 230 p. illus., maps. 24 cm.

A concise but comprehensive account of the design, manufacture and use of mines, torpedoes, and sabotage weapons.

Poolman, Kenneth, 1924–
The Alabama incident. London, W. Kimber [1958]

203 p. illus. 23 cm.

A popular account lacking documentation but generally fair and accurate.

Porter, David Dixon, 1813–1891.
Incidents and anecdotes of the civil war. By Admiral Porter ... New York, D. Appleton and co., 1885.

357 p. front. (port.) 22½ᶜᵐ.

Informal and informative, but not an always accurate or unbiased first-hand account of the war.

Porter, David Dixon, 1813–1891.
The naval history of the civil war, by Admiral David D. Porter. Illustrated from original sketches made by Rear-Admiral Walke and others. New York, The Sherman pub. company, 1886.

1 p. l., xvi p., 1 l., 843 p. incl. illus., port., maps, plans. front., plan. 28½ cm.

Comprehensive, partisan, egotistical, sometimes inaccurate, but always interesting.

Porter, John W   H
A record of events in Norfolk county, Virginia, from April 19th, 1861, to May 10th, 1862, with a history of the soldiers and sailors of Norfolk county, Norfolk city and Portsmouth, who served in the Confederate States army or navy. By John W. H. Porter ... Portsmouth, Va., W. A. Fiske, printer, 1892.

366 p. illus. 24ᶜᵐ.

Credits the author's father, John L. Porter, with the idea that led to the redesign of the Merrimack.

Pratt, Fletcher, 1897–1956.
Civil War on western waters. [1st ed.] New York, Holt [1956]

255 p. illus. 22 cm.

An interesting and generally accurate account of operations on the Mississippi and its tributaries; and appendix lists characteristics of the warships.

Preble, George Henry, 1816–1885.
The chase of the Rebel steamer of war Oreto, Commander J. N. Maffitt, C. S. N., into the bay of Mobile, by the United States steam sloop Oneida, Commander Geo. Henry Preble, U. S. N., September 4, 1862 ... Cambridge, Printed for private circulation, 1862.

60 p. 24 cm.

A compilation of letters, reports, and petitions for Preble's reinstatement in the navy; contains details not found in ORN or other usual sources.

Preble, George Henry, 1816–1885.
History of the United States navy-yard, Portsmouth, N. H. Prepared by order of the Hon. Secretary of the Navy, under the direction of the Bureau of yards and docks, by Geo. Henry Preble, rear-admiral, U. S. N. Washington, Govt. print. off., 1892.

219 p. 2 fold. plans. 24 cm.

Material on the industrial side of the navy.

Roberts, Walter Adolphe, 1886–
Semmes of the Alabama, by W. Adolphe Roberts. Indianapolis, New York, The Bobbs-Merrill company [c1938]

320 p. front., plates, ports., facsims. 24 cm.

A light, readable, and sympathetic biography.

Robinson, William Morrison, 1891–
The Confederate privateers, by William Morrison Robinson, jr. ... New Haven, Yale university press; London, H. Milford, Oxford university press, 1928.

xvi, 372 p. front., plates, facsims. 24 cm.

A clear, well-documented and interesting account that includes sections on submarines and sea-going partisans.

Robinton, Madeline (Russell) 1909–
An introduction to the papers of the New York prize court, 1861–1865, by Madeline Russell Robinton, PH. D. New York, Columbia university press, 1945.

203 p. 23cm.

Gives brief, thoughtful discussions of its subject and explains general documents, procedures, and specifics of the more interesting cases.

Rochelle, James Henry, 1826–1889.
Life of Rear Admiral John Randolph Tucker, commander in the navy of the United States ... with an appendix containing notes on navigation of the upper Amazon river and its principal tributaries, by Captain James Henry Rochelle, and containing a biographical sketch of the author ... Washington, The Neale publishing company, 1903.

112 p. front., port. 22½cm.

An extremely short and superficial biography; includes a sketch of the author, who was also a Confederate naval officer.

Roe, Francis Asbury, 1823–1901.
Naval duties and discipline, with the policy and principles of naval organization. By F. A. Roe ... New-York, D. Van Nostrand, 1865.

2 p. l., [iii]–vi, [7]–223 p. 19½cm.

A clear exposition of the duties of, and advice to, U. S. Naval officers of 1864.

Roske, Ralph Joseph, 1921–
Lincoln's commando; the biography of Commander W. B. Cushing, U. S. N., by Ralph J. Roske and Charles Van Doren. [1st ed.] New York, Harper [1957]

310 p. illus. 22 cm.

A dramatically written account, apparently factual but without a shred of documentation.

Sands, Benjamin Franklin, 1811–1883.
From reefer to rear-admiral; reminiscences and journal jottings of nearly half a century of naval life, by Benjamin F. Sands ... 1827 to 1874. New York, Frederick A. Stokes company [1899]

1 p. l., vii–xv, 308 p. front. (port.) 19½ cm.

Describes the destruction of the Norfolk Navy Yard and service with the blockaders off Cape Fear and Galveston; more interesting and rewarding on Sand's pre-war service.

Sands, Francis Preston Blair, 1842–
... "Lest we forget." Memories of service afloat from 1862 to 1866. Prepared by Companion Acting Master Francis P. B. Sands ... and read at the stated meeting of April 1, 1908. [Washington, 1908]

26 p. 23cm. (Military order of the loyal legion of the United States. Commandery of the District of Columbia. War papers. 73)

Blockading of the North Carolina coast, with much on Joe Fyffe.

Sands, Francis Preston Blair, 1842–
... My messmates and shipmates who are gone, 1862–1865. By Companion Francis P. B. Sands ... Read at the stated meeting of January 4, 1911 ... [Washington, 1911]

22 p. 23cm. (Military order of the loyal legion of the United States. Commandery of the District of Columbia. War papers. 83)

Spritely stories, particularly about the antics of the legendary Joe Fyffe.

Sands, Francis Preston Blair, 1842–

... "A volunteer's reminiscences of life in the North Atlantic blockading squadron, 1862–'5," prepared by Companion Acting Master Francis P. B. Sands ... and read at the stated meeting of April 4, 1894. ₍Washington, 1894₎

27 p. 23ᶜᵐ. (Military order of the loyal legion of the United States. Commandery of the District of Columbia. War papers, 18 ₍i. e. 20₎)

Duty off the North Carolina coast, including attacks on Fort Fisher, with accounts of raids by Cushing and Lamson.

Savannah (*Privateer*)

Trial of the officers and crew of the privateer Savannah, on the charge of piracy, in the United States circuit court for the southern district of New York. Hon. Judges Nelson and Shipman, presiding. Reported by A. F. Warburton ... New York, Baker & Godwin, printers, 1862.

xxii, 385 p. 23½ cm.

Contains procedure, testimony, arguments, and findings of this critical case.

Scharf, John Thomas, 1843–1898.

History of the Confederate States Navy from its organization to the surrender of its last vessel. Its stupendous struggle with the great Navy of the United States; the engagements fought in the rivers and harbors of the South, and upon the high seas; blockade-running, first use of iron-clads and torpedoes, and privateer history. By J. Thomas Scharf ... New York, Rogers & Sherwood; San Francisco, A. L. Bancroft & co.; ₍etc., etc.₎ 1887.

x, ₍11₎–824 p. front., illus. (incl. plans, diagrs.) plates, ports. 24 cm.

The best on its subject in spite of the inclusion of some unevaluated or conflicting opinions by participants.

Scheliha, Viktor Ernst Karl Rudolf von, 1826–1899.

A treatise on coast-defence based on the experience gained by officers of the corps of engineers of the army of the Confederate States, and comp. from official reports of officers of the navy of the United States ... By Von Scheliha ... London, E. & F. N. Spon, 1868.

3 p. l., ₍v₎–xviii p., 1 l., 326 p. col. front., illus., XII (i. e. 15) fold. pl. (incl. maps, plans) 26ᶜᵐ.

A treatise by a Prussian coast artillery officer in Confederate service; contains good descriptions of forts, submarine mines and obstructions.

Schley, Winfield Scott, 1839–1911.

Forty-five years under the flag, by Winfield Scott Schley ... New York, D. Appleton and company, 1904.

xiii, 439 p. front. (port.) illus., plates, map, fold. chart. 22 cm.

Contains brief accounts of service aboard the Niagara, Winona, Monongahela, and Richmond.

Selfridge, Thomas Oliver, 1836–1924.

Memoirs of Thomas O. Selfridge, jr., rear admiral, U. S. N., with an introduction by Captain Dudley W. Knox ... New York & London, G. P. Putnam's sons, 1924.

xii, 288 p. front. (port.) plates, maps (part fold.) 23½ᶜᵐ.

An interestingly written but brief account of Selfridge's service at Hampton Roads, in Western waters, and at Fort Fisher.

Semmes, Raphael, 1809–1877.

The cruise of the Alabama and the Sumter. From the private journals and other papers of R. Semmes and other officers. 2d ed. London, Saunders, Otley, 1864–

v. ports. 21 cm.

Mainly extracts from Semmes's journals; a basic source for later works.

Semmes, Raphael, 1809–1877.

Memoirs of service afloat, during the war between the states. By Admiral Raphael Semmes ... Baltimore, Kelly, Piet & co.; ₍etc., etc.₎ 1869.

1 p. l., vi, xi–xvi, 17–833 p. front., 6 col. pl., port., diagrs. 24½ cm.

A first-hand, subjective account by the captain of the C. S. Sumter and Alabama; interestingly written; reprinted under various titles.

Semmes, Raphael, 1809–1877.

Rebel raider, being an account of Raphael Semmes's cruise in the C. S. S. Sumter; composed in large part of extracts from Semmes's Memoirs of service afloat, written in the year 1869. Selected and supplemented by Harpur Allen Gosnell. Chapel Hill, University of North Carolina Press, 1948.

vii, 218 p. illus., ports., maps. 24 cm.

Annotated extracts from that part of Semmes's Memoirs of Service Afloat which treats of the Sumter.

Simms, Joseph M

... "Personal experiences in the volunteer navy during the civil war." Prepared by Companion Acting Ensign Joseph M. Simms ... and read at the stated meeting of December 2, 1903. ₍Washington, 1903₎

29 p. fold. map. 23ᶜᵐ. (Military order of the loyal legion of the United States. Commandery of the District of Columbia. War papers. 50)

Mainly concerned with the first and second attacks on Fort Fisher; Simms was an ensign on the Minnesota.

Simpson, Edward, 1824–1888.

A treatise on ordnance and naval gunnery, compiled and arranged as a text book for the U. S. Naval academy. By Lieut. Edward Simpson ... 2d ed., rev. and enl. New York, D. Van Nostrand, 1862.

493 p. illus., 5 pl. (part col., part fold.) diagrs. 23½ cm.

A highly conservative textbook in use at the Naval Academy in 1860 but already superseded by new inventions.

Simpson, Evan John, 1901–

Atlantic impact, 1861, by Evan John [pseud.] London, Heinemann [1952]

296 p. illus. 21 cm.

The Trent Affair viewed from many angles; highly analytical.

Sinclair, Arthur.

Two years on the Alabama, by Arthur Sinclair ... with **over thirty illustrations. 3d ed.** Boston, Lee and Shepard, 1896.

vi p., 1 l., 352 p. front., plates, ports., facsim. 24½ᶜᵐ.

One of the best accounts; interesting, reliable, comprehensive, and thoughtful; contains brief biographical sketches and muster rolls.

Smith, Franklin Webster.

The conspiracy in the U. S. Navy department against Franklin W. Smith of Boston, 1861–1865 ... [New York, Press of the American publishing company] 1890.

cover-title, 2 p. l., 100 p. 20ᶜᵐ.

A poorly organized political defence of Smith on charges of defrauding the government in the sale of tools, supplies, etc.

Smith, Franklin Webster.

The United States against Franklin W. Smith. A review of the argument of the judge advocate, by Franklin W. Smith. Boston, Printed by A. Mudge & son, 1865.

1 p. l., 144 p. 23½ᶜᵐ.

Unbearably dull but contains good information on court martial procedure and shop and contract practices in the Boston Navy Yard.

Smith, Joseph Adams, 1837–1907.

An address delivered before the Union league of Philadelphia on Saturday evening, January 20, 1906, by Rear Admiral Joseph Adams Smith ... at the presentation by the Art association of the painting representing the battle between the Kearsarge and Alabama. Philadelphia [Press of J. B. Lippincott company] 1906.

1 p. l., 31, [1] p. front. 24ᶜᵐ.

An account of the battle given by a participant forty years later; contains little of value.

Soley, James Russell, 1850–1911.

... Admiral Porter, by James Russell Soley ... New York, D. Appleton and company, 1903.

vii p., 1 l., 499 p. front., plates, ports., maps, facsim. 19½ cm.

A thoughtful biography that nevertheless glosses over Porter's capacity for intrigue.

Soley, James Russell, 1850–1911.

... The blockade and the cruisers, by James Russell Soley ... New York, C. Scribner's sons, 1883.

viii p., 1 l., 257 p. incl. maps. fold. map. 19 cm. (The Navy in the civil war. I)

An early but solid and informative work; still one of the best in its field.

Soley, James Russell, 1850–1911.

The sailor boys of '61, by James Russell Soley ... Boston, Estes and Lauriat [1888]

381 p. incl. front., illus., pl., port. 22½ᶜᵐ.

One of the best-balanced, early histories of the naval side of the Civil War.

Spears, John Randolph, 1850–1936.

... David G. Farragut, by John Randolph Spears ... Philadelphia, G. W. Jacobs & company [1905]

10 p., 1 l., [11]–407 p. front. (port.) maps, plans. 19½ cm.

Flowery, readable, and inaccurate.

Spears, John Randolph, 1850–1936.
The history of our Navy from its origin to the present day, 1775–1897, by John R. Spears ... New York, C. Scribner's sons, 1897–99.

5 v. front., illus., plates, ports., maps, plans, facsims. 20½ cm.

Volume IV contains a superficial and somewhat inaccurate treatment of the Civil War navies.

Sprunt, James, 1846–1924.
Chronicles of the Cape Fear river, 1660–1916 [by] James Sprunt. 2d ed. Raleigh, Edwards & Broughton printing co., 1916.

xi, 732 p. fold. plans, maps (part fold.) 24½ cm.

A disjointed and repetitious work that contains some first-hand accounts not found in earlier publications.

Sprunt, James.
Derelicts; an account of ships lost at sea in general commercial traffic and a brief history of blockade runners stranded along the North Carolina coast, 1861–1865, by James Sprunt ... Wilmington, N. C., 1920.

xii, 304 p. front. 21½ cm.

Undocumented accounts written or recorded by a former purser on blockade runners.

Sprunt, James, 1846–1924.
Tales of the Cape Fear blockade, being a turn of the century account of blockade-running. With an editorial map showing the lower Cape Fear and coast of Brunswick County with plantations, places, fortifications, and wrecks of blockade-runners, 1861–1865. Edited by Cornelius M. D. Thomas. Wilmington, N. C., Printed by J. E. Hicks for the Charles Towne Preservation Trust, 1960.

134 p. illus. 18 cm.

A meandering account, largely reproducing other printed works, but including some of the author's personal experiences.

Starbuck, Alexander, 1841–1925.
History of the American whale fishery from its earliest inception to the year 1876.

(*In* Report of the commissioner [of fish and fisheries] for 1875–1876. Washington, 1878. 22 cm. 1–779 p. incl. plates. VI pl.)

Includes list of whalers captured by the Shenandoah and Alabama.

Steedman, Charles, 1811–1890.
Memoir and correspondence of Charles Steedman, rear admiral, United States navy, with his autobiography and private journals, 1811–1890, ed. by Amos Lawrence Mason ... Cambridge, Priv. print. at the Riverside press, 1912.

xxi, 556 p. front., plates, ports., maps. 23½ cm.

Written by a South Carolinian who remained in the U. S. Navy and commanded ships in the Port Royal, St. Johns, Charleston areas.

Stern, Philip Van Doren, 1900–
The Confederate Navy: a pictorial history. [1st ed.] Garden City, N. Y., Doubleday, 1962.

252 p. illus. 29 cm.

A satisfactory picture book based on those few photographs which survive, plus drawings of varying authenticity; Stern points out some of their errors.

Stuyvesant, Moses Sherwood, *d.* 1906.
Navy record of M. S. Stuyvesant. St. Louis, Press of Perrin & Smith [1906?]

cover-title, 26 p. 23 cm.

Brief but helpful for the part Stuyvesant played as a junior officer aboard the Cumberland and Weehawken.

Taylor, Thomas E.
Running the blockade. A personal narrative of adventures, risks, and escapes during the American civil war, by Thomas E. Taylor. With an introduction by Julian Corbett ... 3d ed. London, J. Murray, 1897.

xxii p., 1 l., 180 p. front., pl., port., fold. map. 21 cm.

Reminiscences of the supercargo of blockade runners, especially the Banshee.

Thompson, Samuel Bernard.
Confederate purchasing operations abroad, by Samuel Bernard Thompson. Chapel Hill, The University of North Carolina press, 1935.

ix, 137 p. 24 cm.

Contains a comprehensive analysis of the financial aspects of naval purchases.

Todd, Herbert Henry, 1893–
... The building of the Confederate states navy in Europe ... by Herbert H. Todd ... ₁Nashville₁ 1941.

30 p. 24ᶜᵐ.

A summary of an unpublished thesis.

U. S. *Naval War Records Office.*
Office memoranda. no. 1–9. Washington, 1889–1902.

9 no. 24 cm.

A potpourri of material, ranging from charts and logs to principal operational and adminis- trative actions.

Totten, Benjamin J   1806–1877.
Naval text-book. Letters to the midshipmen of the United States navy on masting, rigging, and managing vessels of war. Also, a set of stationing tables; a naval gun exercise, and a marine dictionary. By B. J. Totten ... Boston, C. C. Little and J. Brown, 1841.

xv, 430 p. incl. illus., pl., tables. 21ᶜᵐ.

Contains technical details on seamanship as taught at the Naval Academy during the Civil War; also includes a useful glossary of terms.

U. S. *Naval war records office.*
... Officers in the Confederate States navy, 1861–65 ... Washington, Govt. print. off., 1898.

157 p. 23½ᶜᵐ.

A summary of the careers of all known Confed- erate naval officers; a revised and corrected edition was issued in 1931.

U. S. *Naval War Records Office.*
Official records of the Union and **Confederate Navies in the War of Rebellion.** ser. 1, v. 1–27; ser. 2, v. 1–3. Wash- ington, Govt. Print. Off., 1894–1922.

30 v. illus., ports., maps (part fold.) 24 cm.

A comprehensive, well-edited source which does, however, contain some errors and omissions; yet it is an essential reference to any study of Civil War navies.

Trexler, Harrison Anthony, 1883–
The Confederate ironclad "Virginia" ("Merrimac") by Harrison A. Trexler ... Chicago, Ill., The University of Chicago press ₁1938₁

vii p., 1 l., 95 p. front. (map) illus. 23½ cm.

A brief but comprehensive and thoughtful account.

U. S. *Naval History Division.*
Civil War naval chronology, 1861–1865. Washington, For sale by the Superintendent of Documents, U. S. Govt. Print. Off. ₁1961–65₁

5 v. illus., maps, ports. 27 cm.

An accurate but unannotated day-to-day break- down of operations and administration on both sides.

U. S. *Navy dept.*
Report of the secretary of the Navy in relation to armored vessels. Washington, Govt. print. off., 1864.

1 p. l., xvi, 607 p. illus., fold. maps. 23ᶜᵐ.

Correspondence among department constructors and commanders concerning the employment and performance of the ships.

U. S. *Naval History Division.*
Dictionary of American naval fighting ships. Washing- ton, 1959–

v. illus. 27 cm.

Gives characteristics and brief histories of the vessels.

U. S. *Navy dept.*
Reports of the naval engagements on the Mississippi river, resulting in the capture of Forts Jackson and St. Philip and the city of New Orleans, and the destruction of the rebel naval flotilla. Washington, Govt. print. off., 1862.

1 p. l., 107 p. 2 pl. (incl. col. front.) 3 fold. maps. 23½ᶜᵐ.

Reports of Welles, Farragut, and Porter; de- tailed but lacking C. S. N. data.

Vail, Israel Everett, 1842–

Three years on the blockade; a naval experience, by I. E. Vail. New York, London [etc.] The Abbey press [1902]

171 p. 20^{cm}.

A light, uninformative account of the comings and goings of an assistant paymaster whose first service was on the Massachusetts.

Vandiver, Frank Everson, 1925–   *ed.*

Confederate blockade running through Bermuda, 1861–1865: letters and cargo manifests. Austin, Univ. of Texas Press, 1947.

xliv, 155 p. front. 24 cm.

An edited collection of business letters and cargo manifests for Bermuda during the war years; the editor's introduction is a masterful presentation of blockade running.

Waddell, James Iredell, 1824–1886.

C. S. S. Shenandoah; the memoirs of Lieutenant Commanding James I. Waddell. Edited by James D. Horan. New York, Crown Publishers [1960]

200 p. illus. 22 cm.

A reproduction of Waddell's 1885 memoirs, with some editing and inadequate annotation; interesting and authoritative, but lacking in candor.

Walke, Henry, 1808–1896.

Naval scenes and reminiscences of the civil war in the United States, on the southern and western waters during the years 1861, 1862 and 1863. With the history of that period. Compared and corrected from authentic sources. By Rear-Admiral H. Walke ... New York, F. R. Reed & co., 1877.

xii, 480 p. pl., port., diagr. 23½^{cm}.

A self-eulogy by a capable central figure in the upper Mississippi; contains many newspaper and unofficial accounts by participants.

Walker, Jeanie Mort.

Life of Capt. Joseph Fry, the Cuban martyr. Being a faithful record of his remarkable career from childhood to the time of his heroic death at the hands of Spanish executioners; recounting his experience as an officer in the U. S. and Confederate navies, and revealing much of the inner history and secret marine service of the late civil war in America. By Jeanie Mort Walker ... Hartford, The J. B. Burr publishing co., 1875.

589 p. incl. front., plates, ports. 21 cm.

A superficial account of Fry's service as a blockade runner and commander of the C. S. Morgan.

Ward, James Harman, 1806–1861.

Elementary instruction in naval ordnance and gunnery. By James H. Ward ... New ed., rev. and enl. New York, D. Van Nostrand; [etc., etc.] 1861.

vi, 209 p. diagrs. 23 cm.

A textbook based mainly on Ordnance Regulations but considerably simplified; gives a good picture of conservative thinking at the outset of the war.

Ward, James Harman, 1806–1861.

A manual of naval tactics: together with a brief critical analysis of the principal modern naval battles. By James H. Ward ... With an appendix, being an extract from Sir Howard Douglas' "Naval warfare with steam." New York, D. Appleton & company, 1859.

208 p., 1 l. diagrs. 24 cm.

Naval Academy textbook which illustrates the pre-war thinking on strategy as well as tactics.

Ward, James Harman, 1806–1861.

Steam for the million. A popular treatise on steam, and its application to the useful arts, especially to navigation. Intended as an instructor for young seamen, mechanics' apprentices, academic students, passengers in mail steamers, etc. By J. H. Ward ... New and rev. ed. New York, H. Dexter & co., 1860.

120 p. diagrs. (1 double) 23½^{cm}.

A simplified explanation of steam propulsion as understood at the outbreak of the war.

Watson, William, *of Skelmorlie, Scot.*

The adventures of a blockade runner; or, Trade in time of war. By William Watson ... Illustrated by Captain Byng, r. n. London, T. F. Unwin, 1892.

xiii p., 1 l., 324 p. pl. 21½^{cm}.

A small sailing vessel makes runs from Mexico and Cuba to Texas.

Wayland, John Walter, 1872–

The Pathfinder of the seas; the life of Matthew Fontaine Maury, by John W. Wayland; with an introduction by William J. Showalter. Richmond, Garrett & Massie, inc. [c1930]

xiii p., 1 l., 191 p. col. front., plates, ports. 23½^{cm}.

A extremely poor biography.

Welles, Gideon, 1802–1878.
    Diary of Gideon Welles, secretary of the Navy under Lincoln and Johnson, with an introduction by John T. Morse, jr. ... Boston and New York, Houghton Mifflin company [1911]
        3 v. fronts. (ports.) 19¼ cm.

The best edition of this excellent diary is that of Howard K. Beale; earlier editions should be used with caution.

Welles, Gideon, 1802–1878.
    Lincoln and Seward. Remarks upon the memorial address of Chas. Francis Adams, on the late William H. Seward, with incidents and comments illustrative of the measures and policy of the administration of Abraham Lincoln. And views as to the relative positions of the late President and secretary of state. By Gideon Welles ... New York, Sheldon & company, 1874.
        viii, [7]-215 p. 19½ cm.

Essentially a revision of Welles's Galaxy articles.

Welles, Gideon, 1802–1878.
    Selected essays. Compiled by Albert Mordell. New York, Twayne Publishers [1959–60]
        2 v. 22 cm.

These essays, written for the Galaxy, 1870-1873, give Welles's views on the loss of Norfolk, the Fort Sumter and Fort Pickens expedition, the capture of New Orleans, and the Trent Affair.

West, Richard Sedgewick, 1902–
    Gideon Welles, Lincoln's navy department, by Richard S. West, jr. Indianapolis, New York, The Bobbs-Merrill company [1943]
        379 p. front., plates, ports. 24 cm.

A satisfactory but somewhat superficial treatment.

West, Richard Sedgewick, 1902–
    Mr. Lincoln's navy. [1st ed.] New York, Longmans, Green, 1957.
        328 p. illus. 24 cm.

A brief, generally satisfactory, but pedestrian treatment.

West, Richard Sedgewick, 1902–
    The second admiral; a life of David Dixon Porter, 1813–1891, by Richard S. West, jr. ... New York, Coward-McCann, inc., 1937.
        xvi, 376 p. front., illus. (incl. maps) plates, ports. 24 cm.

The best biography of D. D. Porter; favorable but not uncritical.

Wheelwright, Charles Henry, 1813–1862.
    Correspondence of Dr. Charles H. Wheelwright, surgeon of the United States Navy. Edited by Hildegarde B. Forbes. [Boston?] 1958.
        xiv, 350 p. ports., 3 geneal. tables. 24 cm.

A medical officer aboard the San Jacinto reports the war's first naval events, including the recapture of Norfolk.

White, Ellsberry Valentine, *b.* 1839.
    The first iron-clad naval engagement in the world; history of facts of the great naval battle between the Merrimac-Virginia, C. S. N. and the Ericsson Monitor, U. S. N., Hampton Roads, March 8 and 9, 1862. By E. V. White ... [Portsmouth? Va., c1906]
        [24] p. plates, port. 26½ cm.

This pro-Confederate account, written by a participant, includes some of his personal experiences.

White, William Chapman, 1903–1955.
    Tin can on a shingle, by William Chapman White and Ruth White. With an introd. by Henry Steele Commager. [1st ed.] New York, Dutton, 1957.
        176 p. illus. 21 cm.

A brief, thoughtful history of the Monitor written from standard sources.

Wilkes, Charles, 1798–1877, *defendant.*
    ... Commodore Charles Wilkes's court-martial. Letter from the secretary of the Navy, transmitting, in answer to a resolution of the House of representatives of May 16, proceedings of the Court-martial which tried Commodore Charles Wilkes ... [Washington, 1864]
        301 p. 22½ cm. ([U. S.] 38th Cong., 1st sess. House. Ex. doc. 102)

Contains material on cruiser operations and navy department administration not found in official records.

Wilkinson, John, 1821–1891.

The narrative of a blockade-runner. By J. Wilkinson ... New York, Sheldon & co., 1877.

252 p. 19½ cm.

A first-rate autobiographical work of a naval officer who was one of the most successful blockade runners of the war.

Williams, Frances Leigh.

Matthew Fontaine Maury, scientist of the sea. New Brunswick, Rutgers University Press [1963]

xx, 720 p. illus., ports., charts, forms. 25 cm.

Emphasizes Maury's scientific career but includes a thorough treatment of his Civil War career.

Wilson, Herbert Wrigley, 1866–

Ironclads in action; a sketch of naval warfare from 1855 to 1895, with some account of the development of the battleship in England [by] H. W. Wilson ... With an introduction by Captain A. T. Mahan ... 5th ed. London, S. Low, Marston and company, 1897.

2 v. 80 pl. (incl. fronts., ports., maps, plans) tables. 23½ cm.

A masterful and penetrating discussion of the major events of the naval war, as seen by an Englishman.

Winslow, William Henry, 1840–1917.

... Cruising and blockading. By W. H. Winslow ... Pittsburgh, Pa., J. R. Weldin & co., 1885.

2 p. l., [7]–207 p. 19½ cm.

A fictionalized biography of a young Union officer; written by a former officer from his own experiences.

Worden, John Lorimer, 1818–1897.

The Monitor and the Merrimac; both sides of the story, told by Lieut. J. L. Worden, u. s. n., Lieut. Greene, u. s. n., of the Monitor, and H. Ashton Ramsay, c. s. n., chief engineer of the Merrimac ... New York and London, Harper & brothers, 1912.

xi p., 1 l., 72, [1] p. incl. front. 18 cm.

Worden and Greene's post-action report (when Lincoln visited the Monitor), and Ramsay's essay written fifty years later.

DIPLOMACY

Norman Ferris

Adams, Charles Francis, 1807–1886.

The address of Charles Francis Adams, of Massachusetts, on the life, character and services of William H. Seward. Delivered by invitation of the Legislature of the state of New York, in Albany, April 18, 1873. New York, D. Appleton and company, 1873.

47 p. 22½ᶜᵐ.

Appraised Seward's personal character and wartime statesmanship as superior to Lincoln's.

Adams, Charles Francis, 1835–1915.

... Charles Francis Adams, by his son, Charles Francis Adams. Boston and New York, Houghton, Mifflin and company, 1900.

vii p., 1 l., 426 p., 1 l. 18 ᶜᵐ.

An unscholarly and slight study; lively but full of errors in fact and judgement; particularly biased toward Seward.

Adams, Charles Francis, 1835–1915.

Before and after the treaty of Washington: the American civil war and the war in the Transvaal; an address delivered before the New York historical society on its ninety-seventh anniversary, Tuesday, November 19, 1901, by Charles Francis Adams ... New York, Printed for the Society, 1902.

141 p. 25ᶜᵐ.

In the course of a comprehensive, sensible discussion of Confederate shipbuilding in England, the author accuses the British of "criminal dereliction" and with acting as "an accomplice in piracy."

Adams, Charles Francis, 1835–1915.

The crisis of foreign intervention in the war of secession, September–November, 1862, by Charles Francis Adams. Boston, 1914.

54 p. 24½ᶜᵐ.

Narrative moves back and forth from Confederate agent John Slidell in Paris to deliberations on intervention by the British cabinet; one of Adams' better productions, but as usual it contains excessive unfounded speculation.

Adams, Charles Francis, 1835–1915.
Studies military and diplomatic, 1775–1865, by Charles Francis Adams. New York, The Macmillan company, 1911.
v, 424 p. 23 cm.

Several chapters touch on wartime Anglo-American relations, but they are too shallow and argumentative to possess much authority.

Adams, Charles Francis, 1835–1915.
Trans-Atlantic historical solidarity; lectures delivered before the University of Oxford in Easter and Trinity terms, 1913, by Charles Francis Adams. Oxford, Clarendon press, 1913.
184 p. 22½ cm.

Lectures on Anglo-American relations during the Civil War that are remarkably opinionated -- considering the paucity of source material on which they are based.

Adams, Ephraim Douglass, 1865–1930.
Great Britain and the American Civil War. New York, Russell & Russell [1958?]
2 v. in 1. illus. 22 cm.

A valuable, ponderous, and pretentious work; concentrates on British diplomacy and public opinion; based primarily on printed official sources and the often unreliable studies of C. F. Adams, Jr.

Adams, Henry, 1838–1918.
The education of Henry Adams, an autobiography. With a new introd. by D. W. Brogan. Boston, Houghton Mifflin, 1961.
xxiv, 517 p. 21 cm. (Sentry edition, 3)

Includes sardonic, stimulating, metaphorical treatment of Adams's wartime life in London.

Adams, Henry, 1838–1918.
Henry Adams and his friends; a collection of his unpublished letters, compiled, with a biographical introduction, by Harold Dean Cater ... Boston, Houghton Mifflin company, 1947.
cxix p., 1 l., 797 p. fronts., ports. 23½ cm.

Contains a few letters of Henry Adams pertaining to Anglo-American relations, 1863-1864.

Adams, Henry, 1838–1918.
Letters of Henry Adams ... edited by Worthington Chauncey Ford. Boston and New York, Houghton Mifflin company, 1930–38.
2 v. fronts. (ports.) 24½ cm.

Includes letters by the private secretary of U. S. minister at London; describes life and society in that city during the Civil War period.

Adams, James Truslow, 1878–1949.
Henry Adams [by] James Truslow Adams. New York, A. & C. Boni, inc., 1933.
246 p. incl. front., plates, ports., double facsim. 22 cm.

Superseded by the much better biography by Samuels (q. v.).

Albion, Robert Greenhalgh, 1896–
Sea lanes in wartime; the American experience, 1775–1942, by Robert Greenhalgh Albion and Jennie Barnes Pope. New York, W. W. Norton and company, inc. [1942]
367 p. tables. 22 cm.

Touches lightly on diplomatic implications of the destruction of Northern merchant shipping by Confederate raiders.

Allen, Harry Cranbrook.
Great Britain and the United States; a history of Anglo-American relations (1783–1952) New York, St. Martin's Press, 1955.
1024 p. maps (part fold.) 22 cm.

Contains a clear 50-page summary of Anglo-American relations during the Civil War; based largely on E. D. Adams' work and a handful of other secondary sources.

American Thanksgiving dinner, at St. James' hall, London. Thursday, November 26th, 1863. London, W. Ridgway, 1863.
94 p. 21 cm.

Reproduces program, menu, and speeches at this occasion, including one of the rare public addresses made by C. F. Adams as minister at London.

Anent the North American continent ... London, W. Ridgway, 1864.

15, [1] p. 21cm.

An anonymous pro-Southern argument for England to join with other European powers and recognize the Confederacy - thus providing an excuse for a Confederate-Canadian alliance.

Anent the United States and Confederate States of North America ... London, J. Ridgway, 1862.

7 p. 21¾cm.

An anonymous appeal for English intervention to end civil war on the basis of a permanent division.

The **Annual** register of world events; a review of the year. 1758–
London, New York, Longmans, Green [etc.]

v. in   maps. 21-23 cm.

These collections of State papers and published documents include summaries of important Parliamentary debates on questions pertaining to the American Civil War and biographies of important people who died during the year prior to publication.

Archibald, *Mrs.* **Edith Jessie (Archibald) 1854–**
Life and letters of Sir Edward Mortimer Archibald, K. C. M. G., C. B. A memoir of fifty years of service by his daughter, Edith J. Archibald; with a foreword by the Rt. Hon. Sir Robert Laird Borden, G. C. M. G. Toronto, G. N. Morang, 1924.

xviii p., 1 l., 266 p. front., plates, ports., facsims. 22½cm.

The British Consul at New York during the Civil War period discusses Anglo-American relations with gusto and authority.

Argyll, George Douglas Campbell, *8th duke of,* 1823–1900.
... Autobiography and memoirs, ed. by the dowager Duchess of Argyll ... Londono, J. Murray, 1906.

2 v. 5 pl. (2 col.) 8 port. (incl. fronts., 1 col.) 23½cm.

Extracts from correspondence tell part of the story of the Duke's stout defense within the British Cabinet of the American Union.

Arnold, *Sir* **Arthur,** 1833–1902.
The history of the cotton famine, from the fall of Sumter to the passing of the Public works act. By R. Arthur Arnold. London, Saunders, Otley, and co., 1864.

xiv, 570 p. 22cm.

Factual contemporary study of the effects of the war on the British cotton textile industry, and the side effects on British foreign policy.

Atkins, John Black, 1871–
The life of Sir William Howard Russell, C. V. O., LL. D., the first special correspondent; by John Black Atkins ... London, J. Murray, 1911.

2 v. 10 pl., 6 port. (incl. fronts.) facsim. 22½cm.

Recounts how war reports in 1861-1862 from a Times correspondent in America affected Anglo-American diplomacy and public opinion.

Aucaigne, Félix, *d.* 1914.
L'alliance russo-américaine, par Félix Aucaigne. 2. éd. Paris, E. Dentu, 1863.

32 p. 24cm.

Discusses visit of Russian fleet to the United States in 1863 with thoroughness and perception.

Austin, Victor, *ed.*
La guerre de secession, 1861–1865. Paris, R. Julliard [1961]

331 p. illus. 21 cm. (Il y a toujours un reporter)

A collection of contemporary comment, domestic and foreign, on the Civil War; extracted from printed works of generally high reliability.

Bailey, Thomas Andrew, 1902–
America faces Russia; Russian-American relations from early times to our day [by] Thomas A. Bailey. Gloucester, Mass., P. Smith, 1964 [c1950]

xi, 375 p. illus. 21 cm.

Interesting treatment of Civil War period drawn from secondary sources.

Bailey, Thomas Andrew, 1902–
A diplomatic history of the American people. 6th ed. New York, Appleton-Century-Crofts [1958]

806 p. illus. 25 cm.

Coverage of the Civil War is fairly complete and highly readable, but Bailey sacrifices accuracy to flamboyance.

Balch, Thomas Willing, 1866–1927.
The Alabama arbitration, by Thomas Willing Balch ... Philadelphia, Allen, Lane & Scott, 1900.

3 p. l., 150 p. 25 cm.

The superficial story of the "Alabama Claims" from that vessel's launching until the Geneva settlement of 1872.

Balme, Joshua Rhodes.
American war crusade; or, Plain facts for earnest men. By J. R. Balme ... London, Hamilton, Adams, & co. [1863]

40 p. 17ᶜᵐ.

A self-professed abolitionist condemns the North's alleged policy of emancipation based on force rather than on reason. Full of odd arguments and curious logic.

Balme, Joshua Rhodes.
Letters on the American Republic; or, Common fallacies and monstrous errors refuted and exposed. Enl. ed. London, Hamilton, Adams [introd. 1863]

vii, 191 p. 17 cm.

Fancy mixes with fact in this blanket condemnation of American institutions.

Balme, Joshua Rhodes.
Synopsis of the American war. By J. R. Balme ... London, Hamilton, Adams & co.; [etc., etc.] 1865.

2 p. l., p. 547–776. 17½ᶜᵐ.

A disgruntled emigrant from America, in what is misrepresented as an impartial factbook, lashes out intemperately and often inaccurately against both North and South.

Bancroft, Frederic, 1860–
The life of William H. Seward, by Frederic Bancroft ... New York & London, Harper and brothers, 1900.

2 v. fronts. (ports.) 21½ᶜᵐ.

This account of Seward's character and personality shows insight, and the treatment of his diplomacy is thorough; but when Bancroft strains to be profound, he is meanly supercilious.

Barrillon, François Guillaume.
Politique de la France et de l'humanité dans le conflit américain, par Barrillon ... Paris, Guillaumin et cⁱᵉ, 1861.

40 p. 25 cm.

The author advocated French intervention to end the Civil War with a final separation of South from North.

Baty, Thomas, 1869–   *ed.*
Prize law and continuous voyage; containing Continuous voyages, by Sir Travers Twiss ... Brief in the Springbok case, by the Hon. W. M. Evarts ... Analysis of the Springbok judgment, by D. C. L. And the memorial on prize procedure of Lee, Paul, Ryder and Murray. Ed. by T. Baty ... London, Stevens & Haynes [pref. 1915–

134 p., 1 l. 21½ᶜᵐ.

A sometimes lucid discussion of the legal issues involved in the American seizure and condemnation of a British ship.

Barrows, Chester Leonard, 1891–
William M. Evarts, lawyer, diplomat, statesman, by Chester L. Barrows. Chapel Hill, The University of North Carolina press, 1941.

x p., 1 l., 587 p. front. (port.) 23½ cm.

The best source for information on Evarts' two trips to England to handle legal problems growing out of the Civil War.

Bayman, *Mrs.* **A   Phelps**
Notes and letters on the American war. By an English lady. London, W. Ridgway, 1864.

1 p. l., ii, [3]–82 p. 20ᶜᵐ.

A masterly defense of the Northern cause and a devastating refutation of arguments in defense of the Southern slaveholders presented in England by A. J. B. Beresford-Hope.

Beecher, Henry Ward, 1813–1887.

Patriotic addresses in America and England, from 1850 to 1885, on slavery, the civil war, and the development of civil liberty in the United States, by Henry Ward Beecher. Ed., with a review of Mr. Beecher's personality and influence in public affairs, by John R. Howard. New York, Fords, Howard & Hulbert, 1887.

857 p. 19 port. (incl. front.) 23 cm.

Contains much of the flag-waving claptrap Beecher purveyed on both sides of the Atlantic during the Civil War.

Beecher, Henry Ward, 1813–1887.

Speeches of Rev. Henry Ward Beecher on the American rebellion, delivered in Great Britain in 1863. Rev. and now first published in America. New York, F. F. Lovell & company [c1887]

2 p. l., 3–368 p. 19cm.

In this series of addresses delivered at popular meetings in England during October, 1863, Beecher glorified himself and rather incidentally the Northern cause.

Bemis, George, 1816–1878.

Hasty recognition of rebel belligerency, and our right to complain of it. By George Bemis. Boston, A. Williams & co. [1865]

viii p., 1 l., 57 p. 24cm.

A reasonable, moderately worded criticism of the British government and its champion, "Historicus," maintaining that recognition of Confederate belligerency was a necessity.

Bemis, George, 1816–1878.

Precedents of American neutrality, in reply to the speech of Sir Roundell Palmer, attorney-general of England, in the British House of commons, May 13, 1864. By George Bemis. Boston, Little, Brown and company, 1864.

viii, 83 p. 21 cm.

The author cited historic cases to show that with regard to Confederate cruisers the British acted contrary to American precedents of neutral maritime law.

Bemis, Samuel Flagg, 1891–

A diplomatic history of the United States. 4th ed. New York, Holt [1955]

1018 p. illus. 25 cm.

The coverage of the Civil War period is as reliable and judicious as secondary sources of widely varying quality permit.

Bemis, Samuel Flagg, 1891–

Guide to the diplomatic history of the United States, 1775–1921, by Samuel Flagg Bemis and Grace Gardner Griffin. Washington, U. S. Govt. Print. Off., 1935. New York, P. Smith, 1951.

reprint: xvii, 979 p. 21 cm.

Contains standard bibliography on Civil War diplomacy, but now, however, thirty years out of date.

Bemis, Samuel Flagg, 1891– *ed.*

The American Secretaries of State and their diplomacy. J. Franklin Jameson, H. Barrett Learned [and] James Brown Scott, advisory board. New York, Pageant Book Co., 1958 [c1928]

10 v. in 5. illus., ports., map. 22 cm.

A mediocre study; sadly needed is a fresh appraisal of Seward's Civil War diplomacy.

Belmont, August 1816–1889.

A few letters and speeches of the late civil war. New York [Priv. print.] 1870.

2 p. l., 126 p. 26cm.

Correspondence of a New York agent of the Rothschild family who wrote continually to influential friends in Europe and who made wartime trips there in behalf of the Union cause.

Beresford-Hope, Alexander James Beresford, 1820–1887.

The American disruption. 1. A popular view of the American civil war. 2. England, the North and the South. 3. The results of the American disruption. In three lectures, delivered by request at Kilndown, Hawkhurst, and before the Maidstone literary & mechanics' institution. By A. J. B. Beresford Hope, esq. 6th ed. London, J. Ridgway; [etc., etc.] 1862.

116 p. 21cm.

A vociferous supporter of the Confederate cause in England favored Southern independence as being in Great Britain's best interests.

Beresford-Hope, Alexander James Beresford, 1820–1887.

England, the North and the South. By A. J. B. Beresford Hope ... 3d ed. London, J. Ridgway; Maidstone, Wickham [etc.] 1862.

40 p. 21½ cm.

The best source for this pro-Southern pamphlet is the same author's American Disruption, which includes other work in the same vein.

Beresford-Hope, Alexander James Beresford, 1820–1887.

A popular view of the American civil war. By A. J. B. Beresford Hope. London, J. Ridgway; Maidstone, Wickham [etc.] 1861.

28 p. 21ᶜᵐ.

On the eve of the Trent Affair crisis, an Englishman advocates an Anglo-Confederate alliance.

Bernard, Mountague, 1820–1882.

A historical account of the neutrality of Great Britain during the American civil war. By Mountague Bernard ... London, Longmans, Green, Reader, and Dyer, 1870.

xv, 511 p. 25 cm.

Learned but one-sided argument by a British authority on international law in favor of the correctness of British policy toward the Civil War.

Bernard, Mountague.

A lecture on alleged violations of neutrality by England in the present war. By Mountague Bernard ... June, MDCCCLXIII. London, W. Ridgway, 1863.

45 p. 20ᶜᵐ.

An Oxford University expert on international law defends the British policy of neutrality.

Bernard, Mountague.

Notes on some questions suggested by the case of the "Trent." By Mountague Bernard ... March, MDCCCLXII. Oxford, J. H. and J. Parker [etc., 1862]

39 p. 20½ᶜᵐ.

A brief recapitulation of the British legal position.

Bernard, Mountague, 1820–1882.

On the principle of non-intervention. A lecture delivered in the hall of All souls' college, by Mountague Bernard ... Oxford & London, J. H. & J. Parker [1860]

1 p. l., 36 p. 23ᶜᵐ.

A warning that the British government should be carefully neutral if Civil War came to the United States.

Bernard, Mountague, 1820–1882.

Two lectures on the present American war. By Mountague Bernard ... November, MDCCCLXI. Oxford & London, J. H. and J. Parker [1861]

95 p. 20ᶜᵐ.

A pedantic discussion of the constitutionality of Southern secession; Bernard predicted that if the North restored the Union, America would survive only as a military dictatorship.

Bigelow, John, 1817–1911.

Les États-Unis d'Amérique en 1863; leur histoire politique, leurs ressources minéralogiques, agricoles, industrielles et commerciales, et la part pour laquelle ils ont contribué à la richesse et à la civilisation du monde entier, par John Bigelow ... Paris, L. Hachette et cⁱᵉ, 1863.

3 p. l., [iii]–xxiv, 551 p. fold. tab. 22ᶜᵐ.

A statistical reference work about America written by the U. S. Consul at Paris to correct misconceptions resulting from Confederate propaganda in Europe.

Bigelow, John, 1817–1911.

France and the Confederate navy, 1862–1868; an international episode, by John Bigelow. New York, Harper & brothers, 1888.

x p., 1 l., 247 p. 19½ᶜᵐ.

An insider's account of Northern efforts to block building and financing of Confederate ironclads in France.

Bigelow, John, 1817–1911.

Lest we forget. Gladstone, Morley and the Confederate loan of 1863; a rectification by John Bigelow ... New York [The De Vinne press] 1905.

65 p. 23ᶜᵐ.

A former U. S. minister at Paris disputed Gladstone's biographer regarding the chancellor of exchequer's American position during Civil War.

Bigelow, John, 1817–1911.

Retrospections of an active life, by John Bigelow ... New York, The Baker & Taylor co., 1909–13.

5 v. fronts., plates, ports., fold. map. 25½ cm.

Bigelow alternated verbatim extracts from contemporary letters, speeches, and dispatches with a sensible, informative commentary on American wartime diplomacy.

Blegen, Theodore Christian, 1891–

Abraham Lincoln and European opinion, by Theodore C. Blegen ... Minneapolis, 1934.

12 p. 24^{cm}.

Author quoted European writers to show Lincoln as not merely a national figure but also a world folk hero.

Bonham, Milledge Louis, 1880–1941.

... The British consuls in the confederacy, by Milledge L. Bonham, jr. ... New York, Columbia university, Longmans, Green & co., agents; [etc., etc.] 1911.

267 p. 24½^{cm}.

Valuable treatise based on primary sources but not on consular dispatches themselves.

Blumenthal, Henry.

A reappraisal of Franco-American relations, 1830–1871. Chapel Hill, University of North Carolina Press [1959]

xiv, 255 p. tables. 24 cm.

An excellent study based on careful use of source materials.

Boynton, Charles Brandon, 1806–1883.

English and French neutrality and the Anglo-French alliance, in their relations to the United States & Russia, including an account of the leading policy of France and of England for the last two hundred years—the origin and aims of the alliance—the meaning of the Crimean war—and the reason of the hostile attitude of these two powers towards the United States, and of the movement on Mexico, with a statement of the general resources—the army and navy of England and France—Russia and America—showing the present strength and probable future of these four powers. By Rev. C. B. Boynton, D. D. Cincinnati, Chicago, C. F. Vent & co., 1864.

576 p. 23^{cm}.

In anticipation of war between U. S. and Anglo-French-Confederate alliance, Boynton exhaustively compared the military forces of each side.

Bradley, Joseph P. 1813–1892.

A memorial of the life and character of Hon. William L. Dayton, late U. S. minister to France. By Joseph P. Bradley, esq. Prepared in conformity with a resolution of the New Jersey historical society. Newark, N. J., Daily advertiser printing house, 1875.

50 p. 22½^{cm}.

Material on Civil War period is mostly eulogistic trivia.

A brief reply to an important question; being a letter to Professor Goldwin Smith from an implicit believer in Holy Scripture. London: Saunders, Otley and co., 1863.

24 p. 20½^{cm}.

A reply to Smith's pamphlet "Does the Bible Sanction American Slavery?" by a religious fundamentalist who supported slavery and defended Southern institutions in general.

Briggs, Herbert Whittaker, 1900–

The doctrine of continuous voyage, by Herbert Whittaker Briggs ... Baltimore, 1926.

x, 11–226 p., 1 l. 24½^{cm}.

A presentation of cases and commentary on questions of international law deeply involved in Anglo-American diplomacy of the 1860's.

Bright, John, 1811–1889.

The diaries of John Bright, with a foreword by Philip Bright, edited by R. A. J. Walling ... New York, W. Morrow & company, 1931.

xii, 591 p. front., pl., ports., facsim. 24 cm.

Bright's energetic assistance to the Union cause in England is illuminated and clarified.

Bright, John, 1811–1889.

... John Bright and the American civil war; ed. by Lawrence V. Roth. [Boston, Old South association, 191–]

28 p. 19½^{cm}.

Contains extracts from Bright's pro-Union letters and speeches that are widely available elsewhere.

Bright, John, 1811–1889.

Speech of Mr. Bright, M. P., in the Town hall, Birmingham, December 18, 1862. Birmingham, Printed by J. Allen and son [1862?]

20 p. 19½^{cm}.

Assails British government for its cotton policies, the Alabama, and neutrality questions -- while upholding the free states of the North as the last hope of the world's working men.

Bright, John, 1811–1889.

Speeches of John Bright, M. P., on the American question. With an introduction by Frank Moore. Boston, Little, Brown & company, 1865.

xv, 278 p. front. (port.) 19½ᶜᵐ.

Probably the Union's greatest English ally repeatedly upholds the Northern cause as a war for worldwide human freedom and democracy.

Bright, John, 1811–1889.

Speeches on questions of public policy, by John Bright, M. P. Ed. by James E. Thorold Rogers ... London, Macmillan & co., 1868.

2 v. front. (port.) 22½ᶜᵐ.

Includes several pro-Northern speeches by Bright not readily available elsewhere.

... **British** aid to the Confederates. [London, British and foreign anti-slavery society, 1863]

8 p. 21ᶜᵐ.

Public letters to Lord Palmerston asking his intervention to stop continued violations of British neutrality in the form of Confederate ship-making and supply operations in England.

Broom, Walter William.

An Englishman's thoughts on the crimes of the South, and the recompence of the North. By W. W. Broom ... New York, C. S. Westcott & co., printers, 1865.

24 p. 22½ᶜᵐ.

A disorganized diatribe against the Southern slave society; and concludes with rejoicing that Christ has triumphed with the downfall of the Confederacy.

Browne, Nathaniel Borodaille, 1819–1875.

An address delivered before the Union league in the 24th ward of the city of Philadelphia, at its opening celebration, May 9, 1863, by N. B. Browne, esq. ... Philadelphia, The League, 1863.

16 p. 22½ᶜᵐ.

An attack on Lord Lyons for being "heart and soul" with the Copperheads; based on an analysis of Lyon's diplomatic correspondence.

Bulloch, James Dunwody, 1823–1901.

The secret service of the Confederate States in Europe; or, How the Confederate cruisers were equipped. With a new introd. by Philip Van Doren Stern. New York, T. Yoseloff [1959]

2 v. illus., ports., maps. 22 cm.

A generally reliable account of Confederate ship-building operations in Europe by the man who directed them.

Butler, Pierce, 1873–

... Judah P. Benjamin, by Pierce Butler. Philadelphia, G. W. Jacobs & company [1907]

459 p. front. (port.) 19½ cm.

This opinionated study of the Confederate Secretary of State sheds little light on the foreign relations of the Davis administration.

Cairnes, John Elliott, 1823–1875.

The American revolution: a lecture, delivered before the Dublin Young men's Christian association in connection with the United church of England and Ireland, October 30th, 1862. By John Elliott Cairnes ... New York, T. J. Crowen, 1862.

15 p. 23ᶜᵐ.

An Irish legal authority attempts to show slavery as the principal issue of the Civil War.

Cairnes, John Elliott, 1823–1875.

England's neutrality in the American contest. By J. E. Cairnes ... London, The Emancipation society, 1864.

23 p. 20½ᶜᵐ.

A reinforcement of arguments in C. G. Loring's "Neutral Relations . . . "; international law, Cairnes felt, was still somewhat unsettled.

Cairnes, John Elliott, 1823–1875.

The revolution in America: a lecture by John Elliott Cairnes, A. M. ... Delivered before the Dublin Young men's Christian association in connexion with the United church of England and Ireland, in the Metropolitan hall, October 30th, 1862 ... [Dublin, Committee of the Dublin Young men's Christian association in connexion with the United church of England and Ireland, 1862?]

43 p. 18½ᶜᵐ.

A discussion of the principles underlying the Civil War from an anti-slavery point of view.

Cairnes, John Elliott, 1823–1875.
The slave power: its character, career, and probable designs: being an attempt to explain the real issues involved in the American contest. By J. E. Cairnes ... ₍American ed.₎ New York, Carleton; ₍etc., etc.₎ 1862.
1 p. l., ₍vii₎–xvi, ₍17₎–171 p. 24 cm.

This Irish legal scholar asserted that the best interests of mankind rested on a thorough defeat of the South and the eradication of slavery.

Callahan, James Morton, 1864–
American foreign policy in Canadian relations, by James Morton Callahan. New York, The Macmillan company, 1937.
x p., 1 l., 576 p. illus. (maps) 22½ cm.

One chapter on the border problems of the Civil War period is outdated by modern research.

Callahan, James Morton, 1864–1956.
American foreign policy in Mexican relations, by James Morton Callahan. New York, The Macmillan company, 1932.
x p., 1 l., 644 p. maps (1 double) 22½ cm.

Seward's Mexican policy receives detailed scholarly treatment in one chapter.

Callahan, James Morton, 1864–
...The diplomatic history of the southern confederacy. By James Morton Callahan, ph. d. Baltimore, The Johns Hopkins press, 1901.
304 p. 20½ cm.

Entirely superseded by Owsley's King Cotton Diplomacy.

Callahan, James Morton, 1864–
... Evolution of Seward's Mexican policy, by James Morton Callahan. Morgantown, W. Va., Department of history and political science, West Virginia university, 1909.
1 p. l., 88 p. 21½ cm.

A hypercritical examination of American policy based on superficial research.

Callahan, James Morton, 1864–
... Russo-American relations during the American civil war, by James Morton Callahan. Morgantown, W. V., Department of history and political science, West Virginia university, 1908.
1 p. l., 18 p. 22 cm.

A pioneer study, based on selected sources, but now outdated.

Carreño, Alberto María, 1875–
La diplomacia extraordinaria entre México y Estados Unidos, 1789–1947. México, Editorial Jus, 1951.
2 v. facsims. 21 cm.

Although based on Mexican manuscripts, this volume's meager treatment of the Civil War period reduces its value.

Case, Lynn Marshall, 1903– *comp.*
... French opinion on the United States and Mexico, 1860–1867; extracts from the reports of the procureurs généraux, compiled and edited by Lynn M. Case ... New York, London, D. Appleton-Century company, incorporated ₍c1936₎
xxiii, 452 p. illus. (map) 23 cm.

An edited compilation of extracts from reports of French officials during the 1860's; especially valuable regarding the economic effects of the Civil War on France.

The **case** of the Trent examined ... London, J. Ridgway, 1862.
24 p. 21½ cm.

Adds little to the voluminous body of writings on the legality of the Trent seizure-- even though the author was rumored to be a famous British jurist.

Casper, Henry Weber, 1909–
American attitudes toward the rise of Napoleon III; a cross section of public opinion. Washington, Catholic Univ. of America Press, 1947.
xv, 242 p. 23 cm.

Qualitatively inferior to White's American Opinion, but more thorough for the Civil War era.

Chase, Salmon Portland, 1808–1873.
    Inside Lincoln's Cabinet; the Civil War diaries of Salmon P. Chase, edited by David Donald. ₁1st ed.₎ New York, Longmans, Green, 1954.

    ix, 342 p. port. 24 cm.

Sheds light on cabinet attitudes toward the Trent Affair and several other foreign relations topics.

Clapp, Margaret Antoinette, 1910–
    Forgotten first citizen: John Bigelow. ₁1st ed.₎ Boston, Little, Brown, 1947.

    x, 390 p. port. 23 cm.

An excellent brief account, but the author would have profited from research in the French archives.

Clark, Charles, *d.* 1881.
    "Principles that ought naturally to govern the conduct of neutrals and belligerents"; a paper read before the Juridical society, 1 February 1864. By Charles Clark ... London, Butterworths, 1864.

    42 p. 20ᶜᵐ.

A somewhat awkward attempt to describe the issues of international maritime law raised by the Civil War.

Clark, Charles, *d.* 1881.
    The Trent and San Jacinto; being the substance of a paper on this subject, read before the Juridical society, on the 16th December 1861. By Charles Clark ... London, Butterworths, 1862.

    46 p. 20½ᶜᵐ.

Rehashes legal principles involved in the Trent seizure.

Clay, Cassius Marcellus, 1810–1903.
    The life of Cassius Marcellus Clay. Memoirs, writings, and speeches, showing his conduct in the overthrow of American slavery, the salvation of the Union, and the restoration of the autonomy of the states ... In two volumes, written and compiled by himself, and illustrated with engravings on steel. vol. i. Cincinnati, O., J. F. Brennan & co., 1886.

    xiii, 15–600 p. pl., 6 port. (incl. front.) 25½ cm.

Provides invaluable reminiscences and extracts from correspondence pertaining to Clay's wartime mission to Russia.

Cobbe, Frances Power, 1822–1904.
    The red flag in John Bull's eyes. By Frances Power Cobbe ... London, E. Faithfull, 1863.

    24 p. 18ᶜᵐ.

Cobbe's contention was that re-soldering the fetters of the Southern slaves would hurt the white population more than completing the work of liberation.

Cobden, Richard 1804–1865.
    A friendly voice from England on American affairs ... New York, W. C. Bryant & co., printers, 1862.

    30 p. 23ᶜᵐ.

Contains a letter from Cobden and a speech by Bright, both friendly to North, and both published in many different places.

Cochin, Augustin, 1823–1872.
    L'abolition de l'esclavage, par Augustin Cochin ... Paris, J. Lecoffre ₁etc.₎ 1861.

    2 v. tables. 22½ cm.

A detailed examination of the peculiar institution which helped form French opinion toward the Confederacy.

Coleridge, Ernest Hartley, 1846–1920.
    Life & correspondence of John Duke lord Coleridge, lord chief justice of England, written and ed. by Ernest Hartley Coleridge ... London, W. Heinemann, 1904.

    2 v. fronts., plates, ports., fold. geneal. tab. 23½ᵐ.

Contains a few extracts from letters that illuminate British policy toward the Civil War.

Coleridge, John Duke Coleridge, *1st baron,* 1820–1894.
    Forty years of friendship as recorded in the correspondence of John Duke, lord Coleridge and Ellis Yarnall during the years 1856 to 1895, ed. by Charlton Yarnall. London, Macmillan and co., limited, 1911.

    xv, 340 p. front., ports. 23 cm.

Contains letters between the Lord Chief Justice of England and the American correspondent of the Manchester Guardian.

Conrad, Earl.
The Governor and his lady; the story of William Henry Seward and his wife Frances. New York, Putnam [1960]
433 p. 22 cm.

Contains invented dialogue and serious misunderstandings of Seward's policies and motives; worthless as history.

Cordner, John.
Canada and the United States: an address, on the American conflict, delivered at Montreal, on Thursday evening, December 22, 1864. By the Rev. John Cordner. Manchester, A. Ireland and co., printers, 1865.
ix, 30 p. 21ᶜᵐ.

Reassures Canadians that the North has no designs on Canada; Cordner attempted to elicit Canadian sympathy for the North's struggle against Southern slavery.

Corsan, W C
Two months in the Confederate States; including a visit to New Orleans under the domination of General Butler. By an English merchant. London, R. Bentley, 1863.
2 p. l., 299 p. 19ᶜᵐ.

Essentially a travel book containing little politics but reflecting a pro-Southern viewpoint about alleged Northern atrocities.

Cortambert, Louis Richard, 1808?–1881.
La guerre américaine; discours prononcé devant l'Institut-Canadien le 6 novembre 1863, par L. Cortambert. Montréal, Presses du journal le Pays, 1863.
11 p. 21ᶜᵐ.

A cautious, pedestrian evaluation of the issues.

Cowell, John Welsford.
Southern secession. A letter addressed to Captain M. T. Maury, Confederate navy, on his letter to Admiral Fitzroy. By John Welsford Cowell, esq. London, R. Hardwicke, 1862.
2 p. l., 99 p. 21½ᶜᵐ.

In six public letters, an Englishman attributes the Civil War almost entirely to Northern attempts to despoil the South through protective tariffs.

Crooks, George Richard, 1822–1897.
Life and letters of the Rev. John M'Clintock ... By George R. Crooks, D. D. New York, Nelson & Phillips; Cincinnati, Hitchcock & Walden, 1876.
410 p. front. (port.) 19ᶜᵐ.

A large number of letters written during the Civil War by an American working for the Union cause in Paris.

Cushing, Caleb, 1800–1879.
The Treaty of Washington: its negotiation, execution, and the discussions relating thereto. By Caleb Cushing. New York, Harper & brothers, 1873.
viii, [9]–280 p. 21 cm.

The U. S. counsel at the Geneva arbitration conference discusses Anglo-American differences arising out of Civil War events.

Dana, Richard Henry, 1851–
The Trent affairs, an aftermath, by Richard Henry Dana. Cambridge, 1912.
20 p. 25ᶜᵐ.

Dana challenged both the data and the conclusions of C. F. Adams's monograph on the Trent Affair with cogent arguments; Adams offered a feeble, petulant rejoinder.

Davis, William Columbus, 1910–
The last conquistadores; the Spanish intervention in Peru and Chile, 1863–1866. [Athens] University of Georgia Press [1950]
ix, 386 p. maps (on lining papers) 24 cm.

Sheds light on Seward's Latin American policy.

De Arnaud, Charles A 1835–
The union, and its ally, Russia. An historical narrative of the most critical and exciting period of our late war. Reminiscences of Col. Charles A. de Arnaud. Washington, Gibson bros., printers, 1890.
cover-title, 32 p. 23ᶜᵐ.

An insider discusses Russo-American relations during the Civil War period; unfortunately he neglects to support his best stories with evidence.

De Leon, Edwin, 1828–1891.
 Thirty years of my life on three continents, by Edwin **De Leon** ... With a chapter on the life of women in the East, by Mrs. De Leon ... London, Ward and Downey, 1890.

 2 v. front. (port.) 23^{cm}.

An egocentric account by the Confederate propaganda chief in Europe.

Duberman, Martin B
 Charles Francis Adams, 1807–1886. Boston, Houghton Mifflin, 1961 [c1960]
 525 p. illus. 22 cm.

Contains the clearest and most accurate short account available of American diplomacy in England, 1861-1865, but weak in depicting the personality of Adams.

Du Bose, John Witherspoon, 1836–1918.
 The life and times of William Lowndes Yancey. A history of political parties in the United States, from 1834 to 1864; especially as to the origin of the Confederate states. By John Witherspoon Du Bose ... New York, P. Smith, 1942.
 2 v., pl., 8 port. (incl. front.) 24½ cm.

Reveals little about Yancey's diplomatic efforts in Europe that is not found in published official records.

Dunning, William Archibald, 1857–1922.
 The British Empire and the United States; a review of their relations during the century of peace following the treaty of Ghent, by William Archibald Dunning ... with an introduction by the Right Honourable Viscount Bryce, o. M., and a preface by Nicholas Murray Butler ... New York, C. Scribner's sons, 1914.
 xl, 381 p. 22½ cm.

A highly readable and generally reliable short survey; lacks documentation.

Durden, Robert Franklin.
 James Shepherd Pike: Republicanism and the American Negro, 1850–1882. Durham, N. C., Duke University Press, 1957.
 249 p. illus. 24 cm.

A failure to employ mss. sources outside the Pike papers themselves keeps this good biography of the U. S. Minister at The Hague from being definitive.

Edge, Frederick Milnes.
 America yesterday and to-day. The United States prior to the rebellion; and the prospects of reconstruction of the South ... London, F. Farrah [1869?]
 viii p., 1 l., [ix]–xv, 224, [ii] p. 12°.

A reissue of an 1860 book entitled "Slavery Doomed," written by a pro-Northern English traveler and news correspondent, and which caused a sensation in England during the Civil War.

Edge, Frederick Milnes.
 The destruction of the American carrying trade. A letter to Earl Russell ... By Frederick Milnes Edge. London, W. Ridgway, 1863.
 27 p. 20½^{cm}.

A warning by an English journalist of a rising tide of American hostility to England.

Edge, Frederick Milnes.
 England's danger and her safety. A letter to Earl Russell ... By Frederick Milnes Edge. London, W. Ridgway, 1864.
 31 p. 20^{cm}.

Edge points out some flaws in Russell's American policy.

Edge, Frederick Milnes
 ... Whom do English Tories wish elected to the presidency? [New York, 1864]
 4 p. 22½^{cm}.

McClellan, of course.

Einstein, Lewis, 1877–
 Napoleon III. and American diplomacy at the outbreak of the Civil War. An address read in French before the Société d'histoire diplomatique at Paris, on the ninth of June, 1905. London, 1905.
 29 p. 23 cm.

An able study, too long neglected.

Evans, Thomas Wiltberger, 1823–1897.
   Memoirs of Dr. Thomas W. Evans; the second French empire, edited by Edward A. Crane, M. D. Napoleon the Third, the Empress Eugénie, the prince imperial. New York, D. Appleton and company, 1905.
   xx, 527 p. front., plates, ports. 21½ cm.

Has good stories about an eminent dentist's close relations with high French officials, and Americans struggling against French public opinion.

Fairbanks, Charles, 1821–
   The American conflict as seen from a European point of view. A lecture delivered at St. Johnsbury, Vt., June 4, 1863, by Charles Fairbanks. Boston, Press of G. C. Rand & Avery, 1863.
   44 p. 23¼ cm.

A rambling discussion of British opinion and policy regarding the Civil War.

Field, Edwin Wilkins, 1804–1871.
   Correspondence on the present relations between Great Britain and the United States of America. Boston, Little, Brown and company, 1862.
   2 p. l., 153 p. 25 cm.

Reflects the positions of most educated opinion in England and America during the first year of the war.

Fischer, LeRoy Henry, 1917–
   Lincoln's gadfly, Adam Gurowski, by Leroy H. Fischer. [1st ed.] Norman, University of Oklahoma Press [1964]
   xvii, 301 p. illus., ports. 24 cm.

The best examination of a Polish nobleman who became a clerk-translator for Seward's State Department while also involved in Radical Republican intrigues.

Fitzmaurice, Edmond George Petty-Fitzmaurice, *1st baron,* 1846–
   The life of Granville George Leveson Gower, second earl Granville, K. G. 1815–1891, by Lord Edmond Fitzmaurice ... 5th impression. London, New York [etc.] Longmans, Green, and co., 1906.
   2 v. fronts., plates, ports. 23½ cm.

Printed extracts from British cabinet correspondence regarding the Civil War.

Fogdall, Soren Jacob Marius Peterson.
   ... Danish-American diplomacy, 1776–1920, by Soren J. M. P. Fogdall, PH. D. Iowa City, The University [1922]
   171 p. 23½ cm.

A general survey that suffers from the author's failure to use diplomatic archives or other manuscript sources.

Forbes, John Murray, 1813–1898.
   Letters and recollections of John Murray Forbes; ed. by his daughter Sarah Forbes Hughes ... Boston and New York, Houghton, Mifflin and company, 1899.
   2 v. fronts., pl., ports., map, fold. facsim. 22½ cm.

Contains correspondence of a wealthy merchant and railroad magnate sent to England early in 1863 to buy ships for the Union.

Ford, Worthington Chauncey, 1858–1941, *ed.*
   A cycle of Adams letters, 1861–1865, ed. by Worthington Chauncey Ford ... Boston and New York, Houghton Mifflin company, 1920.
   2 v. fronts., plates, ports. 22 cm.

Selected wartime correspondence of the Adams family, stressing military intelligence but also revealing many facets of the American minister's diplomacy.

The **foreign** enlistment acts of England & America. The "Alexandra" & the rams. By Vigilans [pseud.] London, Saunders, Otley, and co., 1864.
   viii, 124 p. 20 cm.

An attack on the British official attitude toward the Confederate warships being built in English ports.

France. *Ministère des affaires étrangères.*
   ... Documents diplomatiques. 1864. Paris, Imprimerie impériale, 1865.
   3 p. l., 185 p. 30½ cm.

Fundamental to any understanding of French attitudes and policies.

France, Mexico, and the Confederate States. **By M. M.** Chevalier. Translated by Wm. Henry Hurlbut. New York, C. B. Richardson, 1863.

16 p. 23^{cm}.

Applauds Napoleon III for embarking allegedly upon Mexican intervention as a step toward bringing about Confederate independence through eventual French participation in the Civil War.

Frothingham, Paul Revere, 1864–1926.
Edward Everett, orator and statesman, by Paul Revere Frothingham ... Boston and New York, Houghton Mifflin company, 1925.

x p., 2 l., 495 p. front., plates, ports., facsims. 23 cm.

Prints some of the many letters exchanged between C. F. Adams at London and Everett, who had formerly been a minister there.

Fuller, Hiram 1814–1880.
The flag of truce. Dedicated to the Emperor of the French. By a White Republican. London, J. Ridgway, 1862.

52 p. 18½^{cm}.

Redundant, flamboyant claptrap, vaguely referring to Christian necessity for an end to Civil War bloodshed.

Gasparin, Agénor Étienne, *comte* **de,** 1810–1871.
L'Amérique devant l'Europe, principes et intérêts, par le Cte Agénor de Gasparin. Paris, Michel Lévy frères, 1862.

viii, 556 p. 21½^{cm}.

The author based this lengthy and eloquent defense of the Union cause on the conviction that Northern success was to be identified with that of universal human rights and justice.

Gasparin, Agénor Étienne, *comte* **de,** 1810–1871.
Reply of Messrs. Agenor de Gasparin, Édouard Laboulaye, Henri Martin, Augustin Cochin, to the Loyal national league of New York, together with the address of the league, adopted at the mass inaugural meeting, in Union square, April 11, 1863. New York, W. C. Bryant & co., printers, 1864.

30 p. 22½^{cm}.

Four prominent pro-Union Frenchmen eloquently proclaim the indignation of the civilized world toward the arrogant anti-democracy of slaveholders.

Gasparin, Agénor Étienne, *comte* **de,** 1810–1871.
... Réponse de mm. de Gasparin, Laboulaye, Martin et Cochin à la Ligue loyale et nationale de New York. New York, Impr. de W. C. Bryant & co., 1864.

20 p. 22½^{cm}.

An abbreviated translation of a pamphlet indicating support of prominent French intellectuals for the Union cause.

Gasparin, Agénor Étienne, *comte* **de,** 1810–1871.
Une parole de paix sur le différend entre l'Angleterre et les États-Unis, par le Cte A. de Gasparin. Paris, Michel Lévy frères, 1862.

31, [1] p. 21½^{cm}.

An attempt to still the clamor in Europe over the Trent Affair and to promote renewed sympathy for the Northern cause.

Gasparin, Agénor Étienne, *comte* **de,** 1810–1871.
The uprising of a great people. The United States in 1861. From the French of Count Agénor de Gasparin, by Mary L. Booth. New York, C. Scribner, 1861.

1 p. l., [v]–x p., 1 l., [9]–263 p. 17 cm.

Perhaps the wisest and most influential pro-Union statement produced by a European during the Civil War.

Gasparin, Agénor Étienne, *comte* **de,** 1810–1871.
A word of peace on the American question. By Count Agenor de Gasparin. London, S. Low, son, and co. [1862]

24 p. 19^{cm}.

An eloquent attempt to swing European opinion toward support to the Northern cause.

Gibbs, Frederick Waymouth, 1821–
The Foreign enlistment act. By Frederick Waymouth Gibbs, c. b. London, W. Ridgway, 1863.

1 p. l., 74 p. 20½^{cm}.

A discussion of how a forty-year-old act applied to American belligerents purchasing supplies and fitting out ships in England.

Gibbs, Frederick Waymouth, 1821–

Recognition: a chapter from the history of the North American & South American states, by Frederick Waymouth Gibbs, c. b. London, W. Ridgeway; [etc., etc.] 1863.

1 p. l., 46 p. 20½ cm.

Gibbs concluded that the Confederacy did not merit British recognition, but that military successes in the months to come might be used as a claim.

Girard, Charles Frédéric, 1822–1895.

A visit to the Confederate States of America in 1863; memoir addressed to His Majesty Napoleon III. Translated and edited with an introd. by Wm. Stanley Hoole. [Limited ed.] Tuscaloosa, Ala., Confederate Pub. Co., 1962.

126 p. port., map, facsims. 22 cm.

Written by a pro-Southern historian.

Goddard, Samuel Aspinwall.

The American rebellion. Letters on the American rebellion. By Samuel A. Goddard, Birmingham. 1860 to 1865 &c. London, Simpkin, Marshall & co.; Boston, Nichols and Noyes; [etc., etc.] 1870.

xvi, 583, [1] p. 22½ cm.

Collected writings of an Englishman who aided the Northern cause in both Parliament and the press.

Gooch, Daniel Wheelwright, 1820–1891.

Recognition of Hayti and Liberia. Speech of Hon. D. W. Gooch, of Mass., delivered in the House of representatives, June 2, 1862. [Washington, McGill, Witherow & co., printers, 1862]

8 p. 24 cm.

A speech in Congress advocating diplomatic recognition of two new Negro republics.

Grandguillot, Alcide Pierre, 1829–1891.

La reconnaissance du Sud. Par A. Grandguillot. Paris, E. Dentu, 1862.

30 p. 23½ cm.

The author took recognition of Confederate independence for granted.

Grattan, Thomas Colley, 1792–1864.

England and the disrupted states of America. By Thomas Colley Grattan ... 3d ed. London, Ridgway, 1862.

47 p. 21½ cm.

England should prepare for war, Grattan states, and should encourage Spain to take the lead in recognizing the South.

Great Britain.

... The case of Great Britain as laid before the Tribunal of arbitration, convened at Geneva under the provisions of the treaty between the United States of America and Her Majesty the queen of Great Britain, concluded at Washington, May 8, 1871 ... Washington, Govt. print. off., 1872.

3 v. fold. map. 23½ cm.

Thousands of pages of printed documents treat of neutral rights, blockade running, Confederate raiders and privateers.

Gt. Brit. *Foreign office.*

... Correspondence respecting the seizure of the British vessels "Springbok" and "Peterhoff," by United States' cruisers in 1863 ... London, H. M. Stationery off., Harrison and sons, printers [1900]

iv, 69, [1] p. 33½ cm.

A compilation of documents, mostly diplomatic notes, bearing on two important Civil War prize disputes.

Green, Samuel Abbott, 1830–

James Murray Mason and John Slidell in Fort Warren, Boston Harbor, with other matter relating to the war of the rebellion, by Samuel Abbott Green. Cambridge, J. Wilson and son, 1912.

14 p. 24½ cm.

An elderly gentleman reminisces vaguely about long visits with imprisoned Southern envoys at Fort Warren.

Guedalla, Philip, 1889–

Palmerston, by Philip Guedalla ... London, E. Benn, limited [1926]

501 p. front., plates, ports., facsim. 24½ cm.

This jaunty, sardonic biography admirably reflects the personality of its subject; valuable for its shrewd insights into the British prime minister's foreign policies.

Gurowski, Adam, *hrabia*, 1805–1866.
Diary ... By Adam Gurowski. Boston [etc.] 1862–66.
3 v. 19ᶜᵐ.

A day-by-day commentary on American foreign policy during the Civil War by an eccentric, shrewdly cynical state department translator who knew Europe better than Lincoln or Seward.

Hackett, Frank Warren, 1841–1926.
Reminiscences of the Geneva tribunal of arbitration, 1872, the Alabama claims, by Frank Warren Hackett. Boston and New York, Houghton Mifflin company, 1911.

xvi p., 1 l., 450 p., 1 l. 21 cm.

Covers certain events of 1870's; unrelated to contemporary diplomacy of the Civil War period.

Hall, Newman, 1816–1902.
The American war. By Newman Hall, ll. d. A lecture, delivered in London, October 20, 1862. New York, A. D. F. Randolph, 1862.

48 p. 19ᶜᵐ.

Author suggests that the Civil War is God's punishment and purification of Americans for allowing human slavery to exist.

Hanna, Alfred Jackson, 1893–
Confederate exiles in Venezuela, by Alfred Jackson Hanna and Kathryn Abbey Hanna. Limited ed. Tuscaloosa, Ala., Confederate Pub. Co., 1960.

149 p. 22 cm.

Scarcely touches wartime diplomatic relations.

Harcourt, *Sir* **William George Granville Venables Vernon**
1827–1904.
American neutrality: by Historicus [*pseud.*] Reprinted from the London Times of December 22d, 1864. New-York, 1865.

11 p. 22½ᶜᵐ.

A defense of English neutrality policy during the Civil War.

Harcourt, *Sir* **William George Granville Venables Vernon** 1827–
Belligerent rights of maritime capture. By Historicus [*pseud.*] ... Liverpool, Printed by Webb and Hunt, 1863.

22 p. 20½ᶜᵐ.

A statement that England should not impulsively assert neutral rights against the American government in cases of blockade breaking.

Harcourt, *Sir* **William George Granville Venables Vernon**
1827–1904.
Letters by Historicus on some questions of international law. Reprinted from 'The Times' with considerable additions ... London and Cambridge, Macmillan and co., 1863.
xiii p., 2 l., [3]–212 p. 22ᶜᵐ.

One of Great Britain's legal geniuses discusses issues arising during the war with discernment and objectivity.

Harris, Thomas Le Grand, 1863–
The Trent affair, including a review of English and American relations at the beginning of the civil war, by Thomas L. Harris ... With an introduction by James A. Woodburn ... Indianapolis, The Bobbs-Merrill company [ᶜ1896]

1 p. l., 5–288 p. 20½ᶜᵐ.

Unscholarly, unreliable, and badly written.

Harvey, Arthur, 1834–
... The reciprocity treaty: its advantages to the United States and to Canada. By Arthur Harvey ... Quebec, Printed by Hunter, Rose & co., 1865.

29 p. 20½ᶜᵐ.

An argument for reciprocity, one of the principal issues of wartime U.S.-Canadian relations.

Haut, Marc de.
La crise américaine; ses causes, ses résultats probables, ses rapports avec l'Europe et la France, par Marc de Haut ... Paris, Dentu, 1862.

4 p. l., 168 p. 24ᶜᵐ.

A call for French intervention in order to assure the permanent division of the American Union.

Hautefeuille, Laurent Basile, 1805–1875.

Quelques questions de droit international maritime, à propos de la guerre d'Amérique. Par L. B. Hautefeuille ... Leipzig, A. Frank; [etc., etc.] 1861.

2 p. l., 74 p. 22ᶜᵐ.

A French jurist tries with considerable success to anticipate those problems of international law, growing out of the Civil War, which would affect French interests.

Headley, John William, b. 1841.

Confederate operations in Canada and New York, by John W. Headley; illustrated with portraits. New York and Washington, The Neale publishing company, 1906.

xv p., 1 l., [19]–480 p. front., ports. 23 cm.

Provides no information about the effects of these raids on diplomacy.

Hill, Lawrence Francis, 1890–

Diplomatic relations between the United States and Brazil, by Lawrence F. Hill ... Durham, N. C., Duke university press, 1932.

x, 322 p. 28½ cm.

An exhaustive study based on printed sources and American archives.

Hobson, John Atkinson, 1858–1940.

Richard Cobden, the international man, by J. A. Hobson ... New York, H. Holt and company, 1919.

415, [1] p. incl. front. plates, ports. 22½ᶜᵐ.

Contains a large portion of Cobden's correspondence.

Hodge, Charles 1797–1878.

England and America ... 2d ed. Philadelphia, W. S. & A. Martien, 1862.

cover-title, 31 p. 23ᶜᵐ.

An attempt to persuade the English people that in supporting the South they have aided an evil cause.

Hughes, Thomas, 1822–1896.

The cause of freedom: which is its champion in America, the North or the South? By Thomas Hughes ... (Being a speech delivered by him at Exeter hall on the 29th of January, 1863.) ... [London] The Emancipation society [1863]

16 p. 17½ᶜᵐ.

A spirited but temperate condemnation of the Southern cause; includes an especially able defense of Cassius M. Clay.

Huse, Caleb, 1831–1905.

The supplies for the Confederate army, how they were obtained in Europe and how paid for. Personal reminiscences and unpublished history, by Caleb Huse ... Boston, Press of T. R. Marvin & son, 1904.

36 p. front. (port.) facsim. 23ᶜᵐ.

A meager but lively description of Confederate purchasing operations in Europe by a Southern agent.

Hyde, Charles Cheney, 1873–

International law, chiefly as interpreted and applied by the United States, by Charles Cheney Hyde ... 2d rev. ed. Boston, Little, Brown and company, 1945.

3 v. 24 cm.

Contains a brief section treating generally, though authoritatively, of developments during the Civil War period.

The Index. A weekly journal of politics, literature, and news; devoted to the exposition of the mutual interests, political and commercial, of Great Britain and the Confederate States of America. v. 1–5; May 1, 1862–Aug 12, 1865. London, 1862–65.

5 v. 39ᶜᵐ.

A newspaper edited in London by Confederate agent Henry Hotze; the policy was to "suggest rather than assert" the justice of the Southern cause.

Jay, John, 1817–1894.

The great issue. An address delivered before the Union campaign club, of East Brooklyn, New York, on Tuesday evening, Oct. 25, 1864. By John Jay, esq. New York, Baker & Godwin, printers, 1864.

32 p. 22ᶜᵐ.

In an election campaign address, the author praises Lincoln, Seward, and Adams for a wise and determined foreign policy.

Jay, John, 1817–1894.

Mr. Jay's letter on the recent relinquishment of the Monroe doctrine. [New York, 1863]

8 p. 23½ᶜᵐ.

Warns U.S. government against acquiescing in the French-Mexican intervention.

Johnston, Robert Matteson, 1867–   *ed.*

Memoirs of "Malakoff" [*pseud.*] being extracts from the correspondence and papers of the late William Edward Johnston, ed. by his son R. M. Johnston. London, Hutchinson & co. [1907]

2 v. front. (port., v. 1) 22½ᶜᵐ.

Reproduces many communications, public and private, of the New York Times correspondent in Paris during the Civil War.

Jones, Robert Owen, 1925–

British pseudo-neutrality during the American Civil War. Washington, 1952.

252 l. 29 cm.

Based largely on the Thomas Dudley consular diapatches; relates Dudley's achievements in Great Britain.

Jones, Wilbur Devereux.

The Confederate rams at Birkenhead; a chapter in Anglo-American relations. Tuscaloosa, Ala., Confederate Pub. Co., 1961.

124 p. illus. 22 cm.

Author employs British manuscript sources to provide the clearest and most authoritative account available of Laird ram incident.

Jordan, Donaldson.

Europe and the American civil war, by Donaldson Jordan ... [and] Edwin J. Pratt ... with an introduction by Samuel Eliot Morison. Boston and New York, Houghton Mifflin company, 1931.

xii, [1], 299, [1] p. front., plates. 23½ cm.

An excellent summary of contemporary English opinion regarding the Civil War up to 1863.

Juridicus, *pseud.*

The recognition of the Confederate States considered in a reply to the letters of "Historicus" in the London Times. By Juridicus ...   Charleston, S. C., Evans & Cogswell, 1863.

41 p. 23½ᶜᵐ.

Egregious twaddle designed to show that the South should have her independence recognized by European powers.

Kelley, William Darrah, 1814–1890.

The Trent case, and the means of averting foreign war. Speech of Hon. William D. Kelley, of Pennsylvania, in the House of representatives, January 7, 1862. [Washington, D. C., Scammell & co., printers, 1862]

7 p. 23½ᶜᵐ.

A discourse upon the horrors of war, with slight reference to foreign affairs.

Kingsley, Vine Wright.

French intervention in America; or, A review of La France, le Mexique, et les États-Confédérés. By Vine Wright Kingsley. New York, C. B. Richardson. 1863.

22 p. 22½ cm.

A clumsy assault on Michel Chevalier's pro-Confederate pamphlet.

Kirkland, Charles Pinckney, 1830–1904.

Liability of the government of Great Britain for the depredations of rebel privateers on the commerce of the United States, considered. By Charles P. Kirkland ... New York, A. D. F. Randolph, 1863.

37 p. incl. tables. 23ᶜᵐ.

A belligerent demand for damages anticipating the later "Alabama claims."

Koerner, Gustavé Philipp, 1809–1896.

Memoirs of Gustave Koerner, 1809–1896, life-sketches written at the suggestion of his children; ed. by Thomas J. McCormack ...   Cedar Rapids, Ia., The Torch press, 1909.

2 v. front., ports. 25 cm.

This loquacious memoir of the U. S. Minister of Madrid, 1862-1865, is more concerned with personal life than diplomatic work.

Laboulaye, Édouard René Lefebvre de, 1811–1883.
Les États-Unis et la France, par Édouard Laboulaye ... Paris, E. Dentu, 1862.

72 p. 23½ᶜᵐ.

A strong statement favoring the North and continued French neutrality; written to reinforce Gasparin's America Before Europe.

Laboulaye, Édouard René Lefebvre de, 1811–1883.
... Separation: war without end. By M. Édouard Laboulaye ... New York, Loyal publication society, 1864.

19 p. 22ᶜᵐ.

A Frenchman argues that Southern victory would lead to reestablishment of English supremacy in Europe.

A **legal** view of the seizure of Messrs Mason and Slidell. New York, 1861.

27 p. 22ᶜᵐ.

An argument that the capture of the Southern commissioners cannot be justified by international law.

Leng, *Sir* **William Christopher.**
... The American war: the aims, antecedents, and principles of the belligerents. A lecture, delivered on the 10th December, 1862, in Castle street church, by William C. Leng ... Dundee, Printed at the Advertiser office, 1863.

38 p. 21ᶜᵐ.

A very able, highly volatile, attack on Southern slaveholding by a staunch friend of the Union.

Loehnis, H.
Die Vereinigten Staaten von Nord-Amerika. Mit besonderer berücksichtigung ihrer finanziellen verhältnisse, von H. Loehnis. Bonn, M. Cohen & sohn, 1863.

2 p. l., 97, [1] p. fold. tab. 21½ᶜᵐ.

A condemnation of Chase's wartime financial program.

Logan, Rayford Whittingham, 1897–
The diplomatic relations of the United States with Haiti, 1776–1891, by Rayford W. Logan. Chapel Hill, The University of North Carolina press, 1941.

xi p., 2 l., 516 p. 24 cm.

A good survey.

Loidolt, Alfred, 1925–
Die Beziehungen Österreichs zu den Vereinigten Staaten zur Zeit des amerikanischen Bürgerkrieges, 1861–1865. Wien, 1949.

Microfilm copy (negative) Made by Photo Section, Vienna University Library.
Collation of the original, as determined from the film: [13], 117, [10] l.

The author uses Viennese sources to provide an informative account of Austrian policy towards the Civil War.

Lord, Henry William, 1834–1893.
The highway of the seas in time of war. By Henry W. Lord ... Cambridge [Eng.] London, Macmillan and co., 1862.

2 p. l., [vii]–viii, 56 p. 19ᶜᵐ.

A pontification of the Trent Affair.

Lorimer, James, 1818–1890.
The rights and duties of belligerents and neutrals with reference to maritime commerce. By James Lorimer ... A lecture delivered to the Leith Chamber of commerce on December 29, 1864. Edinburgh, Printed by T. Constable, 1865.

28 p. 22ᶜᵐ.

A Scottish lawyer and novelist criticizes the British government for letting the Alabama escape.

Loring. Charles Greely, 1794–1867.
England's liability for indemnity: remarks on the letter of "Historicus" [i. e. Sir William Vernon-Harcourt] dated November 4th, 1863; printed in the London "Times", November 7th; and reprinted in the "Boston daily advertiser", November 25th. By Charles G. Loring. Boston, W. V. Spencer, 1864.

vii, 46 p. 24ᶜᵐ.

A preliminary argument of what later became essentially the U. S. case in the Alabama claims arbitration.

Loring, Charles Greely, 1794–1867.
Neutral relations of England and the United States. By Charles G. Loring. Boston, W. V. Spencer, 1863.

iv, 116 p. 24½^{cm}.

A reprint of articles from the Boston <u>Daily Advertiser</u> ably arguing that England often violated her own neutrality policy during the Civil War.

Lothrop, Thornton Kirkland, 1830–1913.
... William Henry Seward, by Thornton Kirkland Lothrop. Boston and New York, Houghton, Mifflin and company [1908]

vi, 446 p. 18^{cm}.

An undocumented short biography of the Secretary of State; its main value lies in an analysis of U. S. foreign policies during the war.

Lowenthal, David.
George Perkins Marsh: versatile Vermonter. New York, Columbia University Press, 1958.

442 p. illus. 24 cm.

Good biography of U. S. Minister to Italy during the Civil War; better on personal life than on diplomatic policy.

Lowrey, Grosvenor Porter
English neutrality. Is the Alabama a British pirate? Philadelphia, H. B. Ashmead, printer, 1863.

32 p. 22^{cm}.

Assertions that the British government should make full compensation for pirates' damages, or else the U. S. should declare war.

Lutz, Ralph Haswell, 1886–
Die beziehungen zwischen Deutschland und den Vereinigten Staaten während des sezessionskrieges ... Heidelberg, C. Winter, 1911.

2 p. l., 93, [1] p. 22½^{cm}.

Contains a careful analysis of German opinion toward the Civil War; prepared mostly from printed sources.

Lyell, *Sir* **Charles,** *bart.,* 1797–1875.
Life, letters and journals of Sir Charles Lyell, bart. ... Edited by his sister-in-law, Mrs. Lyell ... London, J. Murray, 1881.

2 v. fronts., pl., ports. 23^{cm}.

Sidelights on Anglo-American relations by a close English friend of the American minister in London.

Lynch, Claire, *sister,* 1898–
... The diplomatic mission of John Lothrop Motley to Austria 1861–1867, by Sister M. Claire Lynch ... Washington, D. C., The Catholic university of America press, 1944.

viii, 159 p. 23^{cm}.

A shallow and sometimes inaccurate treatment of Motley's mission; based on a poor selection of sources.

MacCarthy, Desmond, 1878–   *ed.*
Lady John Russell; a memoir, with selections from her diaries and correspondence, ed. by Desmond MacCarthy and Agatha Russell; with twelve illustrations, of which six are in colour. New York, John Lane company, 1911.

xi, 325, [1] p. 12 pl. (6 col., incl. front., ports.) 23 cm.

These extracts from the manuscripts of the foreign minister's wife only hint at revelations about British policy toward the war.

Macdonald, Helen Grace, 1888–
... Canadian public opinion on the American civil war, by Helen G. Macdonald, PH. D. New York, Columbia university; London, P. S. King & son, 1926.

237 p. 22½ cm.

This thorough but prosaic study covering both popular and official opinion in Canada is based upon a wide variety of sources.

McHenry, George, *of Philadelphia.*
The cotton trade: its bearing upon the prosperity of Great Britain and commerce of the American republics, considered in connection with the system of Negro slavery in the Confederate States. By George McHenry ... 2d ed. London, Saunders, Otley, & co., 1863.

4 p. l., [vii]–lxix p., 1 l., 292 p. incl. tables. 22½^{cm}.

A vitriolic attack by an expatriated Northerner upon the Lincoln administration; heavy with statistics.

McHenry, George.

... A paper containing a statement of facts relating to the approaching cotton crisis. By George McHenry. Richmond, Dec. 31, 1864. [Richmond, 1865]

87 p. 22½ᶜᵐ.

A reiteration of arguments set forth in the author's Cotton Trade; supported by some additional data.

McInnis, Edgar.

The unguarded frontier, a history of American-Canadian relations, by Edgar W. McInnis ... Garden City, N. Y., Doubleday, Doran & co., inc., 1942.

5 p. l., 384 p. 22 cm.

The portion treating of the 1860's lacks documentation and seems based on meager research.

Magnus, *Sir* **Philip Montefiore,** *bart.,* 1906–

Gladstone, a biography. New York, Dutton [1954]

482 p. illus. 22 cm.

Sheds little light on Gladstone's odd role in British policy during the Civil War.

Malet, *Sir* **Edward Baldwin,** 1837–1908.

Shifting scenes; or, Memories of many men in many lands; by the Right Honourable Sir Edward Malet ... [2d ed.] London, J. Murray, 1901.

xii, 335, [1] p. 21 cm.

Includes offhand remarks about the work routine of the Washington legation; written by a British attache.

Marquardsen, Heinrich von, 1825–1897.

Der Trent-fall. Zur lehre von der kriegscontrebande, und dem transportdienst der neutralen. Von dr. Heinrich Marquardsen ... Erlangen, F. Enke, 1862.

xii, 194 p., 1 l. 22ᶜᵐ.

A somewhat distorted explanation of issues involved in the Trent Affair; designed for the German public.

Marshall, Carl Richter, 1928–

Der amerikanische Bürgerkrieg, von Österreich ausgesehen. Wien, 1956.

Microfilm copy (negative) of typescript.
Collation of the original; 1 v. (various pagings)

A thorough treatment of Austrian public opinion on the American War.

Martin, *Sir* **Theodore,** 1816–1909.

The life of His Royal Highness the Prince consort, by Theodore Martin ... London, Smith, Elder, & co., 1875–80.

5 v. 2 pl., 10 port. (incl. fronts.) facsim. 22½ᶜᵐ.

Except for the famous selection on the Trent Affair in Vol. V, this work lacks material pertinent to the Civil War.

Marx, Karl, 1818–1883.

The Civil war in the United States, by Karl Marx and Frederick Engels. New York, International publishers [*1937]

xxv, 325 p. 22 cm.

A compendium of newspaper articles and correspondence, in which the authors of the Communist Manifesto interpret the American Civil War as essentially a struggle between free and slave labor systems.

Mason, Virginia, 1833–1920, *comp. and ed.*

The public life and diplomatic correspondence of James M. Mason, with some personal history by Virginia Mason (his daughter). 2d thousand. New York and Washington, The Neale publishing company, 1906.

ix, 603 p. incl. front. (port.) 24ᶜᵐ.

Most of the wartime dispatches of the Confederate envoy to Great Britain are printed here, with little attempt at explanation.

Massie, James William, 1799–1869.

America: the origin of her present conflict, her prospect for the slave, and her claim for anti-slavery sympathy; illustrated by incidents of travel during a tour in the summer of 1863, throughout the United States, from the eastern boundaries of Maine to the Mississippi. London, J. Snow, 1864.

(American culture series, 135:5)

Microfilm copy (positive) made in 1960 by University Microfilms, Ann Arbor, Mich.
Collation of the original: viii, 472 p. fold. map.

An assertion that slavery caused the Civil War, which can end only with its extinction.

Maxse, Frederick Augustus, 1833–1900.
Pro patriâ: being a letter addressed by Captain Maxse, R. N., to the "Morning post" upon the subject of our American attitude ... London, Chapman and Hall, 1863.

8 p. 20½ᶜᵐ.

England will serve its own interest, Maxse writes, by recognising the Confederacy and thus striking a fatal blow against the evil of democracy.

Maxwell, *Sir* Herbert Eustace, *bart.*, 1845–1937.
The life and letters of George William Frederick, fourth earl of Clarendon, K. G., G. C. B. By the Right Hon. Sir Herbert Maxwell ... London, E. Arnold, 1913.

2 v. fronts., pl., ports. 23ᶜᵐ.

Correspondence of a Tory foreign affairs expert printed in Vol. II illuminates the British cabinet's policy toward the war.

Meade, Robert Douthat, 1903–
Judah P. Benjamin, Confederate statesman ₍by₎ Robert Douthat Meade. New York, London ₍etc.₎ Oxford university press, 1943.

ix p., 2 l., 432 p. front., ports. 22 cm.

The best biography of the Confederate Secretary of State.

Meier, Heinz K   1929–
The United States and Switzerland in the nineteenth century. The Hague, Mouton, 1963.

208 p. 25 cm.

A 20-page chapter on U. S.-Swiss relations during the Civil War contains the most thorough and reliable survey of the subject.

Merson, Ernest, 1819–
La guerre d'Amérique et la médiation, par M. Ernest Merson. Paris, Dentu, 1862.

111 p. 24½ᶜᵐ.

A declaration that mediation in the Civil War to assure Southern independence was not only a right but a duty of France.

Miall, Charles S.
The proposed slave empire: its antecedents, constitution, and policy ... By Charles S. Miall. London, E. Stock, 1863.

32 p. 21½ᶜᵐ.

Contains cogent anti-slavery arguments.

Mill, John Stuart, 1806–1873.
The contest in America, by John Stuart Mill ... 2d ed. Boston, Little, Brown and company, 1862.

32 p. 20ᶜᵐ.

Mill argued that the Civil War was a contest between ideas of freedom and slavery, and that British intervention for the sake of cotton would be to "make Satan victorious."

Mixed commission on British and American claims under article XII of the Treaty of Washington, 1871.
British and American claims. ₍British claims₎ no. 1 ₍to 478₎ Memorials, demurrers, briefs, and decisions. ₍Washington, 1873₎

34 v. maps, tables. 22ᶜᵐ.

Ponderous compendia of diplomatic documents, testimony, and other official information bearing on the American Alabama claims and the British counter claims presented at the Geneva arbitration; a basic source.

Monaghan, James, 1891–
Diplomat in carpet slippers: Abraham Lincoln deals with foreign affairs ₍by₎ Jay Monaghan. ₍Indianapolis₎ Charter Books; ₍distributed by the Macfadden-Bartell Corp., New York, 1962₎

505 p. 21 cm.

Puffery, undocumented references, suppositions and insinuations try to show that Lincoln's hand firmly guided American foreign policy during the Civil War.

Montagu, *Lord* Robert, 1825–1902.
A mirror in America. By Lord Robert Montagu ... London, Saunders, Otley, & co., 1861.

108 p. 21½ᶜᵐ.

An intemperate attack on the North as a threat to England's long-term selfish interests.

Montague, Ludwell Lee, 1907–

Haiti and the United States, 1714–1938, by Ludwell Lee Montague ... with a foreword by J. Fred Rippy ... Durham, N. C., Duke university press, 1940.

xiv, 308 p. illus. (maps) 23½ᶜᵐ.

One of several acceptable surveys.

Moore, John Bassett, 1860–1947.

A digest of international law as embodied in diplomatic discussions, treaties and other international agreements, international awards, the decisions of municipal courts, and the writings of jurists ... By John Bassett Moore ... Washington, Govt. print. off., 1906.

8 v. 24 cm.

Provides detailed coverage to many disputes of international law arising between the U. S. and England during the Civil War.

Moran, Benjamin, 1820–1886.

The journal of Benjamin Moran, 1857–1865; edited by Sarah Agnes Wallace & Frances Elma Gillespie. Chicago, University of Chicago Press ₍1949, v. 1, ᶜ1948₎

2 v. (1488 p.) ports. 24 cm.

Expertly edited, gossipy, vitriolic, private diary of a secretary in the American legation in London.

Moreau, Henry, 1826–

... Plaidoirie de mᵉ Henry Moreau pour les États-Unis d'Amérique, appelants, contre m. Battarel, syndic de la faillite L. Arman, intimé. Audience des 11 et 12 juillet 1871. Paris, Typ. de Renou et Maulde, 1871.

78 p. 27 x 21ᶜᵐ.

Presents arguments and supporting documents accompanying U. S. claims for damages against French suppliers of arms to the Confederacy.

Morley, John Morley, *viscount,* 1838–1923.

The life of Richard Cobden, by John Morley ... London, Macmillan and co., limited, 1908.

2 v. 18½ cm.

Extracts from Cobden's correspondence faintly indicate his efforts to sway the U. S. to free trade and emancipation during the Civil War.

Morley, John Morley, *viscount,* 1838–1923.

The life of William Ewart Gladstone, by John Morley. New ed. in one volume ... New York, The Macmillan company, 1932.

3 v. in 1. front., 1 illus., pl., ports. 22ᶜᵐ.

Disappointingly slight coverage of the Chancellor of the Exchequer's part in rushing the British cabinet toward intervention in favor of the Confederacy.

Morse, Samuel Finley Breese 1791–1872.

The present attempt to dissolve the American union, a British aristocratic plot. By B. New York, Printed for the author, 1862.

42 p. 22½ cm.

Evidence that the author was a better artist and inventor than he was a convincing pamphleteer.

Motley, John Lothrop, 1814–1877.

The causes of the American civil war. By John Lathrop ₍!₎ Motley ... New York, D. Appleton & company, 1861.

24 p. 23ᶜᵐ.

Argues the constitutional case against Southern secession in an unsuccessful attempt to influence opinion.

Motley, John Lothrop, 1814–1877.

The correspondence of John Lothrop Motley ... ed. by George William Curtis ... New York, Harper & brothers, 1889.

2 v. front. (port.) 26½ cm.

A valuable compilation of the personal correspondence of the American minister at Vienna.

Motley, John Lothrop, 1814–1877.

John Lothrop Motley and his family; further letters and records, ed. by his daughter and Herbert St. John Mildmay ... London, John Lane; New York, John Lane company, 1910.

xi, 321 p. front., plates, ports. 22ᶜᵐ.

Supplements Curtis's edition of Motley's correspondence.

Mowat, Robert Balmain, 1883–
  The diplomatic relations of Great Britain and the United States, by R. B. Mowat ... London, E. Arnold & co., 1925.
    xi, 350 p. 23ᶜᵐ.

The account of the Civil War period, based on secondary sources, has been superseded by the works of H. C. Allen and others.

Müller, George, 1918–
  Der amerikanische sezessionskrieg in der schweizerischen öffentlichen meinung ... von George Müller. Basel, Helbing & Lichtenhahn, 1944.
    216 p. 24ᶜᵐ.

Contains good work on Swiss public opinion about the Civil War, but uses no U.S. sources to show causes and effects.

Musson, Eugène
  Lettre à Napoléon III sur l'esclavage aux états du Sud, par un créole de la Louisiane. Paris, Dentu, 1862.
    vii, 160 p. 24ᶜᵐ.

An apologia for slavery.

Nemo, *pseud.*
  Remarks on the policy of recognizing the independence of the southern states of North America, and on the struggle in that continent. By Nemo. London, E. Wilson, 1863.
    31 p. 21ᶜᵐ.

A brief contribution to the great mass of literature in England favoring recognition of the Southern Confederacy.

Newman, Francis William, 1805–1897.
  Character of the southern states of America. Letter to a friend who had joined the Southern independence association, by F. W. Newman ... Manchester [Eng.] Union and emancipation society's depôt, 1863.
    14 p. 21ᶜᵐ.

Compares Southern slaveholders with thugs, cannibals, and buccaneers.

Newton, Thomas Wodehouse Legh, *2d baron,* 1857–1942.
  Lord Lyons; a record of British diplomacy, by Lord Newton ... New York, Longmans, Green, and co.; [etc., etc.] 1913.
    2 v. fronts., pl., ports. 22½ cm.

An informative collection of the private and official papers of the British Minister at Washington during the war.

Noel, Baptist Wriothesley, 1798–1873.
  Freedom and slavery in the United States of America. By Baptist Wriothesley Noel ... London, J. Nisbet & co., 1863.
    vi, 242 p. 18½ cm.

An attack on slavery in the South.

Noel, Baptist Wriothesley, 1798–1873.
  The rebellion in America. By Baptist Wriothesley Noel ... London, J. Nisbet and co., 1863.
    xviii p., 1 l., 494 p. 20ᶜᵐ.

A lengthy, poorly written, overly dramatized argument for English intervention to end the Civil War.

Notes on American affairs. By E. L. London, Houlston & Wright, 1863.
    30 p. 18ᶜᵐ.

Supports the Confederacy with one-sided argumentation.

Nouette-Delorme, Émile.
  Les États-Unis et l'Europe; rupture de l'union, reconnaissance du Sud, abolition de l'esclavage, par Émile Nouette-Delorme. Paris, E. Dentu, 1863.
    30 p. 25ᶜᵐ.

Briefly surveys some of issues of Franco-American relations midway during the Civil War.

O'Brien, Joseph J
 Lincoln's secret ally, a brief history of Russia's aid in civil war, by Joseph J. O'Brien.   New York city, ᶜ1944.
   cover-title, ₍A₎–B, 12 numb. l., 1 l.   4 pl. (incl. port., music)   29 x 23½ᶜᵐ.

A useless hodgepodge of facts, out of context, with legends about Russo-American relations during the war.

Ollivier, Émile, 1825–1913.
 … L'empire libéral; études, récits, souvenirs …   Paris, Garnier frères, 1895–₍1918₎
   18 v.   front. (port., v. 6)   maps (part fold.)   18½ᶜᵐ.

Voluminous memoirs contain a French reformer's recollections of his friendship with Americans and his sympathy for the Union.

Onesimus Secundus, *pseud.*
 The true interpretation of the American civil war, and of England's cotton difficulty; or, Slavery, from a different point of view, shewing the relative responsibilities of America and Great Britain.   By Onesimus Secundus.   London, Trübner & co., 1863.
   iv, ₍5₎–47 p.   20½ᶜᵐ.

From the perspective of literal interpretation of scriptures, the author evaluates the emancipation act as a gigantic error.

Osterweis, Rollin, 1907–
 Judah P. Benjamin, statesman of the lost cause, by Rollin Osterweis; foreword by Horace D. Taft …   New York, London, G. P. Putnam's sons, 1933.
   3 p. l., v–xi, ₍1₎ p., 3 l., 19–205 p.   front., plates, ports., facsim.   21ᶜᵐ.

A flamboyant, undocumented biography.

O'Sullivan, John Louis, 1813–1895.
 Peace the sole chance now left for reunion. A letter to Professor S. F. B. Morse … from John L. O'Sullivan …   London, Printed by William Brown & co., 1863.
   25 p.   21ᶜᵐ.

A former U.S. diplomat preaches secession doctrines.

Owls-glass, *pseud.*
 Rebel brag and British bluster; a record of unfulfilled prophecies, baffled schemes, and disappointed hopes …   By Owls-glass.   New York, The American news company ₍ᶜ1865₎
   1 p. l., ₍v₎–vi, ₍7₎–111 p.   19½ᶜᵐ.

A jingoistic exercise in British-baiting, padded out to excessive length with extracts from English and Confederate periodicals.

Owsley, Frank Lawrence, 1890–1956.
 King Cotton diplomacy; foreign relations of the Confederate States of America. 2d ed., rev. by Harriet Chappell Owsley.   ₍Chicago₎ University of Chicago Press ₍1959₎
   xxiii, 614 p.   tables.   23 cm.

A massive study of Confederate diplomacy; the author's careful scholarship and thoroughness far overshadow his pronounced Southern bias.

Palmerston, Henry John Temple, *3d viscount.* 1784–1865.
 … Gladstone and Palmerston; being the correspondence of Lord Palmerston with Mr. Gladstone, 1851–1865, edited with an introduction and commentary by Philip Guedella.   ₍London₎ V. Gollancz ltd., 1928.
   367 p.   front., plates, ports., facsims.   24 cm.

Includes verbatim copies of cabinet memoranda and correspondence treating of such critical topics as the 1862 intervention crisis.

Papers relating to the condemnation of the British barque "Springbok" and her cargo, by the District prize court of New York, U. S.; with the opinions of the press thereon …   London, Printed for the owners, 1864.
   2 p. l., ₍3₎–112 p.   21ᶜᵐ.

An appeal to British public opinion against the condemnation of an English blockade runner by an American prize court.

Parker, Joel, 1795–1875.
 The domestic and foreign relations of the United States.   By Joel Parker.   Cambridge ₍Mass.₎ Welch, Bigelow, and company, 1862.
   74 p.   23½ᶜᵐ.

A Harvard Law School professor discusses Anglo-American relations for the year 1861 from a pro-American perspective.

Parker, Joel, 1795–1875.
  International law. Case of the Trent. Capture and surrender of Mason and Slidell. By Joel Parker. Cambridge [Mass.] Welch, Bigelow, and company, 1862.

  66 p. 23½ᶜᵐ.

Asserts that the Trent Affair should have been treated as primarily a political and not a legal question.

Pecquet du Bellet, Paul.
  The diplomacy of the Confederate Cabinet of Richmond and its agents abroad; being memorandum notes taken in Paris during the Rebellion of the Southern States from 1861 to 1865. Edited with an introd., by Wm. Stanley Hoole. Tuscaloosa, Ala., Confederate Pub. Co., 1963.

  130 p. 22 cm.

An undocumented expose of activities of Confederate agents and supporters in France, by a Southern propagandist residing in Paris.

Pemberton, William Baring, 1897–
  Lord Palmerston. London, Batchworth Press [1954]

  363 p. illus. 22 cm.

A weak, unoriginal treatment of the Prime Minister's part in forming British policy toward the "American question."

Perkins, Dexter, 1889–
  ... The Monroe doctrine, 1826–1867, by Dexter Perkins ... Baltimore, The Johns Hopkins press, 1933.

  xi, 580 p. 20ᶜᵐ.

The author shows less understanding of Seward's policies than of those of foreign governments.

Phillimore, John George 1808–1865.
  Case of the seizure of the southern envoys. Reprinted, with additions, from the "Saturday review" ... London, J. Ridgway, 1861.

  26 p. 24½ᶜᵐ.

A lawyer's brief ardently supporting the British government's demands in the Trent case.

Pierce, Edward Lillie, 1829–1897.
  Memoir and letters of Charles Sumner. By Edward L. Pierce ... Boston, Roberts brothers, 1877–93.

  4 v. fronts. (ports.) plan, facsims. 23 cm.

Correspondence printed herein only hints at the insidious role of the chairman of the Senate Foreign Relations Committee during the Civil War period.

Pike, James Shepherd, 1811–1882.
  First blows of the civil war; the ten years of preliminary conflict in the United States. From 1850 to 1860. A contemporaneous exposition. Progress of the struggle shown by public records and private correspondence. With letters, now first published ... By James S. Pike ... New York, The American news company [c1879]

  xlv, 526 p. 22½ᶜᵐ.

Written by Lincoln's minister at the Hague.

Pope, Samuel, 1826–
  The American war: secession and slavery; a lecture delivered at Tunstall, Staffordshire. Manchester [Eng.] Manchester Union and Emancipation Society [1863?]

  16 p. 17 cm.

A witty tract in behalf of the North.

Pratt, Julius William, 1888–
  A history of United States foreign policy. New York, Prentice-Hall, 1955.

  808 p. illus. 24 cm.

The brief section on Civil War diplomacy was drawn from a dozen or so secondary sources.

Putnam, George Palmer 1814–1872, *ed.*
  ... Letters from Europe touching the American contest, and acknowledging the receipt, from citizens of New York, of presentation sets of the "Rebellion record," and "Loyal publication society" publications. New York, Loyal publication society, 1864.

  27 p. 23½ᶜᵐ.

A collection of letters from European friends of the American Union, thanking the Society for sending publications and reaffirming support of the North.

Reed, William Bradford 1806–1876, *supposed author.*

The diplomatic year: being a review of Mr. Seward's foreign correspondence of 1862. By a northern man. Philadelphia, 1863.

68 p. 22½ᶜᵐ.

An effort to demolish the Secretary of State's reputation through an unjust and intemperate analysis of his published diplomatic correspondence.

Reed, William Bradford 1806–1876.

A review of Mʳ Seward's diplomacy. By a northern man ... ₁Philadelphia? 1862?₁

60 p. 22½ᶜᵐ.

An anonymous attack on the Secretary of State's diplomacy during 1861.

Reid, Hugo, 1809–1872.

The American question in a nut-shell; or, Why we should recognize the Confederates. By H. Reid ... London, R. Hardwicke, 1862.

31 p. 18½ᶜᵐ.

The kernel of this pro-Southern pamphlet is rotten.

Reid, Stuart Johnson, 1848–1927.

Lord John Russell, by Stuart J. Reid ... New York, Harper & brothers, 1895.

xvi, 380, ₁1₁ p. front. (port.) 19½ cm.

A short biography in which Victorian gentility impairs accuracy and thoroughness.

Reid, *Sir* **Wemyss,** 1842–1905.

Life of the Right Honourable William Edward Forster; by T. Wemyss Reid ... London, Chapman and Hall, limited, 1888.

2 v. fronts. (ports.) 2 pl. 23ᶜᵐ.

Badly written, with inadequate treatment of Forster's role as defender of the Union cause in Parliament; still the best available biography.

Remarks on Mr. Motley's letter in the London Times on the war in America. Charleston, Presses of Evans & Cogswell, 1861.

23 p. 22ᶜᵐ.

An old man ventures feebly to refute Motley's pro-Union analysis of the constitutional issues of secession.

Responsabilidades contraidas por el gobierno nacional de Mexico con los Estados-Unidos, en virtud de los contratos celebrados por sus agentes . 1864–1867. Mexico, Impr. del gobierno, 1867.

80, ₁16₁, 32 p. 8 fold. tab. 23ᶜᵐ.

Contains extracts from the official papers of the Mexican Minister to the U. S. during the Civil War.

The right of recognition. A sketch of the present policy of the Confederate States. By a recent tourist ... London, R. Hardwicke, 1862.

30 p. 21½ᶜᵐ.

Contrasts Southern "country gentlemen" with "Yankee rowdies" and urges official British recognition of the Confederacy.

Rimestad, Christian Vilhelm, 1816–1879.

... Zwei weltbegebenheiten. Deutsch von Henrik Helms. Leipzig, L. Wiedemann ₁1862₁

3 p. l., 280 p., 1 l. 16½ᶜᵐ.

Contains an unsympathetic discussion of the problems of democracy in America during the first year of the Civil War.

Rimskiĭ-Korsakov, Nikolaĭ Andreevich, 1844–1908.

My musical life; translated from the rev. 2d Russian ed. by Judah A. Joffe; edited with an introd. by Carl Van Vechten. New York, Tudor Pub. Co., 1935 ₁ᶜ1923₁

xxiv, 390 p. ports., music. 25 cm.

Includes the composer's reminiscences about his visit with the Russian fleet to war-torn America.

Rippy, James Fred, 1892–
The United States and Mexico, by J. Fred Rippy ... New York, A. A. Knopf, 1926.

xi, 401 p., 1 l. 2 maps (1 fold.) 22½ cm.

Still a good general survey, although some of the author's conclusions need adjustment to recent research.

Robbins, Edward Young.
The war in America; and what England, or the people of England, may do to restore peace. By E. Y. Robbins. Addressed to all philanthropists, and lovers of peace in England. New York, M. B. Brown & co., printers, 1863.

cover-title, 28 p. 21 cm.

No permanent peace in America can exist, states Robbins, until slavery is removed by total emancipation; an effective pro-Union tract.

Robertson, James Rood, 1864–1932.
A Kentuckian at the court of the tsars; the ministry of Cassius Marcellus Clay to Russia, 1861–1862 and 1863–1869 [by] James Rood Robertson. Berea College, Ky., The Berea college press [c1935]

286 p. plates, ports. 23½ cm.

The most authoritative treatment of Clay's mission available, but better on personality than on policy.

Robertson, William, *of Rochdale.*
Life and times of the Right Hon. John Bright; by William Robertson ... New York [etc.] Cassell & company, limited [c1889]

1 p. l., [vii]–viii, 604 p. front. (port.) 21 cm.

Contains nothing important to American Civil War diplomacy not more fully covered in Bright's own published speeches.

Robertson, William Spence, 1872–
Hispanic-American relations with the United States, by William Spence Robertson ... ed. by David Kinley ... New York, London [etc.] Oxford university press, 1923.

xii, 470 p. illus. (maps) 25½ cm.

A readable survey by one of the foremost authorities on the subject.

Robinton, Madeline (Russell) 1909–
An introduction to the papers of the New York prize court, 1861–1865, by Madeline Russell Robinton ... New York, 1945.

2 p. l., 7–203 p., 1 l. 22½ cm.

A valuable aid in treating Anglo-American differences over the blockade.

Roebuck, John Arthur, 1801–1879.
Life and letters of John Arthur Roebuck ... with chapters of autobiography; ed. by Robert Eadon Leader. London & New York, E. Arnold, 1897.

viii, 392 p. 2 port. (incl. front.) 22½ cm.

Sparse coverage of Roebuck's role as a champion of the Southern cause in the English parliament.

Russell, Addison Peale, 1826–1912.
Thomas Corwin, a sketch by A. P. Russell ... Cincinnati, R. Clarke & co., 1882.

128 p. front. (port.) 18½ cm.

A laudatory biography weak on Corwin's mission to Mexico.

Russell, John Russell, *1st earl,* 1792–1878.
Selections from speeches of Earl Russell 1817 to 1841, and from despatches, 1859 to 1865. With introductions ... London, Longmans, Green and co., 1870.

2 v. 23 cm.

In Vol. II Russell contributes a lengthy explanation of his policy in regard to the Alabama case.

Russell, John Russell, *1st earl,* 1792–1878.
Recollections and suggestions 1813–1873, by John earl Russell ... Boston, Roberts brothers, 1875.

vi p., 1 l., 392 p. 21 cm.

Contains Russell's own retrospective statement on British foreign policy toward the war, but badly written and not wholly reliable.

Russell, John Russell, *1st earl,* 1792–1878.
   The later correspondence of Lord John Russell, 1840–1878; edited by G. P. Gooch ... London, New York [etc.] Longmans, Green and co., 1925.

   2 v. fronts. (ports.) 22½ᶜᵐ.

This admirable edition contains some of the British foreign minister's writings about the Civil War, but much more remains unprinted in the Russell MSS.

Sargent, Fitzwilliam, 1820–
   England, the United States, and the southern confederacy. By F. W. Sargent ... 2d ed. rev. and amended ... London, Hamilton, Adams, and co., 1864.

   viii, 184 p. 21½ᶜᵐ.

An ardent appeal to the English to support the North in achieving slavery's abolition.

Savage, Carlton, 1897–
   Policy of the United States toward maritime commerce in war. Washington, U. S. Govt. Print. Off., 1934–36.

   2 v. 24 cm.

A collection of documents, with expert commentary included; many apply to vital issues of maritime law arising during the war period.

Schmidt, Louis Bernard, 1879–   *ed.*
   Readings in the economic history of American agriculture, edited by Louis Bernard Schmidt ... and Earle Dudley Ross ... New York, The Macmillan company, 1925.

   xii p., 1 l., 591 p. 22½ cm.

Contains Schmidt's classic article on "The Influence of Wheat and Cotton on Anglo-American Relations During the Civil War," which represents Northern wheat as a greater economic force in the world than Southern cotton.

Schurz, Carl, 1829–1906.
   The reminiscences of Carl Schurz ... illustrated with portraits and original drawings. New York, The McClure company, 1907–08.

   3 v. fronts., plates, ports., maps. 23½ cm.

Recollections of Civil War diplomacy by a brilliant, fascinating U.S. minister at Madrid, 1861-1862.

Schurz, Carl, 1829–1906.
   Speeches, correspondence and political papers of Carl Schurz; selected and ed. by Frederic Bancroft on behalf of the Carl Schurz memorial committee ... New York [etc.] G. P. Putnam's sons, 1913.

   6 v. front. (port.) 23½ cm.

Helpful for American diplomacy in Spain and Germany.

Schwab, John Christopher, 1865–1916.
   The Confederate States of America, 1861–1865; a financial and industrial history of the South during the civil war, by John Christopher Schwab ... New York, C. Scribner's sons, 1901.

   xi, 332 p. fold. tab. 23 cm.

Includes well-documented, scholarly treatment of Confederate foreign loan program, tariff policy, and financial aspects of blockade.

Sears, Louis Martin, 1885–
   John Slidell, by Louis Martin Sears ... Durham, N. C., Duke university press, 1925.

   4 p. l., 252 p. front. (port.) 20 cm.

Offers a scanty summary, not thoroughly researched, of Slidell's mission to France.

The **seizure** of the "Peterhoff"; being a statement of the facts, the reason, the law and the consequences. With the correspondence. London, E. Wilson, 1863.

   32 p. 20ᶜᵐ.

This work adds little to a mature understanding of the complicated international law involved in this U. S. maritime seizure of British mails.

Selborne, Roundell Palmer, *1st earl of,* 1812–1895.
   Memorials ... by Roundell Palmer, earl of Selborne ... London, Macmillan and co., ltd.; New York, The Macmillan co., 1896–98.

   2 v. in 4. 4 pl., 11 port. (incl. fronts.) 23ᶜᵐ.

Over 100 pages in Vol. II treat informally and pridefully of the Solicitor-General's part in maintaining British neutrality during the Civil War.

Seward, Frederick William, 1830–1915.

Reminiscences of a war-time statesman and diplomat, 1830–1915, by Frederick W. Seward, assistant secretary of state during the administrations of Lincoln, Johnson, and Hayes ... New York and London, G. P. Putnam's sons, 1916.

x p.; 2 l., 489 p.   front., plates, ports.   23½ cm.

The assistant secretary discusses in sketchy, episodic fashion the State Department's role in the Civil War.

Seward, William Henry, 1801–1872.

The diplomatic history of the war for the union, being the 5th volume of the Works of William H. Seward. Ed. by George E. Baker.

(*In his* Works. Boston, New York, 1853–84.   24½ cm.   v. 5)

Lacking private correspondence and containing few official dispatches not previously printed by the State Department, this volume adds little to official sources.

Seward, William Henry, 1801–1872.

William H. Seward; an autobiography from 1801 to 1834. With a memoir of his life, and selections from his letters ... By Frederick W. Seward. ₍New ed.₎ New York, Derby and Miller, 1891.

3 v.   fronts., plates, ports., fold. map.   24ᶜᵐ.

This careful selection of extracts from letters (many of which have since disappeared) forms a defense of the Secretary's diplomatic record.

Shaffner, Taliaferro Preston, 1818–1881.

The war in America: being an historical and political account of the southern and northern states: showing the origin and cause of the present secession war. With a large map of the United States, engraved on steel. By Colonel Tal. P. Shaffner ... London, Hamilton, Adams, and co. ₍1862₎

vi, 418 p.   front. (fold. map)   18½ cm.

A mass of statistics and pro-Southern theories about the causes of the war; the Northern tariff, states Shaffner, was the chief villain.

Shaw, Frederick John 1863–

Anglo-American relations, 1861–1865, by Brougham Villiers ₍pseud.₎ and W. H. Chesson. London, T. F. Unwin, ltd. ₍1919₎

vii, 214 p., 1 l.   21½ cm.

Haphazard, sporadic, and largely undocumented essays on various Anglo-American wartime feelings.

Shippee, Lester Burrell, 1879–

Canadian-American relations, 1849–1874, by Lester Burrell Shippee ... New Haven, Yale university press; Toronto, The Ryerson press; ₍etc., etc.₎ for the Carnegie endowment for international peace: Division of economics and history, 1939.

xi p., 2 l., 514 p.   maps (1 fold.)   25ᶜᵐ.

Written from primary sources and good on such topics as the San Juan boundary disputes.

Sideman, Belle Becker, *ed.*

Europe looks at the Civil War, an anthology, edited by Belle Becker Sideman and Lillian Friedman. New York, Orion Press ₍1960₎

323 p.   24 cm.

Interesting anthology of European commentary on the Civil War that sheds little light on diplomatic policies.

Simmons, *Sir* **John Linton Arabin,** 1821–1903.

Defence of Canada considered as an imperial question with reference to a war with America. By J. L. A. Simmons ... London, Longman, Green, Longman, Roberts, & Green, 1865.

27 p.   21ᶜᵐ.

A British military expert outlines the handicaps England would face in war involving Canada and the United States.

Simpson, Evan John, 1901–

Atlantic impact, 1861, by Evan John ₍pseud.₎ London, Heinemann ₍1952₎

296 p.   illus.   21 cm.

A short, dramatic, shallow account, lacking documentation and containing serious inaccuracies of the Trent Affair.

Sinclair, Peter.

... Freedom or slavery in the United States, being facts and testimonies for the consideration of the British people. By Peter Sinclair. 2d ed. London, J. Caudwell; ₍etc., etc.,₎ 1862₎

cover-title, 160 p.   21½ᶜᵐ.

Contains nonsensical arguments.

Skelton, Oscar Douglas, 1878–

The life and times of Sir Alexander Tilloch Galt, by Oscar Douglas Skelton. Toronto, Oxford university press, 1920.

4 p. l., 586 p. front., plates, ports., maps, facsim. 24½ᶜᵐ.

Biography of a Canadian statesman active in economic aspects of Canadian-American relations during the 1860's.

Smiley, David L 1921–

Lion of White Hall; the life of Cassius M. Clay. Madison, University of Wisconsin Press, 1962.

294 p. illus. 22 cm.

Well-researched and colorfully presented biography that does not go deeply into foreign policy problems of the Civil War period.

Smith, George Barnett, 1841–1909.

The life and speeches of the Right Honourable John Bright, M. P. By George Barnett Smith ... New York, A. C. Armstrong & son; ₍etc., etc.₎ 1881.

2 v. in 1. 2 port. (incl. front.) 22ᶜᵐ.

Mediocre biography with little on foreign relations and Bright's part therein.

Smith, Goldwin, 1823–1910.

The civil war in America: an address read at the last meeting of the Manchester Union and emancipation society. By Goldwin Smith. London, Simpkin, Marshall & co.; ₍etc., etc.₎ 1866.

1 p. l., 96 p. 19½ cm.

The North's victory was one for free Christianity, which Smith contrasted with religious despotism in Europe.

Smith, Goldwin, 1823–1910.

Does the Bible sanction American slavery? By Goldwin Smith. Cambridge, Sever and Francis, 1863.

107 p. 19 cm.

The answer, from an Oxford University abolitionist, is "No."

Smith, Goldwin, 1823–1910.

England and America. A lecture read before the Boston fraternity, and published in the Atlantic monthly for December, 1864. By Goldwin Smith. Boston, Ticknor and Fields, 1865.

56 p. 22½ᶜᵐ.

Advocating close friendship between the two countries, Smith discusses with perception many of the abrasive issues that have divided the two.

Smith, Goldwin, 1823–1910.

A letter to a Whig member of the Southern independence association. By Goldwin Smith. Boston, Ticknor and Fields, 1864.

64 p. 18ᶜᵐ.

A powerful, well-presented argument against British favoritism of the South.

Soulsby, Hugh Graham, 1904–

... The right of search and the slave trade in Anglo-American relations, 1814–1862, by Hugh G. Soulsby, PH. D. Baltimore, The Johns Hopkins press, 1933.

185 p. 24½ cm.

Adds little to previous work by Mathieson and Milne on the Civil War period.

The southern bazaar, held in St. George's hall, Liverpool, October, 1864. Report of proceedings. London, R. Bentley; Liverpool, Webb and Hunt ₍1864₎

51 p. 20 cm.

Confederate propaganda that hardly hides the desperation of Southerners in England late in 1864.

Spence, James, *b.* 1816.

The American union; its effect on national character and policy, with an inquiry into secession as a constitutional right, and the causes of the disruption. By James Spence. 2d ed. London, R. Bentley, 1862.

xvi, 366 p., 1 l. 23ᶜᵐ.

Very popular English pro-Southern argument of superficial plausability but full of distortions and untruths.

Spence, James, *b.* 1816.

On the recognition of the Southern confederation. By James Spence ... London, R. Bentley, 1862.

48 p.   21 cm.

A warped and weak presentation in which Spence called for European recognition of the Confederacy so that England might obtain cotton.

Spence, James, 1816–

Southern independence: an address delivered at a public meeting, in the city hall, Glasgow, by James Spence, 26th November, 1863. London, R. Bentley; [etc., etc.] 1863.

39 p.   20½ cm.

A facile entreaty for British intervention in behalf of the South by one of the Confederacy's most able English advocates.

Stark, Francis Raymond, 1877–

The abolition of privateering and the declaration of Paris ... New York, 1897.

165 p.   23½ cm.

A summary good only for introductory purposes; research very shallow.

Stephen, *Sir* **Leslie,** 1832–1904.

The "Times" on the American war: a historical study. By L. S. London, W. Ridgway, 1865.

107 p.   21 cm.

A master of stiletto-style literacy criticism surveys the venerable London Times' treatment of the American Civil War and leaves that newspaper's reputation bleeding.

Stevenson, Elizabeth, 1919–

Henry Adams, a biography. New York, Macmillan, 1955.

xiv, 425 p.   illus., ports.   22 cm.

Contains a short, clear, sensitive account, based on printed sources, of Henry Adams's tenure in London as son and private secretary to the U. S. minister.

Stock, John, 1817–1884.

The duties of British Christians in relation to the struggle in America; being the substance of a discourse delivered in Morice square Baptist chapel, Devonport ... 7th June, 1863, by the Rev. John Stock ... London, E. Stock; [etc., etc., 1863]

28 p.   17½ cm.

A shallow sermon, favoring the North, and encumbered with religious mummery.

Stratheden, William Frederick Campbell, *2d baron,* 1824–1893.

Speech of Lord Campbell in the House of lords, on the right of the neutral powers to acknowledge the southern confederacy, March 23rd, 1863. London, J. Ridgway, 1863.

28 p.   20½ cm.

Advocates that Great Britain join France in recognizing the independence of the Confederacy.

Sturtevant, Julian Monson, 1805–1886.

English institutions and the American rebellion. Extracts from a lecture delivered at Chicago, April 28, 1864, by J. M. Sturtevant ... Manchester, A. Ireland & co., 1864.

32 p.   21½ cm.

Prevented from giving public addresses in England on the Civil War, Sturtevant asserts that English liberties will be dependent on American freedom.

Sturtevant, Julian Monson, 1805–1886.

Three months in Great Britain. A lecture on the present attitude of England towards the United States, as determined by personal observation. By J. M. Sturtevant ... Chicago, J. A. Norton, 1864.

1 p. l., 43 p.   20½ cm.

An able, contemporary summary of the changing state of English opinion towards the U. S. midway through the Civil War.

Sumner, Charles, 1811–1874.

Our foreign relations: showing present perils from England and France; the nature and conditions of intervention by mediation; and also by recognition; the impossibility of any recognition of a new power with slavery as a corner-stone; and the wrongful concession of ocean belligerency. Speech of Hon. Charles Sumner, before the citizens of New York, at the Cooper institute, Sept. 10, 1863 ... New York, Young men's Republican union, 1863.

80 p.   23½ cm.

The Massachusetts abolitionist senator castigates England at great length for allegedly aiding the Southern rebellion.

Sumner, Charles, 1811–1874.

Les relations extérieures des États-Unis par Charles Sumner ... Préface et traduction par A. Malespine. Paris, E. Dentu, 1863.

31 p. 24½ cm.

Friends of the North in Paris published Sumner's celebrated speech protesting British and French favoritism toward the South.

Tansill, Charles Callan, 1890–

... The United States and Santo Domingo, 1798–1873; a chapter in Caribbean diplomacy, by Charles Callan Tansill ... Baltimore, The Johns Hopkins press, 1938.

viii p., 1 l., 487 p. 23½ cm.

The section on the Civil War lacks both breadth and understanding.

Taylor, William, 1821–1902.

Cause and probable results of the civil war in America. Facts for the people of Great Britain. By William Taylor ... London, Simpkin, Marshall & co. [etc.] 1862.

30 p., 1 l. 22 cm.

Suggests that the Civil War is God's chastisement of the American people for their sins and his means of ending slavery.

Temperley, Harold William Vazeille, 1879–1939, ed.

Foundations of British foreign policy from Pitt (1792) to Salisbury (1902); or, Documents, old and new, selected and edited, with historical introductions, by Harold Temperley ... and Lillian M. Penson ... Cambridge [Eng.] The University press, 1938.

xxx, 573 p. 24½ cm.

Very brief extracts from papers of British cabinet members illuminate several dark corners of British policy toward the American Civil War.

Tennant, Charles 1796–1873.

The American question, and how to settle it ... London, S. Low, son, and co., 1863.

2 p. l., 313 p. 19½ cm.

Tennant advocated that France and England intervene in the Civil War and force a permanent division of the Union.

Thomas, Benjamin Platt, 1902–

... Russo-American relations, 1815–1867, by Benjamin Platt Thomas ... Baltimore, The Johns Hopkins press, 1930.

185 p. 24½ cm.

A short chapter surveying the Civil War period adds nothing (except by way of summary) to familiar published material.

Thompson, Samuel Bernard.

Confederate purchasing operations abroad, by Samuel Bernard Thompson. Chapel Hill, The University of North Carolina press, 1935.

ix, 137 p. 24 cm.

Based on American sources only, this monograph provides a solid introduction to a topic that still lacks definitive treatment.

Thornton, Willis.

The nine lives of Citizen Train. New York, Greenberg [1948]

xii, 327 p. illus., ports. 21 cm.

A neglected biography of a colorful figure, active in behalf of the North in England during the Civil War.

Thouvenel, Louis, 1853–   ed.

Le secret de l'empereur; correspondance confidentielle et inédite échangée entre M. Thouvenel, le duc de Gramont et le général comte de Flahault, 1860–1863, publiée avec notes et index biographique par L. Thouvenel ... Paris, Calmann Lévy, 1889.

2 v. 23 cm.

Correspondence between French diplomats on the Trent and Mexican affairs; gives only a hint of French foreign policy during the war years.

The Times, *London.*

The history of the Times. London, 1935–52.

4 v. in 5. illus. (part fold., part mounted) ports. (part mounted col.) facsims. (part fold.) 26 cm.

A questionable premise offered here is that during the Civil War the London Times exerted great influence in favor of British neutrality and peace with the United States.

Train, George Francis, 1829–1904.
    The downfall of England. By George Francis Train. And a sermon on the civil war in America. Delivered August 17, 1862, by Archbishop Hughes, on his return to America from Europe. Complete and unabridged. Philadelphia, T. B. Peterson & brothers, 1862.

    1 p. l., 19–30 p. 24^{cm}.

A self-made Yankee exhibits both his jingoism and his ignorance.

Train, George Francis, 1829–1904.
    Geo. Francis Train, unionist, on T. Colley Grattan, secessionist. Boston, Lee & Shepard, 1862.

    48 p. 23^{cm}.

A diatribe much after the fashion of Train's many speeches to English working people in favor of the Northern cause.

Train, George Francis, 1829–1904.
    Geo. Francis Train's great speech on the withdrawal of McClellan and the impeachment of Lincoln ... New York, American news co., 1864.

    32 p. 23^{cm}.

Another example of why the author was a popular pro-Union speaker among England's lowest classes, but was detected by most educated Englishmen.

Train, George Francis, 1829–1904.
    My life in many States and in foreign lands, dictated in my seventy-fourth year. London, Heinemann, 1902.

    xxi, 348 p. illus., ports. 20 cm.

Includes a self-important account of author's pro-Northern agitation in England.

Train, George Francis, 1829–1904.
    Train's Union speeches. "Second series." Delivered in England during the present American war. By George Francis Train ... Philadelphia, T. B. Peterson & brothers; London, J. A. Knight, 1862.

    1 p. l., [19]–90 p. 24½^{cm}.

A collection of flamboyant harangues by a master at stirring up public opinion, though less apt at directing it.

Treat, Payson Jackson, 1879–
    ... The early diplomatic relations between the United States and Japan, 1853–1865, by Payson Jackson Treat ... Baltimore, The Johns Hopkins press, 1917.

    ix, 459 p. 20 cm.

About one-half of this book provides a thorough treatment of the Civil War period; well-grounded in source materials.

Treat, Payson Jackson, 1879–
    Japan and the United States, 1853–1921, by Payson J. Treat. Boston and New York, Houghton Mifflin company, 1921.

    4 p. l., 282, [2] p. 21½ cm.

This undocumented work is less useful than Treat's volume of a decade earlier.

Tyrner-Tyrnauer, A   R   1897–
    Lincoln and the emperors. [1st ed.] New York, Harcourt, Brace & World [1962]

    176 p. illus. 21 cm.

Based on data in the Austrian archives and secondary sources; an attempt to place the Civil War in a world perspective.

U. S. *Dept. of state.*
    Correspondence concerning claims against Great Britain, transmitted to the Senate of the United States in answer to the resolutions of December 4 and 10, 1867, and of May 27, 1868 ... Washington, Govt. print. off., 1869–71.
    7 v. fold. tab. (v. 7) 23½^{cm}.

The most voluminous compilation of official papers on Anglo-American diplomatic relations for the Civil War period, published at the time of the Johnson-Clarendon convention dealing with the Alabama claims.

U. S. *Dept. of state.*
    Correspondence relative to the case of Messrs. Mason and Slidell. [n. p., 1861?]

    cover-title, 15 p. 22½ cm.

Reproduces only a small portion of the pertinent diplomatic correspondence, which has all been reprinted many times since.

U. S. *Dept. of State.*
Foreign relations of the United States. Diplomatic papers. ₁1861₎–
Washington, U. S. Govt. Print. Off.
v. fold. maps. 24 cm. annual.

Non-confidential dispatches that passed between the State Department and U. S. ministers abroad during the war.

U. S. *Dept. of state.*
... Foreign service list ...

Washington, U. S. Govt. print. off. ₁18 ₎–19
v. 21½–34 cm.

A handy guide covering the Civil War period.

U. S. *Dept. of state.*
... Insurgent privateers in foreign ports. Message from the President of the United States in answer to a resolution of the House of the 24th of February ... ₁Washington, 1862₎
211 p. 24½ cm. (37th Cong., 2d sess. House. Ex. doc. no. 104)

Some 200 pages of documents pertain to European reception of Confederate shipping in the war's first days.

U. S. *Dept. of state.*
... The present condition of Mexico. Message from the President of the United States in answer to resolution of the House of the 3d of March last, transmitting report from the Department of state regarding the present condition of Mexico. ₁With accompanying documents₎ ₁Washington, 1862₎
434 p. 23 cm. (U. S. 37th Cong., 2d sess. House. Ex. doc. no. 100)

Contains over 400 pages of documents relating to U. S.-Mexican relations during 1861 and to the European intervention in Mexico of that year.

U. S. *Supreme court.*
United States reports ... Cases adjudged in the Supreme court ..: v. ₁1₎–   ₁Sept. 1754₎–
Washington ₁etc.₎ 1798–19
v. 23 cm.

Gives an excellent coverage of Civil War prize cases before the U. S. Supreme Court, including those relating to the Bermuda, the Springbok, and the Peterhoff.

Urquhart, David, 1805–1877.
Analysis of M. Thouvenel's despatch. By David Urquhart, esq. (From the Free press of Jan. 1, 1862.) ₁London, "Free press office," 1862₎
6 p. 32ᶜᵐ.

Tries to prove that the French foreign minister's protest relative to the Trent Affair was incoherent, nonsensical, and inaccurate.

Urquhart, David, 1805–1877.
Answer to Mr. Cobden on the assimilation of war and peace. Also analysis of the correspondence with the United States, showing the Declaration of Paris to have been violated by England and France. By David Urquhart ... London, Hardwicke, 1862.
64 p. 20½ᶜᵐ.

A disorganized but thorough analysis of printed materials bearing on Declaration of Paris negotiation; later writers have added little.

Urquhart, David, 1805–1877.
The right of search: two speeches by David Urquhart. (January 20 and 27, 1862.) Showing: In what it consists. How the British empire exists by it. That it has been surrendered up. With an introduction on Lord Derby's part therein ... London, Hardwicke, 1862.
113 p. 22ᶜᵐ.

Anti-British government diatribe asserting that the historic right of search has been given up under pressure from the Lincoln administration.

Van Alstyne, Richard Warner, 1900–
American diplomacy in action, a series of case studies ₁by₎ Richard W. Van Alstyne ... Foreword by Graham H. Stuart. Stanford University, Calif., Stanford university press; London, H. Milford, Oxford university ₁1944₎
xvi, 760 p. maps (1 fold.) 23½ cm.

Treatment of Civil War diplomacy is superficial, sparse, and perpetuates legends.

Vandiver, Frank Everson, 1925–   *ed.*
Confederate blockade running through Bermuda, 1861–1865: letters and cargo manifests. Austin, Univ. of Texas Press, 1947.
xliv, 155 p. front. 24 cm.

Essential for any study of the routing of English supplies for the Confederacy.

Victor, Orville James 1827–1910.

The American rebellion. Some facts and reflections for the consideration of the English people ... By an American citizen. London, Beadle and company [°1861]

48 p. 18°ᵐ.

Pro-Union pamphlet of mediocre quality.

Victoria, *queen of Great Britain,* 1819–1901.

The letters of Queen Victoria, a selection from Her Majesty's correspondence between the years 1837 and 1861, published by authority of His Majesty the king; ed. by Arthur Christopher Benson, M. A. and Viscount Esher ... New York, Longmans, Green, and co., 1907.

3 v. 40 port. (incl. fronts.) 4 fold. geneal. tab. 23½ cm.

From the handful of communications touching on the American Civil War printed here, it is difficult to assess the Queen's role in relation to it.

Victoria, *queen of Great Britain,* 1819–1901.

The letters of Queen Victoria. Second series. A selection from Her Majesty's correspondence and journal between the years 1862 and 1878, published by authority of His Majesty the king. edited by George Earle Buckle ... London, J. Murray, 1926–28.

3 v. fronts., plates, ports. 23 cm.

Even less space is devoted here to Anglo-American relations during the Civil War period than in the first series.

Vigil, *pseud.*

American difficulties. Letters by Vigil ... London, Houghton, 1861.

44 p. 21°ᵐ.

Treats of commercial aspects of the American conflict.

Walbridge, Hiram, 1821–1870.

Our maritime and neutral rights. Address of Gen'l Hiram Walbridge, at the grand corporation banquet, by the municipal authorities of the city of New York, in commemoration of the anniversary of Washington's birthday, at the St. Nicholas hotel, February 22, 1862. [New York?] Gibson brothers, printers [1862?]

cover-title, 15 p. 21½°ᵐ.

A rambling attempt to reveal ulterior purposes in British policy toward the U. S.

Walker, Robert James, 1801–1869.

American slavery and finances. By the Hon. Robert J. Walker ... [3d ed., with appendix] London, W. Ridgway, 1864.

9 v. in 1. 20½°ᵐ.

A collection of pamphlets contrasting Confederate and Federal finances.

Ward, *Sir* **Adolphus William,** 1837–1924, *ed.*

The Cambridge history of British foreign policy, 1783–1919, ed. by Sir A. W. Ward ... and G. P. Gooch ... Cambridge, The University press, 1922–23.

3 v. 24½ cm.

A restrained brief account is included regarding the British policy toward the "American Question. "

Washburn, Charles Ames, 1822–1889.

The history of Paraguay, with notes of personal observations, and reminiscences of diplomacy under difficulties. By Charles A. Washburn ... Boston, Lee & Shepard; New York, Lee, Shepard, and Dillingham, 1871.

2 v. fronts., illus., plates, ports., maps. 23½°ᵐ.

Quaint recollections of the author's tenure as U. S. minister to Paraguay during the Civil War period.

Weed, Thurlow, 1797–1882.

Life of Thurlow Weed including his autobiography and a memoir ... [Boston, New York, Houghton, Mifflin and company; etc., etc., 1884]

2 v. fronts., pl., ports. 24½°ᵐ.

Weed's account of his visit to London soon after the Trent Affair contains much information on Anglo-American relations -- in spite of his tendency toward self-congratulations.

Welles, Sumner, 1892–

Naboth's vineyard; the Dominican Republic, 1844–1924, by Sumner Welles ... with a foreword by the Hon. L. S. Rowe ... New York, Payson & Clarke ltd., 1928.

2 v. fronts., plates, ports., fold. map. 23 cm.

The best available treatment of 19th century U. S. -Dominican relations.

West, Warren Reed, 1894-
... Contemporary French opinion on the American civil war, by W. Reed West ... Baltimore, The Johns Hopkins press, 1924.

viii, 9–159 p. 25 cm.

An excellent survey, drawn from printed Confederate documents, published French official debates and French periodicals.

White, Elizabeth Brett.
American opinion of France from Lafayette to Poincaré, by Elizabeth Brett White ... New York, A. A. Knopf, 1927.

xvi p., 1 l., 346 p., 1 l. 24½ cm.

One chapter expertly describes American attitudes toward France during the Civil War.

Wilks, Washington, 1825?–1864.
English criticism on President Lincoln's anti-slavery proclamation & message. By Washington Wilks. [London, J. Kenny, printer, 1863]

8 p. 17½ᶜᵐ.

A trivial production.

Willard, Joseph 1798–1865.
Letter to an English friend on the rebellion in the United States, and on British policy. Boston, Ticknor & Fields, 1862.

28 p. 24ᶜᵐ.

A criticism of the "selfish policy of England" in wartime Anglo-American relations.

Williams, James, d. 1869.
The rise and fall of "The model republic". By James Williams ... London, R. Bentley, 1863.

xiv, 424 p. 23ᶜᵐ.

A clumsy attack on democracy and the American Union by a former U. S. minister to Turkey and pro-Southern writer.

Willson, Beckles, 1869–
America's ambassadors to England (1785–1928) a narrative of Anglo-American diplomatic relations, by Beckles Willson ... London, J. Murray [1928]

xiv, 497 p. 36 port. (incl. front.) 23 cm.

Two dozen pages on the Civil War are inaccurate, shallow, and unscholarly.

Willson, Beckles, 1869–
Friendly relations; a narrative of Britain's ministers and ambassadors to America (1791–1930), by Beckles Willson ... Boston, Little, Brown, and company, 1934.

viii p., 4 l., [3]–350 p. front., ports. 22½ᶜᵐ.

A chapter entitled "The Civil War and Lord Lyons" is distorted, undocumented, and inaccurate.

Willson, Beckles, 1869–1942.
John Slidell and the Confederates in Paris (1862–65) by Beckles Willson ... New York, Minton, Balch & company, 1932.

xiii, 296 p. front., plates, ports. 21 cm.

A lively but unscholarly and overly imaginative piece of writing.

Winks, Robin W
Canada and the United States: the Civil War years. Baltimore, Johns Hopkins Press [1960]

xviii, 430 p. 24 cm.

An admirably well-researched and carefully written book that is by far the best on the subject.

Woldman, Albert A
Lincoln and the Russians. [1st ed.] Cleveland, World Pub. Co. [1952]

311 p. 22 cm.

Consists for the most part of extracts from the correspondence of the wartime Russian minister in Washington; very little on Russo-American relations.

Wolseley, Garnet Joseph Wolseley, *viscount*, **1833–1913.**
The American Civil War, an English view. Edited, with an introd., by James A. Rawley. Charlottesville, University Press of Virginia ₁1964₎

xxxvii, 230 p. 24 cm.

Only one in this series of pro-Southern essays has bearing on British public opinion during the war.

Worden, John.
The plain English of American affairs. By John Worden. London, A. W. Bennett, 1863.

63 p. 22ᶜᵐ.

Treats in cumbersome fashion of the causes of the American Civil War.

Yarnall, Ellis, 1817–1905.
Wordsworth and the Coleridges, with other memories, literary and political, by Ellis Yarnall. New York, The Macmillan company; London, Macmillan & co., ltd., 1899.

ix, ₁1₎. 331 p. 22½ cm.

Includes gossip and observations regarding friends of the Union cause in England.